1978

William A. Maesen
30 March 1976

Principles
of
Personality

Principles of Personality

Jerry S. Wiggins
University of British Columbia

K. Edward Renner
University of Illinois

Gerald L. Clore
University of Illinois

Richard J. Rose
Indiana University

ADDISON-WESLEY PUBLISHING COMPANY

Reading, Massachusetts
Menlo Park, California
London
Amsterdam
Don Mills, Ontario
Sydney

This book is in the
ADDISON-WESLEY SERIES IN PSYCHOLOGY

Portions of this text originally appeared in the authors' earlier text, *The Psychology of Personality*, copyright © 1971 by Addison-Wesley Publishing Company, Inc.

ISBN 0-201-08618-2
ABCDEFGHIJ-MA-79876

Preface

In this text, we have attempted to provide the student with a broad and balanced introduction to the field of personality study. Theory, research, and substantive issues are integrated within a single comprehensive framework. The central thesis of the book is that personality is best considered from many, often conflicting, points of view. Four alternative viewpoints—each with its own methods and assumptions—are used to bring order to the events which are the concern of personality study. The biological, experimental, social, and psychometric-trait viewpoints represent the major conceptual frameworks in terms of which contemporary psychologists function. These four viewpoints are applied to three substantive topics that have considerable theoretical and practical significance for the study of human behavior: dependency, aggression, and sexuality. The alternate treatments of each topic from four distinct viewpoints provide the student with a sense of diversity and breadth that is characteristic of the field of personality. Representative research findings from experimental, correlational, and field studies are presented simply, yet in sufficient detail to enable the student to develop an appreciation of the nature of personality research.

We have also included concise treatments of the major contemporary theories of personality: psychoanalytic theory, social learning theory, cognitive-developmental theory, and self theory, and we have suggested the contribution of each theoretical viewpoint to the understanding of dependency, aggression, and sexuality. Although there is some discussion of the historical background of each theory, the emphasis is on theories of personality rather than on prominent historical figures.

The final section of the book presents examples of contemporary models of personality, a topic that other introductory personality texts do not treat. The student is introduced to the role of analogy in the construction of miniature personality theories through considering models of the human as rat (Skinner), scientist (Kelly), actor (Goffman), and computer (Loehlin). We consider the primary virtue of the present text to be the *organization* of the material into a comprehensive and, we hope, convincing framework from which to view all the interrelationships. This organization, supplemented by the overriding philosophical viewpoint of constructive alternativism, permits an introduction to the field of personality study that is, in our opinion, broader and closer to the field itself than that contained in any other single work.

In the years following the appearance of our earlier text, *The Psychology of Personality* (1971), we have received comments and constructive suggestions from students and instructors at many different institutions. It has been suggested that the earlier text is best suited for the full-semester or two-quarter course in which the textbook is the principal reading assignment. There appears to be a need for a shorter, less detailed textbook that can be used in courses of relatively short duration and in courses where additional readings are emphasized. It has also been suggested that the earlier text is best suited for upper-division students, psychology majors, and even beginning graduate students. Hence, there appears to be a need for a somewhat more readable text that meets the needs of lower-division students and majors in fields other than psychology. The present text was designed to be a more concise, readable, and up-to-date version of the earlier one.

The present text differs from our earlier one in other ways as well. In it we present the essential features of each of the viewpoints of personality study with less emphasis on conceptual and methodological issues more likely to be of interest to specialists in the field. In our treatment of the substantive topics of aggression, dependency, and sexuality, we have tried to select examples of research that are particularly relevant or of high interest value, with less concern for encyclopedic coverage. The most notable changes have been made in our presentation of the theories of personality. The chapters on social learning theory, cognitive-developmental theory, and self theory have been revised for greater appeal to the student reader and to reflect the changes that have occurred in these still-evolving theoretical perspectives. The chapter on psychoanalytic theory has been completely rewritten from a perspective more familiar to most beginning students than the metapsychological approach used in the earlier text.

When we wrote our earlier text, we felt that the field of personality was moving in the direction of becoming both more cognitive and more humanistic, and we attempted to give emphasis to these emerging trends. The ensuing years have more than borne out this judgment and, consequently, we have written the present text on the assumption that the field of personality will continue to move in these directions.

We are deeply indebted to Dr. Richard Runyon for his help in all phases of the writing of this book. Dr. Runyon is a proven author of undergraduate psychology texts, whose ability to communicate clearly and directly to students has impressed several of us. Thus we were delighted when he agreed to work with us as a watchdog for the student reader and as a coordinator of our collective exposition. We would also like to express our gratitude to those colleagues and undergraduate students who were thoughtful enough to provide us with unsolicited words of criticism and praise for our earlier text. We hope that the present reader will benefit from their helpful comments.

January 1976

J.S.W.
K.E.R.
G.L.C.
R.J.R.

Contents

SECTION 1   INTRODUCTION   1

1   Orientation   2

Central assertion   5

Constructive alternativism   5

Events   5
Constructs   6
Evaluation of constructs   6
Multiple constructs imposed upon single events   6
Range and foci of convenience   7
Relativism   8

Four viewpoints in personality study   8

Plan of the book   10

Suggestions for further reading   10

2   Emergent Points of View   12

The biological viewpoint   14

Evolutionary perspective   15

Behavior genetics   18
  Biological individuality   18
  Genetics and behavior   19
  Methods and data of behavior genetics   21
    Maternal effects   21
    Human research: twin and family studies   23
    Karyotype analysis   27
  Principles of behavior-genetics analysis   28
    Susceptibility: genetypic-experiential interaction   29
    Selective exposure: genotypic-experiential correlation   31
Early experience   32
  Prenatal experience   32
  Early postnatal experience   33
    Enrichment   35
    Deprivation   36

The experimental viewpoint   **36**
Learning processes   37
  Classical conditioning: an approach to feelings   37
    Stimulus generalization   38
    Discrimination   39
  Instrumental conditioning: an approach to actions   40
    Escape and avoidance learning   40
    Reward   43
  Incentive learning: an approach to values   44
Perceptual processes   45
  Adaptation level   46
    Incentive contrasts   46
    Social contrasts   46
  Needs and perception   47
Cognitive processes   48
  Decision-making   48
  Cognitive structures   49
    Cognitive types   50

The social viewpoint   **52**
Models   53
  Learning and unlearning by observation   53
  The conditions for imitation   55
    Aspects of the observer: emotional arousal   56
    Aspects of the model: rewards and punishment   57
    Interpersonal aspects: similarity between observer and model   58
Roles   59
  The nature of roles   59
  Role expectations   59
  Role as an alternative to personality   60
  Role playing   61

Cultures   64
  The study of cultures   64
  Objective measures   65
  The study of variables across cultures   67

The psychometric-trait viewpoint   **70**

The nature of personality measurement   71
  Continuous versus discrete scales   71
  Bipolar versus unipolar scales   71
  Interval versus ordinal scales   72
  Traits as constructs   73
Construct validity   74
  Substantive considerations   74
  Structural considerations   75
  External considerations   75
Methods of trait measurement   76
Observational methods of trait measurement   76
  Control of environment   76
  Presence of observer   77
  Rating scales   77
  Peer ratings   79
  Interviews   80
Self-report methods of trait measurement   81
  Rational personality inventories   81
  Forced-choice personality inventories   82
  Empirical personality inventories   84
Indirect methods: projective techniques   87

Summary   **91**

Suggestions for further reading   **93**

SECTION 2   DEPENDENCY   **97**

3   Dependency: The Biological Viewpoint   **98**

Evolutionary perspective   **100**

Behavior genetics   **102**

Infant twin studies of dependency and socialization   103
Twin studies with older children   107
Longitudinal stability of passivity and dependency   108

Early experience   **110**

Initial studies of Spalding   110
Imprinting in mammals   112
The effect of rearing mice with rats   112

Rearing experiences and social behavior in monkeys   113
Institutionalization and social behavior in humans   114

Summary   **116**

Suggestions for further reading   **117**

4   Dependency: The Experimental Viewpoint   **118**

Learning processes   **120**

Feelings of dependency   120
  Positive feelings of dependency   120
  Human positive feelings of attachment   122
Dependent behaviors   124
  Instrumental conditioning   124
  The use of punishment   126
Dependency values   127

Perceptual processes   **129**

Social perceptions   129
Field dependency   130

Cognitive processes: forced dependency   **131**

Summary   **134**

Suggestions for further reading   **135**

5   Dependency: The Social Viewpoint   **136**

Models   **138**

The effect of dependency on imitation   138

Roles   **140**

Dependency and age changes   140
Birth order   141
  Dependency-producing behavior of mothers   141
  Birth order, fear, and affiliation   145

Cultures: Dependency and type of subsistence economy   **146**

Summary   **149**

Suggestions for further reading   **150**

6   Dependency: The Psychometric-trait Viewpoint   **152**

Observational methods: a peer nomination measure of dependency   **154**

Rationale and development   154
Construct validity   156

Self-report methods: forced-choice dependency scales

Construct validity 1ь

Requesting help and reassurance from others 160

Responsivity to verbal approval and disapproval 161

Social suggestibility 162

Social conformity 164

Indirect methods: a fantasy measure of dependency 165

Fantasy dependency and social conformity 165

Fantasy dependency and psychosexual orality 166

Summary 169

SECTION 3 AGGRESSION 171

7 **Aggression: The Biological Viewpoint** 172

Evolutionary perspective 174

Aggression and human evolution 175

Ethology and human aggression 176

Behavior genetics 178

Correlated responses to selection 179

Analysis of pure strains 179

Human studies: the Y chromosome and aggressiveness 181

Male hormones and the XYY karyotype 183

Neurological abnormalities and the XYY karyotype 183

Some reservations and alternative hypotheses 184

Twin studies and longitudinal evidence 185

Longitudinal stability of aggressiveness 185

Twin studies 185

Early experience 186

Hormonal effects 186

Effects of social rearing 187

Aggression and ethology reconsidered 191

Summary 193

Suggestions for further reading 194

8 **Aggression: The Experimental Viewpoint** 196

Learning processes 198

Classical conditioning 198

An animal illustration 198

Extension to human behavior 199

Instrumental conditioning   200
    An animal illustration   200
    Extensions to human behavior   200
The value of aggression   203
    An animal illustration   203
    Extension to human subjects   204

Perceptual processes: binocular rivalry   **204**

Cognitive processes   **207**

Summary   **209**

Suggestions for further reading   **209**

9 Aggression: The Social Viewpoint   **210**

Models   **212**

The imitation of aggression by children   212
Justified aggression   214

Roles: aggression and the police officer's role   **217**

Race   220
Status   220

Cultures   **221**

Culture versus instinct   221
    An aggressive tribe   222
    Pacifist tribes   222
Aggression between cultures   223
    Aggression and cultural differences   223
    Social distance among East African tribes   224
    The enemy as dissimilar   226
The contact hypothesis   227

Summary   **229**

Suggestions for further reading   **230**

10 Aggression: The Psychometric-trait Viewpoint   **232**

Observational methods: a peer-nomination measure of aggression   **234**

Rationale and development   234
Construct validity   235

Self-report methods: the expression and control of aggression   **237**

Intensity   237
Control   238
    Appropriate control   238

Undercontrol   238
Overcontrol   238
MMPI aggression scales   239
CPI self-control scale   241
Self-control and intensity of aggression   242

Indirect methods: relationship between fantasy and overt aggression   **245**

Maternal attitudes   246
Aggression anxiety   249

Summary   **250**

Suggestions for further reading   **252**

SECTION 4   SEXUALITY   **253**

11   Sexuality: The Biological Viewpoint   **254**

Evolutionary perspective   **256**

Behavior genetics   **259**

Selective breeding   259
Analysis of pure strains   259
Mechanisms   259

Early experience   **260**

Experience and sexual reactivity   260
  Prenatal and neonatal effects   260
    Masculinization of the female   260
    Feminization of the male   261
  Postnatal experience   261
    The reproductive cycle of the ring dove   262
    Synchronization of estrous in mice and women   262
    Sexual responsivity in humans   263
Early experience and development of sexual identity   265
  Klinefelter's syndrome   267
  Turner's syndrome   268
Early experience and sexual response   269
  Imprinting process   270
  Development of asexuality   270

Summary   **272**

Suggestions for further reading   **273**

12   Sexuality: The Experimental Viewpoint   **276**

Learning processes   **278**

Classical conditioning: love   278
Instrumental conditioning and incentive processes: sexual behaviors   281

Perceptual processes   **284**

Cognitive processes   **285**

Relative impotence and frigidity   285
Psychosocial aspects of sexual dysfunction   286

Summary   **288**

Suggestions for further reading   **288**

13   Sexuality: The Social Viewpoint   **290**

Models   **292**

Arousal   292
Satiation   293
Behavior   293

Roles: sex identification   **295**

Imitation   295
Theories of identification   297
Cognitive-developmental factors   301

Cultures   **302**

Sex roles across cultures   302
The status of women   304
   In primitive cultures   304
   In technological cultures   306
   The female role in the mass media   308

Summary   **309**

Suggestions for further reading   **310**

14   Sexuality: The Psychometric-trait Viewpoint   **312**

Observational methods   **314**

Special problems of observation   314
The Kinsey interviews   314
   Content of the interviews   315
   Recruitment of interviewers   316
   Recruitment of subjects   317
   Maintaining confidentiality   318
   Establishing and maintaining rapport   320
   Checks on accuracy   320
The Masters-Johnson observations   321
   Recruitment of preliminary sample   322

Recruitment of primary sample   322
Laboratory procedures   323
Significance of the research   324

Self-report methods   **325**

Sexual experiences   325
  Guttman scales   326
  Quantification of sexual experience   327
Sexual preferences   329
  Preference for sexual activity   329
  Heterosexual somatic preferences: men   331
  Heterosexual somatic preferences: women   334

Indirect methods   **337**

Fantasy measures of sexual imagery and guilt   337
Inhibition and arousal of sexual imagery and guilt   338
  Study A   338
    Experimental group   338
    Control group   338
    Results   338
  Study B   339
    Experimental group   339
    Control group   339
    Results   340
  Study C   340
    Experimental group   340
    Control group   340
    Results   340

Summary   **341**

SECTION 5   THEORIES OF PERSONALITY   **343**

15   Psychoanalytic Theory   **344**

Background and orientation   **346**

Historical perspective   346
  The origins of psychoanalysis   346
  Psychoanalysis and the biological viewpoint   348
  Psychoanalysis and the psychometric-trait viewpoint   350
  Psychoanalysis and the experimental viewpoint   351
  Psychoanalysis and the social viewpoint   352
Philosophical perspective   353
  The active and the passive human   353
  Shifting philosophical perspectives in psychoanalysis   355

Central assertion and principal constructs   **356**

The id and associated constructs   356
  Unconscious processes   356
  Instinctual drives   358
The ego and associated constructs   359
  Adaptation and coordination   359
  Defense mechanisms   360
    Repression   361
    Projection   362
    Reaction formation   363
    Rationalization   364
The superego and associated constructs   364
  The socialization process   364
  Adult moral life   366

Range and focus of convenience   **367**

Applications to selected topics   **368**

Dependency   368
Aggression   369
Sexuality   370

Summary   **371**

Suggestions for further reading   **372**

16   Social Learning Theory   **374**

Background and orientation   **376**

Historical perspective   376
  The concept of habit   376
  The early social learning group   377
  The later social learning theorists   377
  Historical comparison   378
Philosophical perspective   379

Central assertion   **382**

Principal constructs   **383**

  Drive   383
  Reinforcement   383
  Cue   384
  Response   384
Social processes and the social context   385
  Observational learning   385
  Situational specificity of behavior   386
  Self-control   387

Range and foci of convenience   **388**

Conceptualizing common human experience   388
   Generalization and discrimination   388
   Conflict   389
Behavior modification   390
Social exchange   391

Applications to selected topics   **392**

Dependency   392
Aggression   395
Sexuality   397

Summary   **398**

Suggestions for further reading   **399**

17   Cognitive-developmental Theory   **402**

Background and orientation   **404**

Historical perspectives: major contributors   404
Philosophical perspective   408
   The active person   408
   Hierarchical growth   409
   Interactionism   409
   Cognitive relativity   410

Central assertion   **410**

Principal constructs   **411**

Orthogenetic development   412
Adaptation   413
   Assimilation and accommodation   414
Stages of growth   416
   An empirical example of a stage sequence: the dream   416
   Basic developmental stages   418

Range and focus of convenience   **419**

Applications to selected topics   **420**

Dependency   420
Aggression   421
Sexuality   422

Summary   **423**

Suggestions for further reading   **424**

18   Self Theory   **426**

Background and orientation   **428**

Historical perspective   428
  Background   429
  Self theory   429
    Nondirective psychotherapy   429
    Self-actualization   432
  Recent developments   432
    Softening of behaviorism   432
    Transcendental meditation   433
Philosophical perspective   433
  The active nature of the human   433
  The scientific study of the human   434

Central assertion   **434**

Principal constructs   **435**

Self   435
  Empirical self   435
  Valuing self   437
An absolute state of psychological health   437
The natural growth tendency of humans   438
Primacy of experience   438

Range and focus of convenience   **439**

Awareness   440
  Self-understanding   440
  Personal satisfaction   440
  Sensitivity   441
Creativity   441
  Creative people   441
  Creativity as freedom   442
  The science of creative intelligence   443

Applications to selected topics   **443**

Dependency   443
Aggression   444
Sexuality   445

Summary   **446**

Suggestions for further reading   **448**

SECTION 6   MODELS OF PERSONALITY   **449**

19 The Human as Rat   **450**

Principal constructs and their translation   **453**

Hours of deprivation = desires and aversions   454

Skinner box = situations 454
Reinforcement = praise 454
Pellet dispenser = mother or socializing agent 455
Secondary reinforcer = promises 456
Shaping = socialization 456
Operant responses = skills 457
Discriminative stimuli = instructions and warnings 457
Schedules of reinforcement = rules 457
Cumulative recorder = reputation and personality description 458

Use of the model in personality study 460

Verbal behavior 462
Gambling 464
Sick talk and sick behavior 464

Practical applications 466

Token economies 466
  The patients 467
  Operant responses 467
  Stimulus control 467
  Contingent reinforcement 467
  Reinforcement 467
  On-ward jobs 469
The technology of teaching 469
  Discriminations 470
  Schedules of reinforcement 471
Social planning and human engineering 473

Summary 476

Suggestions for further reading 477

20 **The Human as Scientist** 478

Principal constructs and their translation 482

Prior facts = past experiences 482
Viewpoint = personal construct system 483
Central assertions = core personal constructs 483
Elaborations of central assertions = subordinate personal constructs 484
Formulation of problem = circumspection 484
Statement of hypothesis = preemption 485
Experimentation = control 486
Results = personal validation 486
Interpretation = channelization 487

Use of the model in personality study 488

Anxiety and threat 488
Guilt 489

Communication   490
Creativity and problem-solving   490

Practical applications   **491**

Assessment   491
  A redefinition of assessment   492
  The Role Construct Repertory Test (RCRT)   492
  Illustrative use of the RCRT in the assessment of thought disorder   495
The clinical setting   497
  Interviewing   497
  Psychotherapy   498
  Fixed-role therapy   498
International understanding   499

Summary   **500**

Suggestions for further reading   **501**

21 **The Human as Actor**   **504**

Principal constructs and their translation   **507**

Parts and routines = positions and roles   508
Scenery and stage props = setting   509
Costumes, makeup, and hand props = appearance   509
Acting = manner   511
Dramatic realization = showing off   512
Cast = team   512
Polite applause = tact   513
Speaking out of character = treatment of the absent, high signs, and
  team collusion   515
Scene changes = privacy   515
The house and the backstage = regions   517

Use of the model in personality study   **518**

The nature of personality   519
Reality and performances   519

Practical applications   **521**

The use of impression management to control one's hospital fate   521
The effectiveness of impression management in the hospital   523

Summary   **524**

Suggestions for further reading   **526**

22 **The Human as Computer**   **528**

Principal constructs and their translation   **531**

Start = stimuli   534

Read in data S = recognition 534
Search = recall 535
Combine = emotional reaction 536
Transform = action 536
Read in data E = environment 537
Consequences loop = consequences 538
Modify memory = learning 538
Print out = introspection 539

Use of the model in personality study **540**

Personality development and change 540
Personality structure 541
Interpersonal behavior 542
Effects of initial attitudes 542
Psychotherapy 543

Practical applications **544**

Prediction and diagnosis of personality characteristics 544
Computer predictions of outcome and performance 544
Automated personality diagnosis and report writing 545
Computer simulation and modeling of expert judges 546
Psychotherapy and attitude change 547

Summary **548**

Suggestions for further reading **549**

References **R1**

Name Index **I1**

Subject Index **I9**

Section 1
Introduction

1
Orientation

I. **Central assertion**

II. **Constructive alternativism**
    A. Events
    B. Constructs
    C. Evaluation of constructs
    D. Multiple constructs imposed upon single events
    E. Range and foci of convenience
    F. Relativism

III. **Four viewpoints in personality study**

IV. **Plan of the book**

V. **Suggestions for further reading**

That people differ from one another is a commonplace observation, but probably the full range of the differences is rarely appreciated. The study of personality is essentially the study of individual differences. This book, then, is about the behaviors and states which differentiate people, including those as diverse as dependency, aggression, and sexuality. In addition, it is about the processes which give rise to variations in behavior and the techniques developed to measure them. Psychologists who study personality are in general agreement that the topic of individual differences is the primary concern of the field, but beyond this basic agreement, their approach to these topics depends on their point of view. The following viewpoints, representative of the field, illustrate the diversity that exists.

> Consider the fact ... that every individual person is endowed with a distinctive gastro-intestinal tract ... a distinctive nervous system, and a morphologically distinctive brain. ... Can it be that this fact is inconsequential, in relation to the problem of personality differences? (Roger Williams, 1960)
>
> The study of personality is the study of how people come to be what they are. Of course people differ widely in what they have learned; each person is indeed unique. But all have learned in accordance with the same general laws. ... The essential point is that there are no laws of personality functioning apart from the laws of general psychology. (Nevitt Sanford, 1963)
>
> The life-history of an individual is first and foremost an accommodation to the patterns and standards traditionally handed down in his community. From the moment of his birth the customs into which he is born shape his experience and behavior. (Ruth Benedict, 1934)
>
> It is in individual differences ... that we find the logical key to personality. ... An individual's personality, then, is his unique pattern of traits. (J. P. Guilford, 1959)

More than one approach to the study of personality is evident in the quotations presented here. In their turn, they suggest that the most fruitful approach to the study of personality is one that emphasizes: (a) inherent biological differences among individuals; (b) the principles of general experimental psychology; (c) the cultural context in which individuals develop; and (d) the underlying personality traits that distinguish one individual from another. While all these statements sound reasonable, they are neither quite in agreement nor exactly contradictory. A common thread in the meanings is that the psychology of personality has as its task understanding how and why people feel and act as they do, especially how and why individuals differ from one another. The purpose of the pages that follow is to report what has been done toward the accomplishment of this end.

CENTRAL ASSERTION

Despite the fact that a common thread can be found in the usages cited, there is no getting around the fact that they represent different points of view. However, it will be the thesis of this book that the problems these discrepancies appear to create are not problems at all, and that each of these meanings has something to recommend it. Stated more formally, *the central assertion of this book is that personality is best considered from many, often conflicting, points of view.*

The topic of personality has obviously been treated by many investigators. They have represented more than one theoretical approach, and they have used a variety of methods of investigation. It is clear that some of these approaches are more fruitful than others, but of those that are useful, it cannot be said that any is best. For this reason, personality will be treated here from four different perspectives—the biological, experimental, social, and psychometric points of view. The case will be made that all are useful, but none is sufficient.

CONSTRUCTIVE ALTERNATIVISM

To assert that many, often conflicting, viewpoints should be considered in the study of personality is to subscribe to a philosophy of science known as *constructive alternativism* (Kelly, 1963). Since this particular philosophy of science is so central to the present book, the best procedure is to explain it at the outset. The basic idea is that the events with which students of personality are concerned exist independently of any ideas or constructs that students may have about the events. The fact that we can know such events only through our constructs about them does not mean that events and constructs are the same things. To clarify this distinction, we must define *events* and *constructs* regarding events, as well as to indicate the manner in which such constructs are to be *evaluated*.

Events

Events are simply those things which happen in the course of time. There is nothing novel in this definition of events, but we should note that events are considered to be *real* happenings and not figments of our imaginations. The events of greatest interest to students of personality are those involving people. Thinking, feeling, acting, and imagining are all events that are studied by personality psychologists. It is assumed, however, that such events exist quite independently of the science of personality, that they always did and always will.

Constructs

Although we assume that events have an independent existence, we come to *know* or understand events only through our concepts or *constructs* about them. A construct is a set of notions or a frame of reference from which events are viewed. The word *construct* is employed in preference to "concept" to emphasize that such frames of reference are constructed by human beings. Thus people construct their own understanding or interpretation of events.

> Man looks at his world through transparent patterns or templets which he creates and then attempts to fit over the realities of which the world is composed. (Kelly, 1963, pp. 8–9)

It is through the imposition of constructs on events that people find "meaning" in the multitude of stimuli that impinge upon them in the course of their lives. Constructs may not always fit the events they are imposed upon, and consequently, they may require revision or replacement. But even poorly fitting constructs are better than no constructs at all, since the only alternative to constructs is chaos.

Evaluation of Constructs

There are many different ways in which a given event can be *construed* (interpreted through a construct), and each person interprets events in a slightly different way. Similarly, there are many different frames of reference or *construct systems* by means of which the events of personality can be interpreted. In a general sense, all these constructions may be true although some may be more scientifically *useful* than others. Constructions of events that are most useful are those that increase the prediction, control, and understanding of the events in question.

Multiple Constructs Imposed Upon Single Events

In the course of the history of scientific investigation, certain constructs and procedures come to be recognized as distinguishable *viewpoints* regarding the events in question. Although different viewpoints tend to focus on different kinds of events, it is not uncommon for several viewpoints to be concerned with the same event. It is at this point that a misunderstanding often arises concerning the relationship of constructs to events. An example will clarify the nature of this misunderstanding.

It is possible to interpret intelligent behavior from a *biological* viewpoint in terms of constructs involving the brain, the central nervous system, and the nutritional condition of the body as a whole. It is also possible to interpret intelligent behavior from a *social* viewpoint in terms of constructs involving social motivation, social reward, and cultural enrichment. But what if the biological psychologist says "Intelligence is a biological phenomenon," and the social psychologist retorts, "Intelligence is a social phenomenon"? Clearly, they are *both* wrong. They confuse events with constructs about events. Events (e.g., intelligent behavior) do not owe allegiance to any particular system of constructs (e.g., biological, social). There are no such things as "biological events" or "social events." There are only events (which may be construed from many different vantage points).

It is quite proper, of course, to inquire whether intelligent behavior is more *fruitfully construed* from a biological construction system than from a social construction system. Here the criteria of prediction, control, and understanding may be invoked and a rigorous evaluation made. It is also proper to raise the question of the relative fruitfulness of the biological and social viewpoints *in general* as they relate to the study of personality. This question is more difficult to answer, however, because it is likely that the two construction systems cover a somewhat different *range* of events and make their greatest contributions at different locations, or *foci*, of events.

Range and Foci of Convenience

Scientific construction systems operate within a limited *range* of events. The major constructs of a viewpoint impose methodological blinders on investigation and achieve their purpose by *ignoring* events that fall outside their range of convenience. Biological constructs can be conveniently applied to certain events but not to others. Social constructs operate within their own range of events, which may or may not include the events that are most conveniently studied from other viewpoints. In general, the most useful constructs are those that may be conveniently applied to a *broad range* of important events.

Scientific construction systems usually have a focal point at which they are most conveniently applied. For some narrow class of events, a particular construct may be highly fruitful in terms of the criteria of prediction, control, and understanding. This focal point is typically the event or events the author had in mind when he or she devised the construct. For example, the construct of repression was particularly useful in understanding the symptoms of upper-middle-class Viennese female neurotics at the turn of the century, since that was the group Freud had in mind when he proposed the construct. The construct of repression may be less useful in understanding the problems of contemporary youth in America, although the construct of identity crisis may be very useful in this context. Clearly, different construction systems have different and possibly nonoverlapping foci of convenience, and this situation requires a *relativistic* approach to the world of events.

Relativism

All events are subject to alternative interpretations by means of a variety of construction systems. The relative fruitfulness of several constructions of the same event may be evaluated by the criteria of prediction, control, and understanding. However, since constructs differ from one another in terms of their ranges and foci of convenience, it would be premature to champion one construction system over another in relation to the field of personality. Instead, it is more appropriate to adopt a *relativistic* view of the relations between constructs and events in this field. The same event should be viewed simultaneously from a variety of construction systems, each contributing its unique version of the "truth." This is the philosophy of *constructive alternativism* as represented by the central assertion of the present book: "Personality is best considered from many, often conflicting, points of view."

FOUR VIEWPOINTS IN PERSONALITY STUDY

A viewpoint, or scientific construction system, involves more than a single construct. A viewpoint is a collection of constructs that fit together logically, and it provides a broad framework for viewing the events of personality study. The elements of a viewpoint are cohesive because they stem from several basic assumptions which, when granted, provide the underlying logical basis for the viewpoint. In this book four separate alternative viewpoints—each with its own basic assumptions—are used to bring order to the events of personality study. These viewpoints represent the major conceptual emphases of contemporary psychology, each with its own methods, procedures, and assumptions. They are:

The biological viewpoint. This viewpoint construes the events of personality study in terms of interactions among the *early experience, genetic*

No One Is Exactly Like Anyone Else

From *All Embarrassed* by William Steig

endowment, and *evolutionary background* of the organism. The reciprocal interaction of behavior with its biological base is the primary focus of this viewpoint.

The experimental viewpoint.   This viewpoint construes the events of personality study in terms of uniform *learning, perceptual,* and *higher processes.* To understand these processes is to understand how particular events influence future behavior through their contribution to the personality of the individual.

The social viewpoint.   This viewpoint construes the events of personality study in terms of the social context in which the person lives and develops. A full understanding of this social context requires an understanding of the contributions of *models,* of cultural *roles,* and of *cultures* themselves.

The psychometric-trait viewpoint.   This viewpoint construes the events of personality study in terms of attributes which reflect underlying trait organizations. Personality-trait measurement is emphasized in the separate realms of *behavior observation, self-report,* and the *indirect assessment* of underlying traits.

Although the full implications of these four viewpoints can hardly be grasped from the abbreviated definitions given above, one can see that the viewpoints differ from one another in at least two ways. First, they represent quite distinct orientations to the study of personality, which are likely to differ in their ranges and foci of convenience. Second, each viewpoint implies and is in part defined by a unique set of methods or tools for observation. Such methodological blinders will, almost of necessity, result in alternative construals of the same events in personality study.

PLAN OF THE BOOK

The four alternative viewpoints that are emphasized in this book represent mainstreams of psychological thought that have evolved during the last century.

In Chapter 2, the nature of each of the four alternative viewpoints is considered in some detail. The central assertion of each viewpoint is stated and elaborated, and the interlocking system of constructs that stem from each assertion is discussed and illustrated. Here the specialized vocabulary and measurement techniques of each viewpoint are presented.

In Sections 2–4, each of three important topics in personality is treated from each viewpoint. The topics of dependency, aggression and sexuality were selected as areas of personality study that have the greatest theoretical and practical significance for the understanding of human behavior. The alternate treatment of each topic from four distinct viewpoints will illustrate both the virtues and the shortcomings of each approach.

Extended construction systems of broad range and scope are referred to as *theories of personality*. The major contemporary theories of personality are introduced for the first time in Section 5. From a consideration of the nature of psychoanalytic theory, social learning theory, cognitive-developmental theory, and self theory, it will become apparent that such extended construction systems attempt an integration of constructs from two or more of the four alternative viewpoints of personality study.

A relatively new approach to personality study, which embodies aspects of both viewpoints and theories, is presented in the final section of the book, on models. *Models* of personality represent constructions from other disciplines (animal behavior, philosophy of science, drama, computer technology) that are applied to the events of personality study. Such constructions have been borrowed from their original foci of convenience and applied well beyond their usual ranges of convenience. The questions raised here concern whether or not it is fruitful to think of the human as rat, scientist, actor, and computer.

SUGGESTIONS FOR FURTHER READING

Allport, G. W. The fruits of eclecticism: Bitter or sweet? In G. W. Allport, *The Person in Psychology*. Boston: Beacon Press, 1968, pp. 3–27. An alternative to the relativistic position adopted in this chapter is the "systematic eclecticism" of Gordon Allport. It is instructive to compare Allport's position with the one adopted in this chapter.

Allport, G. W. *Personality: A Psychological Interpretation*. New York: Holt, 1937. This is the classic personality text which, despite its age, still serves as an excellent introduction to the field. Allport provides almost fifty definitions of "personality" and suggests a scheme for classifying them.

Kelly, G. A. *A Theory of Personality*. New York: Norton, 1963. The first chapter of this book contains a detailed statement of the philosophy of constructive alternativism. It is highly readable and should serve to clarify the material in the present chapter.

2
Emergent Points of View

I. The biological viewpoint
A. Evolutionary perspective
B. Behavior genetics
1. Biological individuality
2. Genetics and behavior
3. Methods and data of behavior genetics
   a. Maternal effects
   b. Human research
   c. Karyotype analysis
4. Principles of behavior-genetics analysis
   a. Susceptibility
   b. Selective exposure
C. Early experience
1. Prenatal experience
2. Early postnatal experience
   a. Enrichment
   b. Deprivation

II. The experimental viewpoint
A. Learning processes
1. Classical conditioning: an approach to feelings
   a. Stimulus generalization
   b. Discrimination
2. Instrumental conditioning: an approach to actions
   a. Escape and avoidance
   b. Reward
3. Incentive learning: an approach to values
B. Perceptual processes
1. Adaptation level
   a. Incentive contrasts
   b. Social contrasts
2. Needs and perception
C. Cognitive processes
1. Decision-making
2. Cognitive structures

III. The social viewpoint
A. Models
1. Learning and unlearning by observation
2. Conditions for imitation
   a. Aspects of the observer
   b. Aspects of the model
   c. Interpersonal aspects
B. Roles
1. The nature of roles
2. Role expectations
3. Role as an alternative to personality
4. Role playing
C. Cultures
1. The study of cultures
2. Objective measures
3. The study of variables across cultures

IV. The psychometric-trait viewpoint
A. The nature of personality measurement
1. Continuous vs. discrete scales
2. Bipolar vs. unipolar scales
3. Interval vs. ordinal scales
4. Traits as constructs
B. Construct validity
1. Substantive considerations
2. Structural considerations
3. External considerations
C. Methods of trait measurement
D. Observational methods of trait measurement
1. Control of environment
2. Presence of observer
3. Rating scales
4. Peer ratings
5. Interviews
E. Self-report methods
1. Rational personality inventories
2. Forced-choice personality inventories
3. Empirical personality inventories
F. Indirect methods

V. Summary
VI. Suggestions for further reading

This chapter introduces the four major points of view that we use to organize the field of personality study. We will state the central assertion of each viewpoint, elaborate it, and explain the consequences to personality theory of adopting each orientation. The *biological viewpoint* emphasizes the evolutionary, genetic, and early developmental foundations of human personality; the *experimental viewpoint* illustrates the manner in which uniform learning, perceptual, and cognitive processes contribute to human individuality; the *social viewpoint* illuminates the importance of the interpersonal and cultural matrix in which the individual learns to assume a role in society; finally, the *psychometric-trait viewpoint* describes the manner in which socially important behaviors manifest underlying personality trait organizations.

THE BIOLOGICAL VIEWPOINT
evolutionary perspective, behavior genetics, and early experience

Central Assertion: *The behavior of an organism can be understood only as the consequence of its history of constitutional–experiential interactions.*

What is an organism? It is at once a product of the evolutionary history of the species in which it claims membership, a product of a unique combination of genes transmitted directly by its parents and indirectly by countless thousands of prior generations of ancestors, and a product of the environmental forces operating upon it from the moment of conception. But first and foremost, an organism is the consequence of the interactions of these constitutional factors with its experience.

Fundamental to the biological viewpoint is a deep appreciation for human individuality. Human variability arises from within the individual as well as from within the species. Functional behaviors have an evolutionary history within the species. The perspective of that history is important in our efforts to understand present behavior. For this reason, the biological approach to personality is set within the context of the evolution of human behavior.

The focus of the biological viewpoint is the origin of behavioral differences. Therefore, anything contributing to behavioral variation is of interest. Assuming that differences in biological constitution always contribute to behavior variation, we take a searching look at two factors known to create biological variation—genetic differences and differences in early experiences.

EVOLUTIONARY PERSPECTIVE

A sexually reproducing population can be regarded as a population of genes—a gene pool. We can describe the population in terms of gene frequencies in the pool. Evolution can then be defined as a change in the gene pool over time. The most important mechanism by which gene frequencies change is *natural selection*. This fundamental principle of evolutionary theory states that variants which increase the probability of survival or adaptation tend to be conserved in the population; variants which decrease the probability of survival tend to be eliminated. Differential selection of genotypes (the genetic structure of the organism) through environmental selection pressure applies not only to morphology (the physical structure of the organism) but also to the organism's behavior. *There is a continuing interaction between behavior and its biological base, so that behavior is both a cause and a consequence of changing gene frequencies.*

Let us develop an account of the origins of man based on Sherwood Washburn's cogent analysis of the interrelationship of tool use, bipedalism and brain development (Washburn, 1960; Washburn and Shirek, 1967). The account is highly speculative of course: the events occurred millions of years ago in little known places and under circumstances about which we can only guess.

The course of evolution is determined by the reproductive success and adaptive ability of a species. Australopithecus, the first step in human evolution, was a small, apelike creature, a vegetarian living in wooded areas and limited to near-tropical regions. The development of two critical behaviors—use of tools and bipedal locomotion—led to further separation from Australopithecus' ape predecessors. Bipedalism was of monumental importance for it freed the hands for carrying tools and weapons and led to the acquisition of skills in their use. Dwindling vegetation required that diets be supplemented with meat; hunting led to the formation of groups, a more complex social life, use of fire, and a greater dispersion of groups in the search for better hunting grounds.

The use of bipedal locomotion put new selective pressures on many parts of the body, including teeth, hand, and pelvis. But the greatest pressure was placed on the brain: therein evolved those functions most critical for the human way of life: attention and memory, language, and thought.

Figure 2.1 traces the development of skull capacity from the first homonid of two million years ago to the Neanderthal of Middle Europe, 75,000 years ago. Skull capacity increased from about 500 cc to 1500 cc, and the amount of brain tissue devoted to higher mental processes showed a steady, dramatic increase.

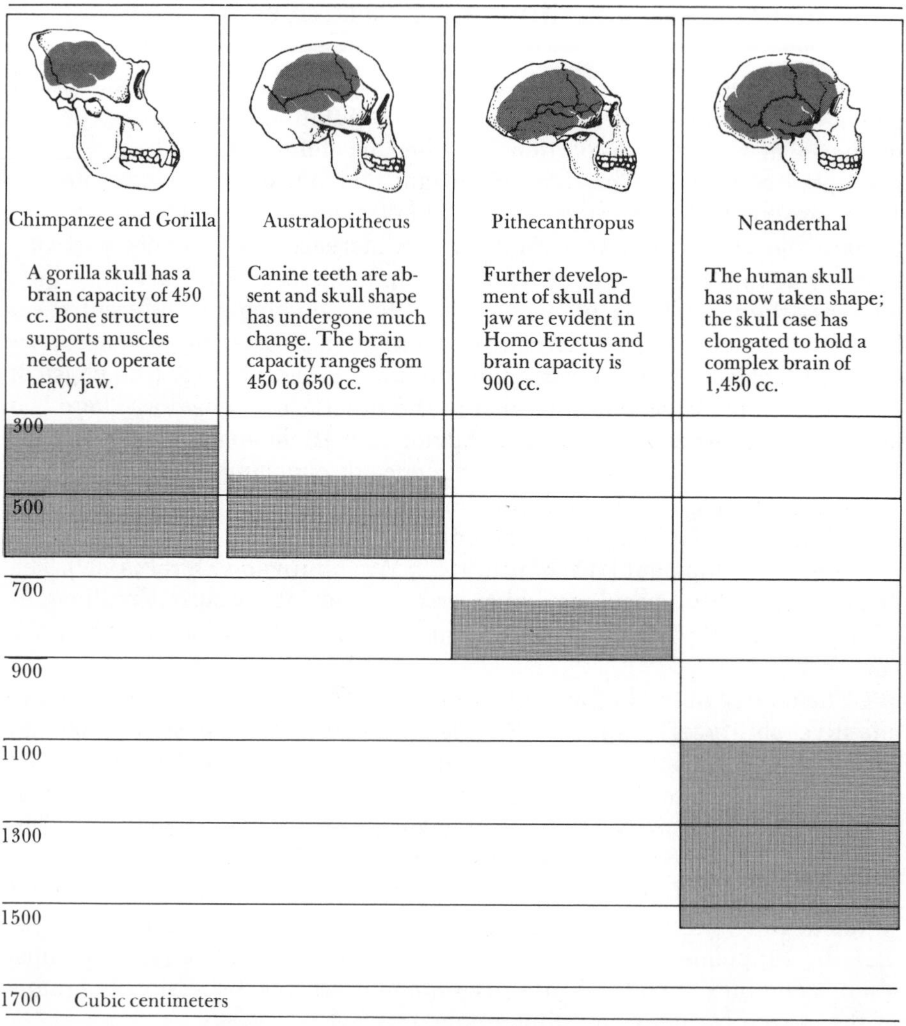

Chimpanzee and Gorilla	Australopithecus	Pithecanthropus	Neanderthal
A gorilla skull has a brain capacity of 450 cc. Bone structure supports muscles needed to operate heavy jaw.	Canine teeth are absent and skull shape has undergone much change. The brain capacity ranges from 450 to 650 cc.	Further development of skull and jaw are evident in Homo Erectus and brain capacity is 900 cc.	The human skull has now taken shape; the skull case has elongated to hold a complex brain of 1,450 cc.

300			
500			
700			
900			
1100			
1300			
1500			
1700	Cubic centimeters		

Fig. 2.1. Evolution of the human brain over several million years. Shaded blocks exhibit range in cubic centimeters of brain size. Shaded portions of skulls trace dramatic development of cortex in response to developing behavior.

Australopithecines and the millions of humans who followed them migrated in response to environmental demands. Their initial movements, probably dictated by availability of local food supplies, must have been very limited. As hunting skills and tool use improved, however, the range of migrating behavior increased. Receding ice sheets enabled them to move into Asia and Europe. The history of their dispersion, read in fossils and artifacts left behind, documents the joint development of human brain and behavior.

Increased brain capacity and specialization of function weren't the only factors in human evolution. Of tremendous importance for the evolution of social behavior and culture was a marked prolongation of individual development: Gestation was greatly prolonged, and infantile characteristics were retained well into life. *This prolongation of relative helplessness was the essential foundation for human socialization.* Along with this came a greater specialization of sex roles as adult females remained with and cared for the young and males joined the hunting groups. The family unit evolved.

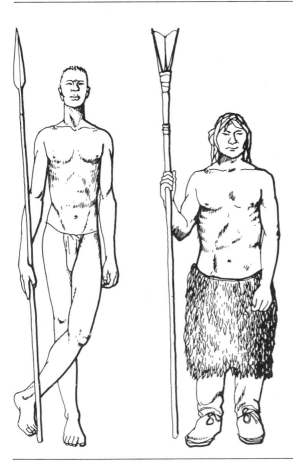

Fig. 2.2. Human adaptation to climate is typified by Nilotic Negro of the Sudan (left) and arctic Eskimo (right). Greater body surface of Negro facilitates dissipation of unneeded body heat; proportionately greater bulk of the Eskimo conserves body heat. (Adapted from W. H. Howells, "The distribution of man." Copyright © 1960 by Scientific American, Inc. All rights reserved.)

With these developments a further change of immense significance occurred. Humans began to transform their environment actively, rather than acting as passive recipients of environmental circumstances. They shaped existing environments and created new ones. Thus *a nongenetic evolution began with cultural transmission of information and change.* Physical conditions and natural resources were brought increasingly under control and, in the process of civilizing themselves, humans dramatically altered their own evolution. The pattern of natural selection was modified and replaced with self-created patterns of cultural evolution. We have taken the crucial step of controlling our own future; it is not yet clear where that step will lead us.

That contemporary humans are their own creation is evident when we consider the entire human family. Within this single species, some 30 social sub-groups exist, each relatively distinct in gene pool and numerous details of physical appearance. Human wanderings spelled selective exposure to widely varying environmental circumstances, leading to selective forces favoring those behavioral and physical traits most adaptive to particular environmental conditions. Figure 2.2 illustrates certain differences that originated in structural adaptation to environment.

BEHAVIOR GENETICS

Biological Individuality

Biological approaches to human behavior begin with the assumption that humans are biologically unique. This assumption follows directly from the fact of genetic uniqueness, and biological individuality has been well documented (Williams, 1956). Throughout the skeletal, muscular, circulatory, endocrine, and nervous systems of the body, there is compelling evidence of incredible morphological variation among individuals. Bodily organs, for example, vary greatly in shape and over a range of six- to ten-fold in size. Endocrine glands display equally wide variation; the thyroid gland varies in weight about six-fold, and protein-bound iodine of the blood, which measures hormonal output, varies to about the same extent. The number of Islets of Langerhans, which are responsible for insulin production, varies over a ten-fold range in diabetes-free individuals. The thickness of the adrenal cortex, where important adrenal hormones originate, varies about ten-fold. All individuals possess distinctive endocrine systems, and hormonal activities vary over a seven-fold range in individuals who are not experiencing known hormonal difficulty.

What are the consequences of such enormous differences in biological makeup? The most basic consequence is to question the search for, and the attempted application of, general laws applicable to the "typical" organism. Thus, in an experiment in psychology, a sample of individuals is studied to estimate the effects of a particular procedure or experimental treatment on the population which the sample of individuals presumably represents. However, there may be a serious defect in this approach: Biological individuality makes it clear that the range of permissible generalization may be very restricted. The outcome obtained with one group of subjects may be quite different from that obtained with a different group. Divergent results obtained by different investigators working on the same problem may be due not only to subtle nuances in procedure, apparatus, or technique; the possibility always exists that there are different subgroups within a species to which genuinely different experimental effects apply. These would appear to be the biological facts of life in the science of psychology.

Genetics and Behavior

The relationship of observable behavior, the phenotype, to the underlying genetic structure, the genotype, is highly complex. Although the genotype remains fixed, its expression in behavior changes with development, learning, and environmental variation. The action of genes depends on the environment and the experience necessary for the genes to be exhibited in the phenotype. Although the environment does not directly alter the genes, it can and does affect their expression in observable behavior.

There are no special sets of genes for behavior control. All genes are merely complex nucleoproteins functioning as a template for the production of proteins in the cell. While some gene action can be described in terms of effects upon particular chemical processes, gene effects in humans are rarely traceable to microchemical action. The consequence is that much behavioral variation known to be heritable cannot be correlated with a specific metabolic pathway, organic structure, or function. That leads to the question: *What is inherited?* This question underlies an important and widely misunderstood issue.

Whatever it is that is genetically transmitted is somehow coded into the chemistry of the individual genes. This genetic encoding influences behavior in such a way that different genotypes, exposed to identical environments, turn out differently. Some of the variance in behavioral traits is therefore due to variance in genetic structure. But let us be clear: *Behavior, per se, is not inherited.* The methods of behavior genetics apply to the study of differences in behavior, especially to differences in the acquisition or modification of behavior patterns. The content of a person's behavioral repertoire is quite certainly a product of that person's experience and learning. One does not inherit the American way of life; one learns it. And the principle involved here is true for all interesting patterns of molar behavior in animals and humans.

> Behavior is a phenotype and like any other organismic character can be related *in at least some of its aspects* to genotype. The fact that a person speaks German may be quite independent of heredity; but the fact that he was able to learn it quickly, the fact that he can pronounce it aptly, and the fact that he uses it with literary skill call in part for a genetic explanation. (Thompson, 1968, p. 196)

The total variability in behavior can be partitioned into three components, those due to heredity, environment, and their interaction. The concept of heritability is commonly used to refer to that portion of behavioral variance due to hereditary differences. Although frequently useful, heritability is a concept whose meaning must be carefully specified. Genes, not behaviors, are inherited. The heritability concept refers to the extent to which differences in behavior can be related to underlying differences in the genes. Where no gene differences exist (as among identical twins or inbred strains of animals), all behavioral variance will be environmental in origin. Where large gene differences exist in the context of controlled environmental variation (as in laboratory comparisons of inbred strains of animals), behavior differences will be largely genetic in origin. And where large differences exist both in genes and in trait-relevant experiences (as in comparisons of measured IQ among different human races), heritability can only be estimated and then only crudely.

The methods of human behavior genetics concern differences in behavior patterns in different people. Using the word "inherited" in this context always implies that the differences in behavior correspond to differences in genes. Thus the entire question of heritability applies to groups of individuals, neither to any one individual nor to any one kind of behavior. Heritability is always a characteristic of populations rather than of individuals.

These comments apply directly to the roles of nature and nurture, i.e., heredity and environment, in the development of human behavior. Every behavioral characteristic is influenced by genes as well as by environment, so that developmental changes must be analyzed in terms of the continuing interaction of the two. Behavioral variation may sometimes be largely attributable to variation in nurture, sometimes to variation in nature. Individual differences important to personality study arise from the reciprocal action of differences in human biological makeup and experiential history.

Methods and Data of Behavior Genetics

Like psychology itself, behavior genetics was practiced long before it was recognized as a formal scientific discipline. Kennel operators have bred dogs for hunting as long as gardeners have cultivated hybrid roses and begonias. That genes make a difference in behavior as well as appearance is familiar to everyone.

Two approaches are used in the experimental study of genotypic influences on animal behavior: *selection* and *the analysis of pure strains*. In selection, or selective breeding as it is often called, one begins with individual differences in behavior (phenotype) and seeks to establish that genetic differences underlie the behavioral variance. Selective mating is practiced over generations in an effort to establish distinct hereditary lines which differ in the behavioral characteristics for which they were selected. That such selection is possible strongly suggests that the differences in behavior which exist in the population are related to underlying differences in the genes.

The selection method can be contrasted with a second, the analysis of pure strains. Here one begins with individual differences in the genotype and seeks to establish consequent behavioral differences. The procedure employs established strains that were originally selected for differences of a nonpsychological nature, such as coat color. The demonstration of behavioral differences between such genetically pure strains, given adequate control of environmental variables, provides a second source of evidence for genotypic control of behavioral variation.

The use of inbred strains is a powerful tool in behavior-genetic analysis. A large number of identical genotypes can be studied in a variety of environments and sophisticated biometrical analysis applied to traits of interest. The mechanics of these procedures are rather complex, but their logic is conceptually clear: Differences between animals of the same strain, or the same hybrid stock, must be environmental in origin, whereas behavioral differences between animals of different strains will be both genetic and environmental. The essence of the analysis is the study of the variability of a behavior pattern within and between strains to determine the extent and nature of genotypic environmental interaction.

Maternal effects. Evidence suggests that anxious mothers tend to have fearful offspring. Does this finding constitute evidence of the genetic transmission of anxiety? Clearly not, since anxious mothers may transmit anxiety to their offspring either prenatally via hormonal mechanisms activated by the anxiety state or postnatally via social modeling. Controls for maternal effects and procedures to estimate their influence are critically important to behavior-genetic study.

Figure 2.3 summarizes techniques for controlling postnatal maternal effects via crossfostering and prenatal maternal effects by reciprocal crossing.

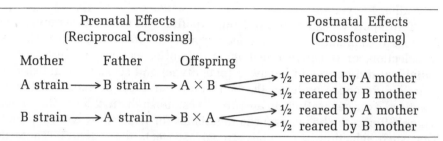

	Prenatal Effects (Reciprocal Crossing)		Postnatal Effects (Crossfostering)
Mother	Father	Offspring	
A strain ⟶ B strain	⟶ A × B	→ ½ reared by A mother → ½ reared by B mother
B strain ⟶ A strain	⟶ B × A	→ ½ reared by A mother → ½ reared by B mother

Fig. 2.3. Design typically used to determine the prenatal maternal effects of a given strain in some aspect of animal behavior. In this example, the two strains under comparison are A and B. Note that reciprocal crossing is used to determine prenatal effects of the maternal strain. Crossfostering allows us to control for and assess postnatal effects of the maternal strain.

Selection studies and analysis of pure strains have demonstrated that gene differences underlie variation in a diverse array of behaviors—activity levels, maze-learning abilities, avoidance-conditioning rates, aggressiveness and dominance, seizure susceptibility, preference for alcohol, response to drugs, and many other behavior dimensions.

One approach is to focus on specific behaviors, of which emotionality is a convenient illustration. Placed in an unfamiliar or noxious environment, rodents display a pattern of behavior involving defecation-urination and an inhibition of gross motor movement. This behavior pattern, known to reflect emotional reactivity, lends itself to objective scoring in a laboratory apparatus called an *open field*. Selection studies for emotional reactivity in rats (Hall, 1938; Broadhurst, 1960) demonstrate rapid divergence of the high- and low-reactive lines. After the first few generations of selective breeding, little overlap remains in the emotional responsiveness of the two selected lines. Careful controls for prenatal and postnatal effects have been employed (Broadhurst, 1961), and neither crossfostering litters nor reciprocal crosses between the two lines reveals significant maternal effects. The importance of gene differences in determining emotional reactivity in rodents is also evident in differences between inbred strains and, more importantly, in dramatic interaction of environmental stimulation with different genotypes. Traumatic, noxious stimulation in infancy may increase or decrease adult emotionality, or it may have no effect whatever, depending on the genotype of the animal studied (Henderson, 1967).

The impact of gene differences for behavior can be appreciated in an alternative way by focusing on specific genotypes, rather than on specific behaviors. This direct approach to genotype-behavior correlation has been illustrated (Jones, 1965) with three inbred strains of mice in which behavior was extensively studied. The three strains—the Bagg albino, the C57 black, and the C3H agouti—were developed by cancer researchers for differing susceptibility to spontaneous mammary cancer. After reviewing behavior differences among the three strains in various tests, Jones constructed miniature behavior profiles to characterize the particular strains. For example, the albinos are emotionally reactive, slow to learn, and quick to extinguish, whereas the C57 mice are emotionally nonreactive and slow to attack but are excellent fighters when provoked:

> ... the blacks ... seem very good all-around mice: comfortable and active in an open field, moderate in appetite, competent in avoidance situations, slow to anger, and tough in a fight. The virtue, however, of the C57 black mouse is not complete: the strain has an unmistakable yen for alcohol. . . .
>
> Though the virtue of the C57 blacks may be blemished, sluggishness of the Bagg albinos seems to be perfect. Not only are they inactive in an open field, poor in avoidance training, and ineffective in battle, they are also slow to copulate with an estrous female.*

Jones then adds that even the albinos may have their points, and he interprets some evidence from a foster-rearing study to suggest that Bagg albino females make superior mothers. The amusing manner in which Jones has sketched these behavior profiles only underscores his serious argument that gene-based differences in behavior appear with striking regularity. With the single exception of seizure susceptibility, every behavior thus far studied shows evidence of the established genetic differences among these three strains.

Human research: twin and family studies.   For obvious ethical reasons, the history and genetic background of human subjects cannot be experimentally manipulated. However the natural occurrence of human twins provides a powerful research method for studying the relative influence of genotypic and environmental contributions to a trait.

Because identical or monozygotic twins arise from the division of a single zygote (fertilized egg), both members of the pair have an identical

---

* From M. B. Jones, "Behavior genetics," in P. F. Regan and E. G. Pattishall, Jr. (eds.) *Behavioral Science Contributions to Psychiatry*, International Psychiatric Clinics, 2, 1965, Little, Brown, and Co., pp. 238–239.

genotype. Any observed differences in behavior must be environmental in origin. By contrast, fraternal or dizygotic twins, which derive from the fertilization and separate development of two independent ova, are genetically as different as ordinary siblings. On the average, they share only 50 percent of their genes in common. Observed differences between fraternal pairs reflect differences in genetic structure *and* social experience.

Comparison of a sample of identical co-twins with same-sexed fraternal pairs, properly matched on appropriate variables, offers a powerful tool in behavior-genetic analysis. Genetically identical pairs are contrasted with genetically dissimilar pairs. All pairs are of the same age and sex, and all pairs have shared a common intrauterine environment. In addition, maternal age, family background, and many other aspects of social experience are intrinsically controlled within pairs.

Comparison between twin samples may be made for either qualitative or quantitative data. For qualitative (all-or-none) data, we measure the trait by independently noting whether it is present or absent in both members. When both members of a twin pair exhibit a trait, or when it is absent in both, the pair is *concordant,* or phenotypically similar. When only one member of a pair possesses a trait, the pair is *discordant.* The extent to which identical and fraternal twin pairs differ in degree of concordance provides a gross estimate of the proportion of phenotypic variance attributable to genotypic differences. A significantly higher concordance rate among identical co-twins for a particular behavior or disease suggests a significant genetic influence in the causal history of that behavior or disease. For a continuous trait that is quantitatively measured, the relative influence of genotypic and environmental contributions to the trait can be estimated by a comparison of variance within fraternal and identical twin-pair samples.

A compilation of concordance ratios for a variety of behaviors, traits, habits, and diseases appears in Table 2.1. Three findings emerge from these data. First, for all behaviors and characteristics listed, concordance in identical twin pairs is greater than that for fraternals; genotypic differences appear to underlie, at least in part, differences in these varied phenotypic behaviors. Second, the extent of the genetic influence varies quite widely for different traits and characteristics. Finally, concordance in identical co-twins is always less than 100 percent even for a characteristic like eye color, and concordance among identical pairs for some traits is quite low, though greater than that for fraternals. In short, genetic and environmental factors always operate for all behavior, but the relative influence of either factor varies from one trait to another.

A number of procedural difficulties arise in twin research that can best be discussed in the context of substantive findings from representa-

Table 2.1 Representative results from twin studies for selected traits, behaviors, and diseases. Percentage concordance is indicated by shaded area; numbers in parentheses indicate the number of twin pairs scored. (Adapted from M. W. Strickberger, *Genetics*, Macmillan, New York, 1968, p. 181. Used by permission.)

	Percent concordance (shaded areas)			
	Identical twins	100	Fraternal twins	100
Hair color	89%	(215)	22%	(156)
Eye color	99.6%	(256)	28%	(194)
Blood pressure	63%	(62)	36%	(80)
Pulse rate	56%	(84)	34%	(67)
Measles	95%	(189)	87%	(146)
Clubfoot	32%	(40)	3%	(134)
Diabetes mellitus	84%	(63)	37%	(70)
Tuberculosis	74%	(190)	28%	(427)
Epilepsy (idiopathic)	72%	(61)	15%	(197)
Paralytic polio	36%	(14)	6%	(33)
Scarlet fever	64%	(31)	47%	(30)
Rickets	88%	(60)	22%	(74)
Stomach cancer	27%	(11)	4%	(24)
Smoking habit	91%	(34)	65%	(43)
Alcohol drinking	100%	(34)	86%	(43)
Coffee drinking	94%	(34)	79%	(43)
Feeblemindedness	94%	(217)	47%	(260)
Schizophrenia	80%	(395)	13%	(989)
Manic-depressive psychosis	77%	(62)	19%	(165)
Mongolism	89%	(18)	7%	(60)
Criminality	68%	(143)	28%	(142)

tive studies. However, one difficulty is so basic to all twin research that it is necessary to review it briefly here. Identical twins are more likely to share similar social-learning histories than same-sexed fraternal twins. They are more likely to dress alike, share common friends, and study together (Smith, 1965). Consequently, greater similarity in behavior among identical twins cannot be interpreted as solely genetic in origin.

Nonetheless, it is not correct to infer that identical co-twins are behaviorally more similar merely because of environmental pressures for similarity. A significant number of parents prove to be mistaken about whether their same-sexed twins are fraternals or identicals, and study of such "misclassified" pairs provides important evidence for the logic of twin research.

Actual twin zygosity, determined by systematic study of a number of genetically controlled blood groupings, can be compared with parental beliefs about their offspring. The frequency of parental misclassification is surprisingly high, ranging from 12–35% among pairs of adolescent twins. Perhaps one-third of all fraternal twins are being reared as identicals (Smith, 1965; Scarr, 1968). An important study of misclassified female pairs (Scarr, 1968) suggests that similarity in both twins' behavior and in parental treatment of them is more a function of genetic relatedness than of parents' beliefs about "identicalness." For example, true identical co-twins are likely to dress alike even if their mother believes them to be fraternal, and these misclassified identical pairs are more likely to dress alike than true fraternal co-twins being reared as identicals.

In principle, the confounding of the effects of shared genes with those of common social experience among identical co-twins could be disentangled by assessing adult similarities in a large sample of identical twins reared apart from infancy. Not surprisingly, however, such a sample does not exist. But an alternative technique, equally powerful and more readily employed, is available through the study of individuals who are adopted in infancy and foster-reared by nonrelatives. Adoption studies separate the genetic transmission of the biological parents from the psychosocial transmission contributed by the foster parents. The strategy and potential of this approach can be illustrated by recent reports on the adult status of foster-reared offspring born to schizophrenic parents.

In one study of this type (Heston, 1966), a group of 47 subjects born to schizophrenic mothers institutionalized in a state mental hospital were matched to 50 foster-reared controls. The controls, whose mothers had no known psychiatric history, were selected from records of the same foundling homes that received the experimental subjects; they were matched for sex, age, type of eventual placement, and length of time in child-care institutions. The adult follow-up was based on a careful review of public records and personal history. The completed dossier for each subject was then independently evaluated by two psychiatrists without knowledge of the biological background of the subjects. Results revealed a heavy concentration of psychiatric disability among the experimental subjects—those born to psychotic mothers. The five subjects independently diagnosed as schizophrenic were all members of the experimental group. Character disorders and other evidence of adjustment difficulties, such as psychiatric discharge from the Armed Services, were also significantly more common among experimental subjects. Similar results have been reported from an adoption study from Denmark (Rosenthal et al., 1968); the Danish findings are particularly important, because they rule out toxic factors in the intrauterine environment as a basis for these results.

In recent years other investigators have employed adoption studies to assess the role of genetic predispositions in alcoholism and criminality (Goodwin et al., 1973; Crowe, 1972); the approach appears to be a powerful method with which to disentangle genetic and environmental determinants of complex behaviors.

Karyotype analysis. The tendency to develop tuberculosis, to dress alike, or to be schizophrenic can be analyzed by twin-family studies. Such studies focus on a specific behavior and are the traditional approach to behavior-genetic analysis. But in a manner analogous to that illustrated with inbred strains of mice, an alternative approach is to focus on a specific genotype rather than on a specific trait. Advances in cytogenetics have provided the means for direct study of human chromosomes, and various nonlethal irregularities in the number and structure of chromosomes occur with sufficient frequency to permit the assessment of their behavioral correlates.

In a typical technique, chromosomes are obtained for study from white blood cells cultivated in a medium facilitating cell division, the division is arrested, and the cells are swollen. Chromosomes are then visible for microscopic examination and can be distinguished one from another by length and structural characteristics. An enlarged photomicrograph is prepared, and the individual chromosomes are cut out and arranged in a standard sequence, called the *karyotype* of the individual (see Fig. 2.4).

The karyotype of the normal human female is designated as 46,XX; that is, cells from the normal female possess 46 chromosomes, consisting of 44 autosomes and two X chromosomes. The karyotype of the normal human male is designated as 46,XY. Karyotypic abnormalities do occur, however, in both autosomes and sex chromosomes, and many, if not all, produce significant behavioral effects. Perhaps the most important of

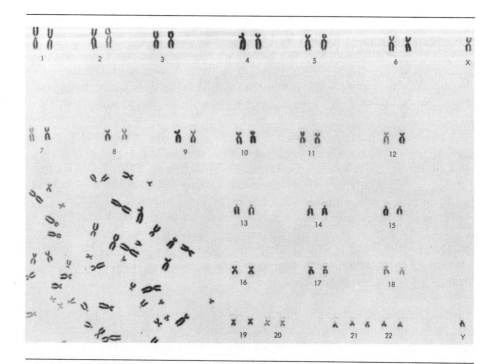

Fig. 2.4. Karyotype of Down's syndrome, or mongolism. (From J. German, "Studying human chromosomes today," *American Scientist*, 1970, **58**, 182–201. Reprinted by permission, *American Scientist*, journal of Sigma Xi, The Scientific Society of North America.)

these is Down's syndrome. This severe and frequent form of mental retardation is a developmental consequence of an additional small autosome identified at Locus No. 21. The discovery of the chromosomal basis for Down's syndrome has stimulated intensive research on karyotype-behavior associations, and results of that research have already contributed to understanding human personality.

Principles of Behavior-genetics Analysis

Behavior-genetics analysis, whether arising from study of inbred strains of animals or from twin and family research in humans, must eventually answer the question: What is the relationship between genes and overt behavior? We know that behavior itself is not inherited. The basic factors in heredity, the genes, are constructed from a spiral molecule of deoxyribonucleic acid (DNA), and genes can act only by controlling the synthesis of proteins. This is obviously a long way from organized behavior. The relationship between genes and their phenotypic behavioral effects is very complex; interactions among genes and between genes and environmental factors occur to modulate and complicate the genotypic-behavior relationship.

What is inherited is not behavior, but a predisposition that biases behavior development. That predisposition may take several forms, but for behavior-genetic analysis, two general principles seem paramount. The first is *differential susceptibility,* or the interaction of the genotype with its environment; the second is *selective exposure,* or the correlation of a genotype with its experience.

Susceptibility: genotypic-experiential interaction.   Several examples have been cited in which the intensity, or even the direction, of an environmental treatment is dependent on the genotype of the organism. Simply stated, the effect of experience depends in part on the genotype to which that experience occurs. As an example, consider the question of differential susceptibility to common diseases in humans.

Refer again to the concordances presented in Table 2.1. A number of diseases of diverse specific causes demonstrate significantly higher concordance in identical twin pairs. For each of these diseases we know that an external, environmental agent is necessary in the history of the disease entity. Yet the twin data in Table 2.1 clearly indicate that different genotypes are not equally susceptible to that environmental agent. Thus, while nongenetic factors play a dominant role in the causal history of these diseases, individuals are differentially susceptible to infection by the microorganisms underlying tuberculosis, polio, or scarlet fever, to the nutritional deficiency in rickets, or to the metabolic disturbance represented by diabetes. Interaction is at the very core of the disease problem. What is genetically transmitted is a predisposition, rather than the disease in any overt sense.

Let us take a brief look at tuberculosis, an infectious disease in which the causative agent is the tubercle bacillus. We shall see that susceptibility to the bacillus varies and that the variation is associated with genetic factors.

Table 2.2 presents percentages of tuberculosis for members of families in each of which there is a tuberculous twin. The risk of developing tuberculosis, which is slightly above one percent in the general population, rises with increasing genetic similarity to a tuberculous patient. The much higher risk for identical co-twins, compared with fraternals, provides evidence that genetic factors are at least partly responsible.

Table 2.2 Percentage of tuberculosis in families of tuberculous twins.*

Relationship to tuberculous twin	N	Percentage affected (risk)
Unrelated (general population)		approx. 1.4
Spouses	226	7.1
Half-siblings	42	11.9
Parents	688	16.9
Siblings	720	25.5
Fraternal co-twin	230	25.6
Identical co-twin	78	87.3

* Derived from Kallmann and Reisner, *J. Heredity*, **34**:293–301, 1943.

Note, however, that Table 2.2 also reveals the part played by the bacillus. Thus the spouse of a tuberculous twin has a risk of approximately seven percent of developing tuberculosis, although spouses are genetically no more alike than are two unrelated individuals randomly selected from the general population, for whom risk is one percent. Similarly, there is a higher risk between two siblings than between parent and child, although siblings are no more alike genetically. These findings, which do not admit of simple genetic explanation, must reflect differences in the probability of exposure.

Nevertheless, more than mere exposure is involved. Concordance among identical co-twins is very much higher than the percentage of household associates of open cases who develop tuberculosis. Some factor other than exposure must influence development of the disease, and that factor must be differences in susceptibility mediated by the genotype. Animal evidence indicates that, given equal exposure to the same bacilli, different genotypes respond differently.

Given that an invasion by the bacillus is necessary for the development of tuberculosis, two findings emerge: (1) not everyone runs an equal risk of exposure, and (2) not everyone is equally susceptible, once exposed. Differences in gene-determined susceptibility interact with exposure to a specific environmental agent in the causal history of the disease.

The circumstances just described for tuberculosis are also true, though less readily demonstrable, for experiences of all types. The effect of any experiential event is modified and refracted by the genotype to which that experience occurs. The notion that individuals are equally and uniformly affected by experience is simply untenable.

Selective exposure: genotypic-experiential correlation.   The great genetic diversity among individuals leads to the second principle of behavior-genetic analysis: The genotype will, in part, determine the nature of experience to which the individual is exposed. Individuals who differ markedly in their appearance, physiological functioning, or behavioral predisposition will be exposed to quite different patterns of experience.

One dramatic example is repeated findings that the rate of maturational development has stable personality correlates. From many lines of evidence we know that gene differences underlie the rate at which an individual moves through the maturational changes of puberty; in turn, the speed with which one developmentally matures is related to a wide variety of personality correlates, including anxiety and social dominance. These data appear to be explicable as an experiential-constitutional correlation in that wide differences in maturational development will, in our culture, inevitably lead to wide differences in social and personal experiences. That the adolescent girl who is very late to mature and acquire secondary sexual characteristics is often dependent and socially anxious must reflect the manner in which her peers and parents respond to her. Conversely, that the adolescent who is early to mature is likely to be socially dominant and relatively free of interpersonal anxiety in both adolescence and adulthood reflects the fact that early biological maturation is the stimulus for granting social responsibility early. One who appears to be an adult is frequently treated accordingly regardless of chronological age. The long-range results of such patterns of social reinforcement are obvious.

We have, then, two principles of behavior-genetic development. The first, differential susceptibility, focuses on the genotype as reactive to experience, while the second, selective exposure, focuses on the genotype as stimulus for experience. Most behaviors of interest to personality study involve a combination of the two processes. An example is the well-documented association between muscular physique and delinquent behavior: About twice as many delinquents as nondelinquents possess muscular physiques. How do we explain such a finding? First, muscular strength, athletic prowess, and physical stamina are relatively direct consequences of gene action. Second, possession of these attributes, at least in certain subcultures, will lead to a history of selective reinforcement for delinquent acts. Thus the ultimate association between constitution and behavior is a direct result of gene action and an indirect consequence of the selective exposure and differential reinforcement history of the delinquent individual. This joint influence of the genotype on developing behavior may be called the "looking-glass" theorem: Differences in physique and behavioral predispositions (arising as relatively direct results of gene differences) create the stimulus for differential social learning, which tends to selectively reinforce the initial predispositions. The developmental consequence is that genotypic differences in behavioral dispositions become strengthened through experience, because they create opportunities for their expression, and the expression gets reinforced.

EARLY EXPERIENCE

That the experiences of one's early life affect later behavior is widely assumed. Parental practices, educational policies, and Sunday-school procedures are predicated on the belief that experiences acquired in childhood have important consequences for adult behavior. Within psychology, the notion that infantile trauma, nurturant affection, and exposure to unusually enriched or deprived environments have consequences for a lifetime of behavior has provided the theoretical impetus for extensive research.

Prenatal Experience

Folklore abounds on the presumed influence of prenatal experience on adult behavior. During the Victorian period, it was common for a pregnant woman to engage in such activities as attending music concerts or reading the literary classics in hopes that her child would acquire special aptitudes in these areas. Although there is no basis to encourage the renewal of this practice, the thalidomide disaster, the infants of drug-addicted mothers, and the well-known consequences of German measles during early pregnancy attest to the disastrous effect on the developing fetus of an abnormal intrauterine environment.

Many external factors modify the intrauterine environment of the developing fetus to influence both structure and function. Relatively direct effects result from drugs, hormones, X-rays, and alterations of maternal diet.

Administration of pituitary growth hormone to pregnant rats significantly increases the number of brain cells, total brain weight, and cortical cell density in their offspring; when mature, these offspring demonstrate superior performance in learning complex mazes. Conversely, protein deficiency in early fetal life decreases the number and size of brain cells (Zamenhof, Van Marthens, and Margolis, 1968). Brains of offspring born to rats maintained on protein-insufficient diets during gestation contain significantly less DNA, and the deficiency in number of cortical neurons may be irreversible. Effects from maternal malnutrition in humans have long been known, and deficits in physical growth and biochemical maturation, together with retarded intellectual and emotional development, are well documented (Eichenwald and Fry, 1969). Protein-calorie deficit during prenatal and early life can cause profound reduction in behavioral responsiveness and concomitant functional abnormalities in the central nervous system.

Of particular interest to personality study are the indirect effects that arise through social experience. For example, psychological stress will elicit in the pregnant mother a neuroendocrine response that will alter the chemical composition of her blood and affect the fetus through placental transfer. Because emotional reactivity is mediated by the endocrine system, studies of the effects of maternal emotion on subsequent behavior of the offspring are of special interest.

That such indirect effects do occur is established by study of emotional reactivity in rodents. The experiences of pregnant mice or rats can have lasting effects on the emotional responsiveness of their offspring. Exposure of a pregnant rat to a buzzer which was associated with shock prior to the rat's mating will significantly elevate emotionality in her offspring (Thompson, 1957). Conversely, systematic gentling of a rat during pregnancy will significantly decrease the adult emotional responsiveness of her offspring (Ader and Conklin, 1963).

Parallel data for human mothers are difficult to obtain, since it is not possible to experimentally manipulate stress levels during gestation. Research is necessarily correlational in design, and it is subject to serious limitations. Nonetheless, some preliminary evidence associating maternal stress with neonate behavior has been obtained. In one reported study (Ottinger and Simmons, 1964), an anxiety questionnaire was administered to a sample of obstetrics patients during each trimester of pregnancy; babies born to mothers scoring at the two extremes of the anxiety scale were compared for amounts of crying during the first few days of life. The amount was significantly greater among neonates born to anxious mothers.

Thus, in a manner analogous to animal research findings which show that induced maternal stress increases emotional reactivity in the offspring, the anxiety level of human mothers during gestation is related to demonstrable differences in neonate behavior. Intensive study of prenatal determinants of human behavior should be given high priority in future research (Joffe, 1969).

Early Postnatal Experience

Personality theories have typically assumed that early postnatal experiences exert a profound impact upon subsequent behavior development. Available evidence in general supports this theoretical assumption. However, our understanding of the effects of early experience remains quite limited. Can the effects of early experience influence adult behavior? By what mechanism(s) does early experience affect adult behavior? Can the effects of early experiences be modified by subsequent learning? Are there critical periods in personality development during which certain experiences must occur? Such questions cannot yet be answered with certainty, but some possible explanatory models for the effects of early experience have been suggested (Fuller and Waller, 1962).

The simplest explanation of the effects of early experience is based on the assumption that first responses preempt others and have continuing priority throughout the organism's life. Alternative behaviors are not tried because the initial response is adequately reinforced. If the concept of a *critical period* is added to that of preemption, we can account for many phenomena in the social development of mammals. The essential assumption of the critical-period idea is that the probability of eliciting a response from a novel stimulus is some function of the organism's age. At certain critical periods, an organism will tend to emit specific responses with very high probability; if such responses are adaptive and reinforced, they may preempt alternative response mechanisms and assume pervasive importance in development.

A second explanatory concept, arising primarily from studies of infantile deprivation, is based on the notion that the organization of perceptual and cognitive processes is possible during only a limited period of early life. An organism deprived of normal stimulation during this period may fail to develop adequate learning in adulthood. Conversely, an unusually enriched and stimulating environment in infancy may promote rapid maturational development leading to superior adult performance. Infantile stimulation has been shown to increase markedly the maturation of hormonal systems, and this accelerated development of physiological processes may underlie the effects of early experience upon subsequent behavior.

A final explanatory concept of the effects of early experience is based on the assumption of age differences in susceptibility to trauma. There is evidence that the nervous systems of young animals are more readily injured by physical agents such as infections or physically noxious stimulation. Although it is difficult to specify the nature and effect of *psychological trauma*, many theorists, including Freud, have maintained that the young organism is particularly susceptible to psychological trauma.

These notions are not mutually exclusive, nor do they exhaust the possibilities. They do suggest the complexity of the effects of early experience, and they indicate that different mechanisms may underlie the effects of different experiential processes. Note also that these hypotheses reveal the biological nature of theories of early experience: each model assumes that *the young organism is somehow differentially susceptible to effects of stimulation*. These theories are logically similar to those in which differential susceptibility in different genotypes is assumed, but the emphasis is now on *ontogenetic* (developmental) differences, rather than *phylogenetic* (evolutionary) differences.

Enrichment.   One of the earliest studies in this area was an informal experiment by Donald Hebb, who took home some laboratory rats and allowed his daughters to rear them as pets (Hebb, 1949). We need to remind ourselves that in a usual laboratory situation the rat is provided with very constant environmental stimulation: Temperature, humidity, light, and social contact are rigorously controlled. By contrast, the pet rats in the Hebb household had a markedly increased interaction with people, as well as greatly enriched exposure to physical objects and environmental stimuli. In adulthood, the pet rats exhibited superior performance in maze abilities when compared with controls reared in the laboratory.

Following that exploratory study, a number of experiments were performed contrasting "free environments" with restricted ones. Results support the original finding that enriched early experience promotes superior adult performance. Further, it is now known that infantile deprivation and enrichment affect the development of nervous tissue as well as the development of behavior. Extensive studies have systematically explored the effects of early infantile stimulation on biological and behavioral development. In many of these experiments, the stimulation consists merely of taking an individual animal out of the litter and placing it in a separate container for a few minutes daily during the preweaning period. Results from this seemingly innocuous procedure affect both structure and function (Denenberg, 1967; Levine, 1962). The handled rats grow up to be heartier adults. They grow faster, live longer, and withstand physical stress better than the unhandled controls. Development is accelerated in a number of ways. In stimulated animals the eyes open sooner, hair grows faster, and the central nervous system matures earlier; and in adulthood, stimulated animals are less disrupted by unfamiliar environments.

A curious finding is that various physical stimuli produce the same effect as gentle handling. Shock, shaking, temperature change, and other sources of stimulation have common effects. Whatever its source, stimulation apparently promotes activity of the adrenal glands, and the accelerated development of the endocrine system affects not only physiological maturation, but adult behavior as well.

Deprivation.   Rearing an animal under severe sensory and social deprivation has dramatic consequences for its development. An infant chimpanzee raised in complete darkness suffers degeneration of the ganglion cells in its retina. If it is left in darkness for as long as a year, the loss of ganglion cells is extensive and permanent. *Function is necessary for development,* and an organism will not develop normally in the absence of normal stimulation. Sensory deprivation has effects on behavior as well as structure. The importance of visual experience for the acquisition of normal perceptual learning has been documented (Hebb, 1949). Animals that are deprived of or restricted in normal visual or auditory input (and humans who have congenital cataracts removed in childhood) clearly demonstrate lasting impairment from early sensory deprivation. Even more dramatic effects arise from social deprivation in infancy; profound consequences for adult sexuality and socialization are commonly found.

Moreover, anthropologists have discovered that in those societies where newborn infants are treated with some rather drastic stimulation such as infant scarification rites, adults are taller, on the average, than members of societies that do not practice such drastic treatments. Conversely, later assessments of intellectual, motor, and personality behaviors in infants who were reared in state orphanages where stimulation was minimal reveal consistent evidence of maladaptive behavior and impaired intellectual and motor functioning. We cannot, of course, immediately conclude that newborn babies should be treated roughly for their own good! Nonetheless, all available evidence indicates that infantile stimulation is essential to normal development, and drastic reductions in amount and variety of stimulation impair normal developmental processes. Such data provide further evidence of the continuous interaction of structure and function previously described within an evolutionary framework.

THE EXPERIMENTAL VIEWPOINT
learning, perception, and cognition

Central Assertion: *Individuals are to be understood in terms of uniform psychological processes.*

Experimental psychology proceeds on the assumption that behavior is lawful and that, for this reason, each person functions psychologically in the same way as every other person. To understand the basic mechanisms of behavior is to understand the transition from past events and experiences to an organized internal structure.

From the experimental viewpoint, three principal types of processes are of central importance for understanding human behavior—learning, perceptual, and cognitive processes. We are all the sum of what we have learned, perceived, and organized conceptually. But the important uniformities we share are derived from the *processes* through which our unique experiences are acquired. The scientific goal is to invent a set of general principles which specifies how responses are learned, how perceptions are organized, and how cognitions operate.

LEARNING PROCESSES

From the moment of birth, the child begins to acquire feelings, actions, and values that will continue over a lifetime. Much will be informal, learned from parents and playmates during the course of socialization; other learning takes place in a formal school setting. The purpose of socialization and education is to instill "appropriate" feelings, behaviors, and values. Thus, the *emotions* we feel, the *actions* we take, and the *values* we hold are acquired through learning processes.

Although experimental psychologists are not in complete agreement on how many different *learning processes* there are, it is useful for purposes of personality study to identify three separate types. *Classical conditioning* has special relevance to the acquisition of feelings; *instrumental conditioning* is most important in the acquisition of actions and skills; and *incentive learning* has relevance for values.

Classical Conditioning: An Approach to Feelings

Many researchers consider classical conditioning the most basic form of learning. It typically involves the learning of an *autonomic response to a stimulus* that was initially incapable of eliciting that response. Since the autonomic nervous system is intimately involved in the emotional life of the individual, the principles of classical conditioning provide a basis for understanding how feelings are learned.

The basic paradigm of classical conditioning is very simple. A neutral event such as a light is presented several seconds before a second stimulus (unconditioned S) which always elicits a response (unconditioned R), such as salivation to food powder. The temporal arrangement of the training conditions is shown below as stage 1. Then in stage 2, the learned association between light and food is illustrated by the broken line and by the fact that salivation appears earlier as a consequence of the presentation of the light. The substitute capacity of the light alone to elicit salivation (a conditioned response) is shown as in stage 3 in the form of a test trial in which food powder is omitted but salivation nonetheless occurs when the light is presented.

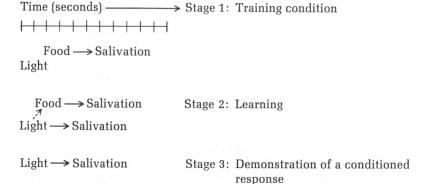

Time (seconds) ─────────⟶ Stage 1: Training condition

Food ⟶ Salivation
Light

Food ⟶ Salivation   Stage 2: Learning
Light ⟶ Salivation

Light ⟶ Salivation   Stage 3: Demonstration of a conditioned
                                      response

Stimulus generalization.   One of the most important principles emerging out of years of animal and human research into classical conditioning is *stimulus generalization.* Organisms conditioned to respond to a given stimulus will also respond to similar stimuli. The greater the similarity to the specific stimulus used in the original conditioning, the greater the strength of the conditioned response. This is known as the gradient of stimulus generalization (see Fig. 2.5).

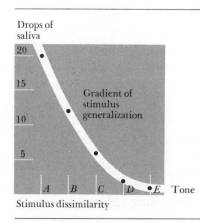

Fig. 2.5. Gradient of stimulus generalization. The number of drops of saliva elicited by the original conditioned stimulus (*A*) is maximum. As the similarity to *A* decreases (*B, C, D,* and *E*), the number of drops of saliva elicited by these stimuli also decreases.

Let us look at an example in which the meaning of words provides the basis for stimulus generalization. Generalization along the dimension of *meaning* is referred to as semantic generalization. In an experiment by Acker and Edwards (1964), the constriction of blood vessels in the finger was conditioned to the stimulus word GOOD for some subjects and to the word BAD for other subjects. Following standard classical conditioning, some subjects heard the word GOOD immediately followed by a loud noise that produced vasoconstriction in the finger. For other subjects the word BAD was used. The pairings of the loud noise with the words were continued until the stimulus words alone resulted in constriction of the blood vessels of the finger.

After such conditioning had taken place, the subjects were presented with a series of words (such as chair, mother, bomb, etc.). Vasoconstriction to the new words was measured. The new words which elicited the strongest vasoconstriction were those which had been independently rated as GOOD (such as mother) by subjects for whom GOOD had been the conditioned stimulus. However, for those subjects for whom BAD was the conditioned stimulus, the strongest vasoconstriction was elicited by words evaluated as BAD (such as bomb). The magnitude of the response was directly related to the meaning of the new word on a GOOD–BAD evaluation dimension.

This experiment demonstrated that the meaning of a word can provide a basis for the generalization of certain internal bodily responses. Such responses, referred to as autonomic responses, are thought to form the basis of emotions. Thus emotional reactions learned in one situation may be generalized or extended to situations that are similar in their personal meaning. For example, anxiety produced by failure in school can generalize to an achievement situation and may further result in loss of interest and a sense of hopelessness.

Discrimination.   We indirectly introduced discrimination when we discussed semantic conditioning among human subjects. You will recall that when the words GOOD and BAD were employed as neutral stimuli, only one was followed by the unconditioned stimulus. As a result of this differential reinforcement, the subject learned the discrimination and responded only to one word—the conditioned stimulus.

Concepts of classical conditioning help us to understand how the discrimination of social cues is achieved. We approach a friend to solicit a favor. When that friend is in a bad mood, we are either ignored or rejected. The cues of moodiness elicit negative feelings (frustration, disappointment), so that moody persons are avoided rather than approached. On the other hand, the social cues of a person in an accessible mood are more likely to be followed by approval of the request and, consequently, positive affective feelings. Conditioned feelings toward the distinctive social stimuli provided by another person may provide helpful guides for interpersonal behavior.

Let us examine an experimental study, using monkeys as subjects, which illuminates the importance of discriminating feelings and associating them with social cues. A team of investigators compared monkeys who had been subjected to total social isolation for the first year of life with normally raised monkeys (Miller, Caul, and Mirsky, 1967). A preliminary assessment of their ability to learn a response that would avoid an electric shock showed that the learning ability of the "isolates" had not been impaired by their social isolation.

In the second stage of the experiment, various pairs of the normal and isolate monkeys were used. As one monkey received electric shocks, his facial expression was shown to the second monkey via closed-circuit television. The picture of the first monkey's face receiving shock was the cue for the second monkey to press a bar. If the second monkey failed to press the bar, he too would receive shock. The normally raised monkeys were able to learn this task but only if the facial expression of a normal monkey was the stimulus. The isolates could not learn the task regardless of whether the first monkey was an isolate or normal. Although these groups had previously demonstrated that they were equivalent in learning ability, their capacities to discriminate social cues were markedly dissimilar.

Instrumental Conditioning: An Approach to Actions

We make personality judgments about others and they about us largely in terms of the typical behaviors and actions in which we engage. These actions are acquired primarily through instrumental conditioning—a process in which rewards and aversive stimulation exercise a selective influence on behavior.

Escape and avoidance learning.   During the course of a lifetime, we are all exposed to aversive and unpleasant circumstances which we will expend considerable effort to *escape* after their onset or *avoid* in anticipation of their occurrence. The avoidance response is usually learned quickly, because it is *instrumental* in producing a desirable consequence (not receiving noxious stimulation). An illustration of the establishment of an instrumental avoidance response appears in Box 2.1.

Box 2.1   Avoidance learning

A box known as a shuttle box is divided into two equal compartments by a small fixed panel low enough to permit a dog to jump over it from one compartment to the other. A gate can be lowered to separate the compartments completely. There is a light in each compartment.

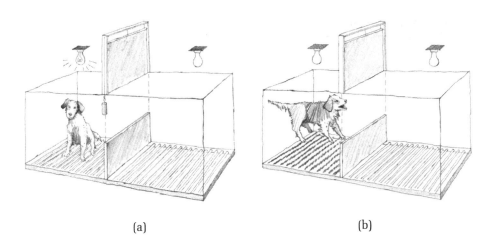

(a)   (b)

The gate is down at the start of the trial, confining the dog to one compartment. The light is turned on in that compartment, and the gate is raised (a). The light signals the coming of an electric shock scheduled for ten seconds later. The dog receives a severe and traumatic electric shock from the floor. It barks and shows signs of pain and distress. The shock continues until the dog accidently jumps over the center panel into the adjoining compartment (b). The gate is then closed. The floor of the adjoining compartment is not electrically charged, so the dog has successfully escaped punishment.

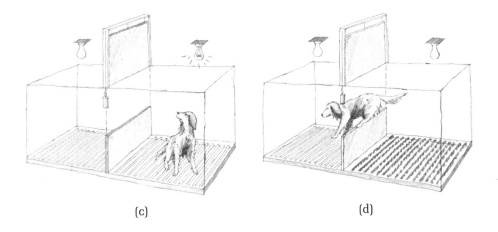

(c)   (d)

After an interval of time the procedure is repeated (c). As before, the light is turned on, the gate is opened, and ten seconds later the shock begins. A repetition of the preceding events again ends with the dog successfully jumping over the panel and landing in the safe adjoining compartment (d). Soon the dog learns to regularly avoid the shock by jumping over the panel when the warning light comes on and therefore before the electric shock begins (e). Ultimately it shuttles back and forth in response to the warning signal.

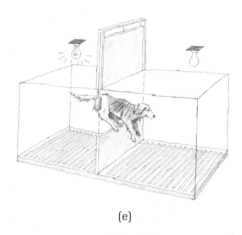

(e)

The progression from escape to avoidance can be easily understood. Because the shock always follows the light, it is reasonable for the dog to "shuttle" without waiting for the painful experience. However, there is an interesting additional aspect of avoidance conditioning. Once conditioning has occurred, the dog will continue to shuttle long after the electric shock has been turned off by the experimenter. Reduction of the pain produced by shock was the initial reinforcement for the shuttling response; now reduction of the fear aroused by the conditioned stimulus serves as adequate reinforcement for maintaining the response. Hence it persists.

There are many direct parallels between avoidance learning and everyday human behavior. The stimulus events which precede an aversive outcome produce negative feelings (via classical conditioning), so we seek to avoid them. However, avoidance responses tend to be self-perpetuating. We avoid a situation or circumstance because we fear an unfavorable outcome. This very avoidance prevents us from reevaluating the situation. Thus, even when the threat or danger is over, the avoidance response persists.

The basic avoidance process provides a means by which to view the internalization of conscience. Indeed, the development of resistance to temptation can be seen as an avoidance response. An experiment by Aronfreed and Reber (1965) illustrates the point. In this study, children were punished for selecting an attractive toy when given the choice of an attractive and plain toy. They soon learned to avoid selecting the attractive toy and choose the plain one. The critical test came when the experimenter left the room. Would the children now reach for the "forbidden fruit"? They did not. Punishment given *in the act of reaching* for the toy had been effective in instilling resistance to temptation.

The explanation of this experiment is based on avoidance-learning principles. Reaching for the forbidden toy constituted a distinctive stimulus event equivalent to the conditioned stimulus used in avoidance conditioning. The disapproval was an aversive event equivalent to the electric shock typically used with animals. The desire for the attractive toy and the act of reaching for it came to signal disapproval and elicit reactions similar to the effect of the external criticism first given by the experimenter. The instrumental act of withdrawing the hand from the attractive toy enabled the child to avoid the disapproval. Thus, there was an internalized "moral" standard produced by fear of the disapproval associated with the initial steps of the transgression. The *timing* of the punishment was critical. When the act of reaching signaled fear, the child made an avoidance response (showed resistance to temptation) with its usual persistance. This sequence illustrates that a uniform process can be applied to the understanding of conscience.

Many naturalistic training situations in which internalization of standards occurs follow the avoidance model. A child with dirty hands approaches the dinner table only to be told that "good children" wash their hands first. Approaching the table with dirty hands soon elicits a feeling of unworthiness, but the instrumental avoidance response of washing restores a sense of righteousness. Cleanliness may come to reassure, as does an avoidance response. A boy may be told, "Oh, no! Dolls are for girls!" If even in the absence of other people he avoids dolls and other objects and activities sex-typed as female, he will feel acceptable to himself.

Reward. Just as punishment may suppress certain behavior and the avoidance of aversive stimulation maintain other behavior, so may reward maintain certain behavior and the loss of reward inhibit other behavior. Most of us have discovered the power of rewards and the withholding of rewards as a means of establishing a measure of control over the behavior of others. The significance of rewards, as of punishment, lies in the persistent and enduring instrumental response patterns which can be established by their use.

One of the most effective methods of behavior control consists of *shaping,* a technique widely employed by animal trainers but not restricted to them. Starting with a motivated organism (hungry or thirsty) and a clear idea of the final behavior that is desired, the trainer provides a reward each time the animal makes a response that approximates the final criterion behavior. As the animal learns successive approximations, the performance criterion required to obtain a reward is made progressively closer to the final desired behavior. Soon the animal learns the response which will dependably produce the reward.

Instrumental learning applies also to the acquisition of personality characteristics. In most social situations the effective rewards are those of attention, approval, and praise from others. Conversely, withholding social attention is equivalent to withholding the food reward in the animal illustration. Selectively giving and withholding social rewards can initially shape and subsequently maintain human behavior, thereby determining the nature and variety of behaviors that an individual has available.

Such training plays an important role in personality development, for the mother is an agent who controls not only the social rewards of attention but also the physical rewards, most of which, whether given or withheld, are contingent on the child's behavior. The selective application of rewards is an extremely important condition for establishing which behaviors are acquired and which characterize the behavioral style of the individual. For example, giving attention whenever a child voices complaints of pain and physical discomfort should establish a person who is likely to use that particular set of responses whenever he or she wants attention. Physical complaints, malingering, and hypochondriacal symptoms are to be understood more in terms of the reinforcements the individual has received for those behaviors than in terms of internal physiological processes.

Incentive Learning: An Approach to Values

Incentive learning concerns the *value* an individual places on an outcome that occurs as a consequence of certain behavior. An important concept is that value is not absolute but *relative* to the individual and the circumstances. A hamburger in the middle of the afternoon when lunch has been missed has a different value from the same food following a hearty meal. The number of hours without eating changes the value of food. Also, its value differs if it can be obtained quickly, rather than after standing in a line, of, say, fifty people.

The subjective evaluations about the value of food given above can be demonstrated very nicely with animals in the laboratory. A rat will cross a grid floor charged with electric shock to gain access to a goal box already containing a food pellet, but it will not cross the same grid if it must wait thirty seconds in the goal box before the pellet is given. However, if the amount of food is increased from one to ten pellets, then the rat will cross the electrified grid to get the food even though it must wait thirty seconds (Renner, 1968). The value of an outcome—in this case food —determines whether the response will be made. In the first case, the immediate delivery of food is more desirable than the shock is bad, but not if the food is delayed. When delay is introduced, only a larger amount of food will offset the combined negative value of the shock and the delay.

In summary, the value of an outcome is relative. Delay is but one form of the "remoteness" of an outcome which will reduce its value. The saying "A bird in the hand is worth two in the bush" reflects the loss of utility due to remoteness. By experimentally determining how the value of an outcome changes in a lawful way as a function of other variables, such as delay, one can describe the factors which control the relative desires and aversions (the values) of an individual. Concepts of incentive seek to specify the uniform processes whereby outcomes take on their particular values.

In illustrating incentive learning and values, we have used examples that involve "acute" conditions, in which a transient state or particular situation such as hours without food, modifies the value of an outcome. However, there is a "chronic" state in which past learning and experiences produce stable individual differences in the evaluation placed on some outcome.

Rats inconsistently fed and starved during infancy will value a food reward more highly as adults than will normally fed animals (Renner, 1967). The early experience produces an expectancy that food may be momentarily withdrawn, and the subject has a chronically elevated value of food, reflected in hoarding and willingness to suffer an electric shock to obtain food. Likewise, experiences which develop in a child the expectancy that delayed rewards may not be given (Mischel, 1966), such as frequent periods of a father's absence from the home (Mischel, 1961), lead to a choice of small immediate rewards over larger but delayed rewards. In the same way, children who are neglected or separated from their mothers may show an "affective hunger" for a long time after the separation or isolation. An affective hunger is an exaggerated need for support and close attention from the mother.

PERCEPTUAL PROCESSES

Historically, interest in perceptual processes has been focused on specific perceptual phenomena, such as optical illusions, and why they occur. However, the study of these basic perceptual processes has contributed much to the study of personality. Perception, as it relates to personality, concerns the processes whereby attention is selectively directed at the external world of situations and people, and meaning is imposed upon those events.

Adaptation Level

The principles of adaptation level (Helson, 1964), which originated in experiments on color constancy and contrast, demonstrate that it is possible to modify the perceived color or brightness of a stimulus without changing the stimulus itself. What is required is an alteration of the luminance and hue of the background color. What a subject perceives will depend on what the stimulus is contrasted with. The same principle applies when the individual refers judgments of objects and situations to internal standards. A 4-ounce pen may be judged heavy and a 26-ounce baseball bat light. This is because we have developed different internal norms against which to judge these objects.

The effects of context upon perceptions are illustrated in two studies, one involving humans and the other white rats.

Incentive contrasts.   A rat will run faster in a runway for a ten-pellet reward than for a one-pellet reward. However, if a rat that has been receiving ten pellets is changed to a one-pellet reward, it will run slower than a rat that has always received one pellet. A one-pellet reward for a rat does not have an absolute value which will maintain performance at some particular level. The speed of running maintained by a given reward depends on the particular context in which it is given and the value the reward has for the animal in comparison with internal norms. One dollar for services rendered is just as likely to be an insult as a reward, depending on the standard of comparison.

Social contrasts.   People perceive one another in part on the basis of the context in which the perception occurs. One determinant of how much an individual likes another is how the other person behaves with respect to the first one. If an individual first expresses negative feelings toward a person, but subsequently becomes more positive, the former will be liked more by the latter than if he or she had been consistently positive all along. Earlier negative behavior results in more positive feelings if the initial negative reaction is followed by a positive reaction. Conversely, if an individual initially says he or she likes a person but gradually shifts to dislike, the former will be disliked by the latter more than if he or she had been consistently negative (Aronson and Linder, 1965).

As with likes and dislikes, context is also important in the perception of other events. If one is alone, the sound of a tree branch rubbing against the rainspout is likely to be interpreted differently at 12:00 noon than at 12:00 midnight. The internal frame of reference used to evaluate a given stimulus, to interpret a particular situation, or to assign a value to a particular outcome can cause the same stimulus event to have radically different meanings.

Work on adaptation level is directed toward identifying how contrast takes place. Adaptation-level researchers seek to specify the determinants of internal frames of references, the manner in which experiences alter the frame of reference and therefore influence the perception of particular stimuli, for example. The ability to specify the mechanisms and processes through which perception takes place makes it possible to predict the meaning that will be imposed upon particular events.

Needs and Perception

Another interesting aspect of perceptual processes in the study of personality concerns the effects of needs on perception. Projective personality tests are based on the assumption that the interpretation of ambiguous stimuli will reflect the particular needs and aspirations of the individual. The experimental work of Murray (1938) and others has demonstrated that the way ambiguous stimuli are perceived can be used to make inferences about an individual's dominant motivations. Motivations can alter significantly the way an event is seen or interpreted. The demand for an unbiased referee at a sporting event is practical testimony to the fact that impartiality is a necessary condition for "objective" perception.

In an early experiment (Sanford, 1936) children were shown mutilated magazine pictures which constituted ambiguous stimuli. The children saw one set of pictures before eating and, about a month later, another set of pictures just after eating. In each case they were asked to free associate to the ambiguous pictures. The subjects made a greater number of responses about eating, food, and meals to the pictures shown when they were hungry than to those shown after they had eaten. The interpretation is that a person's motivational state will influence how external events are perceived.

More recent and systematic experimental studies have confirmed the general finding that the perception of ambiguous stimuli will be influenced by the characteristics of the individual doing the perceiving. Adult subjects who are hungry will produce more food imagery than will subjects who are not hungry when telling stories to pictures of low relevance to food (Epstein, 1962). This general relationship between a need and its systematic and uniform effect on perception has been shown for a variety of other needs as well, including sex, sleep, fear, achievement, and many more (Murstein, 1963).

Because people are in conflict about many of their needs, a demonstration of the direct influence of needs on perception often requires the use of ambiguous stimuli which have low relevance for the need being measured. For example, the person who must stay awake needs to inhibit his desire for sleep, and a chaste person needs to deny strong sexual impulses to avoid guilt. Thus defensive operations are more likely to be aroused by pictures of food shown to a subject who must go without food or of nudes shown to an adolescent troubled with the management of sexual desires. This complexity is not a limitation, but precisely what is to be expected if perceptual processes are to reflect in a meaningful way the full range and complexity of human personality. The assumption is that the relationship between needs and the defensive aspects of personality and perception occurs in a uniform way and that these processes can be specified.

COGNITIVE PROCESSES

In this section, we look at the approach of experimental psychology to the study of higher processes. We shall see that studies on decision-making seek to specify the uniformities which exist among people in their cognitive processes. Human cognitive activity is assumed to occur in a lawful and orderly way. Identifying the processes through which decisions are made is a direct route to understanding human rationality, both descriptively (as it exists) and prescriptively (how it may be improved). The concepts of schema and of cognitive structure are developed to describe the basic elements of these higher processes. The study of the uniform processes resulting in the formation, organization, and operation of cognitive structures is experimental psychology's approach to the conscious human experience of making decisions and selecting courses of action.

Decision-making

Theoretically, every human decision depends on two factors. *What is at stake?* That is, what has the decision-maker to gain or lose as a result of the decision? *What are the odds?* In other words, if the individual selects a particular course, what is the probability of receiving the gains or losses of that particular response? The task of making a decision should be easy once an individual knows what is at stake and what the odds are. Each possible act has a value reflecting what the decision-maker may gain or lose as a result of that act, a value based on taking into account the possible outcome of the act and the probabilities. The decision should be simply to select the act which has, on the average, the greatest expected value or the smallest loss. This is the principle of maximizing one's gains and minimizing one's losses.

A problem in making real-life decisions is that the exact probability of an outcome is seldom known. The probability must be estimated, a decision made, and a consequence endured. That particular experience, and others like it, form the basis for estimating the probability of that outcome the next time a similar decision must be made. Over the course of time, probability estimates are revised to reflect the experience of the person (see Edwards, Lindman, and Phillips, 1965). The uniform processes by which such estimates are made and revised must also be identified if decision-making is to be understood. Again, the basic assumption of general experimental psychology is that through laboratory studies in which subjects must revise their probability estimates on the basis of experience, the uniform mechanisms and processes of this aspect of decision-making can be isolated.

Cognitive Structures

An invented notion like other concepts about human processes, cognitive structures provide an abstract description of the way in which thinking and remembering may take place.

A basic unit of a cognitive structure is a *schema*, or category for classifying events. The concept of cognitive structure as composed of schemata, or categories, is analogous to a storage or file system. There is an overriding organization which specifies how the elements are related to each other; there is a larger but limited number of specific niches in which an experience must be placed in order to be remembered. The specific form of any experience will be determined by the characteristics of the filing system. Likewise, thinking and thought processes occur in the context of the particular dimensions and organization which exist. Of particular interest are questions of how schemata are formed, how they are changed, and what constraints they place on the capacity of the organism for thinking and remembering.

Sir Frederick Bartlett (1932), an early investigator in this area, proposed the idea of a schema. Bartlett used a method which he termed serial reproduction. A subject is asked to read a story or prose passage twice. After a period of 15–30 minutes, the subject attempts to reproduce the passage verbatim. The result, called the first reproduction, is then given to a second subject who reads it several times and, after a period of 15–30 minutes, tries to reproduce it from memory. The second reproduction is then used in a similar fashion, and so on through a series of reproductions. Bartlett found that with each successive repetition, the story changes in significant ways to fit the expectations of the individual. Summarizing his results, Bartlett wrote:

> In fact, the one overwhelming impression produced by this more "realistic" type of memory experiment is that human remembering is normally exceedingly subject to error. It looks as if what is said to be reproduced is, far more generally than is commonly admitted, really a construction, serving to justify whatever impression may have been left by the original. It is this "impression," rarely defined with much exactitude, which most readily persists. So long as the details which can be built up around it are such that they would give it a "reasonable" setting, most of us are fairly content, and are apt to think that what we build we have literally retained.

In his research Bartlett used many different types of prose passages as well as pictorial material. An example of the pictorial material and the results obtained by serial reproduction is shown in Fig. 2.6.

Bartlett proposed that the schemata for thinking and remembering, together with their organization, are socially determined on the basis of the person's experiences. While investigating the memory of the natives of Swaziland in South Africa, a settler proposed a study that demonstrated their capacity to retain information that was personally and socially important. Most of Swazi culture revolves around the possession and care of cattle. The settler guaranteed that his herdsman could give a prompt and absolutely literal description of all the cattle the settler had bought a year earlier. Although he had retained written records of the deals, the settler himself could not remember the details. The native herdsman was asked to list the cattle his employer had bought the previous year, adding whatever details he cared to give. He rapidly recited a list of the nine animals purchased and provided a description of each, the price paid, and from whom it was purchased.

Bartlett felt that his illustration was by no means an isolated case. The Swazi herdsman had the capacity to recall the individual characteristics of his cattle. Animals were not marked, and if they strayed into other herds, they were returned to the proper owner on the basis of recognition by the native herdsman. The native herdsman could recall the cattle freshly and vividly. Obviously an adequate set of categories, or schemata, existed for the storage and eventual retrieval of such information.

Cognitive types.   Recent research on cognitive structures has attempted to deal with personality characteristics of individuals with different types of such structures. For example, the degree to which an individual is cog-

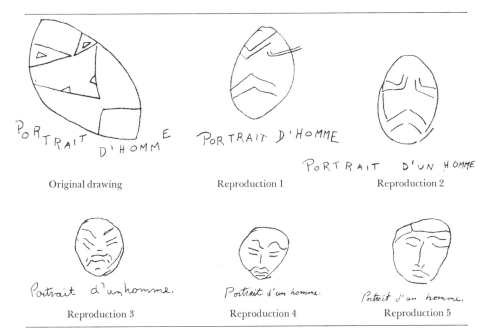

Fig. 2.6. Serial reproduction of a drawing. The first subject studies the original drawing for a period of time and is asked to reproduce it from memory. The result is then shown to another subject, and the process repeated through a series of reproductions. Though the series in this example is a very short one, all the characteristics of the original which have any peculiarity are lost. The face is tilted upward immediately, becomes oval and then round, and acquires eyes, a nose, and a mouth, all of conventional form. (From Frederick C. Bartlett, *Remembering*, Cambridge University Press, 1932, p. 178.)

nitively complex or cognitively simple can be assessed. A cognitively complex person has many different dimensions, intricately related in a hierarchical fashion. The cognitively simple person, on the other hand, has relatively few dimensions and categories.

The cognitively complex person is more creative, able to deal with the world more accurately, and not given to oversimplification and distortions. The cognitively simple person lacks the necessary cognitive structures for dealing differentially with the world and is consequently more concrete and less flexible, missing the nuances. Identification of the principal types of cognitive structures and their correlates is the way one approaches the topic from the psychometric viewpoint. General experimental psychology, however, centers primarily on the uniform processes by which these cognitive structures are formed and the ways in which they operate to determine memory and thinking.

THE SOCIAL VIEWPOINT
models, roles, and cultures

Central Assertion: *Personality can be fully understood only by considering the social context in which the person lives and develops.*

Like the seventeenth century philosopher Spinoza, we shall assert that the human is a social animal. Consequently, we shall argue that nothing is as important as other people in determining the nature of the individual. From the social point of view personality will be seen both as developing out of a social context and as defined by it. Only by comparison of one person with others can we conclude that anyone is crazy or intelligent or tall or ugly or anxious. A person's standing in terms of all of the dimensions in which individuals differ, including personality dimensions, is meaningful only in a comparative sense.

The effect of rewards and punishments on behavior was demonstrated earlier in the chapter; what will be emphasized here is that, unlike the experimental animal whose rewards are frequently delivered by a mechanical device, we generally receive our rewards and punishments from interaction with other people. These social rewards and punishments may be praise, attention, censure, and insults, or more subtle events such as glances, smiles, glares, and smirks. Furthermore, from a consideration of the social context in which the person develops, new principles of learning emerge. It is apparent that one of the primary ways one learns is by observing and imitating the behavior of others who serve as *models*.

The effect of other people on an individual can be seen in other ways in addition to learning. An individual's very identity depends on others and his or her *role* with respect to them. A teacher is a teacher only if there are students, and a doctor is a doctor only because there are people who are sick. People may find it difficult to identify themselves without referring to groups of others and to the roles they play within such groups.

In some respects the most pervasive influence on personality may be the least obvious—the *culture* in which the person lives. The simple fact that most individuals have intimate contact only with their own culture and are surrounded by others who have developed in the same society makes an appreciation of cultural variation uncommon, but cross-cultural research suggests that aspects of people assumed to be universal and natural do in fact vary from one culture to another.

Specific areas of concern from the social point of view, then, include *models, roles,* and *cultures.*

MODELS

Learning and Unlearning by Observation

Many of the things we have learned to fear have never actually hurt us. Rather, much of our fear and avoidance learning results from observing evidence of fear in others. Such social learning is quite efficient since it means that one can learn from other people's misfortunes. A common example of such fear learning, although one which is not necessarily advantageous, is the vicarious conditioning that takes place by hearing, reading, and watching suspenseful drama. After a childhood diet of entertainment in which various fear-producing things happen at night, one can hardly escape a conditioned apprehension of dark places.

The fact that emotional reactions can be conditioned through vicarious experiences raises the intriguing possibility that existing maladaptive fears might be eliminated in a similar manner. Such a possibility is of more than casual interest because of the obvious therapeutic possibilities. Fears are usually difficult to eliminate. Feared situations tend to be avoided, and contact with feared objects is minimized, with the result that even unfounded fear will be unlikely to be extinguished or supplanted by positive feelings. However, if it were possible to unlearn the apprehension through vicarious rather than direct experience, the therapeutic problem would clearly be simpler.

Children 3 to 5 years old who displayed a fear of dogs were used as subjects in an experiment to test just this possibility (Bandura and Menlove, 1968). The extent of their fear was determined by a standardized behavioral test, which consisted of a graded series of 14 performance tasks requiring increasingly close contact with a cocker spaniel. A score of 2 points was assigned for each graded task accomplished willingly and a score of 1 point for each done with signs of reluctance and hesitation. Out of a possible 28 points most of the children scored only 7 or lower, indicating marked fears. Interestingly, the more fearful subjects were also significantly more likely to come from a family in which one or both parents also reported a fear of dogs.

Over a period of several days after the pretesting phase, the children saw 8 different 3-minute films. For some of the subjects, the movies pictured a 5-year-old boy in progressively closer contact with the cocker spaniel. This *single-model* group saw a variety of scenes, such as the dog drinking from a baby bottle, eating a sucker held by the model, and jumping for food in his hand. On the final day the last films showed the model's approach responses to the dog in the playpen, interspersed with several humorous sequences. A second group of children in a *multiple-model* condition saw similar scenes, but instead of only one child and one dog, several male and female models of various ages were shown interacting with different kinds and sizes of dogs. Finally, a third group, serving as a *control* condition, watched irrelevant movies about Disneyland and Marineland which were equal in length to the experimental films.

On the day after the sequence of movies was completed, the avoidance test was readministered to all groups. Compared with their pretest behavior, both the single- and multiple-model groups displayed significantly less fearful avoidance of the dog, but the control subjects remained unchanged. In addition, to determine the durability of these changes, the test was conducted a third time one month later. As shown in Fig. 2.7, the increased ability of the children to approach the dog was still apparent even after a month.

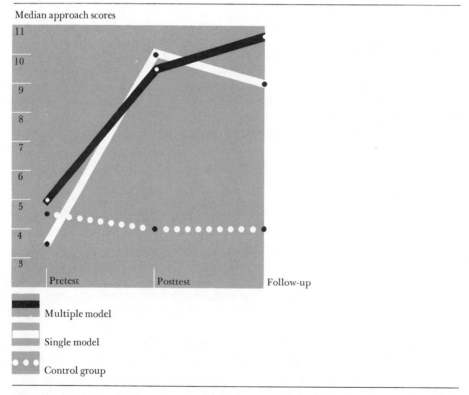

Fig. 2.7. Median approach scores obtained by children in each of three conditions at different phases of the experiment. (From A. Bandura and F. Menlove, "Factors determining vicarious extinction of avoidance behavior through symbolic modeling," *Journal of Personality and Social Psychology*, 1968, **8**, 99–108. Copyright 1968 by the American Psychological Association. Reprinted by permission.)

Although both kinds of films were effective, children who had seen the multiple-model films continued to improve even after the posttest. By the follow-up session, they were significantly more bold than they had been just after treatment. In addition, the groups were compared on the number of children who completed the most difficult task (remaining confined with the dog in the playpen). In the follow-up, twice as many in the multiple-model condition as in the other two groups completed this final task. Thus, observing more than one model interacting with more than one dog was superior in eliminating all avoidance behavior to observing one model and one dog. Finally, the investigators stress the importance of having a graded series of scenes progressing from harmless to ordinarily fear-producing situations, rather than confronting the child initially with an active, jumping dog.

Many of the examples of modeling that we will discuss involve behavior which is easily manipulated and safely produced in the laboratory. Presumably, any behavior is susceptible to such social influence. Among various examples of imitation are the occurrence of panic behavior in crowds when the sight of others rushing to the exits sets off a chain reaction. An equally imitation-inducing counterinfluence against panic is the sight of others making an orderly exit.

On a simpler level, such actions as yawning and laughing are highly susceptible to a model's influence, and crying and thirst are also open to the influence of others' behaviors. In addition, innumerable social behaviors are subject to imitation. One is more likely to make a contribution when the plate is passed in a theater or a church if everyone else in one's row also gives. In like manner, an effective strategy for getting volunteers is to top a circulated list with a few false signatures or to plant some friends in the audience to raise their hands. The same dynamic is sometimes used by realtors and used-car salespeople. As the indecisive customer considers a particular house or car, it helps to have a stooge arrive to profess great interest in the same item. Similarly, on a slack day shrewd restaurant owners may find it beneficial to park their own cars visibly in front of their restaurants. These crowd effects result from the tendency to imitate models, whether planted or genuine. They are the essential ingredient in any really successful group function like a rally, an auction, a county fair, or a religious revival.

The Conditions for Imitation

If the range of imitative behaviors is unlimited, the range of models to be imitated is equally so. The individual meets countless potential models, only some of whom are ever imitated. Observers differ in their proneness to attend to and imitate another's behavior, and some of the model's behaviors are more likely to be imitated than others. All the variables which determine imitation have not been studied, but some that have been investigated will illustrate their diversity. We shall first consider *aspects of the observer*, especially emotional state, then *aspects of the model* and his or her behavior, especially the rewards and punishments which are seen to follow that behavior, and finally *interpersonal aspects*, namely the similarity of the observer and the model.

Aspects of the observer: emotional arousal.   Several aspects of the observer which influence the probability of imitating another person have been studied. People who are low in self-esteem, people who are incompetent at a particular task, and people who are emotionally aroused and uncertain—all tend to watch others closely and follow their actions.

In the classic study on the effects of emotional arousal and uncertainty or imitation, subjects were told that the effects of a vitamin compound were being studied (Schachter and Singer, 1962). Although there were a number of different conditions, two are of particular interest. The subjects in both conditions received injections of adrenaline. The informed group was told of the actual side effects to be expected, such as shaking of the hands, pounding of the heart, and flushing of the face. The uninformed group remained ignorant of the side effects. While each subject was supposedly waiting for the vitamin injection to take effect, a stooge who was with him engaged in euphoric age-inappropriate behavior, such as playing basketball with wads of paper, making paper airplanes, and playing with a hula hoop. (In a repetition of the study, he displayed anger about the conduct of the experiment instead.)

The results showed that in the absence of a satisfactory explanation for their felt emotional states, the subjects who were *uninformed* about the effects of the injection were somewhat more likely to model their behavior and feelings after those of the stooge. In other words, in a state of uncertainty about the origin and meaning of their emotional arousal, subjects tended to rely on the available social cues provided by the model. Consequently they tended to become angry when the model was angry and euphoric when he was euphoric.

Although findings of this sort are obtained under controlled laboratory conditions in which their generality cannot be assumed, the results hold promise of being broadly applicable. For example, it is probable that emotional arousal contributes, through its effect on imitativeness, to the intensification and prolongation of mob behavior, hysterical outbursts of adolescents during personal appearances of celebrities, and the physical demonstrations characteristic of religious revival meetings.

Aspects of the model: rewards and punishment.   In addition to such observer characteristics as emotional state, aspects of the model that influence imitation have been studied. One of the most important features
appears to be the perceived consequences of the model's behavior—
whether or not it leads to rewards or punishment. We see advertising
every day that attempts to influence our behavior in this way. In television
commercials, models drink Pepsi, swallow aspirin, or drive Mustangs in
attempts to foster imitation in the viewer. To help the imitative process
along, vivid nonverbal expressions of pleasure accompany the act of
drinking, swallowing, or driving.

In these examples the models appear to experience some rewarding
consequences from their behavior. Such situations are sometimes termed
instances of *vicarious reward* for the observer: he is not rewarded directly
but may have some empathic or vicarious experience of reward merely by
watching another person's apparent pleasure. It is not clear at present
whether or not a vicarious-reward experience alone can increase responding. A belief on the subjects' part that they too will be rewarded if they
follow the model's actions may be essential. In most imitation situations
such a belief is probably present, whether or not it is essential.

To determine the effect on imitation of positive and negative consequences to the model, an experiment was conducted on a street corner in
New York City. Ninety-five passers-by participated in the experiment
without knowing it (Hornstein, Fisch, and Holmes, 1968). The procedure
consisted of placing on the street an envelope with a man's wallet, which
obviously contained some money ($2.00). A note wrapped around the
wallet indicated that someone else had previously found the wallet and
intended to return it, but in the meantime had apparently lost it. The object of the investigation was to determine the conditions under which the
subject would imitate the apparent good intentions of the previous finder
by mailing the wallet back to the owner.

In half the cases the note stressed that returning the wallet had been
a rewarding experience for the first finder. In the other half of the cases
the note stressed that returning the wallet had been accompanied by negative feelings. After beginning with the same two sentences, this note
stressed the inconvenience, annoyance, and bother of taking responsibility for the wallet. In addition to varying the model's feelings, some of the
notes indicated that the previous finder had been a visitor from a foreign
country. Although ungrammatical in structure, the letter expressed great
pleasure in helping others (the positive form) or the inconvenience and
bother of returning the wallet (the negative form).

The experiment basically consisted of exposing passers-by to the
action of a foreigner or a nonforeigner who reported positive or negative

feelings about helping behavior. (There were also neutral conditions, but for the sake of simplicity they have been omitted from the present discussion.) Two unobtrusively located observers recorded a number of characteristics of the persons who picked up the wallet. They reported that no sex, age, or apparent socioeconomic class was disproportionately represented.

Of the wallets that were dropped, 40 percent were returned intact. The primary finding was that when the model's note said that returning the wallet was a rewarding experience, there were significantly more returns than when the note reported negative feelings. In addition, if negative feelings were expressed, it did not matter whether the model was a foreigner or not. In the rewarding condition, finders were less likely to imitate the foreign than the nonforeign model.

Interpersonal aspects: similarity between observer and model. Beyond aspects of the observer or the model alone, there are *interpersonal* factors, or aspects of both persons in combination, that influence imitation. For example, several studies have demonstrated increased imitation when the model is of a *higher status than the observer.* Thus children are more likely to imitate adult models than peer models (Flanders, 1968). In some advertisements the consumption of the product and the accompanying signs of satisfaction are bolstered by presenting a model whose status is high relative to that of the viewer. The athlete's testimony for razor blades or the actress' appeal for a charity are examples.

Still another advertiser ploy is to picture not a consumer who is famous or of high status but one who is *similar to the observer.* In the previously mentioned study, there was a hint of the possibility that observers are more likely to imitate a similar model. Another investigator has manipulated the similarity variable more directly (Rosekrans, 1967).

Ninety Boy Scouts participated in the experiment individually at their regular troop meeting place. The task was to play a war strategy game which involved moving a toy army along roads on a board with three-dimensional terrain. The object of the game was to surround the enemy in a strategic position. Before they began playing, however, they saw a movie of another boy playing the same game.

The movie showed the boy moving the pieces with a certain strategy, sometimes breaking the rules of the game, and speaking as he played. In one version of the film, the boy wore a scout uniform and was described as similar to the subjects. In another version, the boy was dressed in street clothes and was described as dissimilar to the subjects. The experiment showed that the subjects who saw the similar boy play the game were much more likely to recall his behavior and imitate his strategy than were those who saw the dissimilar model.

ROLES

The Nature of Roles

Besides imitating models, we all take on a multitude of different roles. A *role is the behavior and expected behavior associated with a position within some social structure.* Some of us are parents, and as parents we are expected to behave in certain ways toward our children. But we are also children to our parents and partners to our spouses. Each of these roles carries different implications for our behavior. In a complex society characterized by extreme division of labor, we may play the role of powerful leader in one group and obedient subordinate in another. Knowledge of these roles and the demands they place on the individual help the personality psychologist understand each person's unique behavior.

Roles are also an indispensable tool in the sociologist's task of analyzing the structure of social units. In every social unit some roles are clearly recognized and have institutional support. Thus military people wear uniforms which distinguish them from civilians, and within the army some are officers and others enlisted personnel. Within each of these categories are further officially recognized subroles, each with distinctive insignia and clearly delineated duties and relationships to one another.

In any social unit, an informal structure also exists that is not officially planned, recognized, or written down in a manual. For example, a role analysis of the informal structure within one midwestern prison revealed the following distinct role differentiations, among others: the Politician, who works in the office of the Deputy or Assistant Warden or as a hall-tender; the Strategic who has a skill valued in the prison industries or who has known certain officials over a period of years (Mitchell, 1966). A description of the roles found in the prison population provides a basis for understanding how the prison functions and malfunctions. To new members of a military or prison society (or any other social grouping), learning the intricacies of the informal structure and their place in it is fully as important as learning the demands of their formal role.

Role Expectations

A term which occurs frequently in the writings of role theorists is *expectation.* Implicit in a role is a set of more or less generally recognized expectations about appropriate behavior. For the most clearly delineated roles, these expectations are widely shared in the society. Accordingly judges are expected to be dignified, priests to be pious, actors to be eccentric, and airline stewardesses to be happy. A considerable amount of the humor appearing in jokes, cartoons, and television comedies derives from people (especially those in distinguished roles) engaging in behavior which violates our role expectations for them. Role-inappropriate behavior can be used as a source of humor in the mass media only if expectations for such roles are widely shared.

Role as an Alternative to Personality

Those who take a given role in society display similarities in their performances regardless of who they are. The fact that a play has a standard script which guides the actions of the players ensures that whenever one sees a production of the play, there will be some uniformity in the performance of each role. Similarly, in real life certain behaviors define such roles as that of the mother, and to the extent that this is true, one expects at least a certain minimal similarity among mothers. In a system characterized by division of labor, each job has a more or less definite job description or set of prescribed actions with certain requisite skills. As a consequence, the differences in behavior between two individuals are partly accounted for by differences in the roles they play and differences in the demands their roles place on them.

People are aware that the behavior they see others engage in is partly role-determined, and therefore they look to *role-inappropriate* or extra-role behavior for cues about the "real" personality. An interviewer may try to put candidates for a job at ease to get them out of the applicant role so that their "own" idiosyncratic behavior will be expressed. The interviewer's problem is that the adequacy of the individual in the role of "job applicant" does not necessarily provide evidence of ability to fill the role of "line supervisor." For similar reasons, the ritualized dating situation is probably an unsatisfactory environment for selection of a marriage partner, because extra-role cues to the prospective mate's personality are minimized. Furthermore, dating roles do not usually have much in common with the marital roles ultimately of interest.

From the perspective of role theory, the question of who people are reduces to the question of what role they play. Individuals appear to have fixed characteristics independent of their situations, when in fact they are merely responding to the demands and expectations of their various roles. From this point of view, personality inheres in the role, not the person. Change a person's role and you change personality. If it seems unlikely that changing jobs would change one's personality, consider that an occupation is only one of the many roles one plays. The apparent person emerges from interaction of all the roles and expectations. For example, there are numerous expectations which people hold about priests.

All the people a priest encounters while in his clerical collar and black clothes, including himself, share these expectations to some extent. He comes to speak, to act, and even to feel in accordance with these common expectations, at least to the extent that he is not involved in roles with conflicting expectations. The demands and expectations of roles account for at least some individual differences that are usually thought of as aspects of personality.

Role Playing

In addition to studying the effect of roles on individual differences, personality psychologists have also studied roles by having someone engage in role playing.

Several years ago a free-lance writer, John Howard Griffin, artificially pigmented his skin and, appearing to be a black man, toured the South by bus. In his book *Black Like Me,* he records other people's expectations of him. After living for a time in the segregated Southern society of the late 1950s, Griffin records numerous instances in which he began to internalize the expectations of others. For example, he describes a situation in which he sat in the front seat of a white friend's car.

> We drove through the darkened streets to his home, talking in a strangely stilted manner. I wondered why, and then realized that I had grown so accustomed to being a Negro, to being shown contempt, that I could not rid myself of the cautions. I was embarrassed to ride in the front seat of the car with a white man, especially on our way to his home. It was breaking the "Southern rule" somehow.*

Griffin's description makes it clear that his feelings about himself had become compatible with the role expectations of others regarding his position.

Role playing is of special interest as an agent of personality change. A name historically associated with the therapeutic use of role playing for personality change is that of Jacob Moreno (1946). He considered role playing a way in which one could experiment with different roles and learn to perform them better. The idea was formalized in a method of therapy known as *psychodrama,* wherein problem situations in a patient's life are enacted. The patient is assigned various roles to learn a better understanding of the situation and alternative patterns of response.

Role theorists have suggested that prolonged enacting of a role can change one's extra-role behavior (Sarbin, 1964). After years of teaching

* From J. H. Griffin, *Black Like Me,* Houghton Mifflin, Boston, 1960, p. 72.

primary school children, a teacher may find that her ability to converse on an adult level has suffered, a problem also encountered by mothers who are occupied day after day solely with their children. In like manner, individuals who have been administrators may develop a tendency to be autocratic in other contexts, and college instructors may pick up the habit of lecturing even in conversation.

The belief that roles and role playing are important influences on personality and behavior has led to research on its therapeutic use. We shall briefly examine an experiment in which the subjects played the role of cancer victims.

In this study, the smoking habits of women college students were chosen as the target behavior to be changed. The experimenter played the role of physician, and the women, all of whom were heavy smokers, played the role of patient. In his role as physician, the experimenter informed the smoker that she had developed lung cancer. For an hour, they acted out several scenes in the doctor's office, focusing on the pain of the illness, hospitalization, and early death. There was also a passive control group, composed of equally heavy smokers, who heard a tape-recording of a role-playing session. Hence the control group was exposed to the same information as the role-playing group, but without direct involvement. Smoking habits and attitudes toward smoking were assessed after two weeks, eight months, and eighteen months. The last two follow-up surveys were conducted in such a way that they were not associated with the original study.

The relative effectiveness of role playing and passive listening, as well as of the government report on smoking, can be seen in Fig. 2.8. Over the entire period the role playing group maintained a somewhat stronger avoidance of cigarette smoking than the passive control group, and after the treatment both groups smoked less than did the untreated controls. The government report also had an inhibiting effect on smoking behavior, but in the absence of any other influences, the untreated controls returned to their prior level by the final follow-up.

An interesting spontaneous indication of the effectiveness of role playing was noted by the final interviewer. When she asked what influence had induced them to reduce their smoking, one out of four subjects mentioned the experiment, indicating that the experience had broken down their feelings of personal invulnerability to lung cancer.

Of course it must be borne in mind that the variable being studied in this experiment was the subject's own report on her smoking behavior rather than direct physical or observational evidence of her use of cigarettes. Nevertheless, some care was taken to disguise the connection between the original role-playing sessions and subsequent follow-up mea-

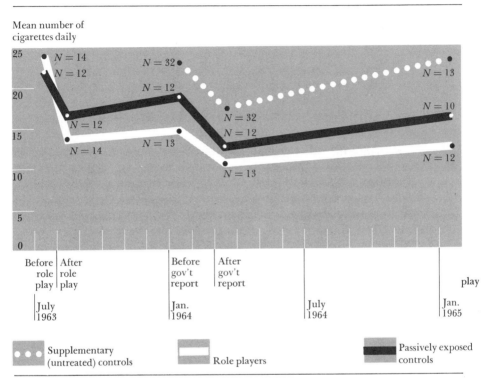

Mean number of
cigarettes daily

Fig. 2.8. Long-term effects of emotional role playing on cigarette smoking. The
number of subjects per group changes because some were not reached. The role
players enacted the role of lung cancer victims. The passively exposed controls
heard a tape recording of a role-playing session but did not participate. The supplementary control group was added following publication of the U.S. Surgeon
General's report which officially linked cigarette smoking and lung cancer. (From
L. Mann and I. L. Janis, "Long-term effects of emotional role playing on cigarette
smoking," *Journal of Personality and Social Psychology*, 1968, **8,** 339–342. Copyright 1968 by the American Psychological Association. Reprinted by permission.)

sures. The experimenters point out that the exact process at work is not
clear. For example, the role playing may have had its long-range effect by
making these subjects unusually sensitive to such later warnings as the
Surgeon General's report.

This experiment was an example of role playing in the sense of pretending to be something that one is not, as in a dramatic production. Note
that playing a real-life role would be expected to have many of the same
effects on extra-role behavior as playing an imaginary role. A somewhat
more general term than role playing is *role enactment,* which denotes the

natural performance of roles in everyday life as well as the dramatic performance of roles on stage or in therapy. Of course, the likelihood that enacting a role will have lasting extra-role effects on behavior probably depends on a number of factors, among which are the duration of the performance, the emotional involvement called for by the role, and the effectiveness of the role enactment (Sarbin, 1964).

CULTURES

In some respects the most pervasive influence on personality may be the least obvious—the whole cultural context in which the person develops. Thus, in addition to models and roles, a third perspective on personality from the social view is that of *cultures*. Commenting on the influence of culture on the individual, anthropologist Ruth Benedict said:

> No man looks at the world with pristine eyes. He sees it edited by a definite set of customs and institutions and ways of thinking...He cannot go behind these stereotypes; his very concepts of the true and the false will still have reference to his traditional customs. (Benedict (1934), 1961, p. 2)

According to this aspect of the social viewpoint, variations in cultural conditions create individual differences among people. In this section we shall look at some of the techniques of cross-cultural research and some of the findings relating cultural variations and personality.

The Study of Cultures

The traditional anthropological approach relies upon the keen observations and descriptions of investigators who live for some time within the cultures they study. They amass a wealth of information based on firsthand observation and personal interviews. The broad scope and great detail of the information collected makes the data difficult to quantify. Thus, in addition to free observations, cross-cultural research teams now employ standardized scales and structured interviews to quantify what they observe and to ensure comparability of their observations. Like all field studies, however, anthropological investigations afford no opportunity to control for the presence of other contaminating variables. For example, coming from one cultural setting to observe another, the anthropologist is a variable. The types of behavior chosen to study, the methods of observation, and the inferences drawn are all influenced by the cultural milieu in which the anthropologist developed. In short, the observer's observations reflect his or her own characteristics as well as those of the society investigated.

How might such a problem be solved? One possibility would be for a second anthropologist from another culture, preferably quite different from that of the first anthropologist, to report on the same society (Campbell, 1964). Aspects of the society that both observers agreed on could be more confidently considered true of the people under study. However, it may have occurred to the reader that, though different, the cultural backgrounds of the two anthropologists might still have many aspects in common. Agreements about a target culture could arise because of these similarities. The more similarity in background, the less will be the error that is eliminated, and the less the advantage of employing multiple investigators.

Another solution is to extend the multiple-observer design to include the study of more than one society. Figure 2.9 illustrates the multiculture-multiobserver method of reducing observer bias.

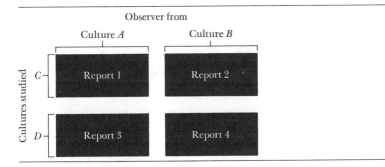

Fig. 2.9.   Diagram of the multiculture-multiobserver method of reducing observer bias. Observations that occur in reports 1 and 3 but are absent from reports 2 and 4 are due to observer A's point of view. Similarly, observations appearing in reports 2 and 4 but not in 1 and 3 show the point of view of observer B. Looking the other way, along the rows, information found in both reports of culture C (reports 1 and 2) but not in reports of culture D (reports 3 and 4) could be considered true attributes of the culture C being studied. (From Donald T. Campbell, "Distinguishing differences in perception from failures of communication in cross-cultural studies," in *Cross-Cultural Understanding: Epistemology and Anthropology*, edited by F. S. C. Northrup and Helen H. Livingston. Copyright © 1964 by the Wenner-Gren Foundation for Anthropological Research, Inc. Reproduced by permission of Harper and Row, Publishers, Inc.)

Objective Measures

One way of avoiding the use of free anthropological observation and its inherently subjective nature is to employ objectively measured behaviors. By ensuring the objectivity and standardization of conditions for observ-

Dr. Margaret Mead with a group of Manus children during a 1938 visit to the Admiralty Islands. (United Press International Photo)

ing and quantifying the behaviors observed in each cultural sample, the investigator can draw quite confident conclusions about similarities and differences among cultures. Let us examine one study in which this method was employed to investigate cultural differences in physical contact (Little, 1968).

The study involved the responses of college students at several foreign universities to a behavioral test using dolls. Each student was given a pair of gray plastic dolls of the same sex and was asked to place them on a piece of 12 by 18-inch paper so that they looked natural for each of 19 specific interactions. Samples of the kinds of interactions suggested are "strangers talking about a pleasant topic" and "an employer reprimanding an employee for errors." The hypothesis under study was that the relative positions in which the subjects chose to place the dolls would reflect their own particular cultural background.

Greeks and Southern Italians were selected as characteristic of *contact cultures,* those with minimal taboos against physical contact between members of the same sex in social situations, and Swedes and Scots were selected as being from *noncontact cultures.* An American sample was also included. The results showed that there was a considerable amount of agreement between the subjects, regardless of their nationality, on the relative interpersonal distance called for by the various hypothetical situations. For example, friends were placed closer than strangers, and pleasant topics produced closer placement than neutral or unpleasant topics. Despite these relative similarities, however, there were significant national differences in absolute distances in placement. On the average, students from contact cultures placed the dolls closer together than did the students from noncontact cultures. Greeks preferred the closest placements, followed by Italians, Swedes, and finally Scots. Americans responded about the same as Italians. Thus the study demonstrates the method of using standard testing situations and responses which can be objectively scored. Clear cultural effects were obtained which substantiate conclusions from casual observation and to some extent conclusions from other studies.

The Study of Variables Across Cultures

Although cross-cultural research yields interesting information concerning differences among cultures, its major function is the study of psychological variables among various cultures to determine the generality of principles and interrelationships.

Child training everywhere begins with the universal characteristics of children and the universal need to socialize the children and shape them into adults. The techniques used in this process vary more across different cultures than within the same culture, and this fact suggests that truly general psychological principles can emerge only when more than one culture is studied. The advantage of cross-cultural study can be seen by analogy with physics. Einstein's theory of relativity holds that the traditional principles of physics fail to be general truths because they were made *relative* to an earthly point of view. The essential methodological lesson for psychology is that scientific research carried out in one place with one method will generate principles *relative* to that place and that method rather than general ones.

A classic example of the faulty conclusions that can arise from culturally limited sampling is apparent in research on the effect of age of weaning on later emotional disturbance. In an effort to determine the nature of the relationship between these variables, Sears and Wise (1950) studied a sample of 80 children living in Kansas City. The investigators found a clear positive relationship between the age of weaning and the degree to which the infant gave indications of emotional disturbance. That is, the later a child was weaned, the more disturbance. Judging from these data, one might conclude that the earlier the child is weaned, the better. However, the normal range of variation in American weaning practices is only from birth to one year of age, and we know from anthropologists that many societies delay weaning until considerably later. The Kurtatchi of the Solomon Islands, for example, do not wean their children until they are over three years old. Information from the Kansas City sample would lead us to assume that Kurtatchi children would show severe emotional disturbance, but according to the anthropologist's report, they show virtually no evidence of such disturbance. Thus little can be concluded from these two studies by themselves, except that the relationship between age of weaning and later emotional disturbance is more complex than was initially suspected. Clearly more information is needed to fill the gap between the weaning ages of one and three years.

Fortunately, a cumulative file of anthropological studies, started at Yale and now available at several colleges across the nation, provides a wealth of organized and catalogued information about several hundred societies from different cultural areas. One study that used these Human Relations Area Files (Whiting and Child, 1953) compiled data on the age of weaning and emotional disturbance for 37 different societies. The range of weaning age in these cultures stretches from 12 months to 6 years. Contrary to the relationship found in the Kansas City sample, weaning and emotional disturbance across these 37 societies are in general negatively related, indicating that children are less rather than more disturbed when weaning is delayed. The results of these studies are not really in conflict, since they represent different segments of the weaning-age continuum. And, as Fig. 2.10 illustrates, the information fits nicely together. There is practically no overlap between ages of weaning in the primitive societies sampled from the Area Files and those in Kansas City, but in combination the two age ranges suggest a conclusion that would not have emerged from either sample alone. Apparently age of weaning and the chance of emotional disturbance are curvilinearly related. Disturbance is likely to increase in the range of weaning age from 0 to 18 months but to decrease as weaning is delayed beyond 18 months (Whiting, 1968). It is

Percent of cases above the median
on amount of emotional disturbance

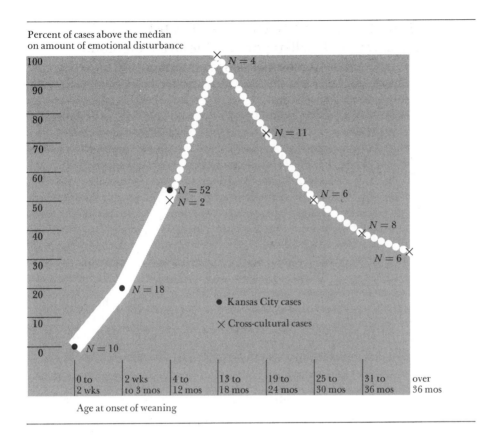

Age at onset of weaning

Fig. 2.10. Relation between age of weaning and amount of emotional disturbance shown by child. Comparable data for 80 individual children from Kansas
City and 37 societies from Human Relations Area Files (Whiting and Child,
1953) are presented. (From J. W. M. Whiting, "Methods and problems in cross-
cultural research," in *The Handbook of Social Psychology,* Vol. II, second edition, edited by Lindzey and Aronson, 1968, Addison-Wesley, Reading, Mass.)

apparent, then, that investigators who limit the range of variability they
study may emerge with only part of the picture, and in many cases (such
as weaning age) the normal range varies considerably from culture to culture. Since mothers are not likely to be willing to vary their child-rearing
practices to satisfy the curious psychologist, drawing on the naturally occurring variations found across different cultures provides a practical way
of studying the full range of the effects of these variables.

THE PSYCHOMETRIC-TRAIT VIEWPOINT
observational, self-report, and indirect methods of personality assessment

Central Assertion: *The behavior of individuals is best understood in terms of attributes which reflect underlying trait organizations.*

The psychometric-trait approach to personality has as its goal the assignment of numbers to human attributes in such a way that the myriad individual differences in behavior with which personality is concerned may be described and explained with greater precision. More concisely, this viewpoint is concerned with the *measurement* of personality traits.

In describing ourselves and others, we frequently employ such adjectives as calm, cautious, carefree, independent, or friendly. If, after dining at an expensive restaurant, a well-dressed man slips a thin dime under his plate and hurriedly departs, the waitress is sure to call him stingy. Stinginess is not behavior but an attribute of behavior. The individual does not "stinge." He behaves in a manner which prompts us to categorize his behavior as stingy. Personality-trait terms refer to attributes or qualities which have been abstracted from behavior by a process referred to as *trait attribution.*

What are the rules and conditions that govern such attribution and to what do such attributes refer? Three characteristics of personality traits are: (1) Any trait attribution is based on the comparison of one individual with others; (2) Qualities that evoked the trait attribution are sufficiently distinctive to permit their differentiation from other qualities; and (3) The qualities attributed to a person are in some way characteristic of that person and will be observed on many occasions rather than just one. They are relatively enduring rather than transitory.

To return to the poor tipper alluded to above, our attributing stinginess to him is based upon norms or standards that we have developed over a period of time concerning the "proper" tip for services at a restaurant; we presume that stinginess can be differentiated from other qualities, such as defiance or orderliness; and we expect to observe similar behavior on other occasions in different situations. In other words, the poor tip does not reflect momentary annoyance with the waitress for poor service.

These three characteristics of personality traits are emphasized in Guilford's well-known definition of a trait: "A trait is any distinguishable, relatively enduring way in which one individual differs from others." (Guilford, 1959, p. 6)

THE NATURE OF PERSONALITY MEASUREMENT

In the area of personality, measurement may be thought of as the mathematical rules which govern the assignment of numbers to attributes of behavior. The *psychometric* (mental measurement) approach to personality places heavy emphasis on the quantification and statistical manipulation of observations of behavioral attributes. A more systematic approach to the assessment of stinginess in our restaurant example would involve the use of several observers, stationed at adjacent tables, who would attempt to provide a quantitative estimate of the personality trait of interest. Since personality traits are always expressed with reference to individual differences, it would be typical for the observers to rate not just one but a number of individuals over the course of a day. Each rater would be provided with a series of rating scales of the following kind:

STINGY __ : __ : __ : __ : __ : __ : __ GENEROUS
$$-3 \quad -2 \quad -1 \quad 0 \quad +1 \quad +2 \quad +3$$

This particular rating scale is only one of a large number of types that might be employed in the assessment of personality traits. The use of this scale rather than another is based on a number of assumptions about the most appropriate rules for assigning numbers to attributes of behavior in this particular rating situation. Among other things, one assumes that the trait in question is best rated by a continuous, bipolar, equal-interval scale. Let us consider the nature of each of these three assumptions.

Continuous versus discrete scales. When we assess stinginess along a seven-place continuum, we assume that the trait itself is *continuous*—that it varies in uninterrupted fashion from small to large amounts and is capable of infinite subdivision (the weight or height of a person is such a trait). We could as well have used 9, 15, or even 100 places on the scale. The number of units employed is restricted only by the discriminating capacities of human observers. Many social phenomena do not lend themselves to continuous measurement, however. If we were to develop a scale of sociability based on the number of social organizations to which a person belongs, we might find that he or she affiliates with 0, 5, 10, 15, etc. It would not make sense to state that the subject belongs to 5.5 groups. Unlike stinginess, group membership is a *discrete* variable in which the basic unit (the group) cannot be further subdivided.

Bipolar versus unipolar scales. The rating scale for assessing stinginess is assumed to be a continuous dimension with STINGY at one pole and

GENEROUS at the other. This *bipolar* conception of a trait is based on the assumption that stinginess and generosity are opposite sides of the same coin. People high on stinginess are low on generosity, and vice versa. Individuals can occupy intermediate positions; if they are neither predominantly stingy nor predominantly generous, they occupy the midpoint (or zero) on the scale.

Although many traits lend themselves to bipolar assessment, others do not. Consider the representations of personality abnormality or maladjustment illustrated in Fig. 2.11. The *unipolar* representation at the top construes maladjustment as extending from "normal" or common behavior to "abnormal" (away from the norm) behavior. This representation of personality abnormality embodies the older statistical view of maladjustment that *any* behavior different from that of most people is by definition abnormal. The bipolar representation at the bottom is more in line with current conceptions of abnormality that emphasize positive aspects of mental health. In the bipolar representation, the healthy personality is not simply one that fails to deviate from the norm. Instead, a pole of self-actualization is represented as a state toward which individuals may grow as they realize more and more of their human potentialities.

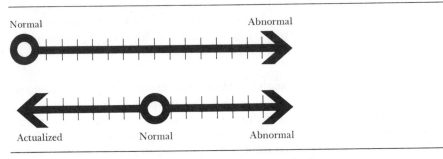

Fig. 2.11.   Unipolar and bipolar representations of adjustment.

Interval versus ordinal scales.   The seven-place bipolar stinginess scale is also based on the assumption that individuals differ in the magnitude of their stinginess and that these differences in magnitude may be represented by a series of equal intervals or units on a scale. An individual who is rated +2 on this scale is considered to differ by a magnitude of two units from an individual rated zero. Not all traits lend themselves to such *interval* measurement. For example, it may readily be said that Tom is stingier than Dick and that Dick, in turn, is stingier than Harry, but it may not be possible to specify the number of stinginess units that separate Tom from Dick and Dick from Harry. Under these circumstances an *ordinal* scale is employed to rank individuals in terms of stinginess: Tom is first, Dick is second, and Harry is third. An ordinal scale implies only rank and not degree, but it is useful in the assessment of certain characteristics that do not lend themselves to interval measurement.

Traits as constructs.   We have defined traits as distinguishable, relatively enduring ways in which people differ from one another, and we have given examples of the mathematical assumptions underlying the psychometric approach to trait measurement. These traits cannot be seen or located in any part of the anatomy. They are constructs that refer to enduring and discriminable differences among people. Individual differences are the primary events of personality study. The psychometric-trait approach to personality focuses on a particular class of such events and construes them according to a set of logical principles that differ from those employed by the biological, experimental, and social viewpoints. The principles that guide most trait approaches to personality study are based on constructs involving the *covariation, stability,* and *structure* of behavioral attributes.

A trait is construed as a *class* of behavioral attributes that encompasses a variety of superficially different behaviors. Consider the following: being purposely late for an appointment, criticizing a friend's manner of dress, striking a child on the head, giving a stranger false directions. Although the physical characteristics of these responses have nothing in common, the attributes of such behaviors may all be instances of the trait of aggression. If we were to compute the *correlations* among such behaviors in a large group of people, we would expect the behaviors to be positively and often substantially correlated. A trait, then, is a collection of diverse behaviors that tend to covary. Thus, the construct of a trait is an organizing principle that permits the integration of data from many levels of behavioral observations.

An individual who is stingy today was probably stingy in the past and is likely to be stingy in the future. It is this relative *stability* of traits over time that allows us to characterize one person as generous and another as stingy. Some traits, such as the basic personality characteristics emphasized in the next sections of this book (dependency, aggression, and sexuality) are assumed to be relatively stable over the major portions of a person's life. Other characteristics (such as optimism, cheerfulness, and apprehensiveness) may exhibit considerable variability within relatively short time periods. Nevertheless, all traits are assumed to have at least some stability from one occasion to another.

Traits are also assumed to be structured or organized classes of behavioral attributes. Whereas the *trait* construct refers to a collection of diverse behaviors that tend to covary, the notion of *structure* refers to the relationships that exist among a collection of traits. In some cases, the correlation between two traits (generosity and sociability, for example) may be high; in other instances (neatness and friendliness) it may be low. This pattern of related and unrelated traits permits specification of the major dimensions of personality. It is possible to compare individuals in terms of these structural dimensions rather than simply one trait at a time.

CONSTRUCT VALIDITY

As indicated in Chapter 1, the usefulness of constructs is evaluated in terms of how well such constructs increase the prediction, control, and understanding of the events in question. Such criteria can also be applied to the psychological test and measurement procedures typically involved in the determination of a personality trait. The question raised is: How well does this particular psychological test measure what it is supposed to measure? Such a question has reference to the *construct validity* of a psychological test (Cronbach and Meehl, 1955). The principal considerations involved in the determination of construct validity have been referred to as *substantive, structural,* and *external* (Loevinger, 1957). Let us briefly look at each.

Substantive considerations. A psychological test that purports to measure a trait may attempt to sample all or most of the superficially unrelated behaviors, or it may be confined to only a limited segment of behavior implied by the trait. For example, a psychological test of adjustment may attempt to sample systematically all important areas of social and personal adjustment that may occur in the life of an individual, or it may sample only such limited areas of behavior as adjustment to college, marriage, or one's boss.

The primary substantive consideration in evaluating the construct validity of a psychological test is one of sampling. What is the universe of content sampled by the test and how was that universe determined? The specification of the universe of content encompassed by a trait should be guided by theoretical considerations. How broadly or narrowly is the trait construed, what behaviors are specifically implied by the construct, and what behaviors are specifically excluded? Psychological tests whose contents are too narrowly or vaguely defined are unlikely to contribute to the prediction, control, or understanding of the trait construct involved.

Structural considerations. A psychological test typically consists of a number of items combined in some fashion to yield a total score that serves as an index of the amount or degree of a trait possessed by the subject. The interrelationships among such items (internal consistency) and the manner in which they are combined to yield a total score (measurement model) are referred to as structural considerations. Although internal consistency or high correlation among items is generally desirable in a psychological test, the degree to which items are correlated may vary with the trait measured. Where the trait encompasses many similar, highly intercorrelated behaviors, the internal consistency will be high. With more divergent behaviors comprising a trait, the internal consistency will be lower. The maximum degree of internal consistency that can be expected from a test measure of a trait is determined by theoretical considerations, including the extent to which such behaviors are thought to be correlated in real-life situations.

The manner in which test items are combined to yield a total score on a test is likewise determined by theoretical considerations. The most common measurement model for personality traits is the *cumulative model,* which specifies that responses to test items be added to yield a total score. The assumption is that the more items answered by the respondent, the more the respondent is characterized by the trait in question. Other available models make different assumptions about the combining of items to yield a total score (Loevinger, 1957).

External considerations. To be of use as a measure of personality, a psychological test must be related to a variety of *nontest* manifestations of the trait in question, such as behavior observed under controlled laboratory conditions and in everyday life. To assert that a test measures the trait construct it purports to measure, it must be demonstrated that important behavioral manifestations of the trait can be *predicted* from scores on a psychological test. If a psychological test really measures extraversion, it should be possible to predict accurately the numbers of social organizations to which an individual belongs from scores on the psychological test. This *external* component of construct validity is the one most heavily emphasized in discussions of test validity, because it has the greatest practical significance. However, a full understanding of the relationship between a psychological test and the trait construct it is supposed to measure is based on substantive, structural, *and* external considerations.

METHODS OF TRAIT MEASUREMENT

A variety of methods are employed to obtain personality-trait measurements. Although there are many possible ways to classify these methods, they may be conveniently grouped under three headings: observational methods, self-report methods, and indirect methods of personality-trait measurement. The remainder of this chapter is devoted to a brief description of the major techniques now used with each of these three methods.

In later sections of the book it will become apparent that the same personality trait may be measured by any or all of the three major methods of measurement. In some situations, the conceptualizations and conclusions drawn concerning a given personality trait will be essentially the same regardless of which of the three methods is employed. In other instances, however, quite differing constructions of the same trait may be obtained when the trait is measured by different methods. The latter situation is compatible with the overall theme of constructive alternativism which pervades this book. Different methods of measurement may lead to different constructions of the same trait. In a sense, then, the use of a given method imposes methodological "blinders" on observations and results in a relative emphasis on certain aspects of an event and a relative neglect of other aspects of the same event. Different methods of personality measurement have different ranges and foci of convenience. In the long run, the discrepant results obtained by different methods of measurement may be reconciled. In the short run, however, such discrepancies are viewed as a natural outcome of constructive alternativism.

OBSERVATIONAL METHODS OF TRAIT MEASUREMENT

Control of Environment

There are three general methods of observation in the behavioral sciences: naturalistic, controlled, and contrived. Traditional anthropological investigation, which we discussed earlier in the chapter, involves the observation of behavior *in situ*, in the absence of artificial constraints. In *naturalistic observation*, the observer has no control over the events to be observed. The method achieves realism but lacks many of the controls necessary to infer causal relationships.

Controlled observation, on the other hand, takes place in the laboratory or under special circumstances created by the observer. To illustrate, a psychologist might manipulate the environment of a playroom by stocking it with objects likely to elicit aggression and then observe the aggressive behavior of children in the presence of these objects. In this and similar situations, the psychologist controls both the stimulating conditions and the categories of possible responses the subject might make. When suitable experimental precautions have been taken, it is possible to make causal inferences about the stimulus conditions which led to a given response. Because of an element of artificiality, the extent to which behavior observed in the laboratory is representative of behavior that occurs in a natural setting is always open to question.

When an apparently (to the subject) natural situation is, in fact, under the control of the experimenter, we speak of *contrived observation*. An example is the Schachter and Singer study discussed earlier, in which subjects thought they had received an injection of a vitamin and were then placed with another subject (actually a stooge) who acted in a euphoric or an angry manner. The contrived experimental situation attempts to retain the rigorous control of laboratory procedures while avoiding the unnatural atmosphere usually created by a controlled setting. In contrived situations, it is extremely important that the subject be unaware that a psychological experiment is taking place.

Presence of Observer

When the observer is clearly visible to or interacting with the subject being observed, we speak of *participant observation*. The presence of the observer may have great impact on the subject's behavior and the method requires trained observers to control and evaluate this impact.

Nonparticipant observation takes place when the observer is not visible to the subject being observed. Such observation may take place with or without the awareness of the subject. When we presume the subject is unaware of the observer, we should establish that this presumption is fact. When the subject is aware of observation, it is important to establish the possible impact of such observation. The presence of a camera or microphone may be more distracting to some subjects than the actual presence of an observer.

Considerations of the degree of control of the environment (naturalistic, controlled, contrived) and whether or not an observer is part of the environment (participant, nonparticipant) allow us to characterize six general kinds of observation. These are indicated in Table 2.3. Although that categorization is not exhaustive, it does represent the major observational paradigms employed in personality research.

Rating Scales

Rating scales are the vehicle whereby raters' impressions of observed personality attributes are transformed into quantifiable form. Such scales provide the observer with a systematic frame of reference for recording

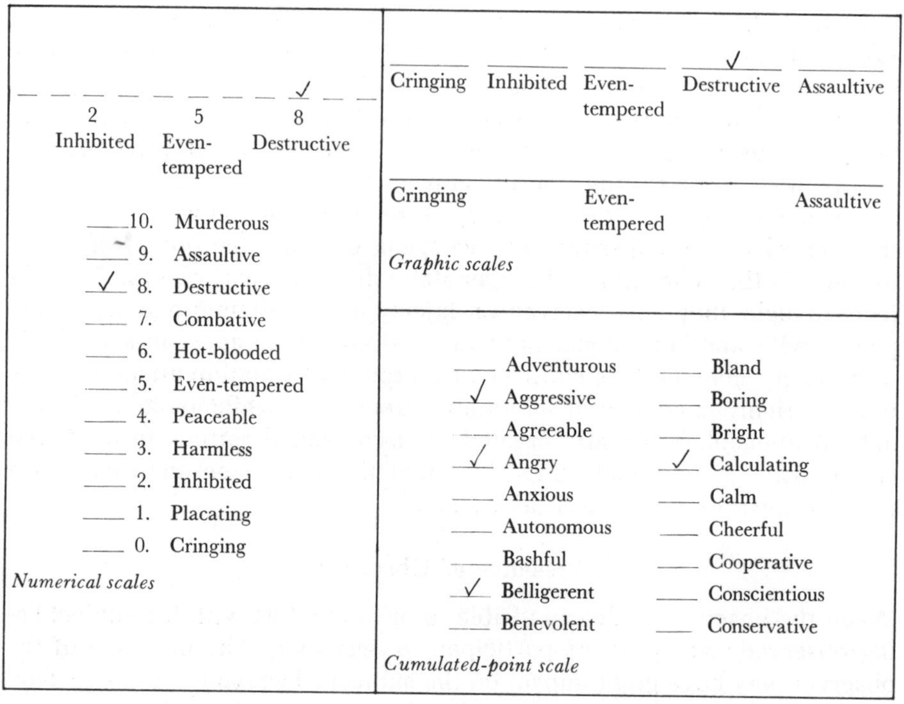

Fig. 2.12. Three types of rating scales for physical aggression. *Numerical scales* provide a direct quantitative assessment of the degree of an observed attribute on an equal-interval scale. Verbal "anchors" are frequently employed to convey the conceptual meaning of the numerical increments. These may be strategically placed along the continuum or presented at every point. *Graphic rating scales* provide a physical representation of the trait dimension in the absence of specific numbers. A graphic scale may be either discrete (above) or continuous (below). On a continuous graphic rating scale, the observer determines the exact point on the continuum which best corresponds to his or her impression of the attribute being rated. A number may be assigned to the rating by physically measuring the distance along the continuum. Finally, the *cumulated-point scales* avoid the possible artificiality that may be associated with the use of both numbers and graphic distances. The observer is provided with a list of verbal statements and asked to check those that apply. On the basis of a predetermined scoring system, one point is added to the total for each critical adjective the observer checks. If the category being rated were one of physical aggression, adjectives such as those checked in the figure would be embedded in the list. The rated score on physical aggression would be the total number of such adjectives checked. Cumulated-point scales are especially useful when several traits are being rated simultaneously.

Table 2.3 Classification of behavioral observations.

	Naturalistic	Controlled	Contrived
Participant	Anthropologist lives with Indian tribe.	Structured interview is orally administered.	Observer poses as peer.
Nonparticipant	Children are observed in classroom through one-way mirror.	Child's reactions to teaching machine are observed through one-way mirror.	Hidden observer watches reactions to "rigged" situation.

sensory impressions of the attribute in question. A variety of rating scales are available for raters of varying degrees of skill to rate different situations. The numerical properties of the rating scale must be appropriate to the phenomenon observed, as determined by the measurement model employed. Fig. 2.12 summarizes and compares three different types of rating scales employed in personality assessment.

Peer Ratings

Peer ratings refer to systematic observations made by friends or colleagues of the person being rated. Extensive contact over a period of time frequently provides peers with information that cannot be obtained from professional observers. Moreover, peer ratings provide insight into the individual's social-stimulus value among associates.

Direct *trait-ratings* may be obtained by asking a group of peers to provide ratings on a list of traits (see Fig. 2.13). Trait ratings are typically

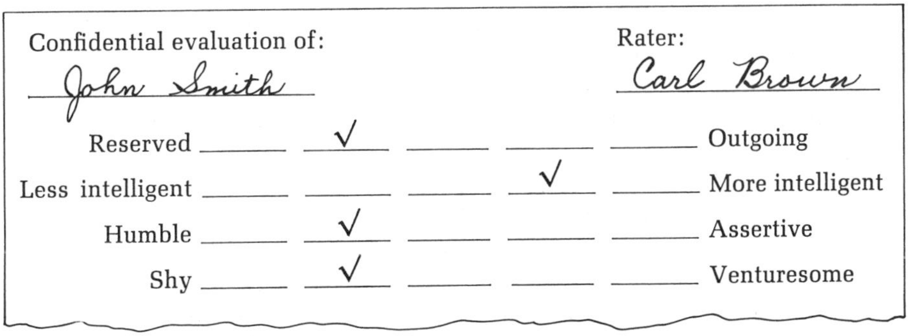
Confidential evaluation of: John Smith
Rater: Carl Brown

Reserved		√				Outgoing
Less intelligent				√		More intelligent
Humble		√				Assertive
Shy		√				Venturesome

Fig. 2.13. Peer trait-rating form.

averaged across all raters to yield the average social-stimulus value of the ratee among the group of peers. Enlisting a number of raters, instead of one, presumably balances out individual biases and misperceptions.

Another approach is the *peer-nomination* technique in which descriptive statements are provided to a group of raters who are asked to nominate those members of their group who fit such statements. Figure 2.14 illustrates a peer-nomination form in which the items are entered in rows and the names of the group members head the columns. Each member of the group is asked to read each item and check the names of any peers to whom the item applies. A ratee's score on a given item is the number of nominations received for that item. In the nomination technique, the rater is not forced to rate a peer on an item which might not be applicable to that peer. Nominations are spontaneous and presumably reflect the real opinion of the rater.

	Jerry Ash	Bob Baker	Joe Grant	John Hall	Tom Jones	Carl Smith	Sam Taber
He cries if you hurt his feelings.						✓	
He's always acting up.							✓
He likes an audience all the time.		✓	✓				
He will always play by himself.				✓			

Fig. 2.14. Peer-nomination form.

Interviews

The personality assessment interview is a semi-controlled, participant observation in which two-way communication occurs between the observer and the subject. Though the technique is highly flexible, it is often difficult to assess the representativeness of the behavior because of the contribution of the observer. Interviews may be unstructured or structured.

The *unstructured interview* is a relatively spontaneous, two-person interaction with broadly stated goals, such as "to form an impression of the person." Because such interviews are not rigidly planned in advance, their success is highly dependent upon the responsiveness of the subject. The interviewer typically takes leads from these responses.

Certain types of interviewing techniques place a high premium on the establishment of "rapport." Nondirective techniques are restricted to supportive statements, such as "You seem to feel that. . . ." An atmosphere is created in which subjects are encouraged to present themselves in their own characteristic fashion. In contrast, the *stress-interviewer* attempts to create a stimulus situation that is maximally uncomfortable for the subject—intimidation, embarrassment, and emotional stress. The purpose is to explore the subject's reactions under stress.

Unlike the unstructured interview, the *structured interview* is a standard stimulus situation designed to elicit specific kinds of information. You are familiar with the public opinion poll in which the respondent is asked such questions as "Would you favor the Democratic candidate over the Republican candidate in the next presidential election?"

Although lacking the flexibility of the unstructured interview, the structured interview provides data that are readily quantified and permits comparison of the results of many interviews. Even with relatively impersonal and factual questions, however, specialized training is required in order to reduce the effects of the interviewer's personality on the responses of the subject.

SELF-REPORT METHODS OF TRAIT MEASUREMENT

In contrast to those methods of personality measurement which involve direct observation of the subject's behavior, self-report methods rely on the verbal report of the subject for information concerning the subject's status with respect to a given personality trait. Of the several techniques available for measurement by self-report, the personality inventory or questionnaire is by far the most popular. Personality inventories differ from one another not in the kind of item employed, but in the rationale for the measurement model that combines items to yield an estimate of an underlying personality trait. A brief review of the major models or kinds of personality inventories follows.

Rational Personality Inventories

Originally, the personality inventory was considered a convenient substitute for a standardized interview. It consists of a number of questions that were presumed, on rational grounds, to relate to the trait of interest. Since hundreds of people could be tested at one time and the responses could be restricted to a yes–no or true–false format, considerable economies could be realized over the face-to-face interview, both in administration time and subsequent scoring.

Historically, the first large-scale use of a personality inventory occurred during World War I. The Woodworth Personal Data Sheet was developed as a technique for the mass screening of men with respect to their suitability for combat (Woodworth, 1920).

The Woodworth Personal Data Sheet consisted of 116 items of the following form:

Are you happy most of the time?   Yes   No

Do you find that people understand and sympathize
with you?   Yes   No

The major trait assessed by the inventory was presumed to be "neuroticism," or lack of personality adjustment. A cumulative scoring model was employed, dictated by the assumption that the more items an individual answered in the "neurotic" direction, the more he had the underlying trait of neuroticism.

Armistice arrived before any large-scale appraisal could be made of the Personal Data Sheet's effectiveness in indicating those unsuitable for combat. Nevertheless, it seems clear that such a rational inventory operates under a number of assumptions which may or may not be valid. Among the assumptions that seem to be involved are: (1) The item has a common "meaning" among subjects and between subject and examiner. (2) Subjects must be able to assess their own internal states accurately. (3) Subjects will honestly report those internal states to the examiner. (4) The items in question are in fact related to the concept of "neuroticism," as used by the examiner.

Subsequent research has demonstrated that most, if not all, of these assumptions are open to serious question. Consequently, other techniques of measurement and item combination have been developed in an effort to minimize sources of bias which exist when the above assumptions are not valid.

Forced-Choice Personality Inventories

Even if we grant that subjects are able to assess their own internal states accurately, it seem unlikely that normal subjects (or even abnormal subjects, for that matter) will spontaneously describe themselves in undesirable terms. Here we are speaking not of a conscious desire to deceive the examiner, but of the normal tendency in our society to put one's best foot foward in self-presentation. Consider the item:

I am certainly lacking in self-confidence.   True   False

Even though this item might be a highly accurate description of the way in which some of us see ourselves, admitting to such a trait is undesirable in our society.

Because of the importance of social desirability as an item characteristic, it has become common to estimate the desirability value of items employed in personality inventories. A format for making such an estimate is illustrated in Fig. 2.15. A number of individuals rate the social desirability of an item on a nine-place equal-interval rating scale, and the separate ratings are averaged to yield a social-desirability scale value for that item. By this rating procedure, the desirability or acceptability of an item may be determined in advance of its application.

Item: "To like to punish your enemies"

Undesirable								*Desirable*
	✓							
Extreme	Strong	Moderate	Mild	Neutral	Mild	Moderate	Strong	Extreme
(1)	(2)	(3)	(4)	(5)	(6)	(7)	(8)	(9)

Fig. 2.15. Social-desirability rating scale (after Edwards, 1957).

The Edwards Personal Preference Schedule (EPPS) is a personality inventory devised with special attention to the social desirability variable (Edwards, 1959). The basic items from which the EPPS was derived express preference for various activities and situations. A group of judges applied the social-desirability rating scale procedure to a pool of items. On that basis, items were grouped in pairs of approximately equal social-desirability values but reflecting different personality traits of interest.

For example, both items of the following pair have high social-desirability scale values that are approximately equal:

A. I like to do things with my friends rather than by myself.

B. I like to experiment and try new things.

In the EPPS, subjects presented with this pair of items are asked to indicate which statement is more characteristic of what they like. They may choose either but must choose only one. Since both items are high in social-desirability value, subjects are unlikely to choose one of the alternatives because it is more socially desirable. Rather, since social desirability is controlled, they will choose the statement that is more characteristic of their personal preferences. In this particular instance, Option A indicates a preference for "affiliation," Option B for "change." Hence the subject is able to indicate preference for affiliation as opposed to change, independently of the social desirability of the statements involved.

The same procedures may be employed to construct pairs of approximately equal social undesirability that reflect different traits of personality. For example, in the following pair, a choice of A indicates a preference for "aggression" and B a preference for "deference."

A. I feel like getting revenge when someone has insulted me.

B. When I am in a group, I like to accept the leadership of someone else in deciding what the group is going to do.

Although both aggression and deference are usually considered undesirable in our culture, the subject may choose without regard to the social-desirability value.

The EPPS consists of 225 such pairs of statements which have been approximately equated for social-desirability values. On the basis of the preferences the statements represent, it is possible to obtain scores on 15 personality-trait dimensions, including achievement, deference, order, and exhibition.

Empirical Personality Inventories

The personality inventories discussed so far have relied heavily on the assumption that the items are, in fact, related to the personality-trait dimension the test constructor had in mind. Such assumptions are subject to test, and indeed, much of the research on personality inventories attempts to evaluate the measurement claims of test constructors.

The *empirical* approach to personality test construction attempts to ensure the relationship between the personality trait of interest and the test item by the manner in which the test is constructed. The technique employed to achieve this end is called the method of "contrasted groups." Starting with two distinct groups of subjects—the *control group*, believed *not* to possess the trait of interest and the *criterion group*, known on independent grounds *to* possess that trait—identical items are administered to both groups of subjects. Those items that show a statistical difference in pattern of response between the two groups are retained for use in an empirical-scale measure of the trait. Two of the most widely used empirical inventories are the Minnesota Multiphasic Personality Inventory (MMPI)* and the California Psychological Inventory (CPI). Let us examine them briefly.

The MMPI was developed for the specific purpose of aiding in the psychiatric diagnosis of abnormal personality types (Hathaway and Mc-Kinley, 1951). The constructors of the MMPI assembled a large pool of about 1000 items which reflected primarily psychiatric content:

I wish I were not bothered about thoughts of sex.   True   False

I believe that I am being plotted against.   True   False

All of the items were administered to a *control group* consisting of 724 "normal" visitors to the University of Minnesota Hospital and to various criterion groups consisting of separate groups of clinically diagnosed psychiatric hospital patients, such as "hypochondriacs," "depressives," and "schizophrenics." The method of contrasted groups was employed to develop the schizophrenia scale of the MMPI in the manner suggested in Table 2.4, where the data represent the percentage of subjects in the normal control group and the schizophrenic criterion group who answered "True" to each of three items. Note that there is little difference between the two groups in the percentage of subjects who answered "True" to the first item in Table 2.4. On the second item, however, a significantly greater percentage of schizophrenics than normal subjects answered "True," and on the third item a significantly smaller percentage. Therefore on the schizophrenia scale developed by this method, the first item was not used, the second was included and scored "True," and the third was included and scored "False." The final schizophrenia scale consisted of 78 items that were answered differently (to a statistically significant degree) by the

---

Table 2.4 Data illustrating the development of a schizophrenia scale by the method of contrasted groups.

Items	Answering "True," %		Difference between groups, %	Final scoring of item
	Control group (724 normals)	Criterion group (50 schizophrenics)		
I like mechanics magazines.	50	51	+1	Not scored
I hear strange things when I am alone.	5	35	+30	True
I get all the sympathy I should.	80	50	−30	False

schizophrenic patients and the normal controls. Individuals who score very high on the schizophrenia scale of the MMPI are said to have patterns of self-report that more closely resemble those of hospitalized schizophrenics than they do those of normal control groups.

Separate scales were developed for eight clinical groups. When employed in a hospital setting, the MMPI requires very careful interpretation by a skilled clinician prior to making a diagnostic recommendation, because there may be factors other than schizophrenia that contribute to a high score on the schizophrenia scale. Nevertheless, unlike the rational or forced-choice personality scales, the empirical method of constructing a test guarantees that scores on the scale are related, to some extent, to the personality dimension of interest.

Unlike the MMPI, the California Psychological Inventory (CPI) was developed to measure "normal" personality traits (Gough, 1957). The original item pool for the CPI consisted of certain MMPI items, to which were added items reflecting traits believed to be critical for interpersonal functioning, for example:

I would be willing to describe myself as a pretty "strong" personality.	True	False
I find it easy to "drop" or "break" with a friend.	True	False

The CPI consists of a series of scales developed to measure specific personality traits such as dominance, sociability, self-acceptance, responsibility, socialization, etc. A variety of procedures were employed in developing the separate scales, although most of them qualify as empirical scales.

In the development of the CPI, heavy stress was placed on peer nominations as a means of defining criterion groups. Groups of normal high school and college students were asked to nominate peers who were high or low on the personality trait in question. For example, in the development of the dominance scale for the CPI, subjects were requested to nominate peers who were high on the trait of dominance (aggressive, confident, self-reliant), as well as those who were low in dominance (retiring, inhibited, lacking in self-confidence). The group of subjects nominated as high served as the criterion group; those nominated as low served as the control group. Items that showed a statistically significant difference between criterion (high-dominance) and control (low-dominance) subjects formed the basis for the dominance scale.

A variety of ingenious variations on the contrasted-group method were used to develop the CPI scales. For example, the constructors developed the scale measuring "Socialization" by contrasting a delinquent group with a normal group matched for age, sex, socioeconomic background, and education. They developed a scale measuring the desire to "make a good impression" by contrasting the responses of subjects instructed to answer the CPI in such a way as to form a favorable impression with the responses of a control group not so instructed. The CPI is widely used as a measure of normal personality functioning. As is true of all empirically-derived scales, those of the CPI possess at least some guaranteed relevance to the personality trait dimensions they are supposed to measure.

INDIRECT METHODS: PROJECTIVE TECHNIQUES

When indirect methods of personality trait measurement are employed, the subject is seldom able to recognize the relationship between the stimulus materials presented and the personality traits in which the examiner might be interested. The relationship between indirect test items and personality traits should, in fact, be "indirect." Indirect methods of personality-trait measurement are related to underlying traits on the basis of certain theoretical assumptions. The most widely employed of such assumptions centers on the concept of projection. Indirect methods whose theoretical rationale embodies that concept are called "projective techniques."

As originally used by Freud, the concept of projection referred to a psychological "defense mechanism" that attributed unacceptable aspects of one's own impulse life to persons or situations in the outside world. Thus, when certain patients described others as hostile, Freud felt that they were "projecting" their own unacceptable hostile impulses onto other people. Such a mechanism was, by definition, unconscious in nature, and it operated without the awareness of the patient. More recently, psychologists concerned with indirect methods of personality measurement have broadened the concept of projection to include the attribution of acceptable as well as unacceptable aspects of one's self to persons or objects in the environment. Projective tests employ stimuli that are purposely ambiguous and lacking in common meaning. When subjects respond or associate to such stimuli, it is assumed that they are "projecting" aspects of their own personality onto the neutral or ambiguous stimuli. Consequently the content, manner of approach, and organization of a subject's response to an ambiguous stimulus is taken as an indication of the content and organization of the subject's own personality traits.

Two of the most widely used projective techniques are the Rorschach Inkblot Test and the Thematic Apperception Test (TAT).

The inkblot test was developed by a Swiss psychiatrist, Hermann Rorschach (1921), to study the perceptual reactions of patients in a mental hospital (see Fig. 2.16). The basic hypothesis of Rorschach's study was that patients suffering from different psychiatric disorders (schizophrenics, neurotics, etc.) would show characteristic differences in their perceptions of ambiguous inkblots. From hundreds of inkblots Rorschach selected a standard set of ten that he felt elicited the widest variety of perceptual reactions. These stimuli were administered to the subject one at a time with the simple instruction "Tell me what this might be." Responses to the inkblots (such as "a bat", "two natives dancing") were classified along several dimensions. The major dimensions of classification involved the location, determinants, and content of the responses.

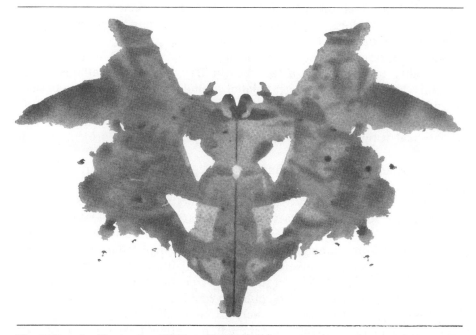

Fig. 2.16. An illustrative inkblot. (Reprinted by permission of Hans Huber, Publishers, Berne, Stuttgart, Vienna.)

The *location* of a response to an inkblot refers to the part of the blot that gave rise to the percept: the whole blot, a large detail, or a small portion of it. The *determinant* refers to formal qualities of the blot that influenced the perception: the shape, color, and shading of the blot and the degree to which movement is attributed to it. The *content* of a response refers to the substantive category in which a response may be classified: human, animal, nature, abstract concepts, and the like. All these dimensions of response classification can be transformed into quantitative form by the use of expert judges' ratings. Once the responses have been classified they form the basis of inferences about personality traits in line with theoretical considerations that link location with cognitive traits, determinants with emotional traits, and content with symbolic preoccupations. Despite the widespread use of the Rorschach test as a basis for making personality interpretations, there is remarkably little evidence to support the elaborate theoretical considerations that relate inkblot responses to more conventional measures of personality attributes.

Another form of projective technique, the Thematic Apperception Test (TAT), was developed as an objective method of systematically investigating a subject's fantasy life (Murray, 1943). The TAT stimulus pictures are less ambiguous than the Rorschach inkblots. In fact, they portray actual persons and scenes taken from photographs and paintings (see Fig. 2.17). The subject is presented with a series of pictures and asked to make up a story for each one, describing what is going on now, how the situation came about, and how it might end. The basic hypothesis is that subjects will "project" their own needs and concerns onto the people they include in the stories, even though the pictures themselves have some "reality" status. This type of personality assessment is to some extent more "direct" than is the Rorschach, though the subject is free to make up any kind of story at all.

The subject's stories are recorded by hand or tape recorder and later analyzed in terms of one of a number of different theoretical systems. The major scoring system involved in TAT analysis is that developed by Murray (1938), the originator of the TAT. In this method of analysis, an attempt is made to identify the "hero" of the story and to indicate the *needs* which the hero is striving to fulfill. At the same time, the analyst tries to identify the *press* (the sources of environmental pressure) that are operating on the hero, often in opposition to his or her needs. The *outcome* of the story frequently provides an indication of the manner in which the basic conflict between the needs of the hero and the press of the environment is resolved. The basic assumption of such an analysis is that the needs of the hero indicate the needs of the subject making up the story. It is generally accurate to say that the needs of the hero reflect the *preoccupations* of the subject. Whether or not those preoccupations are expressed by the subject in overt behavior is a much more complex and controversial subject.

Although the TAT has been used as a basis for drawing elaborate theoretical inferences similar to those made from the Rorschach test, it

Fig. 2.17. An illustrative TAT card. (Reprinted by permission of the publishers from Henry A. Murray, *Thematic Apperception Test,* Cambridge, Mass.: Harvard University Press. Copyright 1943 by the President and Fellows of Harvard College.)

has proved most useful in research designed to study relatively circumscribed need or trait systems. Research designed to explore a small number of carefully defined needs has often yielded positive evidence of the construct validity of TAT measures. The achievement motive, or need for achievement, has been intensively studied in this respect (McClelland *et al.,* 1953). Dependency, aggression, and sexuality have also been the subjects of extensive TAT research, as will become apparent in later chapters devoted to those topics.

SUMMARY

In this chapter we undertook a general survey of the four points of view around which the book is organized.

The *biological* viewpoint focuses on natural units of behavior as they have evolved during human adaptation to changing environments. This evolutionary perspective stresses both phylogeny, the development of behavior within the human species, and the ontogenetic development of each particular person. Therefore, the adaptive significance of a behavioral response in the natural human environment is emphasized more than the precision with which that response can be defined or measured in the laboratory. Selective pressures that give rise to human behavior and the contemporary pressures working to modify it are of central concern.

Techniques from behavior genetics provide basic experimental tools for the biological viewpoint. Much work of interest is necessarily performed on lower animals, where selective mating and controls of maternal effects permit careful delineation of biological factors in behavior development. Parallel procedures for human research include twin-family methods and the study of adopted individuals. Results from these studies reveal that gene differences affect variation in a diverse array of physical and behavioral traits. Because all gene effects on behavior are indirect, however, it is rarely possible to specify the mechanism of action. Two general principles may summarize the behavioral result of gene variation. The effect of any experience depends, in part, on the genotype to which that experience occurs (differential susceptibility), and the genotype determines, in part, the nature of experience to which any individual is exposed (selective exposure).

Just as different organisms are differentially susceptible to experience, the responsiveness of any particular organism varies over time. Prenatal factors in behavior development and theory and research on early experience constitute a third focus of the biological viewpoint. There is evidence of critical periods in development such that experiences within these periods are of particular importance to personality study. And there is general evidence, albeit often indirect, that experience in early infancy is critically important in personality development.

Experimental psychology proceeds on the assumption that uniform processes underlie human behavior. Although the content of the personality of different individuals is highly distinctive and unique, people share uniformity in the way in which that content was acquired. The understanding of human behavior and the possibility for control over it rest in understanding the processes whereby specific content is acquired.

From the point of view of general experimental psychology, the description of behavior concerns the mechanisms through which experiences have their effects. An individual learns to be what he or she is. The "self" or the "I" or the "me" is a collection of experiences which find organization within the person and eventual expression in behavior through uniform learning, perceptual, and higher processes.

The natural units of personality and the possibilities for the prediction, the control, and the understanding of human behavior lie in the mechanisms and processes whereby the unique content of each person is acquired. The study of personality in such a context is indistinguishable from the procedures and methods of general experimental psychology.

In the section on the *social* viewpoint, it was asserted that humans are social animals and that important personality characteristics are both socially defined and socially determined. The research on personality from the social viewpoint was organized around three constructs: *models, roles,* and *cultures.*

In the discussion of models, we contended that one of the primary ways individuals learn to be as they are is by imitating models. The wide range of behavior subject to the influence of models includes everything from suicide to yawning. However, it is clear that not all observers imitate all models. Among the critical factors are such aspects of the observer as emotional arousal, such aspects of the model as whether or not the model is rewarded or punished for the behavior, and such interpersonal aspects as the similarity of the model to the observer.

"Role playing" usually refers to the make-believe enactment of a role for a brief period of time, as in a dramatic production. The process was discussed as an agent of behavior and personality change.

In the discussion of cultures, it was asserted that one of the most pervasive but least appreciated determinants of an individual's behavior is the cultural context of development. Traditionally, the study of other cultures depended on the observations of investigators who lived in the field for extended periods. Although the information gathered by this method is rich in detail, it is contaminated by the cultural bias of the observer and it is consequently difficult to quantify. However, the bias can be reduced if additional investigators from different cultures participate and if they describe additional target cultures. One can place relative confidence in attributes that different observers agree are characteristic of one target culture but are not characteristic of another.

The *psychometric-trait* approach to personality study asserts that the behavior of individuals is best understood in terms of attributes which reflect underlying trait organizations. A trait may be thought of as any distinguishable, relatively enduring way in which one individual differs from others. The measurement of such traits is guided by mathematical rules specifying the manner in which numbers are assigned to attributes of behavior. Because traits are constructs, there are many different mathematical rules under which numbers may be assigned to such behavioral attributes. Which rules are selected will depend on the manner in which traits are construed. The principles that guide most trait approaches to personality study are based on constructs regarding the covariation, stability, structure, and dynamics of behavioral attributes.

A variety of methods are employed to obtain personality-trait measurements. These methods may be conveniently classified under three headings: observational, self-report, and indirect methods. The use of a given type of method imposes methodological "blinders" on observation and results in a relative emphasis of certain aspects of an event and a relative deemphasis of other aspects of the same event. Consequently, differing constructions of the same trait may be obtained when the trait is measured by different methods. This situation is quite compatible with the overall view of constructive alternativism, which is the overriding theme of this book.

SUGGESTIONS FOR FURTHER READING

The Biological Viewpoint

Glass, D. C. (ed.). *Biology and Behavior Series. Neurophysiology and Emotion,* 1967; *Genetics,* 1968; *Environmental Influences,* 1968. New York: Rockefeller University Press. Proceedings of three conferences relating biological ideas and methods to the study of behavior.

Jaffe, J. M. *Prenatal Determinants of Behaviour.* Oxford: Pergamon, 1969. A review of research in the area including Jaffe's studies on effects of gestational stress in rodents.

McClearn, G. E., and J. C. Defries. *Introduction to Behavioral Genetics.* San Francisco: W. H. Freeman, 1973. A recent and scholarly work that fulfills the promise of its title.

Young, J. Z. *An Introduction to the Study of Man.* New York: Oxford University Press, 1971. An eminent zoologist traces human evolution and surveys human behavior within a biological framework. A widely acclaimed work.

The Experimental Viewpoint

Renner, K. E., and J. B. Tinsley. "Self-punitive Behavior," in G. Bower (ed.), *The Psychology of Learning and Motivation,* Vol. 10. New York: Academic Press, 1976. This chapter elaborates the concepts of incentive motivation by using them to analyze the problems of self-destructive and maladaptive behaviors.

Seligman, M. E. P. *Helplessness*. San Francisco: W. H. Freeman, 1975. In this book an experimental psychologist who has done important work on classical conditioning extends the boundaries of the laboratory to a variety of clinical phenomena.

Skinner, B. F. *About Behaviorism*. New York: Knopf, 1974. In this book Skinner presents his version of the experimental viewpoint, which emphasizes those aspects of experimental psychology developed through the experimental analysis of behavior. "Behaviorism" is the name given to the specific methodology developed by Skinner.

The Social Viewpoint

Bandura, A. (ed.). *Psychological Modeling: Conflicting Theories*. Chicago: Aldine-Atherton, 1971. A collection of research articles by numerous authors as they originally appeared in the journals along with Bandura's 60-page discussion of conflicting views.

Biddle, B. J., and E. J. Thomas (eds.). *Role Theory: Concepts and Research*. New York: Wiley, 1966. An edited book with a variety of previously published articles on all aspects of the concept of role as it has been used in sociology and psychology.

Al-issa, I., and W. Dennis (eds.). *Cross-cultural Studies of Behavior*. New York: Holt, 1970. This collection includes examples of fascinating cross-cultural work by both psychologists and anthropologists on mental health, psycholinguistics, and perception, in addition to child rearing and personality.

The Psychometric-trait Viewpoint

Cattell, R. B. *The Scientific Analysis of Personality*. Baltimore: Penguin, 1965. Cattell is a major personality theorist whose work is based on psychometric-trait concepts. This very readable introduction to his work illustrates the wide range of phenomena that can be embraced by the psychometric-trait approach.

Edwards, A. L. *The Measurement of Personality Traits by Scales and Inventories*. New York: Holt, 1970. A presentation of the basic concepts underlying self-report methods and a description of the major instruments. For students who have some background in statistics.

Fiske, D. W. *Measuring the Concepts of Personality*. Chicago: Aldine, 1971. An excellent intermediate-level treatment of the role of measurement in personality theory and research. Theoretical issues in personality measurement are presented clearly with a minimum of technical details.

Guilford, J. P. *Personality*. New York: McGraw-Hill, 1959. This introductory text is written exclusively from the psychometric-trait viewpoint. It is a useful compendium of all major trait dimensions that have been studied in personality research.

Kelly, E. L. *Assessment of Human Characteristics*. Belmont, Calif.: Brooks/Cole, 1967. A brief and highly readable introduction to personality measurement and assessment. Covers a number of topics not included in the present text.

Mischel, W. *Personality and Assessment*. New York: Wiley, 1968. A highly influential and controversial attack on the trait concept in personality. This book raises a number of very basic issues that are still unresolved in contemporary personality assessment.

Wiggins, J. S. *Personality and Prediction: Principles of Personality Assessment*. Reading, Mass.: Addison-Wesley, 1973. An advanced textbook which provides a comprehensive survey of the principles underlying the prediction of human behavior in socially relevant contexts. This book should be of interest to students seeking a more detailed treatment of personality measurement procedures.

Section 2
Dependency

3
Dependency : The Biological Viewpoint

I. **Evolutionary perspective**

II. **Behavior genetics**
   A. Infant twin studies of dependency and socialization
   B. Twin studies with older children
   C. Longitudinal stability of passivity and dependency

III. **Early experience**
   A. Initial studies of Spalding
   B. Imprinting in mammals
   C. The effect of rearing mice with rats
   D. Rearing experiences and social behavior in monkeys
   E. Institutionalization and social behavior in humans

IV. **Summary**

V. **Suggestions for further reading**

EVOLUTIONARY PERSPECTIVE

The introduction to the biological viewpoint in Chapter 2 sketched a history of the joint development of the human brain and human behavior. From a primitive creature able only to shape and use the crudest of stone tools emerged Homo Erectus, whose brain and behavior were highly sophisticated. That human brain and human behavior developed together seems quite certain; equally certain is the fact that they affected each other's development in a most complex interaction.

The emergence of a large brain created profound changes in the nature of human behavior. Simultaneously, dramatic changes occurred in human development. The mother-child relationship in humans is unique among all primates. The nature of this unique relationship is, in part, a product of the evolving development of brain and behavior. In other primates the baby is born with its central nervous system in an advanced state of development, and the young organism is abandoned by its mother relatively soon after birth. But the brain of the human fetus, although capable of immensely complex development later, must first be small enough so that birth can occur. In humans the evolution of bipedal locomotion decreased the size of the bony birth canal at the same time that their use of tools began to selectively create their larger brain. This "obstetrical dilemma" (Washburn, 1960) was solved by the delivery of the fetus at a much earlier stage of development. A marked deceleration of growth and maturation, neoteny, began to occur. And as we have argued before, *it is this prolonged duration of relative dependency that provides the essential framework for human socialization.*

The degree to which neoteny occurred in the evolving human species is apparent in the contrast of a human infant with an infant chimpanzee. Before birth the brain of a monkey fetus increases rapidly in size and complexity; when born, the animal's brain has already attained 70% of its final adult size, and the remaining growth is quickly completed during the first half year of life. Our own species, by contrast, has a brain that at birth is less than 25% of its final adult size. The growth continues for some six years after birth, and the entire process of maturational development is not complete until after the twentieth year of life. Infant monkeys and chimpanzees are playful and exploratory, but the phase dies quickly. In contrast, the human infant, with a longer childhood during which to learn from social modeling of parents and other adults, extends infancy directly into adult life. This remarkable developmental lag provides the framework for the imitative learning that we now call culture.

The extensive neoteny of the human infant developed over thousands of years. Bipedalism, tool use, and the selection for a larger brain were

Ken Heyman

jointly responsible for this dramatic evolutionary change. But once it began to occur, many important consequences followed. Because of the extreme dependency of the young and the demands made by them, females found themselves almost continually confined to the home base. The slow-moving mother, either pregnant or caring for her young, could not hunt; she was obligated to remain behind and care for her slowly developing baby. Thus the roles of the sexes had to become more distinct. Hunting parties had to become all-male groups. But this development demanded another evolutionary change: for a primate male to go off on a hunting trip and leave his female unprotected required a major shift in social behavior. The result was the development of the stable pair-bond. Male and female paired, thus solving a number of problems in one stroke: The females remained bonded to individual males and were faithful to them while the males were away on the hunt; serious sexual rivalries between males were reduced, and stable, nonaggressive associations between males could be maintained; and most important, in terms of our own cultural values, the development of the stable pair-bond breeding unit meant that the offspring also benefited (Morris, 1967). *The task of rearing and training the grossly immature and slowly developing young demanded—and provided —a cohesive family unit.* The female, assured of her male's support, was able to devote herself to maternal duties. The male, certain of the female's loyalty, could go on the hunts and at the same time avoid fighting over her. The net result was that their offspring were provided with a maximum of care and attention.

It is particularly important to understand that these changes are basically *biological,* rather than simply or solely cultural. *The developing species was changing genetically.* And biological evolution provided the essential framework for the culture transmission that we now value so highly in human affairs.

BEHAVIOR GENETICS

The biological immaturity of the human infant retards the initiation and development of most psychological dimensions and traits of interest. Social behaviors, including dependency, affiliation, and interpersonal responsiveness, are not observable until considerable biological maturity has been attained. At an age when they can first be reliably assessed, behaviors of greatest interest to personality study have already been profoundly influenced by the experiential history of the subject. For these reasons, behavior-genetic analysis of dependency and sociability in humans has turned to relatively simple behavior sequences; such behaviors theoretically provide the foundation for the development of the complex behaviors of true interest.

INFANT TWIN STUDIES OF DEPENDENCY AND SOCIALIZATION

An excellent example of this approach is some recent work with infant twins by Freedman (1965). This work has focused on two objectively measurable responses: social smiling and the fear response to strangers. During the first five months of the baby's life, social orientation was scored on the basis of visual fixation of the face and frequency of social smiling. Fearfulness was scored primarily on the basis of fear of the investigator. Social orientation and fearfulness are of obvious adaptive significance and may be considered to reflect basic tendencies to socially approach or avoid another. The influence of the genotype on these dispositions might be regarded as prototypic of the effect of gene differences on later, more complex behaviors.

Freedman (1965; Freedman and Keller, 1963) studied 20 pairs of infant twins of the same sex. Mental and motor abilities and personality development were assessed at monthly intervals throughout the first year of life by means of standardized mental and motor scales. Neither the investigators nor the parents knew the zygosity of these twins until the end of the experiment. At the conclusion of the study, blood serum analyses revealed 11 fraternal twin pairs and 9 identical pairs.

Results of the experiment can be summarized in a single sentence: Identical twins were more alike on every behavior dimension studied. Within-pair differences were significantly greater for fraternal twins on *all* tests and rating scales. Figure 3.1 presents the average within-pair differences during the first year for the Bayley Mental and Motor Scales combined to form a single distribution. It is readily apparent that identical twin pairs exhibit less difference on these standardized scales ($p = .01$). Figure 3.2 presents analogous data for the Bayley Infant Behavior Profile, which is a rating scale consisting of 21 items covering 12 categories of behavior. The Behavior Profile includes ratings of responsiveness to persons and objects, fearfulness, goal directedness, activity level, and reactivity. Again, identical co-twins exhibit significantly greater behavioral similarity.

The methodological sophistication of this study warrants special attention. First, since neither examiners nor parents were certain of zygosity until the end of the study, any differential treatment of identical and fraternal twins by parents, as well as any differential rating bias by the investigators, can be effectively ruled out. Parents were often mistaken

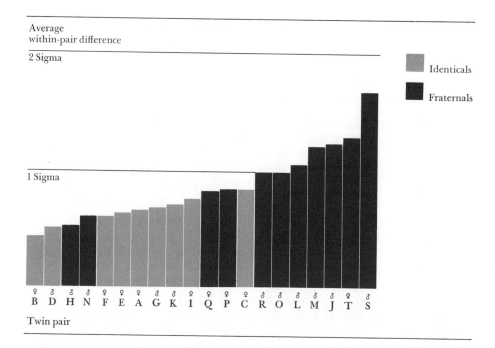

Average
within-pair difference

Fig. 3.1. Bayley Mental and Motor Scales averaged to form a single distribution; average within-pair differences in the first year. (Figures 3.1, 3.2, and 3.3 from "Inheritance of behavior in infants," D. G. Freedman and B. Keller, *Science*, 1963, **140**, 196–198. Copyright 1963 by the American Association for the Advancement of Science.)

in their assumptions about their infant twins: For 6 of the 9 identical twin pairs, parents assumed that twins were fraternals; obstetricians were incorrect 9 out of 19 times in their assumptions concerning zygosity. Thus *all but 3 of the 20 pairs of twins were being reared as fraternals.* We can therefore conclude that the observed behavior differences between the two sets of twins were not created by differences in parental attitude; that is, identical co-twins are not more alike merely because they are being reared more alike.

Second, experimenter bias was equally well controlled. Monthly motion pictures were taken in which the co-twins in each pair were filmed separately in the same situation. At the conclusion of the study the assembled filmstrips of one twin were shown to one group of four professional judges, and the films of his co-twin were shown to a second group. The judges rated each child on the Infant Behavior Profile, with no knowledge as to whether he was an identical or a fraternal twin. The

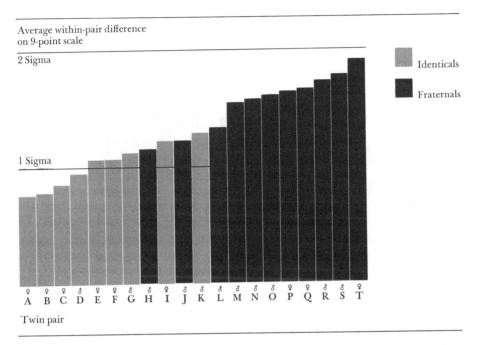

Average within-pair difference
on 9-point scale

Fig. 3.2. Average within-pair differences in the first year on the Bayley Infant Behavior Profile.

scores were averaged for each infant, and the difference within each twin pair was then determined. Figure 3.3 shows the results, and again intra-pair differences among fraternal twins are significantly greater. Free from any obvious contamination from either experimenters or parents, these data clearly demonstrate the contribution of the genotype to the development of differences in motor, mental, and personality behaviors.

This conclusion is strengthened by results from a longitudinal study of the development of infants in the Louisville Twin Study (Wilson, 1972). Similarity of monozygotic and dizygotic twins was assessed through the first 24 months with the Bayley scales. The over-all concordance of fraternal twins is significantly less than that of identical pairs, and Wilson's results indicate that the spurts and lags in early human development are, in part, under genetic control.

To summarize, the genotype plays a role in the differential development of positive social orientation and fear of strangers. Other evidence suggests that the smiling response is innately organized: blind infants smile in response to social stimulation, and the smile is accompanied by orientation of the blind infant's eyes to the caretaker's face, (Freedman,

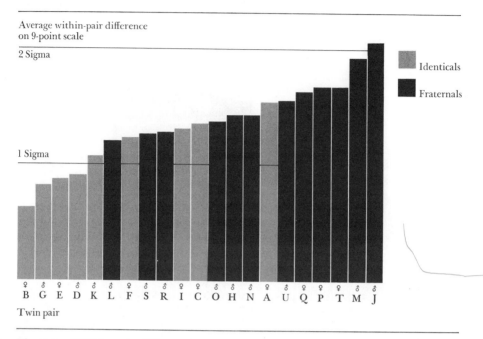

Fig. 3.3. Within-pair differences on the Bayley Infant Behavior Profile. Ratings are based on eight months of filmed behavior.

1964; Wickler, 1973). Because the social smile is the first expression of pleasure with another person, while fear of strangers is normally the first expression of fear of another, individual differences in smiling and fear of strangers are of considerable significance. The two phenomena are universal in our species, and they have been important in human adaptation and evolution.

It is not yet apparent *how* the genotype contributes to individual differences in social orientation or fearfulness. But some provocative data have recently been reported in a study of patterns of response to physical contact in young infants. In a sample of 37 babies (Schaffer and Emerson, 1964), 9 babies consistently and without modification resisted being cuddled and held by their mothers; these noncuddling infants resisted the restriction of movement that is necessarily involved in interpersonal contact with the mother. Babies who were cuddlers appeared to be less active, less resistive, and less restless than did the noncuddlers, and they slept longer. Thus there appear to be stable individual differences among human infants in their desire or need for physical contact; such differences *profoundly influence the course of an infant's development through their effects on parents and caretakers* (Korner, 1971; Lewis and Rosenblum, 1974).

TWIN STUDIES WITH OLDER CHILDREN

If we define sociability broadly enough to include social introversion-extraversion, social anxiety, friendliness to strangers, and social spontaneity, we may consider a behavior dimension extending from shy, intrapunitive, introspective, and anxious withdrawal from others to friendly, extraverted, self-confident engagement in interpersonal relationships. Twin studies have consistently shown evidence that the genotype contributes to individual differences in sociability defined in this manner. A representative study is that recently reported by Scarr (1966). Fifty-two pairs of twin girls between the ages of six and ten were studied. The sample included 28 fraternal pairs and 24 identicals. The twins and their mothers were tested in their homes by two experimenters; the mothers completed a 300-item Adjective Check List for both daughters, and after each test session, the experimenters independently rated the twins on several of the Fels Child Behavior Scales. Some relevant results are given in Table 3.1. Social apprehension, friendliness, and affiliation show significantly higher within-pair similarity for the identical co-twins.

An important methodological aspect of this study involved an analysis of twin similarity in cases where the mother was *mistaken* regarding

Table 3.1 Correlations for selected social-dependent behaviors in identical and fraternal twin girls.

	Correlation identical twins	Correlation fraternal twins
Adjective Check List dimensions		
Need affiliation	83	56
Anxiety	56	03
Need change	70	−12
Need autonomy	40	11
Fels Child Behavior Scales		
Rated anxiety	88	28
Rated friendliness	86	36

Correlations based on Adjective Check Lists completed by twins' mothers and ratings on the Fels scales by two experimenters. (Data adapted from Scarr, 1968, 1969)

the zygosity of her twin daughters. Scarr (1968) demonstrated that identical co-twins who were (mistakenly) being reared as fraternals were as alike as identical pairs whose mothers correctly judged their zygosity. Fraternal twins were less alike, even in those cases where they were being reared as identicals. Although the number of such misclassified pairs was not large, the preliminary results are provocative, for they provide striking evidence of the influence of the genotype on the development of social behaviors.

Thus the evidence that hereditary factors importantly influence the development of socialization is considerable. And that evidence is important in any effort to account adequately for variation in dependency and affiliative behaviors. However, it is equally apparent that social learning profoundly modifies the genotypic effects. The form, frequency, and meaning of most social behaviors are modulated by cultural norms. Interesting evidence of this fact can be found in the longitudinal study of dependency, to which we now turn.

LONGITUDINAL STABILITY OF PASSIVITY AND DEPENDENCY

The stability of passive and dependent behaviors has been intensively studied within the larger framework of ongoing longitudinal studies conducted by Kagan and Moss (1962). One of the earlier reports from that research (Kagan and Moss, 1960) was specifically concerned with the stability of dependency from childhood into adulthood.

A sample of 27 males and 27 females, for whom longitudinal data were available from years three to ten, were assessed by means of detailed interview techniques when they were in their twenties. Each subject was interviewed on several occasions for a total of about five hours; the interviewer had no knowledge of any of the earlier longitudinal data on the subject. Following completion of the interviews, each subject was rated on a 7-point scale for six variables dealing with adult passive and dependent behaviors. The variables included: (1) the extent to which security was a factor in job choice and job stability; (2) the extent to which the subject sought emotional support, stability, and guidance from spouse or sweetheart; and (3) the extent to which subject sought advice, support, and nurturance from parents.

Childhood behavior was independently evaluated by a second judge who had no knowledge of the adult status of the subjects. Narrative reports, based on observations of the subject at nursery, the Research Institute, camp, or school, and at home while interacting with his or her mother, formed the basis of the childhood evaluation. All material for each subject during the period from age six to ten was studied, and the child was then rated on a number of childhood variables that involved passive dependency, including behavioral passivity, emotional dependency on female adults, and tendency to seek assistance from female adults.

Table 3.2 presents some of the correlations between childhood and adult ratings of passive and dependent behaviors.

Table 3.2 Stability of selected passive-dependent behaviors from childhood to adulthood.

Childhood variables (ages 6–10)	Adult dependency variables							
	Dependency in vocation		Dependency on love object		Dependency on parents		Withdrawal to failure	
	M	F	M	F	M	F	M	F
Passivity	11	73	25	36	20	54	21	52
Emotional dependence	21	08	18	37	02	51	35	37
Instrumental dependence	19	39	06	58	14	32	09	39

Correlations of selected passive-dependent behaviors observed in childhood with dependency themes elicited in interviews in adulthood. Tendency of correlations to be much higher in females suggests that passive dependency is culturally reinforced in women. (Adapted from J. Kagan and H. A. Moss, "The stability of passive and dependent behavior from childhood through adulthood," *Child Development,* 1960, **31**, pp. 581–582. Copyright 1960, The Society for Research in Child Development, Inc.)

The major result is that passive and dependent behaviors were fairly stable for females but not for males. For girls the ratings of passivity during ages 6 to 10 correlated significantly with the adult ratings of a dependent orientation in vocational choice, dependency on love object, dependency on parents, and withdrawal to failure. Childhood passivity was inversely correlated with adult conflict over dependent behavior. That is, females who were passive as children were apt to accept their dependent behavior in adulthood and show minimal anxiety over their dependent motives.

For the men there were only two significant correlations between the childhood dependency ratings and those based on the adult interview. (Kagan and Moss, 1960, pp. 581–582)

This striking difference between males and females in the longitudinal stability of passive-dependent behavior is evident in several studies. What produces it? Kagan and Moss argue that *the differential stability of dependency is a product of sex-role training:*

...passive and dependent behavior is less punished in females than in males. Further, females are often encouraged to be passive while men are expected to be independent and autonomous in the face of frustration. Parental and peer group punishment for passive and dependent behavior should result in some inhibition of this behavior in males. Thus, we would not expect this class of behavior to be as stable for men as for women. (Kagan and Moss, 1960, pp. 584–585)

This is a reasonable argument, and it derives support from complementary findings on other behaviors. If cultural training in sex-role behavior does produce differential stability, this result should be evident in all behaviors subject to such training. In our culture, for example, *aggressiveness should show the converse pattern*: stability in males, but not in females. As we shall see in Chapter 7, this *is* the pattern found in longitudinal studies of aggressiveness.

EARLY EXPERIENCE

Longitudinal study of the stability of dependency reveals the interaction of early dispositions with later cultural training. This continuing interaction of experience with constitution is well exemplified in the study of social behavior of animals. The major focus of this study, which we shall now analyze in some detail, is called *imprinting*.

Initial Studies by Spalding

The first systematic observations on imprinting were reported nearly a century ago by Douglas A. Spalding, who initiated a series of studies on the later effects of early experiential deprivation. He reportedly (Haldane, 1954) showed that hand-reared swallows kept in cages too small to permit flying flew perfectly on their first opportunity, but that a gosling reared away from the water refused to enter a pond when first taken to one at the age of several months.

In 1872, Spalding read a paper entitled "Instinct, with original observations on young animals" to the British Association. It was published the next year; in 1954 it was reprinted in a contemporary journal. In the paper, a genuine classic, Spalding clearly described imprinting:

> Chickens as soon as they are able to walk will follow any moving object. And, when guided by sight alone, they seem to have no more disposition to follow a hen than to follow a duck, or a human being. Unreflecting onlookers, when they saw chickens a day old running after me, and older ones following me miles and answering to my whistle, imagined that I must have

some occult power over the creatures, whereas I simply allowed them to follow me from the first.*

Spalding was especially concerned with the instinctive nature of the response of following in the chick. To study it, he developed an ingenious procedure (reproduced by Gray, 1961) to deprive the newly hatched chick of visual experience. Spalding wrote that he

> ... had recourse to the following expedient. Taking eggs just when the little prisoners had begun to break their way out, I removed a piece of the shell, and before they had opened their eyes drew over their heads little hoods, which, being furnished with an elastic thread at the lower end, fitted close round their necks. The material of the hoods was in some cases such as to keep the wearers in total darkness; in other instances it was semi-transparent. . . .
> In this state of blindness—the blindness was very manifest—I allowed them to remain one to three days. The conditions under which these little victims of human curiosity were first permitted to see the light were then carefully prepared. (Spalding, 1954, p. 3)

The results of that classic experiment revealed the responses we now call imprinting; they were

> ... very plainly exemplified in the case of the chicken that, after being un-hooded, sat complaining and motionless for six minutes, then I placed my hand on it for a few seconds. On removing my hand the chicken immediately followed it by sight backward and forward and all around the table. (Spalding, 1954, p. 3)

Following Spalding's initial studies, the phenomenon of imprinting was discussed by William James and other early psychologists; in more recent years, imprinting has been widely investigated in the laboratory. The discussion here is based largely on reviews by Gray (1966) and Sluckin (1965).

Gray has defined imprinting via a consideration of its function, which is to socially attach the young animal to its own species. After the attachment is effected, the young animal will be taught what it needs to be taught, and in adulthood it will court and mate one of its own kind. Thus the function of imprinting is to provide a "social anchor for all life's experiences" (Gray, 1966). *Imprinting is, then, a learned establishment of a social bond securing the inexperienced animal to the parent or to a parent-surrogate.* Imprinting is a learning-of-the-parent. As such, it may well provide the foundation for socialization.

* From D. A. Spalding, "Instinct, with original observations on young animals," *Macmillan's Magazine*, 1893. Reprinted in *British Journal of Animal Behavior*, 1954, **2**, p. 6. Used by permission of Macmillan.

Imprinting in Mammals

Laboratory studies of imprinting have almost exclusively used the domestic chick or other species of birds. Some suggestive evidence from the study of mammals has been obtained, but controversy exists as to whether or not imprinting, in the sense defined above, occurs in mammals, especially humans. However, as Gray (1958) has argued, available evidence does suggest that the human infant's first social response is directed toward learning its parents. Further, the processes of socialization appear to be essentially the same in all mammals, and in all there are specific and distinct periods of social development. Behavioral experiences during these periods profoundly influence later social responses.

Modification of adult social behavior, arising as a result of atypical early experience, has been reported in mouse, monkey, and human. We shall briefly cite representative experiments.

The Effect of Rearing Mice with Rats

A recent study relevant to the issue of imprinting in mammals has been reported by Denenberg, Hudgens, and Zarrow (1964). The investigators reared four groups of male mice under different social conditions and then assessed the social preferences of the mice in adulthood. (1) Mice in the first group were fostered to a lactating rat mother during the first days of life and thereafter lived only with rats. (2) A second group, reared by mice, had experience only with rats after weaning. (3) Mice in a third group, the controls, spent all their lives with other mice. (4) A final group was composed of isolates reared by mice but allowed no experience with peers; each litter was reduced to one pup, which was reared in social isolation after weaning.

At maturity, males from the four groups were compared for social preference of rat versus mouse. The animals were individually placed in the stem of a T-shaped unit; each arm of the T ended in a wire-mesh cage. A male mouse was placed behind one mesh wall and a male rat behind the other. The test animal was placed in the unit for ten minutes on four consecutive days, and the amount of time spent in each chamber was recorded. Table 3.3 summarizes the experiment and provides relevant results.

All but one of the 33 animals from Group 1, which had never seen a mouse until the test, socially preferred rat to mouse, and results were nearly as dramatic for the mice in Group 2. Thus social interaction with rats, before or after weaning, significantly modifies a mouse's social behavior in adulthood.

Table 3.3   Adult social preference in mice reared with rats.

Group	Rearing mother	Peers in infancy	Peers after weaning	Social preference test
1	Rat	Rats	Rats	97
2	Mouse	Mice	Rats	86
3	Mouse	Mice	Mice	27
4	Mouse	None	None	17

The social preference results are the percentage of animals that spent more time in the chamber containing the stimulus rat than in the one containing the stimulus mouse. (From Denenberg *et al.*, "Mice reared with rats: modification of behavior by early experience with another species," *Science*, 1964, **143**, pp. 380–381. Copyright 1964 by the American Association for the Advancement of Science.)

Rearing Experiences and Social Behavior in Monkeys

Provocative studies of imprinting-like phenomena, some similar to those just described for mice, have been reported in primates. The effects of different rearing experiences on the social development of rhesus monkeys have been investigated by Sackett (1967; 1968). Results indicate that rearing conditions during the first year markedly influence the social preferences of a mature monkey. In addition, there is evidence of innate releasers (presumably encoded into the genotype) for some important social responses (Sackett, 1966).

In his studies of social behavior, Sackett uses an apparatus called the "Self Selection Circus." The Circus is a free-choice apparatus composed of six choice compartments surrounding an inner compartment that serves as starting point; the device permits a monkey to choose freely among social stimuli by making differential approach responses.

Behavior very similar to that identified as imprinting has also been obtained in the Circus apparatus (Sackett, Porter, and Holmes, 1965). Pre-adult monkeys (3.5 to 4.5 years old) were given a choice between a human adult female and a caged monkey of the same age and sex.

Among the groups tested were: (1) *partial isolates*, separated from others at birth and given intimate physical contact with a human female for 30 days, then housed in partial isolation from other monkeys; (2) *together-togethers*, separated at birth, provided with human female care for 30 days, then reared with age-mates for remainder of first year; (3) *mother-peer* animals, housed with mother and peers for first year; and (4) and (5) *six-month and one-year total isolates*, kept in total social isolation from birth to the sixth or twelfth month. After the first year, all monkeys had extensive social experience with peers.

Table 3.4 Choice behavior in monkeys as a function of rearing conditions.

Rearing condition	Social preference		
	Human	Monkey	Center
Partial isolate	226	36	38
Together-together	27	165	108
Mother-peer	11	191	98
Six-month isolate	4	99	197
One-year isolate	0	126	174

Social preference results are the mean duration (in seconds) in each compartment. (From Sackett et al., "Choice behavior in rhesus monkeys: effects of stimulation during the first month of life," Science, 1965, **147**, pp. 304–306. Copyright 1965 by the American Association for the Advancement of Science.)

Results from this experiment are summarized in Table 3.4, which gives the mean lengths of time spent in the compartments occupied by the human and the monkey, as well as in the center start area, for the five groups of animals. Partial isolates preferred the human (imprinting?), but the two total isolate groups, who had had neither human nor monkey contact in early life, spent most of their time in the center—away from either social choice.

Institutionalization and Social Behavior in Humans

One of the problems inherent in efforts to identify imprinting in humans is the obvious fact that they are unable to walk immediately after the neonatal stage. Thus, if imprinting does occur, it must occur in responses other than following. Gray (1958) has proposed that the smiling response in the human infant is the motor equivalent of the response of following in lower animals. He argues that the social smile does not appear until about the sixth week of age, and when it does, the response is *released* by the human face or a stimulus configuration similar to the human face. And as noted in the discussion of Freedman's infant twin studies, smiling is apparently the first social response in the human child.

Is there a critical period for imprinting in the human? Gray has summarized evidence from studies of institutionalized infants which suggests that such a critical period may exist. A particularly important study on the effects of institutionalization has been reported by Goldfarb (1947). Goldfarb compared two groups of adolescents who had been adopted at about three years of age. Those in one group had been admitted to the institution before the sixth month of age, in the other at six months or older. Among other results, he found that 11 of the 15 adolescents admitted before the sixth month had severe behavioral troubles in adolescence, whereas only 4 of the other group of 15 were similarly maladjusted. Gray argues that, like the chick, the human infant must pass the period of fear, and that what occurs during that period is of crucial importance for subsequent socialization. While there remains some controversy over the true nature of early imprinting-like responses in the human, there is no question that social apathy, emotional withdrawal, and heterosexual maladjustment frequently result from institutionalization during the critical period of the first six months of life (Gray, 1958).

Everything thus far suggests that imprinting is particularly important in the development of socialization and later adult sexual preferences of the individual animal. An interesting ancedote reported by Gray will summarize this argument. Gray relates that as a graduate student, he and a colleague, Roger Kelley, happened onto a demonstration of imprinting more dramatic than anything they had been able to obtain in the laboratory. Meeting in an animal room where there was a day-old chick not needed for any experiments, they decided to put it in with a kitten to discover what would happen.

Chick and kitten got along as well as chick and kitten ever will; but existence had its ragged edges. The chick tried to adjust. It paid little attention to its grain. Social facilitation obtained and it ate what the rest of the "flock" ate. It became a healthy meat-eating chicken. It also became adept at dodging the kitten's paw. Like kittens everywhere, this kitten liked to roll a ball. It didn't matter much that his ball had little legs on the end and protested its treatment in chick language.

After a month or so the kitten caught distemper and died. The chicken grew up and became a rooster without the least interest in its own kind. Finally, one day Roger and I thought we might test it for the later effects of imprinting, of which we were not too certain. For one thing, we would have to use a strange cat. There was one available, an old alley cat enticed from the streets of Chicago. We put the rooster in a room. It began exploring. We put the alley cat in the room. The rooster made interesting noises and began shuffling toward the cat. The cat hissed and went under a chair. The rooster came along and began "preening" the cat's switching tail. The cat snarled at this thing that had never frequented its alleys and went under the desk. The rooster stooped and followed. The cat had hysterics and bolted down the hall. The rooster hooted and ran out the door after the cat. We caught it and put it back in its cage. It went unwillingly. We had no problem putting the cat back into its cage.

I finally gave the rooster away to a bank teller when he picked up some young chicks that were no longer needed. The teller lived on a farm outside Chicago and his daughter kept pets, he told me (as I told him what a pet the rooster was) and yes, she kept cats, she had quite a few of them. The teller scanned the rooster's obvious virility, looked at the chicks that might be the start of a laying flock for a suburban farmer, and accepted the rooster on one condition. Did I think he would be a good breeding animal?

I looked at the floor and answered as truthfully as I could. I thought he would try. So the rooster went to the country and chances are he had an active and perhaps happy life. I would rather not think about the cats and what kind of life they may have had. (Gray, 1966, pp. 48–49)

SUMMARY

From an *evolutionary perspective,* human behavioral dependency is understood within the context of maturational immaturity. A critical feature of human evolution was a marked prolongation of individual development. This deceleration of growth, called neoteny, applies to behavior as well as to physical structure. Neoteny is clearly evident in the systematic variation across species in rate development. Species with more complex adult behavior and social organization demonstrate greater retardation of infant development. This finding suggests that the more imitative learning required for successful socialization in a species, the more time will be available for the learning to occur. The human infant demonstrates a remarkable developmental delay in both biology and behavior. Infancy is extended directly into adulthood, and behaviors often regarded as distinctively human—playfulness, inventiveness, curiosity—may be by-products of human biological neoteny. The process of neoteny also led to profound changes in human social organization. The increasingly more immature infant made increasing demands on the parents; the role of the sexes became distinguished, and the nuclear family unit evolved. The developing human was changing genetically, and biological evolution provided the foundation for human socialization.

Dependency has obvious adaptive significance. We therefore expect that *behavior-genetic analysis* will reveal that gene mechanisms underlie the expression of dependent behaviors. The expectation has been confirmed, although the actual analysis is difficult. The biological immaturity of the human infant so retards the development of adult social behavior that when such behavior can first be measured, experience has already profoundly influenced its development. For that reason, behavior-genetic analysis of dependency has focused on simple responses which appear early in development and which theoretically provide the foundation for later and more complex social behavior. Infant twin studies of social smiling and the fear response to strangers were cited as representative of this approach. These infant studies convincingly reveal the contribution that gene differences make to the development of dependency, and studies of adolescent and adult twins document the influence of the genotype on dimensions of dominance and extraversion.

Individual differences in dependency and affiliative behavior are, of course, due to variation in experience, as well as to variation in genes. Differences in the cultural reinforcement of passive dependency create differences in the stability of such behaviors over time. Affiliation and social preference are particularly influenced by *early experience*. Atypical experience during critical periods in early life produces atypical adult behavior. Extensive research on imprinting, the learning of a social bond to the parental figure, has underscored the influence of early experience on adult social preference. The typical social behavior of a species apparently develops as a result of early rearing with natural parents and peers. Rearing an animal with members of another species, or with artificial parent-surrogates, produces compelling evidence that early social experience determines adult social preference. Imprinting-like phenomena have been found in mammals, including humans. Monkeys who receive extensive early exposure to a human prior to social isolation later prefer the human to their own kind. And human infants reared in institutional settings, with peer and parental deprivation, exhibit lasting difficulties in adult socialization.

Thus the biological viewpoint suggests that human dependency has evolved as a product of biological immaturity; that because dependency serves adaptive functions, biological mechanisms exist to maintain it; and that dependency and socialization, partly encoded into the genotype, are dramatically affected by early social experience.

SUGGESTIONS FOR FURTHER READING

Freedman, D. G. *Human Infancy: An Evolutionary Perspective.* Hillsdale, New Jersey: Lawrence Erlbaum Associates, 1974. An analysis of human infancy from an ethological, evolutionary perspective, this book provides convincing evidence of genetic variance in social behavior of newborns.

Lewis, M., and L. A. Rosenblum (eds.). *The Origins of Human Behavior: The Effect of the Infant on Its Caregiver.* New York: Wiley, 1974. A series of papers that reveals the stimulus role of the infant in mother-infant interaction.

Sluckin, W. *Imprinting and Early Learning.* Chicago: Aldine, 1965; *Early Learning in Man and Animal.* Cambridge, Mass.: Schenkmann Publishing Co., 1972. Two scholarly reviews of early learning and imprinting with special attention to critical periods in personality growth.

4
Dependency: The Experimental Viewpoint

I. **Learning processes**
   A. Feelings of dependency
      1. Positive feelings of dependency
      2. Human positive feelings of attachment
   B. Dependent behaviors
      1. Instrumental conditioning
      2. The use of punishment
   C. Dependency values

II. **Perceptual processes**
   A. Social perceptions
   B. Field dependency

III. **Cognitive processes: forced dependency**

IV. **Summary**

V. **Suggestions for further reading**

The task of this chapter is to illustrate how the class of behaviors called *dependency* may be viewed in terms of the uniform psychological processes postulated by experimental psychology. Dependency will be considered from the standpoint of learning, perceptual, and cognitive processes.

LEARNING PROCESSES

Dependency includes a wide range of behaviors and human reactions. *Feelings of dependency* are best seen in terms of classical conditioning, *dependent behaviors* in terms of the processes of instrumental conditioning, and finally, *dependent values* in terms of incentive learning and incentive motivation.

FEELINGS OF DEPENDENCY

Subjectively, perhaps the most salient aspects of dependency are the feelings of isolation, fear, and loneliness which weigh on people when they are isolated from others or separated from a nurturant and supporting surrounding. The dependent person seeks a supporting context and is left with feelings of helplessness when separated from the objects on which security depends. The tears of the "junior camper" away from home for the first time illustrate feelings of dependency. However, new adventures —separation from the family or a new encounter in a strange place— need not be aversive. For some individuals such situations may bring forth feelings of excitement, buoyancy, or what might be characterized as freedom and independence. This range of emotional reactions defines one aspect of the topic of dependency.

Positive feelings of dependency. Dependence or independence reflects in part the degree of attachment toward some particular stimulus object, such as a mother. Feelings of attachment can be inferred initially in terms of the relationship between an infant and its mother. Harlow (1958) has shown that infant monkeys removed from their natural mothers form strong attachments to inanimate surrogate mothers, particularly those with special tactile qualities. In what has become a classic study, Harlow showed that monkeys raised with terry cloth "mothers," which provided warmth and tactile stimulation, became attached to the surrogate mothers. In the context provided by classical conditioning, the terry cloth mother becomes associated with warmth and pleasurable feelings. "Her" mere presence is sufficient to elicit feelings of security and well-being.

Harlow compared the number of hours per day that an infant monkey spent with a warm terry cloth mother surrogate with the number spent with a wire mother surrogate which provided food. The infant monkeys spent so much of their time with the terry cloth mothers, that Harlow concluded, ". . . the primary function of nursing as an affective vairable is that of assuring adequate and intimate contact of the infant with the mother" (p. 677). Harlow concluded further that "contact comfort" is the motivational agent for affectionate and attachment responses.

One function of the mother is to provide a source of safety for an infant in times of fear and danger. In a test for feelings of attachment in an open-field situation, Harlow placed infant monkeys in a strange room containing multiple stimuli known to elicit curiosity and manipulatory responses in baby monkeys. On some occasions the terry cloth surrogate mother was present in the room, on other occasions absent.

When the terry cloth mother was present, the infant monkey clutched her, rubbed its body against her, and frequently manipulated her body and face. The infant used the surrogate mother as a source of security. It explored objects in the room and then returned to the mother before embarking on new behaviors in the strange room, as shown in Fig. 4.1.

The behavior of the same infant monkeys was quite different, however, when the terry cloth mother was not in the room. Emotional distress was high, and the infant monkey froze in a crouched position, as shown in Fig. 4.2.

Fig. 4.1. Initial response of an infant monkey (left) to strange objects in an open-field test. In the presence of the cloth mother (right) the infant begins to explore the objects in the room, using the cloth mother as a source of security. (From H. F. Harlow, "The nature of love," *American Psychologist*, 1958, **13,** 673–685. Photos courtesy of Wisconsin Regional Primate Research Center.)

Fig. 4.2. In the absence of the cloth mother, the infant hides its head (left) and remains inactive and frightened, failing to explore the objects (right) as it had done when the cloth mother was present. (From H. F. Harlow, "The nature of love," *American Psychologist,* 1958, **13,** 673–685. Photos courtesy of Wisconsin Regional Primate Research Center.)

If emotional dependency is seen as social attachment, its opposite is independence from feelings of social attachment. Monkeys raised in isolation from both people and other monkeys may become attached to a wide variety of available physical objects, such as diapers and metal tubes (Sackett, 1968), but they are incapable of developing *social* attachments and behaviors. They will not mate, interact appropriately with other monkeys, or care for their children (Harlow *et al.,* 1966). They are "independent" of feelings of attachment to other monkeys and other living organisms.

In a recent study, a rather amusing and novel effort was made to provide "monkey psychiatry" for disturbed infant monkeys who had been separated from their mothers until the age of six months, at which age "therapy" began (Suomi, Harlow, and McKinney, 1972). The therapy consisted of providing monkey therapists who had been trained to engage in both play and clinging behavior with the isolates. By the time they reached two years of age, the disturbed monkey showed almost complete recovery in behavioral defects that had been considered incurable. The authors concluded, ". . . we are aware of the existence of some therapists who seem inhuman. We find it refreshing to report the discovery of non-humans who can be therapists." (p. 392)

Human positive feelings of attachment. Feelings of dependency on a trusted figure and the nostalgia of returning home at Christmas serve as illustrations of the conditioning of positive affect to objects which have provided security in the past. Dependency, in the sense of conditioned feelings of attachment, is neither appropriate nor inappropriate. Rather, such feelings are the inevitable consequence of the normal course of socialization.

But people do not stay dependent forever on their early sources of security and their familiar surroundings. The process of growth involves shifting one's activities to include larger groups of people and an ever-widening range of behaviors. These transitions result from the formation of a large number of instrumental responses which provide the person with a sense of competence for dealing with his or her world and thus provide alternative sources of feelings of security. Independence is the freedom from relying for security on old cues of attachment, and it reflects the successful acquisition of instrumental sources of security. Thus instrumental behaviors can produce outcomes that are satisfying and engender feelings of well-being. The instrumental behavior shifts the origins of such feelings from external figures to one's own actions. However, in the absence of instrumental security, as in times of distress or frustration, the old cues of attachment are available and likely to be used as a reliable source of security. A person who finds himself in such a situation can risk a failure because alternative sources of support exist.

By contrast, the isolated or rejected child, who is reared devoid of contact comforts and therefore of the resulting feelings of social attachment, has no social base of security from which to derive emergency support when there is a loss of instrumental security. The under-mothered organism is independent of attachments to others, but at the expense of a base of security for comfort and attachment. For a person lacking feelings of attachment, presenting to self and others an impression of complete instrumental control may be especially important, because there is no substitute security available. The excessive behavioral independence is required to protect against the lack of external sources of support.

Excessive feelings of attachment may be just as difficult a burden to bear as having no reserve source of security in the form of conditioned emotional feelings of attachment. The over-mothered, sometimes called "smothered," person is not free to acquire the instrumental skills which provide a substitute for the security of the mother. The suppression of such behaviors by punishment or by the withdrawal of attention causes a pattern of behavior in which few responses are tried and the opportunity to learn that one's actions can be instrumental in controlling and manipulating the environment is restricted. Under these circumstances, the base of security remains with the figure on whom attachment and contact comfort were built, because no other form of security has been substituted.

In summary, feelings of dependency may be seen as conditioned positive affects, referred to here as attachments. In the normal course of development, a class of stimuli centering on the mother becomes capable of eliciting feelings of security and well-being. There will be individual differences in the degree to which such conditioning takes place and in the specific cues which have been paired with such feelings. Eventually, instrumental behaviors are acquired which provide the individual with a new source of security within the self. In situations or times of frustration and uncertainty, the person may rely on the old feelings of attachment to reestablish security and confidence. Independence of such feelings of attachment may result from rejection or under-mothering, leaving the individual with no emergency source of support and an exaggerated need for displaying independence. In contrast, excessive mothering may interfere with the development of instrumental security and leave the individual with emotional dependence on others for feelings of security.

DEPENDENT BEHAVIORS

Another aspect of dependency concerns behaviors which are called dependent. These behaviors include such things as asking for help versus doing it one's self, seeking advice versus deciding for one's self, waiting for others versus going alone, etc.

Instrumental conditioning.   Consider any specific behavior which would be characterized as dependent, such as seeking help, crying, asking advice, waiting for others, etc. Conceptualized within the framework of instrumental learning, these behaviors are established and maintained by the selective application of reward and punishment. For humans, most rewards and punishments which are contingent on instrumental behavior are social in nature. Particular behaviors are acquired as a direct consequence of the outcomes which are contingent on those behaviors.

It can be shown that many behaviors judged as dependent are established and maintained through the selective application of positive reward. For example, a child who cries frequently in response to minor mishaps and then requires comfort from mother or teacher (a mother substitute through stimulus generalization) will be judged as dependent. Hart *et al.* (1964) illustrate how such behaviors are controlled by reinforcement in an experiment conducted on a nursery school child named Bill.

Whenever Bill stubbed his toe, bumped his elbow, fell down, or was frustrated or threatened, he would cry until comforted by a teacher. In order to determine the frequency of Bill's crying episodes, one teacher carried a counter on which she recorded the number of times Bill cried aloud enough to be heard 50 feet away for five seconds or longer. The record showed that over a ten-day period Bill was crying five to ten times every morning.

The experimenters felt that Bill's dependent behavior was being maintained by the reinforcement provided by the attention it drew. The teachers were instructed to ignore Bill's crying, that is, not to go to him, speak to him, or look at him while he was crying. If a teacher was close to Bill when he began to cry, she was to turn her back and busy herself with another child. The attention of the teachers was not removed completely, however. It was instead made contingent on a more appropriate response by Bill to a fall, scrape, or frustration. "Appropriate" responses included verbal responses, such as saying "Stop that" to another child, or actions that dealt directly with the source of the frustration. He also received attention when he worked or played without crying. Within five days after attention had been withdrawn for crying behavior and made contingent on appropriate behavior, the frequency of Bill's crying decreased to between zero and two episodes a day.

In order to demonstrate more clearly that the crying behavior had been maintained originally by the selective application of attention, the investigators instructed the teachers to revert to their old pattern of giving attention. The number of crying episodes immediately increased. After Bill's reversion to his old crying pattern, the training procedure was reintroduced; four days later Bill's crying had stopped completely. The data for this experiment are shown in Fig. 4.3.

Frequent crying, as well as other dependent behaviors, may be a simple function of adult attention. The pain of a push, an insult, or a frustration can be quickly and effectively eliminated by seeking the security provided by contact comfort. Such acts are called dependent because the organism becomes dependent on another stimulus object to provide relief from discomfort. As such, dependent behaviors interfere with the person's establishing independent behaviors.

In the course of normal growth, children must acquire appropriate instrumental actions for dealing with their world. They must make a transition from running to mother to establishing direct behaviors which relieve the frustration but do not evoke rejection or other punitive consequences from their associates. The number of skilled instrumental responses for handling frustration must grow and be built from the crude interactions between young children to the highly ritualized responses of adult discourse. The individual who makes prolonged use of dependent behaviors inappropriate for the adult world misses important learning experiences and retains a repertoire of responses ill-suited to the independent person.

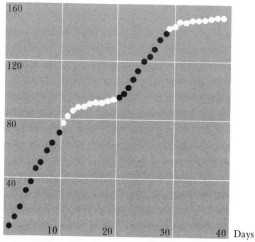

Fig. 4.3. A record of the cumulative number of Bill's crying episodes over a 40-day period. The first 10 days show the high frequency of crying before the attention given in response to Bill's crying was withdrawn. The second 10 days show the reduction of crying when attention was given for constructive activity but withheld for crying. During the third 10 days, the crying episodes returned when attention was once again given for crying. Finally, the last 10 days show the reduction in crying when the training conditions were once again reinstated and attention was used to reinforce constructive activity but was withheld for crying. (Adapted from Hart et al., "Effects of social reinforcement on operant crying," *Journal of Child Psychology*, 1964, **1**, 145–153.)

A study by Heathers (1953) illustrates how a dependent or independent style of behavior may emerge as a function of the subject's reinforcement history. Heathers had six- to twelve-year-old children walk a plank supported by springs and raised eight inches off the ground. At the start of each walk, the experimenter touched the back of the child's hand and waited to see whether the child would accept or reject help. The children who accepted help were those whose parents had encouraged them to go to others for support. They were children whom the experimenters had judged to be held back by their parents from age-appropriate skills more than was true of the children who rejected the helping hand.

The use of punishment.   Theoretically, one could use punishment instead of reward to establish dependent behaviors. Punishment would be given for instrumental acts that are independent and withheld for dependent ones. Although it is theoretically possible to establish dependency in this way, punishment can have other effects, particularly if it is severe and extensive. Punishment does not indicate what response an organism *should* make, and so, in order to be effective, it must be combined in a consistent manner with positive reward; that is, punishment can be used to suppress unwanted behavior, positive reward to encourage desired behavior. If punishment is given frequently, severely, and exclusively, however, there may be such a generalized inhibition of responses that the subject emits no behavior in the presence of the socializing agent, making differential reward for desired behaviors impossible.

Walters and Parke (1967) have suggested that these negative effects of punishment can be overcome if the aversive stimulation is well timed, consistent, sufficiently intense, and coupled with information concerning alternative prosocial behavior that is reinforced when it occurs.

The principal point is that dependent and independent behaviors—like other behaviors—are established and maintained through the consequences they produce. A child who can escape punishment and gain praise by dependent behaviors is apt to acquire a repertoire of responses which force other individuals to give the assistance the child feels he or she needs. On the other hand, independent behaviors can be fostered in an atmosphere where reward is freely given, which ensures that a wide range of responses will be emitted. The parents may then differentially reward those behaviors which are age-appropriate and withhold reward for age-inappropriate dependent behaviors.

DEPENDENCY VALUES

A further aspect of dependency concerns the value of approval and praise from other persons. Such things as an individual's susceptibility to social reinforcement or need to conform are a function of those factors which change the value of approval. In studies of social isolation, in which subjects have been deprived of contact with other human beings or simply deprived of approval, they are more sensitive to receiving praise and approval from others when they return to a social situation (Gewirtz, 1967). Isolation is one way of enhancing the value of praise and attention, just as increasing periods of time without food is a way to enhance the value of a food reward for a rat.

The particular positive or negative value of an outcome is a function of other variables. The subject may show attachment or dependent behavior in some situations but not in others, simply because a particular situation has temporarily (e.g., through isolation) changed the need for social approval. In this sense, dependency is an acute state, which may be aroused or reduced through deprivation manipulations. In addition, dependency can be a chronic state, in which particular experiences create stable individual differences in the value of attention from a figure to whom feelings of attachment have developed.

Ainsworth and Bell (1968) reported a series of experiments in which children were separated from their mothers for various periods of time. The experimenters were interested in observing each child's exploratory behavior during the mother's absence and attachment behavior after her return. During the absence of the mother, exploratory behavior was dampened, and the child typically became increasingly frightened of the situation. On her return, the child showed an increase in attachment behavior.

Such experiments have special interest because they parallel similar but more stressful experiments carried out with monkeys. Infant monkeys separated from their mothers for various periods of time, sometimes several months, show stress reactions, they search for their mothers, and their interest in play and exploration is depressed. During separation the typical infant shows more intense response to frightening stimulation than it does during the mother's presence. When the mother is restored, the infant monkey clings to her more and explores less than it did before separation. The dependent and clinging effect may last for three or more months (Kaufman and Rosenblum, 1967).

The response of the infant monkeys to experimental separation is similar to the behavior of young children separated from their parents for several days or weeks because the child was hospitalized or placed in a residential nursery. The separation produces acute distress, which may give way to despair or depression. If separation continues, affective reactions may brighten in responsiveness to the environment, but when reunion occurs, the child's attachment behavior returns and reaches a level more intense than before separation. The heightened level may persist for a prolonged period of time, usually much longer than the separation itself (Ainsworth and Bell, 1968).

When children's attachment behavior is heightened as a result of separation they attend less to other people and to their environment, and presumably they learn less. They show prolonged periods of clinging and whining and not wanting to let their mother out of their sight. Efforts by the parents to punish such behavior frequently increase its intensity and duration. Long-term follow-up studies (Bowlby et al., 1956) indicate that this kind of behavior—often described as overdependent—may in some cases be a long-lasting effect of extended periods of separation.

It is clear that separation—much like early deprivation of food—can serve to heighten permanently the value of a mother's comfort. The threatened loss of such comfort makes it all the more valuable, and as a consequence, attachment and dependency responses are more likely. Of course, we are all dependent on approval from others to some degree. The degree of dependence on such approval can range from one extreme, the immobilizing concern of an individual who is buffeted about by the beliefs and opinions of others, to the other extreme, the independence of individuals whose only reference point for behavior lies within themselves. The values themselves, however, are acquired and may be seen as one aspect of incentive learning.

PERCEPTUAL PROCESSES

Events in the external world have only the particular meaning imposed upon them by the person. How a particular event will be perceived is influenced by many factors. Its meaning is determined in part by the context in which it occurs—what we previously termed adaptation level. Particular motivational states can influence how an event is perceived. It is possible to experimentally manipulate specific variables, such as context, motivation, expectancy, etc., and to determine how these factors will influence the perception of some stimulus. As applied to personality, the task is to relate these perceptual processes to the consistencies of behavior shown by people.

SOCIAL PERCEPTIONS

Kuethe (1962a, 1962b, 1964) developed an experimental technique in which subjects were asked to place a variety of felt cutouts on a background. He found that the subjects grouped them into consistent patterns. For example, they placed human figures together, geometric figures together, and a child closer to its mother than to its father. Kuethe used the consistencies in such groupings to demonstrate that the felt-figure-placement technique is sensitive to existing social patterns and expectations. These perceptual expectations reflect the meanings about human relationships that are learned through social experience and that mediate social behavior. He concluded that the figure-placement technique provided an index of these underlying processes, which determine the way in which the subject perceives the world, i.e., the relationship between particular objects.

An extension of the procedure is to show the subject a particular pattern of figures, remove it, and then ask him to replace the figures, from memory, exactly as they were. Weinstein (1967) found that the distances between two figures (a man and a woman) were underestimated by children who felt accepted by their parents. On the other hand, emotionally disturbed children, who presumably had been rejected and punished by their social relationships, showed the opposite kind of constant error (Weinstein, 1965). That is, they overestimated the distance between a pair of human figures. The suggestion is that emotional distance can be translated into physical distance in such a reconstruction task. The error of underestimating the distance between figures provides an index of the way in which needs influence how the world is perceived.

The data of Kuethe and Weinstein illustrate the relationship between dependent values and the actual perception of events. Perceptual processes are in part determined by the social expectation which is used for interpreting and classifying information. Individuals with feelings of attachment need to be closer to a nurturant adult than does a person who has been rejected, and they reorganize their perceptions and recollections so that individuals are moved closer to each other. The individual meaning of what a person sees is dictated not by the absolute properties of the stimulus event itself, but rather by the context in which it is perceived. The perception of events is influenced by one's needs, and the events themselves may be seen differently whenever the context is changed.

FIELD DEPENDENCY

In collaboration with others Witkin has conducted a series of studies on the capacity of a person to retain a perception of the orientation of his or her body in space. This characteristic, termed the perception of the vertical, is a dimension in which persons differ, one from another. Consistently discovered differences led to a series of studies in which aspects of personality were related to this perceptual process. Witkin *et al.* (1954) asked their subjects to sit in complete darkness facing a luminous, upright rod surrounded by a square luminous frame, each of which could be independently rotated. Both rod and frame were presented to the subject out of line with the true vertical position. Without changing the frame, the subject had to move the rod until it appeared to be vertical.

Some subjects rotated the rod toward the angle of the tilted frame and reported that the rod then appeared to be upright. For those subjects the perception of vertical was mainly determined by the visual field surrounding it. In this and similar perceptual situations, such subjects find it difficult to overcome the influence of the surrounding field. This characteristic of their perceptual process has led to their being designated as field-dependent subjects.

Other subjects are able to bring the rod close to the true vertical. These subjects perceive it independently of the surrounding field and determine verticality with respect to their own body position. In general, such people are able to distinguish a stimulus from the context in which it occurs. Thus these subjects are designated as field-independent.

The perception of the external world, as in the rod and frame test, seems to signify something about the inner structure of individuals and their sense of identity. A self which is not segregated from the field (field-dependent) is characteristic of people who are fused with their surroundings. The self is defined by the external situation, and it is dependent. Perceptual independence from the field, however, is characteristic of a relatively well-developed conception of the self, which sets it apart from the surroundings. Differentiation of the self—or independence—finds its manifestation in both behavioral and perceptual processes.

COGNITIVE PROCESSES: FORCED DEPENDENCY

The concept of cognitive structures, introduced in Chapter 2, helps to explain not only differences in cognition but also differences in other areas of personality. Both dependent behaviors and a global, field-dependent perception of the world reflect the acquired internal organization which is the basic element of higher processes in humans. Higher processes reflect both the internal organization of the emotions, behaviors, and values, and the acquired perceptual distinctions and discrimination required to maintain the specific results of learning. Thus the specific behaviors and selective perceptions of dependence-independence become a matter of cognitive style when considered in terms of their internal organization and the intellectual functions of an individual.

In many situations people are forced to be dependent on other persons. In some cases one is dependent on another for commodities that are necessary for survival, as the city dweller is dependent on the farmer for food. In other cases the forced dependency is of a social nature, as when an employee needs the boss's approval to gain a promotion. However, in most adult business or social interactions there is a mutual dependency because each party has something the other needs. Thus, while the city dweller needs food, the farmer needs clothing, machinery, and other goods made in the city. Of course, the relative degree of power one person has over another in such situations varies. Typically, the boss's approval has considerably more value to the employee than does the individual employee's service to the boss. One function of labor unions has been to distribute the power more equally.

Prisoner's dilemma games. In a prisoner's dilemma game, two people must depend on each other in order to maximize their gain or minimize their loss. The game derives its name from the dilemma faced by a pair of suspects who are arrested for a crime. They are separated, and each is told that cooperating with the police by providing evidence necessary to convict the other will get him or her off free. If neither talks, both face some possibility of a light sentence on the limited evidence available; if both talk, both will be convicted but with reduced sentences for their cooperation; however, if one talks and the other does not, the former will go free for having turned state's evidence and the latter will face a maximum sentence. The payoffs are shown in Box 4.1(a). Each person must make the decision without knowledge of the other's decision.

In the laboratory version of the task, positive outcomes are typically used, but the basic payoff structure remains the same as shown in Box 4.1(b). It should be clear from both versions of Box 4.1 that mutually cooperative choices (Act 2) are best for both persons. If one player makes exploitive choices (Act 1), the partner is likely to make exploitive choices also, thus reducing the long-term winnings of both.

Discovering the factors which determine the choice a person will make and the conditions which will enhance cooperation are of obvious importance. For example, it is to the advantage of both of two nations to disarm and not to invest resources in, say, an antiballistic missile system; it is to their mutual advantage to spend their resources for other items. Yet the choice of nations, reflecting the repeated findings obtained with individuals in the laboratory, is to select the noncooperative (competitive) choice, even when the stakes are real money. In fact, as the stakes get higher, the level of cooperation decreases (Gumpert, Dutsch, and Epstein, 1969).

In the laboratory, it has been found that a number of factors enhance cooperation, including predisposition to be cooperative, larger payoffs for cooperation, a public commitment to cooperate, an opportunity to know and like the partner, and a unilaterally cooperative partner. In general, conditions which enlarge trust provide the best context for establishing mutual dependency. Unfortunately, dependency permits exploitation, for they are opposite sides of the same coin. The possibility of exploitation appears to have subjective appeal, because people choose the noncooperative alternative even though in terms of the objective value of the out-

Box 4.1   **Prisoner's dilemma**

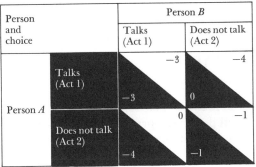

a) Prisoner's version of the decision matrix,
   in which the outcomes are negative.

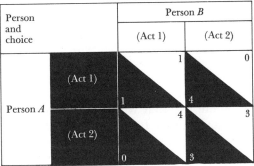

b) Laboratory version of the decision matrix,
   in which the outcomes are positive.

The shaded areas of the figure show the number of years in prison that A will
receive, the unshaded areas the number B will receive, depending on which, if
either, turns state's evidence (talks) or remains silent (does not talk). The minus
sign indicates that the outcomes are aversive to the subject. If neither talks, both
risk one year in prison. If both talk, both can expect three years. But if A talks
and B does not, A will go free and B will get four years in prison, and vice versa.
Each must decide without knowledge of the other's decision.

In the laboratory version of the prisoner's dilemma game, the outcomes are
desirable. The shaded areas represent the payoff in money for A, the unshaded
areas for B, given each possible combination of choices made by the two players.
In the basic version of the game, each must choose without knowledge of the
other's decision. Modifications of the rules have been introduced in the laboratory, such as allowing communication between the two, to study the factors
which will enhance or interfere with establishing a cooperative and mutually
dependent relationship.

come it costs them money. Forced dependency which arises out of natural social and economic situations seems to foster competition rather than cooperation among people.

SUMMARY

In this chapter the class of behaviors identified as dependent were viewed in terms of the uniform psychological processes provided by experimental psychology. Learning processes provide a conceptualization of how feelings of attachment develop through the mother, as a conditioned stimulus, paired with the contact comfort she provides her child. Thus the mother, as well as related stimuli through generalization, provides a source of security for venturing into the world. These feelings of dependency are the natural result of normal socialization. Over the course of development, instrumental skills are acquired which provide an internal source of security and independence. However, if the instrumental training fosters dependent rather than independent behaviors, then reliance on others is maintained. The need for approval and support from others changes in accordance with the situation. When a person is isolated or separated, the value of social support increases and renders him more dependent on others.

The perception of the events of the external world is influenced by one's experiences. People develop mechanisms for selectively attending to their world so that they recognize what is familiar and what will fulfill their needs. In fact, dependence-independence can be seen as a cognitive style. The learning experiences which result in the acquisition of dependent behaviors are internally organized in such a way that there is a global perception of the world and thus poor separation of the events from their context and of the self from the social settings. By contrast, the acquisition of independent behaviors is reflected in a more complex cognitive structure, which is analytic and which allows for perceptual differentiation of objects from their context and of the self from the social setting.

Forced dependent relationships, in which one person needs help or assistance from another or two people need mutual assistance from each other, often exist as a natural occurrence of human economic and social systems. Such relationships usually lead to noncooperation because of the opportunity for exploitation that exists in a dependency situation. A condition of prior trust seems necessary for a cooperative mutual dependency to arise.

SUGGESTIONS FOR FURTHER READING

Gewirtz, J. L. (ed.). *Attachment and Dependency.* New York: Halsted, 1972. This book offers numerous articles on the experimental studies of dependency, including chapters by Ainsworth, Cairns, and Yarrow, whose work has been cited in the text.

Lewis, M., and L. A. Rosenblum (eds.). *The Effects of the Infant on its Caregiver.* New York: Wiley, 1974. The reciprocity of the relationship between infant and "caregiver" is the theme of this book, which emphasizes the psychological processes of interdependence.

5
Dependency: The Social Viewpoint

I. **Models**
   A. The effect of dependency on imitation

II. **Roles**
   A. Dependency and age changes
   B. Birth order
      1. Dependency-producing behavior of mothers
      2. Birth order, fear, and affiliation

III. **Cultures: Dependency and type of subsistence economy**

IV. **Summary**

V. **Suggestions for further reading**

By now it should be clear that the kinds of actions classified as dependent are varied. They might include touching, clinging, holding on to or standing near others; seeking attention or praise from others; asking for help, guidance, or unnecessary permission from others; or perhaps trying to join a group. Regardless of the particular behavior involved, dependency is intrinsically social in nature since all dependent actions have in common one person orienting toward or attending to another. Beyond recognizing its social nature, we will consider, in an exploration of dependency from a social point of view, its relationship to the topics of *models, roles,* and *cultures.*

MODELS

Part of the general thesis of the social viewpoint is that much of what a person learns, much of what becomes characteristic of an individual, is acquired by the observation of others, that is, by observational learning or imitation. If this assertion has any general explanatory value, then the exposure of an observer to a model who behaves dependently should promote the expression of such characteristics in the observer. Laboratory research bearing directly on this question is scarce, but one study of a sample of parents and their sons is suggestive (Bandura and Walters, 1963). Ratings of the parents on dependency were made from transcripts of interviews with them, and ratings of the sons' dependency were obtained from direct observation. Comparing the ratings, the investigators concluded that the parents who displayed a high degree of dependency in their relationships with other adults had children who also behaved dependently in social situations. Similarly, the children of parents who showed little interpersonal dependency also showed little dependency in their social contacts. While it was not possible to determine how much of the effect was specifically due to modeling, the study demonstrates that dependent patterns of behavior in parents are repeated in children.

The Effect of Dependency on Imitation

In addition to the likelihood that dependent behaviors are acquired through modeling, the tendency to imitate a model may in turn be influenced by dependency. Since dependency involves orienting toward and attending to other people, it seems likely that dependent individuals would be particularly prone to model their behavior after the actions of others. This hypothesis has been tested in an experiment in which 52 nursery school children were the subjects (Ross, 1966). The activity in the experiment consisted essentially of teaching the children one at a time to run a play post office. The experimenter was really interested not so much in the intentional learning of the correct behavior but in the extent to which the children imitated various incidental and irrelevant things she had done and said while teaching them the job. Her hypothesis was that children high in dependency would be more likely to imitate the model's behavior, regardless of its relevance to the task, whereas those low in dependency would be more task-oriented and independent of the model's irrelevant behavior. Her expectation was that the low-dependent subjects would do better at learning the postmaster's job itself since they would have less to learn in the same time than would the high-dependent subjects, who were more likely to attend to all of the teacher's behavior.

Ross used several different measures to determine the dependency of the children in her experiment. The primary measure consisted of ratings of all the children by five teachers at the nursery school on five scales of dependent behaviors. The scales were concerned with how much the child showed instrumental dependency, sought reassurance, sought physical proximity, and displayed attention-getting behavior. An independent check on the validity of the ratings showed that the investigator clearly established groups which differed in their tendencies to act dependently.

The task to be learned included seven different sets of behavior, including such things as collecting and giving change, operating the cash register, following letter regulations (kind of stamp, postmark, where to mail), dialing the telephone, and answering the telephone. In the course of teaching these behaviors, the experimenter did numerous unlikely and irrelevant things. For example, when answering the phone, she picked up a pencil from the counter and stuck it behind her right ear, said "Doodle, doodle, doodle," crumpled paper and threw it in a basket, etc. These and other irrelevant responses were repeated in exactly the same way each time the experimenter went through the tasks.

The subject's learning was tested by having first the experimenter and then another child enter as customers to mail various types of letters and packages and to pay with differing types of money (coins, bills). Finally, the subject was asked to teach another child to be postmaster. The scorers who observed the testing were psychology students who were unaware of the hypothesis to be tested or of the classification of the children. To ensure the reliability of the observations there were two different scorers working independently of each other; these scorers agreed 94% of the time.

The results of the experiment show, as hypothesized, that the *high-dependent* children imitated more of the incidental responses which were irrelevant to the job than did the low-dependent children. In contrast, the *low-dependent* children learned more of the correct behavior, presumably because they were oriented less to the model and more to the tasks than were the high-dependent subjects. In addition to the primary results, the investigator found that the high-dependent children liked the more passive consumer role better, but the low-dependent children preferred to be in control as postmaster. Later interviews with the mothers and independent classification of the interviews showed that the mothers of the low-dependent subjects were very much interested in their children's achievement in the situation, whereas the mothers of the high-dependent subjects were concerned more with their children's social skills.

The experiment performed by Ross supports the hypothesis that high dependency increases the likelihood of imitating the observed actions of others. In addition, it suggests that, by virtue of being more oriented to the teacher than to the task, dependent children may learn some tasks less well than their more independent counterparts.

ROLES

An individual fills a number of different positions or roles both simultaneously and over the course of time. Some of the positions are achieved by virtue of having accomplished or failed to accomplish certain goals, but others are simply ascribed, or given. We shall be concerned here more with the latter, with positions and their accompanying role behaviors over which one has no control. These positions are ascribed because of such automatic factors as age, sex, or birth order.

DEPENDENCY AND AGE CHANGES

A distinction is sometimes made between task-oriented and person-oriented dependency. The distinction is a useful one, since task-oriented dependency changes considerably with age, whereas person-oriented dependency remains more constant. As individuals mature, they ought to be able to conduct their affairs without constant reliance on the advice and aid of others, but they also ought to continue to be involved in interdependent relationships with other people.

From western heroes to city detectives, movies and television have glorified emotionally independent characters. But in real life the failure to seek and maintain stable interdependent relationships with others is usually a sign of maladjustment rather than adequacy. Of course, growth is expected to be accompanied by an increased preference for and ability to handle interdependent relationships as opposed to those involving one-sided dependency. In other words, one ought to become able to provide nurturance for others as well as to seek it for one's self.

In order to determine just what changes in the form of dependency expression do occur with growth, one investigator had observers watch groups of nursery school children of different ages (Heathers, 1955). The observers noted instances of dependent behavior in groups of two-year-old and four-year-old children and indicated for each whether the dependency was directed toward the teacher or another child in the group. They found that the younger children were more likely than were the older to make direct affection-seeking responses, such as clinging to the teacher or sitting on her lap; older children were more likely to seek approval or attention. In addition, the observers' records indicated that the two-year-olds directed their dependency toward the teacher significantly more often than did the four-year-olds, who were more likely than the younger to express dependency toward peers. From this study it can be seen that as children grow older, the objects of emotional dependence change as well as the mode of obtaining nurturance from others.

BIRTH ORDER

Birth order is a variable which has attracted a great deal of attention in recent years. Like age and sex, birth order has the advantage among psychological variables of being free of measurement problems; all subjects are readily classifiable on the basis of simple and direct questions. Of course, it is not the order of one's birth in itself that is a consideration of interest; rather it is the distinctive child-rearing treatment and role expectations that accompany one's ordinal position in the family and the long-term differences they are likely to produce.

Dependency-producing Behavior of Mothers

It has been theorized that differences in dependency may underlie many of the observed effects of birth order (Schachter, 1959). There is evidence that the behavior of parents toward the first child is more extreme and more inconsistent, factors which have been postulated to lead to the development of dependency. Hilton (1967) conducted an experiment to test the hypothesis that birth order and dependency are related and, if they are, to determine the role of maternal behavior toward the child in the relation-

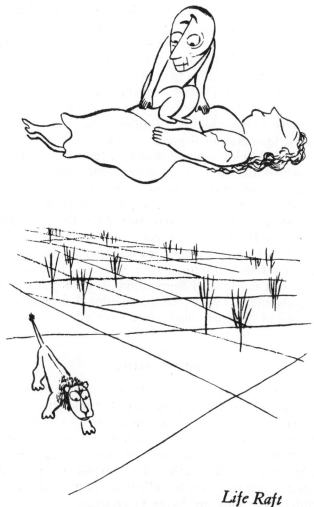

Life Raft
From *All Embarrassed* by William Steig

ship. The subjects were 20 only children, 20 firstborns, and 20 later-borns, all four years old. All except the only children were from two-child families with siblings of the same sex. The 60 mothers were solicited by mail and telephone to bring their four-year-olds to participate in a study of independent thinking.

The procedure involved having each child work a series of puzzles for five minutes while the mother looked on. Half the mothers were told that their children's performances were below average and half that they were above average. During a five-minute intermission, each mother was left alone with her child while their interaction was observed by two unseen judges, who rated the behavior of mother and child. To ensure the objectivity of the ratings, the judges did not know the children's birth order, and they also did not know whether they were in the success or failure group. Since their behavioral observations showed no differences between the firstborn and the only children, those two groups were evaluated as one. Together these firstborns showed considerably more dependent behavior than did later-born children. They were significantly more likely than later-borns (1) to run to their mothers during the intermission, even though instructed to remain seated, (2) to persist in this behavior when instructed to return, and (3) to ask for direct help or reassurance on the task.

The ratings of the mothers' behavior also showed consistent differences. The mothers of the firstborn children were significantly more likely to interfere with their activities during intermission, suggesting that they work on the puzzle and directing them how to do it. Figure 5.1 shows the

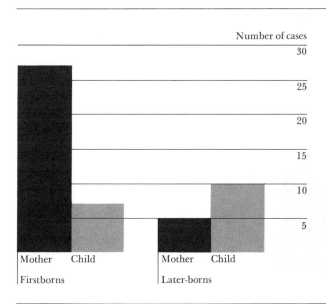

Fig. 5.1. During a five-minute intermission some children practiced on the puzzle. For firstborns the practice was generally initiated by mothers whereas later-borns initiated their own practice. The difference was taken as evidence of the tendency of mothers to interfere more with their firstborn children (after Hilton, 1967).

number of mothers and children who initiated practice on the puzzle during the intermission. There is clear evidence that with firstborns the mother tended to initiate practice but with later-borns there was a greater tendency for the child to initiate practice. Furthermore, even though told to remain seated and participate as little as possible, 18 mothers disregarded the instructions and gave direct help to their children. Of that number, 15 were mothers of firstborn children.

Hilton's experiment afforded the opportunity to observe mothers' reactions to their children under conditions of failure and success and therefore to study extremes in their responses. Of the ten who made excessive supportive or critical comments, nine were mothers of firstborns, and those who made overt demonstrations of love, such as hugs and kisses, were also significantly more often the mothers of firstborns. Finally, in addition to this evidence of immoderation in maternal behavior, Hilton found that firstborn children were treated more inconsistently. When the children were doing well, the mothers of firstborns were more demonstrative than those of later-borns, but unlike the latter, who maintained a constant level of affection, they showed a significant decrement in affection

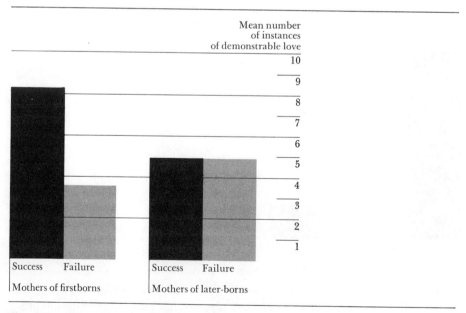

Fig. 5.2. The affection level for mothers of firstborns was dependent on the children's success or failure at the task, but that of the mothers of later-borns was more constant. This effect suggests that mothers of firstborns are more inconsistent in their affection (after Hilton, 1967).

under conditions of failure. Figure 5.2 shows the constancy of affection enjoyed by later-borns and the relative inconsistency of affection received by firstborn children.

The results of this experiment indicate that firstborn children are more likely than later children to be high in dependency. The relationship presumably indicates that reactions to the first child in a family are more likely to be dependency-producing. Consistent with existing hypotheses regarding the origin of dependency, the firstborn children in this study received more *interference* and more *extreme* and *inconsistent* reactions than did the later-born children.

In line with this evidence of differential tendencies of firstborns and laterborns to depend on others, we shall look again at the relationship between fear and affiliation.

Birth Order, Fear, and Affiliation

Several findings suggest that firstborns find the prospect of physical pain, including electric shock, more fear-inducing than later-borns do. When firstborns and later-borns have been exposed to a sample shock, observers have judged the former to react more strongly than the latter, and the firstborns themselves have reported the shock as more painful than have the later-borns.

Other studies that have further investigated this characteristic have determined that firstborns are less likely than later-borns to participate in relatively dangerous sports (Nisbett, 1968). That conclusion was drawn from a variety of sources, including information from 2000 Columbia undergraduates, a smaller number of Pennsylvania State and Yale students, the New York Giants professional football team, and the New York Mets baseball team. The proportion of firstborns to later-borns is substantially smaller among those who play such dangerous sports as professional or intercollegiate football, rugby, or soccer than among those who either do not play sports or play such nondangerous sports as baseball or basketball. Others have shown that firstborns express more fear than later-borns in hazardous driving situations. There is also evidence that during the Korean War, fighter pilots who were firstborns were less likely to be highly effective and become aces.

These investigations document the greater fearfulness of firstborns, but what about the hypothesis that firstborns are more prone to deal with their fears by affiliating with or depending on others? An unusual opportunity to study this possibility arose when on the night of November 9–10, 1965, New York City experienced a power failure that resulted in a massive blackout of the northeastern states. Three enterprising psychologists give the following account of collecting data on the extent of people's fears and affiliative reactions.

> The power failure occurred in New York City at about 5:30 p.m., at a time when darkness was falling and the city was at the peak of its evening rush hour. The blackout lasted until the early hours of the next morning.... The authors arrived in Manhattan shortly before midnight. On the basis of radio information that the major bus terminal for Manhattan had restored some of its operations and thus provided one of the few outlets from the city, it was decided to begin data collection there.
>
> At the terminal there was some dim emergency lighting. A large number of people were standing, sitting, or lying on the floor attempting to rest. The authors identified themselves and requested help in completing a questionnaire about the blackout and their personal experiences of it. Data were obtained from 15 men and 8 women.
>
> At about 1:30 a.m., in an effort to sample another area, we moved toward mid-town and discovered that one hotel was operating with adequate illumination from an emergency power plant. The atmosphere here was more lively than it was in the terminal. Data were obtained from 50 men and 27 women at this location. The overall cooperation rate at both sites was approximately 70%. (Zucker, Manosevitz, and Lanyon, 1968, p. 355)

The results of the study indicated a significant tendency of more first-borns than later-borns to indicate, as predicted, that they had been anxious in the situation. In response to questions about their preference for being with others during the blackout, the expected difference in favor of firstborns was found only among females. Finally, the investigators compared the reported anxiety of the firstborns who had spent the time alone with the anxiety of those who had been with others. If firstborns reduce stress through affiliation, then those who affiliated would be expected to report less anxiety. That expectation was confirmed, but only for men.

CULTURES
dependency and type of subsistence economy

The roles of the firstborn and later-born child have been discussed as roles which frequently give rise to individual differences in dependency. In this section, the kind of subsistence economy will be explored as a cultural factor in dependency. The research project presented utilizes an objective measure of dependency administered in the field to members of widely differing cultures. However, before describing the primary study of interest, we will consider a project which served as background for the study.

One set of investigators were interested in the relationship between the type of subsistence economy of a society and the personality of its members (Barry, Child, and Bacon, 1959). To obtain information about a variety of subsistence level cultures, they consulted the Human Relations Area Files. Specifically, they distinguished between hunting or fishing societies and pastoral or agricultural groups. Their hypothesis was that successful hunting and fishing societies would require individualistic, assertive, and venturesome members, but the members of agricultural societies would tend to be conscientious, compliant, and conservative.

By rating information on a sample of societies from the Area Files on the food-accumulation dimension and also on several aspects of their socialization practices, the investigators obtained evidence to demonstrate that socialization or child-rearing practices do differ as a function of the type of subsistence economy in the society. However, even though agricultural societies tended to have child-rearing practices which *ought* to lead to dependency as a personality characteristic, there was still no direct evidence that such personalities are actually more common in agricultural than in hunting societies.

Therefore, as a further test of the hypothesis, another investigator (Berry, 1967) employed objective measures of dependency when studying two cultures differing greatly in their economies—the Eskimos as an example of a hunting and fishing culture, and the Temne of Sierra Leone as an example of an agricultural society.

As a measure of dependency or conformity to group norms, Berry used the Asch line-judging task. Six test sheets, each counting nine horizontal lines, were presented at a distance of four feet. A standard line appeared at the top, followed by eight lines varying progressively in length. After two sample problems, the subject was told:

> Here is another sheet with nine lines on it, one here at the top, and eight beneath it. This time I am going to give you a hint. Most Temne (or Eskimo) people say this line (experimenter pointed to number 6) is equal in length to the one at the top. Which one do you say? (p. 416)

Although on that particular test trial the line suggested as the norm was correct, on each of the next three trials an incorrect line five lines away from the correct one was indicated as the norm. The distance of the subject's choice away from the correct line toward the falsely designated line provided an objective measure of his dependence on the group norm. The subject's dependency score was the number of lines away from the correct line, summed over the three trials. Since it is of course possible that the observed differences in line-judging accuracy arose from differences in visual acuity rather than from differences in dependency, the investigator matched the groups on far and near visual acuity to eliminate that alternative explanation of his results.

From each society a sample of 122 subjects were tested in their own language through a native interpreter. The instructions had been pretranslated and then translated back into English to ensure that the meaning was the same in both languages. The samples in each society were divided into those who followed the traditional rural occupations and those who were in transition to Western life, e.g., attending school or working for wages. Test data for a sample of equal size from Scotland were also included for comparison. The Scottish sample was divided into urban and rural subgroups.

As predicted, the results showed that the agriculturally oriented people of the Temne society were significantly more prone than the Eskimos to depend on the group norm in making their judgments. The cultural basis of their dependency on the group is suggested by the reaction of one Temne, who commented, "When Temne people choose a thing, we must all agree with the decision—this is what we call cooperation" (p. 417). On the other hand, the Eskimos' livelihood does not require such dependence on the group; they live almost solely by hunting and fishing, skills which require independence. Typically, Eskimo subjects said nothing during the testing but often gave a quiet, knowing smile as they indicated a line close to the correct one. Finally, the comparison sample from Scotland showed an intermediate degree of dependence not too different from the test scores of the Eskimos.

The results of Berry's study supported the expectations from the earlier study using the Area Files (Barry, Child, and Bacon, 1959), as well as other reports of anthropologists characterizing the Eskimo as self-reliant, individualistic, and fearful of dependency and incompetence. Similarly, the results agree with characterizations of the Temne as a people who punish individuality and deviations from socially accepted behavior.

The comparisons between the traditional-rural and the transitional-urban subgroups in each society showed that this dimension was not important; rather, the author concluded that the culturally rooted characteristics of dependence or independence carry "into the transititional period (where economic life is no longer at a subsistence level), thereby demonstrating the persistence of psychological and cultural patterns in the absence of their ecological origins." (p. 418)

The two societies studied in this experiment are perfect examples of high and low food-accumulating economies, and the differences in group dependency on the line-judging task are quite clear. Nevertheless, it is not certain that these variables are causally related. The problem is that the study involved only two cultures, which necessarily differ from each other not only in the food-accumulation dimension but in a variety of other ways as well. Thus, although no better explanation of the results has been advanced, it is still quite possible that the differences in dependency were due not to their respective economies at all but to one or more of the other differences between the two societies. Of course, the same kind of difficulty arises in any cross-cultural experiment; one cannot control or balance out the effects of confounding or contaminating variables when comparing complex societies. Nevertheless, any future evidence of the same relationship for additional cultures at each end of the food-accumulation dimension would ensure that the observed phenomenon was not peculiar to those two cultures alone.

SUMMARY

The relationship of models, roles, and cultures to dependency has now been considered. Experimenters have demonstrated that dependent behavior patterns in parents also appear in their children, but studies of the precise role of models in this process have been limited. However, there has been some research on the effect of dependency on a child's tendency to model an adult. When nursery school children were taught to run a pretend post office, those previously rated by teachers as high in dependency learned fewer task-relevant behaviors and more incidental or task-irrelevant behaviors than did low-dependent children.

In addition to the role of dependency in modeling, the effect of fear on dependency has been the subject of research. In these studies subjects anticipating severe electric shocks were more likely than control subjects to prefer spending a waiting period with another person to spending it alone. Furthermore, fearful subjects preferred waiting with someone in the same emotional state to waiting with someone in a different state. Presumably affiliation with others in the same state is preferable because it provides an opportunity to validate the appropriateness of one's own emotional reactions. Researchers have referred to this searching for consensual validation as a process of social comparison.

In the section on roles, we considered the effects of age roles and birth order on dependency. Whereas task-oriented dependency is expected to decrease with age, person-oriented dependency (in the form of interdependent relationships with others) is expected to be present at all ages. In a study of nursery school children, two-year-olds expressed dependency through affection-seeking responses directed toward the teacher, while four-year-olds made approval- or attention-seeking responses which they directed toward peers. Thus both mode and object of dependency expression change with age.

Dependency is one of the primary characteristics hypothesized to differentiate firstborn and later-born children. In support of this contention, one investigator found that firstborns were more likely than later-borns to engage in such dependent behaviors as running to their mothers and seeking reassurance during a problem-solving task. In addition, mothers of firstborns interfered more than mothers of later-born children and were more extreme and inconsistent in their affection.

In other birth-order research, firstborns were found to be more fearful of physical pain. As a consequence they are relatively infrequent participants in dangerous sports. In line with this finding, data collected during a blackout of New York City showed that firstborns reported more anxiety than later-borns did. Female firstborns were more likely than female later-borns to prefer company during the blackout and male firstborns who affiliated with others during the crisis were less anxious than firstborn males who spent the time alone. Thus both laboratory and field studies provided support for the hypothesis that first-borns are more dependent.

As an example of cross-cultural research on dependency, a conformity study conducted in two widely different cultures was cited. The project was intended to test the hypothesis that the kind of subsistence economy of a society influences the personality of its members. Using the Asch line-judging task, the experimenter found that subjects from a cooperative farming society (Temne) depended more on the group judgment to form their individual judgments than did subjects from a hunting and fishing society (Eskimo). The results are consistent with the notion that the requirements for life in an agricultural society are more likely to foster dependency on the group, whereas successful hunting and fishing requires assertiveness and independence.

SUGGESTIONS FOR FURTHER READING

Gewirtz, J. L. (ed.). *Attachment and Dependency*. New York: Halsted, 1972. Containing contributions prepared especially for it, this volume represents an unusually comprehensive picture of current views on the development of interpersonal relationships.

6
Dependency: The Psychometric-Trait Viewpoint

6
Dependency: The Psychometric-Trait Viewpoint

I. **Observational methods: a peer nomination measure of dependency**
   A. Rationale and development
   B. Construct validity

II. **Self-report methods: forced-choice dependency scales**
   A. Construct validity
      1. Requesting help and reassurance from others
      2. Responsivity to verbal approval and disapproval
      3. Social suggestibility
      4. Social conformity

III. **Indirect methods: a fantasy measure of dependency**
   A. Fantasy dependency and social conformity
   B. Fantasy dependency and psychosexual orality

IV. **Summary**

OBSERVATIONAL METHODS
a peer nomination measure of dependency

The Peer Nomination Inventory is a specialized instrument that was designed for the observational study of adjustment in preadolescent (8- to 12-year-old) boys. This instrument is unique in that it attempts to define adjustment in terms of social reputation among relatively young children. It also illustrates many of the difficulties and complexities involved in trying to measure the trait of dependency by observational methods.

Rationale and Development

The items which constitute the final form of the Peer Nomination Inventory were derived from actual statements made by 8- to 12-year-old boys about peers who were experiencing adjustment difficulties. To collect the statements, 252 boys from seven different schools were individually interviewed in the presence of a tape recorder. The boys were asked to describe typical behaviors of their peers who were "not getting along too well with the other kids or with the teacher." The interviews elicited 3,290 behavior statements that were considered representative peer descriptions of maladjustment in the school situation. The statements were typed on individual cards, and their content was rated by three psychologists working independently. The raters were asked to classify each statement in one of several categories. The description of the *dependency* category was as follows:

> The boy, by implication or act, attempts to secure attention, approval or affection from adults or peers by physical proximity, verbal demands or any device that tends to focus attention on himself. (Wiggins and Winder, 1961, p. 650).

This procedure produced 444 separate statements that the three raters unanimously agreed on as belonging in the category of "dependency." These statements were then examined by two clinical psychologists, who further subcategorized them into different aspects of dependency and attempted to eliminate obvious duplications. The clinical psychologists agreed on nine subcategories in the pool of dependency items: (1) general physical proximity, (2) immaturity, (3) general attention, (4) conformity, (5) help-seeking, (6) obsequiousness, overfriendliness, (7) dynamic inferences, (8) negative attention-getting, and (9) masochistic negative attention-getting. The investigators then selected a preliminary pool of 60 dependency items that were representative of the nine subcategories and that involved a minimum amount of content overlap.

The 60 dependency items were used to construct six different forms of the Peer Nomination Inventory, each of which contained 10 dependency items as well as items from other personality-trait categories. On a typical form, illustrated in Fig. 6.1, dependency items appear as rows and the names of boys in a given class appear as columns. Subjects are instructed to consider the possible applicability of each dependency item to each peer name. The rater enters a check in the appropriate box under the name of any boy he considers well described by a given item.

	Jerry Ash	Bob Baker	Joe Grant	John Hall	Tom Jones	Carl Smith	Sam Taber
He likes an audience all the time.							✓
He feels a lack of attention.		✓	✓				
He's trying hard to get popular.							
He wants everything done for him.						✓	
He acts as if he's sort of a baby.				✓			

Fig. 6.1.   Peer Nomination Inventory format.

After the six preliminary forms of the inventory were administered to numerous boys in different classes and schools, a procedure known as *item analysis* was conducted. The 12 best dependency items were selected from the pool of 60. These items showed the most consistency among themselves, were used sufficiently often to make them practical, and were highly correlated with teacher ratings made on the same items.

As a further check on the properties of items, the final form of the Peer Nomination Inventory (which included the 12 dependency items as well as items measuring other traits) was administered to large groups of boys in various classes and schools. This additional testing procedure demonstrated that the items retained their original satisfactory properties. Approximately a year later, when the same form was administered to classes that included 339 boys who had been in the original study, it was found that the individual dependency items had remained relatively stable.

In its current version, the Peer Nomination Inventory yields for each boy a dependency score based on percentages of peer nominations of him on items in that category. This scoring method allows for comparability of ratings obtained in different-sized classrooms. Consider a class of 21 boys. Since subjects do not rate themselves, there are 20 raters for each boy. If five nominate Johnny Jones for the item "He feels a lack of attention," Johnny receives a score of 5/20, or 25%, on that item. With 12 dependency items in the inventory, a single boy's dependency score could vary from 0 to 1200 (i.e., from no nominations on any item to 100% on all 12). Note that the scoring model employed is *cumulative.* The underlying assumption is that the higher the percentage of peers who nominate the subject and the more items on which they nominate him, the more dependent is the social behavior of the boy in the opinion of his peers. The resulting score is a composite of peer opinion which gives a subject's *social-stimulus value* with respect to the personality trait of dependency.

Construct Validity

The manner in which the Peer Nomination Inventory was constructed reflects the concern of the test authors for the substantive and structural aspects of construct validity. The universe of content sampled by the test may be thought of as all possible statements related to dependency that might be emitted by 8- to 12-year-old boys when asked to describe peers who are experiencing adjustmental difficulties. Obviously, the authors could not consider all such possible statements, but they made an effort to obtain a representative sample of such statements and to ensure that different categories of dependency were represented in the final version of the instrument. The primary structural considerations were those involving the interrelationships among test items, their stability over time, and the manner in which items were combined to yield a total score. The constructors of the inventory employed item-analysis procedures that tended to maximize the intercorelations among dependency items and to ensure their relative stability over time. The cumulative-scoring model under which items were combined is based on a construal of social-stimulus value that emphasizes the continuous and cumulative social "impact" of a boy on his peers.

As emphasized in Chapter 2, it is not enough to demonstrate that a psychological test represents an appropriate universe of content and that the items in the test are related to one another in the manner specified by the theory of the trait in question. Construct validity requires that the test be related to a variety of nontest manifestations of the trait, such as behaviors observed under controlled laboratory conditions and in life situations. As an example of checking the external validity of the 12-item Peer Nomination Inventory dependency scale, let us look at an experiment in which an attempt was made to predict controlled observations of dependent behavior from dependency scores.

The Peer Nomination Inventory dependency scale was administered to boys in 27 classes in several elementary schools (Winder and Wiggins, 1964). From each class two high-dependency boys, two medium-dependency boys, and two low-dependency boys were selected on the basis of their ratings by classmates. In addition, a seventh boy with a history of adequate classroom performance was selected from each class to play the unwitting role of a "successful" stooge in the experimental session.

Each group of seven boys was taken to an experimental room arranged as shown in Fig. 6.2. The experimenter introduced himself as a "toy manufacturer" who was interested in obtaining boy's reactions to a new line of interesting toys. Two additional raters, already present in the experimental room were told by the experimenter to remain and finish their "work" which consisted of rating sheets attached to clip boards. The subjects were seated around the large table, and another table containing attractive toys was in full view of all.

The experimenter explained to the boys that they could play with the toys when they had completed a simple maze game. Each subject was

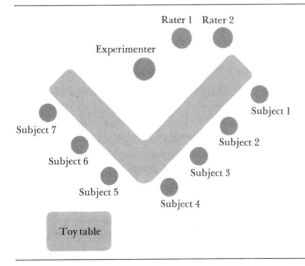

Fig. 6.2.   Experimental arrangement for dependency study.

given a booklet of seven paper mazes to complete, all of a type previously determined to be appropriate for this age group. However, for each of the six experimental subjects, one of the mazes was impossible to complete. Its position in the test booklet varied from subject to subject. The seventh subject (the stooge) received a booklet containing seven solvable mazes. When the unwitting stooge finished his seven mazes, the experimenter took him to the other table and encouraged him to play with the toys. Meanwhile, the raters independently observed all subjects at one-minute intervals according to a predetermined rating schedule. The dependent behaviors included in the schedule were such items as "seeks information," "seeks approval," "asks for help," "seeks reasurance," etc.

The experimental strategy of providing the subjects with an unsolvable task which prevented them from playing with the attractive toys gave rise to a great deal of dependent behavior in all subjects. After a fixed time interval, the experimenter asked the subjects to turn in their papers and told them they could play with the toys.

The experimental hypothesis was that subjects who had been classified as high, medium, and low by the Peer Nomination Inventory dependency scale would show respectively high, medium, and low amounts of dependent behavior in the experimental situation. It was tested on a total of 162 boys—54 each in the classifications of high, medium, and low de-

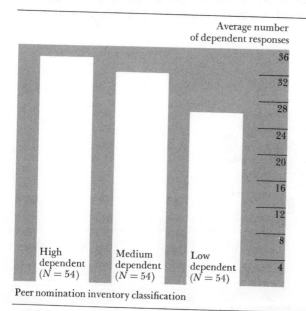

Fig. 6.3. Average number of dependency responses observed in subject groups classified by the Peer Nomination Inventory (after Winder and Wiggins, 1964).

pendency. The average number of dependent behaviors observed in the time interval for the three groups of subjects is presented in Fig. 6.3.

As one can see from simple inspection, the average number of dependent responses observed in the experimental situation is related to subjects' scores on the Peer Nomination Inventory dependency scale. Whereas the 54 high-dependency subjects made approximately 34 dependent responses, the low-dependency subjects made approximately 27. These results are statistically significant and would be expected to occur by chance in only one out of a 1,000 instances. This study provides clear evidence for the construct validity of the Peer Nomination Inventory dependency scale with respect to experimental studies of dependency.

SELF-REPORT METHODS
forced-choice dependency scales

As noted in Chapter 2, the Edwards Personal Preference Schedule (EPPS) is a forced-choice, self-report inventory that measures 15 manifest needs or personality traits emphasized by Murray (1938). Items are presented in pairs that have been approximately equated for social desirability, and subjects must select the statement in each pair that is more characteristic of what they like. Murray's system of personality classification is a complex one in which many fine distinctions are made. Thus, there is no single category of dependency in the EPPS but rather two subcategories which reflect different aspects of dependent behavior: autonomy and deference. Descriptions of both of these needs, as well as some typical EPPS items from the need scales, are presented in Box 6.1. Dependent people are lacking in autonomy (score low on the scale) and have a high need to defer to others (score high on the scale). Usages of the word "dependency" differ, and any particular usage may reflect a relative emphasis on one or the other of these two aspects of the trait.

Construct Validity

As a psychological-trait construct, dependency implies a wide variety of behaviors that are considered manifestations of the underlying trait. Evidence for the construct validity of the autonomy and deference scales of the Edwards Personal Preference Schedule should include demonstrations that the scales are related to the behavioral manifestations implied by the construct of dependency. It is expected, for example, that dependent individuals will rely on others for approval and help, will value verbal reward and social reinforcement, will be suggestible, and will tend to conform under group pressure to do so. Evidence from a number of stud-

---

Box 6.1   Edwards Personal Preference Schedule dependency scales*

Autonomy: To be able to come and go as desired, to say what one thinks about things, to be independent of others in making decisions, to feel free to do what one wants, to do things that are unconventional, to avoid situations where one is expected to conform, to do things without regard to what others may think, to criticize those in positions of authority, to avoid responsibilities and obligations.

Sample items
I like to do things in my own way and without regard to what others may think.
I like to avoid responsibilities and obligations.
I like to say what I think about things.
I like to be able to come and go as I want.
I like to avoid situations where I am expected to do things in a conventional way.

Deference: To get suggestions from others, to find out what others think, to follow instructions and do what is expected, to praise others, to tell others that they have done a good job, to accept the leadership of others, to read about great men, to conform to custom and avoid the unconventional, to let others make decisions.

Sample items
I like to follow instructions and to do what is expected of me.
I like to read about the lives of great men.
I like to praise someone I admire.
I like to accept the leadership of people I admire.
When I am in a group, I like to accept the leadership of someone else in deciding what the group is going to do.

---

ies suggests that the autonomy and deference scales are related to all these behavioral manifestations of dependency.

Requesting help and reassurance from others. From the administration of the Edwards Personal Preference Schedule to a large group of students at the University of Colorado, 20 subjects were selected as dependent (low autonomy–high deference) and 20 as independent (high autonomy–low deference). All subjects were given a difficult Chinese block puzzle to assemble in a 15-minute period. They were informed that the experimenter would be willing to give them as much help as they needed and that whenever help was requested, the experimenter would place the next piece of the block puzzle in place.

Two direct behavioral ratings of dependent behavior were made. The *suggestion score* was the number of requests a subject made that the experimenter put the next piece of the block puzzle in place. The *corroboration score* was the number of times the subject made comments asking for reassurance (e.g., "Is this correct?") A statistical analysis of the two scores indicated that the dependent subjects had both higher suggestion scores and higher corroboration scores than did the independent subjects. The results were interpreted as indicating that the EPPS dependency scales measured the behavioral manifestation of dependency of requesting help and reassurance from others (Bernardin and Jessor, 1957).

Responsivity to verbal approval and disapproval. It is to be expected that dependent subjects will be highly responsive to social reinforcement that takes the form of verbal reward or praise for their behavior. Cairns and Lewis (1962) conducted a study that evaluated the extent to which the dependency scales of the Edwards Personal Preference Schedule are related to subjects' tendencies to value verbal reward. From a larger group of male freshmen at the University of Pennsylvania, 30 dependent (low autonomy–high deference) and 30 independent (high autonomy–low deference) subjects were selected for study. The procedure followed was a verbal conditioning task in which all subjects were requested to make up sentences from combinations of words presented to them. When a subject selected the word to be conditioned, the experimenter showed approval by glancing up at him and murmuring "Mm—hmm." On completion of the experiment, each subject was presented with an 11-place rating scale and asked to judge the pleasantness of the "Mm—hmm" of the experimenter. The results indicated that the dependent subjects valued the verbal reinforcement of the experimenter considerably more than did the independent subjects. Thus the dependency scales of the EPPS appear to be predictive of the differential sensitivity to approval of high- and low-dependent subjects.

Although dependent individuals are sensitive to approval and likely to value it highly, they are also sensitive to disapproval and likely to react adversely to it. Bernardin and Jessor (1957) employed the dependency scales of the EPPS to investigate the hypothesis that the performance of dependent subjects is more likely to be disrupted by verbal disapproval than is the performance of independent subjects. From the administration of the EPPS to a larger sample, 20 subjects were selected as being dependent and 20 as independent. Ten dependent and ten independent subjects were tested under the experimental condition of negative verbal reinforcement, while the other half were tested under a control condition in which no negative reinforcement was given. All subjects were blindfolded and asked to learn a finger maze which consisted of a raised welding rod fastened to a wooden base with 20 choice points between start and finish.

Under the experimental condition, the experimenter made comments such as: "You're going very slowly," "Your performance is not very good," "I thought you could do much better than this," etc. In addition, the experimenter said *"No!"* each time the subject made an error. Measures of learning included: (a) the number of errors made in each trial, (b) the time spent on each trial, and (c) the amount of improvement in later trials over earlier trials.

The results clearly indicated that dependent subjects under the experimental condition of negative verbal reinforcement (a) made significantly more errors per trial, (b) took significantly longer per trial, and (c) showed significantly less improvement in later trials than did independent subjects who were tested under the same condition. In addition, it was found that the quality of performance for dependent experimental subjects was significantly lower than that of the dependent control subjects who did not receive negative verbal reinforcement. The results of this study were interpreted as indicating that the dependency scales of the EPPS serve as indices of the differential sensitivity of dependent individuals to verbal disapproval.

Social suggestibility.   Suggestibility has long been thought of as a behavioral manifestation of the underlying trait of dependency. The most frequently employed laboratory measures of suggestibility are those associated with hypnosis. Although once considered an exotic practice or a parlor game, hypnosis has now become a standard laboratory procedure for assessing the degree of susceptibility of a subject to social influence.

The Stanford Hypnotic Susceptibility Scale (Weitzenhoffer and Hilgard, 1959) is a set of standard laboratory procedures for assessing hypnotic susceptibility. It begins with an attempt to induce a very mild state of suggestibility and ends with an attempt to induce a hypnotic trance. The first item is known as the Postural Sway Test. The subject stands erect with heels and toes together, hands by sides, eyes closed. The experimenter makes suggestions such as: "You are falling backward, swaying backward, falling backward, swaying backward, falling backward, falling backward, falling backward, backward ... you are falling, falling, falling ... *Fall!*"

Does dress reflect conformity to group norms? Can you speculate about the degree of "sameness" suggested by the similarities in costume in each of these groups of people? ▶

J.-P. Laffont/Sygma

Lang and Lazovik (1962) attempted to relate scores on the Edwards Personal Preference Schedule to the Stanford Hypnotic Susceptibility Scale in a sample of 46 college student volunteers. The results indicated that scores on the EPPS deference scale were positively related to scores on the Postural Sway Test and to those on all remaining items of the Stanford Hypnotic Susceptibility Scale. These results lend support to the construct validity of the EPPS deference scale as an index of one of the behavioral manifestations of dependency (i.e., suggestibility). Although autonomy was not correlated with suggestibility in the Lang and Lazovik study, such a relationship was found in another study. Zuckerman and Grosz (1958) administered the Postural Sway Test to 27 student nurses who had also taken the EPPS. They reported that the autonomy scale on the EPPS was significantly related to degree of postural sway.

Social conformity. The dependent person is thought of as one who will conform to a majority opinion or to group pressure. A basic laboratory procedure for studying conformity to group pressure was devised by Asch (1952). Gisvold (1958) employed a modification of the Asch laboratory conformity test to study the construct validity of the autonomy and deference scales of the Edwards Personal Preference Schedule as indices of social conformity. Student volunteers participated in the study in groups of four.

The four subjects in a group entered the experimental room and sat on chairs that were partitioned from one another, so that no subject could observe the behavior of the other three. The only person the subjects could see was the experimenter, who was seated in front of them at a small table. On each trial, the experimenter displayed two large cards: the card on the left showed a straight line and the card on the right showed three parallel comparison lines. The subjects were asked to indicate which of the three comparison lines was of the same length as the standard line. They did so by holding up one of three card numbers corresponding to their choice of a comparison line.

Each subject was led to believe that he was the fourth subject to make his judgment. In all instances, the three "preceding judgments" made available were in agreement. On some trials, the three "judgments" were correct; i.e., they indicated the correct matching of lines. On the critical conformity trials, however, the three "judgments" were in agreement but were incorrect; i.e., they showed the choice of a line that was clearly not of the same length as the standard. The conformity score derived from such a laboratory test is simply the number of trials on which the subject conforms by giving an incorrect answer in response to the pressure of the three other "judges." Although the other "judges" were actually fictional, the subjects accepted their judgments as real and conformed in varying degrees. Two weeks later all subjects were given the Edwards Personal Preference Schedule.

Analysis of the results of this study indicated that subjects who scored low on the autonomy scale tended to give many conformity responses, whereas subjects who scored high on the autonomy scale tended to give few, if any, conformity responses. Although the analysis showed a slight positive relationship between deference scale scores and conformity responses, the relationship was not statistically significant and could have occurred by chance. Nevertheless, this study provides supportive evidence of the relationship between the EPPS autonomy scale and conformity to group pressure.

INDIRECT METHODS
a fantasy measure of dependency

The Thematic Apperception Test (TAT) provides an indirect method for assessing dependency on the level of fantasy. Stories made up by TAT subjects may be analyzed for the presence of help-seeking or concern about social reward and support on the part of the hero. In obtaining indirect fantasy measures of personality traits, such as dependency, one is never certain of the exact relationship that exists between fantasy and overt behavior. There is some evidence to suggest that such a relationship is a function of the degree to which the trait is sanctioned or considered acceptable in our culture. When the trait under consideration is culturally sanctioned, one expects a fairly direct and positive relationship between fantasy measures and overt behavioral measures. Since help-seeking and social dependence are, to some extent, viewed positively in our culture, one would expect to find a fairly direct relationship between TAT measures of dependency and measures of overt dependent behaviors.

Fantasy Dependency and Social Conformity

The last-mentioned hypothesis was subjected to a test in a study conducted by Kagan and Mussen (1956). Under the hypothesis that there would be a positive association between TAT dependency themes and overt measures of dependent behavior, the authors attempted to relate TAT dependency to social conformity in the Asch social conformity situation. Male undergraduates were instructed to write stories to eight TAT cards which were then scored for fantasy dependency. Two types of theme were scored as instances of dependent fantasies: (a) those in which the hero sought help from another person in solving a personal problem and (b) those in which the hero was disturbed over the loss of a source of love and support. The subjects' stories were independently scored by the two authors, who achieved 93% agreement in their classifications of dependent fantasies.

In the experimental conformity situation, each subject was taken individually into a small room in which there were four other "subjects." The four were, in fact, paid stooges who had been preinstructed on how to behave. The experiment was presented as a test of vision, and the subjects' task was to match lines of various lengths to a standard. On each of 12 trials the subjects were asked to call out their choices. The order was always the same, and the naïve subject was fourth. The stooges were always in complete agreement, but on seven trials their responses were incorrect, on five correct. The measure of social conformity employed was the number of trials on which the naïve subject agreed with the factually incorrect responses of the paid stooges. Naïve subjects who conformed to the incorrect group judgment on one or more of the seven incorrect trials were classified as yielders; those who did not so conform on any of the trials were classified as nonyielders. Of the 27 naïve subjects, 16 were classified as yielders and 11 as nonyielders.

The TAT stories given earlier by the subjects were used as a basis for classifying the subjects on dependency. Subjects who gave more than the average number of dependency themes were classified as high-dependent, those who gave less than the average as low-dependent. The statistical analysis of the results was based on the number of times high-dependency subjects were classified as yielders and the number of times low-dependency subjects were classified as nonyielders. The data given in Fig. 6.4 show that of the subjects who gave more than the average number of TAT dependency themes (high-dependent), 100% yielded to group pressure on one or more of the conformity trials. Of the subjects who gave less than the average number of TAT dependency themes (low-dependent), only 35% yielded to group pressure on one or more of the conformity trials. These results are statistically significant and would be expected to occur by chance only once in 100 times. Clearly, there is a relationship between fantasy dependency as measured by the TAT and conformity as measured by the Asch laboratory situation.

Fantasy Dependency and Psychosexual Orality

Because it is presumably a measure of fantasy rather than of overt behavior, the TAT lends itself readily to the testing of research hypotheses derived from psychoanalytic theory. An interesting example of such a test may be found in a study reported by Scodel (1957). According to Freud

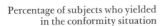

Percentage of subjects who yielded
in the conformity situation

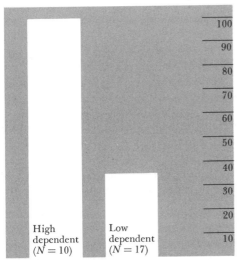

100

90

80

70

60

50

40

30

20

High   Low
dependent   dependent   10
(N = 10)   (N = 17)

Thematic apperception test classification

Fig. 6.4. Percentage of subjects who yielded in groups classified by the Thematic Apperception Test. (After J. Kagan and P. H. Mussen, "Dependency themes on the TAT and group conformity," *Journal of Consulting Psychology*, 1956, **20**, p. 30. Copyright 1956 by the American Psychological Association. Reprinted by permission.)

(1905), the personality trait of dependency is closely linked with the notion of *orality*, since breast feeding by the mother represents the first significant interpersonal relation or object attachment for the infant. The significance of the early breast-feeding experience for later adult personality development has been repeatedly stressed by psychoanalytic writers. According to one psychoanalyst (Tridon, 1949), men who were nursed at the breast in infancy are attracted in adulthood to women with well-developed breasts, whereas men who were bottle-fed tend to prefer thin, boyish-looking girls. The assumption here is that men who are attracted to women with large breasts are concerned with gratifying their oral-dependency needs. Hence it would follow that men who prefer large-breasted women are more dependent than men who prefer women with small breasts. Although such a notion is subscribed to by many clinicians of Freudian persuasion, Scodel (1957) was the first to submit it to systematic test.

Five male graduate students rated 101 full-length pictures of nude females (obtained from photography and art magazines) along a dimension of breast size. The following rating scale was used:

1. Considerably above average breast size.
2. Slightly above average breast size.
3. Average breast size.
4. Slightly below average breast size.
5. Considerably below average breast size.

When the judges' ratings were averaged, it was possible to classify 32 pictures as large-breasted and 33 as small-breasted. Five different judges then rated each picture on a six-place scale of attractiveness. To minimize the possible contribution of facial attractiveness, masking tape had been placed over the face in each picture. On the basis of these attractiveness ratings, 10 large-breasted and 10 small-breasted pictures were selected; both groups fell within the same general range of attractiveness. The experimenter then constructed a set of slides, each of which presented a large-breasted and a small-breasted figure approximately equated for attractiveness and other characteristics, such as position, view, etc. Ten additional pairs of pictures were included in the series in an attempt to disguise the purpose of the study.

The subjects were 169 male students who were recruited from an introductory psychology course at Ohio State University. The subjects were tested in small groups, ranging in number from 5 to 15. At the beginning of the session, the subjects were presented with seven TAT cards which had been chosen on the basis of their likelihood of eliciting dependency themes. The experimenter then told the subjects that they were to participate in a study designed to find out what female body types the typical American male generally prefers. They then looked at 20 pairs of slides and were asked to indicate which of the two figures they preferred on each trial.

Two psychologists independently scored the TAT stories according to the scoring procedure for dependency followed by Kagan and Mussen (1956). A score for dependency was given if the hero sought help from another person in solving a personal problem or was disturbed over the loss of a source of love and affection. The psychologists achieved 93% agreement in the scoring of the TAT stories.

The subjects' ratings of the slides were used as a basis for classifying them into three groups. The 28 subjects who had selected no more than three of the large-breasted females were defined as the small-breast-preference group. The group defined as having a preference for large breasts comprised the 35 subjects who had selected eight or more of the females so classified. The 57 subjects who had selected from four to six large-breasted figures constituted a middle group, considered to have no strong preferences in either direction.

Contrary to expectation, subjects in the small-breast-preference group gave significantly more dependency themes on the TAT than did either the subjects preferring large breasts or those in the middle group. There are at least two possible explanations for the unexpected result. The first involves a problem common to all TAT research, namely, that the relationship between fantasy and overt behavior is poorly understood. Consequently, it is possible that subjects who give a large number of dependency themes in fantasy stories actually have fewer dependency conflicts than do subjects who are not able to discharge their dependency needs in fantasy. The second possible explanation, the one given by Scodel, is based on a social-learning approach to dependency. In this view, large-breast preference is regarded as the consequence of continuing satisfaction of dependency needs rather than of their frustration. Additional evidence on this issue, which is related to the broader topic of human sexuality, will be presented in Chapter 14.

SUMMARY

The trait construct of dependency provides an organizing framework from which to view a variety of superficially different behaviors as manifestations of a single underlying trait. This chapter provided illustrations of typical findings and problems encountered in the measurement of dependency by observational, self-report, and indirect methods of personality assessment. The primary emphasis was on the procedures employed for establishing the construct validity of psychological-test measures of dependency.

We considered in detail the development and validation of a peer-nomination measure of dependency in order to illustrate the importance of substantive, structural, and external considerations in the evaluation of the construct validity of an observational method. A universe of content was clearly specified, and efforts were directed toward a balanced and representative sampling of that universe in the selection of test items. Theoretical considerations relating to the social-stimulus value of dependency as a component of peer reputation guided the interrelationships among test items and the manner in which items were combined to yield a total score. We presented evidence for the external validity of the peer-nomination measure of dependency from a study in which controlled observations of dependent behavior were predicted from peer nomination scores.

The autonomy and deference scales of the Edwards Personal Preference Schedule provide self-report measures of two aspects of dependency. Dependent subjects are expected to score low on the autonomy scale and high on the deference scale. Conversely, the pattern of response of independent subjects is expected to reflect high autonomy and low deference. Evidence for the construct validity of the autonomy and deference scales should include demonstrations that the scales are related to a variety of behavorial manifestations of the trait of dependency. We described a number of experimental studies that provide positive evidence that the autonomy and deference scales of the Edwards Personal Schedule are predictive of such diverse manifestations of dependency as: (a) requesting help and reassurance from others, (b) responsivity to verbal approval and disapproval, (c) social suggestibility, and (d) social conformity.

The Thematic Apperception Test provides an indirect method for assessing dependency on the level of fantasy. Stories told by TAT subjects may be analyzed for the presence of help-seeking or concern about social reward and support on the part of the hero. When such themes are scored independently by two judges, the judges typically agree in a high percentage of their ratings of fantasy dependency. In obtaining indirect fantasy measures of personality traits, one cannot specify with certainty the nature of the relationship that exists between fantasy and overt behavior. There is some evidence to suggest that this relationship is a function of the degree to which the trait is considered acceptable in our culture. Since dependency is, to some extent, viewed positively in our culture, it is expected that the relationship between TAT measures of dependency and overt dependent behaviors will be a direct and positive one. Such a result was found in a study which investigated the relationship between fantasy dependency and social conformity in a laboratory setting.

Section 3
Aggression

7
Aggression: The Biological Viewpoint

I. **Evolutionary perspective**
   A. Aggression and human evolution
   B. Ethology and human aggression

II. **Behavior genetics**
   A. Correlated responses to selection
   B. Analysis of pure strains
   C. Human studies: the Y chromosome and aggressiveness
      1. Male hormones and the XYY karyotype
      2. Neurological abnormalities and the XYY karyotype
      3. Some reservations and alternative hypotheses
   D. Twin studies and longitudinal evidence
      1. Longitudinal stability of aggressiveness
      2. Twin studies

III. **Early experience**
   A. Hormonal effects
   B. Effects of social rearing
   C. Aggression and ethology reconsidered

IV. **Summary**

V. **Suggestions for further reading**

EVOLUTIONARY PERSPECTIVE

If we search for causes of human aggressiveness, we must begin with our ancestry. The emotional patterns which underlie aggressive behaviors evolved thousands of years ago.

We have previously described the intricate and facilitative relationship between bipedal locomotion, tool use, and the development of the human brain. Further process in this evolutionary development resulted in a dramatic reduction in the size of teeth and the facial skeleton; changes in diet, necessitated by a sharp reduction in available fruit, led to the development of hunting. *This carnivorous adaptation of the humanoid apes and their effective employment of lethal weapons were crucially important to their survival.* Their evolutionary success was predicated, in part, on their predatory and carnivorous adaptation to their new environment, which was in turn based on their upright stance, developing brain and hand, and adoption of lethal, manual weapons.

As humans became carnivorous, they also became terrestrial, and in so doing, they must have gone through a "behavioral transition from a retreating to an attacking pattern" (Freedman and Roe, 1958). Aggressive behaviors have adaptive significance for survival value. This fact, readily evident when we assess the behavior of lower organisms, can be documented by behavior-genetic studies of aggressiveness in rodents. Aggressiveness is no less significant in humans:

> Man takes pleasure in hunting other animals. Unless careful training has hidden the natural drives, men enjoy the chase and the kill. In most cultures torture and suffering are made public spectacles for the enjoyment of all. The victims may be either animal or human. This behavior is strikingly similar to that of many carnivores, and no parallel behavior has been observed among wild primates; in fact, our whole conception of wild and tame is a reflection of the human hunting attitude, with a feeling that it is normal for animals to fight and flee.*

Prehistoric humans were hunters. Their survival depended on evolving behavior and attitudes supporting their hunting abilities. That contemporary humans have learned to kill and, all too frequently, enjoy seeing others suffer may be seen in the light of these facts of human ancestry. Human aggressiveness and cruelty may be understood in terms of our carnivorous and cannibalistic origins (Dart, 1953). Of course it is pain-

---

* From S. L. Washburn and V. Avis, "Evolution of human behavior," in A. Roe and G. G. Simpson (eds.), *Behavior and Evolution,* Yale University Press, New Haven, 1958, p. 433. Reprinted by permission.

fully clear that the aggressive dispositions which served evolutionary development a million years ago have become our most basic and difficult problem. But to understand and control human aggression, we should begin with knowledge of our origin.

Aggression and Human Evolution

Aggressive behavior has adaptive significance for humans no less than for other animals. Human origin is closely associated with the beginning of hunting and the skilled use of weapons. The evolutionary break represented by the South African Australopithecus resulted from the carnivorous adaptation. That, together with upright stance, led to changes in teeth and facial skeleton and to the creation and employment of lethal weapons. From a weaponless scavenger emerged a walking, tool-using hunter. And in this development of hunting lies the birth of aggression and territoriality (Leakey, 1967).

Based on the paleoanthropological evidence, aggression, associated with a predatory, carnivorous adaptation to the environment, was a major key in human evolution. As argued in Chapter 3, the human brain evolved after—and largely as a consequence of—this development.

> In broad anthropological perspective, then, it may be argued that man's nature and skills and, ultimately, human civilization, owe their existence to the kind of predatory adaptation first achieved by the carnivorous Australopithecinae on the grasslands of southern Africa. . . .*

There is a second way in which aggressive patterns of behavior contributed to human evolution. In the human, as in other animals, aggressiveness is closely associated with dominance and the maintenance of stable hierarchies within groups. Dominance hierarchies appear to have played a crucial role in the rapid development of the complex human brain. For brain development to have occurred as rapidly as it did, some special type of breeding system was necessary. A polygamous system based on a dominance hierarchy seems most likely (Fox, 1967); in such a system, the chances that any individual male would breed and contribute to the gene pool would depend on his status within the dominance hierarchy. Perhaps half of all males would not breed, and their genes would be selectively excluded from the pool. Continuing selection would occur, since only the stronger, more intelligent, and more social males would succeed in reproducing themselves.

---

* From D. Freeman, "Human aggression in anthropological perspective," in J. D. Carthy and F. J. Ebling (eds.), *The Natural History of Aggression*, Academic Press, New York, 1965, p. 116. Reprinted by permission.

Ethology and Human Aggression

One approach to the study of human behavior, implicit in the comments above, begins with an appreciation of our animal origins and our primate nature. This biological approach, rooted in naturalistic observation of animal behavior, is called *ethology*. The approach of the ethologist has high relevance to an understanding of human aggression (Tinbergen, 1968). Consider, for example, the common observation of dominance hierarchies in an animal species. Once established, the hierarchy serves important functions, because most overt fighting is avoided through conventionalized displays of threat and submissive posturing. The dominant animal threatens; the subordinate submits. Actual conflict is avoided. Analogously, pecking orders typically exist in human organizations, and dominance hierarchies are readily established in human groups. Maintained by emotional cohesion, the hierarchy is strengthened by any external threat which promotes aggression against the common enemy.

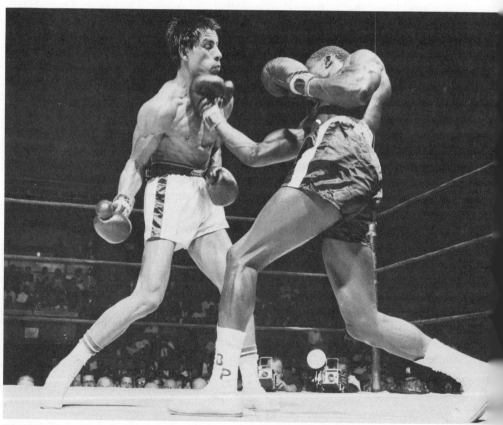

N.Y. Daily News photo

A detailed description of this process in human behavior, with an analysis of its evolution and function, is available. Tiger (1969) suggests that social aggregation is the basic prelude to aggression. He argues that the social structure of the male group provides the model and sanction for aggression. Reduced to essentials, Tiger's argument is that aggression is a natural, predictable outcome of the association of men in groups. Social aggregation is not necessarily followed by aggression; rather, aggression is effectively stimulated by the association of males.

> Men in continuous association aggress against the environment in much the same way that men and women in continuous association have sexual relations.*

As one compelling illustration of his argument, Tiger cites William Golding's widely acclaimed novel, *Lord of the Flies*. Golding portrays the violent and savage relationships that develop among a group of English schoolboys shipwrecked on an isolated island. Forced to manage for themselves in order to survive, the boys disagree fiercely. The initial dominance hierarchy is overthrown, and violence results. One boy is killed, and when the group is finally rescued, the original leader is being hunted with cries of "Kill the beast! Cut his throat! Spill his blood!" *Lord of the Flies,* of course, is fiction. Its validity as a statement of human nature might be dismissed, were it not for the dramatic consequences that resulted from an effort to film the novel. The careful attempt to create Golding's story was almost too authentic.

> . . . The experiment in Stanislavskian acting had to be controlled. The children threatened violence, felt deep antipathies for each other, and created a situation very close to the book's. . . . (Tiger, 1969, p. 163)

The director of the film, Peter Brook, later described the situation.

> Many of their off-screen relationships completely paralleled the story, and one of our main problems was to encourage them to be uninhibited within the shots but disciplined in between them. . . .
>
> My experience showed me that the only falsification in Golding's fable is the length of time the descent to savagery takes. His action takes about three months. I believe that if the cork of continued adult presence were removed from the bottle, the complete catastrophe could occur within a long weekend.†

---

* From L. Tiger, *Men in Groups,* Random House, New York, 1969, p. 160. Published in Great Britain by Thomas Nelson and Sons. Reprinted by permission.

† From P. Brook, "Filming a masterpiece," *The Observer,* London, July 26, 1964, p. 23. Reprinted by permission.

Let us recapitulate. Dominance hierarchies are common to the social behavior of human and animal. It is suggested that aggression arises as a natural product of this social process. The mechanisms which lead to aggressive violence are the same mechanisms which underlie normal social aggregation. Emotional bonds between members of a group are strengthened by real or symbolic enemies. Given a dominance hierarchy maintained by emotional bonds and strengthened by the perceived presence of an enemy, violence may erupt (Tiger, 1969, p. 165).

Crucial to Tiger's argument is a point we shall later consider at length: *aggression depends on events in the social environment.* Aggression-dominance is a tendency of men in groups, but the emergence of violence is triggered by external circumstances—circumstances which are social in character and which vary over time and across cultures:

> Aggression and violence ... are not individually motivated behaviour patterns. They are "released" or "directed" by social activity, and particularly effectively so by the social interactions of males. Furthermore, the *gestalt* of a group's social interactions—which perhaps we call its culture—and the wider social system within which the group exists, provide the models and sanctions for aggressive and violent behaviour. The claim, then, is that male bonding is both a function and cause of aggression and violence. These, in turn, are defined, mediated, and expressed through local-cultural social patterns. (Tiger, 1969, p. 172)

BEHAVIOR GENETICS

In many species, including our own, aggressiveness has direct adaptive value. Dominance hierarchies and territorial behavior space out the population and maintain an optimal relationship between a social group and its environment. Further, success in fighting is often directly related to reproductive dominance. Therefore we should anticipate that selective factors favoring aggressive behaviors act on the gene pool.

For example, one experiment (Lagerspetz, 1961) provides evidence of successful selection for fighting abilities in the mouse. Male mice of an albino strain were selected for high and low aggressiveness and mated to the sisters of the most and least aggressive mice. Aggressiveness was measured by pairing animals in a cage for brief periods and scoring aggressive behavior on a seven-point rating scale. At one extreme of the scale the animal showed no interest in his test partner and, if attacked, tried to escape; at the other extreme, there was fierce wrestling and the animal bit his test partner hard enough to draw blood. At least seven trials were made with each animal, and the mean of the observed scores served as the measure of aggressiveness for that animal. Selection effects appeared as early as the second generation; by the seventh generation the two lines of animals differed very significantly in aggressiveness. Cross-fostering experiments suggest that the difference between the two strains was not due to early postnatal maternal effects (Lagerspetz and Wuorinen, 1965).

Correlated responses to selection. In general, selection for a specific behavior will have correlated effects on other behaviors. Since the aggressive behavior pattern contains elements of high motor activity, we anticipate a positive correlation between aggressiveness and activity level. And since selection for emotionality produces a correlated response in aggressiveness, we are led to hypothesize that selection for aggressiveness will lead to a correlated response in emotionality. Both expectations are confirmed in the present experiment. *Aggressive animals are more active and they are less emotional.*

Further, animals selectively bred for aggressiveness and nonaggressiveness differ on several neurochemical variables. A comparison between animals from the thirteenth and fourteenth generations of the selection study revealed that animals from the aggressive line have heavier forebrains, and their brains contain significantly greater concentrations of several neurochemicals commonly thought to be important in the expression of aggressiveness (Lagerspetz, Tirri, and Lagerspetz, 1968).

Analysis of pure strains. A substantial number of studies reveal significant differences among inbred strains of rodents in the latency, amount, and duration of fighting (Scott, 1966). Many of these studies have also routinely assessed the influence of postnatal maternal influences via crossfostering experiments. A general conclusion from all available data is that cross-fostering does *not* markedly modify the genotypic differences in aggressive behaviors. Rearing a pup from a highly aggressive strain with a foster mother from an extremely submissive strain typically produces only a negligible effect on the animal's adult aggression.

Strain differences are also evident in behavior associated with aggressiveness, particularly social dominance. For example, strain differences are readily apparent in a laboratory measure of competitive dominance among inbred strains of mice (Lindzey, Winston, and Manosevitz, 1961).

Research on aggressiveness among inbred strains of rodents further documents the interaction of experience with the genotype. Adult aggressiveness is determined by a complex interplay of genetic and environmental effects. Thus early experiences which profoundly affect adult aggressiveness in one strain of mice have no effect on adult fighting in another strain (Ginsburg, 1967).

Similarly, the interaction of genotype with degree of adult crowding has been investigated by Vale and his colleagues (Vale, Vale, and Harley, 1971). Five different strains of mice were separately placed in cages in which population densities of two, four, and eight animals were maintained for ten days. Although several different physiological and behavioral measures were taken, the attacking response revealed a clearcut interaction of genotype with population density. As can be seen in Fig. 7.1, the B strain of mice showed a sharp augmentation in attacks with increasing population density. The remaining strains showed increases that varied from zero to slight.

Finally, DeFries and McClearn (1970) investigated the role of aggressive behavior in the transmission of genes to the next generation. Three

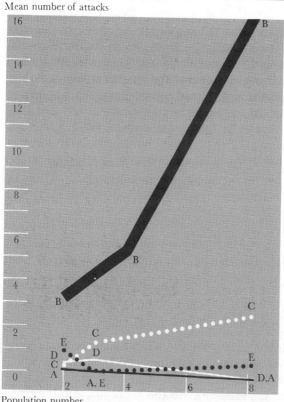

Fig. 7.1. Effect of increasing population number on attacking response for each of five strains of mice.

female and three male mice were placed in three cages that were inter-connected by a Y-shaped plastic tunnel. Within a relatively short period of time, dominance-submissiveness relationships were established among the male mice. The behavior of the dominant animal was marked by mo-bility. In contrast, the submissive mice tended to remain in a single cage, venturing out on pain of punishment by the dominant mouse. In an analy-sis of 61 litters born to animals in this social situation, it was found that the dominant male sired from 91 to 95 percent of the offspring. As ex-pressed by McClearn (1974), "This represents a stupendous Darwinian fitness, and clearly shows the extent to which aggressive behavior will be naturally selected in situations of this type" (p. 93).

Human Studies: The Y Chromosome and Aggressiveness

Because of various accidents during cellular division, sperm and ova with more or fewer than the usual number of chromosomes can be produced. When involved in fertilization, such gametes produce humans with a de-ficiency or an excess of chromosomal material. Evidence is accumulating that these chromosome errors are usually associated with behavioral disturbance.

Direct study of human chromosomes from photomicrographs prepared from blood cells led to the discovery that Down's syndrome, a severe form of mental retardation commonly called mongolism, is associated with an extra chromosome. Stimulated by this finding, continuing study has identified several other behavioral syndromes that are associated with chromosomal errors. Of interest here are very recent investigations which suggest that aggressive behavior is associated with an extra Y chromo-some in males. Instead of the normal 46 chromosomes, these men have 47, and the extra one is a second Y; *their karyotype*, or chromosome con-stitution, *is 47,XYY*.

Some years ago, it was suggested, from clinical evidence, that de-linquent behaviors were unusually common among male patients with various sex-chromosome anomalies (Court-Brown, 1962). Subsequently, a systematic search for sex-chromosome errors was made among men in security institutions for the mentally retarded (Casey et al., 1966). Such errors were found to be ten times as frequent in those men as in the normal population; chromosome examination revealed that many of the men studied possessed an extra Y chromosome. Finally, in addition to their asocial behavior and mental retardation, most of them were unusu-ally tall.

These preliminary findings suggested that delinquent aggressiveness and height were associated with the extra Y chromosome. And acting on that assumption, investigators have undertaken chromosome surveys of men in security institutions in a number of countries. The available evidence, though too recent and still too limited to permit firm conclusions, suggests that the extra Y does relate to aggressiveness, but the association may be largely indirect.

The major study to date is one reported by investigators (Jacobs et al., 1965; 1968) at a Scottish State Hospital provided for individuals subject to detention and requiring special security because of their presumed violent and dangerous tendencies. About two-thirds of the inmates had been referred directly from the courts, and all but a handful had a criminal record. Chromosome results were reported for 315 of the 342 men at the institution; sixteen, or 4.7%, exhibited some chromosome error, and nine of them had the karyotype 47,XYY.

Clinical and behavioral study of the nine men with the extra Y is particularly interesting (Price et al., 1966; Price and Whatmore, 1967). They were compared with a control group of 18 men randomly selected from the hospital population and known to have normal (46,XY) karyotypes. Both the XYY group and their controls were characterized as demonstrating serious personality disorder, but two further comparisons do reveal marked differences.

The first finding of interest was that the XYY men had been convicted of their first offense at a significantly earlier age than the controls had been. In fact, three men in the XYY group had been initially convicted before the age of ten. A second, more interesting comparison came from an examination of siblings of the two groups. Among the 31 siblings of the nine XYY males, only one had a criminal conviction and it was for a single offense. By contrast, among the 63 siblings of the 18 control males, 12 had criminal records, and the total number of convictions for that group was 139 (Price and Whatmore, 1967). This marked difference in family history has important implications: it suggests that the criminal behavior of the normal men may be understood in terms of social learning theory, whereas for the men with an extra Y chromosome, some genetic predisposition seems likely.

From all these studies of the XYY males identified at the Scottish State Hospital the picture emerged of psychopathic individuals lacking in any ordinary capacity for feeling, apparently without much depth of emotion, who seemed incapable of making any rational plans for the future, and who on the whole pose behavioral problems from childhood.... These individuals, drawn from all the social classes, stood out as the black sheep of their families and as the apparently inexplicably erring sons in otherwise reasonably well-adjusted families. This picture strongly favours the idea that the additional Y chromosome genetically predisposes the 47,XYY male to the development of a psychopathic personality and to consequent aberrant behaviour and antisocial conduct.*

Male hormones and the XYY karyotype.   A direct effect of the YY chromosome constitution on behavior might arise from a double dose of male hormones. The extra Y could lead to an earlier triggering of androgens (with organizing effects on the neural tissue) or to an elevated level of them. This possibility has recently been investigated in a preliminary way. In one study (Ismail *et al.*, 1968) urinary testosterone assays were performed on a series of patients with sex-chromosome abnormalities. Included in the sample were the nine males with a 47,XYY complement from the Scottish State Hospital. A control sample comprised 14 patients from the same hospital with a normal chromosomal constitution and six male patients with anomalies of the X chromosome. In addition, a study was made of normal men and women together with a small series of phenotypic females with sex-chromosome abnormalities.

Results indicated that individuals with the XYY constitution had a mean testosterone output level that was significantly higher than that of normal control males. However, the meaning of this finding is unclear; the value was not significantly different from that of hospital controls with a normal karyotype. The presence of an extra X chromosome in males was associated with lowered testosterone output.

Another study assessed urinary gonadotrophin excretion in men with a 7,XYY karyotype (Papanicolaou, Kirkham, and Loraine, 1968). That investigation was directed to pituitary function in the XYY constitution. For each of the three subjects investigated, serial assays for follicle-stimulating hormone (FSH) and luteinizing hormone (LH) were made.

The LH assays revealed levels considerably higher than the normal range. The suggestion is made that in men with the 47,XYY karyotype, the testes are relatively insensitive to stimulation by pituitary LH; in order to overcome this insensitivity, the anterior pituitary produces abnormally large quantities of LH.

> The normal reciprocal relationship existing between the pituitary and the gonads does not appear to operate in 47,XYY males, since an abnormally high LH output in these subjects is associated with urinary testosterone readings which are above the normal range. (Papanicolaou *et al.*, 1968, p. 610)

Neurological abnormalities and the XYY karyotype.   Diffuse abnormality of the electroencephalogram (EEG) is a finding commonly reported in indi-

---

* From W. M. Court-Brown, "Males with an XYY sex chromosome complement," *Journal of Medical Genetics*, 1968, **5**, 348–349. Reprinted by permission.

viduals with a history of asocial aggressiveness. The meaning of the finding is not clear, because a substantial minority of normal individuals have
EEG records that exhibit mild, diffuse abnormalities. Nonetheless, many
theorists believe that neurological difficulties, though of an admittedly unknown nature, characterize many, if not most, psychopathic criminals.
Therefore, several investigators have made neurological studies on XYY
males.

One of these studies was made on a United States sample obtained
from tall patients in security hospitals and institutions for the mentally
retarded (Daly, 1969). Among 210 such patients, 10 were found to have
the XYY karyotype; two additional cases were obtained from clinical settings. Daly reports that only one of the 12 patients was free of abnormal
neurological signs. Six exhibited body asymmetry, and 10 demonstrated
a tremor in voluntary movements. There is other evidence, obtained primarily from European samples, that abnormal EEG records characterize a
large proportion of those individuals in security institutions who have
excess chromosome material (Forssman and Hambert, 1967).

Some reservations and alternative hypotheses.   The evidence summarized above is impressive; however, the relationship between the extra Y
chromosome and aggressiveness is far from established. Critically necessary are better estimates—requiring much more data!—on the frequency
of the XYY karyotype in the normal population and among prisoners convicted of nonviolent crimes. In addition, there are serious problems with
much of the research thus far reported (Kessler and Moos, 1970). Differences in sampling, in the adequacy of controls, and in laboratory methods
make it difficult to compare and evaluate results obtained to date. The
methodological problems are serious and pervasive.

This reservation is underscored by a recent comprehensive review of
research on the 47,XYY male (Owen, 1972). The critical finding that linked
the extra Y chromosome to aggressiveness was the increased prevalence
of the 47,XYY karyotype in criminal and institutional populations. Owen
points out that much of the evidence is based upon impressions from clinical data and the rate of occurrence of the 47,XYY male may be greater
in the general population than previously estimated. Recent studies have
failed to sustain the high rates previously reported and raise the distinct
possibility that earlier studies may be in error. He concludes, "No consistent personality or behavioral correlation has been successfully predicted from the XYY complement." (p. 209)

These remarks suggest that the high incidence of the XYY karyotype in
criminal populations may reflect an indirect relationship between the
extra Y chromosome and behavior. If we assume that continuing research

firmly establishes a higher frequency of YY males in institutionalized samples, we must still ask why it occurs. Does it reflect a direct contribution of the Y chromosome to behavior (via androgens or through some subtle neural change)? Not necessarily, since it could arise as an indirect consequence of the social-learning history of a male who, excessively tall and mentally dull, provokes fear and is readily labeled delinquent. If this hypothesis is true, the relationship between the extra Y chromosome and aggressiveness would represent the outcome of a history of selective learning. The genetic effect would be no less real, but it would be largely indirect.

To summarize, the correlational evidence relating the 47,XYY karyotype to aggressiveness should be evaluated in terms of the two principles of behavior-genetic development discussed in Chapter 2. The relationship may be a direct one, such that the XYY male is unusually predisposed to aggressive acts; alternatively, an indirect relationship mediated by selective exposure to certain learning experiences may adequately account for the data. Only further research will resolve the uncertainty.

Twin Studies and Longitudinal Evidence

Longitudinal stability of aggressiveness.   In Chapter 3 we examined the longitudinal stability of passive dependent behaviors from childhood to young adulthood. These traits proved to be highly stable in women but not in men. The apparent explanation for that result (Kagan and Moss, 1962) lies in social learning. The hypothesis is that behavior traits will be stable over long time periods only if congruent with cultural expectation. Behaviors incongruent with culturally defined roles (e.g., dependency in men or aggressiveness in women) will not be socially reinforced, and they will therefore exhibit poor stability over time. For those reasons we expect aggressiveness to exhibit a pattern opposite to that of passive dependency—stability only in males.

The relevant data, derived from the longitudinal study described in Chapter 3, are presented as Table 7.1. Correlations between several dimensions of aggression observed from birth to age 14 and the intensity of aggression elicited in adult interviews are consistently higher in males.

Twin studies.   Further evidence that sex-role training affects aggressiveness can be found in twin studies (Gottesman, 1963). Identical male twins closely resemble each other on dimensions of dominance and aggression, and differences between male fraternal and identical twins are large. Presumably, genes predisposing male aggressiveness are socially reinforced so that gene differences are exaggerated through experience. Differences

Table 7.1   Stability of aggressiveness from infancy to adulthood.

Childhood variable	Age	Correlations Males	Females
Aggression toward mother	0–3	−.02	.19
	3–6	.39	.10
	6–10	.37	.23
	10–14	.77	.24
Behavioral disorganization	0–3	.35	.04
(loss of control when frustrated)	3–6	.30	−.06
	6–10	.42	.12
	10–14	.52	.08

Correlations of rated aggressiveness based on childhood observations
with ratings of anger arousal obtained from adult interviews. The pattern of correlations reveals higher stability for aggressiveness in males,
presumably as a product of differential reinforcement in the culture.
(Adapted from H. Moss and J. Kagan, "Report on personality consistency and change from the Fels longitudinal study," *Vita Humana*, 1964,
7, p. 130. Used by permission of S. Karger, Basel/New York.)

in aggressiveness are much smaller between female identical and fraternal twins; since aggressiveness has been culturally punished in women,
gene differences are presumably masked.

EARLY EXPERIENCE

Fundamental to the biological viewpoint is the assertion that all behavior
develops through genetic-environmental interaction. The expression of
genetic effects in behavior can be dramatically modified by experience.

An adequate understanding of aggression requires an appreciation of
the concept of interaction. The longitudinal research and twin studies
cited above suggest that aggressive predispositions can be potentiated or
suppressed by environmental training. We shall next review selected research on early postnatal experience to elaborate that suggestion.

Hormonal Effects

In many species of animals there are large sex differences in aggressiveness. Unless protecting their young, females will usually not fight despite
severe provocation. In contrast, males in most species fight readily even in

the absence of external provocation. Further, males given injections of testosterone in infancy exhibit an increase in adult fighting, but males castrated before puberty rarely fight. Such observations, well established for many species, suggest that hormonal processes underlie the observed difference in fighting, and it has often been hypothesized that male hormones act on the neonate to organize the neural structures that subserve aggressiveness.

Direct evidence on that hypothesis has recently been reported by Edwards (1968), who virilized day-old female mice and studied their adult aggressiveness. Three groups of mice were tested: (1) males treated with peanut oil at birth, (2) females treated with oil at birth, and (3) females treated with testosterone at birth—the experimental group. At 60 days of age, all three groups received injections of small amounts of oil daily and were tested for fighting. None fought. Throughout the subsequent five weeks, all animals received daily injections of testosterone in increasing dosages; each week they were also tested for fighting in paired competition.

All pairs of males fought, and more than 90% of the virilized females exhibited fighting during one or more tests. In contrast, only one pair of female controls—those who had received oil at birth—ever fought. Figure 7.2 summarizes the results. Female mice who were administered male hormone in the first 24 hours following birth resembled normal male mice in the tendency to fight. Female controls failed to fight even under massive doses of testosterone.

The Edwards experiment reveals the dramatic effect of neonatal testosterone on adult fighting. The results imply that the usual difference observed between normal male and female mice is due to the stimulation the male receives from testicular hormones early in life.

A more recent study indicates that the effect of administering androgen to female mice interacts with genotype (Vale, Ray, and Vale, 1972). It was found that androgen increased the fighting behavior of females from strains in which the males are aggressive. However, little change was found in the aggressive behavior of female mice from strains in which the male is passive.

Effects of Social Rearing

Mice and rats reared in groups, whether in the laboratory or in natural colonies, fight less than do animals brought together after early social isolation. Group-reared animals will fight strangers, however, and their early social experiences affect the intensity of their fighting. Social rearing conditions can profoundly modify aggressive dispositions, and because

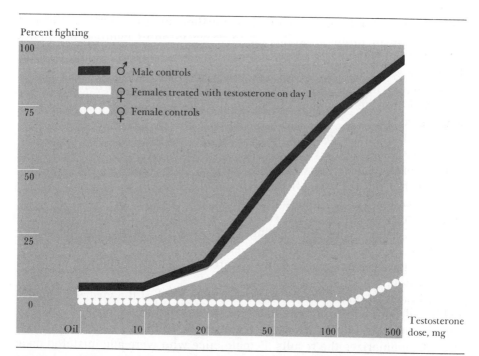

Percent fighting

Fig. 7.2. Effects of neonatal testosterone on adult fighting in mice. The figure plots the percentages of pairs in each group who fought at increasing dosages of testosterone. (From D. A. Edwards, "Mice: fighting by neonatally androgenized females," *Science*, 1968, **161**, 1028. Copyright 1968 by the American Association for the Advancement of Science. Used by permission.)

these facts may have important implications for human aggressiveness, we conclude this chapter with a review of relevant animal research.

The critical finding which emerges from these animal experiments is that behaviors widely considered to be "in the nature of an animal" can be eliminated, fostered, or reversed if an appropriate environment is provided during early development. Fighting between and within species cannot be considered a genetically fixed, species-specific behavior. It is dramatically altered by early social experience.

The earliest demonstrations of these effects were made by Kuo:

> . . . We had no difficulty in making kittens play, eat, and sleep together with puppies. . . . Similarly, a friendly, even "affectionate," relationship was established between dogs and birds.

The experimental procedures of these studies are quite similar and simple. A single, newly hatched Asian song thrush, usually considered a predatory bird, was reared in the same cage with one or a number of smaller birds. . . . At night, this new hatchling was placed as closely as possible with the smaller birds, which roosted together. In the study of dogs, a newborn puppy was raised and hand-fed in the same room with a number of friendly birds of different species. . . .

The Asian song thrush and the masked jay thrush have both been long known in China as predatory birds. . . . When hungry, they . . . kill and eat . . . smaller birds. . . . However, when they were reared according to the procedures described above . . . [they] became very friendly with the smaller birds. They ate together, sat together, groomed each other, the large birds letting the smaller ones snatch meat, insects, etc., from their beaks. And, on cold nights, they would spread out their wings and let the little birds roost under them.*

Similar effects have been obtained in rodents. Adult rats frequently attack and kill mice housed with them. Because the killing occurs in the absence of prior exposure to mice and requires no previous fighting experience, it is often regarded as instinctive. Yet the killing response can be eliminated by early interaction between the two species (Denenberg, Paschke, and Zarrow, 1968). Experimental rats were housed with small groups of mice from the time they were weaned until they were 57 days old. At 90 days of age, each rat was individually housed with a single mouse for 24 hours. The rats' behavior was compared with that of control rats, who were normally reared without any interaction with mice prior to testing. While 45% of the control rats killed one or more mice, no experimental rat killed a mouse. Further, the change in aggressiveness generalized: experimental rats had early social interaction only with mice from a black strain; yet even when they were tested with white mice, no killing resulted.

Interaction between mice and rats reduces the aggressiveness of both. Mice reared with rats from birth exhibit social preference for rats and show little or no aggression toward their own species in adult tests.

The methodology of the studies cited is of particular interest. Both test and control animals were from an inbred strain. Genetic variation was thus eliminated, and all mice shared a similar prenatal environment. The experimental variable was postnatal experience. Test animals were cross-fostered to a lactating rat mother on the first day of life. The female rat, who had been rearing her own young for several days, readily accepted the mouse baby, nursing it as if it were her own pup. Such a methodology permits a rather unique separation of genetic and prenatal factors from effects arising in early social experience.

---

* From Z. Y. Kuo, *The Dynamics of Behavior Development,* Random House, New York, 1967, pp. 65–66. Reprinted by permission.

Four experiments using that method have measured adult fighting in control and experimental mice. Combining the experiments (Denenberg, Hudgens, and Zarrow, 1964; Hudgens, Denenberg, and Zarrow, 1968; Denenberg and Zarrow, 1970) yields this comparison: 29 of 63 pairs of control mice (reared by mouse mothers with normal littermates) fought at least once in the test situation; in contrast, only 5 of 115 pairs of experimental mice (cross-fostered to rat mothers) fought with each other. The difference, 46% versus about 4%, indicates the dramatic effect of early social learning on adult fighting. Fighting between adult mice is a species-specific behavior with an adaptive function and a genetic basis. Yet the incidence of fighting ranges from 0% to 78% as a function of social rearing (Hudgens et al., 1968).

In further studies, the experimental mice were exposed to rat peers before or after weaning. A general finding is that for mice reared by rat foster mothers, peer-group relationships have no effect on aggressiveness. These mice tend not to fight, whether they have been reared in isolation or with peers before weaning. Thus it is the rat mother who is critical in reducing fighting. Finally, other evidence indicates that physiological changes are produced by the foster-mother experience. The adrenocortical response to novel stimulation is significantly modified in the experimental mice reared by foster rat mothers.

The findings noted led to a final series of experiments designed to isolate the effect of the rat mother on the mouse's behavior. The rat mother could be influencing her foster mice offspring through either her maternal behavior or biochemical factors present in her milk supply. To resolve the uncertainty, the investigators placed a mouse mother and a rat "aunt" together. Nonlactating adult female rats, termed "aunts," were placed with pregnant mice; the expectation was that the rat "aunt" would take over many of the maternal caretaking tasks while the mouse nursed the young. Pilot studies indicated that the procedure did work; the adults behaved maternally toward the pups, and the mouse mother maintained sufficient contact with them to provide adequate nursing.

Two experiments in which this technique was used have been reported. The first (Denenberg et al., 1969) revealed that mice reared in the presence of a rat "aunt" had a decreased hormonal response to stress. The "aunt"-tended group had a lowered adrenocortical response to novelty. The effect of the rat "aunt" was as powerful as that produced by a rat foster mother; hence the physiological change must have been due to behavioral interactions between female rats and mice offspring, rather than to biochemical differences in the milk of the rat and mouse mothers.

The final, crucial question is whether a rat "aunt" will also reduce aggressiveness in mice. The relevant experiment (cited in Denenberg and

Zarrow, 1970) used three groups: (1) control mice reared by mouse foster mothers; (2) experimental mice reared by rat mothers; and (3) experimental mice reared by natural mothers in the presence of rat "aunts." When tested for adult aggressiveness, both experimental groups exhibited significantly less fighting than did controls, and they did not differ from each other as groups.

> This experiment clearly eliminates the rat-milk factor and establishes that the social interaction between rat-aunt and the mouse baby is sufficient to bring about fundamental changes in the aggressive behavior and the activity pattern of the species.*

Aggression and Ethology Reconsidered

This chapter has been centrally concerned with the origin of aggressive behavior. We have reviewed relevant facts from ethology, behavior genetics, and studies of early experience. What can we conclude? Consider this statement:

> We generally describe the most repulsive examples of man's cruelty as brutal or bestial, implying by these adjectives that such behavior is characteristic of less highly developed animals than ourselves. In truth, however, the extremes of "brutal" behaviours are confined to man; and there is no parallel in nature to our savage treatment of each other. The somber fact is that we are the cruellest and most ruthless species that has ever walked the earth. . . .†

A recent essay on human aggression begins with a phrase coined by the philosopher Thomas Hobbes: *Homo homini lupus*—"Man is (like) a wolf (to his) fellow man" (Kaufmann, 1970). Hobbes was suggesting what Storr has concluded: humans possess—or are possessed by—a savage cruelty to their fellows.

It can hardly be argued that our aggressiveness constitutes our greatest behavioral problem. Humans are the only animals who engage in systematic mass murder, and we are the only species in which aggression threatens survival. The issue, however, is not whether we are aggressive but why.

Is aggression an inevitable component of life? Is it an instinctive force which, analogous to hunger or sex, possesses internal energy and must

---

* From V. H. Denenberg and M. X. Zarrow, "Rat pax." Reprinted from *Psychology Today* Magazine, May 1970, p. 67. Copyright © 1970, Ziff-Davis Publishing Company. All rights reserved.

† From *Human Aggression* by Anthony Storr, p. ix. Copyright © 1968 by Anthony Storr. Reprinted by permission of Atheneum Publishers.

find periodic release? This conception of aggression (Lorenz, 1966) assumes an energy model; aggressive acts are taken as evidence of an internal drive process and cathartic relief is assumed to follow the discharge of surplus aggressive energy. We find no compelling evidence that such a drive process exists (Ziegler, 1964; Scott, 1966; Berkowitz, 1969; Kaufmann, 1970). There are internal mechanisms which, properly stimulated, reliably lead to fighting. But the stimulation is external; it is neither instinctive nor spontaneous. And as the animal studies reveal, social rearing can eliminate fighting behaviors that appear to be instinctive. In short, though a trigger for aggression does exist, it need not be pulled.

Furthermore, that animals find fighting rewarding and that fighting can reinforce operant behavior do not demonstrate the existence of a spontaneous trigger. To assume so would be to assume that "most people find the odor of roses pleasant (because) there is spontaneous internal stimulation to go out and smell the flowers" (Scott, 1966, p. 696).

Bearing further on this question is the recent discovery, in the Phillipines, of a small tribe in which aggression appears to be singularly absent (MacLeish, 1972). The Tasadays are a friendly, gentle people who possess no weapons and feed on vegetables gathered from the land. Evidence of this sort is cited by Ashley Montagu to counter the view of Lorenz that man is basically an aggressive animal (Montagu, 1974).

Aggression is not an instinctive drive controlled by a spontaneous internal trigger. It is socially learned behavior. Aggression always occurs in a social context, and the context determines the initiation, form, and intensity of the aggressive act. The energy model of aggression is erroneous. And televising violence every Saturday morning to provide cathartic release of children's aggression is a particularly pernicious form of that erroneous conception (Wertham, 1966). Such modeling can only facilitate aggressive behavior in a child.

Aggressive behaviors are universal to the species; they can and have served adaptive functions, and they are subserved by internal biological processes which, once triggered, are slow to subside. But the trigger exists in the external social environment. It need not be pulled. Aggressiveness is neither instinctive nor fixed, and we can be optimistic that it will yield to social control.

> ... We may definitely conclude that species-specific behavior patterns as well as fundamental physiological processes, both of which have a strong underlying genetic basis, can be modified dramatically by appropriate social experiences in early life. How genes express themselves is a function of the environment in which the organism grows and develops. The fact that an organism has genes that may ultimately contribute to aggressive behavior does not mean that those genes will necessarily have to express themselves

in that manner. We feel that appropriate rearing conditions can have a marked effect in modifying presumably inborn aggressive tendencies, and that they may even keep the tendencies from being expressed. (Denenberg and Zarrow, 1970, p. 67)

SUMMARY

This chapter has viewed aggressiveness from the biological perspective. Much of the material has been addressed to the determinants of aggression and to a consideration of its function and social control. A major theme, as always, is that of interaction: aggression rests on biological mechanisms, but it is molded through social experience.

From the biological perspective, aggressiveness serves valuable functions. Aggressive dominance has played a critical role in the origin and preservation of the human species. Early humans must have initially existed in small groups, and the formation and maintenance of such groups required stable dominance hierarchies. With increasing socialization and evolving competence, aggression became increasingly dangerous, and aggressive acts have now become conventionalized in humans and other animals. Aggression is contained through a stable dominance hierarchy maintained by ritualized displays of threat. This pattern ensures that the population of a given area will maximally adapt to the area's resources. Evidence of dominance hierarchies among humans, their formation and function, was cited from fiction—in the novel *Lord of the Flies* —and from fact—in the filming of the novel.

In lower animals, aggressive dominance directly relates to breeding advantage, so that behavior differences in aggressiveness directly modify the gene pool. Behavior-genetic analysis reveals the role of gene differences in producing behavior variation in aggressive competition. Selective breeding studies with rodents demonstrate a rapid response to selection for aggressiveness, and animals bred for aggressiveness are less emotional and more active. Twin studies and longitudinal research reveal evidence of genetic factors in human aggressiveness, but these studies also indicate that social and cultural rearing can mask such genetic effects.

Further evidence of interaction of genetic mechanisms with social learning appears in the analysis of humans with an extra Y chromosome. Early studies suggested an elevated incidence of chromosome errors in institutional populations. In particular, there was suggestive evidence that males who carry an extra Y chromosome (karyotype 47,XYY) are over-represented in delinquent and criminal populations. More recent studies, however, suggest that the incidence of the extra Y chromosome may not be as great in institutional settings as previously reported. Moreover, the incidence of XYY males in the general population appears to be greater than previously believed.

The chapter concluded with a review of effects of early postnatal experience on aggressive behavior. Animal studies indicate that administration of male hormones during critical periods of early life profoundly increases adult aggressiveness. Such evidence suggests that differences in aggressiveness commonly observed between male and female animals are, in part, due to differences in neural organization produced by early hormonal stimulation.

The effects of social rearing on aggressive dispositions were shown through studies which indicate that aggression is significantly modified by early social experience. Although fighting between adult mice is a species-specific behavior with an adaptive function and a genetic basis, its incidence depends on conditions of early social rearing. Similarly, adult rats frequently attack and kill mice housed with them, but the killing response can be eliminated if rats are given early social experience with mice. Such experiments led us to conclude that aggression is better construed as a socially acquired behavior than as an instinctive drive controlled by an internal trigger. Aggression is neither instinctive nor spontaneous, and we can be optimistic that it will yield to social control.

SUGGESTIONS FOR FURTHER READING

Carthy, J. D., and F. J. Ebling (eds.). *The Natural History of Aggression.* New York: Academic Press, 1965. A set of essays that offer an evolutionary perspective on human aggression.

Johnson, R. N. *Aggression in Man and Animals.* Philadelphia: W. B. Saunders, 1972. A synthesis of theory and research on aggressive behavior in many species. An excellent integration of diverse views.

Lorenz, K. *On Aggression.* New York: Harcourt, 1966. The major work by Europe's distinguished ethologist and Nobel laureate. A starting point for serious study of the determinants of human violence.

Montagu, M. F. A. (ed.). *Man and Aggression.* 2nd ed. New York: Oxford University Press, 1973. A collection of readable essays that offer a useful critique of Lorenz's conception of human aggression.

Whalen, R. E. (ed.). *The Neuropsychology of Aggression.* (*Advances in Behavioral Biology,* Vol. 12). New York: Plenum Press, 1974. A recent series of papers reviewing conceptual and methodological problems and present data on the biology of aggression.

8
Aggression: The Experimental Viewpoint

8
Aggression: The Experimental Viewpoint

I. **Learning processes**
   A. Classical conditioning
      1. An animal illustration
      2. Extension to human behavior
   B. Instrumental conditioning
      1. An animal illustration
      2. Extensions to human behavior
   C. The value of aggression
      1. An animal illustration
      2. Extension to human subjects

II. **Perceptual processes: binocular rivalry**

III. **Cognitive processes**

IV. **Summary**

V. **Suggestions for further reading**

Aggression will now be viewed through the constructs of experimental psychology: learning processes, perceptual processes, and cognitive processes. These processes are the uniform ways in which the content of personality is acquired and manifests itself in behavior.

LEARNING PROCESSES

Classical Conditioning

An animal illustration.   A male Siamese Fighting Fish will present an aggressive display when confronted by another male. The display will become an attack if the other fish does not flee. Both display and attack serve the purposes of protecting territory and spreading the species over the feeding area. The ethology of such behaviors has been discussed in the biological materials already presented.

The aggressive display can in fact be evoked in a Siamese Fighting Fish by its own image in a mirror. The instinctive and reflexive occurrence of such a display in response to a self-image lends itself readily to the application of classical-conditioning procedures in a laboratory situation. Two investigators (Thompson and Sturm, 1965) demonstrated that the aggressive display could be elicited by a conditioned stimulus. Recall that the stimulus to be conditioned precedes an unconditioned stimulus, which uniformly elicits a particular response. In the Thompson and Sturm experiment, a mirror image was the unconditioned stimulus that produced an aggressive display in the Siamese Fighting Fish.

A fish tank was constructed in such a way that it could be illuminated by either a red or a green light located at one end of the tank. The lights were to serve as the conditioned stimulus. The investigators placed a one-way mirror along one side of the fish tank. Plain white lights were located behind the one-way mirror and on the opposite side of the tank. The fourth side was open for viewing the fish and recording its behavior. When the light behind the one-way mirror was turned off and that on the opposite side of the tank turned on, the mirror became highly reflective and the fish could see its own image. Reversing the illumination terminated the mirror effect.

All the necessary components were thus available for the procedure known as differential classical conditioning. At intervals of time, which varied between 30 and 240 seconds, either the red or the green stimulus light was turned on. Ten seconds after the green light (the conditioned stimulus) was presented, the illumination of the mirror was adjusted so that the fish could see its image (the unconditioned stimulus) for 15 seconds. The red light (the differential stimulus) was never followed by the image. Observers recorded the occurrence of the aggressive display during the 10-second interval that followed each presentation of the red or the green light. The demonstration of a classically conditioned response would require that the aggressive display occur after the green light was presented, but before the fish saw its mirror image 10 seconds later. However, such a display should not occur after the red light, which was never followed by an image. Those circumstances were obtained; the Siamese Fighting Fish reliably presented the aggressive display to the green light but not to the red light.

Extension to human behavior.   Is it warranted to make the generalization that the fish felt angry at the sight of a green light? If we were to take the view that the fish's aggressive display is akin to human emotion and arousal, then we would conclude that in the presence of green the fish became angry. Let us consider how such a viewpoint is consistent with human experience.

Most people have at some time experienced irrational emotions of one kind or another. For example, one may continually associate the landlord who collects an unreasonably high rent with the making of a payment which, by depleting one's resources, precludes the satisfaction of other strong desires and produces resentment and anger as a consequence. The resentment and anger which can then be aroused by the thought or sight of a landlord—any landlord—represents the generalized component of a conditioned emotional response. The landlord is a mild example. Perhaps the intense anger of some blacks at white police officers should not be surprising when we consider that blacks have personally suffered or witnessed differential interpersonal treatment, arrest standards, and bail levels, in comparison with whites, while being required to contain the rage such differential treatment aroused. Most of us can find some class of events which elicits irrational anger—i.e., an anger directed at an innocent bystander who represents a stimulus class that has been a source of what we regarded as unjustified frustration and provocation.

The conditioned feelings of anger toward a specific object are the potent sources of planned and directed aggressive acts. Aggressive behaviors cannot be adequately dealt with directly so long as the conditioned aggressive feelings elicited by some stimulus class remain unchanged. The remedy to destructive and violent behaviors that are the instrumental expressions of conditioned anger will not come from having more police or stricter rules of discipline. The answer lies in correcting the social experiences which continue to associate a particular class of stimuli with unjustified frustration.

Consideration of two additional aspects of aggression—learned aggressive behaviors and the satisfaction or reduction of feelings of anger—will complement what has been said so far about the relationship between the processes of classical conditioning and feelings of anger. The "instrumental" and the "satisfaction" aspects of aggression will be considered separately in the next two sections. One should bear in mind that the distinction among feelings, behaviors, and values is arbitrary with respect to human aggression, because all these processes contribute to the complex notion of aggression as one normally thinks of it.

Instrumental Conditioning

An animal illustration.   As we have seen before, the frequency of occurrence of a particular behavior can be modified by the outcomes contingent on the behavior. In an experiment with pigeons (Azrin and Hutchinson, 1967), a food reward was given for attacks against another pigeon. The proportion of time spent attacking was directly related to the giving and withholding of the rewards. When the food was removed, the attacking behavior stopped, but when it was again given for attacking, the behavior increased in frequency. The data for this experiment are shown in Fig. 8.1.

When an animal is punished, the two most typical consequences are aggressive behaviors and the tendency to look for some means to escape. In a series of studies on the reinforcement of aggression in pigeons (e.g. Azrin, Hutchinson, and Hake, 1967), it was found that the subjects rapidly learned a biting-attack response if it led to escape from or avoidance of an electric shock.

In an avoidance paradigm, it will be recalled, a signal warns that an aversive situation is to follow. An avoidance response on the part of the subject terminates the signal and permits avoidance of the aversive event. Since attacking is a natural response to pain in many organisms, that behavior is rapidly acquired when the subject learns that it terminates a warning signal and prevents aversive stimulation.

Extensions to human behavior.   Bandura and Walters (1963) have written about rewarding aggressive behaviors as follows:

> Let us now consider a father who devotes some of his time to playing punchball with his young son. He punches the ball himself and then, with or without verbal encouragement, elicits a similar response in the boy. He responds to the boy's punching with approval. The boy punches harder and is again positively reinforced. Indeed, a competition in prowess is likely to develop. In the course of the play, the father provides the model for the hitting response and reinforces the response when it is made. In fact, the

Percentage of time
spent attacking

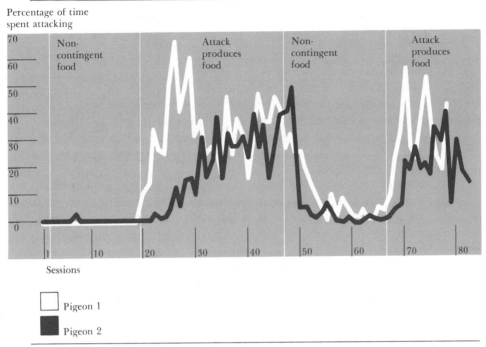

Sessions

Pigeon 1

Pigeon 2

Fig. 8.1. The percentage of time spent attacking a target pigeon by each of two pigeons. Under the "noncontingent food" condition, the pigeon received food every 30 seconds, independently of its behavior. Under the "attack produces food" condition, food was delivered for the first response of attacking the target pigeon after a 30-second interval had elapsed. Thus food would not be received unless an attack was made. When the food was given only for attacking, there was a steady increase in the frequency of such responses. When food was given on a regular basis, independently of the subject's behavior, attack responses were reduced. (From N. H. Azrin and R. R. Hutchinson, "Conditioning of the aggressive behavior of pigeons by a fixed-interval schedule of reinforcement," *Journal of the Experimental Analysis of Behavior,* 1967, **10,** 397. Copyright 1967 by the Society for the Experimental Analysis of Behavior, Inc. Used by permission.)

father is likely to provide differential reinforcement for intensity responses, since weak hitting responses are frequently interpreted as a sign of lack of virility. Once the intense hitting response has been established, it can be elicited in various situations, some frustrative and some nonfrustrative.

In the course of development, then, a child is provided with many opportunities to acquire responses of high magnitude in nonfrustrative situations; these responses may remain relatively high in his response hierarchies and can thus be readily mobilized to cope with the various situations that have been classed as frustrating. While the fact that these responses are not elicited more frequently may be in part due to expectations of punishment, it is probably due just as much, if not more, to good discrimination learning, which results from differential reinforcement.*

To study experimentally the reinforcement of aggressive behaviors, Bandura and Walters constructed a Bobo clown doll that could be punched. Automatic equipment recorded the frequency and intensity of hitting responses; a marble dispenser provided rewards for the punching responses. The intensity and the persistence of hitting behavior followed the standard pattern produced by rewards for increasing the strength and persistence of other behavior.

The positive reinforcement which may accrue through the avoidance of an aversive stimulus by aggressive behavior is even more striking. If a child who is taunted by another child makes an attacking response which terminates the aversive stimulation provided by the antagonist, then the attacking behavior has been rewarded through the withdrawal of punishment. In the typical avoidance paradigm, a distinctive cue—called a CS—is presented before the aversive stimulation occurs. In social situations, the CS would be one or more of those social cues which serve as forewarnings that aversive stimulation (for example, taunting) may occur. The individual who can successfully attack provoking sources and thus escape—or better yet, avoid—the aversiveness of the provocation thereby receives a reward for instrumental acts of aggressive behavior.

Individuals who are typically described as "aggressive" emit verbal and physical attacks to cues and to situations which do not evoke aggressive responses in most people. Many such aggressive acts may simply be avoidance behaviors that have been reinforced and therefore maintained because they remove, block, or otherwise drive away a source of anticipated aversive stimulation.

By generalizing from animal research, we would expect a human aggressive behavior initially established as a means of avoiding aversive stimulation to be exceptionally resistant to extinction or change, because that individual habitually makes a forceful response to cues associated with an unpleasant situation. To the extent that the aggressive response successfully removes a perceived source of frustration, the behavior is rewarded for that individual and is likely to be retained.

However, if a person responds to most social cues with aggressive displays that drive away social contacts, certain experiences—e.g., emotional warmth expressed by others—that might be effective in changing behavior will simply not occur. Aggressive persons may be lonely, but the lack of

---

* From A. Bandura and R. H. Walters, *Social Learning and Personality Development,* Holt, Rinehart and Winston, 1963, p. 117. Reprinted by permission.

the emotional warmth they desire cannot be a punishment for their aggressive behavior unless they first engage in nonaggressive behavior and learn the contingencies. A wide range of response variation ensures a wide sampling of possible outcomes and contingency relationships and, above all, permits adjustment to change, awareness of new contingencies, and a restriction of overgeneralization. Consequently, protective aggressive responses restrict the social adaptability of an organism although protecting a narrowly defined psychological territory.

Children who are positively rewarded—as in the case of punching the Bobo doll—will have certain kinds of behavior high in their response repertoire. If they emit such behaviors in many situations, there is an increased likelihood that they will emit them in situations where aversive stimulation is present. If the behaviors are successful in eliminating the sources of aversive stimulation, then two kinds of positive reinforcement —one based on direct reward and one on the avoidance of a negative event—can combine to facilitate the occurrence of aggressive behaviors.

An additional point to consider is the effect of differential reinforcement in shaping and directing behaviors. The child who punches the Bobo doll and receives praise from his father has that act strengthened. Once well-aimed punches are in the repertoire of the organism, they are available for use on other occasions. The stage is now set for discrimination training based on differential reinforcement. The child who has learned to aim a well-directed punch at the Bobo doll may aim a similar punch at the neighborhood child who is teasing him. The act may reduce aversive consequences provided by the other child, and perhaps elicit further praise from the father. However, if he directs the blow at the father's nose, a swift retaliatory response will probably serve primarily to inhibit such behaviors toward the father. Thus an act made available to the organism but differentially rewarded may become narrowed in its use. Through differential rewards and punishment, the child learns the targets at which it may be aimed (e.g., the neighborhood kid) and those at which it may not (e.g., the father's nose).

The Value of Aggression

An animal illustration.   A final experiment by Azrin (Azrin, Hutchinson, and McLaughlin, 1965) illustrates how aggressive behaviors will have differential utility or value under different circumstances. When a monkey is hurt, it has a strong natural disposition to attack any living or inanimate object which is accessible. Azrin provided his monkeys with a chain which could be pulled to produce such an object. When painful electric shocks were delivered, there was a high frequency of chain-pulling responses and attacks on the object. The opportunity to attack following a painful situation was a reinforcing event. The chain-pulling response seldom occurred in the absence of a painful electric shock; in the absence of pain, attacking is neither valued nor exhibited.

Extension to human subjects.   After a painful, frustrating, or humiliating experience, the opportunity to behave aggressively—even toward an inanimate or distant object—will be more attractive and more likely to occur than would otherwise be so. However, it is generally assumed that the threat of retaliation provides an effective barrier against the acting out of aggressive impulses. Baron (1973) conducted a study in which the level of anger and the threat of retaliation were carefully varied. Subjects were exposed to conditions that aroused little or no anger or relatively high levels of anger. They were subsequently afforded the opportunity to aggress against the instigator of anger by delivering various intensities of electric shock. These subjects were, in turn, placed on one of three conditions of retaliation: low, moderate, and high probability of retaliation. It was found that in the non-angry condition, the threat of retaliation was an effective barrier to aggressive responses (i.e. turning the shock levels high). However, when anger was high, the threat of retaliation had little or no effect upon the levels of shock chosen by the subjects. According to Baron, ". . . this finding appears to suggest that threatened punishment may be much less effective as a technique for the prevention or control of common aggression than has previously been suggested, serving to substantially inhibit such behavior only where aggressors offer no provocation, or very mild levels of this factor." (1973, p. 112)

PERCEPTUAL PROCESSES
binocular rivalry

The meticulously dressed individual notices and removes a small speck of dandruff from a shoulder. Another individual notices that of two boxes of equal size and price, one contains 575 toothpicks and the other 600. A speck of dandruff and a small printed number giving the numerical count of toothpicks are not equally distinctive stimuli for different individuals. The differential distinctiveness of a particular stimulus reflects the fact that perception is necessarily selective. We cannot notice everything; we see some things but not others. Our perceptual processes are selectively tuned much more by psychological factors than by the physical distinctiveness (frequency, brightness, size, etc.) of a stimulus. Since selective attention can alter what individuals notice and thereby what they do, the study of perceptual processes is one way to understand people better. The selective aspect of perception is illustrated by work on binocular rivalry.

The research on binocular rivalry uses an instrument known as a stereoscope, which presents separate pictures to each eye of the subject. When two photographs of the same object taken at slightly different angles are viewed through the stereoscope, the subject obtains a three-dimensional effect. Since the duration of exposure can also be controlled, one may determine the threshold of vision, i.e., the minimum amount of time needed to see a picture, by making the exposure to the stimuli very short. In a binocular-rivalry situation, two completely different pictures are presented, one to each eye. The duration of exposure is so short that the subject does not have time to see both pictures or to realize that each eye is receiving a different one. Since only one of the pictures can be assimilated, there is rivalry between the two to determine which one will be seen.

In a study by Toch and Schulte (1961) a picture of violence was presented to one eye and a neutral picture to the other. The subjects were students who had completed or were currently entering a three-year police-administration training program. More subjects finished with the training program course than those just beginning it reported seeing the violent pictures. The experience of the training procedure had selectively increased the subjects' attention or the likelihood that they would see violence.

Studies on binocular rivalry show that the past experiences of an individual will influence, through perceptual processes, what he or she sees. For example, a familiar figure will predominate over a less familiar figure. In one study, Bagby (1959) showed subjects paired photographs of Mexican and American scenes. Mexican subjects tended to see the Mexican scenes, whereas Americans reported seeing the American scenes more often.

In reviewing these and other studies on binocular rivalry, Moore (1966) concluded that specific past experiences, such as training, sensitize a person to the perception of related content. As suggested by the police example cited above, an elevated perception of violence may result from training which exposes one to violent material. In some populations, such as criminals and institutionalized offenders, the elevated perception of violence is correlated with the tendency to behave aggressively. Moore noted that in Western culture the expression of aggressive behavior is related to sex. Males learn to be more active, overtly aggressive, and socially assertive than females. In addition, the learning of aggression is a continual process so that sensitization to the cues of aggression should increase with age.

To test that hypothesis, Moore used photographs like those shown in Box 8.1 in a binocular-rivalry situation. He used male and female subjects

---

Box 8.1   Binocular rivalry.

In the binocular rivalry study by Moore (1966) stereograms were used in which the picture projected to one eye was nonviolent and the picture projected to the other eye showed violence. One of the pairs used by Moore is shown below. The verbatim responses of the subjects were scored in accordance with the standards given beside the stereograms.*

Stereogram pair used in the
experiment by Moore (1966)

Points Description

2   Clearly the violent stereogram is described by the subject, for example, "A man with a knife in his back."

1   Fusion is described with a sensible percept including violent content (a compromise response), for example, "A mailman with a knife in his back."

1   Clearly the violent stereogram is described, but not in violent terms (a compromise response), for example, "A man with arms out in front and a stick out in the back."

0   Clearly the nonviolent stereogram is described by the subject, for example, "A mailman with pouch and letter in his hand."

0   Fusion is described with a sensible or incomprehensible percept, but *not* including violent content, for example, "A man running with his arms going in all directions."

Six different stereograms were used, each shown twice; thus a subject could theoretically receive a score from 0 to 24. The actual scores ranged from 0 to 11. Two judges, scoring all the responses independently, achieved nearly perfect agreement, as shown by a correlation between their ratings of .98. The perception of violence was greater for males than for females, and it increased with age for both sexes.

---

* From M. Moore, "Aggression themes in a binocular rivalry situation," *Journal of Personality and Social Psychology*, 1966, **3**, 685–688. Copyright 1966 by the American Psychological Association. Reprinted by permission.

ranging from third grade pupils through college freshmen. His expectations were confirmed in that males saw significantly more violence than did females, and the tendency increased with age for both males and females. In discussing the work on binocular rivalry, Moore writes:

> From the point of view presented in this paper socialization is similar to the process underlying the fact that advanced police-administration students reported seeing more violent stereograms than novices in the same training program (Toch and Schulte, 1961)—a process of education into the policeman's reality. As children mature they are educated into a reality that is a slow motion facsimile of the police training situation—a reality where they become increasingly familiar with the abundance of aggression loose in the world. Finally then, the sex and developmental differences found in this study represent learned variant sensitivities of males and females to aggressive situations and feelings which they must know about to operate effectively within a social and cultural context. (p. 688)

Binocular-rivalry situations can be used to learn about the way past experiences influence perceptual sensitivities and selective attention to the world. The perceptual processes, which provide the information about the environment, are built from one's past experiences.

COGNITIVE PROCESSES

Traditional views of aggression, including those of Freud and some of the leading contemporary ethologists, take the position that aggression is a relatively automatic response to frustration and threat. In the recent past, many psychologists have been especially interested in the motive force behind aggressive action. Where does it come from and what happens to it after an aggressive act?

In recent years, however, much of psychology has shifted its interest toward the role of cognitions in all behaviors, including aggression. Thus, with respect to aggression, the role of a person's interpretation of another's action is important in determining whether or not aggression occurs. Aggression is far more likely to occur if the action of another is perceived as a deliberate and malicious attempt to inflict pain.

The same set of potentially frustrating circumstances can be experienced differently by two different people or by the same person at different times. What makes the difference is largely how the person thinks about the circumstances. In this regard, Feshback (1964) writes:

> A student may be annoyed and disappointed at receiving a failing grade. But if he should discover that the instructor is pleased by his failure, he is likely to become furious. A week's solitary confinement in a narrow

cell with room barely wide enough to sit is a tremendously frustrating and painful experience. Prisoners become angry and bitter when subjected to this experience as a punishment. But the same experience when endured in connection with voluntary participation in a research project designed to assess the psychophysiological effects of confinement in a space capsule will elicit far less hostility.

The fact that people can display aggressive feelings and behavior toward someone long after a frustrating event has sometimes been taken to indicate that the aggressive energy resided within the person from the time of the original event until expressed. Theorists were concerned with questions about the dynamics of aggressive energy: What happens when it is not expressed and what substitute outlets are there for such energy? The traditional catharsis view, expressed by Freud, maintains that engaging in aggressive behavior uses up or spends aggressive energy, and conversely, that energy once generated must be expressed at some point either directly or indirectly. Thus psychoanalysts interpret various psychological symptoms, fantasies, slips of the tongue, obsessional thoughts, and so forth, as indirect expressions of aggressive energy.

There is another possibility, however. It appears likely that aggressive motivation does not persist until expressed. Indeed that expression of it may often do more to maintain it than simply ignoring the aggression-inducing situation. Physiological studies show that all angered subjects, regardless of whether or not they vent their hostility, display rapid declines in arousal. Why then do people get angry long after the original insult? According to Bandura (1973), they do so because they engage in self-arousal by reinstating the original event through fantasy or through rumination. If the person becomes distracted by something else, anger dissipates rapidly, but it can be revived later by conjuring up the anger-provoking incident. A person who expected an invitation to a social function but did not receive the invitation is angered by the social slight. Other events distract the mind from anger, but it is reinstated whenever the insult comes to mind. Plans for retaliation interrupt the night's sleep. The next morning's mail brings the invitation. Anger arousal drops immediately and no need is felt to express aggression against someone in order to dissipate a lingering aggressive drive. Why did the anger arousal go away? The individual in question no longer had a reason for thinking about the thing that had caused anger.

Anecdotal evidence, however, does suggest that people feel relief after viewing violence on television or in the movies. Bandura suggests that the relief comes not from a cathartic drainage of aggressive impulses, but because the absorbing activities provide distractions from self-generated ruminations. He proposes that relief could as readily be obtained by reading an absorbing book or attending an interesting talk.

SUMMARY

Many emotional reactions, including the emotions of anger, can be classically conditioned, in both animals and humans. "Irrational anger," described as feelings of hostility toward a person or situation that is merely passive and is not frustrating or hurting the individual, is probably best seen as a conditioned emotional response. The person or situation that elicits the feeling, though benign, may be related to a class of stimuli associated with directly evoked anger and aggression. The actions of verbally or physically hurting another are simply instrumental responses and, like other instrumental responses, follow the laws of instrumental conditioning. The responses themselves are sensitive to differential reinforcement. Thus an aggressive response may be made in one instance but not to the same insult in another, depending, for example, on how powerful the person who does the insulting is in each instance. The behavior and the feeling need not, of course, be in a one-to-one correspondence. A variety of situations and circumstances can change the value of hurting another person. The chance to hurt another will have greater value if the other is seen as having caused a person pain or loss of self-esteem. Otherwise there is little motivation to aggress.

Social learning plays a very important role in human aggressiveness. The situations which evoke anger and many of the possible responses to hurt another person are not always physical, but rather secondary, arising from learned social experiences. The learning which takes place defines the dimensions and the situational constraints on aggression. These learned social expectations, in turn, influence the way events are perceived. People whose experiences have sensitized them to aggression, such as police officers, may selectively perceive aggression more readily than will others.

SUGGESTIONS FOR FURTHER READING

Bandura, A. *Aggression: A Social Learning Analysis.* Englewood Cliffs, N.J.: Prentice-Hall, 1973. This book on aggression provides a deeper analysis of the role of cognitive processes, as well as a review of social learning principles to be discussed in the next chapter.

Singer, J. L. (ed.). *The Control of Aggression and Violence.* New York: Academic Press, 1971. This is a collection of articles by individuals who have made important contributions to research on aggression. Coverage of origins and expressions of aggression includes learning, perceptual, and cognitive processes.

9
Aggression: The Social Viewpoint

I. **Models**
   A. The imitation of aggression
      by children
   B. Justified aggression

II. **Roles: aggression and the police
    officer's role**
   A. Race
   B. Status

III. **Cultures**
   A. Culture versus instinct
      1. An aggressive tribe
      2. Pacifist tribes
   B. Aggression between cultures
      1. Aggression and cultural
         differences
      2. Social distance among East
         African tribes
      3. The enemy as dissimilar
   C. The contact hypothesis

IV. **Summary**

V. **Suggestions for further reading**

In the biological chapter it was asserted that a particular person's propensity for aggressive behavior is partially a biological given. The experimental viewpoint stressed that beyond genetic and early experience factors, individual differences in the expression of aggression are learned. With this background the social view will emphasize the intrinsically interpersonal nature of aggression, since aggressive thoughts and acts are both elicited by and expressed toward social objects. Here we shall consider the social factors in aggressiveness, maintaining that the models individuals have been exposed to, the social roles they play, and the cultural context in which they act are all indispensible determinants of aggression.

MODELS

The Imitation of Aggression by Children

The importance of models has been more clearly documented for aggression than for any of the other areas of behavior considered in this book. Of this research, an experiment conducted by Bandura, Ross, and Ross (1963a) is probably the most frequently cited. The primary object of the study was to demonstrate the transmission of novel aggressive responses from an adult to children solely by having the children *see* the adult's behavior. To accomplish this, nursery school children were seated one at a time in the corner of a room, where they played with paper and scissors. In the opposite corner an adult (a male in some conditions and a female in others) played with Tinker Toys. At some point the adult model began making a series of aggressive responses toward a large inflated doll called a Bobo doll. The model sat on the doll, punched it in the nose, threw it into the air, struck its head with a mallet, and kicked it about the room (see Fig. 9.1). These responses were accompanied by distinctive verbalizations such as "Hit him down," "Kick him," and "Pow!"

A second goal of the study was to determine whether realism in the presentation of the model influences imitation. Thus, in addition to the group that saw the *live* performance of the aggressive acts already described, other nursery school children saw a *film* of the model's behavior, and still others saw a *cartoon* version of the same actions shown on a simulated television set. Finally, as a control condition, a fourth group saw no model at all.

After the initial session, the subjects in all conditions were frustrated; that is, they were allowed to play with an array of highly attractive toys

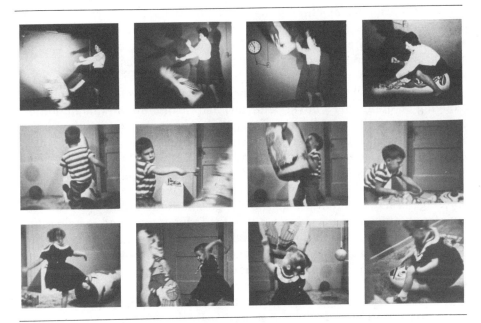

Fig. 9.1. Photographs of children reproducing the aggressive behavior of the female model they had observed on film. (From A. Bandura, D. Ross, and S. A. Ross, "Influence of film-mediated aggressive models," *Journal of Abnormal and Social Psychology*, 1963, **66**, 8. Copyright 1963 by the American Psychological Association. Reprinted by permission.)

just long enough to get involved, whereupon the experimenter came and took them away saying, "These are my best toys; I don't just let anyone play with them." The frustration session was included to ensure that at least some aggression occurred. Note that the experiment could not be considered a test of the effects of frustration on aggression, because all the groups, including the control subjects, were frustrated.

To determine the effects of the models on the children's behavior, each child was taken to another room where he was allowed to play with other toys, among which was the Bobo doll. There his behavior was observed for 20 minutes by two raters through a one-way mirror. Without knowing which group the subject was in, the raters tallied the number of the model's aggressive responses the child imitated.

The most pertinent finding was that nursery school children who were exposed to the aggressive behavior of an adult did imitate the behavior. Children in all three experimental groups (live, film, and cartoon) reproduced more of the model's responses than did the control subjects, who had seen no model at all. The live and filmed models were both more effective than the cartoon version. In addition to tallying instances of exact modeling, the observers tallied the number of nonimitative aggressive acts. They concluded that seeing others act aggressively makes all kinds of aggressive behaviors more probable as well. The children's responses to the Bobo doll in this experiment demonstrate both *modeling* (copying of the model's novel behavior) and *disinhibition* (stimulation by observation of the model to perform their own repertory of aggressive acts). In addition, two other processes were illustrated in these results. As noted in Chapter 2, observers tend to imitate models similar to themselves, and in this study boys tended to imitate the male model whereas girls were more responsive to the female. Furthermore, the boys made more aggressive responses than did the girls, a finding that has been frequently obtained and that is relevant to the topic of male and female roles.

The finding that imitation is selective has received support in a series of on-going studies. Unlike most modeling research, in these studies the nursery school children and their models maintained sustained relationships (Yarrow and Scott, 1972; Yarrow, Scott, and Wexler, 1973). Some of the teachers served as nurturant (i.e. warm and supporting) and others as non-nurturant models. In one study, it was found that nurturant models did not facilitate the imitation of aggressive behavior but did facilitate the imitation of nurturant behaviors. In contrast, non-nurturant models facilitated the imitation of aggressive behaviors (Yarrow and Scott, 1972).

Justified Aggression

A laboratory experiment by Berkowitz (1964) that showed increased aggressive behavior in college students after they had watched a violent movie sequence is especially relevant to the effects of filmed aggression. Initially two male subjects at a time were given an intelligence test, but one of them was actually a confederate of the experimenter. In some pairings, the confederate frustrated the other subject by making inflammatory remarks, such as "You're certainly taking a long time with that." In others, the confederate remained neutral toward the subject. At various intervals during the study, the experimenter took both subjects' blood pressure to support the cover story that the study concerned physiological reactions to various tasks.

After taking the intelligence test, the subjects watched a brief movie sequence and answered some questions about it. The seven-minute excerpt from *The Champion* was a fight scene in which Kirk Douglas received a serious beating in the ring. The primary experimental manipulation concerned the nature of the story leading up to the fight scene. Each

The Museum of Modern Art/Film Stills Archive. Copyright 1949, United Artists Corporation.

subject was given a synopsis of the early part of the film. For half of the subjects the character played by Douglas was portrayed as an unprincipled scoundrel. The assumption was that the subjects hearing that story line would perceive the beating as *justified* retribution for the protagonist's misdeeds, and later questioning revealed that they had little sympathy for him. For the other half of the subjects, the description of the character was more favorable. According to that version, he had behaved badly but only because he had been victimized when he was young, and he was now about to turn over a new leaf. When questioned later, those subjects did display sympathy for the protagonist.

The third task in the experiment provided a socially acceptable situation in which to express aggression. Subject and confederate were separated, and the subject was told that his coworker was going to make a creative floor plan for a house which he would be asked to judge. He would indicate his judgment of the plan's creativity by the number of electric shocks he gave to the coworker by depressing a telegraph key. If he judged the plan highly creative, he was to deliver one shock, if poor, more than one, and the worse the plan, the greater the number of shocks. To ensure that the shocks reflected real hostility rather than responses to differences in creativity, the same house plan was shown to all subjects.

The results showed that in the *frustrated* group (those earlier insulted by their coworkers), the subjects who had seen the *justified* aggression in the film delivered *more shocks* to their coworkers than did those who had seen the unjustified aggression, and the shocks were of *longer duration* (see Fig. 9.2). The roles of both *justification* and *frustration* in aggression can be seen in the results. The subjects who had not been frustrated expressed less aggression and were no more likely to be influenced by justified than by unjustified aggression. However, a subject who had been frustrated and who had witnessed justified aggression against the movie villain was very prone to aggress against the momentary villain in his own life. According to Berkowitz, the movie influenced the subjects' judgment about the propriety of aggression.

Incidentally, this study is interesting in part because it points to a possible fallacy in the technique employed in motion pictures to discour-

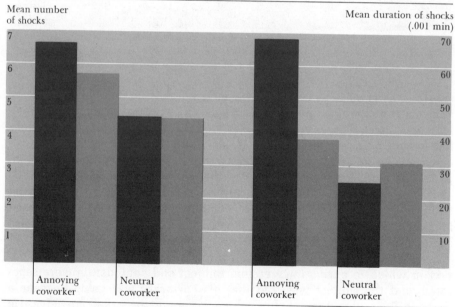

Fig. 9.2. Responses of subjects invited to commit aggression after seeing prize-fight film varied according to synopsis they heard beforehand. One synopsis (black bars) called Douglas' beating deserved; the other (shaded bars) said it was undeserved. After the film the subjects were told they could give electric shocks to an annoying or neutral coworker based on his "creativeness" in doing a task. Seeing a man receive what had been described as a well-deserved beating apparently lowered restraints against aggressive behavior. (From L. Berkowitz, "The effects of observing violence." Copyright © 1963 by Scientific American, Inc. All rights reserved.)

age the imitation of criminal behavior. The usual way to accomplish this objective is to end the movie by punishing the villain with "justified" aggression. Thus the film may provide a model for justified aggression.

In addition to the research already reviewed, there have been other experiments that produced related findings. A study of nursery school children showed that those exposed to an aggressive cartoon movie were later more aggressive toward a toy than were those in a control group that had watched a less aggressive film (Lövaas, 1961). Another series of experiments using adults as subjects showed that greater aggressive behavior (i.e., more intense shocks) followed exposure to a movie of a knife fight than to an innocuous movie (Walters and Llewellyn Thomas, 1963; Walters, Llewellyn Thomas, and Acker, 1962).

These studies seem to demonstrate convincingly that seeing aggressive behavior by others tends to elicit aggression in the viewer, even when the presentation of the aggressive model is in the context of entertainment. An alternative possibility was that watching the violent movies would have served as a substitute outlet for the viewers' aggressive tendencies, leaving them less aggressive than before; however, that result did not occur. Indeed, one experiment (Hokanson, Burgess, and Cohen, 1963) has shown that even if angered people commit aggressive acts themselves, their aggressive tendencies are not satisfied unless the actions are directed at the person who has frustrated or angered them. The investigators used systolic blood pressure as a measure of anger arousal. According to that measure, arousal was not much reduced when aggression was directed toward similar substitute targets; only direct aggression to the frustrater was satisfying.

Of course, one ought not to conclude from this research that a one-to-one relationship will exist between observed and expressed aggression, with the result that an immediate hostile display will consistently follow the seeing of violent films. The conditions under which the normal person's predisposition to inhibit hostility will allow him or her to express aggression overtly are presumably rare. Among other factors, the target, as the blood-pressure study shows, must appear relevant to the person's anger or must be disliked for some other reason.

ROLES
aggression and the police officer's role

In Chapter 8, we reviewed a study on the perception of aggression by cadets in a police training school. In that study aggressive and nonaggressive pictures were presented in a binocular-rivalry situation, and it was found that over the course of their training the police officers came to perceive the aggressive pictures significantly more often than the nonaggressive ones. That study serves not only as an illustration of the relationship between aggression and perception but also as an example of the effects of learning an aggressive role on individual aggressiveness. Responding to aggression and being aggressive in certain situations are part of the set of behaviors which make up the police officer's role.

Although physical aggression toward other members of the same society is generally prohibited, even killing is legal in some places and under certain circumstances. In an attempt to enforce the rules of the group, whether that group is a single family or a whole society, certain members of it are sometimes empowered to behave aggressively. In society at large, the necessity of having some form of police as well as the necessity of strictly controlling such a source of legal aggression is well illustrated by the frontier experience in this country. However, in frontier situations there was typically only a fine line between those who enforced the law and those who were outlaws. Indeed, some of the most notorious killers of the day, such as Bat Masterson and Wyatt Earp, were employed as marshals in frontier towns in the hope that their reputations would deter other bad men from coming (Raine, 1944). Some of the bloodiest scenes from the American past are those in which such individuals or vigilante groups killed in the name of law enforcement.

The experiment, cited in the previous section on models, suggested that aggression is more likely to be imitated when it is seen as justifiable. Although the results of such studies cannot be generalized to the markedly different stimulus situations of interest in this section, it seems quite apparent that the claims of "justifiability" may add an extra measure of force and brutality when violence is carried out in the name of law and order.

The important point to be made here is that legalized and justified aggression can clearly endanger the very order it is intended to maintain unless it is carefully controlled. Perhaps for this very reason the role of the police has been clearly defined in most societies. Police officers usually wear uniforms to differentiate them from other citizens; they are permitted to carry only certain kinds of weapons and to use them only in specified situations. In addition, a military form of organization with a hierarchy of ranks is usually adopted to ensure greater control and clear lines of responsibility.

The concept of role is particularly useful in understanding social acceptance of aggressive behavior. Certain highly aggressive acts are considered both legal and appropriate, provided that the person behaving in this way fills the role of police officer. The events to be considered here represent failures to keep the aggressive behavior of the police within acceptable or role-appropriate limits, and as we shall see, we can also more easily understand these occurrences by considering role variables. The most dramatic examples of role-inappropriate aggression, those that occur during riots and mass demonstrations, are well known, but the ordinary application of undue force has also been studied.

To determine the prevalence of police mistreatment of citizens and the conditions under which it occurs, Reiss (1968) carried out a large-scale sociological project in the summer of 1966. For seven weeks 36 observers watched the police at work in Boston, Chicago, and Washington, D.C. With police cooperation, they rode along in patrol cars and observed booking and lockup procedures in high-crime precincts. They recorded all instances in which physical force was used by the police, but only those which were clearly cases of unnecessary force were considered in the analysis. Instances in which mere restraint was exercised, such as holding a suspect by the arm, were eliminated from consideration, although the legitimacy of such action was in many cases questionable. Only instances in which the police officer struck someone with hands, fist, feet, or body or used a weapon were considered forceful. Actions of this sort, if found to be unjustifiable, would be grounds for arresting the officer and charging him with assault. A forceful incident was judged "unwarranted" or "improper" if it included any of the following circumstances: (1) the police officer physically assaulted a citizen without making an arrest (proper use involves an arrest); (2) the citizen did not by word or deed resist; (3) the police officer could easily have restrained the citizen in other ways; (4) a large number of police were present and could have helped subdue the person; (5) the citizen was handcuffed and did not attempt to flee or resist violently; or (6) the citizen did resist but the force continued after he or she was already subdued.

Included in the 1,394 observed encounters with suspects were 37 different situations in which 44 citizens were victims of improper force. In 15 of the situations no one was arrested, and in 8 of these 15 the suspects had made no verbal or physical resistance at all. Arrests were made in the other 22 encounters. In the arrest cases, 13 suspects were assaulted in the station house when at least 4 other police officers were present. In 2 cases prisoners were assaulted in the absence of any verbal or physical resistance, and in 2 others force was used on handcuffed offenders in the field. Finally, in 5 instances the citizen did resist arrest, but force was applied even after the citizen had been subdued.

The injuries to the 44 citizens varied in seriousness. About half were described as appearing "little more than physically bruised," but in 3 instances the assaulted individuals had to be hospitalized. About a third of the assaults occurred in the station house. Of the 3 individuals requiring hospitalization, 2 were worked over in the lockup.

In three-fourths of the cases of undue force, there were witnesses besides the observer present, but in only one case were the witnesses sympathetic to the victim. That instance is the only one of the assaults on which a formal complaint was ever filed. In half of the cases at least one other police officer was present but did not use force; apparently the presence of other police officers at times acted as a stimulus for aggression rather than serving as an inhibition. For example, Reiss states:

> One man brought into the lockup for threatening a policeman with a pistol was so severely beaten by this policeman that he required hospitalization. During the beating, some fellow policemen propped the man up, while others shouted encouragement. (p. 18)

Such group participation suggests that, though illegal, this behavior is acceptable within police culture. Such acceptance is sometimes found in police administrators as well. One administrator was more concerned about the fact that his officers would allow themselves to be observed applying undue force than about the behavior itself.

Race.   One of the questions asked by the investigators was whether there is more police brutality toward blacks than toward whites. They reported that in largely black precincts, three-fourths of the policemen express prejudice against blacks, and only 1% indicate sympathetic attitudes. Contrary to expectation, however, their behavior did not follow suit. Of the 643 white suspects observed, 27 were assaulted, whereas force was used on only 17 of the 751 black suspects encountered. From these data we can infer a rate of undue force per 1000 suspects of 41.9 for whites and 22.6 for blacks.

Moreover, racial prejudice did not appear to be a primary factor in the application of undue force. To the contrary, most of the police officers aggressed against members of their own race. Of the citizens assaulted by white officers, 67% were white, and 71% of the citizens assaulted by black officers were black.

Status.   It appears that in the particular cases observed in this study race was not the primary stimulus to aggression among the police; but if race was not an important factor, what was? Who are the most probable targets of police brutality? The investigators concluded that two facts about the victims stood out; namely, all were *suspects* and all were from the *lower class.* Though there were fewer citizens of middle and upper status apprehended, a sizable number were among those observed, and none was treated with unnecessary force.

Here the explanatory usefulness of sociological concepts like *status* and *role* becomes apparent. Middle- or upper-middle-class citizens often find it hard to accept claims of police brutality not only because they have never experienced it, but perhaps also because their own experience with the police is frequently just the opposite. In a citizen of the middle or upper-middle class, the average police officer is usually addressing someone of a higher social status. In that relationship the expected role behavior for police officers is to explain their actions courteously, sometimes even apologetically if the status gap is great. On the other hand, if the status gap is reversed so that the hapless individual is of a lower caste as well as being a law breaker, the typical police role may be disrespectful at best.

The investigators concluded from their data that the incidence of excessive force in major metropolitan areas "is far from rare." In fact, about one in ten policemen in high-crime areas sometimes use unnecessary force. It seems highly unlikely that these figures, based as they are on observed and recorded instances, are exaggerated. The more likely direction of bias, if any, would be toward underestimation, although the investigators believe the figures are accurate since the officers had been told that the main interest of the observers lay in citizen behavior toward police. In addition, most of the observers were in fact sympathetic to police problems, and the officers saw them as a source of additional help if it was needed.

CULTURES

Thus far the function of models and societal roles as determinants of individual differences in aggressiveness has been considered. At the cultural level of analysis, the most obvious form of aggression is warfare between people in different cultures—tribes, societies, nations, religions, and ideologies. Given the eternal presence of war, a question which inevitably arises concerns the origin and nature of human aggression.

Culture versus Instinct

In the biological chapter on aggression, the work of the ethologist Konrad Lorenz (1966) was discussed. According to the research on animal behavior reviewed by Lorenz, humans and rats are both exceptions to the norm in the animal kingdom because they frequently kill members of their own species. Born without the natural weapons of a tiger or a wolf, humans were a relatively harmless species, at least until they learned how to fashion artificial weapons. Accordingly the human species experienced no evolutionary pressure to generate the innate inhibitions against killing within the species that are apparent in other killer animals.

It has been argued that humans, realizing the dangerous possibility of self-destruction with weapons, developed *internal* moral restraints to killing ingroup members, restraints which each culture carefully teaches its progeny. To bolster the moral lessons, we have also devised *external* legal restraints which prescribe severe punishment for the act of murder. Nevertheless, the definition of murder is restricted in general to the killing of a member of the same tribe or society. Killing an outgroup member is not murder, and it may even be considered heroism. These conjectures assume that the division of the population into ingroups and outgroups causes aggression. A contrary view put forth by Lorenz argues that the cause of human aggression is not that men are split into political groups; rather, they are split into groups because such division provides the stimulus that allows them to release their aggression.

An aggressive tribe. The foregoing conjectures seem to point to a killer instinct in humans, and the field researches of cultural anthropologists find much to support the apparent universality of human aggression. Indeed, in a review of Lorenz's book *On Aggression*, the anthropologist Geoffrey Gorer (1966) cites the example of a people in the eastern highlands of New Guinea to whom almost anyone is considered a potential victim. Prohibitions against killing here extend only to certain specified kinfolk and a few relatives of one's wife or wives; all others are considered legitimate prey. The anthropologists who studied these people report that the only way for a man in this culture to achieve power and prestige is by killing. As further evidence of their extreme behavior, Gorer notes that these bushmen usually eat their prey and that they usually rape female victims, sometimes before and sometimes after death. One might infer that the mutual practice of cannibalism between these tribes would have ensured their rapid extinction, but it is reported that they rarely kill more people than they can eat, and they tend to leave weaker groups alone to allow them to propagate.

Pacifist tribes. But if there are cultures which seem to be instinctively aggressive, there are also a few examples of cultures which show virtually no interpersonal aggression. Among such pacifist cultures are the Arapesh, also of New Guinea, the Lepchas in the Himalayas, and the pygmies in the Congolese rain forest (Gorer, 1966). These tribes and a few others like them, even though they possess weapons, show no tendency to dominate, hurt, or kill either one another or their neighbors. All these societies are small and technologically backward, and they inhabit remote and inaccessible regions. When invaded by outsiders, they have always chosen to retreat to more inaccessible regions rather than to fight. According to Gorer, they are all hunters, but they do not idealize bravery and aggression as admirable traits that signify masculinity. Indeed, he finds it highly significant that very little distinction is made between the ideal characters of men and of women. He says:

> No child, however, grows up with the injunctions, "All real men do ..." or "No proper woman does ... ," so that there is no confusion of sexual identity; no cases of sexual inversion have been reported among them. The model for the growing child is of concrete enjoyment, not of metaphysical symbolic achievements or of ordeals to be surmounted. They do not have heroes or martyrs to emulate or cowards or traitors to despise; their religious life lacks significant personalized gods and devils; a happy, hard-working and productive life is within the reach of all.*

This atmosphere contrasts sharply with the highly aggressive ideal of masculinity found among the New Guinea cannibals, or, says Gorer, among all peoples who value military success and who practice killing their enemies and "inferiors." He also suggests a possible significance in the finding that these peaceful tribes all tend to immerse themselves in eating, drinking, sex, and laughter—sensual pleasures often discouraged in highly military societies.

Aggression Between Cultures

Aggression and cultural differences. The simple fact that most individuals have intimate contact only with their own culture and are surrounded by others who have developed in the same society makes an appreciation of cultural variation uncommon. The characteristics of one's own culture are usually thought of as more or less universal. As Benedict (1934) points out, humans seem always to have overemphasized their own primacy and importance. Until the Copernican theory took root, we believed that our earth was central and different from other planets, and until Darwinian thought became established, we believed ourselves to have been specially created and to be unrelated to other animals. But almost all people still assume that their own race and certainly their own culture are primary. Indeed, a number of the tribal names by which primitive people know

---

* From G. Gorer, "Man has no 'killer' instinct," *New York Times Magazine*, November 27, 1966, p. 107. Copyright © 1966 by The New York Times Company. Reprinted by permission.

themselves (for example, Zuni, Déné, and Kiowa) are merely their native terms for "the human being," that is, themselves.

Social distance among East African tribes. To determine what cultural factors are most important in producing the negative feelings toward others that are often basic to aggressive behavior, Brewer (1968) analyzed survey data collected from 30 tribes in East Africa. Structured interviews, usually in the appropriate native language, were obtained from 50 members each of tribes from Kenya, Uganda, and Tanzania. The investigator considered three major variables as possible determinants of positive and negative feelings toward the members of other tribes, namely, (1) perceived educational and economic *advancement*, (2) perceived *similarity*, and (3) the physical *distance* between the tribes. The purpose of the study was to determine how the respondent's own tribe related to 13 outgroups. Among other things, the interviews required the subjects to respond to a series of 48 traits, both positive and negative, with the name of the outgroup tribe for which each trait was most characteristic. From the adjectives applied by all respondents to a given tribe (progressive, backward, wealthy, poor, etc.), the investigator classified each group as to its *advancement* in the eyes of other tribes. In addition, from the respondents' indications of the outgroup tribes most and least similar to their own tribe, he calculated the *perceived similarity* of each tribe to the others. The *distance* of an outgroup tribe referred to the number of other tribes that lived between the territory of the outgroup and that of the ingroup. Finally, the measure of positive or negative feelings toward members of an outgroup tribe consisted of four *social distance* items:

1. Would you willingly agree to work with a _____ ?
2. Would you willingly agree to have a _____ as a neighbor in your house?
3. Would you willingly agree to share a meal with a _____ ?
4. Would you willingly agree to become related to a _____ by marriage?

The interviewer recorded the responses to each question and quantified the answers by giving 0 for "No," 1 for "Don't know," and 2 for "Yes." Thus a score of 2 on each, a total of 8, indicated a willingess to have intimate contact with a member of the outgroup, and a total score of 0 indicated strong negative feelings or a desire to keep considerable *social distance* between one's self and the other person.

The results of the survey indicate that all three of the variables studied were important determinants of preferred social distance. The most important of the three was *perceived similarity;* when respondents perceived another tribe as dissimilar to their own, they preferred a relatively large social distance. The influence next in importance was *physical distance.* Although Brewer had thought it possible that nearby tribes would be disliked because of competition over scarce resources, the reverse proved to be true. The greater the actual physical distance between the tribes, the greater was the preferred social distance. The relationship between physical distance and social distance is graphed in Fig. 9.3.

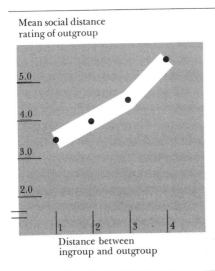

Mean social distance
rating of outgroup

5.0

4.0

3.0

2.0

|1 |2 |3   · |4

Distance between
ingroup and outgroup

Fig. 9.3. Social distance as a function of physical distance. (From M. B. Brewer, "Determinants of social distance among East African tribal groups," *Journal of Personality and Social Psychology,* 1968, **10,** 279–289. Copyright 1968 by the American Psychological Association. Reprinted by permission.)

Although the correspondence between physical distance and social distance is quite reliable, there are of course exceptions to the rule, as in the case of the Kisii tribe of Kenya, who did not like nearby tribes. Brewer notes:

> The Kisii are geographically separated from the other Kenya Bantu tribes to which they are most similar, and of their three immediate neighboring tribes, two (Kipsigis and Marai) are traditional enemies of the Kisii, with a record of quite recent hostilities, and the other (Luo) is looked down upon by the Kisii because they do not practice the Kisii custom of circumcision. (p. 287)

Thus, as this example illustrates, the amount of military and social conflict between neighbors *can* drastically alter the usual relationship between nearness and social distance.

The third variable studied, economic and educational advancement, was also significantly related to social distance. It was not clear prior to the study whether the advanced tribes would be admired because they were successful or disliked because they were a source of frustration for the less advanced groups. The results (Fig. 9.4) showed that all the tribes were generally willing to accept close relations with members of more advanced tribes. Actually, so long as an outgroup tribe was seen as similar, its advancement was not very relevant, but among dissimilar tribes advancement was important. Tribes that were seen as both dissimilar and backward were particularly disliked.

Mean social distance
rating of outgroup

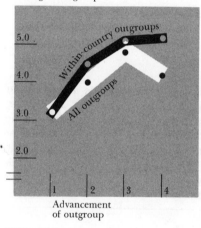

Advancement
of outgroup

Fig. 9.4. Social distance as a function of outgroup advancement. (From M. B. Brewer, "Determinants of social distance among East African tribal groups," *Journal of Personality and Social Psychology,* 1968, **10,** 279–289. Copyright 1968 by the American Psychological Association. Reprinted by permission.)

The Brewer study constituted a very large undertaking, with 1,500 subjects spread over 30 tribes. The subjects were interviewed one at a time where they lived and usually in their native language. The results showed that in general these East Africans were willing to associate on intimate terms with people who appeared to be similar to themselves, who lived nearby, and who were relatively advanced, and they correspondingly preferred greater social distance from dissimilar, remote, and backward tribes.

The enemy as dissimilar. The finding that people who seem dissimilar from one's self in important ways are disliked has been obtained quite regularly with American as well as East African subjects. It is also true that those who are already widely disliked come to seem increasingly different from one's self, regardless of the true facts. For example, in 1942, when the United States was allied with China in a war against Japan, one investigator showed American subjects a sample of 56 photographs of Chinese and Japanese faces (Farnsworth, 1965). He found that they were unable to accurately distinguish the Chinese from the Japanese faces, but more importantly, the ones they selected as "Chinese" were also the ones they said looked "most Caucasian" to them.

Of course, the relationship between similarity-dissimilarity and liking-disliking can also be used to manipulate attitudes toward other cultures. The propaganda technique of presenting a nation's allies as similar and its enemies as highly dissimilar is probably as old as warfare itself. For example, in 1943 Russia and the United States were allies against Germany, and in that year the magazine *Life,* in an issue devoted to Russian-American cooperation, proclaimed that The Great Russians were "one hell of a people," who "look like Americans, dress like Americans, and think like Americans." (Quoted in Boller, 1967, p. 191) And on the same theme, another popular magazine said in 1944:

> Out of closer contacts in this war, we are discovering that in spite of external differences, Russians are in many ways like ourselves. In history, geography, industry ... and consequently in the characteristics of the people ... there are striking parallels and resemblances between America and Russia. (Williams, 1944, p. 45)

However, by 1951 Russia was no longer considered an ally, and in the *Reader's Digest,* to cite only one example of many, Russians were seen as "toughened and obedient industrial soldiers.... The average Russian is a clumsy member of the machine age ... totally responsive to iron commands." (O'Daniel, 1951, p. 54)

We have looked at some of the many potential sources for negative attitudes between ethnic and national groups. A question that remains concerns how the relations between cultures and subcultures can be improved. One frequently employed solution is known as the contact hypothesis.

The Contact Hypothesis

In cultures where two or more groups are divided and segregated and in which negative feelings and overt aggression exist between them, the suggestion is sometimes made that the schools and living conditions be reorganized to ensure contact on the assumption that contact will reduce intergroup prejudice. An open and quite researchable question concerns the extent to which mere contact will produce the desired result. Various international exchange programs currently operate on just that principle. Of course, it is clear at the outset that *mere* physical contact is not sufficient, since at times violent outbreaks also occur following such contact. Thus the question becomes: What kind of contact, if any, would be effective?

In a review of a large number of studies, Amir (1969) has summarized the conditions under which international and interracial contact proved effective in reducing negative feelings. The settings in which these contacts occurred included housing, military units, work situations, classrooms, camps, and hospitals, and the findings show that only some contacts produced positive changes of attitudes, whereas others fostered changes in a negative direction. Amir concluded that positive changes are most likely to occur when members of the majority group encounter members of the minority who are either *equal in status* or of a higher status than themselves. Recent data in support of this idea come from research conducted at an interracial summer camp (Bray, Itkin, Murphy, and Clore, 1975; Eaton and Clore, 1976). The setting was unusual in that blacks and whites shared every status level within the camp equally. Half of the campers, the counselors, and the camp administrators were of each race. The results showed that after a week of such intimate and equal-status contact, the children had changed their racial attitudes and no longer used race as a criterion when choosing friends within the camp. In addition, as part of an Indian initiation ceremony in which they could imitate either black or white models, the children were more likely at the end than at the beginning of the week to imitate opposite-race adults they had never met before.

Some of the other conclusions summarized by Amir are that positive changes are fostered (1) when contact is *pleasant* or rewarding, (2) when contact is *intimate* rather than casual, and (3) when the setting involves important activities or activities from which common *superordinate* goals emerge, goals which are more important to each group than are their own separate goals.

Among the conditions under which contact may do more harm than good are those that produce *competition* between groups; those that are unpleasant, involuntary, or tense; those that lower the status of one of the groups; those in which members of a group are in a state of frustration (defeat, failure); those in which one of the groups has moral or ethnic standards objectionable to the other; and those in which the minority group members are lower in status than the members of the majority group.

It is clear from this partial list of findings that just integrating schools, armed forces, or housing projects or just exchanging students between two countries may not produce dramatic changes. However, such conditions are essential first steps before the intimate contacts between equals that do change attitudes can take place.

SUMMARY

This chapter began by discussing the role of models in aggression. An experiment was cited showing that children imitated novel aggressive responses they saw others make, whether the models were live, filmed, or in cartoon form. Moreover, evidence was also presented to show that the imitation is selective. In one study, it was found that nurturant models facilitated the imitation of nurturant behaviors whereas non-nurturant models facilitated the imitation of aggressive behaviors.

An important variable in the likelihood of imitating an aggressive model is perceived justification of the observed action. We discussed an experiment showing that exposure to filmed aggression seen as justified was more likely than unjustified aggression to be followed by aggressive behavior toward a frustrating coworker.

The section on roles considered two different uses of the concept. The first observation was that, although aggressive behavior toward others in the society is generally prohibited, the position of police officer is one in which certain kinds of aggressive behavior constitute part of the approved role behavior. In practice it is sometimes difficult to control and limit aggressive behavior that is seen as role-appropriate and labeled as "justifiable." However, various formal aspects of the police role and of police organization exist in part to keep the use of force under control. The second use of the concept of role appeared in a sociological study of the prevalence of unnecessary force in three major metropolitan police departments. The assaults observed were all against lower-class citizens without regard to race. It was suggested that the relative status of police officers and middle-class citizens makes it likely that most of such citizens would never be the victims (or even believe in the existence) of police brutality. Some aggressive behavior is part of the police officer's accepted role. In addition, one in the police role is most likely to aggress unnecessarily against citizens in the dual roles of *suspect* and *lower-class citizen*. Thus both the police role itself and the roles of those encountered (lower class versus middle class) help explain the aggressive behavior.

In the section on cultures we sought an explanation of the unique tendency for humans to kill within their own species. No definitive answer to the question of instinctual versus cultural origins of aggression is available, since anthropologists have discovered both exceedingly aggressive and totally pacifistic groups.

In an attempt to investigate aggression between cultures or, more exactly, negative feelings toward members of other cultures, a large study of East African tribes was undertaken. The research showed that tribesmen were least willing to accept intimate contact with members of tribes that were perceived as dissimilar, were geographically distant, and were not advanced. A similar tendency for most people in wartime to see allies as similar and enemies as dissimilar was also noted. Finally, we investigated the hypothesis that contact between members of different cultural groups will create positive feelings. Cross-cultural contact is most likely to have beneficial results when it is rewarding and intimate, when the minority group members are of higher status than the majority, and when the work of the two groups accomplishes mutual goals.

SUGGESTIONS FOR FURTHER READING

Bandura, A. *Aggression: A Social Learning Analysis.* Englewood Cliffs, N.J.: Prentice-Hall, 1973. In this book Bandura gives a thoroughgoing social learning analysis of aggression, emphasizing modeling as discussed in this chapter and the role of cognitive processes or self-arousal of anger as discussed in the previous chapter.

Freud, S. Why war? In J. Strachey (ed.), *Collected Papers,* Vol. 5. London: Hogarth Press, 1950, pp. 273–287. In 1932 an institute of the League of Nations arranged for Freud and Einstein to correspond on the topic "Why war?". This brief essay is Freud's answer to Einstein's letter to him. It is interesting not only as a historical curiosity, but also as an example of Freud's application of his system to a practical problem.

10 Aggression: The Psychometric-Trait Viewpoint

10
Aggression: The Psychometric-Trait Viewpoint

I. **Observational methods: a peer-nomination measure of aggression**
   A. Rationale and development
   B. Construct validity

II. **Self-report methods: the expression and control of aggression**
   A. Intensity
   B. Control
      1. Appropriate control
      2. Undercontrol
      3. Overcontrol
   C. MMPI aggression scales
   D. CPI self-control scale
   E. Self-control and intensity of aggression

III. **Indirect methods: relationship between fantasy and overt aggression**
   A. Maternal attitudes
   B. Aggression anxiety

IV. **Summary**

V. **Suggestions for further reading**

OBSERVATIONAL METHODS
a peer-nomination measure of aggression

The Peer Nomination Inventory was described in Chapter 6 as a special-ized observational instrument designed for the study of adjustment in pre-adolescent boys. An aggression scale was developed for the Peer Nomina-tion Inventory at the same time that the dependency scale was developed. Because the general method of scale development was described in Chap-ter 6, only a brief review will be given here.

Rationale and Development

In individual interviews, 8- to 12-year-old boys were asked to describe typical behaviors of peers who were experiencing adjustmental difficulties in school. Verbatim behavior statements made by the boys were tran-scribed to cards, and their content was rated by three psychologists. The description of the aggression category given to each rater was as follows:

> The boy by implication or act, is hurtful or destructive. His behavior may be described as quarrelsome, antagonistic, negativistic, disruptive, defiant, etc. (Wiggins and Winder, 1961, p. 650)

The 597 behavior statements which the judges unanimously agreed reflected aggression were further sorted into subcategories of aggression by two clinical psychologists. The subcategories included: physical ag-gression, socially condoned aggression, verbal aggression, indirect aggres-sion, etc. Sixty aggression items considered representative of these sub-categories were administered in preliminary forms of the Peer Nomination Inventory to 8- to 12-year-old boys in 10 different elementary schools. On the basis of item-analysis procedures, the 12 best items were selected to constitute the final aggression scale (Table 10.1).

The aggression items, like those for dependency, are administered in a special sociometric format in which the items appear as rows and the names of the boys in a given class appear as columns. The percentage of classmates who indicate that an item applies to a given boy is tabulated, and the sum of the percentages for the 12 items yields that boy's social-stimulus value with respect to the personality trait of aggression. The substantive and structural considerations of construct validity that guided these procedures were described in Chapter 6. The next section will be concerned primarily with external considerations of construct validity.

Table 10.1   Peer Nomination Inventory Aggression Items.*

He's always acting up.
When he doesn't get his way, he gets real mad.
If someone gets in his way, he shoves them out of the way.
He's just plain mean.
He's really wild.
He makes fun of people.
He doesn't pay attention to the teacher.
He seems to have a chip on his shoulder.
He tries to get other people in trouble.
He always messes around and gets in trouble.
He says he can beat everybody up.
He likes to pick on little kids.

---

* Reprinted with permission of authors and publisher from J. S. Wiggins and C. L. Winder, "The Peer Nomination Inventory: an empirically derived sociometric measure of adjustment in pre-adolescent boys." *Psychological Reports,* 1961, **9**, 643–677, M5-V9. Available as a separate from journal at $1.50 per copy.

Construct Validity

The Peer Nomination Inventory aggression scale was administered to boys from 29 different classes in several elementary schools. From each class, six boys were selected whose scale scores indicated that they were high, medium, or low on aggression with respect to their classmates. Thus, from each class two boys who scored high on aggression, two medium, and two low were selected. Although the entire class participated in each study, only those six were observed by raters.

All boys from each class participated in a "special physical education project," which took place on the playground of the school. The project involved foursquare, a game popular among boys of that age. A player standing in one of four squares of a court hits a hard rubber ball into one of the other three squares, and the player in that square returns it. Although the game is not likely to instigate high levels of aggression in its ordinary four-player form, the particular variation chosen for study, "group foursquare," provided maximum stimulation for aggressive behavior.

The number of courts available for "group foursquare" permitted approximately half the boys to play while the other half waited in line for their turn. At two-minute intervals, a whistle was the signal for the boys to shift positions as indicated by the arrows in Fig. 10.1. This minor variation on a standard game created a situation in which the probability of

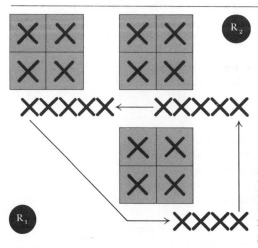

Fig. 10.1. Experimental arrangement for aggression experiment. Subjects are indicated by X and raters by R (after Winder and Wiggins, 1964).

aggressive behavior was extremely high. The boys waiting in line, eager to play the game, grew restless. When they were finally allowed to participate, however, they were interrupted after two minutes and forced to rotate to the end of another line on a new court. Two observers rated each of the experimental subjects on a time-sampling basis. The categories for observation included such items as: (a) physical aggression (kicking, striking, pushing, etc.); (b) verbal aggression (name calling, shouting, arguing); (c) resistant and oppositional behavior (breaking rules, resisting direction, ignoring instructions); and (d) ease of provocation (readiness to become irritated, annoyed, provoked).

The experimental hypothesis was that subjects classified as high, medium, and low by the Peer Nomination Inventory aggression scale would show corresponding amounts of aggressive behaviors in the experimental situation. The hypothesis was tested on a total of 174 boys, 58 in each category. The average number of aggressive behaviors observed in the time interval for each of the three groups of subjects is presented in Fig. 10.2.

Note that the averages for aggressive responses observed in the experimental situation are related to the subjects' scores on the aggression scale. Whereas the subjects with high scores on aggression averaged approximately 35 aggressive responses in the experimental situation, the medium-scoring subjects averaged about 29 and the low-scoring only 25 aggressive responses. These results are statistically significant; they would be expected to occur by chance in only one of a thousand instances. Although a single experiment cannot establish the validity of a personal-

Peer Nomination Inventory classification

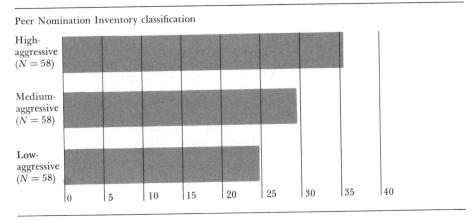

Fig. 10.2. Average number of aggressive responses observed in subject groups classified by the Peer Nomination Inventory (after Winder and Wiggins, 1964).

ity-trait scale, the construct validity of the Peer Nomination Inventory aggression scale is considerably enhanced by this experimental study of aggression.

SELF-REPORT METHODS
the expression and control of aggression

The personality trait of aggression has assumed critical social importance in recent years. The incidence of senseless murder and violent assault in the larger cities has become an issue of central concern to all citizens. The prediction and understanding of the extremes of aggressive behavior are therefore necessary, not only for a complete understanding of the psychology of personality, but for the enjoyment—and perhaps preservation —of life as we know it.

Intensity

Aggression varies both in kind (verbal, physical, indirect) and in intensity. The kind that most concerns society at present is physical aggression. However, within the category of physical aggression itself there are recognizable degrees of intensity. One such subdivision distinguishes *mild, moderate,* and *extreme* intensities of physical aggression (Megargee, 1966). Mild physical aggression, which is not likely to seriously injure the victim, is characteristic of most schoolyard scuffles. Moderate physical aggression is likely to injure (but not maim) the victim, and some "justification" for the aggressive response is usually involved. Extreme physical aggression is aggression which has reached homicidal intensity and in which the victim is likely to be killed or permanently maimed.

From society's viewpoint, the intensity of aggressive behavior is more important than its frequency. Thus individuals may frequently be involved in acts of mild aggression without being considered particularly harmful to society. On the other hand, a single act of murder is enough to classify an individual as extremely aggressive. The intensity of aggressive behavior and the frequency with which it is expressed are, in turn, functions of the degree of control that individuals have over their aggressive impulses.

Control

In order to establish and maintain effective interpersonal relationships, an individual must regulate and control the expression of aggressive impulses toward others. Since aggressive behavior is not always maladaptive, the individual must strike a balance between total inhibition and total absence of control. From the standpoint of personality adjustment, three types of control may be distinguished.

Appropriate control. Since most forms of antisocial aggression will be punished by society, an individual must maintain the degree of control necessary to avoid explosive outbursts of aggression. On the other hand, many social situations require assertiveness, and our society recognizes "justifiable aggression" as an adaptive form of self-defense. Hence the well-adjusted person maintains a balance between appropriate assertiveness and inhibition of antisocial aggressive impulses.

Undercontrol. Individuals who are unable to inhibit aggressive impulses will strike out at others under minimal provocation. Because they lack the controls necessary for effective social adjustment, such individuals will experience difficulty in establishing and maintaining effective interpersonal relationships, and they are likely to be arrested for their antisocial behavior.

Overcontrol. Because aggressive behavior is generally viewed as undesirable by our culture, it may seem that the more control individuals exercise over their aggressive impulses, the more readily they will be accepted by society. However, individuals who are overcontrolled are unable to be appropriately assertive when such behavior may be adaptive. More important, the individual who rigidly inhibits all assertive impulses has no outlets for the expression of frustrations. Consequently, the chronically overcontrolled individual may be operating under a great deal of tension built up by unexpressed hostility. In the work of Megargee, to be considered next, it is apparent that the chronically overcontrolled individual may be the most dangerous from the standpoint of society.

MMPI Aggression Scales

The Minnesota Multiphasic Personality Inventory (MMPI) item pool has served as a basis for the construction of a number of scales designed to measure the expression and control of hostility. Most of these scales were developed by the method of contrasted groups, although some were the product of rational procedures. An adjustment-to-prison scale was developed by contrasting item responses of a group of prisoners who were characterized by assaultiveness, fighting, and belligerence with those of a group of prisoners who had not exhibited such aggressive behaviors (Panton, 1958). A hostility-control scale was developed by contrasting the item responses of patients rated by their therapists as maintaining effective control over their aggressive impulses with the item responses of patients similarly rated as lacking such control (Schultz, 1955). In addition to these two, there are ten other MMPI scales and combinations of scales designed to reflect different aspects of the control and expression of hostility (Dahlstrom and Welsh, 1960). To the extent that these scales possess construct validity, one would expect them to be able to predict or directly classify individuals characterized by different degrees of expression and control of aggressive behaviors.

As a test of the construct validity of MMPI indices of hostility and control, Megargee and Mendelsohn (1962) administered 12 such scales to the following four groups of subjects who clearly differed in degree of expressed hostility. The extremely assaultive group consisted of incarcerated criminals who had been convicted of crimes involving murder, mayhem, and assault with a deadly weapon. The moderately assaultive group consisted of men convicted of crimes involving battery, or the use of force or violence, but not of the more serious crimes committed by the first group. As a control group for assaultiveness, the investigators selected a group whose criminal records were characterized by the absence of an assaultive component. The majority of these prisoners had been convicted either of robbery or of nonviolent sex offenses. As a further control, they selected a group of normal subjects who were comparable, in terms of socioeconomic background and geographical location, but who had never been convicted of any criminal charge.

Wayne Miller, © Magnum Photos, Inc.

When the average scores on each of the twelve MMPI indices of hostility and control were compared among the four groups, the overall results were both discouraging and perplexing. Many of the scales failed to show any significant differences whatsoever among the four groups. Some scales provided slight means by which to separate criminals from noncriminals, but they were generally lacking in discrimination between the assaultive and nonassaultive criminal groups. Scales such as these would of course have very little practical value as measures of hostility. In addition to being generally discouraging, the findings of this study were perplexing, in that when scales did show differences among the four groups, *the differences were in the opposite direction from that antici-pated.* A conclusion drawn from this single study would have to be that assaultive criminals are better controlled and less hostile than both non-violent criminals and normals.

Studies reporting negative results (the absence of any relationships) are not uncommon in the area of self-report personality scales. Many scales are simply lacking in construct validity; i.e., responses to the scales do not represent manifestations of the underlying trait of interest. How-ever, studies reporting reversals (relationships in the opposite direction from that expected) are less common. Reversals may indicate that the trait under investigation was improperly construed in its original form, and further investigation may lead to a revision. The study described next (Megargee, 1966) illustrates the manner in which constructs may be modi-fied by empirical findings.

CPI Self-control Scale

Although most California Psychological Inventory (CPI) scales were de-veloped by the method of contrasted groups, four scales (including that for self-control) were developed by the technique of internal consistency analysis. That technique is a variant of the rational method, in which items are selected on the basis of their apparent relevance to the trait of interest and on the basis of their high correlations with one another. It was resorted to when obtaining large samples of criterion subjects for contrasted group analysis was not feasible. As defined by Gough (1957), the dimension of self-control measures the degree and adequacy of self-regulation and self-control, as well as freedom from impulsivity and self-centeredness. Those who score high on the self-control scale tend to be described as calm, patient, practical, inhibited, strict, and conscientious. Individuals who score low on the self-control scale are described as im-pulsive, excitable, irritable, self-centered, aggressive, and uninhibited.

Starting with a pool of items whose content suggested self-control (or its opposite, impulsivity), Gough administered them to groups of subjects and then selected additional items that showed a relationship to the items of self-control content. Subsequently, he showed that the final self-control scale was related to ratings and peer nominations on the dimension of impulsivity. Illustrative items from the CPI self-control scale are presented in Table 10.2.

Table 10.2 Illustrative items from the California Psychological Inventory self-control scale.*

Item	Scoring
At times I feel like smashing things.	False
At times I have a strong urge to do something harmful or shocking.	False
I have never done anything dangerous for the thrill of it.	True
I have very few quarrels with members of my family.	True
Sometimes I feel as if I must injure either myself or someone else.	False
At times I feel like picking a fist fight with someone.	False
I am often said to be hotheaded.	False
I find it hard to keep my mind on a task or job.	False
I like to go to parties and other affairs where there is lots of loud fun.	False

* Reproduced by special permission from Consulting Psychologists Press—*The California Psychological Inventory* by Harrison G. Gough. Copyright 1956. Published by Consulting Psychologists Press Inc.

Self-control and Intensity of Aggression

In an attempt to clarify the puzzling results of his earlier study, Megargee (1966) conducted a follow-up study on a group of institutionalized male juvenile delinquents. The boys were classified for aggressiveness on the basis of the severity of their offenses, as indicated in Table 10.3. Subjects in the extremely assaultive group had been apprehended for severe assaults involving lethal weapons. Subjects in the moderately assaultive group had been involved in crimes of violence with no apparent homicidal intent. Control groups included subjects who had been detained for property offenses and subjects who had been classified as incorrigible. The property offenders had no history of assaultive behaviors; the incorrigibles had no history of physical aggression, although the presence of verbal aggression was especially likely. All subjects were administered

Table 10.3 Groups compared on California Psychological Inventory scales (after Megargee, 1966).

Group	N	Average age	Typical behaviors
Extremely assaultive boys	9	14.4	Killed mother with rifle; slashed victim with knife; shot father with pistol; attempted to shoot victim.
Moderately assaultive boys	21	15.3	Hit victim with brass knuckles; hit victim with wrench; kicked victim when down; struck woman with blunt object.
Offenders against property	20	15.4	Committed auto theft, burglary.
Incorrigibles	26	15.2	Demonstrated unruliness, defiance, unmanageability in the home.

the CPI, along with interviews, behavior ratings, and indirect measurement methods.

The results for the CPI self-control scale are given in Fig. 10.3. As predicted, the extremely assaultive group had self-control scores that were

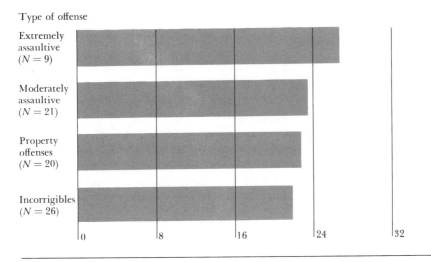

Fig. 10.3. Average self-control scale score for subject groups classified by type of offense (after Megargee, 1966).

significantly higher than those of the moderately assaultive and nonas-saultive delinquent groups. In fact, the average self-control score for the extremely assaultive group (26.5) was higher than the average self-control score for normal male high school students (25.3), as reported in the test manual for the CPI (Gough, 1957).

Actually, the self-control scale was only one of seven CPI scales on which the extremely assaultive group scored significantly higher than the other groups; the other six are listed in Table 10.4. In comparison with the moderately assaultive and the two nonassaultive groups, the extremely assaultive group attained significantly higher scores on scales measuring responsibility, well-being, tolerance, achievement via independence, in-tellectual efficiency, and flexibility. On the basis of the CPI results in this study, it appears that extremely assaultive persons have a greater degree of self-control, are more responsible, are relatively free from worries, are more tolerant, are more intellectually independent and efficient, and are more flexible in their thinking and social behavior.

The results suggesting that the extremely assaultive group are more controlled and generally healthier than the moderately assaultive and de-

Table 10.4 California Psychological Inventory scales on which the extremely assaultive group scored higher than other groups.*

CPI scale	Personality dimension
Responsibility	Persons of conscientious, responsible, and dependable disposition and temperament.
Well-being	Persons who minimize their worries and complaints and are relatively free from self-doubt and disillusionment.
Tolerance	Persons with permissive, accepting, and nonjudgmental social beliefs and attitudes.
Achievement via independence	Persons whose interest and motivation facilitate achievement in any setting where autonomy and independence are positive behaviors.
Intellectual efficiency	Persons who have attained a high degree of personal and intellectual efficiency.
Flexibility	Persons whose thinking and social behavior are flexible and adaptable.

* Reproduced by special permission from Consulting Psychologists Press—*The California Psychological Inventory* by Harrison G. Gough. Copyright 1956. Published by Consulting Psychologists Press Inc.

linquent groups were not specific to the CPI. In a study of the predetention behavior of the members of the extremely assaultive group, for example, it was found that they had experienced fewer previous incarcerations and had better school attendance and conduct records. During the first ten days in custody, the extremely assaultive subjects were rated by their counselors as significantly more cooperative, amiable, and friendly than the moderately assaultive subjects. Finally, the extremely assaultive group was rated higher on a specially devised adjective-checklist measure of overcontrol than the three other delinquent groups, all of which had essentially similar scores. Typical adjectives in the checklist were: meek, self-controlled, conscientious, and withdrawn.

The results of the Megargee study have practical relevance for the detection and control of antisocial aggression. Megargee (1966) suggests that there are at least two types of aggressive personalities. The *undercontrolled aggressive* are lacking in controls for aggression and likely to engage in many crimes involving moderately assaultive behavior. The *chronically overcontrolled* are unlikely to express any aggression at all. Because they exercise such rigid controls over their aggressive impulses, however, when such impulses do erupt, they are likely to result in extremely assaultive, murderous behavior.

A review of newspaper accounts and case histories of extremely assaultive individuals strongly suggests that such individuals are likely to be characterized by extreme overcontrol: "In case after case the extremely assaultive offender proves to be a rather passive person with no previous history of aggression." (Megargee, 1966, p. 2) Newspaper reports of puzzling, senseless, and shocking crimes of extreme violence frequently describe the criminals as polite, softspoken, unemotional, and mild-mannered. The concept of overcontrol may well describe the dynamics of many of these cases. Clearly, much more research of the kind conducted by Megargee is needed to illuminate the dynamics of aggression underlying extremely assaultive acts.

INDIRECT METHODS
relationship between fantasy and overt aggression

Thematic methods, such as the Thematic Apperception Test, provide an index of the extent to which an individual is preoccupied with the expression of a given personality trait on the fantasy level. When the trait in question is relatively acceptable socially (e.g., dependency), a fairly direct relationship will occur between the amount of fantasy preoccupation and the extent to which the behavior is expressed overtly. However, when the trait in question is viewed as undesirable by our society or by segments of it (e.g., aggression), the relationship between fantasy pre-occupation and overt expression will be more complex. The attempts of numerous investigators to establish the relationship between fantasy and overt expressions of aggression constitute one of the more interesting chapters in the history of personality-trait measurement. Although our current understanding of this complex relationship is far from complete, a number of studies have provided us with considerable insight into the nature of variables which influence it. We shall next consider several studies that illustrate these complex relationships.

Maternal Attitudes

Lesser (1957) administered a peer-nomination measure of aggression to 44 middle-class boys in fifth and sixth grades, who ranged in age from 10 to 13 years. It consisted of 15 items (e.g., "Here is someone who is always looking for a fight."), which were presented to all boys in a given class. The boys were asked to indicate the names of classmates whose behavior was described by the item. Each boy's overt-aggression score was based on the number of times he was named by his classmates.

Lesser administered to the same boys a modified TAT, which con-sisted of a set of ten pictures portraying two boys in a variety of interac-tions. Each boy's fantasy aggression score was based on the number of times aggressive acts (fighting, injuring, assaulting) appeared in the stories he composed. The stories were scored independently by two judges, who attained a high degree of agreement in scoring aggressive themes.

When the overt-aggression scores from the peer-nomination test were compared with the fantasy-aggression scores from the modified TAT, no relationship at all appeared to exist between the two; that is, no relation-ship could be detected between overt and fantasy aggression in this group of 44 middle-class boys. Such a negative finding is fairly common for the trait of aggression. However, because both fantasy and overt expressions of aggression are known to be influenced by other variables, the possibil-ity existed that the apparent lack of relationship masked more subtle re-lationships within the same data.

To explore the latter possibility, the investigator interviewed each of the mothers of the 44 boys in their homes. The focus of the structured interview was on maternal attitudes and child-rearing practices relating to the support or prohibition of aggression in children. An illustrative in-terview item was: "A child should be taught to stand up and fight for his rights in his contacts with other children." On the basis of responses to such items, the mothers were divided into one group whose attitude toward aggression was encouraging ($N = 23$) and another whose attitude was discouraging ($N = 21$).

The relationship between fantasy aggression (TAT) and overt aggression (peer-nomination test) was then examined separately for the 23 boys whose mothers encouraged aggression and for the 21 boys whose mothers discouraged it. In the former group, a substantial and positive relationship was discovered: the more fantasy preoccupation with aggression, the more overt aggression. In the group of boys whose mothers discouraged aggression, a substantial and negative relationship was found: the more fantasy preoccupation with aggression, the *less* overt aggression. Clearly, the variable of maternal attitudes was operating in such a manner as to obscure the actual relationships that existed between fantasy and overt expressions of aggression in young boys. What at first appeared to be a negative result subsequently turned out to be two relationships that canceled each other within the entire group.

The complex relationship between parent-child interactions and the expression of aggression was further illuminated in a study performed by Kagan (1958). The subjects were 118 middle-class boys in the first, second, and third grades, whose ages ranged from six to ten. Teachers rated all the boys on a five-point scale indicating the tendency to start fights at the slightest provocation. On the basis of those ratings, the experimenter selected a group of extremely aggressive boys ($N = 21$) and a group of extremely nonaggressive boys ($N = 21$) made up respectively of the three most and the three least aggressive boys in each of the seven classrooms studied.

The two groups of boys were administered a modified TAT, which consisted of 13 pictures, each showing either an adult (man or woman) interacting with a boy or two boys interacting with each other. The stories the boys produced were scored for the aggression categories of fighting, property destruction, stealing, swearing, and physical aggression toward an adult, as well as for themes which indicated dependency on an adult figure, anger toward a parent, and parental anger toward a child. Finally, all boys were asked three questions:

1. Who is the boss in your house, your mother or your father?
2. If your mother said one thing and your father said something different, who would you listen to, your mother or your father?
3. Let's make believe you were bad at home and your mother and father were both home; who would punish you, your mother or your father?

(Kagan, 1958, p. 314)

Some of the results of the thematic scoring and the interpretation of the answers to the questions concerning the maternal role are presented in Fig. 10.4. Because only one of the five categories of fantasy aggression,

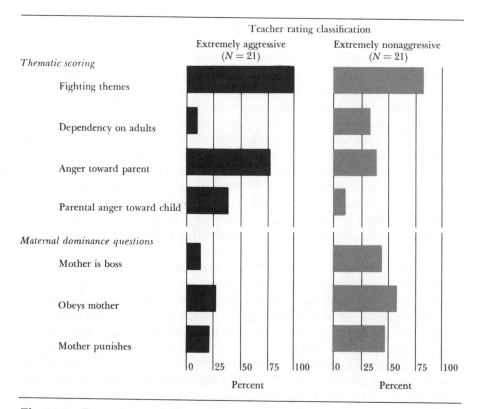

Fig. 10.4. Percentages of thematic responses and responses to maternal dominance questions in subject groups classified by teacher ratings of aggressiveness (after Kagan, 1956; 1958).

that of fighting, showed any differentiation between the two groups of boys, only that aggressive theme is included in the figure. Whereas all the extremely aggressive boys reported one or more fighting themes, only 81% of the extremely nonaggressive boys did so. Although this difference suggests a trend, it is not a large or statistically significant one, and the other four categories of fantasy aggression showed even less difference. Hence it must again be concluded that little or no relationship appears to exist between the overt and fantasy expression of aggression in middle-class boys.

However, when we consider the other thematic scoring categories, we find that significant differences in fantasy exist between the two groups. Scores for the thematic category of dependency on adults show that 33% of the nonaggressive boys but only 9% of the aggressive boys give such themes. Since the relationship between fantasy and overt expression of dependency tends to be generally positive, it may be inferred that extremely aggressive boys are less dependent on adults than extremely non-aggressive boys.

When we examine the scores for the thematic categories of anger toward parent and parental anger toward child, we again find differences between the aggressive and the nonaggressive boys. It appears that extremely aggressive boys are preoccupied, on the fantasy level, with parent-child interactions in which aggression is openly expressed. In contrast, the extremely nonaggressive boys give fewer stories of that type.

Perhaps the most interesting results are those relating to the role of the mother in the family unit. The three questions the boys were asked relate to the relative dominance of the mother and the extent to which she assumes the role of disciplinarian. It is clear from Fig. 10.4 that the non-aggressive boys perceived their mothers as the dominant member of the family unit and as its disciplinarian. We cannot say with certainty that those boys came from homes in which the mother was actually the dominant member of the family unit, but we can conclude that they perceived their mothers in that role.

It is known from other studies that mothers are generally less encouraging of aggression than are fathers. Consequently, boys who come from homes in which the mother is perceived as the dominant or influential figure will tend to be less aggressive than those from homes in which the father is so perceived. Again, although little or no relationship was found between overt and fantasy expressions of aggression in this group of middle-class boys, some of the factors which influence that relationship were clearly identified.

Aggression Anxiety

Boys from middle-class families, particularly those in which the mother discourages aggression, are apt to experience considerable guilt or anxiety concerning the expression of the trait. *Aggression anxiety* will operate to inhibit the expression of aggression in both fantasy and overt behavior. Given a measure of aggression anxiety, we should be able to predict not only the extent to which a boy will be preoccupied with fantasy aggression, but that to which his fantasy aggression will be expressed in overt behavior. We can measure indirectly the presence of aggression anxiety by scoring responses to thematic materials for themes that reflect it. When both aggression and aggression anxiety are scored from the same thematic stories, it is possible to express the potential for overt aggression as the ratio between these conflicting tendencies:

$$\frac{\text{Fantasy aggression}}{\text{Aggression anxiety}}$$

The ratio of fantasy aggression to aggression anxiety (FA/AA) provides an index of the extent to which aggression is allowed expression. Such an index can be expected to be positively related to measures of overt aggression.

Lesser (1958) obtained peer-nomination measures of aggression for 72 middle-class boys in fifth and sixth grade classes. Each score served as an index of overt aggression. The same boys were administered a modified TAT consisting of pictures showing two boys in a variety of interactions. Each story was scored for the presence of both fantasy aggression and aggression anxiety. The latter was considered present when a story included a definite instigation to aggression, but aggressive behavior did not occur, for example, when one of the figures in the story, faced by an instigation to aggression by the other, left the situation without expressing aggression.

In this particular sample of middle-class boys, a slight positive relationship was found between fantasy and overt aggression, as well as a slight negative relationship between aggression anxiety and overt aggression. Although small in magnitude, both relationships were statistically significant. By combining the two scoring categories from the thematic test, Lesser was able to compute a ratio expressing the amount of fantasy aggression in relationship to the amount of aggression anxiety: FA/AA. This ratio was found to be substantially and positively related to overt aggression as measured by the peer-nomination technique.

Whereas the experimenter found only relatively slight relationships between thematic categories of aggression and overt aggression, the combination of thematic measures into a ratio resulted in a substantial relationship between fantasy and overt expressions of aggression. This result suggests that studies of fantasy aggression should not be restricted to the simple tabulation of the number of aggressive themes given to TAT stories. When the variable of aggression anxiety is taken into account, substantial relationships may be demonstrated between fantasy and overt expressions of aggression.

SUMMARY

This chapter provided illustrations of typical findings and problems encountered in the measurement of the trait construct of aggression by observational, self-report, and indirect methods of personality assessment. A brief description was provided of the manner in which the aggression scale of the Peer Nomination Inventory was developed. Evidence for the external validity of that scale came from a study in which controlled observations of aggressive behavior were predicted from peer-nomination scores.

Aggression varies both in kind (verbal, physical, indirect) and in intensity (mild, moderate, extreme). The kind that is of greatest concern to contemporary society is extreme physical aggression. A related concern is that of the appropriate degree of control that individuals should maintain over their aggressive impulses. A number of MMPI scales reflect different aspects of the control and expression of aggression. In at least one study, MMPI measures of aggression and control were unable in general to discriminate between assaultive and nonassaultive criminal groups. Where differences did occur, it appeared that assaultive criminals were better controlled and less aggressive than nonassaultive criminals and normals.

In an attempt to clarify that puzzling result, the CPI and other test measures were administered to groups of institutionalized juvenile delinquents who had been classified according to the assaultive component of their offenses. The results for the CPI self-control scale indicated that the extremely assaultive group had significantly higher self-control scores than did the moderately assaultive group and the other non-assaultive delinquent groups. These findings and others were discussed from the standpoint of the construct of overcontrol. The possibility exists that overcontrolled individuals are more dangerous to society than are undercontrolled individuals.

The Thematic Apperception Test provides a measure of the extent to which individuals are preoccupied with aggression on the fantasy level. However, because the trait of aggression is viewed as undesirable by most segments of our society, the relationship between fantasy preoccupation with and overt expression of aggression is highly complex. In middle-class boys, the relationship between fantasy preoccupation with aggression and its overt expression is typically near zero. However, research has demonstrated that for boys whose mothers encourage aggression, fantasy and behavioral measures of aggression are positively and substantially related. For boys whose mothers discourage aggression, the relationship is negative and substantial. It has also been demonstrated that aggression is least likely to be expressed in behavior by boys whose mothers occupy the dominant role in the family unit.

Aggression anxiety serves to inhibit the behavioral expression of aggression. Experimenters have indirectly measured the presence of aggression anxiety by scoring responses to thematic materials for themes that reflect it. When both aggression and aggression anxiety are scored from the same thematic stories, it is possible to express potential overt aggression as the ratio between these two conflicting tendencies. The ratio of fantasy aggression to aggression anxiety is predictive of overt aggression in middle-class boys.

SUGGESTIONS FOR FURTHER READING

Megargee, E. I., and E. S. Menzies. The assessment and dynamics of aggression. In P. McReynolds (ed.). *Advances in Psychological Assessment,* Vol. 2. Palo Alto, Calif.: Science and Behavior Books, 1971, pp. 133–156. This chapter surveys the methods that have been employed in the assessment and prediction of aggressive behavior. Observational, self-report, and indirect methods are described, as are a variety of miscellaneous techniques.

Murstein, B. I. *Theory and Research in Projective Techniques.* New York: Wiley, 1963. A comprehensive summary of theory and research related to the Thematic Apperception Test. Chapter 11 is devoted to a consideration of the relationship between fantasy and overt aggression.

Section 4
Sexuality

11
Sexuality:
The
Biological
Viewpoint

I. **Evolutionary perspective**

II. **Behavior genetics**
   A. Selective breeding
   B. Analysis of pure strains
   C. Mechanisms

III. **Early experience**
   A. Experience and sexual re-activity
      1. Prenatal and neonatal effects
         a. Masculinization of the female
         b. Feminization of the male
      2. Postnatal experience
         a. The reproductive cycle of the ring dove
         b. Synchronization of estrous in mice and women
         c. Sexual responsivity in humans
   B. Early experience and development of sexual identity
      1. Klinefelter's syndrome
      2. Turner's syndrome
   C. Early experience and sexual response
      1. Imprinting process
      2. Development of asexuality

IV. **Summary**

V. **Suggestions for further reading**

EVOLUTIONARY PERSPECTIVE

Let us begin our discussion of human sexual behavior by referring again to our evolutionary history. We have previously described how the primitive human was forced to hunt because of decreasing supplies of available food. Humans had to hunt in order to survive. The marked environmental pressures created by this struggle for survival led to increased size and complexity of brain mass. And as described in Chapter 3, humans needed a longer period of childhood, not only to grow a larger brain, but also to educate and train it. In turn, the increased dependency of the child required the female to stay behind with her infant while the males bonded into hunting groups. This circumstance, as noted in Chapter 7, forced the males to cooperate with one another on the hunt, reduced intraspecies aggression, and produced profound changes in the nature of human socialization. These changes did not occur in sequential order; rather, they developed gradually and concurrently, each modification facilitating all others. *It is against the background of evolving human structure and behavior that we must seek to understand our present sexual practices.*

Changing environmental pressures required humans to develop a stable pair-bond relationship between the sexes. Sexual rivalries were too dangerous among the males once they were armed with weapons and had learned to use them effectively. Further, the increasingly immature infant produced heavy demands on the parents, so that parental behaviors necessarily developed with the duties shared between mother and father (Morris, 1967).

What were the factors that helped humans develop the stable pair-bond relationship? How did we learn to develop the family as we know it? A crucial factor was the prolongation of childhood. During the long growing years of adolescence, human children have the opportunity to develop deep emotional relationships with their own parents—relationships more powerful and more enduring than any other species experiences. The imitative learning that occurs during that period of life has profound consequences for adult sexual behavior; it provides the essential foundations for sexual attraction and interdependence. But not only did humans have to learn to fall in love, they had to learn to stay in love: the relationship had to endure for the increasingly longer period required to rear a family. To state it another way, the shared activities of pair bonding had to become more rewarding. Or as Morris (1967) has put it, sex had to become sexier.

How did this development occur? Largely through a remarkable evolutionary change in sexual response. Sexual drive became relatively permanent in both sexes, and human sexuality, unlike that of other mammals, was freed from a strict dependence on physiological factors. The human female experiences sexual desire throughout her monthly cycle. Since she ovulates only once each cycle, mating at other times has no propagative function. Thus most sexual behavior in our species is not concerned with producing offspring, but rather with maintaining the family unit by providing the mutual rewards of sexual satisfaction.

Human sexual behavior, as we now know it, evolved through the ever-increasing importance of psychological, rather than physiological, factors in promoting and regulating sexual motivation. During the course of evolutionary development, humans have moved further and further away from strict dependence on physiological factors underlying sexual behavior. This progression can be demonstrated most clearly through a comparison of the role of the ovulation cycle in the sexual behavior of the human female and of the female chimpanzee. In Fig. 11.1, rhythms of sexual desire in a group of American women are compared with cycles of coital behavior of female chimpanzees. The data for these two primate species are almost directly opposed; and though desire cannot be identified with behavior, the comparison clearly suggests that the factors governing sexual behavior in the human and in the chimpanzee are quite distinct. In lower mammals, the female's sexual drive is quite rigidly tied to reproductive function. The control is maintained via hormones from the ovaries. And in most of such animals, the duration of the female's receptive period is predetermined by hormonal rhythms and is not affected by the occurrence of fertile mating. Apes and monkeys show a clear-cut rhythm of sexual behavior; the highest number of coital acts occur when ovulation is imminent (Michael and Herbert, 1963). In dramatic contrast, most women experience their strongest sexual desire at times when ovulation is *least* likely (Ford and Beach, 1951; Hampson and Hampson, 1961).

If the human female's sexual drive were closely associated with ovarian hormones, as in other mammals, desire would be strongest when ovulation is about to occur, for then the concentration of the hormone, estrogen, shows a marked increase. And *in a biological sense, the relationship between desire and fertility would obviously be most adaptive; it would lead to more frequent intercourse in the woman's fertile period, thereby favoring perpetuation of the species.* Why, then, do only a small minority of women experience greatest desire at that time?

This important question provides the foundation for considering the role of social learning in human sexual behavior. Freed of the limitation of cyclical sexual drive, sexuality has become progressively more depen-

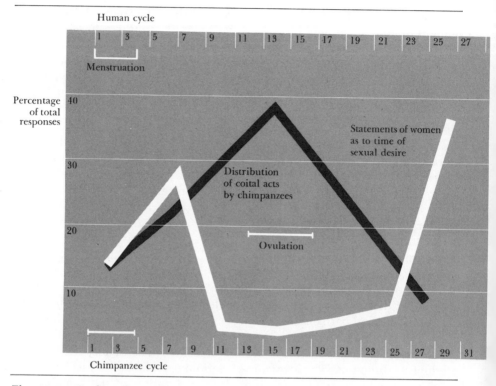

Fig. 11.1. Cycles of erotic desire described by a group of American women compared with cycles of coital behavior as shown by female chimpanzees. (Adapted from C. S. Ford and F. A. Beach, *Patterns of Sexual Behavior*, Harper, 1951. Used by permission of Harper and Row, Publishers, Inc.)

dent on experience; we are now bound by cultural taboos and stimuli rather than by hormones. That the human female's sexual behavior is not adaptive in a biological sense is understood, given our cultural taboos regarding menstruation and our social regulation of pregnancy. And in general, the increasingly more important role of the brain rather than the sexual glands in promoting and regulating human sexual behavior has made psychological factors crucially important in that behavior. The fundamental difference between human beings and other primates in their sexual practices is due primarily to the lessening of hormonal control and the dramatic increase in the extent to which social stimuli influence human eroticism (Ford and Beach, 1961).

BEHAVIOR GENETICS

Sexual behavior is preeminently of selective importance in evolutionary development. The animal most successful in mating will usually contribute the most genes to the next generation, so that the genes of the most successful individuals will become most frequent in the gene pool. We may therefore expect to find evidence of genotypic influence on the specific behaviors and motives of courtship and sexual responsivity.

Selective breeding. Rasmussen (1952) has directly assessed the contribution of the genotype to sexual motivation in rats. He selected animals for high versus low sexual responsiveness. By the fifth generation of selection, male rats of the high-drive strain would cross an electrically charged grid to reach a receptive female six times more frequently than would rats of the low-drive strain.

Similar results have been obtained in other species. Thus in domestic cockerels selected for high versus low mating speeds, the two strains separated without overlap as early as the second generation (Wood-Gush, 1960). Manning (1961) produced similar results in two strains of the fruitfly, *Drosophila melanogaster*. Males from the fast-mating line began to court as soon as they were placed with a female, in contrast to the "slow" males who required some time to adapt.

Analysis of pure strains. Strain comparisons of inbred lines in several species reveal the marked contribution of the genotype to variation in sexual responsiveness. In either guinea pigs (Goy and Jackway, 1959; 1962) or mice (McGill and Blight, 1963) strain differences in various behavioral measures of response exhibit high heritability.

Mechanisms. The physiological mechanism(s) through which genes exert their effects on sexual responsiveness is largely unknown. We do know, however, that in lower animals sexual responsiveness closely covaries with the blood level of sex hormones. Thus it appears probable that genetic effects are mediated by hormonal processes. Two major possibilities seem likely: genes directly affect the *concentration* of hormones or they alter the *neural responsiveness* to sex hormones. To date there is fragmentary but inconclusive evidence in support of both possibilities (Wood-Gush and Osborne, 1956; Goy and Jackway, 1959).

EARLY EXPERIENCE

EXPERIENCE AND SEXUAL REACTIVITY

The emphasis on constitutional-experiential interaction, which characterizes the biological approach to personality, is a most important perspective from which to examine sexual behavior. The intricate relationship of experience to those neural and glandular processes underlying mating and sexual responsiveness has been documented in humans and in numerous other species. As an introduction to the complex empirical and theoretical issues involved, we shall briefly review prenatal effects and then examine postnatal influences in humans and animals.

Prenatal and Neonatal Effects

Patterns of adult sexual behavior are established in early life. A critical part of this behavioral organization occurs in the neonatal period. The neural tissues that mediate sexual behavior are organized prenatally by hormones. Acting upon developing neural structure of the fetus and neonate, hormones determine the nature and pattern of adult sexual response.

Masculinization of the female. The organizing effect of hormones on sexual behavior was first demonstrated in guinea pigs (Phoenix et al., 1959). Female animals born to mothers who had received testosterone during pregnancy were hermaphroditic: their external genitalia were indistinguishable from those of newborn males, although internal organs were female. The adult sexual behavior of these females was more like that of normal males than like untreated female controls. Similar masculinization occurs in a female rat treated with testosterone shortly after birth. In both species, the magnitude and persistence of this effect are time-dependent: permanent masculinization results only when testosterone is administered within a critical period.

A possible parallel to these experimental animals may be found in human females with the adrenogenital syndrome, hermaphrodites whose condition arises from exposure in utero to excess androgens from the adrenal cortex.

> Some of these patients, in adulthood, have reported experiences more typically reported by normal males than by females, namely, erotic arousal with a strong genitopelvic component from the stimulation of visual and narrative perceptual material. (Money, 1965a, pp. 69–70)

Feminization of the male.   The converse effect, feminization of a male, occurs in an animal deprived of male hormones during critical developmental periods. Male rats castrated shortly after birth display feminine behavior in adulthood as a consequence of the lack of neonatal androgen (Feder and Whalen, 1965). Male rats given neonatal injections of estrogen, the female hormone, show impaired development of accessory sex organs and inadequate and bizarre sexual behavior as adults (Levine and Mullins, 1964).

A parallel is again suggested by human hermaphrodites. Individuals with the testicular feminizing syndrome are genetic males (karyotype 46, XY), and their initial embryonic differentiation is male; consequently, internal organs are male. But because the neural tissue is insensitive to androgen, the fetus is feminized by the estrogens circulating from the mother, and the external genitalia are completely female. As adults, individuals with this syndrome have normal feminine appearance. And because they are reared as girls, their gender role is feminine (Money, 1965a). Although they possess the chromosome constitution of a genetic male, these individuals can achieve a normal female adjustment (Money, Ehrhardt, and Masica, 1968). They are incapable of reproducing, but prenatal feminization has produced normal feminine appearance and fostered the development of attitudes, interests, and sexual behaviors typical of an adult female.

It is appropriate to caution (Money, 1965a) against facile comparisons of species; the inferential leap from guinea pig or rat to human is a large one, and the human syndromes described above may, in fact, bear little similarity to the animal experiments. But this does not negate the important fact evident in both laboratory study of animal and clinical observation of human: within a critical period, prenatally or shortly after birth, sex hormones exert a profound—often permanent—effect on adult sexual behavior.

Postnatal Experience

In higher mammals, and especially in humans, sexual reactivity is regulated by psychological stimuli more than by physiological ones. A major consequence of this fact is that adequate sexual response requires extensive social experience. Thus the now classic studies by Harlow show that chimpanzees deprived of social experience normal to the species exhibit ineffectual and abnormal sexual responses in adulthood. The balance of this chapter, as well as portions of the next, documents the role of early experience in the development of sexual behavior. We begin with several illustrations of the interrelationship of experience, sexual hormones, and sexual behavor.

The reproductive cycle of the ring dove.   A series of recent experiments (Lehrman, 1965) has examined the continuous interaction of environmental and hormonal factors in the reproductive cycle of the ring dove. This small relative of the domestic pigeon exhibits a regular, predictable series of behaviors that constitute its reproductive cycle. A male and a female of the species, which have had recent breeding experiences with other birds, display characteristic patterns of courtship, nest-building, and incubation when they are placed together in a cage containing suitable nesting material. Observation of the birds clearly reveals that these regular behavioral responses are not solely reactions to external stimuli; a parallel set of stimuli arise from changes in the internal condition of the animals. The behavioral changes are associated with dramatic changes in the anatomy and physiological state of the birds.

Thus the oviduct weight of the female dove will increase some 400% during the reproductive cycle, and equally striking changes occur in the condition of the ovary, the crop, the pituitary gland, and other internal structures. But neither behavioral nor anatomical change will occur unless the male and female doves are placed together in an appropriate cage. Systematic research has analyzed the origin of this cycle and elucidated the mechanisms by which it is regulated and maintained.

This research indicates that stimuli coming from the mate's behavior and from the nesting environment induce in the female a readiness to incubate, and that such readiness in turn depends on hormonal stimuli. Presumably, therefore, external stimuli exert their influence by stimulating the secretion of hormones in the glandular system of the female bird. And indeed, it can be shown that the stimuli provided by a male dove will induce ovulation in the female. Even when the male is physically separated, his behavior will induce ovarian activity; that is, if the female dove is placed in one part of a cage containing an experienced male separated by a glass partition, her oviduct weight rises more than threefold within a week's time. However, if the male has been castrated two months before the beginning of the experiment, the increase in oviduct weight is significantly smaller (Erickson and Lehrman, 1964). Thus *the stimulating effect of the male* does not merely arise from his presence but *depends,* at least in part, *on behavioral characteristics which are dependent on his hormone system.*

Synchronization of estrous in mice and women.   It has been well documented that external social stimuli influence the estrous cycles of female mice. If female mice are crowded into living quarters, they become anestrous. The onset of first estrous in juvenile mice is accelerated by contact with a mature male. A group of adult female mice, strangers to one another, will synchronize their estrous in the presence of a male, or in response to his odor. Recent research suggests that human females may also synchronize or suppress their menstrual cycles in response to social stimulation (McClintock, 1971). A significant increase in the synchronization of menstruation was observed among roommates in a college dormitory. The effect is not due to common diet, nor, apparently, does it reflect friends' awareness of one another's menstrual cycle. And, in parallel to mouse data, interaction with males shortens the ovulation cycle in college women. Some of McClintock's subjects reported that they become more regular and have shorter cycles the more often they date; women who report that they see males less than three times per week experienced significantly longer cycles than those who dated more often.

Sexual responsivity in humans.   The role of experience is central in the initiation, development, and maintenance of human sexual behavior. It is, in fact, difficult to distinguish physiological factors from those psychological influences that regulate erotic responsiveness. In marked contrast to lower mammals, whose sexuality is a direct function of the amount of appropriate hormone available to them, human sexual behavior is largely independent of chemical factors. As indicated in Fig. 11.1, the correlation between fertility and sexual receptivity, which is rigid in lower mammals and still apparent in subhuman primates, is virtually absent in the human female. Many other data reveal the progressive relaxation of hormonal control of human sexual behavior. For example, whereas ovariectomy (removal of the ovaries) permanently abolishes sexual behavior in rats, cats, dogs, or guinea pigs and tends to reduce it in adult chimpanzees, *in the human female, neither an ovariectomy nor the natural menopause impairs retention of full sexual responsiveness.* If such behavioral changes do occur, they rest on psychological rather than physiological changes consequent to either the natural or the surgical menopause. In a classic survey of comparative and cross-cultural research, Ford and Beach (1951) summarized evidence revealing the dominant role of psychological factors in regulating sexual responsiveness in the human female. They argued that case histories provide one source of such evidence, as illustrated by the following example:

> A young woman, married at 21, engaged in intercourse with her husband once or twice a week for five years until the first child was born. During the first year or two she felt sexual desire but never reached climax. After five years of marriage her desire and responsiveness had grown to be as strong

as those of her husband. At this time, however, she discovered that he was unfaithful, and for two years she refused to have intercourse. Following this lapse sexual relations were resumed; but although the wife was easily aroused, she was usually unsatisfied and rarely attained climax. Several years later, after removal of both of her ovaries, her capacity for complete response returned. At that time the habitual pattern of sexual relations included half an hour of foreplay, and a total of an hour to an hour and a half of coitus. She usually had five or six orgasms; less than two left her unsatisfied.

This single case history illustrates several general points.... The first is that full sexual responsiveness including regular orgasm may not appear in the physiologically normal woman until she has had a considerable amount of sexual experience. The second point is that normal reactivity to erotic stimulation may be lost under circumstances which have no demonstrable effect upon reproductive physiology. The emotional trauma resulting from discovery of her husband's extramarital affairs created a block in this woman's sexual response, with the result that climax became difficult or impossible to attain even though her ovaries were secreting normal amounts of sex hormones....

The third and final point illustrated by the example ... is that complete and satisfactory sexual relations are possible in the human female despite the total absence of ovarian hormones.*

It should be evident that human sexual behavior is relatively independent of those hormonal mechanisms which, in lower animals, closely regulate sexual reactivity. It is a serious error, however, to conclude that humans are totally free of hormonal influences. For example, there is evidence of a relationship between pituitary hormones and sexual behavior in adult women (Schon and Sutherland, 1963). The data derive from study of the psychological reaction to hypophysectomy, the extirpation of the pituitary gland. Hypophysectomy is occasionally performed in cases of advanced carcinoma presumed to be dependent on endocrine factors. Because the spread of breast cancer is thought to depend on estrogens and pituitary hormones, in certain cases the pituitary is removed. After surgery, hormones necessary for life are replaced, but gonadal hormones are not. Consequently menstruation ceases, and urinary level of gonadal hormones become unmeasurable. *Women who have undergone this surgical procedure show a marked decrease in sexual desire and responsiveness.*

Additional evidence of the effect of hormones on eroticism comes from the clinical study of hypogonadal men for whom androgen therapy is begun and subsequently terminated. In such cases, the absence of

---

* From C. S. Ford and F. A. Beach, *Patterns of Sexual Behavior*, Harper, 1951, p. 230. Reprinted by permission of Harper and Row, Publishers, Inc.

androgen markedly decreases sexual desire. Finally, there are synthetic hormones which have been found to have androgen-depleting or anti-androgen effects. These drugs appear to lower the plasma level of testosterone, and thus act as "chemical castration." When administered to male sex offenders they reportedly lower sexual drive and regulate behavior so as to keep the individual out of jail (Money and Ehrhardt, 1972).

We are left with two facts: disturbances in sexual functioning can and do occur as a result of psychosocial factors, despite the presence of an adequate hormonal supply; conversely, severe hormonal deprivation typically leads to a marked diminution in response. In short, while social factors often play the dominant role in the expression of human sexuality, hormonal processes also play a part. Here then—as always—social and biological factors are interrelated in the determination of human behavior.

EARLY EXPERIENCE AND DEVELOPMENT OF SEXUAL IDENTITY

We have seen that experience is critically involved in human sexual re-activity. We now consider whether the same is true of sexual identity. The variables of sexual differentiation include the following: *genetic sex,* as revealed either by nuclear cell pattern or chromosome count; *hormonal sex,* the relative predominance of androgen and estrogen; *morphological sex,* the form and structure of internal reproductive organs and external genitals; *sex of assignment and rearing,* the nature of social learning; and *psychological sex,* or gender role. Usually, of course, there is congruence for all these variables; but there are clinical conditions in which contradictions exist. The individuals involved in such cases are by definition hermaphroditic, since a contradiction exists between their predominant external genital appearance on the one hand and the chromatin pattern, hormonal pattern, or internal reproductive structures on the other. Psychological study of such individuals has revealed the surprising prepotency of psychological determinants of psychosexual orientation. We shall first discuss the biological basis for sexual differentiation and then assess the development of sexual identity.

From a biological, genetic framework, sexual identity is revealed through two indicators: *nuclear sex* and *chromosomal sex.* Some 20 years ago, a body of darkly staining chromatin was found in the cell nuclei of normal females but not in those of males. This material is now called sex chromatin, or the Barr body (for its discoverer). The procedure is to scrape a small amount of tissue from the inside of the mouth, fix and stain it, and then examine it under a light microscope. Several hundred cells are counted, and the number showing the Barr body is expressed as a percentage. A Barr body is visible in at least 20 percent of the nuclei of cells

H. Armstrong Roberts Company

from normal females but in less than one percent of the cells of normal males. A person with no chromatin bodies is labeled "chromatin negative," and one with more than 5 percent chromatin bodies is "chromatin positive." Various evidence now indicates that *the Barr body represents the second X chromosome of the female cell.* Hence the Barr body, or nuclear chromatin, serves as a screening test—a histologic marker of genetic sex identity.

The second biological indicator of sexual identity, the *karyotype,* derives from direct study of human chromosomes. A photomicrograph of the chromosomes, obtained by techniques described in Chapter 3, is arranged into a standard sequence. The karyotype of the normal female is 46,XX; that is, the normal female possesses 46 chromosomes, consisting of 44 autosomes and two sex chromosomes, both X. The normal male has a karyotype symbolized as 46,XY.

In all higher animals, sex determination follows a chromosomal mechanism. In the typical instance, the female has two X chromosomes, the male one X and one Y. This is the pattern of sex determination in mammals, including humans. A rare but interesting genotypic anomaly is that of organisms which have only one X chromosome and no Y, that is, XO organisms. This genotype occurs in the fruitfly, Drosophila, where the XO organism is an infertile male. A second karyotypic abnormality is one with two X chromosomes and one Y chromosome (XXY); in Drosophila, this organism is a fertile female. As these observations indicate, the Y chromosome in the fruitfly is *not* involved in sex determination; instead, sex determination apparently depends on the balance between the amount of X-chromosomal material and the other chromosomes (autosomes).

In the human, just as in Drosophila, the normal female possesses two X chromosomes, and the normal male possesses one X and one Y chromosome. Despite the formal similarity of the chromosome-determining mechanism in human and fruitfly, however, different behaviors are associated with these two genotypes. The XO human is an infertile female, whose condition is now known as *Turner's syndrome.* And the XXY human is an abnormal, sexually dystrophic male, whose anomaly is called *Klinefelter's syndrome.* Thus, in contrast to Drosophila, *the Y chromosome in the human does have a sex-determining action.*

Klinefelter's syndrome.   The karyotypic abnormality of Klinefelter's syndrome is the presence of an extra sex chromosome. Instead of the 46,XY pattern that would be expected, given their phenotype, the affected subjects have 47,XXY; they are usually chromatin positive and have more than 20% chromatin bodies. Because internal and external genital differentiation is male, however, the condition is seldom recognized until puberty.

A frequently reported finding is a slight but significant reduction in intellectual functioning. In population studies of the frequency of chromatin-positive males, an incidence of 2.06 per 1,000 has been found; by contrast, study of male mental defectives has shown a frequency of 9.71 chromatin-positive males per 1,000.

> ... there seems little doubt that there is a significant association between the chromatin-positive male phenotype and mental impairment. Increase in chromatin-positive males has also been found in certain surveys of penal institutions ... taken together, these data suggest that Klinefelter's syndrome provides a small but identifiable and significant segment of the society's adverse biologic heritage. (Federman, 1967, p. 33)

Turner's syndrome.   Extensive clinical observations of human hermaphrodites clearly indicate that *psychological sex* (gender role) *is not attributable to any single physical variable of sex*—that is, gonads, external genitals, or internal reproductive structures. Then where does the gender role originate? Clinical evidence suggests that our concepts of gender role and sexual orientation arise as a correlate of the kinds of learning experience we have had. Although an important part of that experience is formed by the somatic variables of sex, *hormonal functioning does not directly or automatically determine maleness or femaleness of gender role*. In fact, some humans have established a gender role consistent with the sex of their assignment and rearing despite obviously contradictory-looking genitals.

Critically important in the development of normal gender role at any age are the psychological responses of daydreaming and fantasying and role-playing games. Available evidence indicates that this component of normal psychosexual development is not dependent on specific sexual hormones.

The point can be demonstrated through the analysis of adolescent girls with Turner's syndrome (gonadal dysgenesis). Turner's syndrome is a disorder of phenotypic females characterized by short stature, sexual immaturity, and various congenital anomalies. However, the central feature is the absence of functional ovaries. Despite the undifferentiated gonads, individuals in this condition exhibit clearly feminine differentiation of both internal and external genitalia. Typically, they show no breast development, and they do not experience menarche. Most of them are chromatin negative, and the usual karyotype is 45,XO. Therefore, the central anomaly is absence of the second sex chromosome. Since they have no functioning gonadal tissue, they undergo no somatic pubertal development unless they are treated with substitute estrogens.

... nine patients ... were studied psychologically prior to substitution therapy. They were therefore totally lacking in any kind of ovarian hormone. Even so, every single one described daydreams and fantasies of romantic courtship, marriage and sometimes of heterosexual erotic play which were indistinguishable from those of normal girls. Thus a significant component of feminine psychosexual orientation was operative in these girls despite the total absence of any estrogenic hormone.*

Clinical study of Turner's syndrome thus indicates that feminine role identity is acquired through experience. Gender role is learned. And we must conclude that human sexual identity and sexual responsiveness are governed more by psychological, social, and cultural stimuli than by the biological and hormonal processes that operate exclusively in lower animals. Because sexual identity is a deep feeling, very intense and very personal, the traditional assumption has been that it must arise from something innate—some instinctive process that is not modifiable by postnatal experiences; this assumption is a serious error (Money, 1965b) that underestimates the power and permanence of learning experiences:

One must make the inference that psychosexual differentiation takes place as an active process of editing and assimilating experiences that are gender-specific and that derive ultimately from the genital appearance of the body. These experiences include apperception—visual, tactile, and proprioceptive —of one's own sexual organs. They also include the multitudinous and cumulative experiences that derive from genital appearance as it has determined the sex of assignment and rearing—experiences that are defined by the gender of personal nouns and pronouns, clothing style, haircut, and a thousand other gender-specific expectancies and attitudes.†

EARLY EXPERIENCE AND SEXUAL RESPONSE

Our discussion of imprinting (Chapter 3) revealed that adult sexual preferences can be modified by early experience; in particular, exposure to certain kinds of models will lead to selective mating practices. In one experiment cited in that discussion (Denenberg, 1964), mice that had been reared with rats showed an adult social preference for rats over mice. Other studies also indicate the role of early experience in modifying adult sexual preference. One series of experiments (Mainardi, Marsan, and Pasquali, 1965) used an apparatus consisting of a box subdivided into three

---

* From J. L. Hampson, "Determinants of psychosexual orientation," in F. A. Beach (ed.), *Sex and Behavior,* Wiley, New York, 1965, p. 121.

† From J. Money, "Psychosexual differentiation," in J. Money (ed.), *Sex Research: New Developments,* Holt, Rinehart and Winston, New York, 1965, p. 12. Reprinted by permission.

adjacent compartments of equal dimensions. The adjoining compartments were connected with each other by holes of such diameter that a mouse with a yoke around its neck could not pass through, but one without a yoke could. The experimental technique consisted of placing an unyoked mouse of one sex in the central compartment and yoked mice of the other sex in the two outside compartments. The experimenter could then assess the free sexual choice of one mouse and investigate the effects of early experience in modifying that sexual preference.

Imprinting processes. In one of the experiments reported by Mainardi and associates, young mice were reared by parents who had been per-fumed with a foreign odor; later in the apparatus described above, their sexual preference was assessed when they were allowed to choose be-tween two mice of the opposite sex, one perfumed and one normal. Fe-males, given a choice of males, strongly preferred perfumed ones. These results, obviously similar to the mechanisms previously described as im-printing, suggest that the *adult sexual preference of a female mouse is strongly influenced by early learning of parental traits.* Interpretation of the results, however, is complicated by the fact that males of the same strain did not respond in the same way.

Development of asexuality. Some fascinating experiments indicating the long-term effects of early environmental experiences on adult sexual be-havior have been reported by Kuo (1967). The experiments developed from an incidental observation:

> Many years ago in Hangchow, our laboratory had a pound with a large num-ber of stray dogs given to us by the City Health Department. These dogs were being used in laboratory courses in physiology and anatomy. Although all of them fought over food, and the males fought over the females in heat as well, there was no serious injury, no prolonged engagement in combat. One day an animal caretaker reported to me that a particular dog, the strongest male in the pound, always lay quietly beside a female in heat, but would leap up and chase away other males who approached the receptive bitch. However, for two days he made no attempt at copulation with the female. Yet, two or three days before, this same dog had a number of fights with males over the possession of this female, and in every case he had been victorious.*

This observation led Kuo to systematically investigate the effects of early punitive training on adult sexual behavior. Male chow puppies were selected for the experiments on the basis of anatomical features suggest-

---

* From Z. Y. Kuo, *The Dynamics of Behavior Development*, Random House, New York, 1967, pp. 73–74. Reprinted by permission.

ing that they would become fearless fighters. Kuo reports that dogs of this type will seldom retreat; if fighting occurs, they will continue until victorious or until severely wounded. The puppies were divided into two groups, and all were isolated as soon as they were able to eat without assistance.

Members of the first group were systematically trained in a situation that always led to a brief fight that ended in favor of the experimental animal. Each puppy ate from a dish too small for two animals in the presence of a timid and weaker but equally hungry puppy brought in to share the dish. Struggle over possession of the food dish was almost inevitable, and in the resulting fight the experimental animal invariably won. Whenever fighting did begin, the experimental animal was rewarded verbally by the human attendant. Kuo reports that after two weeks of such training, the experimental pups were intolerant of the presence of any other animal near the food dish. And after months of such training, they would attack any dog introduced into their living quarters, even when there was no competition for food. When the dogs were about a year old, females in heat were introduced into the living quarters as intruders. Kuo reports (p. 76) that of the twelve chows in the group, nine invariably attacked any female in sight, whether she was sexually receptive or not. Although the other three rushed to attack the receptive bitches at first sight, upon approaching, they began to sniff rather than to attack. All three, however, continued to attack any intruding male dog on sight.

The second group of chow puppies received very different training. One of each animal's hind legs was wired so that a mild electric shock could be administered whenever the pup showed any undesirable response, such as urination inside the living quarters. Shock was always administered concurrent with the verbal reprimand "No, no." In time, the verbal reprimand became a powerful conditioned stimulus for withdrawal responses. Throughout most of the training period, each puppy in this group was allowed to stay with a friendly and fully grown bitch. Play between the pup and the female was not interfered with, but any responses resembling sexual approaches were immediately stopped by the attendant's reprimanding "No, no." Ultimately, play activities similar to sexual responses were eliminated, and at that point, females in heat were introduced into the experimental cages. Kuo reports (p. 77) that within weeks all pups in the group learned to discriminate between males and females, becoming vicious to the males but friendly to the females, even allowing the latter to eat from the same dish. Behavior toward the females is described as friendly but asexual, regardless of the state of receptivity of the female. The dogs' behavior is best described in Kuo's own words:

Like the dog in the pound, they would act as if they were bodyguards of the females in heat. They would lie beside the receptive bitch whenever she rested on the floor and would jump up to attack or drive out any male approaching her. Whenever there were one or more males sniffing outside the wire net, the trained dog would dash to the mesh, attempting to attack the other dogs through it. . . . If we were to employ anthropomorphic language to describe the behavior of the two animals in such a situation, it would run something like this: The female acts like a sexually starved, seductive, or even sexually demanding lady-in-waiting of the ancient Chinese Imperial Palace, whereas her guard appears like a dull, uninterested, unresponsive eunuch. (pp. 77–78)

SUMMARY

This chapter has evaluated sexual reactivity and sexual identity from the three facets of the biological viewpoint: evolutionary perspective, behavior genetics, and effects of early experience.

The distinctive quality of human sexual reactivity is that it is primarily controlled by social convention rather than by hormonal processes. The human is the only species in which sexual responsiveness is free from a rigid dependence on hormonal mechanisms. From the evolutionary perspective, the shift in the determinants of sexuality—the transition from instinctive drive to social motivation—was a key development in the emergence of humans. To illustrate this shift, sexual responsiveness in human females was contrasted with that of our primate relatives. In contrast to the chimpanzee, sexual reactivity in women exhibits no dependency on ovarian hormones; neither natural menopause nor surgical removal of the ovaries necessarily reduces sexual responsiveness.

The consequences of that evolutionary change are several. Continuous sexual receptivity triggered the development of the nuclear family, which became crucial as the human infant became increasingly more dependent. In addition, the shift in control of sexuality from sexual glands to the cortex has made social learning essential to human sexuality. The result is that custom and convention control our sexual behavior; this fact, in part, defines our humanity and generates our neuroticism.

Differential reproduction is the basis of evolutionary change, and it must be anticipated that gene differences will affect many specific behaviors of courtship and sexual reactivity. Behavior-genetic analysis has demonstrated this relationship. Animal studies (selective breeding and the analysis of inbred strains) reveal large genotypic components in sexual behavior.

The neural tissues that mediate sexual behavior are organized in early life by sexual hormones. Experimental administration or deprivation of hormones during critical periods profoundly affects the structure of sexual organs and the adequacy of adult sexual behavior. Clinical parallels to these animal data are found in observation of human hermaphrodites. Females exposed to excess androgens and males feminized by maternal estrogens illustrate that permanent behavioral effects result from prenatal hormonal stimulation.

Because sexual reactivity in higher mammals is regulated more by psychological than by physiological stimuli, adequate sexual behavior requires extensive social experience. To document that fact, experimental studies with animals and clinical observations of humans were reviewed. Phenomena similar to those usually called imprinting were discussed; atypical social experience in early life leads to atypical adult sexuality. And the nature of sexual attraction is at least in part a product of early social exposure.

Concluding with a discussion of the role of social experience in determining human sexual identity, the chapter reviewed the psychological study of Turner's syndrome, a disorder in phenotypic females who possess the karyotype 45,XO. Lacking a second X chromosome, such women have no functional ovarian tissue, and they therefore have no natural estrogens. Nonetheless, individuals with Turner's syndrome, studied prior to supplementary therapy, are unmistakably feminine in their sexual identity.

Thus the theme of this chapter is the familiar one of interaction. Sexual reactivity and gender identity rest on a genetic background that has an evolutionary history; but they are profoundly altered by prenatal stimuli and early social experience.

SUGGESTIONS FOR FURTHER READING

Bardwick, J. M. *Psychology of Women: A Study of Bio-Cultural Conflicts.* New York: Harper and Row, 1971. A provocative effort to integrate diverse data to explain the origin and development of sex differences.

Ford, C. S., and F. A. Beach. *Patterns of Sexual Behavior.* New York: Harper and Row, 1951. A major survey of comparative and cross-cultural variations in sexuality. A contemporary classic.

Money, J., and A. A. Ehrhardt. *Man & Woman Boy & Girl: The Differentiation and Dimorphism of Gender Identity from Conception to Maturity.* Baltimore: Johns Hopkins University Press, 1972. Reviews sexual differentiation through a brilliant integration of clinical data with laboratory research. Hailed as the most important work on sexuality since Kinsey.

Rosenberg, B. G., and B. Sutton-Smith. *Sex and Identity.* New York: Holt, 1972. An introductory overview of the determinants and meaning of gender differences and the relationship of gender to identity.

Wickler, W. *The Sexual Code: The Social Behavior of Animals and Men.* Garden City, N.Y.: Anchor Press, 1973. A review from microbes to mammals, advancing the thesis that sexual behavior patterns function to secure social bonds.

12
Sexuality: The Experimental Viewpoint

12
Sexuality: The Experimental Viewpoint

I. **Learning processes**
   A. Classical conditioning: love
   B. Instrumental conditioning and incentive processes: sexual behaviors

II. **Perceptual processes**

III. **Cognitive processes**
   A. Relative impotence and frigidity
   B. Psychosocial aspects of sexual dysfunction

IV. **Summary**

V. **Suggestions for further reading**

LEARNING PROCESSES

Classical Conditioning: Love

Harlow's work with monkeys was discussed in Chapter 4 on dependency, in which the idea of contact comfort was presented as a basis for feelings of security. Warmth and comfort were provided by a terry cloth mother surrogate, and thus paired with contact comfort, the surrogate became a source of security for the infant monkey. Though providing security, however, the surrogate was not enough, as we shall see. Some of the monkeys so raised were isolated from all physical contact with other monkeys during the first year of life. They could hear and see other monkeys but, most important, were allowed no physical contact or interactions with them.

Harlow reports (1962) that as the monkeys grew older, they appeared to be less and less normal:

> We have seen them sitting in their cages strangely mute, staring fixedly into space, relatively indifferent to people and other monkeys. Some clutch their heads in both hands and rock back and forth—the autistic behavior pattern that we have seen in babies raised on wire surrogates. Others, when approached or even left alone, go into violent frenzies of rage, grasping and tearing at their legs with such fury that they sometimes require medical care. (p. 6)

The consequences of this early social isolation were pervasive, affecting even subsequent mating and mothering behavior. For example, when these "isolates" were paired at one year of age and permitted to grow together to sexual maturity, not a single pregnancy ensued. Even subsequent attempts to mate these monkeys with experienced breeders met with no success. The females avoided the larger males and attacked the smaller ones. The males raised by cloth surrogate mothers were no more successful. Even attempts by the experienced females to direct their inadequate sexual behavior were ineffective.

Success was finally achieved for the experimental females. Harlow found two male breeder monkeys who succeeded in impregnating the females using "gentle understanding" in one case and direct physical methods in the other. Similar success was denied their male counterparts, who maintained their monastic celibacy even under very provocative conditions.

In addition to interference with normal heterosexual behavior, there were other, even more profound effects on the cloth-raised monkeys. The females who finally became pregnant proved incapable of being good mothers. They crushed their babies against the floor of the cage, knocked them away forcefully, and refused to nurse them. The treatment of her infant by a surrogate-raised mother and the infant's behavior are illustrated in Fig. 12.1.

The failure of the surrogate-raised monkeys to engage in normal heterosexual behavior and to be adequate mothers was not a result of their being raised in a laboratory. Other monkeys born in the same laboratory and raised by monkey mothers displayed appropriate sexual behavior and provided normal maternal care for their infants. Even cloth-raised

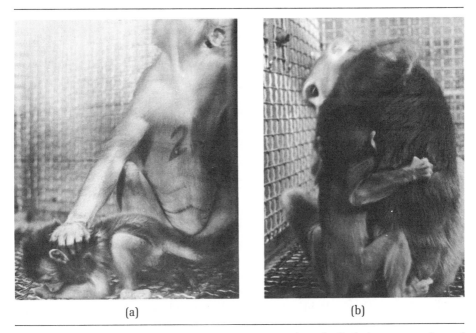

(a)   (b)

Fig. 12.1. (a) The unmothered mothers constantly rebuffed the approaches of their infants and, in addition, frequently engaged in cruel and unprovoked attacks. They struck and beat their babies, mouthed them roughly, and pushed their faces into the wire-mesh floor. (b) In strong contrast to the frailty of the maternal affectional system was the vigor and persistence of the infants' bondage to the mother—time after time, hour after hour, the infants returned, contacted, and clasped the mother in spite of being hit, kicked, and scraped unceremoniously off the mother's body. (From Harlow and Harlow, 1962. Reprinted with permission from the *Bulletin of the Menninger Clinic*, **26**, 213–214, copyright 1962 by The Menninger Foundation. Photos courtesy of Wisconsin Regional Primate Research Center.)

monkeys were able to engage in sexual behavior and provide maternal care for their young if, from the time of birth, they were allowed to play and interact with other monkeys. Whether raised by cloth surrogates or by natural mothers, monkeys can show appropriate behavior if they have the opportunity to form normal infant-infant affectional patterns. Although the surrogate-raised monkey's sense of security in an exploratory situation is based on the contact comfort provided by the surrogate, the monkey is unable to engage in normal affectionate behavior unless it has contact with other monkeys and thereby develops feelings of love and affection for its own kind. Both love and love-making require physical contact.

This latter observation is not restricted to monkeys. Like observations have been made with dogs (Scott, 1958) and sheep (Scott, 1945). Recall also our discussion in Chapter 2 where we described a study (Miller, Caul, and Mirsky, 1967) in which isolated (unloved) monkeys, unlike their normal counterparts, appeared incapable of sending or receiving, by facial expression, a warning of impending shock. In Chapter 4 on dependency, we noted a similar inefficiency of affective discrimination in human contact in the early years, which may result from such isolation or lack of attention as experienced in an orphanage. Lack of opportunity to acquire the necessary conditioning may cause the flattening and the reduced discriminability of affective states.

For affection to develop, it is essential that various affective states be consistently and reliably provoked in the presence of distinctive and discriminable cues. Out of such experience arise classically conditioned feelings and states appropriate to the social situation. Such feelings are necessary for the adequate development of heterosexual affection and of the capacity for mothering and for loving. Sexuality, in its most inclusive sense of courting, mating, and performing parental behaviors, requires affectionate and sensitive interaction with a member of the opposite sex in the same species.

Long and enduring relationships are, in turn, strengthened by what Masters and Johnson have termed the pleasure bond (1974). According to their observations, the search for pleasure, in the broadest and most comprehensive sense of the word, is a lifelong quest. Children learn to give pleasure to their parents just as they hope to receive pleasure from them. In marriage, an emotional commitment is made between partners in which mutual pleasures set the seal. The quality of marital relationships is, in fact, determined by the disparity between the shared pleasures and the inevitable displeasures that all humans experience in their social interactions. "When there is more displeasure than pleasure in a marriage, a husband and wife are more aware of the obligations of marriage than they are of its rewards. Their bond is characterized as a commitment of obligation." (p. 53)

On the other hand, where the pleasure exceeds the displeasure, there is a commitment of mutual concern rather than obligation. Both marriage partners will meet their commitments because they feel *impelled* rather than *compelled* to do so.

Obviously, the quality of sexual relations constitutes an important element in the pleasure bond. Where sexual relations are mutually satisfying, strong affectional ties develop between partners. These positive feelings generalize to nonsexual situations and improve the quality of all the transactions that occur between the partners.

Instrumental Conditioning and Incentive Processes: Sexual Behaviors

Rewards are often recommended for use in attempts to establish behavior, because they emphasize what is to be done. On the other hand, punishment is the effective agent in the establishment of most inhibitions, because it emphasizes what must not be done. Sexuality includes not only acts but omissions of acts.

Moreover, the classical conditioning of affective responses seems to provide the basis on which adequate heterosexual instrumental behavior develops. Here we will consider the role that reward plays in shaping and directing the execution of heterosexual behaviors and the conditions and circumstances under which such behaviors occur.

As the work of Harlow (1962) has shown, early physical contact with other animals is an important and necessary condition to a later ability to engage in appropriate sexual behaviors. Presumably, immature forms of play and physical contact provide the pleasurable states that reinforce the instrumental responses necessary for carrying out and engaging in later sexual activity. With a variety of animals, early rough and tumble play is prerequisite to the later development of appropriate sexual behaviors. With humans a similar form of gradual shaping occurs as a result of the practice and execution of a variety of instrumental responses, directed at first toward peers of both sexes and later toward members of the opposite sex. Both males and females go through a graded series of experiences and instrumental acts in a highly regularized way. The sequence usually begins with hand-holding and incidental, playful touching, and it then progresses through kissing to the more demanding instrumental acts of courting, mating, and love-making. A person with experience in acts late in the sequence has usually experienced and practiced all the earlier acts as well.

The most remarkable feature of sexual behavior in the human is that it is a complicated collection of instrumental social actions. The acts are far more complicated than the assumption of a posture, as in monkeys, or the provision of a display, as in birds; the human sexual display and posturing includes not only the preparatory grooming and presentation of one's self but the instrumental capacity to manage the interaction with another person and to control the social setting. Such acts are practiced in miniature in a variety of nonsexual settings, and the skills are acquired in accordance with the rewards and punishments they yield. Only much later in life are the bits and pieces combined into larger units for the expression of sexuality, ranging from mere indications of gender to actual courting behaviors. At that point, the outcome of any sexual encounter—whether at a low- or a high-intensity level—provides reinforcement for the molar instrumental response units that are formed from previous learning. Such combinations then begin to take the form of the individual's instrumental sexual response system, i.e., his or her sexuality.

For a variety of reasons, some individuals of both sexes are unable to perform one or more of the behaviors required to achieve orgasm. It is illustrative to briefly examine the applications of learning techniques employed by Masters and Johnson to alleviate such sexual dysfunctions as impotence, premature ejaculation, retarded ejaculation, and inorgasmic potential in women (1970; 1974).

To begin with, a husband and wife are treated together. The reason is quite straightforward: sexual intercourse is an intense and intimate personal-social relationship in which the satisfaction of both partners is dependent upon their ability to work together as a team so as to achieve mutual sexual arousal and satisfaction. Indeed, mutual satisfaction is the foundation of the pleasure bond.

During the first few days of the two-week course, the partners are encouraged to spend periods of time in their room, unclothed. They are instructed to touch, fondle, and massage each other. The purpose is to allow each partner to discover the specific body areas which provide maximum sensual pleasure. However, touching the genital regions and the wife's breasts is specifically forbidden during this stage of therapy. The emphasis is completely upon exploration in giving pleasure without the imposition of overt sexual performance pressures that may be anxiety-producing to one or both of the partners. In many ways, the procedures are reminiscent of shaping (see Chapter 2): "Instead of being suggested . . . to go all the way from A to Z sexually on any specific occasion, it is suggested that marital units go from A to B one day, possibly from A to C or D the next. . . ." (1970, p. 205)

The withholding of genital contact during the first few days of therapy serves an additional purpose—by increasing the deprivation level, the incentive value of the reinforcement increases. The point is illustrated in a study in which male subjects described the frequency with which they had orgasms and the period of time which had elapsed since the most recent sexual experience (Epstein, 1962). The procedure was based on the assumption that persons whose most recent orgasm places them early in their interim cycle are relatively satiated compared to those who are about due. Epstein found that his college male subjects who were not inhibited about sex (had low sex guilt) showed a direct relationship between sexual responses on a projective test (Thematic Apperception Test) and their level of sexual deprivation. When other male subjects were exposed to life-size projections of nude women, there was a direct relationship between sexual deprivation and the measured level of sexual arousal. Events and situations which increase the sexual drive, either through deprivation or extra stimulation, can serve to enhance the kinds of objects perceived as sexually relevant and potential sources of sexual gratification.

In the Masters and Johnson sexual therapy, the period of nongenital contact also serves as encouragement for the dysfunctioning male and his marital partner. In the absence of performance expectations, penile erections occur quite spontaneously during the sensate focus phase of treatment. These spontaneous erections set the stage for manipulative play (teasing technique) with the erective reaction. In sessions lasting up to a half hour, the marital couple engages in slow, nondemanding sexual play during which the male may undergo several erections and losses of erections. Thus, the male gains some measure of control over his erective capacity and the female is sexually stimulated by the opportunity to produce an erection in her partner.

By the time the marital couple is ready for coital experience, they have become quite adept at communicating, often in a nonverbal fashion, their likes and dislikes, pleasures and aversions. They have, in effect, developed a feedback system which selectively rewards and encourages behavior that enhances each other's sexual pleasures. The female, for example, is encouraged to guide the hand of the male to the vaginal area that she wishes to have stimulated, thus obviating clumsy and sometimes painful manipulation.

Throughout all of the therapy period, one theme predominates: the individual should value sexual experiences. Unless each partner is able to internalize a value system that regards sex as pleasurable and desirable, the ability to perform the skills necessary for satisfactory sexual relations will be impaired. In short, the pleasure arising out of the activity is sufficient justification for the activity.

PERCEPTUAL PROCESSES

Schachter (1967) has proposed that physiological changes may serve as a stimulus or cue which is cognitively interpreted as feelings. Such feelings, however, elicit cognitive efforts to define the nature of the situation which precipitated them. Specific emotional behavior results when those feelings can be attributed to some perceived condition or situation in the external environment.

In short, internal events can function as cues or stimuli which have a cognitive representation and which then provide constraints for the perception and interpretation of external stimulus events. Valins (1966) suggests, in light of Schachter's research, that if the subject were pharmacologically aroused and shown a slide of a nude female, he would interpret his internal sensations as due to the nude stimulus and thus would label the girl as more attractive than he would if he had been injected with a placebo. However, Valins suggests that if it is the cognition of the internal event which influences emotional behavior, then the same influence should be observed when the subject thinks he has reacted to a given stimulus. For example, if a subject thought his heart rate had changed when he looked at the slide of a nude girl, he would perceive the girl as more attractive or appealing because of the cognition: "That girl has affected my heart rate."

To test his hypothesis, Valins showed male subjects ten slides of nude females while they were hearing sounds they thought were their own heart beats. For one group of subjects, the heart rates increased markedly to five of the slides but not to the other slides. A second group of subjects heard a marked decrease of their bogus heart rates to five of the slides and no change to the other five. Of the slides to which the subjects heard a change, whether increase or decrease, they rated the girls as more attractive both during the experiment proper and in an interview conducted four to five weeks later. In addition, as a remuneration for participation in the experiment they more frequently chose a picture of a nude which had been accompanied by a change in heart rate.

A cognitive process—in this case a fairly explicit one induced by a pronounced change in heart rate—influenced the perception, i.e., the kind of meaning imposed on the slides. In a similar fashion, our acquired values, feelings, behaviors, and cognitions provide internalized constraints which help to determine the way in which a person perceives the external world. The perceptual processes will operate in concert with one's acquired dispositions and cognitions. A particular female slide, for example, will be seen as sexually provocative to the extent that the internal constraints permit the interpretation or perception of the situation as sexually relevant.

COGNITIVE PROCESSES

Sexuality or sexual expression is typically thought of as primarily a reflexive or emotional response. However, higher processes play an important role in any consideration of sexuality. One's cognitive system of beliefs imposes important constraints not only on perceptions but also on sexual effectiveness and the functioning of the biological system. The important work of Masters and Johnson (1966; 1970) provides empirical documentation for the role of higher processes as corroboration of what has been reported clinically for some time.

Relative Impotence and Frigidity

The inability to function sexually with success is referred to as impotence in the male and frigidity in the female. Impotence or frigidity is relative, however, not something a person either has or does not have. There are situations and circumstances in which any person can function effectively in sexual performance and others in which he or she cannot.

In the Masters and Johnson research program, some 7,500 complete sexual-response cycles were studied in female subjects, and more than 2,500 ejaculatory experiences of male subjects were recorded. The measurements were made during automanipulative, artificial coital, and coital activities. The highest concentration of failures occurred during the orientation program, when potential subjects were introduced to the study and to the demands that would be made on them. The orientation provided for a trial participation so that the investigators could evaluate the subjects and the subjects themselves could evaluate their suitability for the study. The demands for a sexual performance under laboratory conditions of observation, recording, and measurement are sufficiently inhibiting for some subjects to cause inability to function sexually.

Among subjects accepted for the study, there were some 321 recorded incidents of failure to attain orgasm during coital activity. More males than females failed (213 versus 108). The primary male failure lay in obtaining or maintaining an erection sufficient for effective sexual performance. These occasional failures were of individual subjects who usually had no difficulty maintaining an erection in an automanipulative situation, during laboratory coital tests, or in the privacy of their bedroom. There were also occasional female failures to reach an orgasmic level.

The distractions of the semipublic laboratory performance can produce constraints which preclude the ability to function sexually. In natural conditions, various circumstances and situations can similarly impose restrictions on sexuality. Preoccupation with other problems or responsibilities is perhaps the major deterrent to male as well as female sexuality.

Masters and Johnson note that the attainment of orgasm in the female has never been afforded the same status as ejaculation by the male. They are unable to account for the extent to which female orgasmic experience is often neglected and therefore not acknowledged as a naturally occurring psychophysiological response. The subjects who volunteered for the laboratory research may of course be atypical in many ways; however, Masters and Johnson report:

> . . . The ability to achieve orgasm in response to effective sexual stimulation was the only constant factor demonstrated by all active female participants. This observation might be considered to support the concept that sexual response to orgasm is the physiologic prerogative of most women, but its achievement in our culture may be more dependent upon psychosexual acceptance of sexuality. . . .
>
> . . . The development of sexual responsiveness to orgasmic level, identifiable subjectively, must be a cumulative result of interaction between the individual female's hereditary endowment and the psychosocial influence to which it is exposed. The element of time must be assumed to be a finally determining factor, as it accrues the experience of social and psychosexual maturation. . . .*

The important concept is that sexual performance to orgasmic and ejaculatory levels is within the physiological range of response under effective stimulation. The occurrence and manifestation of this sexuality is dependent on many social and psychological factors which provide the definition of effective stimulation and the limiting constraints and inhibitions for sexuality.

Psychosocial Aspects of Sexual Dysfunction

Most forms of disordered sexual potency in the male and sexual responsiveness in the female qualify as psychosomatic disorders. The impotency or frigidity itself is the target symptom or overt expression of what is best conceptualized in a psychosocial context.

---

* From W. H. Masters and V. E. Johnson, *Human Sexual Response*, Little, Brown and Company, Boston, 1966, pp. 139–140. Reprinted by permission.

Treatment of sexually dysfunctioning individuals, as advocated by Masters and Johnson, starts out with the basic premise that sexual activity to the point of orgasm is a natural function that is the physiological prerogative of everyone. Moreover, most sexual dysfunction is psychosocial in nature, stemming from the internalization of cultural constraints and prohibitions. It follows then that a major goal of sex therapy is to alter the person's cognitions about sex. For the male, these altered cognitions include the acceptance of the female as an active and joyful participant in sexual intercourse, rather than as a passive recipient of masculine favors. For her part, the female should regard herself as an equal partner in a shared psychosexual experience rather than a person to whom the male is doing something.

The treatment of sexual dysfunction, then, focuses on both the cognitive and physical aspects of sex. Note that there is no requirement that all underlying psychological conflicts be resolved prior to undertaking sexual therapy. As in behavior modification, emphasis is upon treating the symptom. If undesirable behaviors have been learned, they can be unlearned. In this context, the behaviors of both male and female may be regarded as operants that can be modified or shaped by appropriate reinforcement. Thus there is a great deal of concern with the mechanical aspects of sex—the loci where stimulation produces varying degrees of arousal, insertion of the penis, copulating positions, etc. However, since anxiety plays a strong role in the dysfunctioning individual, cognitive elements are not neglected. The person is encouraged to think about sex as a normal, pleasurable activity. Such thoughts are accompanied by physical pleasure, as in the sensate focus stage. Through classical conditioning, sex comes to be associated with desirable rather than anxiety-producing sensations and feelings.

The type of approach that Masters and Johnson have taken to sex represents a new view of sex that would have been unthinkable a couple of decades ago. To some it represents a bold new departure toward the full realization of the potential that exists in all of us. To others, such as psychiatrist Natalie Shainess, the "sex experts" debase sex (1973) because, among other things, they treat the problem rather than the individual. Further, she objects to the research on both ethical and methodological grounds.

Notwithstanding some cogent objections, the new era in sex relations heralded by Masters and Johnson is compatible with the experimental viewpoint. It regards sex as behavior which has much in common with other skills. For example, any one of us can learn to play tennis with some degree of skill. The techniques of grips, positions, distributions of weights can be taught. With skill in tennis also comes greater enjoyment. In sexual behavior, techniques can also be imparted that provide maximum pleasure and freedom for each partner. From the experimental viewpoint, this is desirable since good sexual behavior enhances love and love, in turn, frees a person for sexual responsiveness. In this sense, training in the mechanics of sex does not debase sex but permits a greater realization of the potential in all of us.

SUMMARY

The expression of human sexuality encompasses the entire breadth of the psychological processes of personality and of an individual's learned dispositions. The sexual act itself is but an extremely specific expression of the entire organization of human emotional, perceptual, and cognitive complexity. The heterosexual-affective system is intimately intertwined; early interaction with parents and peers provides for the development of the highly differentiated affective reactions and feelings necessary for love and social attachments. These attachments, in turn, establish conditions for love-making and ensure the continuation of the affective interactions essential to the fostering of future love and social attachment. In addition, these early interactions provide an opportunity for the acquisition of the many instrumental responses, such as touching, joking, smiling, helping, holding, etc., which are later combined in the more complex social acts of courting and mating.

In humans, the learned dimensions in terms of which sexuality is conceptualized set limits on the conditions under which sexual expression and satisfaction can occur. Contemporary culture is removing cognitive inhibitions, as is exemplified by the work of Masters and Johnson. The sexual act has been exhaustively studied under a variety of conditions, and treatment programs are available for impotent males and inorgasmic females. Such treatment involves strong cognitive components, since individuals must learn to value sexuality and sensual pleasures if they are to gain sexual freedom.

SUGGESTIONS FOR FURTHER READING

Masters, W. H., and V. E. Johnson. *Human Sexual Inadequacy.* Boston: Little, Brown, 1970. Masters and Johnson report the techniques they developed for investigating and treating human sexual inadequacy. Their work pioneered a new kind of "behavioral" treatment program, which has altered popular, professional, and scientific views of sexuality.

Masters, W. H., and V. E. Johnson. *The Pleasure Bond: A New Look at Sexuality and Commitment.* Boston: Little, Brown, 1974. Masters and Johnson's studies have focused attention upon sexuality as a topic for serious scientific investigation. They have now considered the social implications of their work, a responsible position for scientists to assume, but one frequently neglected. The reader will find this book interesting in its own right as part of the literature of the sexual revolution, especially if the reader is also familiar with their research.

13
Sexuality: The Social Viewpoint

I. **Models**
  A. Arousal
  B. Satiation
  C. Behavior

II. **Roles: sex identification**
  A. Imitation
  B. Theories of identification
  C. Cognitive-developmental
     factors

III. **Cultures**
  A. Sex roles across cultures
  B. The status of women
     1. In primitive cultures
     2. In technological cultures
     3. The female role in the
        mass media

IV. **Summary**

V. **Suggestions for further reading**

MODELS

In recent years a storm of controversy has raged about the easy accessibility in the media of explicit sexual materials. Although many issues are involved, the main thrust of inquiry has focused on two questions: (1) What constitutes obscene and pornographic material? (2) What are the effects on various aspects of behavior of exposure to these materials? The Supreme Court decision of 1973 provided an answer, however unsatisfactory, to the first question—obscenity is defined by local customs and traditions. The answer to the second question is being sought by increasing numbers of researchers in the behavioral sciences. Does the viewing or reading of sexually explicit material lead to sexual arousal? If it does, is there a satiation effect with continued exposure or does chronic exposure create voracious sexual appetites in the viewers? What about the effects upon behavior? Does exposure to obscene and pornographic materials lead to increased frequency of sexual contacts, alter the nature of the contacts, and encourage, through imitation, sexual offenses by those considered most vulnerable to erotic materials, the juvenile population? These are a few of the questions to which we shall address our inquiries in this section.

Arousal

On the basis of common sense, we might suppose that the more explicit and detailed the erotic situations represented, the greater the sexual arousal. Byrne and Lamberth (1970) investigated the relationship between degree of explicitness and amount of sexual arousal. They presented 19 sexual themes in three media—photographic, literary, and imaginary. In the imaginary condition, subjects read a description of each of 19 erotic situations such as "oral-genital contact, two males" and were asked to imagine "What they would be like" in movies, books, etc.

The subjects were 42 young married people. The males and females among them did not differ from each other in overall arousal to the pornography presented, although there were differences in response to certain themes. The most interesting finding was that less sexually explicit media generate more sexual arousal than more sexually explicit media. Whereas males judged photographic slides and written materials equally arousing, and females judged literary materials more arousing than photographic, both males and females reported the highest levels of arousal when they were asked to imagine sexual themes without visual aids. In fact, the levels of arousal were almost twice as high as those reported in response to literary stimuli.

The greater arousal value of imagination was also observed in a study of films with erotic sequences deleted or edited. It was found, for example, that persons reported higher levels of arousal to films which deleted a rape scene, but implied its occurrence, than to an identical film which retained the sequence (Tannenbaum, 1970).

Satiation

Does repeated exposure to sexually explicit materials lead to a high level of chronic sexual excitement, or does the process of satiation set in, whereby the erotic material loses the capacity to arouse the viewer?

This question was investigated in a study employing 23 male university students (Howard et al., 1970). During every weekday over a period of 3 weeks, each subject spent 90 minutes alone in a room that contained a large collection of both erotic and nonerotic film and textual materials. Subjects were free to read whatever they wished during these daily sessions. Level of psychosexual stimulation was assessed by both self-reports and physiological measures (penile volume, urinary acid phosphatase, and heart rate). Interest in the materials was measured in terms of the proportion of time that subjects spent in reading or viewing erotic versus nonerotic materials.

During the opening sessions of the experiment, interest in the erotic materials was high. Subjects spent most of their time reading or looking at erotic materials. High levels of psychosexual arousal were indicated by the physiological measures. As the experiment progressed, however, both interest in the erotic material and the physiological measures of arousal evidenced large and statistically significant declines. The addition of novel sexual material following the eleventh session led to a marked increase in arousal, but this was followed immediately by a return to the declining levels of stimulation. Although complete satiation of interest and arousal did not occur in this experiment, there was little doubt that the subjects' interests were moving in the direction of satiation. In fact, 9 weeks after the exposure sessions ended, all subjects reported boredom with erotic materials. A number of subjects also declined private opportunities to view erotica.

Behavior

Although exposure to erotic stimuli clearly leads to heightened psychosexual arousal in most males and females, it is not clear whether this stimulation also leads to additional sexual behavior. Two recent surveys, one conducted in the United States (Abelson et al., 1970) and the other in Sweden (Zetterberg, 1970), have shown that degree of exposure to erotic material and frequency of sexual activity are associated. This finding, of course, does not establish a causal relationship between the two. At least three different possibilities exist: (1) high frequency of sexual behavior predisposes the individual to seek out erotic materials; (2) early and frequent exposure to erotic materials influences the user to seek out early and frequent sexual contacts; (3) the two variables—frequency of exposure to erotic materials and frequency of sexual behavior—are related to a third variable. For example, an individual might be a member of a peer group that encourages or discourages both activities.

We pointed out in Chapter 2 that surveys do not establish causal relationships but experimental procedures do. Until recently, it was unthinkable to investigate sexual behaviors of humans in an experimental setting. In the past few years, however, sexual behavior has come increasingly under laboratory study. The broadest generalization arising from these studies appears to be that exposure to erotic material may activate sexual behavior on a temporary basis (Kutchinsky, 1970; Mann et al., 1970) but does not produce mid- or long-term effects. Rather, it appears that well-established patterns of sexual behavior are quite stable and not readily modified by sexually explicit stimuli. In other words, a person who is sexually active before viewing erotic materials will remain so after exposure (Byrne and Lamberth, 1970). Conversely, individuals with relatively low rates of sexual activity prior to exposure will remain relatively inactive subsequent to exposure (Amoroso et al., 1970).

Moreover, for what they're worth, crime statistics among juvenile offenders do not support the view that the greater availability of sexually explicit materials during recent years has lead to an increase in sexual offenses among those under 18 years of age. Table 13.1 presents arrest

Table 13.1 Number and percentage change in juvenile arrests in 1960 and 1971. (Source: *The American Almanac—The Statistical Abstract of the U.S.*, 1974. Bureau of Census.)

Offense	1960	1971	Percent change
All offenses, sexual and nonsexual	404,507	833,562	106.07
All sex offenses	8,802	7,917	−11.18
Forcible rape	1,192	2,359	+97.90
Prostitution and commercialized vice	123	343	178.86
Other sex offenses	6,587	5,215	−20.83
All non-sex offenses	395,705	825,645	108.65

data among juveniles in 1960 and 1971. Note that the total number of arrests for all nonsexual offenses increased by more than 108%. There is, however, an actual decline in the number of arrests for all sexual offenses, although rape and prostitution evidence a large increase.

Surprising as it may seem, presently available research concerning the relationship between early exposure to erotic material and tendency to become a sexual offender justifies one conclusion: when compared to normal controls, adult sex offenders experienced little exposure to sexually explicit material during adolescence (Cook and Fosen, 1970; Johnson et al., 1970). Goldstein and his associates found little adolescent experience with photographic depictions of human coitus among adults committing sex offenses. The normal adult males encountered such depictions with far greater frequency during their adolescent years (Goldstein et al., 1970). As a broad generalization, it appears that sex offenders differ from other adults in both the frequency and the kinds of erotic material experienced during adolescence. The experiences of sex offenders are largely limited to less explicit erotica.

ROLES
sex identification

The topic of sex includes not only sexual behavior as such but also maleness and femaleness, or sex role. This section will be concerned with sex roles and with the social factors which encourage enduring sex differences in behavior. Consistent with the previous emphasis on models as an important influence on personality development, modeling will be stressed as a primary means of acquiring the set of behaviors which constitute sex roles.

Imitation

Once children are grown, it is common for parents to note with satisfaction—and for children to realize with dismay—the countless ways in which the children have modeled their behavior after that of their parents. It is likely that during childhood children's behavior is not so much dependent on what they are told to do as on what they observe others, including parents, actually doing. For example, it is common to see young girls scolding their dolls with the same words and gestures used by their mothers to scold them, behavior which is not likely to have been directly taught. For that matter, the very practice of giving dolls to girls and me-

Photograph by Harold M. Lambert

chanical toys to boys probably serves to foster in children the imitative development of interests and behavior which are respectively character-istic of the mother and the father and of males and females in general. Parents provide models, give distinctive toys, assign different chores, and communicate different aspirations and expectations to male and female offspring. According to a social-learning view of sex-role development (Mischel, 1966), the members of the two sexes tend to take on different roles and engage in behaviors peculiar to their own sex as a consequence of this differential treatment.

Theories of Identification

Of course the extent to which a child develops the behavioral characteristics of one parent rather than the other varies considerably. *Identification,* a term originating with Freud, has come to refer to the tendency of a child to adopt one of the two parents as a primary model. Explaining why the child imitates the same-sex or the opposite-sex parental figure presents an interesting problem, and as a consequence, several theoretical positions have been advanced to account for which parent a child will identify with. One explanation emphasizes the role of primary rewards administered by parents and the resulting *secondary-reward value* that the parent's behavior acquires (Mowrer, 1950). When the parent satisfies the child's primary needs for food, water, and physical contact, various characteristics of the parent develop secondary-reward value because of their constant association with these primary satisfactions. Once the mother or father's behavior has acquired a reward value of its own, the child is in a position to earn rewards merely by reproducing or imitating that behavior.

Freud's concept of *anaclitic identification* also assumes that the child first develops a dependent relationship with an adult (usually the mother). Then, as the child develops, the mother normally withdraws her nurturance but the child, fearing the loss of her love, introjects or adopts her characteristics as a way of holding on to her.

The *status-envy theory* of identification holds that the child will identify with the adult in the family who receives the most rewards (Whiting, 1960). In this view affection, attention, food, and care are considered resources for which the child competes with others. It is assumed that children will envy the primary adult consumer of those things to the extent that they feel deprived of them, and that they will come to identify with the adult by playing the role of that person in fantasy. This approach is primarily based on another of Freud's concepts, *defensive or aggressive identification*. Freud believed this process, which concerns only boys, to be a product of the resolution of the Oedipus complex. The son is said to identify with the father and take on his characteristics in order to keep the father, his rival, from punishing him for his incestuous desires toward his mother. Thus fear of punishment motivates defensive identification in the same way that fear of loss of love underlies anaclitic identification.

In addition to the first explanation (secondary reward) and the second (status-envy), there is another possible explanation: children may identify with the most powerful parent. In contrast to the status-envy position, in which the person who *receives* rewards is imitated, a *social-power theory* holds that the person who *controls* the rewards will be identified with.

To test the relative merit of the social-power, status-envy, and secondary-reward theories of identification, an experiment was conducted with nursery school children as subjects (Bandura, Ross, and Ross, 1963b). Each child was exposed to two models, a male and a female, so that the trio formed a laboratory version of a family. There were two basic kinds of family situations simulated. In the first, one adult took the role of controller of the resources and rewards, and the other adult took the role of consumer. The latter received rewards from the former while the child was ignored. In the second kind of situation, one adult again controlled the resources but rewarded the child to the exclusion of the other adult. Half the subjects in each condition were boys and half were girls; and to study same-sex and opposite-sex identification, half the boys and girls in each condition had a male model as controller (as in a husband-dominant family), and half had a female as controller (as in a wife-dominant family). Table 13.2 gives the pattern of the experiment.

In each condition the adult controller had two boxes of highly attractive toys. In the *Adult consumer condition* the other adult asked for and received permission to play with the toys. While the child was left with

---

Table 13.2 Design of the sex identification experiment.

		Adult consumer condition	Child consumer condition
	Controller	Male adult	Male adult
Husband-dominant family	Consumer	Female adult	Child*
	Ignored	Child*	Female adult
	Controller	Female adult	Female adult
Wife-dominant family	Consumer	Male adult	Child*
	Ignored	Child*	Male adult

* In half the situations, the child was male; in the other half, female.

a few uninteresting playthings, the controller offered the consumer miniature pinball machines, mechanical sparkling toys, kaleidoscopes, dolls,
and other toys. The controller played darts with the adult consumer and
throughout the 20-minute period gave various social rewards in the form
of praise, approval, and positive attention. During the course of the interaction, the consumer demonstrated by such practices as asking permission
that the controller had power over these prized resources and demonstrated by verbalizing positive affect that he or she enjoyed being the
consumer. The *Child consumer condition* was quite similar except that the
child had the opportunity to play with the toys and receive social rewards
from the controller while the other adult read a book and was ignored.

Finally, in order to test the capacity of the various models (controller,
consumer, and passive adult) to elicit imitation, the controller announced
a surprise game that everyone could play. The game consisted merely of
guessing which of two boxes contained a picture sticker, but in the course
of their turns, the two adult models provided the child with a variety of
novel responses to imitate. For example, each model selected a "thinking
cap" with a different-colored feather. The controller selected one with a
green feather, said "Feather in the front," and put the hat on with the
feather forward. Then the other adult selected a hat with a yellow feather,
remarked "Feather in the back," and put the hat on in that manner. The
child's behavior could be scored for imitation of hat choice, verbal response, and hat placement. Among other responses which the child could
later choose to imitate, the investigators described some made by the controller.

> As soon as the experimenter gave the signal for the first trial, the controller
> remarked, "Forward march" and began marching slowly toward the desig-
> nated box repeating, "March, march, march." When he reached the box he
> said, "Sock him," hit the doll aggressively off the box, opened the lid and
> yelled, "Bingo," as he reached down for the sticker. He then remarked,
> "Lickit-sticket," as he pressed on the picture sticker with his thumb in the
> upper right quadrant of a 24 × 24 inch sheet of plain white paper.... (Ban-
> dura, Ross, and Ross, 1963b, p. 530)

The consumer performed a parallel but different series of responses with
different verbalizations.

After the adult models had their turns, the child who had been observing them took a turn. The models left the room, but unknown to the
child, raters made a checklist of the responses copied. As usual, more
than one independent rating was made on some of the subjects to check
on the reliability of the scoring.

To the extent that the experimental arrangement was really analogous
to a family in terms of its power relationships, the imitation scores sup-

ported the social-power theory of identification. *Regardless of whether the child or the rival adult was rewarded by the controller, the model with the rewarding power was imitated much more than either the rewarded or the ignored competing model.* There was no support for a defensive or status-envy type of identification with the rival adult consumer; the rewarding adult (controller) was clearly preferred as a model. This preference was generally maintained even when the child and the powerful adult were of opposite sexes, as would be the case in cross-sex identification. However, girls were more prone to imitate men than boys were to imitate women. In fact, when the man was ignored and a boy was rewarded by the woman, there was a slight tendency for the boy to model him rather than the rewarding woman and express sympathy for him. The greater tendency of girls than of boys to show cross-sex modeling reflects the greater cultural tolerance for masculine behavior in girls than for feminine behavior in boys and the higher status of male-role behavior. The investigators stress that the clue to explaining cross-sex identification probably lies in the power distribution within the family and the consequences for acquiring sex-role behavior through modeling.

Of course, the children did not exclusively choose one of the two adults to model. Although they usually did choose one as the primary source of behavior, they displayed responses made by both the dominant and the subordinate models. Similarly, it is unlikely that in the real family situation children become merely junior versions of one or the other parent; rather they represent an original blend of the parents' responses and characteristics.

An additional observation made by the experimenters was that some of the children apparently believed that only the male adult could really possess the resources they had seen. Even when the woman dispensed the rewards and the man was ignored and denied permission to play, the children believed that the things really belonged to him. They made numerous comments, such as "He's the man it's all his because he's a daddy. Mommy never really has things belong to her." (p. 533) Clearly the culturally defined role differentiations for men and women had already been well instilled in these subjects.

Recent studies of interactions of children with their teachers have revealed subtle but important transactions that differentially affect the identification of boys and girls. In one study, it was found that female teachers dispense positive reinforcement to boys and girls about the same proportion of times. However, since the teachers have instructional contacts with girls with greater frequency than with boys, boys experience fewer positive transactions with their teachers than do girls (Biber, Miller, and Dyer, 1972). Indeed, similar types of pupil-teacher interactions were found among preschool boys and girls and their teachers (Lee and Wolinsky, 1973). Both female and male teachers expressed greater frequency of disapproval of the boys than of girls. However, male teachers provided a greater number of positive reinforcements to boys and were more likely to assign them leadership positions. As a result, the boys showed a strong tendency to affiliate with male teachers and regarded themselves as being preferred to girls by male teachers. The girls, on the other hand, saw themselves as being preferred over boys by teachers of both sexes.

Cognitive-developmental Factors

Before concluding that sex typing is solely a matter of imitating the behavior of the dominant parent, one should note that there are apparently other factors. By and large, children seem to choose the same-sex parent as their primary source of identification, and this choice obviously is not solely dependent on the same-sex parent's being the most powerful member of the family. Although it is clear that the boy's early behavior is elaborated into that of a masculine man or an effeminate man by imitation, some investigators hold that the most important factor in the identification process is the boy's realization that he is a boy and the girl's that she is a girl (Kohlberg, 1966a).

An alternative view to the social-learning approach is a cognitive-developmental one. According to the imitation or social-learning view, a boy becomes attached to his father because the father is the major rewarder and punisher, and as a consequence he imitates the father and finally achieves a sex-typed identity. But a cognitive-developmental approach holds that children start with a sex-typed identity, or categorization of themselves as boys or girls, and it is for this reason that the father is modeled by a boy and the mother by a girl.

Children identify themselves by gender, and between three and seven years of age they develop basic and more or less universal conceptions of gender role. It has been found that during this period children develop constant gender categories (e.g., they no longer assume that mother will grow up to be a daddy or that boys grow up to be mothers, etc.); they become aware of genital differences between males and females; and they develop masculine-feminine stereotypes (e.g., boys fight more than girls; girls get hurt more easily than boys). According to this alternative point of view, parental dominance can play a role, but more as a means of facilitating the normal sex-appropriate modeling than as a basic determiner of model choice. The child may engage in cross-sex behavior to the extent that the same-sex parent is notably passive.

CULTURES

In the previous section on roles, several factors in sex-role development or identification were discussed with special emphasis on the function of models and imitation. Continuing to consider sex roles, the present section will stress the nature and content of male and female roles from a cross-cultural perspective.

SEX ROLES ACROSS CULTURES

In every human group, males and females by definition have different *primary* sexual characteristics. The sexes are less distinct but still notably different in secondary sex characteristics—men tend to be taller, heavier, hairier, and to have a higher muscle-to-fat ratio (D'Andrade, 1966). Partly from these gross physical differences, the sex roles, or kinds of behavior typically expected of men and women, have emerged. Table 13.3 shows that there is some degree of cross-cultural consistency in the duties typically performed by men, by women, and by both sexes equally (Murdock, 1937). General differences seem to exist for all activities except dairy operation, soil preparation, fowl tending, and shelter erection. Males appear to be engaged typically in tasks which are strenuous and cooperative and which require long periods of travel, whereas female activities tend to be physically easier, more solitary, and less mobile.

The primitive division of labor presented here is basic to the traditional family structure. As indicated in Chapter 3 on dependency from the biological viewpoint, evolutionists have speculated that this family structure may have stemmed naturally from two problems: (1) the pursuit of large game required group cooperation and absence from the home; (2) the newborn human developed exceedingly slowly. Given these conditions, the man's greater strength and the initial biological attachment of the child to the mother made it highly likely that males would go on the hunt and females would care for the children. In addition, these conditions might also explain the development of marriage or stable pair bonding in humans. One explanation stresses that cooperation was essential for the hunt and that marriage arrangements had obvious survival value in minimizing intragroup conflicts over sexual partners. Indeed, some suggest that the development of clothing may have served a similar function. Removable clothing allows the sexually stimulating aspects of the body to be uncovered in the mate's presence but covered in the presence of other group members.

From speculations about the development of culture and from animal and anthropological evidence, one can construct some reasonable ideas

Table 13.3   Cross-cultural data from 224 societies on subsistence activities and division of labor by sex.*

Activity	Men always	Men usually	Either sex	Women usually	Women always
	Number of societies in which activity is performed by				
Pursuit of sea mammals	34	1	0	0	0
Hunting	166	13	0	0	0
Trapping small animals	128	13	4	1	2
Herding	38	8	4	0	5
Fishing	98	34	19	3	4
Clearing land for agriculture	73	22	17	5	13
Dairy operations	17	4	3	1	13
Preparing and planting soil	31	23	33	20	37
Erecting and dismantling shelter	14	2	5	6	22
Tending fowl and small animals	21	4	8	1	39
Tending and harvesting crops	10	15	35	39	44
Gathering shellfish	9	4	8	7	25
Making and tending fires	18	6	25	22	62
Bearing burdens	12	6	35	20	57
Preparing drinks and narcotics	20	1	13	8	57
Gathering fruits, berries, nuts	12	3	15	13	63
Gathering fuel	22	1	10	19	89
Preservation of meat and fish	8	2	10	14	74
Gatherings herbs, roots, seeds	8	1	11	7	74
Cooking	5	1	9	28	158
Carrying water	7	0	5	7	119
Grinding grain	2	4	5	13	114

* From G. P. Murdock, "Comparative data on the division of labor by sex," *Social Forces*, 1937, **15**, 551–553. Used by permission.

about the origin of family life and of male and female roles. In so doing, the layman sometimes falls prey to an easy but fallacious conclusion, the gist of which is: "Traditional male-female roles are 'natural' and any deviation from them is 'unnatural.' " Those who put forth arguments against sexual equality of opportunity in employment based on evolutionary assumptions (Tiger, 1969; Ardrey, 1969) sometimes fall into the same trap as those who argued that society should not be changed because it has evolved naturally. Of course, those who see the status quo as justified by its "naturalness" must also accept pressures for social reform as equally "natural." Since a third of all married women in the United States hold positions outside the home, it is clearly fallacious to conclude that gainful employment is not "natural" for women. The traditional sex roles and family structures were responses to certain conditions, and presumably to the extent that conditions change, other role arrangements become appropriate. The classic statement of this fact is Margaret Mead's description of the sex-role variations in three New Guinea tribes:

> We found the Arapesh—both men and women—displaying a personality that, out of our historically limited preoccupations, we would call maternal in its parental aspects, and feminine in its sexual aspects. We found men, as well as women, trained to be cooperative, unaggressive, responsive to the needs and demands of others. We found no idea that sex was a powerful driving force either for men or for women. In marked contrast to these attitudes, we found among the Mundugumor that both men and women developed as ruthless, aggressive, positively sexed individuals, with the maternal cherishing aspects of personality at a minimum. Both men and women approximated to a personality type that we in our culture would find only in an undisciplined and very violent male. Neither the Arapesh nor the Mundugumor profit by a contrast between the sexes: The Arapesh ideal is the mild, responsive man married to the mild, responsive woman; the Mundugumor ideal is the violent aggressive man married to the violent aggressive woman. In the third tribe, the Tchambuli, we found a genuine reversal of the sex-attitudes of our own culture, with the woman the dominant, impersonal, managing partner, the man the less responsible and the emotionally dependent person. These three situations suggest, then, a very definite conclusion. If those temperamental attitudes which we have traditionally regarded as feminine—such as passivity, responsiveness, and a willingness to cherish children—can so easily be set up as the masculine pattern in one tribe, and in another to be outlawed for the majority of men, we no longer have any basis for regarding such aspects of behavior as sex-linked.
>
> We are forced to conclude that human nature is almost unbelievably malleable, responding accurately and contrastingly to contrasting cultural conditions.*

THE STATUS OF WOMEN

In Primitive Cultures

As Mead's observations indicate, it is difficult to talk about what is "natural," since almost every form of role variation can be found in nature. Nevertheless, there is also a degree of regularity in male and

---

* From M. Mead, *Sex and Temperament,* William Morrow and Company, 1935, pp. 190–191. Reprinted by permission.

female roles across cultural lines. For example, a review of research on husband and wife roles (Stephens, 1963) noted the widespread nature of social inequality between men and women. (1) In most societies men hold all important jobs, including formal leadership of the group. Only one of the societies he considered—the Haida of the northwestern United States —allow women a voice in politics. Even in Puritan New England, women played no part in public life. (2) Women are frequently excluded from social gatherings and public places. For example, the Egyptian women of the village of Silwa are considered unclean and are therefore not permitted to enter the mosque, and a wife among the Rajputs of Khalapur in India may not leave her own courtyard except on special occasions. (3) *Polygyny* (more than one wife) is rather common among world cultures, while the opposite, *polyandry* (more than one husband), is very rare. (4) It is quite common for a newly married couple to move a great distance to be near the husband's family *(patrilocal residence)*, but couples rarely move far from the husband's home to be near the wife's family *(matrilocal residence)*. (5) A double standard of acceptable sexual behavior is almost universal. In one sample of cultures considered, 13 have premarital sex restrictions which are stronger for girls than for boys, and none have stricter rules for boys than for girls. In eight instances, men are permitted adulterous relationships, whereas women are expected to be faithful. In two others that permit adultery for both, the rules are stricter for women, and in no societies in the sample are they stricter for males than for females.

It seems clear from these generalizations that an unequal status is one of the most likely components of the woman's role in any culture and in any age. This pattern is nowhere more evident than in the formalized signs of deference women are expected to make toward men in some societies.

In 8 of the societies reported on by Stephens (1963) wives must kneel or crouch before their husbands; in 33 the women must walk behind their mates; in 5 the husband gets his choice of food; in 11 he sits on a stool, chair, or bench while his wife sits or kneels on the floor; and in 12 he has a seat of honor while dining. Against this background of subservience, there are only 3 or 4 societies in the sample in which men defer to their wives. For example, among the Berbers of North Africa the wife rides while her husband walks behind, but the only other examples are found in Europe and America. "Good manners" in Western countries require a variety of ritualized deferential practices by men toward women, such as standing when women enter the room, holding doors and chairs for them, and serving them first.

A useful distinction can be made between deference and power (Stephens, 1963). Whereas a *deference* custom is some ritual expression of a presumably unequal relationship, *power* has to do with who actually dominates and who submits, who decides, who commands, and who obeys. In general power is actually, as well as formally, in the hands of the husband. In a sample of 96 cultures, only 4 or 5 could be called *matriarchies,* in which women customarily rule within the home—Tchambuli (New Guinea), Modjokuto (Java), Jivaro (Brazil), Berbers (North Africa), and perhaps the Nama Hottentots (South Africa). There were also some societies in which husbands and wives appeared to have about equal power.

In Technological Cultures

Of course, most of the societies discussed here are primitive or isolated communities. But among the technologically advanced countries, there are also wide cultural variations in the definition of a woman's proper role and in the goals considered appropriate for women to strive for. A review of statistics in this area shows that in the Soviet Union, one of four physicians is a woman, in Britain one of six, but in the United States only one of sixteen (Dornbusch, 1966).

Philip Bailey/Stock, Boston   Patricia Hollander Gross/Stock, Boston

Furthermore, as of 1973, women made up only 19% of managerial and administrative personnel and 41% of professional and technical workers. On the other hand, as recently as 1950 women constituted only 24% of individuals receiving bachelor's degrees and 29% of those receiving master's degrees. As of 1971, these statistics had improved markedly to 42 and 40%, respectively (see Fig. 13.1).

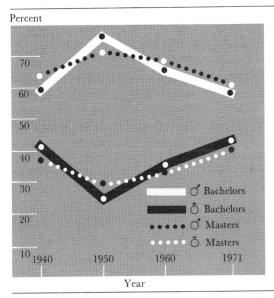

Fig. 13.1. Percent of students receiving Bachelor's and Master's degrees, by sex and by year. (Based upon tables in "The American Almanac," 1974, prepared by the Bureau of Census, U.S. Dept. of Commerce.)

In addition to statistics about actual attainment, there is evidence that expectations held by women themselves reflect differences in sex roles. Even women in professional occupations have a lower level of occupational commitment (Dornbusch, 1966). Only about 25 percent of a group of student nurses studied expressed displeasure at the idea of never working at nursing after marriage, and about 70 percent of female teachers reportedly view their job merely as an adventure. Usually women hold low-paying jobs and earn less than their male counterparts in the same occupations. Furthermore, in support of the idea that women should not receive equal consideration in employment, a variety of myths without basis have been perpetuated:

Women are supposedly more likely to be sick, to be absentees, and to quit their jobs. In fact, men lose more work days through illness than women do, the sex rates for absenteeism are identical, and only the rates for quitting show women markedly higher. Even this latter result cannot be used to defend keeping women out of high-status jobs, for the quit rates turn out to be purely a function of the skill level of the job. When the researchers control for skill level, the sex difference disappears.*

The Female Role in the Mass Media

In the section of this chapter on identification, the roles of parents as sex-role models were stressed, but parents are not the only models for sex roles. As in the case of aggression and sexual behavior, the mass media unavoidably teach by offering the reader or viewer more models than are provided by real life. Betty Friedan (1963), a journalist, studied the content of four major women's magazines over a period of years to obtain evidence of what she feels is a highly restrictive popular model for women. She notes that in 1939 the majority of heroines of the fiction that appeared in these magazines were career women. Although the stories contained the boy-meets-girl theme, it was often not the major theme. Instead, the heroine was usually trying to attain some goal or was concerned with some problem in the world. She was almost never solely a housewife, and the story usually ended before she had children. But by the end of 1949, Friedan reports, only one in three fictional heroines in the same magazines had a career, and by 1959 career women no longer figured as heroines.

Of course, what Friedan is concerned about is that for millions of American women who read these magazines, almost all of whom have been through high school and nearly half to college, little mention is made of the world beyond the home. For our purposes, the broad exposure of traditional female models in this and other media and its function of bolstering culturally prescribed role definitions are noteworthy.

It should be clear from the foregoing that a nearly universal component of the female sex role is subordination and inequality. A saying of the Reindeer Chukchee of Siberia is short but to the point: "Being women, eat crumbs." (Bogoras, 1909, p. 548, as quoted in Stephens, 1963, p. 288) It is not surprising, then, that in cultures that have tried to reorganize society, such as those in China and in Israel (with the kibbutz plan), a basic feature of reorganization is the equalization of status for men and women.

---

* From "Afterword" by Sanford M. Dornbusch in The Development of Sex Differences, edited by Eleanor E. Maccoby (Stanford: Stanford University Press, 1966), p. 216. Reprinted by permission.

SUMMARY

The treatment of sex from the social viewpoint centered on two different topics—sexual behavior and male/female sex roles. The section on *models,* dealing with sexual behavior, presented recent research relating to arousal, satiation, and behavior.

In one study relating degree of explicitness to amount of sexual arousal, it was found that less sexually explicit media generate more sexual arousal than more sexually explicit media. Moreover, repeated exposure to sexually explicit materials does not appear to lead to a chronic level of sexual excitement. Rather, there appears to be a tendency toward satiation of both arousal and interest. Finally, exposure to erotic material may activate sexual behavior on a temporary basis but does not produce mid- or long-term effects. The presumed relationship between early exposure to erotica and a tendency to commit sexual offenses is not supported by available research. To the contrary, it appears that adult sexual offenders had less exposure to erotic materials during adolescence than did normal subjects.

The remainder of the chapter was concerned with male and female roles. Specifically, in the *roles* section, the process by which children come to identify with or imitate one parent or the other was considered. Two current theories of this process have much in common with Freud's conceptions of identification. The *secondary-reward theory* asserts that children will reproduce the characteristics of the parent that rewards them more, because such actions acquire secondary-reward value. The *status-envy theory*, on the other hand, holds that the child will imitate the parent who receives more rewards, role-playing that parent in fantasy. A third possibility, the *social-power theory,* is that the child will model the adult who *dispenses* more rewards, even if the rewards are not given to the child. An experiment involving simulated family units supported the social-power explanation, because the children imitated the powerful model who controlled the rewards, regardless of whether that adult rewarded the child or another adult. The results suggest that the explanation of cross-sex identification lies in the power distribution within the family. However, this social-learning view, which stresses the flexibility of sex-role learning, is challenged by the cognitive-developmental position. The latter approach emphasizes that children choose to identify with the same-sex parent, primarily because children categorize themselves as boy or girl. This theory suggests that cross-sex identification will occur only when the opposite parent is highly dominant.

Cross-cultural research on the content of sex roles shows considerable uniformity in the differentiations made between men's and women's work. Presumably these roles, as well as the family structure of which they are a part, are rooted in the historical necessities which required that humans both care for their offspring and hunt food. The ability of investigators to offer naturalistic explanations for highly different sex roles sometimes suggests that their content is inevitable and unchanging, but the existence of contrary examples in some cultures argues against such a rigid view. Nevertheless, a review of cross-cultural studies of the woman's position discloses that most women are bound by social, political, and sexual restrictions more severe than those prescribed for men in the same culture. As measured by both formalized signs of deference and actual power, only a few cultures appear to give women rather than men the upper hand. What is true for underdeveloped societies is also true for technologically advanced countries. Contemporary American women occupy a less advantageous position in employment and in education than their counterparts in some other advanced countries. One commentator on the position of women in the United States has emphasized that most females in the mass media enact relatively restricted roles and therefore provide limited models for other women.

SUGGESTIONS FOR FURTHER READING

The Journal of Social Issues, 1973, Vol. 29, No. 3. The Society for the Psychological Study of Social Issues published this issue devoted entirely to research on the effects of pornography and on how pornography is dealt with in the legal system.

Maccoby, E. E. (ed.). *The Development of Sex Differences.* Stanford: Stanford University Press, 1966. A collection of chapters written for this volume giving theoretical accounts of the development of sex differences from various viewpoints. This book is already a classic. It has a useful annotated bibliography.

Maccoby, E. E., and C. N. Jacklin. *The Psychology of Sex Differences.* Stanford: Stanford University Press, 1974. The authors give a comprehensive review of the psychological literature on sex differences in intellectual and social functioning. An annotated bibliography is included.

The Report of the Commission on Obscenity and Pornography. New York: Bantam, 1970. Summaries of the many volumes that made up the final report of a commission appointed in 1967 by President Johnson to study the problem of pornography. This 700-page paperback version has information on all aspects of the problem including a summary of the behavioral studies funded by the commission, some of which are discussed in this chapter.

14
Sexuality: The Psychometric-Trait Viewpoint

14
Sexuality:
The
Psychometric-
Trait
Viewpoint

I. **Observational methods**
  A. Special problems of observation
  B. The Kinsey interviews
    1. Content of the interviews
    2. Recruitment of interviewers
    3. Recruitment of subjects
    4. Maintaining confidentiality
    5. Establishing and maintaining rapport
    6. Checks on accuracy
  C. The Masters-Johnson observations
    1. Recruitment of preliminary sample
    2. Recruitment of primary sample
    3. Laboratory procedures
    4. Significance of the research

II. **Self-report methods**
  A. Sexual experiences
    1. Guttman scales
    2. Quantification of sexual experience
  B. Sexual preferences
    1. Preference for sexual activity
    2. Heterosexual somatic preferences: men
    3. Heterosexual somatic preferences: women

III. **Indirect methods**
  A. Fantasy measures of sexual imagery and guilt
  B. Inhibition and arousal of sexual imagery and guilt
    1. Study A
      a. Experimental group
      b. Control group
      c. Results
    2. Study B
      a. Experimental group
      b. Control group
      c. Results
    3. Study C
      a. Experimental group
      b. Control group
      c. Results

IV. **Summary**

Sexuality is, at once, possibly the most important and certainly the least understood dimension of human personality. Until very recently, the social, religious, ethical, and legal barriers to research on human sexuality had been so effective that only a handful of courageous scientists dared to approach the subject. Consequently, the current state of knowledge regarding human sexual behavior is considerably less certain than that regarding other aspects of human personality. The situation is rapidly changing, however. Recent advances in methods and techniques for the study of human sexuality, as well as an increasingly favorable and enlightened public view of sex research, have made possible many rapid advances in this previously underdeveloped field.

OBSERVATIONAL METHODS

SPECIAL PROBLEMS OF OBSERVATION

The obstacles to the application of observational methods to human sexuality are almost unbelievably severe. In most societies, for example, sexual behavior is considered a private and highly personal experience that should not be shared with others. Consequently, there is an understandable and natural reluctance on everyone's part to discuss or report the details of one's own sexual behavior. Similarly, the prospect of having one's sexual behavior directly observed by a scientist is almost certain to arouse strong feelings in almost everyone in our society. It is therefore all the more remarkable that during the past two decades, hundreds of normal and representative subjects have consented to have their sexual behavior assessed by both interview and direct behavioral observation techniques.

The interview studies of Kinsey and associates (1948; 1953) and the behavioral observation studies of Masters and Johnson (1966) are unquestionably among the most monumental studies that have ever been conducted in the science of human behavior. Although not without certain technical shortcomings, these two large-scale studies should serve as models of excellence for the application of observational methods to the study of human behavior.

THE KINSEY INTERVIEWS

During the last 30 years, Alfred C. Kinsey and his associates—the latter participating in the beginning and then carrying on Kinsey's pioneering work after his death—have conducted individual interviews with more than 18,000 people. In each interview, direct and detailed questions were asked concerning the intimate details of the respondent's sexual behavior. Of the 18,000 subjects interviewed, fewer than ten have refused to complete a history once they started (Pomeroy, 1963). Clearly, the interviewing techniques and procedures developed by this highly skilled scientific team would repay the consideration of all who are concerned with observational methods.

"Mr. Tilby is in the Kinsey Report."

Rea, True, November 1948

Content of the Interviews

The purpose of the Kinsey interviews was to obtain as much information as possible about all aspects of the sexual histories of the subjects. In all, 521 items were included as possible areas of exploration. However, since subjects were questioned in detail only about those items that they had specifically experienced, the actual number of items covered in a given interview was closer to 300.

Nine broad areas of sexual history were covered: (1) social and economic data, (2) marital history, (3) sex education, (4) physical and physiological data, (5) nocturnal sex dreams, (6) masturbation, (7) heterosexual history, (8) homosexual history, and (9) animal contacts. The number of specific items covered within each area varied considerably, the greatest number being in the heterosexual and homosexual history categories. Examination of the full list of 521 items covered (Kinsey, Pomeroy, and Martin, 1948, pp. 63–70) should be sufficient to convince the reader that few items of possible relevance to sexual history were omitted. Clearly, the Kinsey interviews constitute the most comprehensive and intensive survey of human sexual behavior conducted to date. To cover such a range of intimate topics in less than two hours required not only special interviewing techniques, but special kinds of interviewers.

Recruitment of Interviewers

Most large-scale survey studies employ students or hourly workers as interviewers. Such interviewers tend to be in the lowest echelon of the research organization of which they are members. In the Kinsey studies, just the opposite was true: each interviewer was both a trustee of the Institute for Sex Research and a member of its policy-making board. The care that went into the selection for this task of professional personnel of the highest caliber can best be illustrated by some statistics. During the 22 years in which the Institute has been in existence, only 9 of some 300 persons considered as possible interviewers have been selected.

One reason for the extreme selectivity resides in the fact that the requirements are almost mutually conflicting (Pomeroy, 1963). In the first place, the interviewer must be happily married yet able to travel extensively. Second, the interviewer must be a highly trained scientist who is nevertheless able to gain rapport and derive enjoyment from working with people from lower socioeconomic groups. Finally, the interviewer must be fully aware of our culture and its Puritan tradition and yet so unaffected by it as not to pass moral judgment on the sexual behavior of others.

The qualities required of a good interviewer were aptly stated by Kinsey himself:

> Learning how to meet people of all ranks and levels, establishing rapport, sympathetically comprehending the significances of things as others view them, learning to accept their attitudes and activities without moral, social, or esthetic evaluation, being interested in people as they are and not as someone else would have them, learning to see the reasonable basis of what at first glance may appear to be most unreasonable behavior, developing a capacity to like all kinds of people and thus to win their esteem and cooperation—these are the elements to be mastered by one who would gather human statistics.*

---

* From A. C. Kinsey, W. B. Pomeroy, and C. E. Martin, *Sexual Behavior in the Human Male*, Saunders, Philadelphia, 1948, p. 35. Reprinted by permission.

Recruitment of Subjects

How does one go about securing the cooperation of 18,000 subjects from all socioeconomic levels and all walks of life in submitting to a sexual-history interview of unprecedented intensity? Many of the more than 200 reviews and critiques of the Kinsey studies criticized the sampling procedures for obtaining subjects and suggested that the results of the study could not be considered truly representative of American society (Himelhoch and Fava, 1955). Too few of the critics paid sufficient homage to the incredible energy, persistence, and ingenuity Kinsey and his associates exercised to secure successfully the cooperation of the subjects they actually recruited.

A large number of interviews were arranged through personal contacts and introductions which required days, weeks, and even years of cultivation of the appropriate community contacts. Frequently, individuals who themselves had given histories became "contacts" for introductions to their acquaintances or other members of their group. On the basis of their experience with the interviews in the course of giving their own sexual histories, such contacts became convinced not only of the integrity of the interviewers but of the overall scientific and social importance of the project. Hence they frequently became proselytizers of their own friends and acquaintances and thus enabled the interviewers to reach segments of society usually closed to social research. Table 14.1 presents

Table 14.1 Principal "contacts" for subject recruitment.*

Bootleggers	Ne'er-do-wells
Clergymen	Persons in the *Social Register*
Clerks	Physicians
Clinical psychologists	Pimps
College professors	Police court officials
College students	Prison inmates
Corporation officials	Prison officials
Editors	Professional women
Farmers	Psychiatrists
Female prostitutes	Public school teachers
Gamblers	Social workers
Headmasters of private schools	Thieves and holdup men
Housewives	YMCA secretaries
Lawyers	YWCA secretaries
Male prostitutes	Welfare workers
Marriage counselors	Women's club leaders

* From A. C. Kinsey, W. B. Pomeroy, and C. E. Martin, *Sexual Behavior in the Human Male,* Saunders, Philadelphia, 1948, p. 35. Reprinted by permission.

a representative list of the contacts who were of the greatest help in re-cruiting additional subjects. The heterogeneity of occupations provides some insight into the heterogeneity of the samples interviewed by the Kinsey team.

The majority of subjects were recruited from social groups of some sort (e.g., church, fraternity, Parent-Teacher Association, factory, etc.). In every instance, the cooperation of the entire group was solicited. Once a significant proportion of a given group had contributed histories, social pressure operated in such a manner that others felt obligated to con-tribute toward the 100% cooperation goal. Securing group cooperation for such an enterprise requires an unusual assortment of skills:

> ... an interviewer must utilize the principles of mass psychology, mix them well with common sense, and all the skills of a patent medicine vendor and a Fuller brush man—while, withal, maintaining the community's esteem for the dignity of a science which has nothing to sell. (Kinsey et al., 1948, p. 38)

Maintaining Confidentiality

The security procedures for maintaining confidentiality in the Kinsey studies rivaled those of any wartime government. The heart of the system was a cryptic code used to record as well as store all data:

> The code was developed with the help of an experienced cryptographer and involves, simultaneously, the use of several devices designed to complicate possible decoding. It is the judgment of the cryptographer who tried to break the final form that decoding would be impossible unless one had access to all of the histories and all of the files for a considerable period of time; and that after identification the data would be practically unintelli-gible because of the difficulty of deciphering such a position code as the one used here. It should be added that the histories are kept behind locked doors and in fire proof files with locks that are unique for this project. (Kinsey et al., 1948, p. 45)

The recording sheet for an illustrative sexual history interview is pictured in Fig. 14.1. By use of the code it was possible to record directly responses to all of the possible 521 items during the course of an interview. Hence no intelligible written document was produced. As a consequence, it was necessary for the interviewer to memorize a large portion of the total code. At the time of last report, only six individuals knew any part of the code and only four had knowledge of the entire code. Presumably, the courts of this country would recognize the right of scientists to pre-serve the confidentiality of data gathered from human subjects. Neverthe-less, Kinsey and his associates were even prepared for the eventuality that they might not do so:

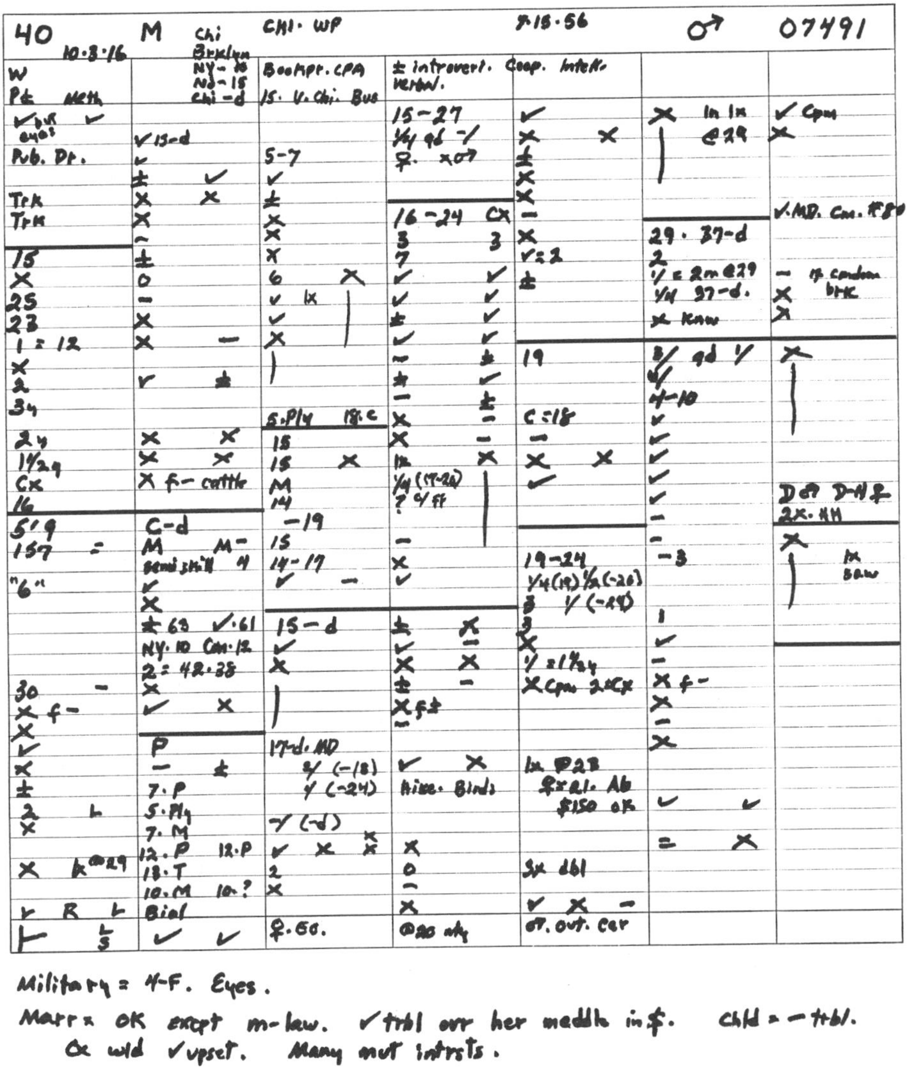

Fig. 14.1. Illustrative recording sheet for sexual history interview. (Courtesy of P. H. Gebhard, Director, Institute for Sex Research, Indiana University.)

If the courts of all levels were to refuse to recognize such a privilege, there would be no alternative but to destroy our complete body of records and accept the consequences of such defiance of the courts. (Kinsey *et al.*, 1948, p. 47)

Establishing and Maintaining Rapport

Subjects were interviewed under conditions of complete privacy and in an atmosphere designed to make them feel as natural and relaxed as possible. In all instances, the subjects were "treated as a friend or a guest in one's own home" with all the respect and propriety that such treatment entails. The typical interview began with informal, everyday conversation, which continued until the subject was clearly at ease. The first interview items were of a nonsexual nature and followed a sequence which took into account the topics that might be most difficult for the particular respondent to discuss. Eye contact was maintained with the respondent as much as possible, and the questions were phrased in a very direct, rather than evasive, manner.

Particular care was taken to phrase questions in the everyday language of the subject. This precaution applied not only to vocabulary level but to type, particularly the specialized sexual vernacular or argot employed by the subject's socioeconomic, ethnic, or sexually deviant group. Euphemisms were avoided. Sexual questions were phrased in such a way that the burden of denial was always placed on the subject. Rather than asking *if* an individual had engaged in a particular activity, the interviewer asked *when* he or she had first engaged in it. This forthright, direct, and "no nonsense" technique tended to reassure subjects that they were dealing with an interviewer who was unlikely to be surprised by any experience they might have had, however unusual.

Checks on Accuracy

Certain features of the interviewing technique itself made it difficult to falsify self-report of sexual histories. Because of the large number of items covered in a single interview, it was necessary to ask questions as rapidly as the subject could possibly comprehend and reply. Since many of the questions consisted of complicated lists of interlocking questions designed to provide cross-checks throughout the history, it is unlikely that a subject who was falsifying could avoid self-contradiction. In certain instances, cross-checking questions were so subtle that their relationship to sexual activity would be recognized only by a skilled psychiatrist. When a given answer was apparently either incorrect or insufficient, the original question was rephrased in such a way that the subject had to prove the answer or expose the falsity of the original response. When it became apparent that the subject was withholding information, the problem was handled directly:

> Look, I don't give a damn what you've done, but if you don't tell me the straight of it, it's better that we stop this history right here. Now, how old

were you the first time this or that happened (or how often did you do it, or how many partners were there)? (Pomeroy, 1963, p. 26)

It is a tribute to the clinical skill of the interviewers that not a single subject refused to continue the interview when so approached.

In addition to the cross-checks in the interview itself, there were a number of additional procedures to assess the validity of the information provided by the respondent. The most common technique was the "retake" in which the identical interview was conducted with the subject on two occasions separated by anywhere from 18 months to seven years. Another source of validity information came from comparison of item responses given by married couples. Whenever both members of a married couple independently reported the same sexual activity, it was possible to compare their responses. In other instances, particularly in institutional settings, such as prisons, sexual partners other than spouses provided cross-checks on the validity of reported experiences. Finally, there were procedures to check the possibility that bias or inaccuracy was contributed by the interviewer himself. Large samples of roughly similar cases were compared among the three principal interviewers (Kinsey, Pomeroy, and Martin, 1948) in order to determine whether different interviewers tended to elicit significantly different sexual histories from comparable individuals. Although such a comparison can never be exact, the obtained results were highly encouraging from the standpoint of interviewer consistency.

THE MASTERS-JOHNSON OBSERVATIONS

During the past 15 years, an extensive investigation of the anatomy and physiology of human sexual response has been conducted by a team of researchers at the Washington University School of Medicine in St. Louis. This program, together with studies of sexual inadequacy and related medical problems, has been coordinated by W. H. Masters and Virginia E. Johnson of the Reproductive Biology Research Foundation. The primary research interest of these investigators may be stated quite simply:

1) What happens to the human male and female as they respond to effective sexual stimulation?

2) Why do men and women behave as they do when responding to effective sexual stimulation?

Recognizing that self-reported sexual histories and anecdotal materials provide only indirect answers to such questions, Masters and Johnson (1966) developed techniques and procedures that would permit the direct observation and recording of sexual response in a laboratory setting. Since there was virtually no precedent for this type of research, years of careful planning and experimentation were devoted to the development of appropriate techniques not only for the observation and physical recording, but also for the interrogation of subjects experiencing effective sexual stimulation. Because the usual problems of human experimentation were intensified by the nature of the particular research program, it was necessary to select a highly specialized sample of subjects for the purpose of technique development.

Recruitment of Preliminary Sample

At the beginning of the research program, the investigators assumed that subjects from the general population would not be available for research of this kind—an assumption which later turned out to be completely unfounded. Consequently, prostitutes were recruited on the basis of their availability, knowledgeability, and cooperativeness, and 118 female and 27 male prostitutes were selected. Their selection was further based on intelligence, diversity of sexual experience and, particularly, ability to verbalize subjective aspects of such experience. The cooperativeness of this highly experienced group enabled the investigators to develop a variety of laboratory techniques which were subsequently applied to a more representative sample. Because of the unrepresentative nature of the preliminary group, however, the data from laboratory observations were not included in the published report.

Recruitment of Primary Sample

The main participants in the Masters-Johnson studies did not constitute a representative sample of the general population. Rather, they were recruited primarily from the academic community associated with a large university-hospital complex, and consequently, they were from the upper socioeconomic and educational brackets. Clinical interviews were conducted with 1273 subjects, from whom 694 were selected for actual participation in the laboratory procedures. The major criteria for selection included: (1) willingness to participate, (2) facility of sexual responsiveness, (3) ability to verbalize details of sexual reaction, and (4) normalcy of reproductive organs (determined by physical examination).

The final sample consisted of 382 females and 312 males. It included 276 married couples and a much smaller number of subjects who were divorced or single at the time the study was initiated. The subjects ranged in age from 18 to 90 years. Because of the milieu from which they had been recruited, a disproportionate number of subjects had acquired some postgraduate education. Because of the predominance of married couples in the sample, the question arose whether the results of the investigation should be reported as "sexual response of married partners." However, in the early phases of the investigation, it was established that there were no basic differences in the anatomy and physiology of sexual response between married and unmarried partners.

Laboratory Procedures

The subjects selected for study participated in an orientation program that thoroughly familiarized them with the purpose and procedures of the research. In a series of interviews conducted by both male and female interviewers, complete medical, social, and sexual histories were obtained. Previous research had shown that the simultaneous presence of both male and female investigators provided an optimal atmosphere for cooperation, trust, and respect. Consequently, a male and a female investigator were present during all phases of the laboratory procedures. The sense of trust and respect developed for the scientists involved in the program was essential for the subsequent laboratory procedures.

A second step in the orientation program involved an intensive physical examination designed to rule out the presence of any gross pathology of a physical nature. After completion of the physical examination, the subjects were introduced to the research quarters, where they examined the various recording and observational devices and learned the details of their operation. After they had been oriented to the research quarters and understood the nature and purpose of the specialized equipment, the subjects were instructed to attempt to initiate sexual activity in privacy in the research quarters. When the subjects had become accustomed to performing in the atmosphere of the research quarters, they then attempted to initiate sexual activity in the presence of the examiners. Over a period of time, the subjects felt more secure in the surroundings and became accustomed to the presence of the investigators and of the highly specialized equipment. When they had achieved full confidence in their ability to respond successfully under such circumstances, they were assigned to one of a number of specialized research projects.

The basic types of sexual stimulation provided were: (1) automanipulation, (2) artificial coition, and (3) natural coition. For some female subjects, automanipulation and artificial coition were accomplished by means of an artificial phallus containing sensitive recording apparatus. This transparent device was created by radiophysicists to allow continuous observation and recording of intravaginal physiological response to sexual stimuli. The major observational techniques included: (1) gross behavioral observation, (2) direct physiological recordings of bodily change, and (3) direct interrogation before, during, and after sexual stimulation. It has

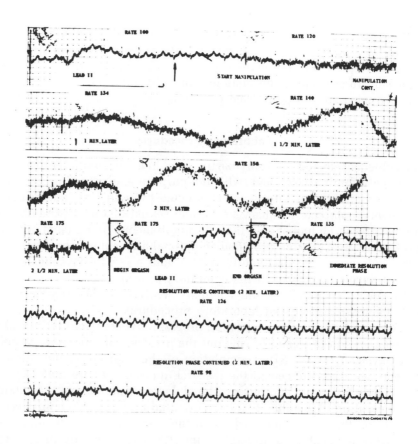

This electrocardiogram of a female study subject during orgasm illustrates the complex recording techniques applied to physiological processes throughout the Masters and Johnson investigations. (From William H. Masters and Virginia E. Johnson, *Human Sexual Response,* 1966. Boston: Little, Brown and Company. Reprinted with permission.)

been conservatively estimated that 10,000 complete cycles of sexual response were studied in the first decade of the research program (Masters and Johnson, 1966, p. 15).

Significance of the Research

The fact that the research emphasis of Masters and Johnson was almost exclusively on the anatomical and physiological aspects of response to sexual stimulation does not mean that their view of human sexuality is a narrowly biological one. Rather, as they state, "Sexuality is a dimension and an expression of personality." (p. 301) However, although human sexuality is not necessarily best construed from a biological viewpoint, the basic anatomical and physiological facts of human sexual response must be established before intelligent psychological and sociological investigations can be conducted.

In the absence of such established facts, a number of psychological and sociological hypotheses regarding sexual response have been developed which presuppose the validity of certain biological assumptions. The careful biological work of Masters and Johnson has established that many of these biological presuppositions are patently false. Consequently, it is likely that many of our current psychological constructions regarding human sexuality represent fallacies rather than viable psychological constructs. The work of Masters and Johnson has established that many current notions concerning, for example, the alleged differences between male and female sexuality, the nature of the female sexual response, and the components contributing to sexual adequacy are without biological foundation. These pioneering studies have illuminated the true "facts of life" on which it is now possible to build psychological theories of human sexuality.

SELF-REPORT METHODS

SEXUAL EXPERIENCES

A tentative hypothesis that can be formed on the basis of the research of Kinsey and associates concerns the cumulative or sequential nature of sexual experience. As the individual has more contact with a partner, his or her repertory of sexual experiences increases in a sequential pattern:

> Petting techniques usually expand in a more or less standard sequence, as the partners become better acquainted. Beginning with general body contact, lip kissing, and the deep kiss, it advances to a deliberate manipulation of the female breast, to mouth contacts with the female breast, to manual stimulation of the female genitalia, less often to the manual stimulation of the male genitalia, to the apposition of naked genitalia, to oral stimulation of the male genitalia, and finally to oral stimulation of the female genitalia. (Kinsey et al., 1948, p. 540)

This sequential pattern of sexual experience may be expected to evolve during prolonged contact with a single partner or in frequent contacts with a variety of partners. Such a cumulative, sequential pattern has definite implications for the type of model employed in the measurement of sexual experiences by self-report methods.

Guttman Scales

The particular model implied was first developed by Guttman (1950) in a study of social attitudes and has become known as the Guttman scale. A Guttman scale comprises cumulative items which form an exact sequential pattern. The pattern is so exact that, given an individual's total score on the scale (i.e., the number of items to which he answers "yes"), one can reproduce perfectly that person's complete pattern of item responses.

Table 14.2 presents the item responses of seven subjects to seven items which form a perfect Guttman scale. A "yes" response is entered as 1, a "no" response as 0. The total score of each individual appears in the final column. Thus Person A, who answered "yes" to one item, has a total score of 1; E who answered "yes" to five items, has a score of 5. Note the perfect sequential pattern that exists among the items. Given an individual's total score, one can reproduce his responses to each of the individual items.

Table 14.2   The responses of seven persons to seven items that form a perfect Guttman scale.

Persons	Items							Total score
	1	2	3	4	5	6	7	
A	1	0	0	0	0	0	0	1
B	1	1	0	0	0	0	0	2
C	1	1	1	0	0	0	0	3
D	1	1	1	1	0	0	0	4
E	1	1	1	1	1	0	0	5
F	1	1	1	1	1	1	0	6
G	1	1	1	1	1	1	1	7
Endorsement percentage	100%	86%	71%	57%	43%	29%	14%	

Consider Person E with a total score of 5; we know that this individual answered "yes" to items 1, 2, 3, 4, and 5, "no" to items 6 and 7. The implication is that an individual who answered "yes" to item 5 must have answered "yes" to items 1 through 4. The pattern holds for every item and every individual in Table 14.2. Therefore, we can conclude that the seven items are arranged in a cumulative order such that answering "yes" to a given item necessarily implies a "yes" answer to all preceding items.

Quantification of Sexual Experience

The hypothesis that sexual experiences are cumulative and may be quantified by means of a Guttman scale has been confirmed in three separate studies conducted under different circumstances, with different samples of subjects, and with different items. Podell and Perkins (1957) employed a structured interview to inquire about the sexual experiences of 100 unmarried college males from Pennsylvania State University. Eleven years later, Bentler (1968) administered a sexual-experiences questionnaire anonymously to 108 college males, most of whom were unmarried. Working in cooperation with the Institute for Sex Research, Brady and Levitt (1965b) administered a sexual-experiences questionnaire to 68 male graduate students, approximately half of whom were married. Despite the differences in subjects, items, and procedures in the three studies, the results were essentially the same: sexual experiences were cumulative in nature and lent themselves to the item patterning of a Guttman scale.

In Table 14.3 Items A through J are the ten items of heterosexual ex-

Table 14.3 Sexual-experiences questionnaire results from three separate studies.

Experience	Brady and Levitt	Podell and Perkins	Bentler
A. Kissing with tongue contact	16	15	16
B. Manual manipulation of clad female breast	15	16	15
C. Manual manipulation of nude female breast	14	14	14
D. Manual manipulation of female genitalia	13	12	12
E. Oral contact with female breast	12	13	13
F. Manual manipulation of your genitalia by a female	11	10	11
G. Heterosexual intercourse: ventral-ventral	10	11	10
H. Oral contact with your genitalia by a female	9	9	8
I. Oral contact with female genitalia	8	8	9
J. Heterosexual intercourse: ventral-dorsal	7	7	7
K. Manual manipulation of your genitalia by a male	6	—	—
L. Manual manipulation of another male's genitalia	5	—	—
M. Oral contact with your genitalia by a male	4	—	—
N. Penile-anal penetration *of* another male	3	—	—
O. Oral contact with male genitalia	2	—	—
P. Penile-anal penetration *by* another male	1	—	—

perience that were common to all three studies. They have been arranged in *decreasing* order of frequency in a Guttman scale; that is, A is the most frequently reported heterosexual experience (ranking sixteenth in two studies) and J the least (ranking seventh in all studies). Although minor variations in relative frequency occurred among the studies, items within a given sample were ordered according to the requirements of a Guttman scale. In the Brady and Levitt study, for example, the vast majority of subjects who admitted to E also admitted to A through D. In all three studies, almost all subjects who admitted to J admitted to all preceding items.

As would be expected from the results of Kinsey, Pomeroy, and Martin (1948), kissing and manual manipulation of the female are among the most frequently reported heterosexual experiences, while oral-genital contacts and intercourse in the ventral-dorsal position (female facing away from male) are among the least frequently reported. Similarly, support was found for Kinsey *et al.*'s hypothesis concerning the cumulative or sequential nature of sexual experiences in that males who reported the least frequent experience (ventral-dorsal intercourse) reported that they had engaged in all sexual experiences which occurred with higher frequencies in the general population. It is also of interest to note that although Item G (heterosexual intercourse: ventral-ventral) is toward the lower (less frequent) end of the scale, it is not at the bottom. In fact, there are three items (H, I, and J) that are consistently more extreme (less frequent) than G. The expression "going all the way," which was popular in the fifties, is clearly not descriptive of activity in more recent times.

A unique feature of the Brady and Levitt (1965b) study was that both heterosexual and homosexual experience items were included in the survey. All sixteen items listed in Table 14.3 were in the Sexual Experience Inventory administered by Brady and Levitt. Items A through J are the heterosexual items common to the three studies, K through P the homosexual ones included only by Brady and Levitt. The male graduate students responded by checking whether they had experienced the activities "sometime in life," "during last five years," or "never." The items of the inventory appeared in a random order on the questionnaire. The table shows that the homosexual experiences are clustered at the extreme end of a cumulative Guttman scale. Reporting any one homosexual experience implies that the individual has experienced all heterosexual items.

It is important to clarify the above findings to prevent misinterpretation. The order of items in Table 14.3 is based on responses indicating that the subjects had experienced the activity "sometime in life." Consequently, it is likely that the reported homosexual experiences occurred primarily around puberty and did not have the same significance that more recent sexual experiences would have. Nevertheless, it is interesting to note that subjects who experienced homosexual contacts early in life tended to experience a greater variety of heterosexual contacts in later life. Thus a male graduate student who experienced penile-anal penetration by another male in early life is likely to have experienced all sexual behaviors appearing in the questionnaire. When the items were analyzed in terms of the response "during last five years," however, the ordering of the heterosexual items (A through J) was preserved, but the homosexual items were admitted to by so few subjects that they no longer formed a useful part of the questionnaire.

SEXUAL PREFERENCES

Preference for Sexual Activity

Preference for various forms of sexual activity may be measured directly by presenting subjects with photographs depicting the various forms and asking them to report the degree of sexual stimulation they experience in viewing each photograph. Levitt and Brady (1965) employed such a procedure in connection with their intensive study of 68 male graduate students. They decided to assess sexual preference for 19 different sexual activities (listed in Table 14.4). From a large pool of photographs specifically depicting such activities, they selected ten 5″ × 8″ photographs to represent each of the 19 sexual themes. In making the selection, they attempted to control such factors as the youth and attractiveness of the individuals depicted, the relative recency of the photograph (choice was restricted to within the last 20 years), and the degree of nudity and the positions of the participants. The 190 photographs were submitted, in sets of ten, to 25 male graduate student volunteers, who were paid for their performance. The photographs were ranked in terms of the degree to which they were sexually stimulating within each activity. The three top-ranked photographs in each category were selected for use in the actual study.

In the experiment proper, the 68 male graduate students (previously employed in the experiences study) were presented with three sets of 19 photographs depicting the activities indicated in Table 14.4. The instructions were as follows:

> Your task is to rate each of the photographs according to the degree to which you find it sexually stimulating. Give each photograph a numerical rating on the scale below. A rating of 0 means that the photograph is not at all sexually stimulating to you. A rating of 5 means that the photo is very highly sexually stimulating. Ratings of 1, 2, 3, and 4 mean varying degrees

of erotic value in ascending order. Thus a rating of 4 means that the photo is less stimulating than 5 but more stimulating than 3, and so forth.*

The average ratings for each set of three photographs in the 19 categories are presented in Table 14.4.

Table 14.4   Mean sexual stimulation values for photographs depicting sexual activities.†

Theme	Average rating
1. Heterosexual coitus, ventral-ventral	4.13
2. Heterosexual coitus, ventral-dorsal	3.70
3. Heterosexual petting, both nude	3.63
4. Heterosexual petting, both partially clad	3.42
5. Oral-genital contact, female on male	3.39
6. Nude female	3.17
7. Oral-genital contact, male on female	3.04
8. Female masturbating	2.72
9. Group activity (two females and one male)	2.69
10. Partially clad female	2.63
11. Oral-genital contact, two females	2.08
12. Petting, two females	1.80
13. Sadomasochism, male on female	1.19
14. Oral-genital contact, two males	.84
15. Sadomasochism, female on male	.81
16. Male masturbating	.79
17. Anal intercourse (two males)	.42
18. Nude male	.13
19. Partially clad male	.04

† From J. P. Brady and E. E. Levitt, "The relation of sexual preferences to sexual experiences," *Psychological Record*, **15**:377–384, 1965. Used by permission.

Since the ratings were made on a five-point, equal-interval rating scale, the higher the rating was, the more sexually stimulating the subjects found the activity depicted. The most sexually stimulating theme was heterosexual intercourse in the conventional ventral-ventral position. Note that the top four themes all involved heterosexual intercourse and heterosexual petting, behaviors which are considered "normal" by our society.

* From E. E. Levitt and J. P. Brady, "Sexual preferences in young adult males and some correlates," *Journal of Clinical Psychology*, 1965, **21**, 348. Reprinted by permission.

In contrast, male homosexual activities and photographs of males alone all received ratings of less than 1.00. Themes depicting female homosexual or autoerotic activity (8, 11, and 12) were rated significantly higher than themes showing male homosexual activity (14 and 17). This result substantiates the widely held belief that heterosexual males are more stimulated by female homosexuality than by male homosexual activity. Heterosexual fellatio and cunnilingus (5 and 7), which are the most common "abnormal" sexual activities (Kinsey, Pomeroy, and Martin, 1948), were relatively stimulating in this group of male graduate students.

Of particular interest are the sexual stimulation values of Themes 6 and 10. The depiction of a nude female (6) is significantly more stimulating than Themes 8, 13, and 15, all of which depict females in some form of sexual activity. The depiction of a partially clad female (10) is no less stimulating than are photographs which would usually be considered pornographic and whose participants are nude. The authors conclude that "a photograph of a partly draped female figure, though it shows neither bare breasts nor pubic area, is likely to be highly stimulating to the young adult male." (Levitt and Brady, 1965, p. 352)

Heterosexual Somatic Preferences: Men

The finding of Levitt and Brady that a photograph of the unclad female figure was highly stimulating sexually for young males is not likely to be viewed as a startling result by most readers of this book. Although there is a remarkably small scientific literature on the subject, it is generally believed that female bodies are the most significant determinants of sexual attractiveness for males. More specifically (and again in the absence of good scientific data), it is generally believed that female breasts, buttocks, and legs are among the body parts most heavily weighted by men in their evaluation of feminine pulchritude. Although wide variations in preference for specific size and shape of these body parts are recognized, their importance as determinants of heterosexual attraction is generally agreed upon.

Of greater interest is the belief that the relative weight a man places on these body parts in arriving at his overall evaluation of feminine attractiveness characterizes or typifies his heterosexual orientation. Thus, under permissive surroundings, men will spontaneously classify themselves or their associates as breast men, buttocks men or leg men, depending on the body part which most determines their heterosexual preference. Further and of considerable interest is the cultural belief that preference for a specific body part implies certain personality characteristics, although there appears to be little agreement as to what such characteristics might be. One of the few examples of an investigation of such a hypothesis was the study of Scodell (1957) described in Chapter 6. Scodell investigated the hypothesis that men who preferred large breasts were more dependent than men who preferred small breasts. In fact, just the opposite proved to be true in the study.

The first systematic investigation of the relationship between men's preferences for specific body parts and personality characteristics was conducted by Wiggins, Wiggins, and Conger (1968). Nude female silhouettes were prepared in such a manner that the size of breasts, buttocks, and legs could be varied systematically. Five different sizes of each body part were employed. Each figure, which varied in one of the selected parts, was presented with every other figure in a forced-choice design that required the subject to indicate which of the two figures he found more attractive. An illustrative stimulus pair of silhouettes is shown in Fig. 14.2.

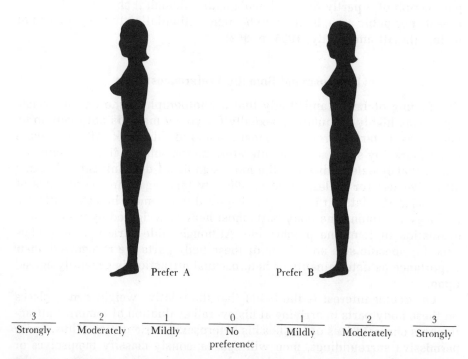

3	2	1	0	1	2	3
Strongly	Moderately	Mildly	No preference	Mildly	Moderately	Strongly

Fig. 14.2. An illustrative stimulus pair employed in the study of male heterosexual somatic preference. (From J. S. Wiggins, N. Wiggins, and J. C. Conger, "Correlates of heterosexual somatic preference," *Journal of Personality and Social Psychology*, 1968, **10**, 83. Copyright 1968, by the American Psychological Association. Reprinted by permission.)

The subjects, 95 male undergraduates from a state university, participated in two experimental sessions which they were led to believe were two distinct experiments. In the first session, the slides were presented to small groups (6–10), and the men were asked to give attractiveness ratings on the scale shown in Fig. 14.2. In the second experimental session, the subjects were administered a battery of tests: the Edwards Personal Preference Schedule, the Minnesota Multiphasic Personality Inventory, a value test, and a biographical inventory requesting information on such topics as college major, socioeconomic and family background, career plans, reading habits, smoking, drinking, dating, and infant feeding experiences. In addition, the subjects were administered the Semantic Differential test (Osgood, Suci, and Tannenbaum, 1957), which determines the "meaning" that concepts have for subjects in terms of the dimensions of evaluation, potency, and activity. In this instance, the concepts of breasts, buttocks, and legs were evaluated along with several filler items.

When the subject's preference ratings for the various sizes of breasts, buttocks, and legs were related to the background and personality characteristics, a number of interesting and significant correlations emerged.

Large breasts. Men who preferred the figure with the largest breasts included in the study were found to be readers of *Playboy* magazine. They tended to date frequently, to have masculine interests, and to read sports magazines. On the EPPS, it was found that large-breast preference was related to needs for independence, heterosexual contact, exhibitionism, and a tendency to be non-nurturant. Large-breast preference was positively related to amount of smoking and negatively related to Endurance on the EPPS. In the meaning ratings given on the Semantic Differential, those who preferred large figures saw all female body parts as "strong" and "good."

Small breasts. On the Semantic Differential, those who preferred the smaller breasts tended to rate breasts as "weak" and legs as "passive." Preference for small breasts was negatively related to the consumption of alcoholic beverages. Those who preferred the small breasts tended to hold fundamentalist religious beliefs and to be mildly depressed. In social relations, those who preferred small breasts tended to be nurturant and lacking in achievement motivation.

Large buttocks. Those who preferred the figure with the largest buttocks employed in the study were characterized by a need for order (neatness, organization, orderliness). On the Semantic Differential they tended to rate buttocks as "passive." They tended to be business majors and were not psychologically minded. In social situations, those who preferred the large buttocks were found to be dependent and given to self-abasement (guilty, self-blaming). Further, their value orientation was found *not* to be stoic in nature. The authors called attention to the similarity of this constellation of personality characteristics to the "orderliness-frugality-obstinancy" syndrome of the anal character described by Freud and later psychoanalytic writers.

Small buttocks. Those who preferred the small buttocks tended not to be self-abasing. They were high on the need for endurance and low on the need for exhibition. An unexpected finding was that those who preferred small buttocks reported that they were breast-fed as infants.

Large legs. Those who preferred large legs tended not to consume alcoholic beverages. On the EPPS they were found to be non-aggressive and self-abasing. They were psychologically minded and characterized by a slow personal tempo. In general the personality pattern associated with large-leg preference suggested one of inhibition and restraint in social situations.

Small legs. Those who preferred small legs were characterized by needs for nurturance, affiliation, and exhibitionism. Such individuals are helpful to others, feel a need for social participation, and like to be the center of attention in social situations. Those who preferred the small legs were socially dependent and tended to be low in endurance. This preference was associated with smoking, but not drinking, and the reading of sports magazines rather than *Playboy* magazine. Whereas preference for large legs appeared to be associated with social inhibition and restraint, preference for small legs appeared to be accompanied by a strong need for social participation.

The results of this study suggest that female breasts, buttocks, and legs are indeed among the determinants of heterosexual somatic preference among males. Further, they suggest that heterosexual somatic preferences are related in a meaningful fashion to other personality dimensions and background characteristics.

Heterosexual Somatic Preferences: Women

It is only very recently that the topic of female preference for male body parts has been systematically investigated. The cultural stereotype of women as less interested than men in the physical components of heterosexual attraction may have discouraged investigation of this topic. There is, of course, a cultural standard of the ideal male physique, which is portrayed in the mass media as a male with massive upper body areas (arms, shoulders, and chest) tapering down to thinner waist, hips, and legs. But this "muscleman" stereotype may have been perpetrated by males themselves, since there is evidence that such physiques are viewed positively by males (Dibiase and Hjelle, 1968; Strongman and Hart, 1968) and that males tend to equate this physique with masculinity (Darden, 1972).

The first systematic investigation of the relationship between women's preferences for specific male body parts and personality and background characteristics was conducted by Lavrakas (1975). Nude male silhouettes were prepared in such a manner that the size of arms, upper trunk, lower trunk, and legs could be varied systematically. Five different sizes of each body part were employed. Each figure, which varied in one of the selected parts, was presented with every other figure in a forced-choice design that required the subject to indicate which of the two figures she found more attractive. An illustrative stimulus pair of silhouettes is shown in Fig. 14.3.

The subjects, 64 female college undergraduates and recent graduates, participated in two experimental sessions. In the first session, the slides were presented and the women were asked to give attractiveness ratings on the scale shown in Fig. 14.3. Following the slide ratings, subjects were ad-

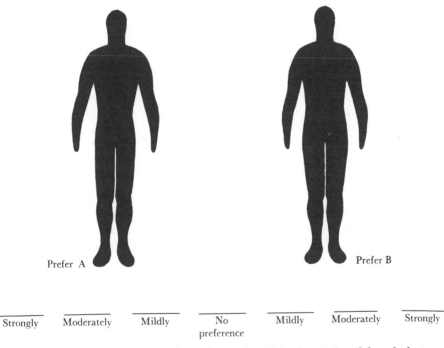

Prefer A   Prefer B

| Strongly | Moderately | Mildly | No preference | Mildly | Moderately | Strongly |

Fig. 14.3. An illustrative stimulus pair employed in the study of female heterosexual somatic preference. (From P. K. Lavrakas, "Female preferences for male physiques," *Journal of Research in Personality*, 1975, **9**, 324–334.) Used by permission.

ministered a sex-role questionnaire describing their real self (Rosenkrantz *et al.*, 1968), part of a background inventory, and a personality questionnaire. In the second session, the subjects completed the Attitudes Toward Women Scale (Spence, Helmreich, and Stapp, 1973), made Semantic Differential ratings of male body parts, completed the sex-role questionnaire describing their ideal male, and finished the remainder of the background inventory.

When the subjects' preference ratings for the various sizes of arms, upper trunk, lower trunk, and legs were related to their background and personality characteristics, a number of interesting and significant correlations emerged.

Overall moderate appearance.   Women who preferred a moderate physique, as opposed to an extreme or muscleman figure, expressed a desire for an egalitarian (androgenous) heterosexual relationship in which traditional masculine-feminine stereotypes are deemphasized. Such women tend, themselves, to have full figures (large breasts and hips). Preference for a moderate physique was correlated with ratings of thighs as "weak" on the Semantic Differential. Those who preferred the moderate figure also tended to have been raised in homes in which both the mother and father were present.

Arms and upper trunk.   Women who preferred a *large* configuration of arms and upper trunk regions expressed a desire for a traditional heterosexual relationship in which sex roles are clearly differentiated. On the Attitudes Toward Women scale, those women who presented themselves as liberated, rather than traditional, also exhibited a preference for large arms and upper trunks. Those who preferred this region to be large tended to rate chest, lower trunk, and thigh as "strong." Preference for this region was also associated with being raised in a family in which only a mother was present and in which there were more sisters than brothers.

Upper trunk.   Women who preferred a *large* upper trunk region reported that the currently most important man in their life also had a large arm and upper trunk region. Preference for a large upper trunk region was also associated with a denial of using marijuana, drugs, or alcohol.

Lower trunk.   Women who expressed traditional attitudes on the Attitudes Toward Women scale tended to prefer a large lower trunk region. Preference for a large lower trunk was expressed by women who themselves tended to be heavy. The currently most important male in the lives of women who preferred a large lower trunk tended to have large upper and lower trunk regions and large arms.

Legs.   Women who preferred large legs tended to be heavy in their own body configuration. Preference for large legs was also associated with a denial of smoking cigarettes, playing cards, and watching television. Those who preferred large legs tended to rate the lower trunk and thigh regions on the Semantic Differential as "strong."

The results of this study suggest that male arms, upper trunk, lower trunk, and legs are among the determinants of heterosexual somatic preference among females. Moreover, they suggest that heterosexual somatic preferences of females are related to feminine and masculine sex-role stereotypes and to physical appearance, personal habits, and family structure.

INDIRECT METHODS

FANTASY MEASURES OF SEXUAL IMAGERY AND GUILT

Because of strong cultural sanctions against the expression of direct sexual material, the relationship between sexual fantasy and overt sexual behavior is especially complex. It should be recalled that although the Thematic Apperception Test provides an indirect measure of personality traits, it does not provide an unconscious measure in the psychoanalytic sense of that term. The TAT is thought to measure preoccupations on the fantasy level, and such preoccupations are subject to processes of inhibition and constraint. Even when it is possible to overcome normal inhibitions against the fantasy expression of sexual material, it is likely that a certain amount of guilt will accompany even that form of expression. Consequently, when sexual preoccupation is assessed by such indirect instruments as the TAT, it is also desirable to obtain a measure of guilt connected with sexual activity.

Thematic Apperception Test stories may be scored for three different levels of sexual imagery. The primary level involves themes related to overt sexual activities, such as sexual intercourse. The secondary level involves themes expressing secondary sexual activity, such as kissing, dancing, fondling, etc. On the tertiary level, characters are perceived as sweethearts, they are in love, and they are involved in such activities as dating, courting, etc., although not engaged in activities of either the primary or the secondary level.

Thematic Apperception Test stories may also be scored for three categories which indicate the presence of sex-related guilt. In the first, the characters are openly ashamed, guilty, embarrassed, or anxiety-ridden over sexual activity. In the second category of guilt, the characters may be punished, ostracized, or criticized for sexual activity. In the third, characters may punish themselves as a result of sexual activity.

INHIBITION AND AROUSAL OF SEXUAL IMAGERY AND GUILT

A series of three pioneering studies performed by Clark (1952) will serve to illustrate the manner in which indirect measurement techniques have been employed in the study of sexuality. The basic design is one in which two groups of persons are subjected to differing degrees or conditions of sexual arousal. The experimental effect of the arousal conditions is then evaluated through an analysis of sexual imagery and guilt in TAT stories obtained after the experimental manipulation. In all cases the TAT stories were scored independently by two investigators for the two variables under study.

Study A

Experimental group.   A group of 40 male volunteers from an introductory psychology class were presented a series of life-size slides of attractive female nudes. They were asked to make ratings of sexual attractiveness for each slide, and the stimulating characteristics of the slides were emphasized. Following the presentation of the nude slides, a different experimenter administered the TAT under the guise of "a test of creative imagination."

Control group.   A group of 38 undergraduate males from the same introductory psychology class were administered a series of slides involving landscape scenes, architecture, fashionably decorated rooms, etc. The slides were presented as part of an "investigation on factors affecting esthetic judgment," and the subjects were asked to make attractiveness ratings of each slide. Following the presentation of the neutral slides, a different experimenter administered the TAT as "a test of creative imagination."

Results.   The TAT results of the two groups under comparison were combined and divided at the median, or middle, of the number of sexual and guilt stories produced. For each of the two groups, then, it was possible to determine the percentage of subjects whose stories fell above the middle of the group on both sexual imagery and guilt. If the experimental manipulation had no effect, one would expect that approximately the same percentage of subjects in each of the two groups would obtain scores above the middle on both sexual imagery and guilt.

The rather striking findings of Study A, presented in the first two rows of Table 14.5, show that the subjects who were exposed to the stimulating nude slides gave significantly fewer sexual themes and expressed significantly less sexual guilt than did the control subjects who were exposed to the neutral slides. Contrary to what one might expect for other dimensions

Table 14.5 Effects of arousal on Thematic Apperception Test sexual themes in three experiments.*

Groups	Treatment	Percentage of subjects above average on sexual imagery	Percentage of subjects above average on sexual guilt
Study A			
Experimental group (N = 40)	Exposed to nude slides		
Control group (N = 38)	Exposed to neutral slides		
Study B			
Experimental group (N = 30)	Attractive female experimenter		
Control group (N = 29)	Male experimenter		
Study C			
Experimental group (N = 35)	Nude slides plus alcohol		
Control group (N = 27)	Alcohol only		

* After Clark, 1952.

of personality, the experimental arousal of sexual stimulation appears to result in a significant inhibition of fantasy expression of sexuality. Perhaps because this inhibition was successful, the aroused subjects also expressed significantly less guilt than did the unaroused subjects in the control group.

Study B

Experimental group. A highly attractive female examiner administered the TAT at night in an office to 30 male freshmen. The girl was attractively dressed, and she wore a brand of perfume thought to be stimulating. When she "had trouble" with the projector and requested assistance, the subjects gathered around her and helped.

Control group. A male examiner administered the TAT to 29 male freshmen under more or less standard conditions.

Results. The third and fourth rows of Table 14.5 show that the presence of an attractive female examiner significantly reduced both the amount of sexual imagery expressed on TAT scores and the amount of associated guilt. Thus it may be concluded that the effects of the experimental arousal were successful and that the experimental results were comparable to those obtained in the experiment involving nude slides: conditions of sexual arousal appear to result in an inhibition of the expression of sexual imagery and consequent reduction in the amount of guilt expressed over sexuality.

Study C

Experimental group. In the course of a beer-drinking party, 35 members of a fraternity were administered a series of slides of attractive nude females as part of the general festivities. Shortly thereafter, the TAT was administered under the guise of a study of "the effects of informal environment and alcohol on a test of creative imagination." The TAT was administered approximately an hour and fifteen minutes after the start of the beer party, and the subjects were permitted to continue drinking during the test.

Control group. At another fraternity beer party, 27 undergraduate males participated in a study of "the effects of informal environment and alcohol on a test of creative imagination." As with the experimental group, the TAT was administered approximately an hour and fifteen minutes after the start of the beer party, and the subjects were permitted to continue drinking during the test. However, no nude slides were shown to this group.

Results. The final two rows of Table 14.5 show that the effects of the alcohol and the informal party conditions were sufficient to overcome the inhibition of sexual expression that ordinarily follows the presentation of sexually arousing slides. Fraternity men who saw the nude slides under beer party conditions expressed significantly greater sexual imagery on the TAT than did fraternity men who did not see nude slides under similar conditions. Of equal importance is the finding that significantly greater sexual guilt also accompanied sexual imagery in the fraternity beer-drinking group who had been sexually aroused. It may be concluded from these data that alcohol ingestion, in an informal party setting, is sufficient to overcome inhibitions against sexual expression after sexual stimulation. Even under such informal conditions, however, sexual expression results in a concomitant increase in sexual guilt as expressed on the fantasy level.

The results of the three experiments by Clark (1952) are consistent with one another and highly informative with respect to the patterns of relationship that exist between sexual arousal and the fantasy expression of sexual themes. It appears that sexual arousal results in an active inhibition of fantasy preoccupation with sexuality, as indicated by a reduction in both sexual imagery and sexual guilt. This inhibition may be overcome, to some extent, by the ingestion of alcohol in an informal social setting. But even under such informal circumstances, increases in fantasy expression of sexual themes are accompanied by increases in fantasy preoccupation with sexual guilt. Such findings are consistent with the observation that sexuality is the dimension of personality most severely inhibited by our society.

SUMMARY

Sexuality is, at once, possibly the most important and certainly the least understood dimension of human personality. Recent advances in methods and techniques for the study of human sexuality, together with an increasingly favorable and enlightened public view of sex research, have made possible many rapid advances in this previously undeveloped field. The interview studies of Kinsey and associates and the behavioral-observation studies of Masters and Johnson are unquestionably among the most monumental studies that have ever been conducted in the science of human behavior. The present chapter provided a description of the sampling and interviewing procedures employed by Kinsey and of the sampling and observational procedures employed by Masters and Johnson.

The research of Kinsey and others suggests that heterosexual experiences follow a cumulative or sequential pattern from petting to intercourse to oral-genital contacts. That cumulative pattern has definite implications for the type of model employed in the measurement of sexual experiences by self-report methods. Such a model forms the basis for a Guttman scale, in which the complete pattern of item responses can be reproduced from a knowledge of the total score on the scale. The hypothesis that sexual experiences are cumulative and may be quantified by means of a Guttman scale has been confirmed in three separate studies, conducted under different circumstances, with different samples of subjects, and with different items. If an individual admits having had a particular sexual experience, it can be assumed with a high degree of certainty that he or she has experienced all or most sexual experiences that are reported with greater frequency in the general population.

Preferences for various forms of sexual activity may be measured directly by showing subjects photographs depicting the various forms and asking them to report the degree of sexual stimulation they experienced in viewing the photographs. A carefully designed study of preferences for sexual activity demonstrated that heterosexual intercourse and heterosexual petting were the most stimulating themes for male graduate students. Of particular interest was the finding that themes depicting nude and partially clad females alone were more stimulating than a variety of themes generally considered pornographic in nature. A study of male preferences for specific female body parts indicated that female breasts, buttocks, and legs are significant determinants of heterosexual somatic preferences among college males. A study of female preferences for specific male body parts indicated that male arms, upper trunk, lower trunk, and legs are significant determinants of heterosexual somatic preferences among college females. Of greater interest was the finding that such heterosexual somatic preferences were related in a meaningful fashion to personality and background characteristics of the subjects whose preferences were studied.

From three studies of the relationship between sexual arousal and the fantasy expression of sexual themes on the Thematic Apperception Test, an investigator concluded that sexual arousal results in an active inhibition of fantasy preoccupation with sexuality, as indicated by a reduction in both sexual imagery and sexual guilt. This inhibition may be partially overcome by the ingestion of alcohol in an informal social setting. Even under such circumstances, however, increases in fantasy expression of sexual themes were accompanied by increases in fantasy preoccupation with sexual guilt. Such findings are consistent with the observation that sexuality is the dimension of personality most severely inhibited by our society.

Section 5
Theories
of
Personality

15
Psychoanalytic Theory

I. **Background and orientation**
   A. Historical perspective
      1. The origins of psycho-analysis
      2. Psychoanalysis and the biological viewpoint
      3. Psychoanalysis and the psychometric-trait view-point
      4. Psychoanalysis and the experimental viewpoint
      5. Psychoanalysis and the social viewpoint
   B. Philosophical perspective
      1. The active and the passive human
      2. Shifting philosophical per-spectives in psychoanalysis

II. **Central assertion and principal constructs**
   A. The id and associated con-structs
      1. Unconscious processes
      2. Instinctual drives
   B. The ego and associated con-structs
      1. Adaptation and coordina-tion
      2. Defense mechanisms
         a. Repression
         b. Projection
         c. Reaction formation
         d. Rationalization
   C. The superego and associated constructs
      1. The socialization process
      2. Adult moral life

III. **Range and focus of convenience**

IV. **Applications to selected topics**
   A. Dependency
   B. Aggression
   C. Sexuality

V. **Summary**

VI. **Suggestions for further reading**

Aside from their profound influence on psychology in general and on the study of personality in particular, the findings of Sigmund Freud and the constructs of psychoanalysis have had a massive impact on the fabric of the society in which we live. Psychoanalysis has been responsible for new ways of viewing such diverse fields as anthropology, sociology, political science, literature, art, medicine, and advertising. When we make a "Freudian slip," uncover a hidden motive in the behavior of a friend, or recognize the sexual significance of certain symbols, we are behaving as members of a society well aware of the teachings of Sigmund Freud.

We will begin this chapter with a brief consideration of the historical context in which psychoanalytic theory arose, and we will show how the principal constructs of psychoanalysis have influenced the four viewpoints of personality study considered earlier in the text. Next, we will discuss the philosophical perspective or view of humankind that has developed as a consequence of psychoanalytic propositions. The central assertion of psychoanalysis will be described, and some of the principal constructs of the theory will be presented. Consideration of the range and focus of convenience of psychoanalytic theory and some illustrative applications to dependency, aggression, and sexuality will follow.

BACKGROUND AND ORIENTATION

HISTORICAL PERSPECTIVE

The Origins of Psychoanalysis

Sigmund Freud (1856–1939) is clearly the founder of psychoanalysis. Nevertheless, he was indebted to a number of contemporaries, as well as to a set of circumstances which made the development of psychoanalysis possible. Though Freud was not interested in medical practice, at the time that career was the only one suitable for the pursuit of his more general interests. Consequently, Freud enrolled as a medical student at the University of Vienna in 1873.

On completion of medical school, Freud entered the practice of neurology and became interested in the treatment of neurological disorders. Three years before Freud received his doctor's degree, the famous French physician Jean Charcot (1825–1893) had established a neurological clinic in France which was attracting the attention of many European neurologists of the day. Charcot's speciality was the treatment of hysterical paralysis, paralysis in the absence of any demonstrable organic pathology. Charcot treated such patients by hypnotizing them and suggesting that their symptoms of neurological disorder would disappear. Freud studied at Charcot's clinic for four months and came away with an enthusiasm for the use of hypnosis in the treatment of hysterical disorders.

A few years prior to Freud's study with Charcot, an extraordinary discovery had been made by Freud's friend and colleague Josef Breuer (1842–1925). Breuer was then treating a young woman (the now famous "Anna O.") who was the victim of a variety of hysterical symptoms, including paralysis and complications in sight, speech, and eating. Although Breuer was treating the patient by hypnosis, she would frequently talk about her symptoms and their origin while in a waking state. Once, when she was relating the details of the first appearance of a symptom, the symptom itself disappeared. Breuer continued to encourage the patient to speak about her illness in a procedure which he called the "talking cure." Freud and Breuer later studied this technique more intensively over a period of three years, during which they combined the methods of hypnosis with the "talking cure." Eventually, Freud abandoned the technique of hypnosis entirely and substituted for it the now well known method of *free association.*

The material provided by Freud's analysis of his patients and of himself led to a tentative account of the origins of hysterical symptoms in female patients. Hysterical symptoms appeared to be related to "forgotten" memories of certain childhood experiences. In particular there appeared to be evidence that many, if not all, of the hysterical women treated by Freud and Breuer had been sexually seduced during childhood by irresponsible adults. The memory of this event gave rise to painful feelings or affects. Through the mechanisms of defense, such unpleasant memories were "dissociated" from consciousness along with their associated unpleasant affects. Because they were outside consciousness, the affects could not then be expressed. Energy from such "dammed-up" affects constituted the basis of hysterical symptoms. Through the process of the "talking cure," the unpleasant memories were recalled, the dammed-up effects released, and the symptoms cured.

The assertion that large numbers of respectable Viennese fathers were actively seducing their daughters was hardly well received by the Victorian society of Freud's day. Even Krafft-Ebing, no stranger to sexual aberrations, considered the idea a "scientific fairy tale" (Jones, 1953). Eventually Freud himself, in an act of unprecedented intellectual courage, repudiated his own theory. He had learned that his patients had *fantasized* their childhood seductions and that the memories in question had no basis in external reality.

From that point on, Freud shifted his interest from external reality to internal, or "intrapsychic," matters. He pursued the theory that painful memories arose from internal *instincts,* or *instinctual drives,* rather than from internal events. Freud's concentration on intrapsychic structures and forces resulted in a relative neglect of such external realities as the social and cultural influences that contribute to personality development. This one-sided emphasis of Freud's psychoanalytic theory was eventually corrected by psychoanalysts such as Heinz Hartmann (1939) and Erik Erikson (1950), who described the manner in which intrapsychic structures and forces were influenced by the social environment in which the individual develops.

Although the development of psychoanalytic theory was complex and often contradictory, three basic psychological constructs can serve to illustrate the influence of Freud's ideas on contemporary views of humans. Running throughout Freud's writing is a distinction among three aspects of psychological behavior which were originally thought to be specific entities, but which are now recognized as vantage points from which to interpret psychological behavior.

The *id,* or unconscious aspect, of the individual was thought to be the reservoir of primitive biological instincts that are continually striving for expression.

The *ego,* or self, was that aspect of experience which is readily available to individuals in their conscious and waking state. The normal functions of memory, perception, thinking, and the like were eventually recognized to be specialized ego structures.

The *superego,* or conscience, represented the internalized values of society which oppose the expression of unacceptable impulses, such as sexual and aggressive instincts. Although moral values may originate in the institutions of society, they operate within each individual via the superego.

The historical influence of the constructs of id, ego, and superego on the development of the field of personality study can best be grasped by considering these constructs in relation to the four viewpoints of personality study we have discussed in this book. Figure 15.1 illustrates the manner in which the constructs of id, ego, and superego have influenced these viewpoints. The diagram emphasizes the major points of development and modifications of psychoanalytic theory as applied to personality study.

Psychoanalysis and the Biological Viewpoint

Because Freud introduced the psychogenic (of psychological origin) view into psychiatry, one might not think of him as a biological psychologist. Actually, however, Freud was one of the most "biological" of all personal-

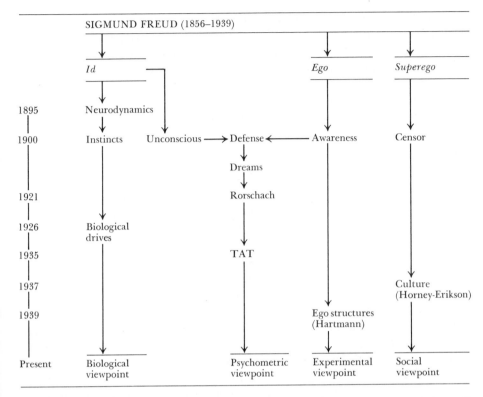

Fig. 15.1. Diagram of the intellectual history of the four current viewpoints of personality insofar as they stem from Freud.

ity theorists. As a medical doctor Freud had been trained in anatomy and physiology, and his specialization was clinical neurology. It is not surprising, therefore, that Freud's first attempt to give an account of human behavior (1895) was based exclusively on neurological constructs. In that early neurodynamic theory, Freud attempted to specify the neurological processes underlying such psychological phenomena as pleasure, pain, memory, motive, learning, and thinking. Even by today's standards that neurological theory is considered a sophisticated one (Pribram, 1962). Freud himself soon abandoned the neurological approach and focused instead on the biological drives that determine psychological behavior.

The origins and causes of all behavior, according to Freud, may be attributed to the action of biological drives arising from specific tissue tensions within the organism. These biological drives are instinctual in nature, and although they may be modified, they cannot be eradicated. In a sense, the whole history of civilization may be viewed as an attempt to reconcile innate human biological drives with the demands of society. The biological viewpoint is so central to psychoanalysis that any variant of the theory which does not accept biological determinism as a central assumption is not properly called psychoanalysis. Those who do not accept that assumption are referred to as Neo-Freudians, rather than Freudians.

Psychoanalysis and the Psychometric-Trait Viewpoint

As can be seen in Fig. 15.1, the biological instincts that reside in the id are unconscious in nature. For the most part, such impulses are unacceptable to the conscious ego, and for this reason the ego attempts to defend itself from awareness of them. Freud was the first to recognize that hysterical symptoms represent a defense against the intrusion into consciousness (ego) of unconscious material from the id.

The elaborate *defense mechanisms* of the ego are dramatically revealed by the analysis of dreams. Many psychoanalysts believe that Freud's *The Interpretation of Dreams* (1900) was his most brilliant and original contribution. It was in this work that Freud demonstrated how an analysis of the *manifest* content of dreams (what we recall on awakening) may lead to an understanding of their *latent* (hidden) meaning as an expression of unconsciousness instincts. Because the superego, or censor, is more relaxed in the dreaming state, the operation of various defenses may be observed more readily than in the waking state. Defenses operate to distort, disguise, or displace the latent content of dreams in such a way that their true meaning does not become subject to conscious awareness and thereby disturb the sleep of the dreamer. Freud referred to dreams as "the royal road to the unconscious." By this he meant that the dreaming state was one of the few occasions on which relatively precise measurements could be made of the operation of various defense mechanisms in transforming the latent meaning of the dreams to their manifest content. Other occasions which provide opportunity for the measurement of defense mechanisms are slips of the tongue, reveries, and the free associations given during psychoanalysis.

Another avenue to the measurement of defense mechanisms was provided when Rorschach (1921) published his inkblot test. As indicated in Chapter 2, Rorschach studied the associations of psychiatric patients to ambiguous inkblots in order to classify the disorders of perception, thought, and association that occur among the mentally ill. The implications of that technique for the study of defense mechanisms were almost immediately recognized by Freudian psychologists. Later, Murray's Thematic Apperception Test was specifically designed to provide more controlled measurements of fantasies than those obtained from the analysis of dreams and free associations (Morgan and Murray, 1935).

The recent history of projective testing is characterized by increased efforts to produce accurate and reliable measures of defense mechanisms. For the most part, these techniques represent improvements over the methods first employed by Freud. Nevertheless, it was Freud who first formulated the problem and thus laid the foundation for the eventual application of the psychometric-trait viewpoint to the study of defense mechanisms.

Psychoanalysis and the Experimental Viewpoint

In the beginning, Freud's studies followed a path quite divergent from that of general experimental psychology. Whereas experimental psychology emphasized laboratory studies of thinking, perception, memory, and learning in normal individuals, Freud emphasized clinical studies of unconscious processes in abnormal individuals. This fact has led some critics to assert that psychoanalysis is opposed to the viewpoint of experimental psychology. It is true that in his early writings Freud tended to neglect the normal aspects of ego functioning, such as thinking, perception, and memory. His reason was strategic rather than ideological, however. Prior to Freud, virtually no one had studied the irrational aspect of individuals represented by their unconscious instincts. To make up for this one-sided emphasis, Freud devoted the bulk of his professional career to the study of the unconscious and the defense mechanisms. Nevertheless, it is clear from Freud's early writings that he intended his psychology to be a general psychology that embraced the normal ego functions of thinking, perception, and memory as well as the less-understood functions of instincts.

In Freud's early writings, the ego was a relatively passive instrument of consciousness which attempted to serve as a mediator between biological drives and the demands of the conscience. The ego attempted this reconciliation between the id and the superego by means of defense mechanisms, or ego defenses. Freud's stress upon the defensive functions of the ego tended to give the somewhat one-sided impression that all, or most, ego functions served only a defensive purpose.

It remained for Heinz Hartmann (1894–1970) to reinstate the normal, non-defensive functions of the ego in psychoanalytic theory and thereby bridge the gap between psychoanalysis and general experimental psychology. Hartmann emphasized certain ego structures (*apparatuses*) which are independent of biological instincts and therefore capable of development in other than defensive ways. Hartmann did not deny the importance of biological instincts as determinants of a large part of human behavior; therefore he remained well within the Freudian camp. By emphasizing normal ego functions, such as perceptual apparatuses, that developed independently of biological instincts, Hartmann made Freudian psychology a truly general psychology.

Hartmann's extension of psychoanalytic theory has proved beneficial to both psychoanalysis and general experimental psychology. Many psychoanalytic investigators are now conducting experimental studies of perception, memory, and thinking in laboratory settings. Similarly, during the past two decades a number of experimental psychologists have attempted to apply laboratory techniques to the study of such psychoanalytic phenomena as conflict, displacement, and defense. In many respects the kinds of investigation stimulated by Hartmann's work are indistinguishable from traditional experimental studies of perception and thought.

Psychoanalysis and the Social Viewpoint

As indicated in the last section, Freud was committed in principle to the task of constructing a general psychology, but in practice he tended to emphasize certain aspects of human behavior rather than others. Perhaps the most neglected determinant of human behavior in Freud's early writings was the social or cultural matrix in which behavior develops and occurs. Freud's early psychology was primarily an intrapsychic (within the individual) psychology and, as such, tended not to concentrate on social and environmental events that occurred outside the organism. In his early writing, Freud spoke of a "censor" which passed moral judgment on the sexual and aggressive instincts of the id. That censor represented society's values in a rather vague manner, and it was not until the development of the superego construct that Freud explained how the values of society came to be internalized within the individual. Regardless of its origin, the superego was primarily an intrapsychic mechanism which tended to operate in a somewhat irrational and infantile fashion. For the most part, Freud neglected rather obvious aspects of the social context in which the organism develops, preferring to concentrate on intrapsychic representations (ideas) of the external social world.

It was that relative neglect of the social and cultural context in which behavior occurred that led many of Freud's disciples to abandon the biological determinism of Freudian psychology in favor of a cultural determinism. Anthropological studies of societies very different from our own had provided evidence that personality is not solely dependent on universal biological drives, but rather that it is formed and shaped by the culture in which it develops. In the same manner in which Freud neglected social and cultural factors in favor of biological drives, the Neo-Freudians tended to emphasize cultural factors to the relative exclusion of biological determinants. The net result was an increased emphasis on social and cultural factors within the general framework of psychoanalytic theory itself.

Karen Horney (1885–1952) was among the first to offer an explanation of the manner in which cultural influences provide a framework within which personality develops. She called attention to the fact that neurotic behavior does not develop solely as a consequence of intrapsychic conflict, but rather may be determined by incompatible emphases within the culture itself. The most detailed exposition of the role of cultural factors in personality development has been that provided by Erik Erikson. For Erikson it is not a question of the individual's adapting to society nor of the society's molding the individual. The individual and the society form a unity which cannot be artificially separated.

PHILOSOPHICAL PERSPECTIVE

The Active and the Passive Human

An ancient philosophical issue first posed by Aristotle (384–322 B.C.) raises the question whether humans are active or passive agents in their environment. This issue became crystallized in the divergent philosophical perspectives of Gottfried Leibnitz (1646–1716) and John Locke (1632–1704). Following Aristotle's line of reasoning, Locke conceived of the mind at birth as a *tabula rasa,* or blank slate. The individual is thus a passive recipient of sensations imprinted by the outside world and can know only such sensations, not the world itself. According to this view, a person's development and eventual destiny are entirely dependent on environmental experiences and the knowledge they give of the external world.

In reply to Locke's assertion *"nihil est in intellectu quod non fuerit in sensu"* (nothing can be in the intellect that was not first in the senses), Leibnitz replied, *"excipe: nisi ipse intellectus"* (nothing—except the intellect itself). For Leibnitz, mind is an active unity that undergoes continuous development in accord with its own laws. Rather than being passive recipients of experiences, people actively construe their environment according to laws of mental development independent of experience.

Box 15.1   Psychoanalytic theorists.

Courtesy of the Bettmann Archive

Sigmund Freud, born in 1856 in Freiberg, a small town in what is now Czechoslovakia, moved to Vienna a few years later. He received his M.D. in 1881 from the University of Vienna. By the turn of the century, his clinical and theoretical writings had attracted worldwide attention; in 1910 Freud and such disciples as Alfred Adler, Ernest Jones, C. G. Jung, and Otto Rank founded the International Psychoanalytic Association. Dissent within the association and a general lack of acceptance by the medical profession made Freud's career a bitter and difficult one. Shortly after the rise of Hitler in Germany, Freud fled to England, where he died in 1939. He was survived by his daughter Anna, who continued to make major contributions to the theory of personality originated by her father.

Heinz Hartmann, born in 1894 in Vienna, received his M.D. from the University of Vienna. His early practice was in the University Psychiatric Clinics, and after a period of time in Berlin, he returned to Vienna to undergo further psychoanalytic training under both Freud and Breuer. In his long and distinguished career, he was affiliated with psychoanalytic institutes in Vienna, Paris, and New York. Hartmann's *Ego Psychology and the Problem of Adaptation* (1939) established him as one of the foremost psychoanalytic theorists of modern times. His emphasis on normal ego functions and the importance of external reality broadened the scope of psychoanalytic theory and brought it closer to Freud's goal of a general psychology.

Erik H. Erikson, born in 1902 of Danish parents in Frankfurt, left a career in art to be educated at the Vienna Psychoanalytic Institute, principally by Anna Freud. At the Harvard Psychological Clinic, he was introduced to other personality theories by Henry A. Murray and, through field trips, to cultural anthropology in association with Margaret Mead. For some time he was on the staff of the Austen Riggs Center and is currently Professor Emeritus of Human Development and Lecturer on Psychiatry at Harvard. His works are widely read and highly relevant to our times, particularly his formulations regarding the *identity crisis* which youth faces developmentally—and in aggravated form in times such as our own.

Shifting Philosophical Perspectives in Psychoanalysis

In his early writings, Freud viewed humans as essentially passive agents. The ego, which is the individual's essential core of being, was the victim of both external reality and instinctual strivings. Freud admitted that instinctual drives were active forces within the organism, but the ego had no independent energies to oppose such forces. Because Freud believed that the ego was a relatively passive victim of reality and instincts, his view was basically a pessimistic one. Under the proper circumstances, people could effect adaptive compromises between their primitive instinctual promptings and the demands of a mainly oppressive society. But the nature of the compromises was dictated by the matrix in which the ego developed rather than by the active long-range goals of the ego.

The extensions of psychoanalysis made by Hartmann and Erikson shifted the philosophical perspective in the direction of Leibnitz's active view of the human. Hartmann postulated inborn ego energies that equip the organism for active adaptation to its environment. Erikson maintained that the ego is an active unity that undergoes continuous development in accord with its own laws. Ego development, to be sure, is influenced by cultural institutions and particularly by child-rearing practices. But people are free to change such institutions and practices to make them more compatible with the long-range goals of the ego.

CENTRAL ASSERTION AND PRINCIPAL CONSTRUCTS

Central Assertion: *Behavior is multiply determined by interacting and interrelated forces originating in the separate domains of the id, ego, and superego. Behavior cannot be construed solely in terms of the principles of mental functioning that govern any one of these systems. Instead, behavior should be viewed as a product of all three. Considering the domains of id, ego, and superego respectively, we might say that for any behavior we must seek multiple causes (instincts, defenses, anxiety) and multiple reasons (irrational, rational, moral).*

THE ID AND ASSOCIATED CONSTRUCTS

Unconscious Processes

In the Western world prior to Freud, the predominant view of human nature was one that emphasized *rationality*. Our ability to plan, to reason, and to perceive the world realistically was assumed to distinguish us from the "lower" animals whose behaviors were governed primarily by instincts and base appetites. This picture of the rational human may be thought of as an inverted pyramid in which higher qualities of logical thought and reason predominate over a small base of vestigial instincts. Freud's most revolutionary contribution to Western thought was his insistence that this picture was totally wrong. In Freud's view, the individual is *mainly* governed by irrational instincts; conscious, rational facilities constitute only a fragment of the total personality.

The psychoanalytic view of the human is illustrated in Fig. 15.2. The bulk of our mental life is unconscious in nature. Our conscious apperception of external reality is only the tip of an iceberg. Because we are aware only of the contents of our consciousness, which relate mainly to the events of the external world, we are ignorant of the contents of our unconscious, which relate to the bodily instincts of our internal psychic world.

This view was so much at variance with the traditional views held by the scholars of Freud's day (and with the intuitions of almost everyone) that it met with understandable resistance. Darwin's *On the Origin of*

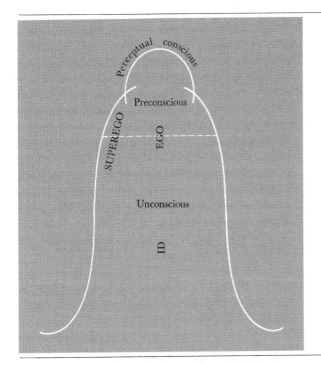

Fig. 15.2. The psychoanalytic view of the human.

Species, published 40 years earlier, had paved the way for acceptance of the view that we share much in common with other animals, including instincts. But the concept of *unconscious* was a real stumbling block in the road to acceptance of the theory. How can we talk about things of which we are, by definition, unaware? If the principles governing our interior mental lives are not rational or logical, how could they be systematic enough to determine our behavior?

Freud's greatest discovery was that the unconscious processes of the id have a "language" and "logic" of their own. This insight followed Freud's recognition that the symptoms of hysterical patients appeared to be communicating a symbolic message that represented instincts in disguised form. Through painstaking analyses of his own dreams and those of his patients, Freud was able to delineate the nature of unconscious processes and to specify their modes of operation. This analysis was extended to the "parapraxes" (faulty acts) of everyday life: slips of the tongue, misreadings, mishearings, temporary forgettings, and mislayings shown not to be accidental but to make sense in terms of the logic of the unconscious.

Unconscious processes are designated as *alogical* to emphasize that they are not simply accidental or faulty in logic, but that they are characterized by the complete *absence* of ordinary logical conventions. For example, the logic of the unconscious is unrestrained by ordinary conventions regarding temporal and spatial coordinates. Our dreams are "timeless" in the sense that characters from different periods coexist side by side; figures long-dead appear in the present, or we may find ourselves in an earlier period of history. Ordinary conventions of space are violated when, in our dreams, we cross a familiar street and find ourselves in a foreign country. It is common in dreams to have two objects occupying the same space, as when two different persons are fused into one character.

Unconscious processes are *primitive* in several meanings of the word. They are held to characterize the interior lives of infants, members of primitive societies, and mental patients who are severely regressed to an earlier developmental stage. The average adult has access to unconscious material only under special circumstances: during dreams and reveries when conscious controls are temporarily suspended, during states of extreme fatigue, and during altered states of consciousness induced by psychedelic substances. The peculiar logic of the unconscious is evident in the magical beliefs and practices of primitive societies and in the bizarre symptoms of mental patients. The ascription of unconscious qualities to the mental life of infants is an inference demanded by the theory.

Instinctual Drives

The id is the reservoir of instinctual drives which energize the organism and give directionality to behavior. Tensions and excitations in the body are transformed into "psychic energy" experienced as an unpleasant state of tension or irritability. The id system operates in such a way that the painful tension brought about by increases in drive level is reduced by the *immediate discharge* of psychic energy. Depending upon the opportunities available for immediate discharge, the psychic energy may be dispelled through reflex actions (behavior), emotional outbursts (feelings), or mental images (ideas).

When the infant is hungry and the mother's breast is available, the reflex action of sucking (behavior) will satisfy the drive and thereby reduce tension. Should the mother be absent, the infant may cry (feelings) and achieve a temporary reduction in tension through the expression of emotion. It is also possible for the infant to form a mental image of the remembered breast (idea) and to discharge psychic energy through this hallucinatory experience. The latter process of discharging energy through a mental representation of the desired object is called *wish-fulfillment,* and it plays a key role in psychoanalytic theory. On the basis of his investigations of dreams, Freud concluded that the hallucinated images of the dream experience represent wish-fulfillments and hence provide clues to the nature of the unconscious instincts which gave rise to them.

The principle whereby increases in tension are reduced by immediate discharge is called the *pleasure principle.* It is important to note that the id system operates according to this principle automatically and without regard for environmental or reality consequences. In the undifferentiated mind of the infant, actions, feelings, and ideas are equivalent; that is, they all provide immediate discharge of energy in accord with the aim of the pleasure principle. Obviously, however, these responses are not equivalent in terms of their adaptive significance for the organism. A baby who only cries or thinks about the breast will eventually starve.

THE EGO AND ASSOCIATED CONSTRUCTS

Adaptation and Coordination

It should be clear from the foregoing account that the survival of the organism is not ensured, and may in fact be endangered, by the pleasure principle of the id system. The pleasure principle is not an adaptive one because it fails to take into account the consequences of actions and because it fails to distinguish among actions, feelings, and ideas as appropriate means for energy discharge. The ego system is concerned with the appropriate and adaptive coordination of instinctual drives with the demands of external reality. Thus, in contrast with the id which follows the pleasure principle, the ego follows the *reality principle.*

In the course of development, the ego system evolves as an organized subsystem of the id. Although its energy source is principally instinctual, the ego is capable of utilizing id energies in the service of the reality principle. For example, the ego system is capable of evaluating whether or not hallucinatory images correspond to events in the external world—it distinguishes between a memory image of the mother's breast and the mother's breast itself. On the basis of this distinction between subjective and objective reality, the ego system is able to delay drive expression until conditions in the external world are appropriate—until the mother's breast is present. The pleasure principle of the id system is eventually satisfied, but in a manner that is more adaptive from the standpoint of the organism's survival.

As the ego system serves the ultimate purpose of the id system (tension reduction) in more efficient ways, it is granted more energy for its operations. These operations of logical thought or problem-solving are familiar to everyone. The delay of immediate instinctual gratification permits "experiments in thought" which serve as temporary substitutes for action. The individual reasons: "If I were to do A, it would have consequence X, which is undesirable; but if I were to do B, it would have consequence Y, which is more desirable than X." By such mental experimentation, individuals can anticipate the consequences of their actions, plan accordingly, and thus locate the most appropriate source of gratification according to the reality principle.

Referring back to Fig. 15.2, notice that the ego occupies the central position among the personality systems. It has access to the external world through the conscious apparatuses of perception. It also has access to instinctual drives because the ego system is itself an organized portion of the id system. And, as will be discussed later, the ego has access to the promptings of the superego. In its efforts to gratify instinctual drives in accord with the reality principle, the ego assumes the role of an executive who must *coordinate* the often conflicting needs and goals of co-workers. Although the system is "in charge" in this sense, its position is not an enviable one. In serving what Freud called the "three harsh masters," the ego system must resort to a variety of Machiavellian maneuvers. A particularly interesting class of such maneuvers is found in the mechanisms of defense.

Defense Mechanisms

As the coordinator of diverse inputs, the ego system is vulnerable to attack on several fronts. Events in the external world may threaten the well-being of the organism, instinctual drives may force the organism to behave in an inappropriate fashion, or certain thoughts and actions may violate the organism's own internal standards. When the ego system is unable to cope with such threats, anxiety is experienced as a warning signal of impending doom. Freud distinguished three types of anxiety according to their source of threat: *objective anxiety* signals a danger from the external world; *neurotic anxiety* arises from the fear of punishment for impulsive actions; *moral anxiety* signals the possibility of guilt feelings when the standards of the superego are violated.

The defense mechanisms of the ego are a class of maneuvers employed in warding off anxiety when the threat to the system cannot be dealt with according to the reality principle. Because they involve falsifications of reality and operate outside of awareness, the ego defense mechanisms provide only a temporary solution to psychological problems. Most of us have used some of these mechanisms on occasion, but their prolonged and extensive use can result in serious problems of adjustment. From among the dozen or so ego defense mechanisms that have been identified, we shall consider regression, projection, reaction formation, and rationalization.

Repression. This is one of the earliest and most fundamental ego mechanisms for warding off anxiety associated with unacceptable thoughts, feelings, or impulses. The ego expends energy to force the threatening material out of consciousness and to keep it out of awareness. Painful feelings of anxiety are temporarily avoided, since the individual is literally unaware of the thoughts or impulses that posed a threat to the ego system. This may not be an effective long-range solution, however, since repressed material in the id system continually strives for expression, either directly or in symptomatic form. Additional ego energy must be expended either to keep the material from erupting into consciousness or to deal with it by means of alternative defensive maneuvers.

A husband humiliates his wife at a party by behaving toward her in an inconsiderate and insensitive way. This gives rise to quite legitimate feelings of anger and a desire to retaliate on her part. These feelings are potentially anxiety-arousing, however, since the woman may fear punishment for retaliatory behavior (neurotic anxiety) or she may feel guilty for having negative feelings that are not compatible with her moral standards concerning marriage (moral anxiety). As a consequence, the hostile feelings are automatically repressed and thereby excluded from conscious awareness. Note that this is not a conscious decision to inhibit angry feelings. Counting to ten before striking out at her husband would be an example of "suppression," not repression, which operates automatically and unawares.

By repressing her anger and behaving sympathetically, the woman is able both to avoid anxiety and to preserve the more positive aspects of her marital relationship. However, by relegating her hostile feelings towards her husband to the id system, she has precluded the possibility of working through this conflict in terms of the rational thought processes of the ego system. The repressed impulse may be expressed in inappropriate ways, or even in symptomatic form. The woman may find herself expressing anger toward close associates in a way that is out of proportion to any provocation that might have been offered. Or she may find herself becoming extremely defensive when anyone suggests that she might have negative feelings toward her husband.

If the woman continues to employ repression as a major defense, it is possible that she will exclude (repress) progressively larger areas of experience related to her negative feelings toward her husband. Her impoverished realm of experience would then make it more difficult to behave realistically with respect to the original conflict. In an extreme symptomatic expression of the repressed impulse, the woman might develop an hysterical paralysis of the arm as atonement for and an expression of a primitive desire to strike her husband. One of the goals of psychoanalytic psychotherapy is to bring repressed conflictual material into conscious awareness so that it may be dealt with in terms of the reality principle. Freud stated this goal succinctly: "Where id was, there ego shall be."

Projection. In this defense mechanism, unacceptable thoughts, feelings, or impulses originating in the id system are attributed to objects or events in the external world. Being unable to cope with the feelings of neurotic or moral anxiety triggered by aggressive or sexual impulses, the individual "projects" these impulses onto other people or organizations in the real world. The aggressive or sexual connotations of the conflict are not denied, but they are easier to cope with when viewed as originating outside rather than inside the organism. This maneuver effectively converts neurotic or moral anxiety into objective anxiety. In general it is easier, psychologically, to cope with threats from without than with threats from within. The external threat remains as a source of objective anxiety, but it can be dealt with by "rational" procedures designed to protect the organism from external harm.

It is common for people to attribute their own shortcomings to others. In most instances, they may illustrate the general principle that we tend to view others as being like ourselves. In projection, however, the origin of the original unacceptable impulse is denied and any residuals of that impulse are rationalized on different logical grounds. In our example of the wife who had unacceptable hostile impulses toward her husband, the impulse "I hate him" could have been transformed to "He hates me" by the mechanism of projection. The husband's inconsiderate and insensitive behavior might then have been construed as a behavioral manifestation of hostile impulses and, more generally, as part of a systematic program of persecution. This maneuver has the advantages of both denying the source of the hostile impulse ("It is his anger, not mine") and providing a rationalization for any residual hostile feelings that may remain ("I am justified in hating him because he persecutes me").

In its extreme form, this line of reasoning is characteristic of paranoid personalities. In order to justify the attribution of unacceptable impulses to others, the paranoid may develop highly systematized modes of thought (delusions of persecution) which seriously impair contact with reality. That there is usually more than a grain of truth involved in any paranoid delusional system tends to sustain the system and make it resistant to therapeutic modification.

The complexity of the mechanism of projection and its relation to pathological conditions such as paranoia are well illustrated in Freud's (1911) analysis of the case of Schreber. Schreber's delusional system revolved around the central notion that it was his mission to redeem the world and that he could do so only if he were first transformed from a man into a woman. Delusions of persecution clustered around these ideas as well. In this case study, Freud discovered what appeared to be a relationship between paranoia and unacceptable homosexual impulses: a relationship that could be understood in terms of the mechanism of projection. In this instance, the unacceptable id impulse is homosexual in form: "I (a man) *love him* (a man)." This proposition is denied by the paranoid personality in terms of a contradiction: "I do not *love* him. I *hate* him." However, this contradiction still leaves the ego open to threat from an unacceptable internal impulse. By the mechanism of projection, it becomes transformed into: "He *hates* (persecutes) *me,* which will justify me in hating him." The unconscious impulse can be accepted because it appears to be the consequence of an external perception. The locus of the impulse is denied and the residuals are rationalized in terms of external reality.

Reaction formation.   This mechanism serves to transform an unacceptable impulse into its logical opposite and to allow expression of the opposite in consciousness. Reaction formations are usually recognizable by the exaggerated and inflexible quality which betrays their instinctual bases. Continuing the example of the woman made anxious by hostile impulses toward her husband, the mechanism of reaction formation could transform this impulse into an oversolicitous concern for the welfare of her husband. The original impulse still remains, but it is disguised by the conscious appearance of its opposite. For example, the woman may become so afraid that something might happen to her husband that she begs him not to leave the house. This illustrates the manner in which a reaction formation may succeed in realizing the original aim of the unacceptable impulse. In this instance, the husband may be victimized more severely by his wife's "concern" than he would have been by a direct expression of hostility.

  Psychoanalytic constructs such as reaction formation may tend to make us unduly suspicious of the motives of others. If a friend is especially nice to us, we may wonder if this represents a reaction formation. Genuine reaction formations can be identified by their exaggerated qualities. We are speaking not of individuals who are genuinely loving, generous, honest, and neat, but of individuals who have these virtues to a fault. They simply overdo it with an intensity that betrays a reaction formation. Frequently reaction formations and direct expressions of the original impulse may stand side by side in the same individual. In situations that are unimportant enough to fall outside of ego surveillance, the overly neat child may wallow in mud or the overly thrifty individual may behave extravagantly. Hence, behavior patterns that are exaggerated, compulsive, and unstable may suggest an underlying reaction formation.

Rationalization.   The operation of this mechanism may be observed in the tendency we all have to reinterpret our own irrational behavior or feelings so that they may appear more reasonable. When we act impulsively and regret it, we are inclined to invent a "good reason" for our behavior which both excuses it and denies its irrational basis. If we are unable to concoct a framework of reinterpretation which places us in a favorable light, we may have to resort to saying, "I wasn't myself." The recognition that we sometimes behave in an irrational or impulsive fashion may give rise to feelings of neurotic or moral anxiety, which can be diminished by rationalization.

The mechanism of rationalization does not prevent unacceptable impulses from being expressed. Instead, it attempts to ward off anxiety that might arise after an unacceptable thought, feeling, or action has occurred. If the woman in our example had expressed her unacceptable hostility toward her husband in an irrational outburst of temper (breaking dishes), she might have attempted to conceal the instinctual basis of this behavior by placing it in a rational context. Since it is difficult to muster a convincing rationalization for obviously impulsive behavior ("I thought that if I got rid of those dishes, we could buy the new ones we wanted"), it is more likely that she would resort to saying, "I wasn't myself." The rationalization that we are temporarily not ourselves or that we temporarily lose our temper calls attention to the uncharacteristic nature of such actions or feelings and thereby denies that they represent our "true selves." Since rationalizations are so much a part of everyday social transactions, it should not be assumed that they have pathological significance. However, excessive rationalization of all behaviors that might potentially be criticized can result in an unrealistic self-view which may lead to difficulties in adjustment.

THE SUPEREGO AND ASSOCIATED CONSTRUCTS

The Socialization Process

According to psychoanalytic theory, there is no inborn sense of morality which distinguishes right from wrong. In the beginning the infant responds only to instinctual drives under the pleasure principle and to external stimuli under the reality principle. Because of its relatively slow rate of maturation, the human organism experiences a prolonged period of dependence on adults for gratification of basic needs. Loss of parental love or support constitutes a realistic threat to the child's existence and gives rise to objective anxiety. The gain of parental love and support, on the other hand, has a definite biological survival value. The superego system is the internalized representation of parental values that enables children to comport themselves in a manner that will be approved by their parents and ensure continued love and support.

The values of society are instilled in the child by the parents through rewards and punishments. Undesirable or improper behavior is punished. Desirable behavior is encouraged and rewarded. The superego develops as a specialized system for obtaining rewards and avoiding punishments from the parents. Because it is finely tuned to the patterns of rewards and punishments meted out by the parents, it becomes an internalized representation of society's values.

Impulses, thoughts, or actions likely to bring parental disapproval give rise to objective anxiety based on the realistic fear of loss of parental support. Instinctual drives from the id system, particularly of a sexual or aggressive nature, must be inhibited to ward off this objective anxiety. The ego system, which is ultimately concerned with the realistic expression of instinctual drives, cannot be counted upon to restrict behavior to that which is morally proper. Thus the superego system must persuade the ego system to suspend the reality principle in favor of a moral principle.

The *conscience* is the specialized subsystem of the superego that attempts to inhibit thoughts, feelings, or actions opposed to parental values. The energizing force of the conscience is moral anxiety, a specialized form of objective anxiety related to issues of value. Moral anxiety, or guilt, eventually becomes a more efficient deterrent to immoral behavior than the original punishments of the parents. Whereas the ego system attempts to effect realistic coordinations through mechanisms of delay and detour, the conscience strives for perfection through uncompromising mechanisms of total inhibition. This resoluteness doth make cowards of us all.

The *ego-ideal* is the specialized subsystem of the superego which incorporates the positive values of society. When children are praised or rewarded for good behavior, they experience a sense of pride and enhanced self-worth. The ego-ideal incorporates the values most approved of by parents, and behavior in accord with these ideals will give rise to a feeling of pride. It should be evident that socialization is best achieved by providing the child with clear guidelines for the kind of behavior considered good or proper. A well articulated ego-ideal provides a standard for comparison that, when met, will lead to ego enhancement. Lacking a clear sense of what is proper, an individual must suffer the pangs of conscience for bad behavior without being compensated for good behavior by the exhilarating experience of enhanced self-esteem.

Adult Moral Life

Because of the effectiveness with which the superego system can inhibit the id and control the ego, it is a force to be reckoned with in the total personality system. Opinions differ on whether this force should be viewed as beneficial or deleterious, and Freud himself was uncertain on this point (Mowrer, 1950). Returning to Fig. 15.2, notice that the superego has access to both the biological instincts of the id system and the realistic perceptions of the ego system. However, its principle of operation is neither irrational nor rational. Instead, it strives for perfection with respect to a moral code incorporated relatively early in life. The values incorporated into the superego are parental values *as perceived by the child*. Once formed, the superego system tends to operate in a relatively automatic and inflexible fashion. Hence the possibility exists that some of the values the superego serves are *archaic* values inappropriate for an adult. Guilty and depressed patients may be the victims of superego systems that incorporate unattainable ego-ideals or prohibitions against behaviors which are

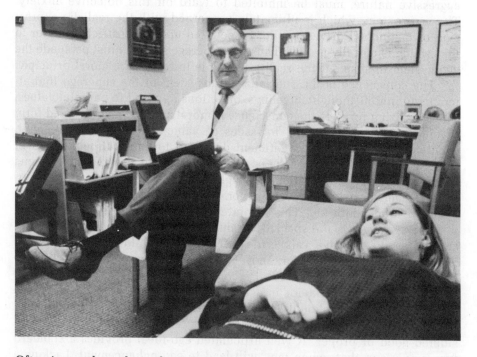

Often in psychoanalysis the patient reclines on a couch and the therapist sits out of the patient's direct line of vision. This technique encourages relaxation and ready access to memory and imagination. (Van Bucher)

necessary and natural. In his early writings, Freud viewed the id system as the "true psychic reality" and felt that the values of society incorporated in the superego imposed unnecessary restrictions on human growth. Perhaps for this reason, psychoanalytic psychotherapy is generally believed to be a procedure whereby individuals may be freed of their "inhibitions" (superego) and thereby lead a more expressive life.

It is natural that psychoanalysts should view the superego system as an unnecessarily repressive force, since the painful symptoms of many of their patients testify to the deleterious effects of a harsh, archaic, or punitive conscience. But it should also be recognized that the three systems of personality operate harmoniously in most normal individuals. In a sense, society's values represent a *social reality* which must be reckoned with for the good of the individual as well as for society. The ego and superego systems may be in conflict if the latter is based on archaic values. But it is possible to perceive society's values realistically, and most of us do. Similarly, although there are some limits on what we are free to do within a society, these need not be so stringent that the realization of natural biological instincts is thwarted. Finally, we should not discount the pleasure we experience as enhancement when we act in accord with our ideals.

RANGE AND FOCUS OF CONVENIENCE

As should be apparent from the variety of constructs employed, the range of phenomena to which psychoanalytic theory may be applied is extremely broad. Although originally conceived as primarily a theory of human motivation, the theory has been progressively extended to embrace virtually all aspects of human behavior. In fact, the intent of both the founder and his subsequent followers was to make psychoanalysis a general psychology. Despite its aspirations to being a general psychology, however, psychoanalysis has made unique contributions in relatively delimited areas. Thus, although the theory postulates ego apparatuses that have energy sources independent of the id, such a construct does little more than *refer* to the empirical facts that have been discovered in traditional laboratory studies of sensation, perception, learning, memory, etc. For example, psychoanalysis has contributed neither a unique theory of learning nor a unique theory of perception. Similarly, although interpersonal attachments and reality considerations are a central part of the theory, such constructs would hardly be meaningful in the absence of the detailed knowledge about social and cultural factors provided by social psychologists and sociologists.

The unique contributions of psychoanalysis lie in the formulation of the drive-defense-conflict paradigm and the central importance the theory assigns to the substantive topics of dependency, aggression, and sexuality. The original focus of psychoanalysis was on abnormal behavior and understanding it in terms of the drive-defense-conflict paradigm. Although abnormal behavior may be viewed as an exaggeration of normal behavior, the theory's primary focus of convenience is still likely to be on abnormal behavior and particularly neurotic behavior. One should bear in mind that almost all the material that has formed the basis for psychoanalytic theorizing has been obtained from observations of neurotic patients. It seems likely that the theory is most conveniently applied within this limited focus.

APPLICATIONS TO SELECTED TOPICS

One of the principal contributions of psychoanalytic theory is the importance the theory assigns to the topics of dependency, aggression, and sexuality. These topics have been the subject of considerable research from a variety of theoretical viewpoints. If nothing else, the emphasis given these topics in almost all subsequent theories of personality attests to the heuristic value of the original psychoanalytic theory. By far the richest and most elaborate theoretical accounts of the nature of dependency, aggression, and sexuality are provided by psychoanalytic theory. Since a full exposition of those theoretical accounts would require several volumes, we can present here only a brief summary of the psychoanalytic position on each topic.

Dependency

The origins of dependent attitudes and behaviors may be traced to the conflicts inherent in the feeding of infants. The breast (or bottle) is probably the first object the infant discriminates, and experiences associated with it lay the foundations for attitudes to the mother herself and eventually toward people in general. As a means of controlling behavior, the mother may feed an infant when it is "good" and not feed it when it is "bad," thereby establishing an early association between love and food on the one hand, between rejection and withholding of food on the other. Thus the slightest rejection by the parent may be anxiety-arousing because of its association with food deprivation. Under these circumstances, the infant may develop a passive-dependent attitude which minimizes the possibilities of offending the parent. This attitude, which is based on a fear of deprivation, may generalize to other individuals and, indeed, to the world at large. Dependent persons expect good things to happen to them when they are good (passive) and to have things taken away from them when they are bad (active).

The essential helplessness of dependent behavior may be censured by the superego or opposed by reality considerations. Thus inhibiting forces may be erected against the direct expression of dependency needs. When dependency needs are *repressed,* they do not register in conscious awareness but may appear in disguised behaviors. Compulsive eating to overcome depression and excessive drinking are thinly disguised symbolic representations of infant feeding experiences. These behaviors may mask strong needs for dependence on others. When *projection* is used as a defense against unacceptable dependency needs, the dependency is attributed to others. Thus, instead of seeking the help of others, the individual may be devoted to helping others as a social worker or crusader for "those who cannot help themselves." *Reaction formations* against dependency needs take the form of exaggerated independence from others. The counterdependent individual will refuse to accept any help from others, even when it is clearly in his or her best interest to do so. Dependent behaviors may be *rationalized* by claims of role-appropriate behavior in relationships in which dependent behaviors have been institutionalized. Hence, it can be asserted that a passive-dependent attitude is appropriate within the context of the "feminine" role, the teacher-student relationship or the supervisor-employee relationship.

Aggression

Unlike social-learning theories, which view aggression as a response to frustrating circumstances, psychoanalysis postulates an instinct for aggression present at birth rather than acquired by experience. Although the case for the survival value of an aggressive instinct may be made along with that for hunger and procreation, it is difficult to specify a tissue system in which the need for aggression might reside. Consequently, Freud's (1920) formulation of a death instinct (thanatos) comparable to the life instinct (eros) has not gained wide acceptance among psychoanalytic theorists. Regardless of whether they are viewed as innate or acquired, however, aggressive impulses are assigned a central role as energy sources in the psychoanalytic theory of personality dynamics and development.

Aggressive impulses are strongly condemned by society, and inhibitions against their expression are instituted early in life, primarily through superego mechanisms. Dream analysis has made evident the manner in which aggressive impulses are distorted, disguised, or displaced so that their true meaning does not become evident to the dreamer. Much of the work of the ego's defense mechanisms is directed toward the avoidance or shunting off of aggressive impulses. When aggressive impulses are re-pressed, they may appear in disguised behaviors. Lateness for an appoint-ment, "accidental" loss of another's valuable property, and enthusiastic "constructive" criticism may be veiled expressions of hostility. The projec-tion of hostility involves the familiar mechanisms of paranoia. "I hate him" is transformed into "He hates me" or "They are plotting against me." Reaction formations to aggressive impulses involve exaggerated and over-solicitous concern for some person's welfare. Exaggerated concern that a child may be injured in playing with sharp objects may disguise an uncon-scious impulse to hurt the child. A familiar example of the rationalization of aggressive impulses occurs in the unconvincing statement that "This hurts me more than it hurts you."

Sexuality

Freud broadened the construct of sexuality to include all instincts or life forces (libido) that contribute to the development and survival of the or-ganism. Thus conceived, sexuality is not limited to the erotic pleasures associated with the stimulation of genital organs. Psychoanalysis broad-ened the construct to include the erotic pleasures associated with eating (oral), defecation (anal), and urination (urethral) as well. Under this broadened view, it was possible to develop a theory of infantile sexuality which described the manner in which conflicts associated with critical stages in the child's psychosexual development shape the adult personal-ity. Parental attitudes and practices regarding such matters as breast feed-ing and weaning, toilet training, and masturbation may produce conflict situations for the child, which may be resolved in an unrealistic manner. The attitudes and feelings associated with these early conflict situations may persist throughout life. The theory of infantile sexuality provided not only a long overdue recognition of the sexual impulses of children, but a coherent and systematic account of psychosexual and psychosocial devel-opment that has few rivals as a complete developmental psychology.

The puritanical attitudes toward sexual matters that characterized the Victorian age in which Freud lived restricted the realm of psychologi-cal investigation to "proper" subjects. Freud was able to demonstrate that precisely those attitudes led to neurotic symptoms and other problems of living in his time. The demonstration that sexual conflicts provided the basis for most neurotic behavior laid the groundwork for an elaborate theory of neurosis (Fenichel, 1945) which has strongly influenced psychi-atric practice throughout the Western world.

In addition to providing a comprehensive account of normal psychosexual development, psychoanalysis has increased our understanding of abnormal or deviant sexual behavior as well. In the course of development, an individual may experience conflicts regarding a given mode of impulse expression. Thus an early object of pleasure which is ordinarily abandoned in the course of development retains its attractiveness as a source of instinctual gratification. Under sufficient temporary stress, the person may return to this primitive mode of gratification and behave in a regressive and often bizarre fashion. Unresolved conflicts of early childhood may stimulate contemporary defenses characterized by ritualistic, symbolic, and peculiar symptoms. These and other psychoanalytic conceptualizations have greatly increased our understanding of the mechanisms operative in exhibitionism, voyeurism, fetishism, transvestism, sadomasochism, and a variety of other deviant sexual behavior patterns.

SUMMARY

This chapter was concerned with the psychoanalytic theory of personality developed by Sigmund Freud and his followers. On the basis of initial attempts to treat hysterical patients, Freud concluded that neurotic symptoms are related to repressed memories of sexual seduction during childhood. Later, recognizing that such memories were fantasies, he turned his attention to sexual instincts, or wishes, as the important elements in neurosis. Running throughout Freud's writing is a distinction among three aspects of psychological behavior originally thought to be specific entities but now recognized as vantage points from which to interpret psychological behavior. The *id*, or unconscious aspect, of the individual was thought to be the reservoir of primitive biological instincts that are continually striving for expression. The *ego*, or self, was that aspect of experience which is readily available to individuals in their conscious and waking state. The *superego*, or conscience, represented the internalized values of society which oppose the expression of unacceptable impulses, such as sexual and aggressive instincts. The historical influence of the constructs of id, ego, and superego on the development of the field of personality study may be seen in the influence these constructs had on the four viewpoints of personality study described in this text. Philosophically, there has been a shift in the psychoanalytic view of human nature. In the early view individuals were passive victims of both external reality and internal drives; in the recent view they are more active agents capable of determining their own destiny.

The central assertion of psychoanalysis holds that behavior is multiply determined by interacting and interrelated forces originating in the separate domains of the id, ego, and superego. Behavior cannot be construed solely in terms of the principles of mental functioning that govern any one of these systems. Instead, behavior should be viewed as a product of all three. The principal constructs related to the id system characterize the nature of unconscious processes and specify the manner in which instinctual drives struggle for immediate discharge under the pleasure principle. The principal constructs related to the ego system are concerned with the manner in which the ego effects adaptive coordinations with the environment under the reality principle and the manner in which defense mechanisms ward off anxiety which signals threats from within and without. The principal constructs related to the superego system indicate the role of incorporated parental values in the socialization of the child and the moral life of the adult.

The unique contributions of psychoanalysis lie in the formulation of the drive-defense-conflict paradigm and the central importance the theory assigns to the substantive topics of dependency, aggression, and sexuality. The original focus of psychoanalysis was on understanding abnormal behavior in terms of the drive-defense-conflict paradigm. Although abnormal behavior may be viewed as an exaggeration of normal behavior, the theory's primary focus of convenience is still likely to be on abnormal behavior and particularly neurotic behavior. One should bear in mind that almost all the material that has formed the basis for psychoanalytic theorizing has been obtained from observations of neurotic patients. It seems likely that the theory is most conveniently applied within this limited focus.

SUGGESTIONS FOR FURTHER READING

Freud, S. The Standard Edition of the Complete Psychological Works, J. Strachey (ed.). London: Hogarth Press, 1953–   . The definitive English-language edition of the works of Freud. This collection, which now numbers 23 volumes, is the primary source for the serious student of Freud.

Freud, S. The interpretation of dreams. Standard Edition, Vols. 4 and 5. London: Hogarth Press, 1953. Freud's early (1900) classic study of the meaning and significance of dreams. Considered by many to be his most important single work.

Freud, S. The psychopathology of everyday life. Standard Edition, Vol. 6. London: Hogarth Press, 1960. The classic early (1901) work on "Freudian slips" and their significance. A good introduction to psychoanalytic reasoning.

Freud, S. The ego and the id. *Standard Edition,* Vol. 19. London: Hogarth Press, 1961. The last of Freud's major theoretical works. Original source material for much of the present chapter.

Freud, S. *The Complete Introductory Lectures on Psychoanalysis* (Translated and edited by James Strachey). New York: Norton, 1966. Two sets of introductory lectures, the first given in 1916 and the second in 1933. Between them they cover the entire range of Freud's observations and theories.

Hall, C. S. *A Primer of Freudian Psychology.* New York: World Book, 1954. A brief and very readable introduction to psychoanalytic theory. A good place to start for those with little previous exposure to the theory.

16 Social Learning Theory

I. **Background and orientation**
A. Historical perspective
  1. The concept of habit
  2. The early social learning group
  3. The later social learning theorists
  4. Historical comparison
B. Philosophical perspective

II. **Central assertion**

III. **Principal constructs**
A. Basic systems of the organisms
  1. Drive
  2. Reinforcement
  3. Cue
  4. Response
B. Social processes and the social context
  1. Observational learning
  2. Situational specificity of behavior
  3. Self-control

IV. **Range and foci of convenience**
A. Conceptualizing common human experience
  1. Generalization and discrimination
  2. Conflict
B. Behavior modification
C. Social exchange

V. **Applications to selected topics**
A. Dependency
B. Aggression
C. Sexuality

VI. **Summary**

VII. **Suggestions for further reading**

BACKGROUND AND ORIENTATION

Social learning theory consists of a group of approaches in which personality development is analyzed by means of principles from learning theory. Although there have been many individual social learning theorists, we shall here emphasize two principal groups. The early group (from 1936 to the 1950s) were concerned with the application of Hull's theory of learning to psychoanalytic phenomena; the later group (from the 1950s to the present) have stressed imitation and other vicarious, symbolic, and self-regulatory behavior.

HISTORICAL PERSPECTIVE

The Concept of Habit

How individuals adapt to their environment has been an important question from Darwin to the present. Exactly how does experience with the environment change the individual?

To answer this question, theorists introduced the concept of *habit* as the means whereby the effects of previous experience influence one's future behavior. That concept fits nicely with Darwin's emphasis on automatic, natural processes. Further, since both men and animals have habits, the concept is also compatible with Darwin's thesis of the continuity of species.

Clark Hull developed his theory of learning around the habit construct, and the social learning theory of the 1930s and 1940s was an application of Hull's system. Social learning theorists used the concept in a very straightforward way, applying it not only to personality development but also to psychotherapy, which they saw as a situation in which relearning takes place. For example, Dollard and Miller (1950) state that "by the same principles that bad tennis habits can be corrected by a good coach, so bad mental and emotional habits can be corrected by a psychotherapist." (p. 8)

The concept of habit did not originate with Hull, however. William James also felt that habit was indispensable to understanding human behavior. Referring to the effects of habit on people, James wrote in 1890 that "by the age of thirty, the character has set like plaster, and will never soften again. . . . An invisible law, as strong as gravitation, keeps him within his orbit." (1950, pp. 121–122)

One of William James's students at Harvard, Edward L. Thorndike, also became an important figure in the history of American psychology. As a student, Thorndike carried out in the basement of James's home experiments on the intelligence of chickens (Boring, 1950). His animal work on instrumental learning provided an important basis for early social learning theory. Like James before and Hull after him, Thorndike was concerned with the principles of habit formation. The cumulative research in that area, together with the writings of John B. Watson and the Russian research on classical conditioning, of which there was increasing awareness in scientific circles, set the stage for the intense interest in the psychology of learning which followed.

The Early Social Learning Group

During the 1930s, Skinner, Guthrie, Tolman, and Hull all produced rival theories of learning. Of these, Hull's had the most immediate effect on personality theory. In 1933, the Institute of Human Relations at Yale brought together a variety of individuals interested in the social and behavioral sciences. The aim of the institute was to integrate the findings of psychology, sociology, anthropology, and psychiatry. Clark Hull had joined the Yale faculty in 1929, and in 1936 he began a seminar in the institute with Neal Miller, John Dollard, and O. Hobart Mowrer. The stimulating atmosphere of the seminar exerted an important influence on the intellectual development of a number of graduate students and young faculty members who participated.

Dollard and Miller made the fullest explication of the early social learning approach formulated in the seminar. Both had been trained in psychoanalysis, Dollard in Berlin and Miller in Vienna. The career of Dollard, who has held professorships at Yale in sociology and anthropology as well as psychology, clearly reflects the interdisciplinary flavor of the enterprise. Essentially, the two men attempted to translate the observations of Freud and of anthropologists into stimulus-response terms. The influences on the thought of Dollard and Miller can be seen from the fact that they dedicated their first book to Hull and their second to Freud and Pavlov and to the students of both.

The Later Social Learning Theorists

The influence of the early work of Dollard and Miller and of Mowrer has declined, and a somewhat different social learning approach to personality has recently emerged. The early spokesmen for the newer theory were Albert Bandura and one of his students, Richard Walters (Bandura and Walters, 1959, 1963; Bandura, 1969). They have rejected the concepts of both Freud and Hull. In fact, their approach represents a reaction to what they consider the too theoretical nature of earlier social learning theory.

The chief contribution of Bandura and Walters has been to emphasize the importance of social factors in learning. They argue that earlier learning approaches to personality relied on a limited range of learning principles established in animal studies and one-person learning situations. They suggest that, when the social context of personality development is considered, the importance of a new kind of learning that is uniquely social in nature (imitation) becomes apparent.

Dollard and Miller also treated imitation in their first book, which was entitled *Imitation and Social Learning* (Miller and Dollard, 1941), but they assumed that imitative responses had to be learned by reinforcement. Believing that imitation was a special type of instrumental learning for rewards, they hardly mentioned it in their later book, *Personality and Psychotherapy* (Dollard and Miller, 1950). In contrast, Bandura and Walters have shown that learning occurs by observation without rewards, and therefore, any person who is observed is potentially a model to be imitated. Thus, to a greater extent than did the earlier social learning theorists, they see models, whether real or symbolically presented, as primary sources of the behaviors which characterize any individual.

Historical Comparison

Social learning theory seeks to explain personality by applying principles from the psychology of learning to the social development of humans. To the extent that principles are borrowed from another area, such as animal learning, and applied unchanged to human behavior, the social learning approach is a model rather than a theory. Indeed, Dollard and Miller's approach is perhaps more a model of personality based on the analogy between animal and human learning than a theory of personality. However, recent social learning theory is increasingly based on human studies in which new principles emerge and decreasingly on analogues from animal learning. Partly for this reason, the social learning position is treated here as a theory rather than a model.

The terms "model" and "theory" are often used interchangeably in science. In this book, *model* connotes the wholesale application of terms and principles from one realm to another, whereas *theory* connotes the indigenous development of concepts and principles to handle the phenomena directly studied. For example, the psychoanalytic theory of abnormal behavior came directly from encounters with patients,* and cognitive-developmental theory grew directly out of the observation of children growing up. On the other hand, the Skinnerian approach to human be-

---

* If Freud's work alone is considered, it would be as accurate to refer to an abnormal or neurotic model, because principles developed to handle observations about patients were applied to personality development in general. However, as indicated in Chapter 15, psychoanalytic theory encompasses more than Freud's work, especially in view of the inclusion of the work done by the ego psychologists.

havior, in accordance with this distinction, is more accurately a model than a theory because it involves the application of animal learning principles to humans.

One difference between theories and models is that the interaction between theory and data is two-way, that between model and data one-way. Evidence provides a corrective for theories and changes them, but it does not do so for models. A model is an analogy that serves a heuristic or hypothesis-generating function, suggesting what to look for in the phenomena under study, but the results of the suggested research do not reflect on the adequacy of the model in its original setting. For example, if the results say that people do not behave like rats, then the model of man as a rat can be discarded; but our understanding of rats themselves is not challenged. Thus the interaction between models and data is only one-way.

Early social learning research was generally directed at demonstrating the accuracy of the analogy between animal and human learning. For example, Miller and Mowrer did experiments in which they tried to show that rats, like humans, displace their aggression from its true source to safer targets. In contrast, the current social learning approach is a theory rather than a model. Bandura and Walters have constructed a theoretical account of personality development in children by drawing on direct study of nursery school children. In addition, their research has done more than demonstrate the relevance of learning to human personality. The two-way interaction between theory and data has made it possible for their experiments to alter our conception of the learning process itself.

PHILOSOPHICAL PERSPECTIVE

Social learning theory falls into the philosophical tradition of British empiricism. John Locke's assumption that complex ideas are made up of associations of more elementary ideas is quite compatible with a theory that stresses learning (the association of stimuli) as the primary influence in personality formation. Consistent with this tradition is the view that people are relatively passive recipients of experience which they then mirror in their own personality. Their behavior depends on the situation they find themselves in and the conditioning they have undergone in that situation. The actions they take will be those they have taken or seen taken previously in that or similar situations, especially if those actions were rewarded before. People are passive, then, rather than active with regard to the control of their own behavior. Indeed, Langer (1969) has appropriately referred to this view as the mechanical-mirror theory of human personality, implying that an individual's personality is a reflection of experience.

Box 16.1   Social learning theorists.

John Dollard, born in 1900 in Menasha, Wisconsin, received his Ph.D. in sociology from the University of Chicago in 1931. Appointed an assistant professor of anthropology at Yale in 1932, in the following year he joined the faculty of the Institute of Human Relations as an assistant professor of sociology. In 1948 he became a professor of psychology and in 1969, professor emeritus. Dollard's interdisciplinary background also included early training in psychoanalysis at the Berlin Institute. The wide-ranging subjects of his ten books and numerous articles further document the breadth of his scholarly interest.

Neal E. Miller, born in 1909 in Milwaukee, Wisconsin, received his Ph.D. from Yale in 1935. He spent the following year in Vienna, where he received training in psychoanalysis. From 1936 to 1942 he was on the faculty of the Institute of Human Relations at Yale. Miller occupied a chair in psychology at Yale from 1952 to 1966, when he went to Rockefeller University. His recent work concerns instrumental conditioning of heart rate and other physiological functions. Elected president of the American Psychological Association in 1959, he was awarded the President's Medal of Science in 1965, then one of only two behavioral scientists to have received that honor. In 1975 Miller was presented the Gold Medal Award by the American Psychological Foundation for his contributions as a "scientific innovator."

Photo by Gene's Studio, Palo Alto, California

Photo by Personal Studio, Waterloo, Ontario

Albert Bandura, born in 1925, received his Ph.D. in clinical psychology from the University of Iowa in 1952. After a year of postdoctoral clinical training, he joined the psychology faculty of Stanford University, becoming a professor of psychology in 1964. In 1974 he served as president of the American Psychological Association. At Iowa Bandura was trained in an atmosphere dominated by Hullian learning theory, but since that time he has worked to change the direction of traditional learning theory to include such social phenomena as observational learning, or modeling. His published works include five influential books, two of which were written with Richard Walters as coauthor.

Richard H. Walters, born in 1918 in Wales, received a B.Phil. in philosophy from Oxford University in 1948. He was a lecturer at the University of Auckland in New Zealand before coming to the United States. As Bandura's first doctoral student, Walters received his Ph.D. at Stanford in 1957. He then taught at the University of Toronto until 1963, when he left to establish a psychology department at the University of Waterloo. Before his untimely death in 1967, he made impressive contributions through his investigations of the effects of punishment, the relation between social motivation and social influence, and the role of reinforcement and modeling in aggression.

The more recent social learning approach characterized by the work of Bandura (1969) fits the same ultimately passive view, but a new active element has also been introduced. Bandura's theory has greatly increased the emphasis on self-instructions, self-reinforcement, and other forms of internal regulation of behavior, and in that way the approach differs from several alternative views. On the one hand, psychoanalytic theorists see people as impelled by powerful internal forces that are both out of their direct control and unknown to them. On the other hand, radical behaviorists see the individual as totally under the control of external stimuli. The current social learning theorists suggest that neither view is accurate. Bandura (1969) holds that there is a reciprocal interaction between behavior and the conditions that control it, so that individuals partly create their own environment. For example, he argues that it is only because individuals do have some control over the outcomes they receive that therapeutic treatment at the individual level is a reasonable strategy. Indeed, if people are completely passive recipients of rewards and punishments, therapeutic intervention should be directed at institutions, families, spouses, parents, and other external factors rather than at the persons requiring help.

CENTRAL ASSERTION

Although some aspects of social learning theory have changed since the early days at the Yale Institute of Human Relations, the general nature of the approach has been the same since 1936. A consistent and integral assumption of this orientation is that experience (rather than instinctual, maturational, or genetic factors) is the important formative influence on behavior; that adaptation to the contingencies of one's own unique environment is the basis of personality. Simply put, the central assertion of social learning theory is that *individual differences in behavior among people are a consequence of variations in the conditions of learning that the individuals have encountered.*

Social learning theory sees normal and abnormal behavior as parts of one continuum rather than as separate behaviors that are fundamentally different or caused by different principles. Thus the explanation of a characteristic act, whether labeled normal or deviant, arises from analysis of the conditions which led to its acquisition and maintenance. Specifically, explanations are couched in terms of the kinds of models that are being imitated and the reinforcement contingencies that are active.

PRINCIPAL CONSTRUCTS

The appeal of social learning theory—or of any successful theory—lies in the explanatory power of its constructs or its ability to tie together diverse phenomena with the thread of a few general principles. The early Yale group deployed an array of simple constructs based on Hull's learning theory (e.g., drive, reinforcement, cue, and response) to account for personality development and change.

These constructs provided a useful starting place. They served as tools that allowed psychologists to reduce complex human behavior to a manageable number of basic processes. This simplification served a desirable function since, as we shall see, it transformed the study of personality into an hypothesis-testing, rather than a descriptive, science.

It should not be surprising that the original set of simple constructs needed to be enriched with new concepts in order to account for the diversity and complexity of human behaviors. These additions have not exactly replaced the original concepts. Rather, the original concepts have assumed a subordinate status. Increasingly cognitive, the new concepts reflect the emergent nature of psychological theory. We have chosen, therefore, to emphasize the similarities, rather than the differences, between the old and new versions of social learning theory. The most recent trends stress the social, cognitive, and symbolic nature of the human while deemphasizing the human as a reflexive automaton.

Drive

Dollard and Miller (1950) define drives as strong stimuli that lead to action. According to this position, learning consists essentially in developing efficient means of reducing drives. Any stimulus can become a drive if it is made strong enough. For example, the faint murmur of distant music has little drive value, but the same sounds loudly blaring in one's ear may be a strong drive. Although any stimulus can act as a drive, certain special classes of stimuli, the primary drives, are the ultimate basis for most motivation. Among them are pain, thirst, hunger, cold, and sex.

Reinforcement

Dollard and Miller substitute the principle of reinforcement for Freud's pleasure principle as the most basic operating rule of the human organism. The principle of reinforcement refers to the tendency for certain events, when they follow a given behavior, to increase the likelihood of that behavior on subsequent occasions. Though the effects of reinforcement are readily observable, the exact process by which it operates is not clear. Like Hull, Dollard and Miller reserve the term for instances of drive reduction. In addition, they assume that such drive reduction is essential if learning is to occur.

In the same way that stimuli associated with drives develop *secondary drive* value, stimuli repeatedly linked to the delivery of reinforcement acquire *secondary reinforcement* properties. Thus money itself has no capacity to reduce primary drives, but through learning it comes to have high reinforcement value. Similarly, research on chimpanzees has shown that, after association with primary reinforcers, poker chips become effective secondary reinforcers.

Cue

Stimuli vary both quantitatively and qualitatively, and whereas the drive value of a stimulus depends on its strength, its cue value depends on its distinctiveness. Since learning involves establishing a bond between a cue and a response, an individual's actions are controlled by the cues that are presented. Thus cues determine when and where one will respond and what response one will make. Dollard and Miller emphasize that the cue which elicits a learned response may be a single stimulus or a complex pattern of stimuli. Even the internal stimuli which serve as drives are distinctive enough to be cues. For example, the stimuli associated with hunger can be discriminated from those which indicate thirst.

Response

Dollard and Miller maintain that before learning can occur, that is, before a given response can be linked to a given cue, the response must be made. Once made, the response can be reinforced and become established. In any situation some responses are more likely than others; that is, there is an initial *hierarchy of responses*. In light of this concept, one can think of learning as a change in the order of responses; through reinforcement an initially weak response becomes the most probable one in the hierarchy.

One of the primary tasks of animal trainers, teachers, and psychotherapists is to arrange situations in which desired responses are made so that they can be rewarded. When the correct response is improbable, the task may require great ingenuity. A solution advanced by Dollard and Miller is to place the individual in a *learning dilemma*. As long as one's old responses are adequate to reduce one's drive, one has no reason to produce new responses; in a new situation, however, if the old responses are not rewarded, then one must attempt new responses that were initially less likely. In such a dilemma, one must either forgo receiving rewards or change one's responses.

SOCIAL PROCESSES AND THE SOCIAL CONTEXT

Although the theory of Bandura and Walters is in many ways similar to that of Dollard and Miller, some important distinctions should be made. For example, both theories use learning principles to explain personality, but as indicated earlier, Bandura and Walters largely ignore both Hull and Freud. They have conducted their research exclusively on human subjects, and they criticize Dollard and Miller's readiness to depend on animal experiments for evidence. Bandura and Walters also deal less with isolated, discrete responses and more with unified behavior than their predecessors did. Last and of most importance, Bandura and Walters place more emphasis on the social conditions of learning and on the role of models in personality development.

Observational Learning

The most distinctive feature of the recent social learning approach is the extent to which modeling or observational learning has been investigated. A highly important aspect of Bandura's (1969) treatment of that research is his emphasis on cognitive and symbolic factors. His theory of observational learning is that the observed behavior of the model and other stimulus events are transformed into images and verbal codes that are retained in memory. Later the images and verbal codes combine with the appropriate environmental cues to guide the overt reproduction of the original behavior. Successful imitation thus requires attention to the model's original behavior, adequate symbolic coding, accurate retention, the motor capacity to perform the acts, and some reinforcement or incentive for imitating.

Traditionally, learning theorists have been divided on whether learning depends on the number of reinforced responses or merely the number of responses alone, regardless of reinforcement. In answer, Bandura and Walters assert that neither reinforcement nor response is required for learning. To support this assertion, Bandura (1965) had three groups of children watch filmed models whose behavior was followed by rewards, punishments, or no consequences. In a free play session afterward, the children imitated the rewarded model most, the no-consequences model next, and the punished model least. However, when later offered a reward for reproducing the behavior they had seen, all three groups of children were clearly able to imitate the responses equally well. They had learned merely by observing, and although external reinforcement determined whether they performed, it did not determine *ability* to perform. Thus, according to Bandura and Walters, reinforcement affects performance but not learning, and *contiguity* (the association of two events in time) is the important condition if learning is to take place. In contrast to Dollard and Miller, who are reinforcement theorists, Bandura and Walters may therefore be labeled contiguity theorists.

The position that reinforcement is unnecessary for making permanent associations (learning) does not mean that this construct is unimportant in current social learning theory. Indeed, a central tenet of the theory is that behavior is controlled primarily by its reinforcing consequences. Spelling out the implications of this assertion for personality development constitutes in large part the substance of social learning theory; simply stated, if people behave in ways that produce reinforcement, then an understanding of a person's behavior requires knowledge of his or her reinforcement history. Generally, the implications can be deduced from the principle that individuals will act to maximize their rewards and minimize their efforts. Thus immediate rewards are preferred to delayed rewards and large rewards to small ones.

However, there is growing evidence that the effects of rewards and delays of reward are intimately related to the cognitions of the individual (Mischel, 1973). To illustrate, Mischel and his colleagues have been systematically exploring the ways in which the meaning and the impact of a stimulus can be modified by *cognitive transformations*. One experimental method is to place pre-school children alone in a chair and have them wait for a preferred but delayed outcome before they can signal with a bell that they will accept a less preferred but immediate reward (Mischel, Ebbeson, and Zeiss, 1972). On some occasions a child will terminate the waiting almost immediately and at other times wait for long periods. The period that children will delay can be altered by having them cognitively transform the nature of the reward. If, for example, sticks of pretzels or marshmallows are placed in front of them, it becomes exceedingly difficult for them to delay gratification. If, on the other hand, they cognitively transform the stimulus by thinking of the pretzel sticks as small brown logs and the marshmallows as cotton balls, they are able to delay gratification for long periods of time (Mischel, 1973).

Situational Specificity of Behavior

In contrast to psychoanalysis, social learning theory sees the causes of behavior (including abnormal behavior) as modifiable reactions to external conditions rather than as complexes, defenses, traits, or other forces within the individual. One consequence of the strongly behavioral view of current social learning theorists (e.g., Mischel, 1968) is to bring them into conflict with traditional approaches to personality which emphasize traits. They view as an untenable assumption the idea that generalized and stable traits can determine behavior in a variety of situations. While learned behaviors do generalize to situations other than that in which they were acquired, everyday behavior is much too flexible to be predicted from a few general traits. Indeed, Mischel (1969) holds that the consistency in behavior that everyone seems to display is in fact illusory, and that the impression that people possess stable, enduring characteristics can be maintained only at the expense of glossing over inconsistencies and ignoring or reinterpreting discrepant actions.

Self-control

Early attempts to apply the principles of conditioning toward modifying behavior and permitting the individual to achieve self-control tended to stress a mechanical and automatic approach. For example, if an individual had an undesirable habit he or she wanted to eliminate, a common behavioral technique was to apply an aversive stimulus to the undesirable behavior in hopes of suppressing that behavior, thereby permitting the desired behavior to occur and receive positive reinforcement.

In recent years, there has been an increasing trend toward incorporating cognitive factors in behavior therapy (Meichenbaum, 1971). One study nicely illustrates this trend. Based upon the observation that impulsive children show less verbal control over their motor behaviors and employ inner speech in a less instrumental fashion than reflective children, Meichenbaum and Goodman (1971) formulated a treatment procedure for teaching impulsive children to talk to themselves as a means of achieving self-control. In brief, the treatment consisted of using the experimenter as a model both for learning a given skill and for practicing talking to oneself about mastering the task. For example, if you provide an impulsive child with a dartboard and a set of darts, he or she will launch them in rapid-fire order. However, Meichenbaum and Goodman taught the impulsive children to talk to themselves, saying such things as "I should count to three between each dart and then take a deep breath." When this is done, the child's score improves. In fact, the self-instructional training procedures resulted in significant improvement in scores on the Porteus Maze, performance I.Q. on the Wechsler Intelligence Scale for Children, and on a test of cognitive reflectivity. When similar procedures were employed with institutionalized schizophrenics, their performance on attention and cognitive tasks was improved (Meichenbaum, 1971).

Studies such as these reveal a trend toward a more individualized approach to therapy in which self-control is placed inside the individual rather than located in and dependent upon external or situational factors.

RANGE AND FOCI OF CONVENIENCE

Because social learning theory is still an emerging trend in psychology, it is impossible to capture its essentials as a static process. The dynamic nature of this approach can be seen in the fact that in its short history it has had three different foci, each one superseding the earlier ones and encompassing the same explanatory power *plus* a wider range.

CONCEPTUALIZING COMMON HUMAN EXPERIENCE

Generalization and Discrimination

Many of Dollard and Miller's constructs refer to phenomena commonly observed in the study of learning; two of the most important are generalization and discrimination. Since no two situations are exactly alike, learning to deal with one's environment would be impossibly difficult if it were not for the fact that behavior learned in one situation generalizes to other similar situations. Although two stimulus situations are not alike, applying the same verbal label to both aids the generalization. For example, parents find that after children have had one painful experience, the label "hot" can serve as a cue-producing response to keep them away from the china cabinet as well as the stove. Of course, getting along in the world requires not only generalizing but also discriminating, or responding differently to similar situations. If two similar stimuli are presented but responses to only one of them are rewarded, an organism can learn to make new discriminations. If the distinction is difficult, verbal concepts and labels can often mediate the discrimination.

Thus the words "pill" and "candy" may help the young child discriminate between two quite similar objects; verbal labels help the individual solve problems that require high-level generalizations and discriminations. With that function of words in mind, Dollard and Miller point out that the difficulty with repression as a solution to emotional problems is that it strips the person of the ability to make fine discriminations and to apply previous learning to new situations. Repression inhibits cue-producing responses associated with the problem area, and it reduces the individual's problem-solving ability to the level of a child or a nonverbal organism.

Conflict

Like Freud, Dollard and Miller suggest that many emotional problems are due to unverbalized or unconscious conflict learned during infancy and childhood. Relying on simple learning principles, Miller (1944) deduced an impressive theory of conflict. He makes five assumptions to account for behavior in a conflict situation, that is, one in which the same goal is both desired and feared. (1) The tendency to approach a goal increases as one nears the goal; the increase is called the *gradient of approach*. (2) The tendency to avoid a negative stimulus also increases with nearness to the stimulus (the *gradient of avoidance*). (3) As one nears the goal, the avoidance tendency increases faster than the approach tendency (see Fig. 16.1

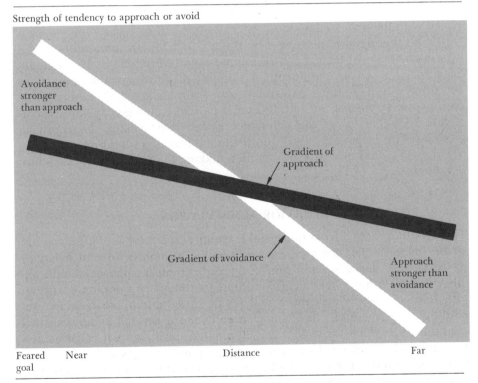

Strength of tendency to approach or avoid

Avoidance stronger than approach

Gradient of approach

Gradient of avoidance

Approach stronger than avoidance

Feared goal   Near   Distance   Far

Fig. 16.1. An approach-avoidance conflict. The tendency to approach is the stronger of the two tendencies far from the goal, whereas the tendency to avoid is the stronger of the two near to the goal. Therefore, when far from the goal, the subject should tend to approach part way and then stop; when near to it, the subject should tend to retreat part way and then stop. In short, the subject should tend to remain in the region where the two gradients intersect. (Adapted from Miller, 1944.)

for a graphic representation of these three assumptions). (4) An increase in the positive or negative drive associated with the goal increases the overall level of the approach or avoidance gradients respectively. (5) When two response tendencies compete, the stronger will occur. According to these assumptions, whether an organism approaches or avoids a goal depends on how far away it is and on the relative strengths of the approach and avoidance drives.

In an ingenious experiment, Brown (1948) found support for all of Miller's assumptions. He tested the theory by measuring the strength with which rats pulled against a harness, either toward a goal after they had been fed there or away after they had been shocked. He showed that both approach and avoidance increased as the animals were placed closer to the goal, that the avoidance increased faster than the approach, and, by varying the hunger and shock levels, that the overall levels of the gradients varied with drive.

Of all the material presented by Dollard and Miller, the conflict model is perhaps the most lasting contribution. From it Miller has deduced guidelines for the proper therapeutic treatment of certain patients, such as neurotics who have unnecessary fears of desirable goals. Of two possible therapeutic strategies for getting such a patient to his goal, Miller recommends trying to lower the avoidance rather than raising the approach gradient. The latter procedure (until the approach gradient exceeded the avoidance) would intensify the conflict, making the situation worse before it got better.

BEHAVIOR MODIFICATION

Therapeutic practice from the social learning standpoint avoids an emphasis on the patient's past and instead attempts to modify current behavior by rewarding desirable and punishing undesirable responses. Traditionally, therapists have been cautioned that treatment of symptoms without attention to underlying causes will result in *symptom substitution*. According to this notion, new and generally more serious symptoms will continue to replace those that are eliminated until the real cause is discovered and corrected. However, Bandura (1969) suggests that the issue has been erroneously dealt with and that any treatment procedure certainly ought to be aimed at causes. The dispute centers on whether one believes those causes to be psychodynamically and historically remote or relatively manipulable and close at hand, rather than on whether one should treat causes or symptoms.

In order to account for the cases in which behavioral treatment appears to be followed by symptom substitution, Bandura (like Dollard and

Miller) suggests that learned strategies for dealing with stress form a *hierarchy of habits*. The therapeutic elimination of the dominant undesirable pattern will be followed by other responses that were initially less probable or lower in the hierarchy. According to this theory, the "mental illness" is gone as soon as the deviant behavior is extinguished, and there is no reason to expect the extinguished response to be followed by other symptoms of some underlying pathology. Of course, the next response pattern in the hierarchy may or may not be more adaptive than the first. If the ensuing pattern is undesirable, the therapist does face the task of eliminating it also, but there is no automatic progression of symptoms from bad to worse. To increase the likelihood that desirable behavior will result from treatment, the therapist should accompany the punishment or withdrawal of positive rewards used to eliminate the problem behavior with the teaching of more desirable patterns.

A second instance in which apparent symptom substitution is likely occurs when elimination of avoidance responses is not paired with reduction of the conditioned fears on which the aversion is based. As long as a groundless fear remains, either the target behavior or some other pointless coping pattern can be expected to reemerge. Thus failure either to foster acceptable alternative behaviors or to extinguish the fear associated with certain stimuli may yield disappointing therapeutic results. Social learning theory does not see such outcomes as evidence of an insidious process of symptom substitution requiring a traditional psychoanalytic depth-psychology approach.

SOCIAL EXCHANGE

As noted earlier in the chapter, many of the variables manipulated on the early practice of behavior therapy were situational in nature. In recent years, there has been a steady shift in research interest to cognitive factors in self-control. One of the leading proponents of the trend, Frederick Kanfer, has distinguished between two broad categories of variables that individuals can employ to modify their own behavior (Kanfer, 1971; Kanfer and Karoly, 1972; Kanfer et al., 1974). The first class, which he terms *alpha* variables, involve environmental or situational determinants. For example, a person who wishes to give up smoking may associate smoking with aversive stimulation, such as electric shock. The second class of variables, termed *beta*, arise from within the individual. They may be self-instructions, vivid imagery, or other controlling responses. For example, smokers may be asked to imagine themselves in a situation in which they are tempted to light a cigarette. They are also to imagine themselves able to avoid electric shock by either refusing to light the cigarette or extinguishing it forcefully the moment it is lit. Surprisingly, in a study which contrasted the effects of the actual delivery of shock to the imagined delivery of shock, the smoking rate of subjects in the "imagine" condition showed a significantly greater decline that was sustained over two follow-up periods (Steffy, Meichenbaum, and Best, 1970).

According to Kanfer and Karoly, "The concept of self- (now termed beta-) regulation is concerned with the processes by which an individual alters or maintains his behavioral chain in the absence of immediate external supports" (1972, p. 406). When a behavioral chain does not run smoothly, individuals begin to monitor their own functioning. Making use of the impact of the external environment as well as of cues arising from their own responses (verbal, proprioceptive, or autonomic), they evaluate their own performance relative to a subjective standard. This standard is referred to as performance promise or contract. In situations involving beta-control, the individual makes a contract (specifies a performance criterion) either covertly or overtly in interaction with another person. Using as the criterion task the length of time a subject will tolerate the submersion of a hand in ice water, Kanfer and his associates have been studying the effects of systematically varying the contract on subsequent performance (Kanfer et al., 1974; Karoly and Kanfer, 1974). They have found, as predicted, that the tolerance of painful exposure to ice water varies with changes in instructional procedures (the nature of the contracts).

APPLICATIONS TO SELECTED TOPICS

Dependency

The early social learning theorists conceived of dependency as one of many drives or needs that are learned during the process of socialization. There are two important premises of this position: (1) dependency has its own motivational properties and (2) these properties are acquired. Initially, behaviors of the child, such as turning toward the mother, smiling, and clutching her, are instrumental in getting hunger, thirst, and other biological needs satisfied; being near the mother is not a goal in itself. However, as the mother continues to be associated with primary-drive reduction, she herself acquires secondary-reward properties. Then her mere presence or the sound of her voice is satisfying to the child and sufficient to stop crying and agitation. At that stage children have developed needs for social contact, so that they are satisfied when they obtain it and tense when they do not.

In contrast to the early social learning theorists, later theorists define dependency in terms of the dependent behaviors themselves (Walters and Parke, 1964). They suggest that dependency, regardless of how it is caused, involves the common components of orienting toward and attending to others. Rather than positing a motivational system specific to dependency, Bandura and Walters (1963) treat dependent behaviors as a category of instrumental responses that are learned as any other behavior is learned. When conceived of as orienting and attending responses, dependency clearly consists of habitual response tendencies that are established by reinforcement and modeling.

The earlier social learning view of Sears (Sears *et al.*, 1953) that dependency is a drive was based on evidence that frustration of children's attention-seeking behavior leads to greater dependency. However, Walters suggests that this finding can be accounted for without hypothesizing a learned drive at all. He notes that parents who sometimes withdraw social rewards or punish their child's dependency at the same time partially or intermittently reward dependent responses. A fundamental learning principle which operates on humans as well as animals is that when all rewards are withdrawn, responses that in the past were only occasionally rewarded are more persistent than those that were always rewarded. Of course, the basic reason that Dollard and Miller needed to posit a special dependency need in the first place was that people often engage in dependency behavior even when they are not getting any primary rewards for it. By invoking the partial reinforcement principle, Walters hypothesizes that parents who intermittently reward dependent behavior are the most likely to produce children who behave dependently *in the absence of any rewards*. By this reasoning, parents who either consistently reward or consistently punish dependent responses should have less dependent children than should those who only occasionally reward and punish such behavior. Thus, without hypothesizing a special motivation, this theory accounts for the fact that children whose parents sometimes deprive them of dependency gratification behave as though they have a high dependency drive.

If the learning of dependency results from the inadvertent rewarding of specific dependent behaviors of the child, then the proper treatment for overly dependent children is to reverse this trend. However, it may not be sufficient merely to withdraw the reward. Sometimes children are dependent because they lack the skills to be independent. As an example, Becker (1971) discusses the case of a seven-year-old girl named Linda who insisted that one of her parents cut her meat for her. The elimination of this overly dependent behavior required the parents to ignore her requests, but it also required that they train her to use a knife and fork so that she could cut her own meat.

Not all examples involved such easily delineated skill deficits as using a knife and fork. Much school work requires self-direction on the part of the child. A child who is overly dependent on directions from the teacher and other students frequently performs poorly. But it is not sufficient to say simply that the child does not know how to work alone. Surely "working by oneself" involves many specific behaviors. In a behaviorally orientated book aimed at showing teachers how to cope with such problems, Swift and Spivack (1975) point out that inability to start working is one prime contributor to academic failure. In the beginning teachers should help the child to overcome this problem by clarifying assignments and giving precise directions so that little initiative is demanded of the student. The teacher might begin by having the child verbalize the instructions and write them down so that student and teacher can review them in the child's own handwriting. Then assignments should be broken down into several smaller lessons. The child should be told that there is a series of tasks to complete, but that there is a sequence and that one task must be done first. In that way, the child does not drown in choices, does not *have* to make a choice. As the youngster becomes successful at moving from one element in the task to another, work plans can be drawn for increasingly longer periods of time. The child can be asked, "How many of these problems do you think you can do this morning?" and can be told that the teacher expects him or her to follow the sequence of steps independently. In such ways the teacher can get the child into the habit of starting the work and following a step-by-step plan.

But of course, there are some stages that are not preplanned, some choicepoints where children must use independent judgment. At such times dependent children may throw up their hands and seek assistance that they would not need if they were in the habit of asking and answering some basic questions themselves. "I can do this *and* that, this *or* that, this and *not* that." To solve a problem one might need to ask "Is this the same kind of problem we did yesterday?" "Are these problems different?" "If they are the same, how did I do them before?" "If they are different, how do they differ?"

In all these examples, particular stages or aspects of the larger problem are focused on one at a time. At each stage the child receives practice at engaging in the behaviors that independence requires. At first they are external, such as writing the instructions, listing on paper the sequence of steps, or asking aloud the questions that need answering, but eventually these become automatic and covert and result in actual independent behavior. Once the child shows instances of such behavior, the teacher can assist the process by labeling it as such and rewarding it. Gradually, the rewards inherent in independence can be expected to maintain the new orientation. The teacher might also arrange situations in which the child has rewarding experiences as a leader instead of a follower—is asked to show a new child around or to teach the others something special. As the child's self-image changes, more and more independent behaviors become attractive and consistent with that self-image.

Aggression

In 1939, a group of learning theorists published a brief book entitled *Frustration and Aggression* (Dollard et al., 1939) which formally stated, in learning theory terms, a hypothesis about aggression that reflected Freud's early views on the subject.

In essence, it said that aggression is a natural and inevitable consequence of frustration. To the authors *frustration* meant any interference with goal-directed activity or any interruption of an ongoing sequence of behavior. The amount of frustration—and consequently the amount of aggression—was hypothesized to depend on three factors: the *strength* of the instigation to make the frustrated response, the *degree* of interference with the response, and the *number* of response sequences interrupted.

Like all such pioneering efforts, the frustration-aggression hypothesis has been modified in the years since its original proposal. As soon as it appeared it attracted critics, and the authors were obliged to revise their initial formulation. The critics pointed out, on the one hand, that reactions other than aggression can be learned as a response to frustration, and on the other hand, that aggressive behavior sometimes occurs in situations that do not involve frustration. Nevertheless, the view that frustration is a basic antecedent of aggression is still a primary assumption, both for the average person and for most social scientists.

In the most recent theorizing about aggression from a social learning point of view, Bandura (1973) has taken aim at the catharsis hypothesis. An integral part of the older frustration-aggression hypothesis as well as of instinct hypotheses, was the idea that aggressive behavior releases or uses up aggressive energy. This was also Freud's basic hypothesis about aggression. Essentially he maintained that aggression gets rid of anger. He theorized that once the person was motivated to aggress, the anger or aggressive energy had to be expressed either directly or indirectly, and that such expressions drained off the pent-up motivation.

Bandura, on the other hand, suggests that such catharsis does not in fact occur and that opposite processes might be at work. In support of his views, Kahn (1966) found that angered students who expressed their resentment to a sympathetic listener increased rather than decreased their feelings of dislike for the person who angered them. Control subjects, who were also angered but merely sat for an equivalent period of time, developed less of a dislike for the other person and were generally less physiologically aroused. From these and other related findings, Bandura concludes that aggressive behavior does not reduce aggressive motivation as maintained by the catharsis hypothesis.

Bandura (1973) acknowledges that the expression of anger can sometimes decrease its incidence, although not through the drainage of the aggressive drive. For example, anger displays can sometimes intimidate antagonists so that they discontinue behaving in provocative ways. Also, there is almost always ambiguity about who did what and to whom. If a person attributes malign intent to the action of another, anger can be aroused during subsequent ruminations so that he acts with inappropriate hostility, as if he had been mistreated on purpose. However, the verbalized resentment may lead to a discussion that clarifies matters and gets rid of any reason for the person to sustain his or her anger.

As with dependency, social learning analyses of aggression focus primarily on the consequences of behavior. As a dramatic illustration of the importance of reinforcement in maintaining aggressive behavior, Patterson, Littman, and Bricker (1967) report a study in which nursery school children were observed over a period of nine months. The researchers found that approximately 80% of the assaultive actions of the children paid off; that is, the children got what they wanted. Considered in this light, theories about inner forces that propel aggressive behavior are unnecessary. Any behavior that is rewarded so handsomely will occur often.

This analysis suggests that effective modification of aggressive behavior would require a change in the pattern of rewards that aggression brings. However, as in the case of dependency, ignoring aggression and withholding the rewards that maintain it is only part of the answer. This is true partly because many of the rewards aggression brings among the child's peers are not under the control of parents and teachers. More importantly, the child's aggressive displays may signal a lack of the social skills necessary to obtain attention through alternative behaviors. Thus, therapy from the social learning approach might include teaching rudimentary social skills or teaching the child to play the games that members of the age-group play. In such cases, once the missing skills have been acquired, the attention and acceptance the child seeks can be obtained more easily by nonaggressive means. Thus the aggressive outbursts lose their functional value. Initially the teacher or parent may need to coax the child, remind him or her of the necessary steps, and reward the proper approach to such situations, but eventually the natural rewards that social acceptance brings ensure maintenance of the appropriate behavior.

On the theory that such skill deficits underlie much of the aggressive behavior of juvenile delinquents, Sarason and Ganzer (1969) have reported preliminary studies that make use of modeling procedures with delinquents to develop social and other skills required for getting a job and developing rewarding interpersonal relationships.

Sexuality

Social learning theorists, in contrast to psychoanalytic theorists, consider sexuality no more important than any other human attribute. Rather than reducing everyday behavior to its presumed sexual determinants, they view sex as a kind of behavior to be explained by more basic principles of learning. Thus sex is involved in neurotic conflicts not because it is more important than other human needs but because it is the most severely attacked and inhibited of primary drives.

Dollard and Miller accept as a frequent and genuine occurrence the Oedipus complex as described by Freud, and they recount in faithful detail his version of its origin. However, they do not accord it the central importance that Freud did. Rather, they are interested in it solely as one in a series of psychological phenomena requiring a social learning explanation. They emphasize that when children handle their genitals, the usual adult response is to punish them or to jerk their hands away. For this reason and others, the child attaches fear to sexual responses, and sex becomes the content of an approach-avoidance conflict. Because the punishment for sexual interest occurs at an early age, however, the conflict is unverbalized or unconscious. The child cannot make the complex discriminations that verbalization would allow and must solve problems in this area at a primitive, trial-and-error level. In addition, even after verbal abilities have developed, the fear that often becomes attached to sexual thoughts motivates the person not to think about them (repression). This process may also eliminate the verbal cues which would have helped solve these problems efficiently.

Bandura and Walters agree that the importance of sex as a psychological variable is due to cultural restrictions. Indeed, they demonstrate that parental inhibitions and anxieties about sex are transmitted to children by both modeling and direct teaching. However, they are less concerned than Dollard and Miller with squaring their social learning account of sexuality with that of Freud. As with dependency and aggression, Bandura and Walters treat sex merely as another class of behavior. In that context, the occurrence of sexual responses is subject to the control of models and of the reinforcements and punishments that follow the responses.

The most recent developments in the area are those of Masters and

Johnson. Theirs is truly a social learning approach to the treatment (1970) and the conceptualization (1974) of human sexuality.

For example, the leading cause of orgasmic dysfunction in the female is presumed to reflect the woman's cognitions concerning acceptable sexual feelings and practices.

> Sociocultural influence more often than not places woman in a position in which she must adapt, subliminate, inhibit, or even distort her natural capacity to function sexually in order to fulfill her genetically assigned role. (1970, p. 218).

The treatment procedures place great stress upon developing her capacity to enjoy and value sensual and sexual experiences and somewhat less stress on acquiring skill in the techniques of love-making. However, a theme that is woven into the very fabric of the treatment procedure concerns the woman's cognitive acceptance of stimulation. This represents a view that sexual pleasure is to be found in the head. In fact, in one of their recent books (Masters and Johnson, 1974) the principal themes are concerned with open communication, shared knowledge, and a sense of mutual commitment.

SUMMARY

Social learning theory seeks to analyze personality development and change by applying principles of learning. In that task the important concept of *habit* has a long history. In the 1930s, Clark Hull formulated a comprehensive theory of habit formation, and Dollard and Miller's social learning approach was an attempt to apply that theory to the psychoanalytic conception of personality. Later social learning theorists, exemplified by Bandura and Walters, have become more eclectic in their approach, abandoning both psychoanalytic and Hullian terminology.

Philosophically, both early and recent social learning theories are in the British empiricist tradition, in which the individual is viewed as an essentially passive recipient of experience that is then mirrored in personality. Thus the central assertion of social learning theory is that individual differences in behavior are a consequence of variations in the conditions of learning that the individuals have encountered.

The principal constructs of Dollard and Miller's theory include *drive* (a strong stimulus which motivates action), *reinforcement* (the reduction of drive), *cue* (a distinctive stimulus which elicits a response), *response* (a motivated action), *secondary drive,* and *secondary reinforcement* (previously neutral cues can acquire drive or reinforcement properties after association with drives or with reinforcements).

Bandura and Walters are more concerned than Dollard and Miller with the role of models in personality formation. Thus one of their principal constructs is *observational learning,* which occurs in the absence of any overt response from the subject. Although they hold that contiguity alone causes learning to occur, Bandura and Walters nevertheless consider *reinforcement* an important construct because behavior patterns are maintained only when they lead to reinforcement. In addition, Bandura and Walters emphasize that *behavior is situationally specific* (rather than stemming from a few general traits), that conditioning creates a means of *self-control* through self-stimulation, and that behavior modification is an effective therapeutic approach. Finally, although the early and later social learning theories are similar in many ways, the later work is somewhat closer to the usual conception of a theory as opposed to that of a model.

The early social learning approach to dependency is based on the conception of *dependency* as a learned drive, whereas more recent formulations define dependency as a cluster of learned behaviors. With regard to *aggression,* the work of the early theorists was guided by the frustration-aggression hypothesis, but Bandura and Walters place more stress on how aggressive acts are learned than on how frustration triggers their occurrence. However, current social learning theorists emphasize that eliminating inappropriate dependent and aggressive behavior often requires teaching new skills in addition to changing the reinforcement contingencies. Dollard and Miller deal with sexuality as one of several areas in which troublesome conflicts are likely to develop early. Bandura suggests that, because sex involves easily definable overt acts, a behavioral or social learning analysis of aberrant sexual behavior is a useful approach. The work of Masters and Johnson places strong emphasis upon the role of cognitive factors in sexuality, stressing that sexual pleasure is to be found in the head.

SUGGESTIONS FOR FURTHER READING

Bandura, A. *Social Learning Theory.* Morristown, N.J.: General Learning Press, 1971. This brief (41-page) module gives a good updated version of Bandura's social learning position. It differs from the original work with Walters in its emphasis on cognitive and self-regulatory processes.

Bandura, A., and R. Walters. *Social Learning and Personality Development.* New York: Holt, 1963. A clear and readable statement of their basic position is given, along with good examples of basic and applied social learning and modeling research. This book is especially good for understanding the shift in social learning theory from the Dollard and Miller tradition.

Dollard, J., and N. E. Miller. *Personality and Psychotherapy.* New York: McGraw-Hill, 1950. In this book the authors detail how they apply Hullian learning theory to reinterpret many of the insights and observations of Freud. This point of view represented the mainstream of the field of personality for well over a decade.

17
Cognitive-developmental Theory

17
Cognitive-developmental Theory

I. **Background and orientation**
    A. Historical perspectives: major contributors
    B. Philosophical perspective
       1. The active person
       2. Hierarchical growth
       3. Interactionism
       4. Cognitive relativity

II. **Central assertion**

III. **Principal constructs**
    A. Orthogenetic development
    B. Adaptation
       1. Assimilation and accommodation
    C. Stages of growth
       1. An empirical example of a stage sequence: the dream
       2. Basic developmental stages

IV. **Range and focus of convenience**

V. **Applications to selected topics**
    A. Dependency
    B. Aggression
    C. Sexuality

VI. **Summary**

VII. **Suggestions for further reading**

This chapter will present an introduction to cognitive-developmental theories of personality. Of the four classes of theory described in this textbook, cognitive-developmental theories are the most recent, and at present, the label "cognitive-developmental" refers more to a set of theoretical assumptions and research strategies than to a specific, well-articulated theory. These assumptions and strategies are cognitive in that they emphasize the processes by which an individual acquires and uses knowledge; they are developmental in that they emphasize an ontogenetic view of personality acquisition.

From the standpoint of cognitive-developmental theory, time is an intrinsic property of all behavioral data. Personality is a reflection not so much of stable individual traits as of age-typical cognitions and world views. Cognitive growth is age-linked. It proceeds through an invariant sequence of stages. In turn, changes in cognitive growth transform the individual's self-perceptions and thereby alter his social reality.

BACKGROUND AND ORIENTATION

In its core assumptions, the cognitive-developmental approach to personality is a refinement of the naive psychology of everyday life (Baldwin, 1969). In interacting with others, we all assume that attitudes, expectancies, beliefs, and memories determine behavior; that is, we all assume that people's behavior is influenced not only by the immediate environment they perceive, but also by the imperceptible environment they know. Cognitive structures and processes, internal and private, modify external response. Further, we assume that what cannot be cognitively represented —what is unknown—can have no influence on behavior. Finally, interactions with children and adults lead us to assume that knowledge develops through experience and is therefore age-linked.

HISTORICAL PERSPECTIVES: MAJOR CONTRIBUTORS

Cognitive-developmental theory is a conceptual marriage of two areas long excluded from the mainstream of American psychology. Perhaps for that reason, major contributions to the theory have been made by three innovators who were themselves out of the mainstream. Donald Hebb, Heinz Werner, and Jean Piaget were all foreign born and trained; each made psychology his career after earlier training and interest in other fields; and though each has profoundly altered our understanding of the human, none could be considered a personality theorist in the usual sense of the term (see Box 17.1).

Hebb's contribution has been twofold. First, he made internal psychological processes intelligible as physiological constructs. By developing a theory in which expectancy, attention, and other cognitive-perceptual processes could be translated into neurophysiological language, he reintroduced cognition into psychology in a rigorous and acceptable manner. Second, Hebb used new physiological data to translate psychological constructs of drive, fear, and arousal into neural mechanisms of midbrain function. He then cogently argued that *the stimulus source for many complex social behaviors is internal* to the organism. The resulting theory (1949) offers a provocative alternative to the input-output model of radical behaviorism: it combines a philosophical position of phenomenology with a methodology of great rigor.

The contribution of Werner lay in his deep commitment to the developmental approach. His work rested on a single basic assumption: ". . . that wherever there is life there is growth and development, that is, formation in terms of systematic, orderly sequence." (1957, p. 125) Werner's creative application of this principle to behavior generated fresh insights into traditional issues and provided the context for diverse research. Much of the research demonstrated that any measured achievement can be reached by different underlying operations, and that it is in the analysis of the underlying operations that the true developmental picture is revealed. For Werner, *behavior*—indeed, life—*is a process, not a product,* and the developmental frame of reference can be fruitfully applied to individual and group behavior.

The monumental work of Piaget began as a theory of knowledge rather than a theory of personality. But early in his study of children's thinking, Piaget created a unique clinical method of *empathic inference* (Elkind, 1970), and the method led to a general theory of development. Following careful observation of a child's thought processes, Piaget attempted to infer how the child must have experienced the situation in order to respond in that manner. Systematic application of the method revealed

. . . that young children believe that the sun and moon follow them when they walk, that dreams come in the window at night, and that everything that moves is alive . . . that number, length, amount, and area change with a change in their appearance.

Now the image of the child suggested by these discoveries is that of a person who, relative to adults, is a *cognitive alien.* . . . The child . . . thinks differently and, figuratively, . . . speaks a different language. It is useful to contrast this image of the child with that promulgated by Freud, [for whom] the child was, relative to adults, an *emotional alien.* . . .

To compare these two images of the child more succinctly we might say that, for Freud, the child is similar to adults in his thinking but differ-

Box 17.1   Cognitive-developmental theorists.

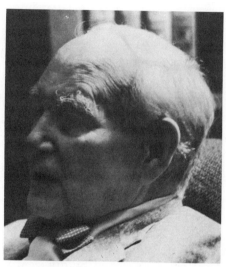

Photo by Chris Payne

D. O. Hebb, one of our most influential and honored psychologists, set out to be a novelist. Failing that, he worked as an elementary teacher and then as a teamster on the Canadian prairies before finally deciding, at age 30, that he wanted to become a psychologist. After receiving a Harvard Ph.D., he worked with Karl Lashley, the physiological psychologist, and Wilder Penfield, the neurosurgeon, before returning to his alma mater, McGill University in Montreal. Hebb's varied experiences, from research on chimpanzees at the Yerkes Laboratories to work with neurosurgical patients at the Montreal Neurological Institute, have given him a perspective of behavior that few others hold. His book, *The Organization of Behavior,* is a contemporary classic, and Hebb's writing exerts a continuing influence on theory and research in the field.

Heinz Werner, born and educated in Vienna, was initially a student of musicology, and many of his later papers dealt with aesthetics. In 1926 his now classic text on the *Comparative Psychology of Mental Development* first appeared and has since gone through numerous editions in many languages. Arriving in the United States in 1933, Werner began a series of influential studies of cognitive-developmental factors in perception, learning, mental retardation, brain damage, language, and aesthetics. He later became the first chairman of the Department of Psychology at Clark University and, during the next 15 years, he published more than 100 articles and five major monographs. Shortly after his death in 1964, the Institute of Development at Clark was renamed the Heinz Werner Institute; there students and colleagues continue his work.

Courtesy of Basic Books

Boston Globe Photo

Jean Piaget, born in Switzerland, published his first paper, an article on a rare albino sparrow, at age 10. On the basis of his early writings, he received an invitation to serve as curator at the Geneva Museum while still in secondary school. Piaget's diverse interests led him to psychology, and after receiving his Ph.D. in zoology, he worked in Binet's laboratory in Paris for several years. There he pursued the clinical study of children's thought processes that has characterized his life's work. For more than four decades Piaget and his Geneva colleagues have systematically pursued that method with findings that have revolutionized psychology and education. Piaget has published more than 18,000 pages, and his influence on contemporary psychology is perhaps second only to Freud's.

Lawrence Kohlberg, America's leading cognitive-developmental theorist, entered the University of Chicago after a hitch in the merchant marine. His doctoral dissertation offered a cognitive theory of moral development as an alternative to psychoanalytic and learning theory accounts. Moral reasoning was hardly a fashionable topic, but the force of Kohlberg's ideas was inescapable. His dissertation provided the impetus for major revisions in theories of development. Just six years later, Kohlberg assumed a professorship at Harvard. He is currently completing a 15-year longitudinal study of the development of moral reasoning and developing teaching procedures to improve moral maturity.

ent from them in his feelings . . . for Piaget just the reverse holds true. . . . The child is similar to adults in his feelings but different from them in his thoughts.*

These differences between Freud and Piaget largely reflect their different foci of study (Hunt, 1969). While Freud was concerned with the development of neuroses in adults, Piaget is concerned with the development of intelligence in children. Thus Piaget's theory emphasizes intellect, not affect. And his observations suggest that a typical child is little concerned with instinctive needs, but, rather, is "looking and listening, manipulating and locomoting . . . continually increasing the complexity of his self-directed activities. . . . It is the fate of these, his own intentions, that control his psychological development rather than the fate of his instinctual needs. . . ." (Hunt, 1969, p. 30)

Thus, from Piaget's approach to a child's construction of reality, a philosophical view of the individual has emerged. To that we now turn.

PHILOSOPHICAL PERSPECTIVE

A theory of personality necessarily assumes a certain model of the individual. Some underlying assumptions about human nature are implicit in the work of personality theorists, and the assumptions determine much of their theories, the type of behavioral phenomena to which they attend, the methods of inquiry that they use, and the forms of explanation that they offer.

The active person.   According to the theories presented in the last two chapters, personality development is an essentially irrational, behavioristic process. For both psychoanalysts and early social learning theorists, the human organism responds in quite automatic ways to stimuli from the external environment. It does so as a consequence of its prior experiences, or it is unconsciously driven to behavior choices by instinctive drives. In either case, the emphasis is on the subject as passive responder to experience rather than initiator of it. By contrast, in this chapter and again in the next, we examine theoretical views of personality in which *the individual is regarded as consciously and rationally making behavior choices and seeking new roles.* In these conceptions, people are the active and initiating determinants of their own behavior choices.

Cognitive-developmental theorists argue that *individuals are less what their experience makes them than what they make of their experience*

---

* From D. Elkind, *Children and Adolescents: Interpretive Essays on Jean Piaget*, Oxford University Press, New York, 1970, pp. 83–84. Reprinted by permission.

(Langer, 1969). Given such an active view of the individual, these theoretical perspectives imply that the self has a key organizing role in social development. Whereas self and phenomenological theories place primary emphasis on human social development, however, cognitive-developmental theories place primary emphasis on biological development as it occurs through continuing social experience.

Hierarchical growth. Cognitive-developmental theories reject the mechanistic philosophy inherent in behavior theory. Social learning views implicitly assume that personality development is *additive;* that is, personality arises through numerous discrete experiences that accumulate over time. But the research of Werner and Piaget suggests that distinctive behaviors are not merely additive; they are emergent. There are some sudden transformations or reconstructions of the behavior of the total organism that are not reducible to lower or earlier functions.

Interactionism. One can recognize three views of development: maturational, environmental, and cognitive-developmental. The maturational view suggests that development is largely an innate process in which stimulation may elicit or maintain but does not create development. Maturational theories stress the notion of unfolding maturational stages in which the order, timing, and patterning of their development is encoded into the genotype.

In contrast to the maturational assumption that mental structures result from innate patterning, environmental theories assume that mental structures result from the patterning of external events. On the other hand, the theoretical structure of cognitive-developmental theories is interactional: *personality results from the interaction of certain structuring tendencies within the organism with the structure of the external world.* The interaction leads to cognitive stages that represent the transformation of early cognitive structures as they are accommodated to or restructured by external experience.

Thus cognitive-developmental theory suggests that growth is self-directed through interaction with social experience. Cognitive theorists reject a strict maturational view because they believe that the structures which organize experience arise themselves through experience. And they reject a *tabula rasa* view because it leaves no room for the modification of experience produced by the structural processes, once acquired. Experience cannot act on the developing human infant without some constraint, because the infant has available only a small number of organized behavioral systems. These systems develop through experience and, once acquired, modify subsequent experiences (Hunt, 1969).

Cognitive relativity. Piaget's descriptions of the growth of reality in the child were based initially on observations of his own children when they were infants. From observations of the child's conception of causality, time, number, and space, Piaget concluded that there is a sequential development of formal thought. Further, for the developing child, thought directs perception. *The world that exists for the child is a function of the child's cognitive construction of it.*

At a higher level, cognitive-developmental theorists conclude that what is true for the child is true for us all. Cultural modes of thought and the formal logic invented for science change as the human construction of reality changes.

One can think of the above argument as a cognitive-relativity hypothesis: *thought directs perception so that reality is a function of our cognitive construction of it.* An even stronger version of this notion is known as the linguistic relativity hypothesis. Here the argument is that the structure and grammatical rules of the language one speaks affect one's perception of the world so as to alter one's knowledge of reality in a profound and pervasive way. And because the concepts symbolized by the constructions of one language are never exactly translatable into another, the thinking processes of those who speak different languages are not identical. In short, the structure of language profoundly affects thought processes. Thought may therefore be relative to the language in which it is conducted. The hypothesis of linguistic relativity finds some support in differences between languages (Whorf, 1956), but available experimental evidence suggests that commonalities among languages are far greater than their structural differences.

We can summarize the philosophical perspective of cognitive-developmental theory as follows: We are what we make ourselves by our own actions; development is a self-constructive process in which the individual is the active agent, not the passive recipient; we do not mirror our experience, we create it, and in the process we change ourselves (Langer, 1969). Reality is a function of our cognitive construction of it, and our cognitive constructions change through experience.

CENTRAL ASSERTION

Personality proceeds through an invariant sequence of stages in its development, and cognitive structuring of the environment is the defining property of each stage. Cognitive-developmental theories assert that between the stimulus situation and the resulting behavioral response lies the construction of a cognitive representation of the environment. The cognitive representation is a coding of information from the stimulus situation, based on the immediate environment as well as stored memories. The *effective environment*, that which arouses and guides overt behavior, is in fact this cognitive representation (Baldwin, 1969), and the representation changes in character with each stage of development.

Cognition is central to the theory, because it is through our cognitive constructions of the world that we come to know it. To understand, we invent and create; we understand an experience or event to the extent that we reinvent it by our own perspective and cognitive actions.

> Knowledge is not a copy of reality. To know an object, to know an event, is not simply to look at it and make a mental copy, or image, of it. To know an object is to act on it. To know is to modify, to transform the object, and to understand the process of this transformation, and as a consequence to understand the way the object is constructed. An operation is thus the essence of knowledge; it is an interiorized action which modifies the object of knowledge. (Piaget)*

Cognitive organization changes with development, and the sequence of changes is assumed to be invariant. The child passes through a series of successive stages, each of which is characterized by a particular mode of cognitive organization. Attainment of an advanced stage is dependent on the attainment of each of the preceding stages. But an advanced stage is not merely an addition to an earlier one; it is a fundamental reorganization of earlier levels.

PRINCIPAL CONSTRUCTS

The theme of the cognitive-developmental approach to personality is that *structure and function are indissoluble.* Development arises through the interaction of behaving organisms with their biosocial environments. Personality development is neither exclusively social nor exclusively maturational; rather, it evolves from the natural history of an individual's life. The model on which these theories rest, adapted from biology (Mehrabian, 1968), is one which emphasizes evolutionary homeostasis: *old structures are assimilated to new functions, and new structures accommodate old functions.*

---

* Quoted in F. G. Jennings, "Jean Piaget: notes on learning," *Saturday Review,* May 20, 1967. Copyright 1967 Saturday Review, Inc. Reprinted by permission.

Orthogenetic Development

The first major construct of cognitive-developmental theory is a principle that derives from the writings of Heinz Werner. The principle character-izes the *direction* of all longitudinal changes associated with behavioral development.

> Wherever development occurs it proceeds from a state of relative globality and lack of differentiation to a state of increasing differentiation, articula-tion, and hierarchic integration. (Werner, 1957, p. 126)

The principle is based on a biological metaphor in that it assumes a psychological parallel to the differentiation and integration of cells and units that occur during biological development (Mehrabian, 1968). That parallel is found in the number and complexity of cognitive categories with which an individual perceives and understands his world. Early in development, a child's cognitions are limited and global; even the basic differentiation of self from environment is incomplete and unstable. With increasing experience, new cognitive categories emerge to permit an ever larger number of possible discriminations. And given the basic theoretical assumption of a cognitive theory that an individual's response in any situation is determined by his cognitive construction of it, such cognitive growth will lead to behavior that is objective and flexible, less egocentric, and more adaptive. The construct of orthogenetic development character-izes a child's intellectual growth from a global, egocentric state to one of sociocentric objectivity. *The evolution of children's ideas is always in the direction of greater objectivity, reciprocity, and relativity,* as is revealed by direct observation of their mental growth.

> Consider, for example, the young child's belief that physical objects are endowed with consciousness and that mental events have physical prop-erties (pre-school youngsters believe that thinking is done with the mouth and that dreams are made of wind). As children grow older they come to distinguish between what is psychic and what is physical and to recognize the properties peculiar to each type of phenomena. Likewise, as children mature they also begin to discover illusions, find that things are not always what they seem, and come to realize that their senses can be deceiving. All of these attainments point to a progressively more objective mode of thought in the sense that children become increasingly able to distinguish between the public world of objects and the private world of thoughts and feelings.
>
> Children's thinking also develops in the direction of greater reciprocity to the extent that they become increasingly able to see the world from the standpoint of others.... If asked, a young boy will readily acknowledge that he has a brother but will vehemently deny that his brother has a

brother. As the child matures . . . he discovers that *being* a brother implies *having* a brother, evidence that he has attained reciprocity of thought.

The final direction taken by mental evolution . . . towards greater relativity . . . can be observed in the evolution of the child's understanding of such relational conceptions as "above," "below," and "on top of." Among young children such relations are thought of absolutely so that if a brick is "on top of a box" they say that the box cannot at the same time be on top of the ground. With increasing age, children gradually discover that "above," "below," and "on top of" correspond to relations between things rather than to properties of things. The late arrival of relative thinking in children helps to account for the fact that prepositions are among the last categories of words to appear in the child's speaking vocabulary. (Elkind, 1970, pp. 48–49)

We must emphasize that *orthogenetic development* not only applies in the narrow sense of ontogenesis (development of an individual organism), but it applies to *any* behavior that can be developmentally ordered. Cognitive developmental theorists have applied the construct to problems of perception, learning, psychopathology, retarded development, aging, and diverse social behaviors. They assume that there is a formal similarity between the organization and structure of behavior processes in young children, in organisms low in the phylogenetic scale, in mature adults in technologically underdeveloped cultures, and in states of lowered consciousness and cases of psychotic regression among adults in advanced societies.

Adaptation

The construct of orthogenetic development described in the last section refers to the *direction* of development through progressive differentiation of cognitive categories. We turn now to the *mechanisms* of development and the constructs used by Piaget to describe cognitive functioning. Piaget's basic idea is that behavior functions remain invariant while the underlying structures systematically change. The change in structures constitutes development.

The core construct, *adaptation,* is taken from biology, and the biological analogy is the ingestion of food by a living organism (Flavell, 1963). Two aspects of adaptation can be distinguished; they are *assimilation* and *accommodation.* Consider the biological example:

First, the organism must . . . transform the substances it takes in in order to incorporate their food values into its system. . . . The process of changing elements in the milieu in such a way that they can become incorporated into the structure of the organism is called *assimilation.* ...

In the process of assimilating foodstuffs to itself, the organism is also ... adjusting itself to them. ... [This] adjustment to the object Piaget labels *accommodation*—i.e., the organism must accommodate its functioning to the specific contours of the object it is trying to assimilate.*

Assimilation and accommodation.   Applied to personality, adaptation refers to the process by which an individual copes with human problems. These processes include the assimilation of experiences to existing structures, as well as the accommodative modification of structures as a function of new experiences. It may clarify the distinction if Piaget's "internal structures" are translated into the cognitive mediating processes described in Chapter 4. Assimilation, then, refers to the modification of incoming stimuli by existing mediating processes; accommodation describes the manner in which mediating processes are themselves modified by continuing experience (Phillips, 1969).

Assimilation is best exemplified by children's play and by psychotic delusions, since experience in both cases is molded (or distorted by fantasy) to fit existing patterns of thinking and feeling. Accommodation is most clearly illustrated in imitation, which behavior is directly shaped to fit the incoming stimulation (Mehrabian, 1968). Most adaptive behavior consists of a balance of the two processes of accommodation and assimilation.

Piaget has studied such adaptive behavior in his classic studies of conservation. Conservation refers to the fact—obvious to an adult—that the mass, weight, and volume of a substance remain unchanged (that is, they are conserved), despite a change in shape or a division into parts. The conservation principle is not at all obvious to young children. For them things are what they seem to be, and immediate sense impressions cannot be subordinated to reason.

To give just one illustration from among hundreds, a child is shown two identical drinking glasses filled equally full with orangeade and he is asked to say whether there is the "same to drink" in the two glasses. After the child says that this is the case, the orangeade from one glass is poured into another which is taller and thinner so that the orangeade now reaches a higher level. Then the child is asked to say whether there is the same amount to drink in the two differently shaped glasses. Before the age of 6 or 7, most children say that the tall, narrow glass has more orangeade. The young child cannot deal with the transformation and bases his judgment on the static features of the orangeade, namely the levels. (Elkind, 1970, p. 15)

---

* From *The Developmental Psychology of Jean Piaget* by J. H. Flavell, p. 45; copyright © 1963 by Litton Educational Publishing, Inc., by permission of D. Van Nostrand Co.

The child's acquisition of an understanding of conservation provides the foundation for Piaget's general theory of development. For in learning the distinction between appearance and reality—in learning to distinguish how things look from how things are—the child is cognitively structuring the world of experience. And that construction is not so much perceived by the senses as conceived by the developing intellect (Elkind, 1970).

Stages of Growth

The fundamental assumption of cognitive-developmental theory is that personality arises through continuing interaction of structuring tendencies within the organism and the structure of the external environment. The interaction produces a sequence of stages. Each stage represents a transformation of an earlier stage, a reorganization of cognitive structures that have been modified by assimilation of experience and adaptive accommodation to it.

An answer to the question "How does personality develop and change?" is given in terms of the invariant sequence of cognitive stages (Pinard and Laurendeau, 1969; Kohlberg, 1969). The characteristics of these stages are as follows: (1) Stages represent *qualitative shifts* in the mode of thinking; they cannot be reduced to an accretion or additive set of responses. (2) These qualitative changes form an *invariant sequence* in development; unique experiences or cultural differences can accelerate or retard rate of sequential change, but they cannot alter its sequence. (3) Cognitive stages are hierarchical integrations; stages form a *sequential order of increasingly more differentiated and integrated structures* (the construct of orthogenetic development). (4) Stages represent a *pervasive reorganization of thought* which determines response to diverse environmental demands; they are "structured wholes," not specific to particular situations.

Do stages exist? In other words, are there cognitive transformations which meet the above definitions? The question is important, because an affirmative answer necessitates an interactional theory of development. If structural stages do exist, children's organization of experience will differ qualitatively from that of their parents (rather than be merely less complete or less complex). Further, if such qualitative differences are common to all children of similar age, the child's mental structure cannot be understood simply as direct imitative learning of adult teaching (Kohlberg, 1969).

An empirical example of a stage sequence: the dream. Kohlberg (1966a; 1969) has presented a simple yet convincing empirical example of a cognitive-stage sequence, the dream. Kohlberg points out that the dream is an experience with which the child is familiar from a very early age but one which is restructured in very different ways throughout development. As the child's structuring of his entire experience develops, his evaluation of the dream changes markedly. Kohlberg's research reveals the sequence of development in children's beliefs about dreams. In the first step, they recognize dreams as not real events. Soon afterward, they understand that dreams are experiences that others cannot see. Still later, children are aware that dreams take place inside themselves and, in the final step, they understand that dreams are thoughts they have caused themselves.

Kohlberg (1969) studied the sequence of development of the dream concept for American children and for children of the Atayal, a Malaysian aboriginal group on Formosa. In these studies, the steps of development in beliefs about dreams were construed as items in a Guttman scale (see Chapter 14). Children who held a belief at a given level were assumed to have passed through all earlier stages of belief. The data provided a striking confirmation of this developmental pattern. Of the 90 American children studied, only 18 failed to conform to the Guttman pattern; of the 15 Atayal children, only 3 deviated from the pattern. This evidence supports the hypothesis of an invariant sequence in the development of the dream concept.

The fact that *adult* Atayal believe in the reality of dreams and equate them with the soul makes development of the dream concept among their children particularly interesting. Despite their parents' belief in the objective reality of dreams, Atayal children develop a subjective concept of dreams that is very similar to that held by young American children. The development of the dream concept among Atayal children is *slower* than among American children, however, and after a relatively subjective concept of dreams is reached at approximately age 11, it begins "reversing" toward the objective concept held by their parents. Such results imply that the sequential development of the dream concept is a product of the child's own cognitive development, rather than of early parental teaching.

But if social learning cannot explain these data, neither can maturational unfolding.

> The apparent invariant universal sequence in the development of the dream concept in the absence of adult cultural support cannot be interpreted as being the direct result of maturational unfolding, since the culture can "reverse" it by specific training, a reversal presumably very difficult to teach for maturational postural-motor sequences. A maturational interpretation is also contradicted by the fact that the Atayal children go through the same sequence more slowly than do their Taiwanese and American age-mates,

presumably because the Atayal exists in a somewhat cognitively impoverished general culture, i.e., they have less *general* experiences.*

In short, an interactional perspective best accounts for the child's development of the dream concept. Furthermore, the development follows an invariant universal sequence that is hierarchical in organization. Analysis of the stages reveals that they provide progressive differentiation on the subjective from the objective: the dream is progressively differentiated, first as unreal, then as internal, and finally as immaterial—a sequence that corresponds to an inner logic of the concept of reality (Kohlberg, 1969).

Basic developmental stages.   Werner and Piaget have identified three basic stages in cognitive development. The first, from birth to about 24 months, is a *sensorimotor period* in which infants are dependent on their bodies for expression and communication. Children come to know objects in their environment by acting upon them—touching, tasting, biting, etc. The responses children make to objects constitute their meaning. By the end of the period, the developing infant is learning to distinguish external from internal stimuli by separating self from nonself. It is this initial development through which the child ultimately attains a sociocentric perspective of reality.

The second stage, from age 2 to about age 11, is a perceptual period, which Piaget refers to as a *period of concrete operations*. During this time, developing children gain skill in manipulating symbolic representations of the environment. They master elementary relationships of space, time, and causality and slowly acquire understanding of conservation of mass, weight, and volume.

The final stage, from approximately age 11 onward, is characterized by cognitive symbolism. Piaget calls it a *period of formal operations*. Growing adolescents achieve understanding of the conservation of area, number, and duration, and they begin to reason by manipulating reality through their symbolic representations of it. They construct their own values and ideals; they invent and evaluate hypotheses about their enlarging world; and they begin to meaningfully plan their future.

To summarize: the child understands the world through a progressive differentiation of categories of experience. In the initial stage, knowledge is action; the first categories of knowledge are sensorimotor. Later, the child integrates sensations arising from sensorimotor experience into perceptual categories. And finally, with development of language skills, perceptual distinctions become the basis for conceptual categorization and true symbolic manipulation of experience.

---

* From Lawrence Kohlberg, "The cognitive-developmental approach to socialization," in David A. Goslin (ed.), *Handbook of Socialization Theory and Research,* © 1969 by Rand McNally and Company, Chicago, pp. 358–359. Reprinted by permission.

RANGE AND FOCUS OF CONVENIENCE

Cognitive-developmental theory springs from apparently limited, if not limiting, origins. Piaget's theory is based almost exclusively on an analysis of thinking processes in a small, selected sample of normal Swiss children. The theory makes no allowance for differences in sex or culture or for unique learning; its single variable is age, and it is a theory of knowledge, not a theory of behavior.

The range of the resulting theory, however, is surprisingly great. Cognitive principles derived from study of Swiss children apply to British, American, Arab, Chinese, and Indian children as well. Constructs invented to understand children's thinking extend to the interpersonal behavior of adults and to the expression of symptoms in psychopathology (Feffer, 1967; 1970). The direction and nature of cognitive development provide a heuristic model of ego development. The conservation of substance across transformations of form parallels the preservation of ego-identity across transformations in role relationships (Kohlberg, 1969).

Nonetheless, the theory has obvious limits. It is, after all, a theory of development; as such it has only limited application to the maintenance and modification of adult behaviors. And the theory is cognitive; it has little to tell us of such raw emotional experiences as rage, shame, or exhilarating joy. Clearly, the focus of the theory remains on epistemology, i.e., how knowledge is acquired.

Cognitive-developmental theorists argue that *learning is dependent on development*—rather than the converse, as is usually assumed. This emphasis on the sequential-stage development of knowledge suggests that the most direct application of the theory lies in education. The implications of cognitive-developmental theory for curriculum planning have been articulated by Hunt (1961; 1968) in what he aptly calls the "problem of the match": the need to match curricular demands to the child's developmental stage. Hunt believes that Maria Montessori's approach solves the problem of the match, because her techniques capitalize on children's spontaneous interests, permitting them to work with materials of interest as their own wishes dictate.

Other investigators are directly engaged in curricular planning from the perspective of cognitive-developmental theory. Some (e.g., Stendler-Lavatelli, 1968) are developing programs explicitly designed to foster the acquisition of cognitive structures; children have direct practice in skills basic to the conservation of number and classification. Others (e.g., Sigel, 1969) are constructing sequential curricula keyed to the child's development, using techniques designed to facilitate decentered functioning. Still others (e.g., Covington, 1970) are exploring cognitive curricula designed to nurture productive thinking. The content of such a curriculum is the thought process itself; its aim is to teach mental strategies as ends in themselves. Children are not learning content; they are not even learning to learn; rather, they are learning to think (Covington, 1970).

APPLICATIONS TO SELECTED TOPICS

The application of cognitive-developmental theories to problems of socialization is of recent origin. Because the theories were created to account for cognitive development (i.e., for the acquisition of knowledge about the world), their extension to social development requires new assumptions. The following account is based largely on Kohlberg's (1969) analysis of the cognitive-developmental approach to socialization.

Kohlberg's analysis requires four assumptions about social-emotional development. (1) Affective development is parallel to cognitive development. (2) There is a fundamental unity to personality organization; social development consists of a continuing restructuring of the self concept. (3) Social cognition is based on reciprocal role-taking; developmental changes in the social self reflect underlying changes in cognitive conception of the social world. (4) The direction of social development is toward an equilibrium between one's own actions and the reciprocated actions of others.

The key theoretical notion is that of stage-sequential development. This idea is of course not unique; it is shared with the psychoanalytic theories of Freud and Erikson (Chapter 15), as well as with the maturational theory of Gesell. What is unique is the emphasis on cognition and the explanation of stages in terms of cognitive transformations.

The issue is one of priority. In contrast to social-learning theory, which views development as a product of learning, cognitive-developmental theory views learning as dependent on development. Given a sequential-stage development of cognition, learning will vary with available cognitive operations. And the developmental stage will determine *what* is learned as well as *how* learning occurs.

We shall conclude this chapter by suggesting some implications of a cognitive-developmental approach for understanding dependency, aggression, and sexuality.

Dependency

A cognitive-developmental approach to dependency is rooted in the human infant's congenital preferences for selected shapes, rhythms, and tactile-kinesthetic stimuli. Such preferences predispose the infant to seek and maintain experiences of certain kinds (Wolff, 1969), and there is fragmentary evidence that human infants seek visual patterns resembling facial gestalts and tactile stimulation such as is found in a mother's embrace. Such *sensorimotor* experiences may be the developmental *precursors of affectional bonding,* from which social dependency emerges.

In common with both psychoanalytic and social-learning perspectives, cognitive-developmental theory suggests that interpersonal dependency arises from the child's imitation of adult models. But the analysis of imitation and its role in the development of dependency differs markedly. Cognitive theorists hold that imitation is intrinsically motivated. Young children imitate interesting and complex behaviors in the absence of extrinsic reinforcements. Thus imitation can be understood in cognitive terms. Further, the construct of dependency itself can be formulated as a function of cognitive inadequacy: people may be most dependent when they feel most inadequate (Mehrabian, 1968).

In cognitive-developmental theory, the sequential relationship of dependency and imitation is the opposite of that suggested by psychoanalysis. In psychoanalytic theory, the child's dependency is related to affective needs, which lead to imitative modeling of parents and ultimately to internalized identification with them. The cognitive-developmental perspective turns this sequence on its head. The child is intrinsically motivated to imitate adult models, and the *imitation leads to dependency,* rather than the converse (Kohlberg, 1969). From this perspective, the child's need for parental approval and guidance is a product of imitation, not its cause.

Aggression

By what processes does the developing child come to behave in accordance with expectations of society? How are normative standards internalized? And what role do rewards and punishment play in the socialization process?

From the cognitive-developmental view, the role of rewards and punishments is not the mechanical one implied by early social-learning theory. Rather, these events provide cues enabling children to cognitively evaluate the adequacy of their responses and develop their sense of morality. Here, as elsewhere, the child's developing cognitions are assigned priority in the socialization process.

Basing his research on earlier studies by Piaget, Kohlberg (1967; 1969) has obtained evidence of stages of development in moral judgment; the trends follow an invariant sequence that has a cognitive base. Thus there are formal *stages of moral development.* The stages are cultural universals: they are found among preliterate villagers from Taiwan as well as

middle-class urban Americans; they are independent of religious education or belief. The stages of moral development are defined by responses
to a set of hypothetical moral dilemmas, and stage definition is based on
25 moral concepts which appear to be cultural universals. Kohlberg believes that any moral judgment can be scored for moral-stage level, and
he has evaluated statements made by Adolf Eichmann as one illustration
(Kohlberg, 1967).

Sexuality

From the perspective of cognitive-developmental theory, the child's
gender identity precedes imitative modeling of the same-sex parent. As indicated in Chapter 13, the boy identifies with his father because he has
sex-typed himself. The developmental shift in the boy's orientation to
his parents is based on his cognitive awareness that he is a boy. The
psychoanalytic idea that the developmental shift is based on castration
anxiety is rejected, and the sequential development of sex-typed identity
is cognitively based. Table 17.1 contrasts psychoanalytic and cognitive-
developmental theory. Study of the imitative preferences of boys aged 4
to 8 suggests that the speed with which a boy proceeds through the cog-

Table 17.1 Contrasting theoretical approaches to the development of sex-typed
identity.*

Neopsychoanalytic identification theory	Cognitive-developmental theory
1. Orientation to father as major re-warder or punisher with associated dependency.	1. Sex-typed identity.
2. Identification or imitation of father.	2. Imitation or identification with father.
3. Sex-typed identity.	3. Orientation to father as major rewarder with associated dependency companionship.

* From Lawrence Kohlberg, "The cognitive-developmental approach to socialization,"
in David A. Goslin (ed.), *Handbook of Socialization Theory and Research,* © 1969 by
Rand McNally and Company, Chicago, p. 458. Used by permission.

nitive-developmental sequence is related to cognitive maturity, but the sequence itself is invariant.

The development of sex-role attitudes and behaviors is the product of cognitive development. Gender identity arises from self-categorization. It is a cognitive judgment about reality, not a product of social learning or cultural training (Kohlberg, 1966b).

SUMMARY

The cognitive-developmental approach represents an effort to apply biological principles to personality. Evolutionary growth and adaptive homeostasis are major constructs. The central theme is that structure and function are indissoluble. Mental and personality growth are viewed as extensions of physical growth, and extreme environmentalism and extreme maturationism are equally eschewed. Personality development is not merely the additive result of discrete experiences, nor is it the simple unfolding of innate structures; it is always an interactional process.

Developmental changes are crucial because they alter internal cognitive structures of the organism; and cognitive structures, once acquired through experience, interpret and transform the organism's subsequent experiences. Thus developmental changes directly influence the acquisition of new responses, for what is learned is based on what is perceived. From a cognitive-developmental perspective, then, learning is a function of development, rather than the converse, and the constructs that explain cognitive development will also apply to personality development.

We reviewed three principal constructs which describe the direction, mechanisms, and stages of development. The first, *orthogenetic development*, states that all growth is in the direction of increasing differentiation. The principle was illustrated by the cognitive growth of a child from a global egocentric state to one of sociocentric objectivity.

A second construct, *adaptation*, describes the mechanisms and nature of development. We distinguished the processes of *assimilation* and *accommodation* and illustrated them by Piaget's studies of conservation in young children.

The final construct, *stages of growth*, was defined as an invariant sequence of integrated cognitive structures that is hierarchical in organization. We reviewed empirical evidence of the existence of such stages in analysis of the dream concept in children of two cultures. Stages in development of the dream concept document a progressive differentiation of subjective experience from objective reality.

Given its limited origins, cognitive-developmental theory has surprisingly wide application. The theoretical constructs invented to account for cognitive growth in childhood have been fruitfully extended to interpersonal behavior of adults. However, the theory remains a theory of cognitive development, and its most important application is to education. We reviewed recent efforts in that area to plan curricula from the perspective of cognitive-developmental research.

The extension of cognitive-developmental theory to socialization depends on an assumption that the nature and direction of affective and social development parallel those of cognitive development. The theory uniquely offers a stage-sequential analysis of personality development in which cognitive transformations define the stages.

From this perspective, dependency is rooted in early sensorimotor experiences. Social dependency arises through imitative modeling, but the imitation is intrinsically motivated, and it can be understood in cognitive terms. Dependency itself is a function of cognitive uncertainty.

Socialization is largely a cognitive process. There are developmental trends in the process of internalizing social expectation; the trends constitute formal stages of moral development that are cultural universals. The introjection of sex-role attitudes is also a process of cognitive development. Gender identity is not a product of social learning. It precedes imitative modeling rather than results from it.

SUGGESTIONS FOR FURTHER READING

Elkind, D. *Children and Adolescents: Interpretive Essays on Jean Piaget,* 2nd ed. New York: Oxford University Press, 1974. An engaging and informative introduction to Piaget's theory and its implications for education.

Furth, H. G. *Piaget for Teachers.* Englewood Cliffs, N.J.: Prentice-Hall, 1970. An effort to apply Piaget's theoretical ideas to early education. Introductory and practical, yet written with passion in the hope of effecting changes that Furth believes necessary.

Ginsburg, H., and S. Opper. *Piaget's Theory of Intellectual Development: An Introduction.* Englewood Cliffs, N.J.: Prentice-Hall, 1969. A brief and well-written monograph that provides what its title claims.

Phillips, J. L., Jr. *The Origins of Intellect: Piaget's Theory.* San Francisco: Freeman, 1969. Another introduction to Piaget's theory with emphasis on the stages of cognitive growth. Numerous illustrations of Piaget's research methods.

18 Self Theory

18
Self
Theory

I. **Background and orientation**
  A. Historical perspective
    1. Background
    2. Self theory
      a. Nondirective psycho-
         therapy
      b. Self-actualization
    3. Recent developments
      a. Softening of behavior-
         ism
      b. Transcendental medita-
         tion
  B. Philosophical perspective
    1. The active nature of the
       human
    2. The scientific study of the
       human

II. **Central assertion**

III. **Principal constructs**
  A. Self
    1. Empirical self
    2. Valuing self
  B. An absolute state of psy-
     chological health
  C. The natural growth tendency
     of humans
  D. Primacy of experience

IV. **Range and focus of convenience**
  A. Awareness
    1. Self-understanding
    2. Personal satisfaction
    3. Sensitivity
  B. Creativity
    1. Creative people
    2. Creativity as freedom
    3. The science of creative in-
       telligence

V. **Applications to selected topics**
  A. Dependency
  B. Aggression
  C. Sexuality

VI. **Summary**

VII. **Suggestions for further reading**

The concept of a "self" has great intuitive appeal. Subjectively, we experience the elation and joy of success and the disappointment of failure. We congratulate ourselves or others for a job well done, but for a careless mistake or costly oversight we may be called irresponsible, either by ourselves or by others. Life is a series of choices which we feel we make; it consists of the courses of actions (or inactions) for which we are held accountable by others and in terms of which we judge others. But it is the self which makes the decision and which suffers the consequent joys and sorrows.

Self theory approaches personality by dealing directly with the experiences and feelings which give rise to the sense of personal existence, to one's self. Thus self theory has its focus within the individual; it is a distinctive philosophical view of the individual and one which is in sharp contrast to behavioristic psychology.

BACKGROUND AND ORIENTATION

Although the mechanical assumptions and experimental methods of modern behavioristic experimental psychology have been the dominant ideology of twentieth-century psychology, they have not been uncritically accepted by all psychologists. In contrast to the dominant trend, self theorists have preserved a humanistic element during this period and have resisted the reduction of human personality to a collection of reflex-like segments which are triggered by events outside the individual. Self theory, because it has been concerned with the total living and functioning person, accepts a philosophical view of the individual which requires internal, as opposed to external, coordinates to be used as the frame of reference for thought about human personality.

HISTORICAL PERSPECTIVE

Self theory is a reaction against the application to people of methods of inquiry developed for physical objects, methods which treat the human psyche as mechanical and chemical processes. It is a reaction against an "empty black box" approach to the human. One of the spokesmen for a humanistic psychology, Gordon W. Allport (1947), in an address to the Division of Personality and Social Psychology of the American Psychological Association, stated that psychoanalytic and contemporary psychology asks us "to believe that an individual's character-structure is, in all essentials, determined by the time his last diaper is changed." He went on to note that "if the chances for peace in the world depend to such a degree upon infant fixations, ought we not disband this division and register as wet nurses to the mewling citizens of tomorrow?" (pp. 185–186)

For Allport and other self theorists (see Box 18.1), personality development is a growing and active process by which individuals take responsibility for their lives and develop in unique and personal ways. The emergence of personal maturity is a continuous and lifelong process of becoming (Allport, 1955).

Background

Early psychology had more in common with philosophy than with contemporary scientific psychology. The early functionalists were more concerned with analysis of the human mind than with an empirical inquiry. William James, in his *Principles of Psychology* published in 1890, devotes a chapter of more than 100 pages to the topic of the "self." For James, a concept of self was necessary to deal with the manifest unity of mental functioning.

However, with the development of the empirical orientation and the experimental methods and concepts of twentieth-century behavioristic psychology, a concept of the self was too dangerous. To assign unifying functions to the self and have "it" serve these functions was to beg the question. The task was to plot the behavior of each subject with reference to external antecedent conditions, and to bypass the need for describing the events against internal referents. The *behavior* was an objective event which could be recorded; the *person* could be left blank, or empty, for scientific purposes so long as reliable and objective antecedent causes and behavioral effects could be demonstrated.

Self Theory

Self theory is thus a reaction against the past 70 years of behaviorism. Many individuals have contributed to self theory, but we will consider in detail only two, both of whom have made an effort to develop a systematic and comprehensive theory of personality.

Nondirective psychotherapy. Carl Rogers began as a psychotherapist rather than as a personality theorist. From the methods he developed for working with his clients (note the choice of the term "client" instead of "patient"), he developed a distinctive view about personality. Like Freud, Rogers built a theory of personality based on his detailed contact with the personal lives of individuals who came to him for help with their prob-

Box 18.1   Self theorists.

Gordon W. Allport was President of the American Psychological Association in 1939. He received his Ph.D. in 1922 from Harvard University and returned in 1930 to Harvard, where he remained as Professor of Psychology until his death in 1967. Allport continually spoke for the need to study individuals in order to gain knowledge of their uniqueness. In 1963 he received the Gold Medal award from the American Psychological Foundation for his contributions to psychology. The American Psychological Association presented Allport with the Distinguished Scientific Contribution Award in 1964, noting in the citation that he has "reminded us that man is neither a beast nor a statistic, except as we choose to regard him so, and that human personality finds its greatest measure in the reaches of time."

Carl R. Rogers was President of the American Psychological Association in 1947. He received his Ph.D. in 1931 from Teachers College of Columbia University. Rogers' theoretical view of personality and his nondirective approach to psychotherapy emerged from his work as director of the counseling service at the University of Chicago from 1945 to 1957. He is now at the Western Behavioral Sciences Institute, La Jolla, California. He received the Distinguished Scientific Contribution Award from the American Psychological Association in 1956, the year the award was initiated.

Courtesy of the International
Center for Scientific Research

Abraham H. Maslow was President of the American Psychological Association in 1968. He received his Ph.D. in 1935 from the University of Wisconsin. Maslow served as chairman of the Department of Psychology of Brandeis University from 1951 to 1961. In 1969 he took a four-year leave of absence from his position as Professor of Psychology at Brandeis to become the first in-residence grant holder of the W. P. Laughlin Foundation, established in 1968 to provide a creative environment for the generation of new ideas which would effect immediate social change. Professor Maslow intended to use the four-year period to develop the philosophy of democratic politics, economics, and ethics which is generated by humanistic psychology, but his work was interrupted by his death in June, 1970.

Maharishi Mahesh Yogi is the major advocate of transcendental meditation and the founder of the "Science of Creative Intelligence." He has established a world-wide organization dedicated to accomplishing seven goals, all of which stress the developments of the full potential of all humanity and the solution of the age-old problems that beset us.

Maharishi graduated from Allahabad University in India as a physics major. Thereafter, he studied many years with Guru Dev, to whom he gives credit for the transcendental meditation movement. He remains an enthusiastic student of science and often draws upon scientific fields for analogies aimed at clarifying concepts. He is almost constantly on the go but when at the headquarters for the movement, in Switzerland, he sits in his office surrounded by flowers.

lems of living. In contrast to Freud, Rogers found that his clients would improve in an atmosphere of unconditional positive regard. He developed the technique of reflecting the client's own feelings back, communicating to the client that the therapist understood—thus the term *nondirective* psychotherapy.

Rogers also asked clients to describe themselves and their ideal self both at the start and at the close of counseling. He found that his clients had a greater discrepancy between self and ideal self than did people without problems, but the discrepancy was reduced by the end of their nondirective counseling experience.

Clients had learned to accept themselves realistically. Through acceptance of themselves, they could also learn to accept their world realistically and find personal satisfaction. Rogers (1959) consistently emphasized the importance of subjective experiences and feelings in determining how an individual goes about the business of living.

Self-actualization.   Abraham Maslow set as his goal the construction of "a comprehensive, systematic and empirically based general psychology and philosophy which includes both the depths and heights of human nature." (1962, p. iv) His life goal was to broaden and enlarge the methods and the jurisdiction of orthodox science so as to make it more capable of taking up the task of achieving positive human fulfillment and self-actualization. He felt that only through science could progress and truth be obtained, and if science was properly extended to include personal and experiential approaches, the science of psychology could yield the basis for psychological health, personal growth, and fulfillment of people as individuals and collectively.

Recent Developments

Softening of behaviorism.   Within psychology there has been a growing interest in the concept of the self and in the kinds of ideas kept alive by Allport, Rogers, Maslow, and others like them. Terms such as "expectancy" and "preference" have been introduced, and the term "self" has been reintroduced, albeit in a hyphenated form, as seen in research on self-concept, self-perception, and self-report. Behaviorism has not taken the larger step of seeking internal, as opposed to external, coordinates; however, it has seen it necessary to label hypothetical internal states which, though marked by external behaviors, are something more. The states are lasting and more general than is a specific behavior; they have a conceptual existence for the psychologists and a hypothetical existence within the person. A self theorist, by contrast, accepts as an appropriate focus the reality, as opposed to the hypothetical existence, of the substance within the person.

Transcendental meditation. A burgeoning activity in this country is the practice of transcendental meditation as advocated by the Indian guru Maharishi Mahesh Yogi. Followers of Maharishi estimate that, as of 1974, 300,000 Americans had learned to meditate, with about 15,000 more joining the fold each month (Campbell, 1974). Essentially, transcendental meditation consists of sitting, with the eyes closed, for about two 20-minute periods a day and thinking about the imagined sounds of a *mantra* (tool for thinking), which is taken from Sanskrit. The avowed goals of transcendental meditation include the development of the full potential of the individual, the improvement of governmental achievements, and the solution of crime and all behavior that leads to unhappiness (Maharishi, 1974).

PHILOSOPHICAL PERSPECTIVE

The Active Nature of the Human

Self theory conceives of the individual as an active agent embodying the power of self-direction toward future goals.

"The future is now," a phrase made popular by the youth revolt of the 1960s, captures the philosophical substance of self theory. In her book *Culture and Commitment* (1970), Margaret Mead notes that the youth who say that the future is now

> . . . give us the way to reshape our thinking. We must place the future, like the unborn child in the womb of a woman, within a community of men, women, and children, among us, already here, already to be nourished and succored and protected, already in need of things for which, if they are not prepared before it is born, it will be too late. (p. 97)

Specifically, human imagination must be freed from the past, from the distortions of reality imposed by social inhibitions, and from the partial truths which are no longer useful in our rapidly changing society. We must be in open communication with experiential reality as it now exists if we are to find the new knowledge on which a viable future can be built. Such is a philosophy in which the future is now and the hope for humankind itself rests on creating an atmosphere in which self-direction can lead to human fulfillment.

The Scientific Study of the Human

The philosophical issue which separates self theory from behaviorism also has a counterpart in philosophy of science. Is it useful or necessary for the study of human behavior to include any concept, such as self, which deals with man's subjective existence? Behavioristic psychology has actively avoided the self as a dangerous concept, because invoking the self to explain the unifying force which gives behavior its direction and purpose begs the question of the scientific study of human behavior.

Self theorists have resisted what they view as an arbitrary definition of science by behaviorists which places the study of subjective experience outside the realm of science. Self theorists claim that the nature of man can be discovered only by extending the boundaries of science to include the study of experience. The scientific community, however, has been unwilling to extend its boundaries. The question concerning the most appropriate boundary definition of science is *not* merely one for philosophers of science for it will also determine what we consider knowledge and the kind of social planning in which we will invest our resources.

Can or should psychology as a discipline accept as both necessary and complementary two views of man on an equal basis, one behavioral and one phenomenological? Psychology has not resolved this problem.

CENTRAL ASSERTION

The essential nature of personality consists in the inner experiences of the individual, the understanding of which provides freedom for action and choice that is necessary for personal satisfaction and human fulfillment.

The central assertion contains four key ideas, which in one way or another find expression in the writings of most self theorists. They see the *inner experiences* of individuals as having more significance for their behavior than external stimuli have. The essence of people is inside—in feelings and in personal experiences.

It is necessary for an individual to *understand* those inner experiences to achieve self-fulfillment. Thus the methods of phenomenology are to be used because they focus on experiences and provide access to the critical material.

It is only through the accurate acceptance and understanding of experience that an individual gains *freedom* for actions and choices. Without the understanding of experiential reality, an individual must necessarily live in a restricted and distorted world. However, with freedom for action can come *personal satisfaction* and *human fulfillment,* because people and situations can be dealt with directly and truthfully. Within such a context, human nature will reach its potential and individuals their destiny within their capabilities.

PRINCIPAL CONSTRUCTS

Self theorists employ several constructs, among which the concept of *self* occupies a central position. But it is the substance of the self, the inner world of experience, which holds the key to personal growth and satisfactions or their lack. Because the self has an existence and can be developed or retarded, we can conceive of a healthy and happy (i.e., self-actualized) state of personal development or of an unhealthy and unhappy (i.e., neurotic) state. There exists a goal for human personality development which is ethically good. There is an *idealized state* which is the biological destiny of humans; it is their due and the expected expression of their *natural tendencies,* given a proper atmosphere for *openness to their experiences.*

SELF

The "self" has been a persistent but troublesome concept, occupying the attention of philosophers and psychologists alike. More than any other single concept, that of a self distinguishes self theory from all other psychological theories. Indeed, the presence of a self in a theory is both a necessary and a sufficient condition for classifying that theory as a self theory. The concept is therefore, by definition, part of and central to all self theories.

Although self has received a variety of definitions, two central aspects have been consistently included: (1) Self as an object, which includes the collection of attributes of the person; William James (1890) called it the empirical self. (2) Self as an organized force with purpose and direction; James called it the "knowing" self.

Empirical Self

The empirical self of James was composed of three constituents: the material self, the social self, and the spiritual self. The material self included the parts of the body, clothes, family and parents, home, and the other material things which define what we are—which give us a material existence. The social self is the recognition we get from our peers. Imagine being turned loose in a situation in which no other person listened or noticed when we spoke; it would be as if we were nonexistent and impotent—recognition by others gives us a social existence. Our spiritual self is our inner or subjective being. It is what we know ourself to be, good at arguing or swift of foot—our pretentions and dreams provide a spiritual existence.

One can find a similar treatment of the concept of the empirical self in the work of most self theorists. For example, Rogers (1959) suggests that a concept of the self, as an object, develops through interaction with the environment. The evaluations made by significant others suggest to people that they are more or less worthy of positive regard, and as a consequence their own self-regard also becomes selective (i.e., conditional on what they do). According to Rogers:

> If an individual should *experience* only *unconditional positive regard*, then no *conditions of worth* would develop, *self-regard* would be unconditional, the needs *for positive regard* and *self-regard* would never be at variance with *organismic evaluation* (immediate and long-range development), and the individual would continue to be *psychologically adjusted*, and would be fully functioning. (1959, p. 224)

Since this chain of events never occurs in actuality, personal doubts about self-worth do develop, and an individual's need for positive regard from others and the need for self-regard are sometimes at odds with immediate behaviors and long-term best interests. Speaking personally, Rogers notes:

> I have, at times, carried on research . . . to satisfy others, to convince opponents and skeptics, to gain prestige, and for other unsavory reasons. These errors in judgment and activity have only deepened the . . . conviction [that a person's activities should be aimed at ordering significant subjective experience]. (1959, p. 188)

A neurotic person, or as Rogers prefers, a defensive or damaged self, seeks self-regard at the expense of openness to experience and to actual reality, and as a consequence limits the appropriateness of behavior and satisfactions because of the discrepancy between self and reality.

He demonstrated that, by providing a climate in which positive self-regard can develop, a change could occur in a person's self-description in the direction of becoming more positive and increasingly similar to the ideal self.

The techniques developed by Rogers and others for achieving self-actualization implicitly recognize the existence of an empirical self, with its various constituents. Schutz (1967) suggests that there is an important connection between bodily, emotional, and mental states. Tense persons display fear in their bodies; the lack of smooth movement and the physiological imbalances of the strain may manifest themselves in digestive disturbances or even in asthma. The body, as the most important element of the material self, will be troublesome and inefficient. Relax the tension and new energy becomes available, a meal becomes digestible, and with it the material self moves closer to realizing its potential. Without skills, without friends, without values to give direction there can be no existence, no self, because these experiences provide the basis for a self which is distinctively human and which encompasses personal identity.

Valuing Self

For Rogers (1964), as for James, the self also has an existence at another level. Rogers feels there is an inner organization of valuing, inherent in the human, which in an atmosphere of freedom directs development toward a condition of self-identity and self-fulfillment in a personal sense and for humankind collectively. This aspect of self is a result of freedom in which the laws of nature may find expression as human nature. These laws are embodied in the laws of biological form and growth; just as the laws of growth in a flower dictate patterns that repeat themselves in all of nature and in aesthetically pleasing objects, so too the individual has an order—a valuing self—which stands against the repressive forces of death in technological rationalism. In this order, in this aspect of self, is the force of hope and a future.

Rogers believes that all mature individuals, across cultures and across time, when they are inwardly free (i.e., mature), will value those objects, experiences, and goals which will make for their own survival, growth, and development and for the survival and development of others. For example, Rogers believes:

> ... that there is an organismic basis for the valuing process within the human individual; that this valuing process is effective to the degree that the individual is open to his experiencing; that in persons relatively open to their experiencing there is an important communality or universality of value directions; that these directions make for the constructive enhancement of the individual and his community, and for the survival and evolution of his species. (1964, p. 160)

AN ABSOLUTE STATE OF PSYCHOLOGICAL HEALTH

Self theory provides its own conception of human adjustment and psychological health. For example, Maslow (1962; 1970) holds that the inner nature of the human can be studied scientifically and that it is possible to discover what that nature is actually like. The key word is *discover;* for him the inner nature of the human species is a biological reality, not an abstraction. It is a reality, according to Maslow, which is intrinsically good, and if encouraged rather than suppressed, it will guide life toward healthy, fruitful, and happy ends. Maslow writes:

> Observe that if these assumptions are proven true, they promise a scientific ethics, a natural value system, a court of ultimate appeal for the determination of good and bad, of right and wrong. The more we learn about man's natural tendencies, the easier it will be to tell him how to be good, how to be happy, how to be fruitful, how to respect himself, how to love, how to fulfill his highest potentiality. This amounts to automatic solution of many of the personality problems of the future. The thing to do seems to be to find out what *you* are *really* like inside, deep down, as a member of the human species and as a particular individual.*

THE NATURAL GROWTH TENDENCY OF HUMANS

The mature, self-actualized person will reach a state of psychological health. Movement toward this state is viewed as the *natural tendency* of humans. Rogers (1959) concluded from his therapeutic contact with clients that a person provided with unconditional positive regard would move toward growth of personality. Within a framework of acceptance, an individual is free to experience reality without distortion and consequently to respond in a meaningful way. The acceptance of reality makes it easier to accept one's self and therefore others without qualifications, thereby realizing the full potentiality of life's experiences. The drive toward self-actualization, originally proposed by Goldstein (1939) as the only drive necessary to account for the unitary character of human motivation, becoming, maturity, or whatever term is used, is considered the only force necessary, the natural growth tendency of human development.

PRIMACY OF EXPERIENCE

Self-actualization can occur only through the open acceptance of one's experiences. It is the phenomenal self that is important, with its focus on personal experiences. Although the importance of openness to experience implies things about the nature of man and the way he is organized, this construct, more than the others, provides the *means* to achieve personal maturity. More than the others, it dictates techniques to be used to rear children, to help others, to gain satisfaction, and even to improve society.

---

* From *Toward a Psychology of Being* by Abraham H. Maslow, Van Nostrand, Princeton, 1962, p. 4. Copyright © by Litton Educational Publishing, Inc. Reprinted by permission.

Since ethics are implicit in self theory, the attainment of certain goals is of considerable importance if people are to improve their lives and if the good is to be achieved. The requirement of openness is thus the central idea behind the procedures which have been developed to achieve self-actualization. In his therapeutic work, Rogers provided his clients with unconditional positive regard to foster the more open acceptance of reality. In fact, Rogers (1951) wrote:

> Psychological maladjustment exists when the organism denies to awareness significant sensory and visual experiences which consequently are not organized into the gestalt of the self-structure. (p. 510) ... Psychological adjustment exists when the concept of the self is such that all the sensory and visceral experiences of the organism are, or may be, assimilated at a symbolic level into a consistent relationship with the concept of self. (p. 514)

In even more dramatic form, Schutz, in his book *Joy* (1967), proposes many techniques for achieving openness to experience as a prerequisite for joy, which is the feeling that comes from the fulfillment of one's potential. According to Schutz, such fulfillment brings to individuals the feeling that they can cope with their environment and a sense of confidence in themselves as competent and lovable. Schutz believes that

> ... obstacles to realizing this potential come from everywhere. The methods used to organize social institutions frequently squelch creativity and impose mediocrity. Society seems to place a premium on relationships featuring hypocrisy and superficiality—relationships that are tolerated rather than sources of happiness.*

Similarly, advocates of transcendental meditation see the prospects of individual fulfillment as synonymous with self-knowledge:

> ... knowledge is directly concerned with fulfillment. For complete fulfillment, complete knowledge is necessary. Complete knowledge should mean total knowledge of the object of inquiry and total knowledge of the subject; total knowledge of both the known and the knower. When the knower does not know himself, then the basis for knowledge is missing. (Maharishi, 1974, p. xiii.)

RANGE AND FOCUS OF CONVENIENCE

The techniques and concepts of self theory have been applied mostly to complex behaviors of a distinctively human quality. These behaviors simultaneously draw on a variety of skills and activities, and they combine

---

* From W. C. Schutz, *Joy: Expanding Human Awareness*, Grove Press, New York, 1967, p. 15. Copyright © 1967 by William C. Schutz. Reprinted by permission.

cognitive, emotional, and motivational dimensions into highly focused, constructive activities. Such activities are not easily studied and cannot be taken into the laboratory except with great difficulty. Thus self theory has as its principal range and focus of convenience those areas in least commerce with behavioristic psychology.

Awareness

One of the strong points of self theory is that it can deal with awareness and can prescribe procedures for gaining awareness. Self theory provides a philosophy and a methodology to deal with the way people think and feel about themselves. There are many ways a person may be made more aware, which together provide self-understanding, personal satisfaction, and sensitivity.

Self-understanding.   A central concept is that people must know themselves and their feelings if they are to respond realistically. Indeed, as we have already indicated, advocates of transcendental meditation consider knowledge of the self a basic condition for all knowledge. Although numerous techniques for acquiring self-understanding are in practice, the sensitivity group has attracted numerous adherents in recent years. In sensitivity sessions, a group of people candidly confront one another with the reciprocal impressions they create. For example, a Houston psychologist, Melvin Sikes, organized groups of community blacks and police officers to thrash out differences in order to promote understanding (Sikes and Cleveland, 1968). Sikes's work has received attention in the popular press as well.

> But as the meetings progressed ... even uncooperative officers began venting their feelings. At one meeting a veteran police sergeant blurted, "I've hated niggers all my life, and every time I see a car with a Texas Southern University (a predominantly Negro school in Houston) sticker on it I'm going to harass the hell out of that driver." To his astonishment he was met with applause and praise for his frankness.... Already Sikes has received reports from the city's Negro districts of increased courtesy and assistance by policemen. "I don't think there is any question that some change toward understanding is taking place," he says. "And with increased understanding comes a change in attitude, and then a change in behavior." *

Personal satisfaction.   How is a sense of personal satisfaction to be obtained? Success and money do not necessarily bring satisfaction. Ulcers,

---

* Reprinted by permission from *Time*, The Weekly Newsmagazine, April 12, 1968. Copyright Time Inc. 1968.

divorce, and psychoneurotic disorders seem to be a peculiarly frequent plague of economic success. Self theorists point out that individuals must know what they want in order to give direction to their lives and to make self-evaluations of their efforts. An open awareness of one's true feelings is necessary for such a process. If a police officer becomes aware of having deliberately and hatefully harassed blacks, the discrepancy between that behavior and the values of ethics and professional duty can then be dealt with directly, and the self can be organized into an integrated set of purposes, once the discrepancy is confronted.

Sensitivity.   Another dimension of awareness is sensitivity to the world and to others. All self theories view mature or actualized persons as having a high degree of sensitivity to the physical world because of the openness of their general style of life. To be psychologically open is to be receptive to all forms of stimulation. The sensitivity to both the world and to others produces an empathy for the feelings and attitudes of others. Thus the basic nature of personality hypothesized by self theory provides a natural and easy framework for viewing sensitivity and empathy with the physical world and with other people.

Creativity

The creative process is no more clearly exemplified than when a person finds new and unique solutions to problems or proposes radically new concepts which cast an issue or topic into an entirely new perspective. Where did the solution or the idea come from? The creative process has been one of the most difficult areas for behavioristic psychology to handle. The answer that creativity is the combination of existing stimulus-response bonds fails to deal adequately with discovery and with problem-solving. When one plots behavior only in terms of external coordinates, as the behavioristic psychologists do, one has difficulty explaining a product which seems to appear from within the individual. Yet self theory finds its greatest power and usefulness in the conceptualization it can provide of the creative process. Creativity is philosophically compatible with self theory, which accepts freedom for action as a characteristic of human personality. Thus creativity is seen not as a troublesome proposition, nor as an unusual occurrence, but rather as the natural expression of inherent human structure.

Creative people.   Creative individuals—writers, scientists, and others from all walks of life—have been studied in depth at the Institute for Personality Research. Barron (1969) found that highly creative people maintain their creativity at some personal expense. Creative individuals are less popular and receive lower evaluations by teachers and peers than less creative but bright individuals; social disapproval in the form of peer and teacher evaluations is a potential force in driving divergent thinking underground. Creative individuals showed a tendency toward divergent thinking during childhood and maintain greater independence, rebelliousness, and tolerance for discomfort than less creative but equally capable individuals do.

Barron treats creativity as something which can be nurtured and increased. But if creativity is to be nurtured, social devaluation of divergent and unusual thought processes must be restricted. Individuals must increase the amount and kinds of environmental stimulation to which they are receptive. Selective perception and attention must be relaxed to realize the potential of the creative process.

Creativity as freedom.   Creativity is thus a form of freedom; it is freedom from the normal constraints that one imposes on one's experiences. Barron (1968) directed his attention to the close relationship between creativity and personal freedom. When people follow the internalized dictates of their parents or the restrictions of established dogma, they are somewhat less free to act according to their own convictions and experiences, but they are at the same time not wholly responsible for the consequences. Although they are not weighted down by the burden of choice, their freedom is nevertheless more limited in fact. Genuine freedom exists when response variability is at a maximum. Freedom occurs in the presence of a broad consciousness of experience, of impulse, and of value. The creative process exemplifies personal freedom.

In his study of self-actualizing people, Maslow saw creativity as spontaneous, effortless, innocent, easy—a kind of freedom from stereotypes and clichés. To Maslow (1962), not only artists, scientists, inventors, writers, etc., could be creative, but anyone who was open to experience and who could avoid the expectations, beliefs, and stereotypes that most people confuse with the real world. He noted:

> ...one woman, uneducated, poor, a full-time housewife and mother, did none of these conventionally creative things and yet was a marvelous cook, mother, wife, and homemaker. With little money, her home was somehow always beautiful. She was a perfect hostess, her meals were banquets. Her taste in linens, silver, glass, crockery and furniture was impeccable. She was in all these areas original, novel, ingenious, unexpected, inventive. I just *had* to call her creative. I learned from her and others like her that a first-rate soup is more creative than a second-rate painting, and that, gen-

erally, cooking or parenthood or making a home could be creative while poetry need not be; it could be uncreative. (p. 128)

The science of creative intelligence.   The Science of Creative Intelligence attempts to learn how all things work in nature. Transcendental meditation is the vehicle by which these universal truths are reached. The basic assumption is that the fundamental principles that underlie all physical and biological reality are paralleled by the operation of the mind. These principles may be grasped intellectually through transcendental meditation. Once this is achieved, students of the Science of Creative Intelligence have an intuitive grasp of the fundamental workings of nature.*

Quite obviously, if this claim were to prove correct, transcendental meditation would represent one of the great breakthroughs in the quest for greater understanding of humans and of the world. While most critics of transcendental meditation do not deny the value of meditation for calming jagged nerves and even permitting remarkable degrees of control over physiological functions, they balk at claims that transcendental meditation permits any special insights into the nature of reality. It has even been suggested that meditation may enhance one class of creative processes while interfering with another:

> To the extent that meditation leads to the kind of arousal and self-reflective behavior typical of right-hemispheric processes, meditation enhances spontaneity and creativity, especially in free association tasks like story telling. On the other hand, too much meditation may interfere with a person's logical, left-hemispheric processes or the sort of problem-solving creativity required by the Wallace-Kogan Test. (Schwartz, 1974, p. 43)

APPLICATIONS TO SELECTED TOPICS

Dependency

Contemporary society has placed a value judgment on the dimension of dependency-independency. The opposite poles are not equally acceptable socially, in that independence is correlated with health and adjustment and dependency with their opposites. In one sense, self theory reverses this value judgment, but in a second sense it supports the judgment. This apparent confusion results because self theory makes conceptual distinc-

---

* Transcendental Meditation, TM®, Science of Creative Intelligence, SCI, and World Plan are service marks of the World Plan Executive Council—United States. Additional information is available from the International Center for Scientific Research, Institute for Social Rehabilitation, World Plan Executive Council—National Center, 1015 Gayley Avenue, Los Angeles, California 90024.

tions which are not typically made by a trait approach to the study of personality.

To the extent that dependency-independency is equated with the relative degree of self-reliance and of competitive individual striving and achievement, self theory evaluates independence negatively. It is precisely these competitive orientations that have alienated humans from themselves. Competition that destroys the communal aspect of interpersonal interaction destroys the most important of the distinctively human qualities. Dependency on fellow human beings is both a natural and a necessary condition. We can most easily see the distinction by realizing that the competitive versus cooperative aspects of the independency-dependency dimension are being defined in terms of behaviors and actions which are external to the individual. Self theory cannot embrace—and must indeed oppose—any view which shifts an evaluative focus of behavior outside the skin of the individual.

However, when the focus is shifted to internal conditions, self theory provides a positive evaluation of independence and a negative evaluation of dependency. Dependency is bad if it is immobilizing, if the individual is not free (independent) to experience and relate fully and openly to other individuals and to the world.

Aggression

Perhaps the most important problem facing contemporary society is how to handle aggression. Never before has the potential for the destruction of the human race been so great or escalated so fast as now. Unfortunately, our understanding of aggression between individuals is sparse and between nations even sparser. The prescriptions available for the reduction of aggression do not match the magnitude of the problem.

Theoretically, open individuals can recognize feelings of anger and hostility, and because they do not need to deny them, they are in a position to deal with the feelings constructively rather than destructively. Such a view of the human would hold promise of a utopia if all people were self-actualized and mature. But every theoretical utopia is free of hate and the destruction of some people by others. Christian religion has preached love for centuries, the flower children have rallied to the cause of peace and love in the sixties and beyond, but no "cultural revolution" has transformed society appreciably toward that goal. Indeed, holy wars to save the savages and armed revolution to save America are extreme aggressiveness in pursuit of a nonaggressive world.

In one sense, however, aggression can be considered not destructive but self-actualizing. For example, Maslow (1962) writes:

Clearly what will be called personality problems depends on who is doing the calling. The slave owner? The dictator? The patriarchal father? The husband who wants his wife to remain a child? It seems clear that personality problems may sometimes be loud protests against the crushing of one's psychological bones, of one's true inner nature. What is sick then is not to protest while this crime is being committed. (p. 7)

Echoing the Declaration of Independence, the Black Panther Party, in its official position statement, noted:

When a long train of abuses and usurpations, pursuing invariably the same object, evinces a design to reduce them under absolute despotism, it is their right, it is their duty, to throw off such government, and to provide new guards for their future security.

Of course, aggression as self-fulfillment is not a new idea, but it does strike a vivid picture of the difference between evaluating and conceptualizing behavior and human problems from internal, as opposed to external, coordinates. The external definition focuses on behavior and must define "revolution" and other similar acts as aggressive; yet, from internal considerations, the same situation may be an act of self-fulfillment for humanity.

A note of hope is found in the teachings of Maharishi. He has stated as a principal goal of the TM movement the elimination of war. Such is the fervor of the advocates of TM that they believe a war would be impossible if only one tenth of the adult population were to meditate regularly.

Sexuality

The harshness of society in its inhibitions to openness of experience is most clearly seen in sexual behavior. The relatively high frequency of female frigidity and the incapacity to enjoy sex for its own sake reflect the psychological constraints society has placed on the fulfillment of a biological potential. Full self-realization requires the capacity to receive gratification through physical contact. Interest in such techniques as nude marathons are based on the need to lose defensiveness over one's body to accept the satisfactions available through physical contact. As Jourard (1968) notes:

The touch is an action which bridges the gulf many people develop between themselves and others, and between their "self" and their body. When I touch someone, I experience his body and my own simultaneously. To be touched is almost an infallible way of having one's attention seized and diverted from anything it was occupied with. . . . Body contact has important implications for psychotherapy, and for healing in general, not to mention its role in maternal care and in the sexual aspects of love. Touching another person is the last stage in reducing distance between people.*

Romantic love is another principal oppressor of sexuality and a block to self-actualization. Establishing sexuality as a special event to be used discriminately is what romantic love usually reduces to in practice. Albert Ellis (1962) notes that a romantic-love notion of sexuality leads a woman to make herself appear sexually desirable in order to use sex as bait, as a manipulating weapon. If she indulges in sexual behavior too easily, it will lose its manipulative power. Such notions interfere with the active and enjoyable expression of human sexuality; romantic love places an interpersonal relationship on a commercial rather than a true and open level. Important, lasting, and satisfying relationships require understanding by each person of the other's feelings and attitudes. Such understanding is interfered with if false and hidden feelings with respect to sexuality permeate the relationship. Indeed, romantic love during the courtship period may well interfere with knowing each other because of the artificiality introduced into the relationship by the romantic-love aspect of sexuality.

SUMMARY

Self theory is the current label given to a philosophical view of humans which emphasizes their capacity for self-direction and freedom of choice. People are seen as active forces of energy pointed toward future goals and self-directed purposes, rather than as creatures being pushed or pulled by other forces that are beyond their control. A mechanistic view of people based on the cause-effect scientific model has been the predominant view in twentieth-century America, and self theory has assumed the role of opposition.

Self theory in general and the more recently popularized varieties of it in particular are moral in an absolute sense. By contrast, other theories of personality are amoral, i.e., irrelevant for dictating *how* people should behave. A strict behavioristic approach will describe the ways in which

---

* From *Disclosing Man to Himself* by Sidney M. Jourard, p. 137. Copyright © 1968 by Litton Educational Publishing, Inc. Reprinted by permission of Van Nostrand Reinhold Company.

a given reaction may be achieved with reference to a set of antecedents (events which are external to the individual). Self theory, because of its emphasis on internal coordinates, rejects a mechanistic psychology as evil, for it enslaves people's thoughts about themselves and limits their freedom and growth.

Self theory assumes the necessity of using a construct of "self" to understand personality. This concept includes the skills and possessions, the friends and recognitions, and the beliefs and values which define who and what we are. The self also includes the integration of these separate aspects into the unified nature shown by an individual's behaviors. Psychological health exists when the self is open to experience and organized so that all aspects of behavior are consistent and serve the further growth and development of the individual. This ideal self is a state of being which is within the biological potential of all people and the natural growth tendency of all. The ideal is seldom realized, however, because of the inhibitions, doubts, and social restrictions which limit freedom of choice and thus thwart self-development. The path to personal growth toward the ideal is through openness to experience, enabling the individual to deal with reality directly and truthfully.

The emphasis on one's own experience and on the achievement of a consistent organization of those experiences as the basis of maturity adjustment illustrates that, to self theory, people must be viewed in terms of coordinates internal to themselves, rather than in terms of external events. With such a focus, self theory offers a convenient way to conceptualize processes, like awareness and creativity, which seem to come from within a person. Creativity is particularly hard for a mechanistic approach to behavior to handle, because there is no clearly describable antecedent event. Since self theory and behavioristic psychology are philosophically incompatible, it is perhaps natural that the material easiest for one to handle is the most difficult for the other.

The implicit identification of self theory with humanism, in the form of a definition of what is ethically good, mature, and adjusted, and with processes such as creativity and awareness may be somewhat misleading. Behavioristic psychology also, at least implicitly, claims that it can deliver humankind to technological perfection through scientific understanding, a feat which, from the standpoint of self theory, is impossible—indeed, even destructive. Thus a philosophical assumption about human nature provides a very important element for the acceptance or rejection of self theory. At the present time, this philosophical assumption is attracting increased attention; whether it will be sufficient to alter the mechanistic view of behavior of twentieth-century American psychology remains to be seen.

SUGGESTIONS FOR FURTHER READING

"The Facts on Transcendental Meditation," *Psychology Today*, April 1974, pp. 37–46. Transcendental meditation is the most important recent development in self theory. A special three-part feature in this periodical carefully examines the movement and its claims. (Though critical in parts, it offers a generally positive evaluation.)

James, M., and D. Jongeward. *Born to Win: Transactional Analysis with Gestalt Experiments*. Reading, Mass.: Addison-Wesley, 1973. This excellent popular book clearly and effectively presents the philosophy and everyday applications of self theory.

Section 6
Models
of
Personality

19
The
Human
as
Rat

I. **Principal constructs and their translation**
   A. Hours of deprivation = desires and aversions
   B. Skinner box = situations
   C. Reinforcement = praise
   D. Pellet dispenser = mother or socializing agent
   E. Secondary reinforcer = promises
   F. Shaping = socialization
   G. Operant responses = skills
   H. Discriminative stimuli = instructions and warnings
   I. Schedules of reinforcement = rules
   J. Cumulative recorder = reputation and personality description

II. **Use of the model in personality study**
   A. Verbal behavior
   B. Gambling
   C. Sick talk and sick behavior

III. **Practical applications**
   A. Token economies
      1. The patients
      2. Operant responses
      3. Stimulus control
      4. Contingent reinforcement
      5. Reinforcement
      6. On-ward jobs
   B. The technology of teaching
      1. Discriminations
      2. Schedules of reinforcement
   C. Social planning and human engineering

IV. **Summary**

V. **Suggestions for further reading**

Trained lions, bicycle-riding bears, dancing dogs, performing elephants, and many more are the standard fare of the circus. Marine shows have also become popular attractions. At Sea Life Park in Hawaii, porpoises have been trained to do an "aerial hula" whenever their trainer gives an auditory underwater signal (See Fig. 19.1). The United States Navy has supported research on porpoises for a number of years, in part because they can accurately locate underwater objects by means of their acute sense of hearing. The Navy has utilized this skill by training porpoises to come to an underwater signal, actually providing a messengerboy for undersea research (Conly, 1966).

Fig. 19.1.   Rocketing in graceful precision, three "educated" dolphins at Marineland of Florida hurtle in unison through an aquatic obstacle course. They sometimes learn to perform this spectacular ballet after only a few days of training. (Jen and Des Bartlett/Bruce Coleman Inc.)

PRINCIPAL CONSTRUCTS AND THEIR TRANSLATION

The performance of circus animals and of porpoises is but a series of highly trained acts. Even the most complicated performances, however, are carried off automatically in response to a cue. The analogy of "the human as rat" lies in the conception of human behaviors as essentially no different from the tricks animals perform. All human behavior may be seen as learned performances, or tricks in response to signals which are present in the environment. The complex and detailed behavior of humans is simply a more refined version of the tricks and the behaviors of the porpoises, just as they, because of their intellectual capacity, represent a more refined version of circus animals.

The laboratory procedures for training animals both formalize the operations and provide a set of interlocking constructs. The principal character, usually a rat, is conceptualized as an *organism,* or S (subject). Thus, even the object of the procedure qualifies as a construct, because it is seen as an interchangeable member of a larger class of objects (organisms) that could be put into the same situations with the same results.

Box 19.1   B. F. Skinner.

B. F. Skinner, born in 1904, received his Ph.D. from Harvard University in 1931. He has taught at the University of Minnesota, Indiana University, where he was chairman of the Psychology Department, and at Harvard, where he has been a professor of psychology since 1948. During his professional career Skinner has won many awards, including membership in the National Academy of Science, a Guggenheim Fellowship, and in 1958 the Distinguished Scientific Contribution Award from the American Psychological Association. He has received several honorary degrees, his first in 1951 from Hamilton College and later degrees from North Carolina State, the University of Chicago, and others.

The organism is the object exposed to particular antecedent conditions so that a specified behavior will be performed on cue.

Hours of Deprivation = Desires and Aversions

The trainer must of course have something the organism wants. When working with rats, he usually withholds food for some period of time, and thus the subject can be described, for example, as 24 hours deprived of food.

People also have a variety of motivations, made up of both desires and aversions. The concept of desire and aversion is a way to capture the intensity with which people want or fear various outcomes. Unlike the rat's, however, many human desires and aversions are of a social and derivative nature. A person may want a new car because it saves the effort of walking or a grade because it gains praise. The source of a desire or an aversion, whether it lies in tissue conditions or social conditions, is not critical. All that matters is that existing motives can be relieved by specific events in the real world.

Skinner Box = Situations

The place of training is important. A skilled animal trainer would not expect good results in a place where there are many distracting events that produce competing behaviors. Laboratory animals are trained in a standard-sized chamber, usually enclosed within another chamber, in which temperature, noise, light, and all other physical events are under control. This device, the Skinner box, bears the name of its developer. Figure 19.2 shows a modified version of a Skinner box developed for use in lecture demonstrations and in student laboratories.

Although we are seldom physically confined as a rat in a Skinner box, we are often bound in time and space by psychological constraints and social barriers. Thus the training for any particular human behavior usually involves a set of limiting conditions which serve the same function as a Skinner box; that is, they restrict the variation of response opportunities available and exclude distractions that are irrelevant to the condition at hand. In essence, we are trained in a variety of "boxes," each one of which may be seen as a separate replication of the basic unit.

Reinforcement = Praise

A hungry animal needs food, and this food may serve as a positive reinforcement. Note, however, that reinforcement is a general term that can be applied to a variety of events, of which food delivery is only one. The determination of whether an object or an event is a reinforcement is

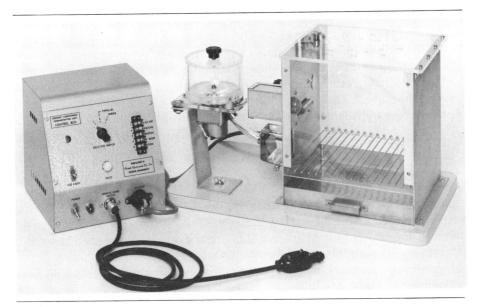

Fig. 19.2. Skinner box. The operant conditioning demonstration and laboratory unit, a modified Skinner-type experimental chamber, consists of the rat cage, with rat lever, stimulus light, and recessed food tray; the pellet dispenser, mounted together with the rat cage on a plywood base; and the control box, containing a 24-volt DC power supply and circuitry necessary for controlling simple schedules of reinforcement. (Photo courtesy of Ralph Gerbrands Co., Arlington, Mass.)

empirical: an event that strengthens a response that precedes it is known as a positive reinforcer. An event (such as electric shock) that strengthens a response by virtue of its reduction or removal is called a negative reinforcer. Finally, punishment is defined as a stimulus applied to a response that lowers the tendency of that response to occur.

Desired behaviors are rewarded and unwanted behaviors are punished. With people, praise is the most common form of positive reinforcement and censure the most common form of punishment. Sometimes the reinforcement is highly formalized and public, as when a medal of honor is given or a criminal is sent to prison; at other times it is spontaneous and private, as when two people share an intimate moment.

Pellet Dispenser = Mother or Socializing Agent

The food reward has to be delivered at the proper time. Ordinarily the delivery is effected by a mechanical device activated by an electrical pulse. Therefore the timing can be very precise, ensuring against errors or omissions. Not only is the mechanical device more reliable than a human, but it also frees the trainer to do other things.

People usually receive reinforcement from other people or from official social institutions. A mother of a young child is an extremely active pellet dispenser, attending and ignoring, smiling and frowning, feeding and spanking her child in a continuous chain of interactions. In a more formalized way, institutions give passing and failing grades to students. A person, particularly in childhood, is literally surrounded by socializing agents who are loaded with "pellets" of various kinds ready for delivery.

Secondary Reinforcer = Promises

The pellet dispenser makes a distinctive clicking sound, which always precedes the appearance of the food reward. The rat soon learns to run to the food dish as soon as it hears the click. Any event that signals a reward is known as a *secondary reinforcer* or *secondary reward,* because it is one step removed from the original or primary reward. The fact that a secondary reward can be readily established by pairing it with the primary reward is extremely important, because secondary rewards can be delivered with greater ease and precision; the primary reward needed to sustain the training can be delivered at a later and more convenient time.

In the realm of human affairs, the socializing agents of the world frequently give stimuli which have earlier been paired with more basic rewards; such stimuli acquire the convenience of signals. In many instances, a nod of approval suffices for a full-blown, overt act of affection. The secondary reward adults commonly use is money, which promises food, security, and tangible goods. We live in a world of tokens, promises, checks, and debts, which can be traded and manipulated symbolically.

Shaping = Socialization

The subject being trained—whether a rat to press the bar or a dog to touch its nose against the cupboard handle—is given food only when it makes a response that approximates what is desired. Each succeeding response has to be at least as good as the previous one to produce the reward. Two ideas are important: (1) the reward is *contingent,* that is, given if and only if the organism makes a desired response; and (2) the criterion for the reward keeps changing. The entire procedure of establishing a contingency between reward and behavior and shifting the criterion to direct the behavior into the desired form is called *shaping.*

Life in such a symbolic world of assets and liabilities requires a highly ritualized set of promises and behaviors, extended at the proper time and in the proper way. We are highly socialized; we have been shaped to produce desired behaviors on cue. The process of socialization requires setting a progressively more stringent criterion for the delivery of contingent rewards until the behavior takes the desired shape and form and is executed at the desired time.

Operant responses = Skills

The act of pressing a bar is the response the animal is being trained to give. It is called an *operant* response, because when given by the organism, it operates upon or changes the environment so as to produce the reward.

People are expected to acquire responses which will operate on the environment to release contingent rewards controlled by the socializing agents. In human affairs, the responses that gain rewards are usually skills of some kind. They are classes of behaviors that effect social rewards.

Discriminative Stimuli = Instructions and Warnings

Imagine that, in the course of training, we were to introduce the following contingencies: red light on, pellet dispenser disconnected. In this situation the lights become events between which the organism must learn to discriminate because they contain information enabling it to avoid unnecessary work. Such an event is called a *discriminative stimulus*.

A skill is not equally applicable in all situations. People learn to discriminate between signs suggesting that the exercise of a particular skill will be profitable and signs warning them that it will not. A person may exercise an appropriate skill even with desire for the particular secondary reward to be gained, because that reward can be exchanged for other secondary or primary rewards that *are* wanted. Thus a person must be alert to environmental instructions that can supply information about present contingencies between skills and reinforcements in order to effectively satisfy desires and aversions.

Schedules of Reinforcement = Rules

A contingent reward must always be given on some schedule. A reward given every time a response is made is on a continuous-reinforcement schedule. Since a rat will perform at a much lower wage scale, however, various other possibilities exist. The principal schedules used in the laboratory are four, and they are of two general types, ratio and interval. When a pellet is given regularly after some predetermined number of presses—for example, 10—the schedule is known as a *fixed-ratio* (FR10) schedule. When the food is given after different numbers of presses but on the average of every tenth press, it is on a *variable-ratio* (VR10) schedule. On an interval schedule, a reward is given for the first response made after some preselected time has elapsed since the last reward. If the time interval is constant, the food is on a *fixed-interval* (FI) schedule; if not, it is on a *variable-interval* (VI) schedule described by the average time interval. Various schedules are of course possible, and many have been explored in the laboratory.

Contingent rewards and punishments are usually distributed according to some system of rules. A mother is unlikely to give her son a second candy bar just after he has eaten a first, no matter how often he asks; rather, she will wait until a sufficient period of time has elapsed, e.g., a day. The candy is thus on an interval schedule of one bar a day, providing the child asks. Other rewards, e.g., piecework pay, are on ratio schedules. The particular rules which are constantly in operation in society are not so by happenstance but have usually evolved because they control behavior in a desired way. Research on schedules of reinforcement can therefore give information about the effects on behavior of various rules for the delivery of contingent outcomes.

Cumulative Recorder = Reputation and Personality Description

The principal reason for taking the analogy into the laboratory is to be able to examine systematically the way many and various events influence the operant response. The frequency of the operant response over time is the primary information needed for analysis. Also of importance is the record of the other events that occurred in the same period, for example, the delivery of a reward or the presence of a discriminative stimulus. A device for making such a cumulative record is shown in Fig. 19.3.

Fig. 19.3. The photo at the top of page 459 shows a cumulative recorder with event marker pen. The paper moves at a constant speed. Each response moves the left pen toward the left margin, creating a step on the graph paper. A reinforcement produces a cross-hatch on the graph. When the pen reaches the left margin, it resets to the extreme right and repeats the process. The pen at the right, an event marker, produces a hatch mark to record the occurrence of some stimulus event. (Photo courtesy Ralph Gerbrands Co., Arlington, Mass.)

At bottom are two cumulative records of an actual experiment. Record (a) shows the first session of a transition from VR 110 to VR 173. The rate of responding falls considerably below what was the final value on VR 110, and even below the early development on VR 110. After 12 sessions on VR 173, however, Record (b) shows a threefold increase in the rate of responding. By this time, intermediate rates of responding have again disappeared, and any deviations from the sustained high rate of responding are abrupt shifts to a zero rate, as at *a* and *b*. (From C. B. Ferster and B. F. Skinner, *Schedules of Reinforcement*, Appleton-Century-Crofts, 1957, p. 399. Used by permission.)

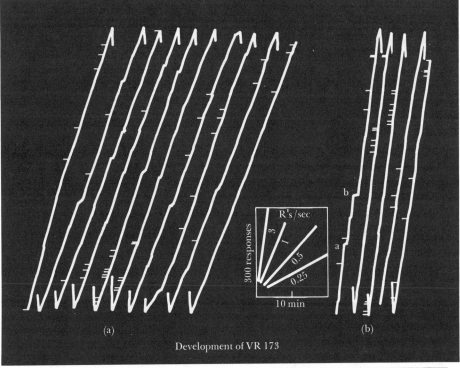

Development of VR 173

If a trainer had a complete cumulative record of every response, reward, and stimulus event in the history of a trainee, there would be a complete reinforcement history. Such a record would be useful in anticipating the probable behavior of the organism under various conditions. In a similar sense, a person's reputation is the cumulative record of the frequency of certain behaviors over time in the presence of specific events. The more detailed this record is, the more fully and clearly it describes the person. The rat is what it does. The human as rat, as an existential reality, is the frequency over time of each of various operant behaviors, within their situational constraints. Like a cumulative record, a reputation summarizes the past and predicts the future.

USE OF THE MODEL IN PERSONALITY STUDY

The analogy of the human as rat is straightforward. A person continuously emits behaviors. If a particular behavior results in the delivery of something the person wants, it will be repeated. When rewards are contingent on specific behaviors, those behaviors can be molded into the desired form and elicited by discriminative cues. Under such conditions, the frequency of the behavior over time, as seen in a cumulative record, becomes routine and predictable, regardless of the species (see Box 19.2). The analogy is illustrated clearly by Skinner (1951) at the end of his article on how to train animals:

> A scientific analysis can, however, bring about a better understanding of personal relations. We are almost always reinforcing the behavior of others, whether we mean to or not. A familiar problem is that of the child who seems to take an almost pathological delight in annoying its parents. In many cases this is the result of conditioning which is very similar to the animal training we have discussed. The attention, approval and affection that a mother gives a child are all extremely powerful reinforcements. Any behavior of the child that produces these consequences is likely to be strengthened. The mother may unwillingly promote the very behavior she does not want. For example, when she is busy she is most likely not to respond to a call or request made in a quiet tone of voice. She may answer the child only when it raises its voice. The average intensity of the child's vocal behavior therefore moves up to another level—precisely as the head of the dog in our experiment was raised to a new height (by shaping the dog to lift its head). Eventually the mother gets used to this level and again reinforces only louder instances. This vicious circle brings about louder and louder behavior. The child's voice may also vary in intonation, and any change in the direction of unpleasantness is more likely to get the attention

Box 19.2   Cumulative record for a pigeon and a man on a fixed-interval schedule of reinforcement. (From B. F. Skinner, *Cumulative Record,* Appleton-Century-Crofts, New York, 1961, p. 126. Used by permission.)

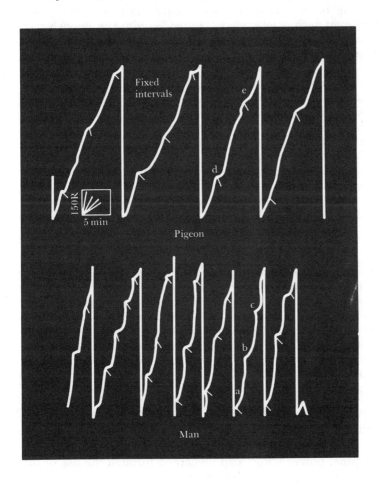

The cumulative records support the contention that schedules can be used to control behavior and that they operate in similar ways for humans and animals. The pigeon was pecking a disk on a fairly short, fixed-interval schedule for food reward; the man was pressing a button to flash a light that would permit him to see a dial. The man's task was to return the dial to zero if it had deflected. His pressing action could be altered by scheduling the frequency of deviations of the pointer, just as the pigeon's pecks could be controlled by scheduling the frequency of the food. The work was done by Holland (1957), who was concerned with the problem of the radar operator who must pay attention over long periods of time.

It is interesting to note that the records of both the pigeon and the man show the typical curvature of a fixed-interval schedule as the subject passes from a low value after reinforcement to a high, fairly constant, terminal rate. Another characteristic of such a schedule is the tendency to run through reinforcement and continue at a high rate for a few seconds after reinforcement; examples can be seen at points a, b, and c for the man and points d and e for the pigeon.

Skinner (1961) goes on to compare the performance of normal men, psychotic patients, and animals under similar schedules of reinforcement but with stimuli and responses appropriate for the subjects. Skinner has been impressed by the uniformity of the effect of schedule across species in such comparisons, and he believes that the insight gained by a functional analysis of behavior will give birth to a new technology, particularly for education. He concludes: "For a long time men of good will have tried to improve the cultural patterns in which they live. It is possible that a scientific analysis of behavior will provide us at last with the techniques we need for this task—with the wisdom we need to build a better world and, through it, better men." (p. 131)

---

of the mother and is therefore strengthened. One might even say that "annoying" behavior is just that behavior which is especially effective in arousing another person to action. The mother behaves, in fact, as if she had been given the assignment to teach the child to be annoying! The remedy in such a case is simply for the mother to make sure that she responds with attention and affection to most if not all the responses of the child which are of an acceptable intensity and tone of voice and that she never reinforces the annoying forms of behavior.*

The model of the human as rat can be used to conceptualize many aspects of human behavior in addition to the fortuitous shaping of obnoxious vocalizations by a child. The use of the model in this way, that is, for the explanation of various aspects of personality, constitutes illustrations of the conceptual power which can be gained through the use of the analogy rather than tests of the model itself.

Verbal Behavior

Skinner published a book entitled *Verbal Behavior* (1957), in which he applied his principles to the acquisition and development of language. The book was an attempt to explain how a person's verbal behavior can be

---

acquired and maintained through the reinforcement contingencies and the other constructs abstracted from the behavior of the rat in a Skinner box, without the addition of any other constructs or internal events. Skinner saw speech as simply a dependent variable, like other behaviors, which can be accounted for by the same functional laws.

People make sounds because they are genetically equipped to do so, and people are susceptible to reinforcements. These two biological facts make language likely, because rewards can be used to shape the form and structure of the sounds emitted. Only when sounds are shaped does vocalization become speech.

Some words, such as commands, have a motivational aspect because they can produce a consequence that directly rewards some motivational state. "Taxi" or "Milk," if received by an appropriate ear—a social "pellet dispenser" such as a taxi driver or a mother—will produce a reinforcing stimulus that satisfies the desire. Such words are operants and, because they produce a reward, will be acquired and emitted in appropriate situations, that is, when discriminative stimuli are present.

The reinforcement for most verbal behavior, however, is not tied directly to a specific motivation, as in the foregoing examples, but comes rather from generalized reinforcements, such as words of agreement, nods, etc. In effect, these responses are verbal tokens or promises, which we have called secondary or social reinforcements. When one of them is delivered for the emission of correct sounds, as when a child says "Mama" for the first time, the probability of repetition of this behavior is increased. Of course, grammar, structure, and complicated discriminative stimuli about when and what to verbalize are acquired later.

The central idea is simply that speech is learned and maintained by speech-contingent reinforcement. At first the reinforcement is usually delivered by others, but later it can be self-delivered. The individual is then both speaker and listener. For example, a musician plays a piece which as a listener he or she finds of excellent quality. He or she can then say "good," which as a secondary reinforcer can be a reward for the performance, just as "bad" can be a punishment. Like other behaviors, verbal behaviors are socially controlled by the contingent reinforcements provided, whether by self or by others. As long as there is consensus among the socializing agents (society), there will be environmental control over the form (grammar) and nature of vocalizations, and they will be successively shaped to conform to the social norm.

Speech is thus a series of complex muscular activities which produce noises. No new concepts, such as intentions, ideas, etc., are needed. In writing about Skinner's (1957) book MacCorquodale (1969) notes: "Thus, the argument in *Verbal Behavior* proceeds, inexorably and relentlessly, to the final overthrow of the speaker as an autonomous instigator" (p. 841). People's last chance for privacy and self-determination, for creativity and personal style, finds its way into the deterministic operant paradigm.

Gambling

Recall that variable-ratio schedule is one in which the number of responses required for reinforcement varies around some average value. Rate of response under such a schedule is typically very steady; however, the rate may become very high (many responses per reward) if the ratio is progressively made more and more demanding as the response is required. The steadily high rate occurs because the responder has no information about when he will receive the next reward.

Gambling devices operate on a variable-ratio schedule. Ratio schedules differ from interval schedules in that the probability of getting a "win" increases as the gambler makes more plays. However, because the wins distribute themselves in an irregular manner, the payoff is unpredictable, and the gambler typically maintains a steady rate of response. Pigeons may peck 12,000 times an hour to obtain a reward given at the rate of one per 110 responses, and even higher ratios sustain substantial rates of responding (Ferster and Skinner, 1957). Refer to Fig. 19.3 for an example of steady responses made on a VR 173 schedule. The schedule of reinforcement exercises considerable control over behavior.

Compulsive gamblers are not in exactly the same position as the pigeon, since they must usually pay more for the opportunity of making a response than they can possibly win. Thus there must be some other factors which get the gambler into the situation to begin with. These could be subjective factors, such as evaluation of the small but fairly certain loss on each play, balanced against the slim chance of a larger win, or realization of the total loss only after a considerable delay from the initiation of playing. But whatever the reasons that get the gambler into the situation, the schedule of reinforcement is designed to maximize the gambler's response rate.

Sick Talk and Sick Behavior

An individual who becomes ill is cast in a role of a sick person. The role has several special features: it excuses the person from working and from performing other daily functions, and it requires that he or she receive attention and care. Usually a person's self-referral for the sick role is accepted at face value, because a given culture or social organization ascribes in fairly uniform manner to the conditions under which one may ask for and obtain the special status of patient.

Psychiatric patients, however, are caught in a more ambiguous position; there is less social acceptance of their role than of the medical patient's. Thus there is more pressure for the psychiatric patient to fulfill a productive social role as father and provider or wife and mother, that is, to perform whatever duties and responsibilities have accrued. To establish eligibility for the role of mental patient, people must negotiate their status, using their illness as an instrument. They must present their illness to others in a form they recognize as legitimate; they may even exaggerate certain behaviors to accomplish that end. In doing so, they may leave themselves no choice but to become sicker (Erikson, 1957). A more detailed account of the role aspect of sickness will be given in Chapter 21, which presents the model of "the human as actor."

For present purposes, the critical issue is what happens in a psychiatric treatment facility from the standpoint of the maintenance or modification of sick talk and sick behaviors. Psychiatric patients frequently develop a "hospital syndrome," consisting of withdrawal, lack of responsibility, and a breakdown of the social behaviors necessary for functioning outside the hospital (Paul, 1969); a chronic condition is the result. Rather than viewing the breakdown as due to causes entirely within the patients, one who performs a functional analysis sees that the environment plays a major role in the development and maintenance of sick talk and sick behavior. The crucial question concerns the way in which the environment of the hospital may interact with the existing complaints of the patients to exaggerate and maintain those behaviors.

Part of the answer lies in the fact that many hospitals are understaffed, and the patient is therefore taught to adjust to a quiet and passive role, with which the attendant and professional staff can more easily cope. Patients learn what is expected of them; in particular, they learn to avoid behaviors that cause them to lose privileges or to be punished. Apathetic cooperativeness is the syndrome that appears to be rewarded by many hospital routines. Energetic self-assertiveness and social experimentation, which may be beneficial and, indeed, even necessary to recovery are disruptive of routine and therefore likely to be punished. The very behavior that keeps chronic mental patients in the hospital has sometimes been inadvertently rewarded by the hospital (Ullmann, 1967).

In a study of psychiatric hospitals, Ullmann showed that the institutions' reinforcement systems often fostered custodial care and the displacement of treatment goals. He found that hospital staff behaviors were controlled by the available reinforcements. For example, when a hospital's funding was based on its average daily patient load, a treatment program that would reduce the resident population, while it would increase the number served, might also make the hospital a "failure" in that it could reduce the funding. Hospitals so funded do, in fact, tend to have chronic

long-term patients. Staff, patients, and the institution itself may develop
behaviors at variance with the institution's purpose if such behaviors are
more frequently reinforced than those which provide the needed services
for which the institution was intended. If given a choice, a worker will
typically perform a task that leaves a record or is visible to the supervisor;
in a hospital, such a task may be writing in a record or putting charts in order rather than attending to a patient, especially if doing the latter would
disrupt routine schedule, for which there is evidence of performance.

PRACTICAL APPLICATIONS

The examples of the use of the model to explain fortuitous child training,
verbal behaviors, gambling, and the maintenance of sick behaviors suggest that the principles derived from the rat in the Skinner box are generally applicable. Thus, from the conceptual powers provided by the analogy of *the human as rat,* we can proceed with practical applications of the
model, acting as though all behavior were under the control of discriminative stimuli and reinforcement contingencies. The power and the usefulness of the model in a practical application will thus be exposed to a
predictive test, since the viability of the analogy can be evaluated only
in terms of the usefulness of applications. If as suggested, particular reinforcement contingencies operate in understaffed psychiatric hospitals to
maintain patients in sick-role behavior, then an obvious application involves modifying those contingencies to support forms of behavior which
more closely approximate the "well" behavior of nonpsychiatric patients.
Such an application in the form of a token economy has been attempted.

Token Economies

The great majority of patients in state mental hospitals remain untreated.
The longer patients remain in the hospital, the more their behavioral problems seem to approach a chronic state (Paul, 1969). Ayllon and Azrin
(1968) note:

> the hospital community is usually geared to providing the biological neces-
> sities of life, and perhaps some minimal level of recreational opportunities,
> but the overall relationship is a parasitic dependency in which the patient
> need not function in order to obtain most, if not all the activities or priv-
> ileges that might still be of interest to him. (p. 3)

The object of a token economy is to strengthen constructive and useful
behaviors of psychotic patients by applying operant principles. Specifically, tokens which can be exchanged for items desired by the patients
serve as contingent reward for constructive behavior. Ayllon and Azrin

(1968) have described in detail the results of the establishment of a token economy, extending and amplifying an earlier report (1965) of their work.

The patients.   The population of the ward on which Ayllon and Azrin established the token economy varied from 43 to 45 female mental patients. None were receiving therapy of any kind, and none had hospital work assignments. All had been hospitalized for long periods of time and were regarded as chronic and untreatable. They ranged in age from 24 to 74, with an average age of 51, and the average period of hospitalization had been 16 years.

Operant responses.   The functional (useful) behaviors selected were objective, observable, and deemed desirable by the hospital staff but none were part of the current behavior patterns of the patients. For example, they included self-grooming, mopping the floor, or developing a potentially marketable skill, such as typing. The selected behaviors were the desired end products; the task was to get the patients to exhibit them. Operant strategy dictates that reinforcement be made contingent on the occurrence of the desired response and that it be brought under the control of a discriminative stimulus.

Stimulus control.   When a mop was made available at some fixed time and place previously specified, it provided an opportunity for reward if it was used. Similarly, grooming aids were made available, always in the same place and only at a specified time. The presence of the mop or the grooming aids at an exact location in time and space signaled the opportunity for the patients to use them.

Contingent reinforcement.   When the patient produced the desired response, she immediately received one or more tokens whose exchange value had been previously explained. The contingent reinforcements could be uniformly and regularly delivered by the hospital staff (pellet dispenser) because there was only one behavior at a time to which they needed to be sensitive. If an attendant had to watch constantly for all possible positive behaviors, many of them would have gone unnoticed and would not have been rewarded promptly, with the result that shaping would have been difficult.

Reinforcement.   Tokens, of course, are secondary rewards. Ayllon and Azrin observed what patients seemed to enjoy and made such pleasures available only on presentation of tokens. For example, a turnstile requiring a token was located at the door of the dining room. Each patient was assigned a free bed in a large dormitory; for tokens, however, the patient could obtain a nicer room with more privacy. Thus tokens had value for the patient because they could be exchanged for desired objects and activities. Some of the pleasures which the tokens could provide are given in Table 19.1.

Table 19.1   Examples of reinforcers available for tokens.*

Reinforcer	No. of tokens daily	Reinforcer	No. of tokens daily
I. Privacy		*IV. Devotional opportunities*	
Selection of room 1	0	Extra religious services on ward	1
Selection of room 2	4	Extra religious services off ward	10
Selection of room 3	8		
Selection of room 4	15	*V. Recreational opportunities*	
Selection of room 5	30	Movie on ward	1
Personal chair	1	Opportunity to listen to a live	
Choice of eating group	1	band	1
Screen (room divider)	1	Exclusive use of a radio	1
Choice of bedspreads	1	Television (choice of program)	3
Coat rack	1		
Personal cabinet	2	*VI. Commissary items*	
Placebo	1–2	Consumable items such as	
		candy, milk, cigarettes, coffee, and sandwich	1–5
II. Leave from the ward			
20-min walk on hospital grounds (with escort)	2	Toilet articles such as Kleenex, toothpaste, comb, lipstick, and talcum powder	1–10
30-min grounds pass	10		
Each additional 30 min	3	Clothing and accessories such as gloves, headscarf, house slippers, handbag, and skirt	12–400
Trip to town (with escort)	100		
III. Social interaction with staff			
Private audience with chaplain, nurse (5 min free)		Reading and writing materials such as stationery, pen, greeting card, newspaper, and magazine	2–5
Private audience with ward staff, ward physician (5 min free); additional time per min	1	Miscellaneous items such as ashtray, throw rug, potted plant, picture holder, and stuffed animal	1–50
Private audience with ward psychologist	20		
Private audience with social worker	100		

* From T. Ayllon and N. H. Azrin, "The measurement and reinforcement of behavior of psychotics," *Journal of the Experimental Analysis of Behavior,* 1965, **8,** 360. Copyright 1965 by the Society for the Experimental Analysis of Behavior, Inc. Reprinted by permission. Additional information and related research can be found in *The Token Economy: A Motivational System for Therapy and Rehabilitation* by T. Ayllon and N. H. Azrin, published by Appleton-Century-Crofts, 1968.

On-ward jobs. Patients were then offered on-ward jobs which were typically performed on other wards by paid hospital personnel. The jobs were available on request, and patients signed up or not as they wished. There were a variety of jobs, requiring different amounts of time and effort, all rewarded by tokens. For example, either washing the coffee urn or filling the salt shakers required about 10 minutes, and each paid 2 tokens. Loading the dishwasher, cleaning the kitchen, and replacing the articles took about 45 minutes and paid 17 tokens. A 15-minute guided tour of the ward explaining the token system to visitors paid 10 tokens. Washing, dressing, and normal grooming could earn up to 5 tokens a day.

Over a 20-day period, 36 of 44 patients participated in the work and on an average day performed some 45 hours of work. In order to demonstrate that the patients performed because of the contingent reinforcement, the experimenters introduced a 20-day period during which each patient received tokens at the start of the day whether or not she performed a job (noncontingent reinforcement). The patient needed only to sign up for a job; she got paid whether or not she did it. Overall performance of work dropped rapidly (though not immediately) to about an hour a day. When the reinforcement contingency was resumed for the next 20-day period, the daily work level immediately returned to about 45 hours. The results of this experiment (Ayllon and Azrin, 1965) are shown in Fig. 19.4.

The valuable lesson the Ayllon and Azrin experiment teaches is that effective contingent rewards that reinforce desired behaviors can provide a means for shaping incapable and dependent patients into functioning and responsible workers. Operant procedures have been used to shape and direct a wide variety of behaviors, ranging from acceptance of toilet training to dieting (for additional examples see Bergin and Suinn, 1975). The psychiatric ward as a large Skinner box has proved to be a remarkably effective analogy; psychotic and long-established bizarre behaviors have given way to functional behaviors. Ayllon and Azrin note:

> Surprisingly, it was found that once the procedures were effective in establishing functional behaviors, many of the symptomatic behaviors were no longer present and could not be studied. One can only speculate, of course, but it appears that the symptomatic behaviors by their very disruptive nature were reduced or eliminated because they could not exist side by side with the functional behaviors. (1968, p. 23)

The Technology of Teaching

B. F. Skinner, in *The Technology of Teaching* (1968), analyzes current educational practices and derives new teaching procedures from the principles of operant conditioning. From his many suggestions based on well-

Performance (total hours/day)

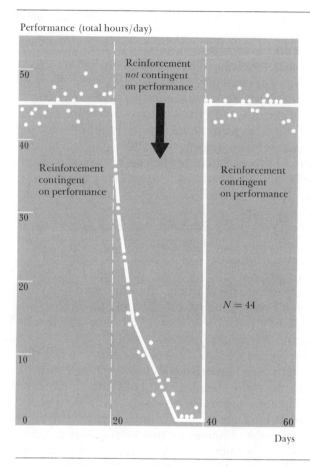

Fig. 19.4. The total number of hours of the on-ward performance by a group of 44 patients. (From T. Ayllon and N. H. Azrin, "The measurement and reinforcement of behavior of psychotics," *Journal of the Experimental Analysis of Behavior*, 1965, **8**, 373. Copyright 1965 by the Society for the Experimental Analysis of Behavior, Inc. Reprinted by permission. See also footnote to Table 19.1.)

researched principles, we have selected several examples that draw on the analogy under discussion.

Discriminations.   A pigeon can be trained to maintain a spot of light at an intensity which makes it just visible. By using a range of different colored lights, the trainer can determine the spectral sensitivity of the pigeon, which happens to be very close to that of humans. Making fine discriminations about the intensity of colored lights is a behavior that can be trained and maintained by a contingent reinforcement. Skinner notes:

> A "discriminating" person can tell the difference between colors, shapes, and sizes of objects; he can identify three-dimensional forms seen from different aspects; he can find patterns concealed in other patterns; he can identify pitches, intervals, and musical themes and distinguish between various

tempos and rhythms—all of this in an almost infinite variety. Discriminations of this sort are essential in science and industry and in everyday life as in identifying the school of a painter or the period of a composer. The remarkable fact is that the necessary contingencies of reinforcement are quite rare in the environment of the average child. Even children who are encouraged to play with objects of different sizes, shapes, and colors and given a passing acquaintance with musical patterns are seldom exposed to the precise contingencies needed to build subtle discriminations. It is not surprising that most of them move into adulthood with largely undeveloped "abilities." Relatively simple machines should remedy the defect.... Pictures or words are projected under translucent windows, which respond to the touch by closing circuits. A child can be made to "look at the sample" by requiring him to press the sample window at the top. He is reinforced for this response by the appearance of material in the lower windows from which a choice is to be made. He identifies corresponding material by pressing one of the lower windows and is reinforced again.... If he presses a wrong window, the choices disappear until he presses the top window again —in the course of which he again looks at the sample. Many other arrangements of responses and reinforcements are, of course, possible. In an improved version of this machine [see Fig. 19.5] auditory stimuli can be generated by pressing sample and choice buttons. If devices of this sort were generally available in nursery schools and kindergartens, children would be far more skillful in dealing with their environment. All young children are now "disadvantaged" in this respect.*

Schedules of reinforcement. Earlier we noted that a variable-ratio schedule is best for maintaining responses at a steady, high rate. Consider the lesson for educational technology which Skinner draws from this effect of schedules on behavior:

A pigeon will continue to respond even though only one response in every hundred, say, is reinforced, but it will not do so unless the contingencies have been programmed. A fresh pigeon is no more likely to peck a disk a hundred times than to pace a figure eight. The behavior is built up by reinforcing every response, then every other response, then every fifth response, and so on, waiting at each stage until the behavior is reasonably stable. Under careful programming pigeons have continued to peck when only every tenthousandth response has been reinforced, and this is certainly not the limit. An observer might say, for example, that the pigeon is "greatly interested in his work," "industrious," "remarkably tolerant to frustration," "free from discouragement," or "dedicated to his task." These expressions are commonly applied to students who have had the benefit of similar programming, accidentally or arranged.

---

* From B. F. Skinner, *The Technology of Teaching*, Appleton-Century-Crofts, 1968, pp. 73–74. Reprinted by permission.

Fig. 19.5. Skinner's machine for teaching visual and auditory discriminations. Correct responses move new material into place. The machine can be used to teach both auditory and visual aspects of verbal behavior, music, etc. (From B. F. Skinner, *The Technology of Teaching*, Appleton-Century-Crofts, 1968, p. 75. Used by permission.)

The effective scheduling of reinforcement is an important element in educational design. Suppose we wish to teach a student to read "good books"—books which, almost by definition, do not reinforce the reader sentence by sentence or even paragraph by paragraph but only when possibly hundreds of pages have prepared him for a convincing or moving denouement. The student must be exposed to a program of materials which build up a tendency to read in the absence of reinforcement. Such programs are seldom constructed deliberately and seldom arise by accident, and it is therefore not surprising that few students even in good universities learn to read books of this sort and continue to do so for the rest of their lives. In their pride, schools are likely to arrange just the wrong conditions; they are likely to maintain so-called standards under which books are forced upon students before they have had adequate preparation.

A program in which exciting results were first common but became less and less frequent could generate the capacity to continue in the absence of reinforcement for long periods of time. Such programs should arise naturally as scientists turn to more and more difficult areas. Perhaps not many effective programs are to be expected for this reason, and they are only rarely designed by teachers of science. This may explain why there are so few dedicated scientists. Maintaining a high level of activity is one of the important achievements of programming. Repeatedly, in its long history, education has resorted to aversive control to keep its students at work. A proper understanding of the scheduling of reinforcement may lead at long last to a better solution of this problem. (1968, pp. 78–79)

Social Planning and Human Engineering

The logical conclusion from evidence supplied by the rat in a Skinner box, the patient in a ward, and the student in an educational setting, is to move toward contingency management of the total social setting of the human as rat. If human behaviors are seen as operants emitted on cue and controlled and maintained by contingent reinforcements, then the fullness of people—the development of their potential—lies in social planning to condition desirable and useful behaviors. Skinner imagined such a utopia in his book *Walden Two* (1948), where the reader may see the fulfillment of the image of the human as rat; within the confinements of his institutions, people occupy the same position the rat occupies within the confinements of its box. The following excerpts are from the description of the nursery of Walden Two to visitors touring the facilities with Frazier, the designer of the community, as their guide.

A young woman in a white uniform met us in a small waiting room near the entrance. Frazier addressed her as Mrs. Nash.

"I hope Mr. Frazier has warned you," she said with a smile, "that we are going to be rather impolite and give you only a glimpse of our babies. We try to protect them from infection during the first year. It's especially important when they are cared for as a group."

"What about their parents?" said Castle at once. "Don't parents see their babies?"

"Oh, yes, as long as they are in good health. Some parents work in the nursery. Others come around every day or so for at least a few minutes. They take the baby out for some sunshine or play with it in a room." Mrs. Nash smiled at Frazier. "That's the way we build up the baby's resistance," she added.

She opened up a door and allowed us to look into a small room, three walls of which were lined with cubicles, each with a large glass window. Behind the windows we could see babies of various ages. None of them wore more than a diaper, and there were no bed clothes. In one cubicle a small red newborn was asleep on its stomach. Some of the older babies were awake and playing with toys. Near the door a baby on all fours pressed its nose against the glass and smiled at us. . . .

"... This is a much more efficient way of keeping a baby warm than the usual practice of wrapping it in several layers of cloth," said Mrs. Nash, opening a safety-glass window to permit Barbara and Mary to look inside. "The newborn baby needs moist air at about 88 or 90 degrees. At six months, 80 is about right."

"... But why don't you put clothes on them?" said Barbara.

"What for? It would mean laundry for us and discomfort for the child. It's the same with sheets and blankets. Our babies lie on a stretched plastic cloth which doesn't soak up moisture and can be wiped clean in a moment."

"... Clothing and blankets are really a great nuisance," said Mrs. Nash. "They keep the baby from exercising, they force it into uncomfortable postures—"

"When a baby graduates from our Lower Nursery," Frazier broke in, "it knows nothing of frustration, anxiety, or fear. It never cries except when sick, which is very seldom, and it has a lively interest in everything."

"But is it prepared for life?" said Castle. "Surely you can't continue to protect it from frustration or frightening situations forever."

"Of course not. But it can be prepared for them. We can build a tolerance for frustration by introducing obstacles gradually as the baby grows strong enough to handle them. But I'm getting ahead of our story. Have you any other point to make, Mrs. Nash?"

"I suppose you'd like to have them know how much work is saved. Since the air is filtered, we only bathe the babies once a week, and we never need to clean their nostrils or eyes. There are no beds to make, of course. And it's easy to prevent infection. The compartments are sound-proofed, and the babies sleep well and don't disturb each other. We can keep them on different schedules, so the nursery runs smoothly. Let me see, is there anything else?"

"I think that's quite enough," said Frazier. "We have a lot of ground to cover this morning."

"... Another thing," said Castle. "What about mother love?"

... "Very real," said Frazier quietly. "And we supply it in liberal doses. But we don't limit it to mothers. We go in for father love, everybody's love —community love, if you wish. Our children are treated with affection by everyone—and thoughtful affection too, which isn't marred by fits of temper due to overwork or careless handling due to ignorance." *

There is of course much more to Walden Two; when the infants graduate from nursery school, they are systematically exposed to frustrations, but at a rate and intensity they can handle and on a carefully worked out schedule. The disruptive emotions, such as hate and jealousy, are eliminated, but the useful ones, such as joy and love, are instilled. Jealousy, for example, does not exist in Walden Two, because it is not

---

* From B. F. Skinner, *Walden Two*, Macmillan, New York, 1948, pp. 77–80. Reprinted by permission.

functional; problems cannot be solved by attacking others, and when a particular emotion is no longer a useful part of the behavioral repertoire, it is eliminated. In Frazier's words, "It's simply a matter of behavioral engineering. . . . The techniques have been available for centuries. We use them in education and in the psychological management of the community." (p. 84) Skinner is quite serious about the possibility of applying operant principles to the task of "engineering" better people. He developed a baby box (Fig. 19.6) for experimentation in less than the total setting of Walden Two and described it in an article in the *Ladies Home*

Fig. 19.6. Skinner's baby box. A closed compartment about the size of a standard crib has insulated wall and on one side a large pane of safety glass which can be raised like a window. The heating is electrical, and special precautions have been taken to ensure adequate temperature control. (From B. F. Skinner, *Cumulative Record,* Appleton-Century-Crofts, New York, 1961, p. 421. Used by permission.)

Journal (Skinner, 1945). Writing later, Skinner (1961) reported that its advantages had been generally confirmed. Of 73 couples who had used his baby box for 130 babies, all but 3 described the device as wonderful. Skinner concluded that the physical and psychological benefits the users reported seem to warrant extensive research on his baby box.

SUMMARY

Animals have been trained to work for people and to provide them with entertainment. Animal training has existed for centuries as both an art and a profession. It remained for B. F. Skinner to make it a science and a model of human behavior as well.

Animal training becomes a science when it is taken into the laboratory and exposed to systematic analysis. In the laboratory, the task is to discover those conditions and circumstances under which training is accomplished most efficiently. Methods, procedures, and results are carefully defined so that information can be conceptualized and communicated and generalizations can be made.

From the results of long study of animal training in the laboratory, Skinner has provided the basis for a functional analysis of behavior. Specifically, behavior occurs because it has some value to the subject. A response that results in food is likely to be made again when the subject is hungry. The relationship between a behavior and a subsequent reward or punishment is one factor determining what response a subject will make again. Stimuli in the environment that provide information about the response-reinforcement contingencies are learned, and thus they gain a measure of influence over behavior. The picture emerges of an animal with a repertoire of skills which are called into action by cues in the environment and maintained by the consequences they produce.

Animal training becomes a model for humans when an analogy is drawn between the rat in the confines of its training box and people in the confines of their social institutions. Like the rat, people emit behaviors, many of which are rewarded. They learn the contingencies between their behaviors and the outcomes they produce, as well as cues that signal the contingencies. Functional behaviors are produced on cue, and we fulfill our moment by performing predetermined acts, just as circus animals perform acts that have been determined by previous response-reward contingencies.

The analogy can be used to describe how speech is acquired, why gamblers persist, and why some psychiatric patients never recover. In each case, human behavior is indistinguishable from animal behavior; it is behavior that has been reinforced. The analogy promises a technology of human engineering, in which information about response-reinforcement contingencies is used to plan psychiatric treatment and educational programs. People, in short, can be trained to perform on cue those acts which are of greatest benefit and value.

SUGGESTIONS FOR FURTHER READING

Crichton, M. *The Terminal Man.* New York: Knopf, 1972. This novel provides a dramatic reminder that the concept of the human as rat is coming increasingly within our technological capacity.

Karlins, M., and L. M. Andrews (eds.). *Man Controlled.* New York: The Free Press, 1972. This edited work reprints a number of important articles about the control of human behavior. Several well known authors are included.

Skinner, B. F. *Beyond Freedom and Dignity.* New York: Knopf, 1971. Skinner directly considers the political and philosophical implications of applying behavioral engineering. The book is a good introduction to the moral dilemmas which will confront us if the potential of the experimental viewpoint is realized.

20
The
Human
as
Scientist

I. **Principal constructs and their translation**
   A. Prior facts = past experiences
   B. Viewpoint = personal construct system
   C. Central assertions = core personal constructs
   D. Elaborations of central assertions = subordinate personal constructs
   E. Formulation of problem = circumspection
   F. Statement of hypothesis = preemption
   G. Experimentation = control
   H. Results = personal validation
   I. Interpretation = channelization

II. **Use of the model in personality study**
   A. Anxiety and threat
   B. Guilt
   C. Communication
   D. Creativity and problem-solving

III. **Practical applications**
   A. Assessment
      1. A redefinition of assessment
      2. The Role Construct Repertory Test (RCRT)
      3. Illustrative use of the RCRT in the assessment of thought disorder
   B. The clinical setting
      1. Interviewing
      2. Psychotherapy
      3. Fixed-role therapy
   C. International understanding

IV. **Summary**

V. **Suggestions for further reading**

This chapter presents a model of personality based on the analogy of the human as scientist. The central claim of this analogy is that psychology holds a unique position among the sciences. The human subjects that psychologists study are themselves engaging in the same methods and tactics by which they are studied: prediction, control, and understanding of their own behavior and that of others with whom they interact.

The model represents a contemporary cognitive approach, emphasizing the manner in which individuals interpret their environment. It deals with people's tendency to transform their perception of the environment to conform to their own cognitive structures and with the impact of these

---

Box 20.1   George A. Kelly.

Photo by Ralph Norman

George A. Kelly (1905–1966) was a diversified, unorthodox, and creative psychologist. After earning a Ph.D. from Iowa, Kelly worked as a clinical psychologist in Kansas and, during World War II, as a military psychologist. Afterward he became a professor of psychology at Ohio State and still later joined the faculty at Brandeis University. Like Freud and Rogers, Kelly developed his approach from extensive contact with clients in clinical settings. In 1955 he published his model of the human in two volumes entitled *The Psychology of Personal Constructs*. The model gave great impetus to cognitive theories of personality, provided new approaches to assessment and psychotherapy, and generated extensive research. The essence of Kelly's position is that he views all people as psychologists; we are all actively engaged in construing events and generating miniature theories to predict, control, and understand our own behavior and that of others. Although not every person is indeed a scientist, all do use the principles of science in everyday life. Kelly did not publish a great deal during his life, but he exerted considerable and growing influence on psychology through his lectures and especially through his personal impact on his many students and on those who knew him. Fortunately, many of Kelly's important papers were collected and published after his death (Maher, 1969), and they provide an excellent introduction to his ideas.

---

cognitions on their behavior. The systematic exploration of the human as scientist was first presented by George Kelly (1955). Kelly's approach is to consider the possibility that all people may be seen as scientists in both their aims and their strategies.

Principal constructs used in describing the scientist and the scientific enterprise itself will be translated into Kelly's constructs, which serve to describe the person and the human enterprise. The translation will have two parts. First, we shall associate a relatively abstract definition of each psychological construct with the definition of the corresponding scientific construct. Second, we shall provide a very simple and familiar example of each psychological construct. The familiar examples of Kelly's psychological constructs are also listed in Box 20.2, to which the reader may find it helpful to refer from time to time.

Box 20.2 Kelly's psychological constructs.

Construct	**Example**
Past experience	A parent will have an opportunity to observe his or her child cry on many different occasions over a period of years.
Personal construct system	From experience with the child crying, a parent will devise ways to interpret crying, perhaps making many different distinctions as to types of crying and situations for crying.
Core personal constructs	The parent may have the general value that a child should not cry unless it is in pain.
Subordinate personal constructs	The parent may elaborate his or her core construct by choosing to ignore crying when it is not due to pain or illness.
Circumspection	The child begins to cry and the parent must interpret that event within his or her construct system by applying various constructs, such as "the child is ill" or "the child wants a piece of candy."
Preemption	The parent concludes that the child is crying for a piece of candy.
Control	The parent can determine the accuracy of the preemption only by acting on the construct and seeing if it correctly fits the event, in this case, by ignoring the child.

Personal validation	The child becomes violently nauseated, faints, develops a high temperature, and dies.
Channelization	The parent may now conclude that the circumspection and preemption were wrong, but that no other changes are needed for dealing with other children. However, the dramatic invalidation may lead to the revision of the subordinate construct that any crying not labeled as sickness should be ignored; or perhaps the parent may even question the wisdom of the core construct or the whole set of dimensions used to distinguish between types of crying and situations for crying.

PRINCIPAL CONSTRUCTS AND THEIR TRANSLATION

Prior Facts = Past Experiences

Few scientific enterprises "start from scratch." Scientists have at their disposal the backlog of existing knowledge and facts that constitute the totality of their discipline and define the units with which they will work. In scientific writings, a "review of the literature" represents an attempt to assemble and organize all previous information available concerning a given subject. Despite the widespread availability of scientific and technical information, however, it cannot be assumed that all scientists will have access to all prior facts. The particular set of facts a given scientist considers is likely to be determined by training, personal experience, and general knowledge of the field.

Just as the scientist does not start from scratch, so people do not; they have at their disposal a backlog of past experiences with which to face each new event. In planning an approach to any activity in life—from organizing a day to selecting a career—people have past experiences to call on. It is the assembly and organization of these experiences which provide the units for finding purpose and transferring direction from the present to the future. Despite the similarities imposed by common cultural constraints, such as those of living in the United States, there is wide variation in experience, and each person's specific past experiences frame a unique approach to life.

Example: A parent will have an opportunity to observe his or her child cry on many different occasions over a period of years.

Viewpoint = Personal Construct System

As we have stressed repeatedly, facts do not exist in a vacuum. They become meaningful only when construed from a particular viewpoint. A viewpoint is a collection of constructs that fit together logically, and it provides a broad framework for viewing the facts of a science. Scientists committed to a given viewpoint are more likely to give credence to facts that may be easily construed within their viewpoint. By making this statement, however, we are not implying that science is "biased" or "subjective," but rather, we are calling attention to the fact that individual scientists hold viewpoints that are determined in large part by their training and experience.

Past experiences in everyday life are also *organized;* they derive their meaning not so much from their objective characteristics as from the way they are interpreted. A personal construct system, similar to a viewpoint, provides a way to name and classify past experience, for example, a happy or a sad experience. Because individuals have different personal construct systems, two people often may have the same past experience but see it as two very different kinds of events. Just as the scientist may invest heavily in certain scientific viewpoints, so people have a tendency to become committed to their own construct systems. This "subjective" aspect of interpreting life simply reflects the fact that the construct systems individuals develop are different.

Example: From experience with the child crying, a parent will devise ways to interpret crying, perhaps making many different distinctions as to types of crying and situations for crying.

Central Assertions = Core Personal Constructs

As noted, viewpoints contain certain central assertions or fundamental postulates. These central assertions—or axioms, as they are sometimes called—represent the basic assumptions a scientist makes about the nature of his or her field. For example, most psychologists subscribe to the assertion that psychology is a natural science. Such a fundamental assertion provides the subject matter of a field with an orientation that is not likely to be changed or modified. Such assertions are taken as the "givens" of a particular viewpoint and are not subjected to direct tests.

Core personal constructs are the fundamental and basic beliefs a person holds. Often core personal constructs are what we ordinarily call *values.* They are the truths which an individual accepts as "given," and they are not subject to direct test. Thus core personal constructs are neither true nor false; rather, they are articles of faith. Individuals cannot change or modify them without at the same time revising much of the personal construct system that is predicated on them. To illustrate: One person may believe that mortal life is but a qualifying test for everlasting life. Another may believe that the only life after death consists in the residue of impact that the forceful exercise of personal power has had on others. Both core constructs are articles of faith; neither is subject to test, nor is either likely to be modified. However, each constrains the way in which personal experiences are to be seen.

Example: The parent may have the general value that a child should not cry unless it is in pain.

Elaborations of Central Assertions = Subordinate Personal Constructs

The implications of central assertions may be elaborated in the form of theorems which presumably follow from a given set of central assertions. Such elaborations or theorems are more tentative than central assertions and may at times be subjected to direct tests. Should available evidence suggest that a given elaboration was formulated incorrectly, some revision in the manner in which the theorem was stated is called for. It may be that a given elaboration did not follow directly from a set of central assertions, and therefore, an alternative elaboration may be derived. For the most part, the demonstration that a given elaboration is incorrect does not imply that the central assertions from which it stemmed are incorrect. Calling a central assertion into question would imply that the entire viewpoint was in error. Such a state of affairs would be highly disconcerting for the scientist.

Subordinate personal constructs serve to clarify the *practical* implications of core constructs. These elaborations are "subordinate" in the sense that they presumably follow from the core constructs and are logically consistent with them. The subordinate constructs are more tentative, however. Because they specify the practical applications of the core constructs, they are subject to revision; that is, a given subordinate construct may be changed if experience suggests that it was incorrectly derived or that it conflicts with another subordinate construct.

Example: The parent may elaborate his or her core construct by choosing to ignore crying when it is not due to pain or illness.

Formulation of Problem = Circumspection

Although it is fairly easy to specify the prior facts that exist with respect to a given scientific problem as well as the viewpoint that a particular scientist brings to bear on those facts, it is difficult to state the precise manner in which a particular scientist formulates a specific problem for investigation. Given the same prior facts and even the same viewpoints two different scientists are likely to arrive at two quite different formulations of the problem for investigation. Reichenbach (1938) used the expression *context of discovery* for this poorly understood step in scientific investigation. Two different scientists, provided with the same facts, may consider different lines of investigation "important" or "interesting."

It is probably true that "creative" scientists are characterized by the ability to select interesting problems. However it occurs, the context of discovery involves an act of creation in which the scientist finds a way to *extend* understanding of a problem by finding a gap in current knowledge. It is through the search for extensions of the range of knowledge that discovery takes place.

Thus far, our description of an individual's experience and personal constructs has been primarily historical in nature. But living is an ongoing enterprise. Past experience flows unending into present and future. Although past experiences, by definition, are events which can be considered after the fact, current decisions and future plans must be made before the fact. These experiences-to-be likewise derive their meaning from the personal construct system. When applied to the future, the constructs allow the person to *anticipate* the nature of an experience. Since the experience has not yet arrived, however, which constructs should be used?

In an effort to anticipate and thus gain a measure of control over the future, people go through a period of circumspection in which they provisionally try out a variety of constructs on some future event to see how well the different constructs seem to work. Sometimes, of course, the period of circumspection is very time-consuming, as when an individual makes a deliberate decision. At other times, particularly on trivial matters, the period may be very brief. The thoughtful person spends a great deal of time in circumspection, the impulsive person very little.

Example: The child begins to cry and the parent must interpret that event within his or her construct system by applying various constructs, such as "the child is ill" or "the child wants a piece of candy."

Statement of Hypothesis = Preemption

Once a problem has been selected for investigation, it is stated in the form of a research hypothesis. Hypotheses must be stated with great precision, and their intent should not be ambiguous. A typical hypothesis takes the form: "If A occurs, then B will occur also." It must be stated with sufficient clarity to encompass all possible outcomes. For example, if A occurs, followed by C, it should be evident that B has or has not occurred. Hence a characteristic of a good hypothesis is that it *delimits* the realm of inquiry. Although many problems may be formulated in a number of different ways, the statement of a hypothesis delimits the realm of investigation to a specific subset of phenomena.

Preemption is a decision as to which constructs are relevant to an experience and in what way. Preemption occurs when an event is construed as "A" and nothing but "A." Once an event has been identified as an instance of the "A" class, it is understandable in terms of properties of the "A" construct. However, properties of "B" or "C" constructs are no longer applicable to the event. In this sense, preemption *delimits* the manner in which an experience can be construed.

Example: The parent concludes that the child is crying for a piece of candy.

Experimentation = Control

The experimental method provides a means of determining the truth or falsity of a research hypothesis. A proper experimental design allows the scientist to hold constant or rule out all variables other than those in which he is interested to determine the exact nature of the relationship that exists among them. It is through experimental design, control, and precise measurement techniques that the scientific method provides unambiguous answers to research questions.

Preemptions are brittle statements, for they can be shattered if the experience-to-be turns out, after the fact, to have been some other kind of experience. Frequently, of course, a person may not choose to determine the accuracy of a preemption, just as a scientist does not perform every possible experiment. But the person who wishes to demonstrate control over an experience must *act* on the basis of his or her preemptions. The effort to control events provides the means whereby the accuracy of circumspection and its preemption may be determined. Control is a bet made with the world that an experience-to-be, when it does arrive, will be of the anticipated type.

Example: The parent can determine the accuracy of the preemption only by acting on the construct and seeing if it correctly fits the events, in this case, by ignoring the child.

Results = Personal Validation

The outcome or results of an experiment should provide evidence of the truth or falsity of the experimental hypothesis. Reichenbach (1938) referred to this phase of scientific investigation as the *context of verification.* Although some ambiguity may exist about the nature of the context of discovery, the context of verification in science is well understood. A given result either occurs or does not occur. Hence a given hypothesis is either accepted or rejected. The results of a scientific investigation are public and verifiable, and there should be little doubt about their nature.

The bet with the world will be either confirmed or not. The result of a well-designed effort to bring external events under the control of a personal construct system is usually clear; the anticipation was either correct or incorrect.

Example: The child becomes violently nauseated, faints, develops a high temperature, and dies.

Interpretation = Channelization

Although the outcome of an experiment may be clear and unequivocal, the *significance* of that outcome is a matter of interpretation. Scientists are prone to interpret the results of an experiment within the context of their own viewpoint concerning the subject matter. Hence the same experimental results may have different implications for scientists with different viewpoints. Each scientist construes outcomes from his or her own viewpoint, and scientific controversies arise from just such different interpretations. Sometimes the results of an experiment require the scientist to revise the formulation of the problem. And when, as happens on occasion, the results of a series of experiments, both the scientist's own and those of others, cannot be reconciled with certain aspects of that viewpoint, the scientist must make revisions in the central assertions and their elaborations.

Although it may be clear to the person that he or she either did or did not correctly anticipate some particular experience, the significance of efforts at control lies in how the outcome is "channelized." The outcome itself now becomes an event which must be interpreted within the construct system. If the experience was anticipated correctly, no problem has been created, and the person may conclude that he or she is good at understanding that kind of experience.

But the person who anticipated the experience incorrectly will seek an explanation of the mistake that makes it possible again to believe he or she has those events under the control of his or her construct system. The simplest and most common reaction is to return to the circumspection and preemption stages to see whether there appears, after the fact, to be a better way to view the experience. This procedure may show that only a revision of the particular name given to the experience is needed. Sometimes, however, the failure at control becomes so repetitive that the person must go back and revise some of the subordinate constructs. Such a course is far more drastic because it changes the actual constructs, and it may require the development of new constructs as well as modifications in the relationships of constructs to one another.

In the normal person, failure is seldom so all-encompassing that core constructs must be revoked. A revision of such scope would require one to reconsider most past experience and to devise a new personal construct system. Such an outcome usually results only under the special circumstances of mental illness.

Extracting the meaning from outcomes that follow efforts at control channelizes life into a dynamic, changing, and ongoing process, just as interpretation propels science into an expanding, unfolding, and unending process.

Example: The parent may now conclude that the circumspection and preemption were wrong, but that no other changes are needed for dealing with other children. However, the dramatic invalidation may lead to the revision of the subordinate construct that any crying not labeled as sickness should be ignored; or perhaps the parent may even question the wisdom of the core construct or the whole set of dimensions used to distinguish between types of crying and situations for crying.

USE OF THE MODEL IN PERSONALITY STUDY

The value of using a model can be illustrated particularly well in the view of the human as scientist. On a variety of topics, Kelly was able to provide unique and interesting perspectives which departed considerably from previous ideas. One of the most distinctive characteristics of Kelly's two-volume work (1955) is the frequency with which old facts or experiences are recast in new shapes with new dimensions and new possibilities. We can consider here but a few of the many unique perspectives Kelly provided when he considered humans as scientists, actively experimenting with gaining control over the events of their lives by the formulations they construct.

Anxiety and Threat

In traditional formulations, personality theorists often link anxiety and threat together. Anxiety, seen as *internal*, is what the person experiences as a reaction to threat, which is seen as *external*—a learned signal that an aversive or painful event may occur. To Kelly, however, anxiety and threat are two very different things.

People experience anxiety when their construct system provides them with no means for dealing with an experience. Thus individuals feel anxious when they cannot name or place some important upcoming experience within their construct system. As an illustration, people we cannot understand often make us anxious because we cannot anticipate what they are going to do. The events that produce anxiety are outside the range of our construct systems. Thus reassurance is not going to reduce a person's anxiety, but new constructs for conceptual control of the events of life will.

By contrast, people experience *threat* when they sense an imminent and fundamental change in their construct system, that is, when important subordinate constructs are no longer tenable. Such a situation can result when efforts at control continue to provide personal invalidation so extensive and so compelling that the validity and usefulness of major parts of the person's construct system are challenged. For example, if too many core constructs are challenged, suicide may result, because the threat calls into question the usefulness of the purposes to which one's life has been devoted; perhaps nothing is more threatening than facing such a realization. Notice that from this view threat, like anxiety, is internal. The experience of anxiety and threat cannot be blamed on someone else; control over one's life and destiny is a personal enterprise.

Guilt

People must interpret their own behavior as well as that of others. In fact, it is only through the application of one's personal construct system to one's own behavior that one's life acquires meaning and purpose. Since one's own behavior is so important, one applies many different constructs to one's own actions. The placement of these behaviors within the personal construct system soon defines the self, and it tells one who one is: honest, hardworking, short, etc.

But sometimes an individual's behavior is discrepant from the placement of the self in the construct system. According to Kelly, the experience of guilt is the dislodgement of self from important constructs. Guilty people have not filled the place they have defined for themselves in their own construct system. Cheating and loafing are incompatible with the construct of the self as honest and hardworking. Guilty people recognize a discrepancy, or invalidating experience, regarding the self.

One must deal with guilt in the same way as with any other invalidating experience. It is of course possible to revise one's basic constructs and conclude that one is in fact a cheater and loafer. Such important constructs are not easily changed, however, and considerable threat is involved, as is well illustrated by the guilt-ridden person's efforts to find "rationalizations" in the form of other constructs and other distinctions that will explain away the apparent discrepancy.

Communication

Communication between two persons can take place only to the extent that each can incorporate the construct system of the other within his or her own system. Thus communication, even in a casual conversation, is a form of role-taking and involves an effort to understand the other's constructs and to apply them to the experiences in question. Misunderstanding occurs when the two persons construe an experience differently. When we can anticipate what another person is going to do or say next, we can assume that we are doing a good job of incorporating his or her construct system.

Kelly emphasized the importance of the psychotherapist's learning to understand the construct system of the patient. In order to help the patient, the therapist must understand the nature of the constructs and dimensions the patient uses to interpret events and experiences. Categorizing the patient's behavior with respect to the coordinates of the therapist's own construct system may help the therapist develop a list of names to call the patient (e.g., anxiety neurotic, schizophrenic, paranoid type, delusions of grandeur, etc.). However, helping and communicating with the patient requires an understanding of the construct system the *patient* is using.

Creativity and Problem-solving

The model of the human as scientist provides valuable insights into the creative process and the activity of problem-solving. According to Kelly, the creative process starts with loosened constructs and terminates with tightened and validated constructs. Problem-solving, though similar to creativity in many respects, follows instead a cycle of circumspection, preemption, and control.

In the *creative process,* people start with a relatively loose construal of events. They may have only a vague feeling that certain elements go together in some way. As *new* constructs begin to take shape, creative thinkers may be hard-pressed to find a suitable symbol for it. They may be able only at first to point to selected elements, with the result that they appear to be somewhat inarticulate. In fact, their friends may conclude that they are talking in very concrete terms about miscellaneous trivia. As creative thinkers tighten up their construct, however, they begin to find more apt symbols. Their listeners then begin to give them credit for being able to perceive matters in a new and interesting way—a heretofore unused dimension or distinction starts to emerge. Thus an idea is likely to take shape before it acquires a suitable symbol. In creative thinking, it is possible to trace the *development* of a new construct from a very loose construal to a tightened construal to a validating encounter.

In *problem-solving,* on the other hand, the person does not invent or create new constructs. The creative process ordinarily involves only one construct, but problem-solving involves the use of several existing constructs. During a period of problem-solving, a person may try many different constructs, thinking circumspectly about the issue at hand and trying out one construct and then another in a provisional way. The issue is finally preempted when the relevant construct is isolated. We may think of problem-solving as an effort at control directed toward gaining validating experiences which can be channelized back into the person's construct system. This cycling process is reflected in the dynamic, constantly changing pattern of human life.

PRACTICAL APPLICATIONS

As is true of the other models described in this book, the model of the human as scientist has been applied extensively to the clinical setting. In fact, Kelly conceived it from clinical practice, and he naturally concentrated on applications in a clinical setting. The entire second volume and much of the first volume of Kelly's major work (1955) contain extensive details on clinical applications. The model has been applied to many phases of clinical practice, from diagnosis (called assessment in this book) to specific treatment. Again, we can present only a few of the many possibilities; the reader should remember that they are only illustrative and do not cover the full range of applications for the model of the human as scientist.

Assessment

Assessment is by now a familiar word in this text. The psychometric viewpoint encompassed the traditional meaning of the term. But when we view humans as scientists engaging in an experiment of life, it no longer makes sense to hang a label on them. The experiments are personal, and the critical questions concern each person and his or her own validating experiences.

A redefinition of assessment.   For Kelly, one gains little understanding of people by placing them in categories. The important task is to understand the *personal* construct system of the specific individual. Thus one does not bring to the assessment setting an *a priori* set of categories—either as diagnostic labels, such as an anxiety neurotic, obsessive-compulsive, etc., or as trait labels, such as anxious, dependent, etc. The assessment must be *content-free,* in the sense that the clinician must try to "subsume" the subject's personal construct system, to find out how the subject sees the world.

The Role Construct Repertory Test (RCRT).   The technique Kelly developed for making a content-free assessment is called the Role Construct Repertory Test. Using that procedure, the clinician asks subjects first to name real persons they know who fit certain role descriptions and then to distinguish those persons from one another in terms of their own evaluations of them. For an illustration of the technique, see Box 20.3 which gives the general form of the test instructions and lists 22 role descriptions.

Box 20.3   The Role Construct Repertory Test

The Role Construct Repertory Test (RCRT) was developed by Kelly (1955) as a procedure for helping his patients to make their personal construct systems explicit. One may understand the nature of constructs as dimensions for distinguishing between people and experiences by following the procedures used in the RCRT. In fact, the personal experience of taking the test is often informative, and the reader may find it interesting to complete the illustrative form provided here.

Instructions

Refer to the descriptions of 22 different persons, and select from among known individuals the *real* person who best fits each description; write that person's name in the grid space above the column with the corresponding number. Now consider the first row only. Three persons (20, 21, 22) have circles under their names. How are two of them like each other and different from the third person? Keep thinking about them until you identify an important likeness of two which distinguishes them from the third person. When you have decided which two are alike, put an × in each of the two circles under their names. Now write on the first line under *construct* the word or phrase that tells how those two are alike. Under *contrast* write the opposite of this characteristic. Now consider each of the other persons who appear at the heads of the columns. In addition to the two persons you have already marked with an ×, which of the others have this characteristic? Put a check mark (√) under the name of each addi-

Name:

Date:

No:

GRID

CONSTRUCT

CONTRAST

1 2 3 4 5 6 7 8 9 10 11 12 13 14 15 16 17 18 19 20 21 22

tional person who has this characteristic. Repeat the procedure for every row on the form.

Description of persons

1. Write your own name in the first blank.
2. Write your mother's first name. If you grew up with a stepmother, write her name instead.
3. Write your father's first name. If you grew up with a stepfather, write his name instead.
4. Write the name of your brother who is nearest your own age. If you have no brother, write the name of a boy near your own age who was most like a brother to you during your early teens.
5. Write the name of your sister who is nearest your own age. If you have no sister, write the name of a girl near your own age who was most like a sister to you during your early teens.

From this point on, do not repeat any names. If a person has already been listed, simply make a second choice.

6. Your wife (or husband) or, if you are not married, your closest present friend of the opposite sex.
7. Your closest friend of the opposite sex, immediately preceding the person listed above.
8. Your closest present friend of the same sex as yourself.
9. A person of the same sex as yourself who you once thought was a good friend but in whom you were badly disappointed later.
10. The minister, priest, or rabbi known to you personally with whom you would be most willing to talk over your personal feelings about religion.
11. Your physician.
12. The present neighbor whom you know best.
13. A person with whom you have been associated who, for some unexplained reason, appeared to dislike you.
14. The person whom you would most like to help or for whom you feel sorry.
15. The person with whom you feel most uncomfortable.
16. A person whom you have recently met and would like to know better.
17. The teacher who influenced you most when you were in your teens.
18. The teacher whose point of view you have found most objectionable.
19. An employer, supervisor, or officer under whom you served during a period of great stress.
20. The most successful person whom you know personally.
21. The happiest person whom you know personally.
22. The person known to you personally who appears to meet the highest ethical standards.

Interpretation of the results

After the form is completed, the material on the GRID can provide answers to a variety of questions about the subject's personal construct system. What is the nature of the constructs? For example, do they make distinctions in terms of physical characteristics (tall-short) or interpersonal characteristics (friendly-mean)? How many different constructs are there? If the pattern of checks and voids for, say, the construct "intelligent versus unintelligent" corresponds exactly to that for the construct "likes me versus does not like me," there is reason to suspect that those constructs are not two but in fact one: "People who like me are intelligent and those who don't are unintelligent." Comparison of the columns rather than the rows uncovers similarities to the subject. Is the self column most like the mother, the father, the successful person, the other males (or females)? The possibilities are numerous. The end product is a sample of the subject's personal construct system and of the way it is used.

Through the RCRT, subjects provide, in written form, their personal construction of the world. Although the format is standardized, all subjects are free to specify the unique dimensions they use for distinguishing among the real people who are part of their daily existence.

Illustrative use of the RCRT in the assessment of thought disorder. Marked disturbances in language and thought are a central feature of schizophrenia. Confusion and blocking of ideas, use of new words with private meanings, and unusual shifts in the direction of thought are quite common. The classic approach to measuring thought processes in schizophrenia uses concept-sorting tasks, but the Role Construct Repertory Test, though a measure of concept-sorting, is distinct in two ways that are relevant here.

First, in traditional measures of concept-sorting, the dimensions of the test are structured preconceptions of psychological theory, and they are imposed on the subject. In contrast, the RCRT requires subjects to invent or interpret concept dimensions according to their personal experience. Because the RCRT is an intra-individual measure of thought processes, it offers a promising methodology for studying deviant thinking.

Second, the content-free nature of the RCRT alters traditional issues of test reliability and internal consistency. From Kelly's perspective, the crucial reliability question is whether a particular sample of an individual's construing is representative: Will the pattern reappear when the individual construes new elements? Here, reliability refers not to properties of the test, but to psychological processes of the subject. Test-retest measures of construct relationships show whether individuals repeatedly apply their constructs consistently.

If we consider the deviant thought processes of schizophrenics from this perspective, two hypotheses emerge:

1. The vagueness of schizophrenic thought may represent instances of *loosened construing.* Interrelationships among constructs common for

most people are weakened or absent in schizophrenics; the confusion that characterizes schizophrenic thought reflects the absence of structure in their construct system.

2. The origin of this weak and inconsistent conceptual structure lies in past experience, specifically in the repeated *invalidation* of personal constructs.

These hypotheses, developed from Kelly's model, provide the basis for a systematic approach to the study of thought disorder. The approach uses the RCRT and assumes that schizophrenics, no less than scientists, construe their experience and personally validate their constructs. To illustrate the approach, we shall describe two experiments.

The first study tested the hypothesis that schizophrenics engage in overloose and inconsistent construing of their experiences (Bannister and Fransella, 1966). Thought-disordered schizophrenics and normal subjects, presented with an array of eight passport-type photographs of strangers, were asked to rank-order the persons photographed on six constructs that normal people usually consider highly interrelated. The constructs were *kind, stupid, selfish, sincere, mean,* and *honest.* As soon as subjects finished the test, they were asked to retake it as if they were doing it for the first time.

Results revealed that the constructs of the schizophrenics were less highly interrelated than were those of the normal subjects, and that their immediate test-retest reliability was much lower. The data support the hypothesis that schizophrenics use overloose and highly inconsistent constructs.

A second experiment (Bannister and Salmon, 1966) indicated that such looseness and inconsistency are most evident in social constructs. Given that constructs differ in the range of phenomena to which they apply, it follows that thought disorder may be more evident in some construct systems than in others. Since schizophrenia is a social phenomenon, thought disorders should be most evident in constructs relating to people.

To test this hypothesis, thought-disordered schizophrenics and normal controls were each administered two forms of the RCRT. The first, a "people" form, used photographs of strangers, and as in the preceding study, the subjects rank-ordered the persons photographed on each of six constructs. They were then immediately retested on the same constructs, but with a new set of photos. In the second form of the test, an "object" form, all subjects ranked a set of 15 objects (e.g., a washing machine) on six constructs (e.g., thin-thick) and then immediately repeated the rank-orderings on a second set of 15 objects.

The schizophrenics did not differ from the normal controls in the consistency or looseness with which they construed impersonal objects. However, they were much less stable than the normals in utilizing constructs about people.

Taken together, the two experiments reveal that thought disorder in schizophrenia is characterized by looseness and inconsistency and that interpersonal construing is its focus. From such results, Bannister has developed a theory of thought disorder based on a *serial invalidation* hypothesis (Bannister, 1963). Because a construct is an implicit prediction, a tightly organized set of constructs leads to specific social expectations; the tighter the construct system, the more likely it is that some expectations will be invalidated. Bannister's hypothesis is that schizophrenics have reacted to such invalidation experiences by a progressive loosening of their constructs. For them, therapy consists of efforts to progressively tighten up their construct systems.

The Clinical Setting

Interviewing. When a therapist and a client meet for the first time, it is necessary for them to get to know one another. Traditionally, the therapist interviews patients in order to make a diagnosis of the past experiences by which they have been victimized. Kelly, however, views psychotherapy as a reconstruction process, in which patients are victims not of their past but only of their construal of it.

Kelly (1955) avoided the traditional word "interviewing" for his discussion of the communication process between therapist and client, preferring instead to speak of *elaborating the complaint and elaborating the personal construct system*. His choice of words alone, perhaps, conveys the distinctive view he held of the human as experimenting scientist. The therapist must come to understand the areas in which the client is experiencing confusion. How are these areas different from other areas? What alternatives exist? When does the confusion occur? Under what conditions is it greatest? What corrective measures have been tried? All these questions serve to clarify the constructs which provide the coordinates for the area of confusion. In a similar way, the client's personal construct system must be elaborated and the core constructs and their subordinate constructs identified. When communication can take place between therapist and client about the client's construction of the world, the two together can plan experiments for testing old constructions and comparing them with new constructions. In the process of elaboration, the therapist seeks to clarify the alternatives so that experiences can be employed to *discover* what is a useful construction rather than to *prove* that an existing construction is adequate.

Psychotherapy.   The psychotherapeutic enterprise is an experiment built upon the model of science:

> The psychotherapist helps the client design and implement experiments. He pays attention to controls. He helps the client define the hypotheses. He helps the client avoid abortive undertakings. He uses the psychotherapy room as a laboratory. He does not extort results from his client to confirm his own systematic prejudices nor does he urge his client, in turn, to seek appeasement rather than knowledge. Finally, he recognizes that in the inevitable scheme of things, he is himself a part of the validating evidence which the client must take into account in reckoning the outcome of his psychotherapeutic experiments.*

Within this context, the *goals* of psychotherapy are:

> (1) that the client has reconstrued himself and certain other features of his world within his original system, (2) that he has organized his old system more precisely, or (3) that he has replaced some of the constructs in his old system with new ones. (Kelly, 1955, p. 941)

Fixed-role therapy.   A discussion of life as an experiment between alternative constructions can be misleading. Life is not a bland, cold, and objective process. The anticipation of future events which provide the validation experiences is important: it is painful to be rejected when the expectation was to be admired. Heavy wagers that are lost may challenge important constructs: such people may lose their role and suffer pangs of guilt; they may experience threat and find their whole construct system endangered.

The therapist, as a good scientist, helps clients design a good research strategy in which systematic reconstruction takes place. One idea Kelly has used is to write a role description for clients that differs from the clients' typical view of themselves. Both then agree that the clients will play this new role for a fixed period of time, say three days. Considerable threat is removed because, in being consistent with their new role, the clients can now do things that they could not do or even consider as long as it was their own construct system that might be threatened by the outcome. The fixed role may be practiced in the therapy room first, with the client and therapist taking turns playing the role and giving it substance. The result of the procedure is often a new appreciation by the client of the range of alternative constructions available, and of the way in which an alternative construction can lead to different behaviors and often to

---

* Reprinted from *The Psychology of Personal Constructs* by George A. Kelly, p. 941. By permission of W. W. Norton and Company, Inc. Copyright 1955 by George A. Kelly.

desired outcomes. Such a brush with reconstruction, under the protective cover of a fixed role, can often provide clients with the personal experience that serves to clarify their place in life as people in control of their own destiny.

International Understanding

Not only individuals must learn to understand one another if they are to communicate as persons, but nations must do so too, if they are to communicate as nations. Of course, nations are made up of people, and it is their leaders who must communicate with one another. Is the problem of leaders of two nations attempting to communicate with each other any different from that of two persons of the same nation attempting to communicate with each other? Perhaps so.

If different nations, with their unique resources and ways of life, acquire unique sets of experiences, then their constructions of nature are also likely to be different. The citizens of each will have different personal construct systems, and each nation itself, as a corporate entity with structure and function, will operate on the basis of a unique construction of events. Such differences have been called "national character." Kelly considers "national construct system" more apt. But from a view of life as an enterprise of cognitive *construal*, international understanding requires more than acknowledgment of national differences; it requires that we rise above the ethnocentrism of thinking that people of all nations should see a given event with constructs identical to our own. Communication requires the ability to "subsume" the construct systems of other people and to see events from the viewpoint of their construct systems.

Although it is a commonplace to acknowledge appreciation of "national character" and to profess the goal of international understanding, such intentions are too often translated into action in the form of trying to get another nation to view an event from the construct system of one's own nation. Little effort has been made to determine the extent to which people from different nations, as well as the corporate enterprise they set up as a nation, have radically different construct systems.

In this respect Kelly was an innovator, spending a year traveling to different nations to study national construct systems. His 1962 paper "Europe's Matrix of Decision" effectively illustrated the practical application of the model of the human as scientist to the understanding of the construction and validation systems of different nations. Using the same kind of content-free techniques (such as the Role Construct Repertory Test) that he had used to elicit the personal constructs of his clients, Kelly elicited and then compared the construct systems of different nations. His work, of course, barely scratched the surface of such a massive undertaking, but the differences he found, even within European nations, seem important enough to support the contention that efforts to explicitly subsume the construct systems of other nations are a prerequisite for international understanding.

SUMMARY

This chapter presented a model of personality that uses the analogy of the human as scientist. The model represents a contemporary cognitive approach emphasizing the manner in which individuals interpret their environment. It deals with people's tendency to make their perception of the environment conform to their own cognitive structures and with the impact of these cognitions on their behavior. Serious consideration is given to the possibility that all people may be seen as scientists in both their aims and strategies.

Scientific enterprises begin with prior facts that represent the totality of the discipline and define the units that will be employed. Facts are construed from a viewpoint consisting of a collection of constructs that fit together logically. Viewpoints contain central assertions that represent the basic assumptions scientists make about the nature of their field. The implications of central assertions are elaborated in the form of theorems, which are more tentative in nature and more subject to direct test. Problems for investigation are formulated in an attempt to extend the range of a field. A hypothesis is a precise statement of a problem that delimits the realm of investigation to a specific subset of phenomena. Through experimental design, control, and precise measurement, scientific experimentation provides evidence of the truth or falsity of the experimental hypothesis. In interpreting the results of an experiment, the scientist may reformulate the problem or revise original assertions and their elaborations.

The model of the human as scientist calls attention to the similarities between scientific and human enterprises. People have at their disposal a backlog of past experiences that represent the totality of their lives to date. These experiences derive their meaning and organization from a personal construct system, which contains core personal constructs representing the person's basic beliefs or values. The practical implications of core personal constructs are elaborated in subordinate personal constructs, which are more tentative in nature and more subject to direct test. In an effort to anticipate the future, people go through periods of circumspection in which they provisionally consider a variety of constructs. A preemption is a decision as to which constructs are relevant to an experience and in what way. The person achieves control over events by making a bet with the world that an experience-to-be, when it arrives, will be of the anticipated type. Personal validation of preemptions occurs when the bet with the world is either confirmed or not. Channelization refers to the interpretation of the outcome in terms of the individual's personal construct system. If they anticipated the experience correctly, people conclude that they understand that kind of experience. If they anticipated it incorrectly, they may need to make revisions within their personal construct system.

On a variety of topics in personality, the model of the human as scientist provides unique and interesting perspectives which depart considerably from previous ideas. The chapter provided examples of the manner in which the model provides new perspectives on the distinction between anxiety and threat, the nature of guilt, the process of communication, and stages involved in creativity and problem-solving.

The traditional goal of assessment is the classification or description of the individual in terms of psychological categories (e.g., neurotic) or traits (e.g., dependent). Within the model of the human as scientist, an attempt is made to understand or subsume the personal construct system of each individual. This goal is achieved through devices such as the Role Construct Repertory Test, which allows individuals to express their own construct system. An example illustrated the manner in which this test has increased our understanding of the thought disturbances characteristic of schizophrenic patients.

As is true of the other models described in this book, the model of the human as scientist has been applied extensively to the clinical setting. The word "interviewing" is avoided in favor of such phrases as "elaborating the complaint" and "elaborating the personal construct system." Psychotherapy is conceived as an experiment built upon the model of science. Fixed-role therapy is a procedure that stems directly from such a scientific model. The chapter ended with a brief description of the application of the model to the broader problems of international understanding.

SUGGESTIONS FOR FURTHER READING

Bannister, D., and F. Fransella. *Inquiring Man: The Theory of Personal Constructs.* Harmondsworth, England: Penguin, 1971. A concise and readable introduction to the model that inquiry and theory-building characterize us all.

Bannister, D., and J. M. M. Mair. *The Evaluation of Personal Constructs.* New York: Academic Press, 1968. Clinical applications of Kelly's ideas to personality assessment and clinical psychology.

Kelly, G. A. *The Psychology of Personal Constructs.* 2 vols. New York: Norton, 1955. Kelly's major work, which provides the basis for the metaphor of human-as-scientist. The first three chapters, containing the central ideas, are also available as a paperback titled *A Theory of Personality,* which was published by Norton in 1963.

Maher, B. (ed.). *Clinical Psychology and Personality: The Selected Papers of George Kelly.* New York: Wiley, 1969. This collection of major papers written by Kelly during the decade 1957–1967 is an interesting extension of the model to psychotherapy and human problems.

21
The
Human
as
Actor

21
The
Human
as
Actor

I. **Principal constructs and their translation**
   A. Parts and routines = positions and roles
   B. Scenery and stage props = setting
   C. Costumes, makeup, and hand props = appearance
   D. Acting = manner
   E. Dramatic realization = showing off
   F. Cast = team
   G. Polite applause = tact
   H. Speaking out of character = treatment of the absent, high signs, and team collusion
   I. Scene changes = privacy
   J. The house and the backstage = regions

II. **Use of the model in personality study**
   A. The nature of personality
   B. Reality and performances

III. **Practical applications**
   A. The use of impression management to control one's hospital fate
   B. The effectiveness of impression management in the hospital

IV. **Summary**

V. **Suggestions for further reading**

The similarity between everyday people and their counterparts on the stage has been noted by numerous commentators on the human condition, but we shall concentrate on the recent and relatively systematic exploration of this analogy undertaken by the sociologist Erving Goffman.

The notion of the human as actor is a natural enough point of view, since the term *personality* itself comes from the Latin word *persona*, which refers to the mask actors in the classical theater held up to denote their character. Also, this conception has much in common with role theory, and apparently the term *role* comes from the *rolls* on which actors' lines were inscribed in the ancient theater. Shakespeare verbalized the role theory, or dramaturgical viewpoint, when he wrote:

> All the world's a stage,
> And all the men and women merely players:
> They have their exits and their entrances;
> And one man in his time plays many parts ...
> *(As You like It*, Act II, Scene 7)

Box 21.1   Erving Goffman.

Photo by Frederick A. Meyer

Erving Goffman is currently a research professor of sociology at the University of Pennsylvania. He received his Ph.D. from the University of Chicago and consequently owes an intellectual debt to such sociologists as Charles Horton Cooley and George Herbert Mead. He has published six books on social behavior which have been widely read and which, according to the magazine *Time*, "cemented his reputation as one of the most illuminating—and disturbing—cartographers of that shadowy terrain where man plays at being a social animal without fully understanding exactly what he is doing." * The simplest statement of Goffman's position is that he views all social encounters as theatrical performances and sees personality not as a collection of traits within an individual but rather as a dramatic effect.

---

* From *Time*, January 10, 1969, p. 50. Reprinted by permission from *Time*, The Weekly Newsmagazine; copyright Time Inc., 1969.

Of course, neither Shakespeare nor Goffman is saying that the world is literally a stage. In choosing a role in a play as an analogue of personality, they are choosing from something relatively simple and concrete that people know something about, the theater, to illuminate an aspect of something complex and ephemeral that they know little about, personality. The value of the dramaturgical analogy is that it helps to make some features of personality clearer, just as any metaphor can communicate certain aspects of an event more vividly. The point is not that the content of plays mirrors interpersonal reality, but that the whole theatrical enterprise models real-life behavior. In a dramatic production words are spoken and behavior engaged in for the purpose of conveying certain impressions to the audience. What Goffman stresses is that people's everyday behavior in the presence of others also involves performances designed to create a particular impression. To explicate the model of the human as actor, we shall be primarily concerned with the strategies and techniques of these performances, or what Goffman calls *impression management,* both as theatrical and as interpersonal strategies.

PRINCIPAL CONSTRUCTS AND THEIR TRANSLATION

When two people enter each other's presence for the first time, each seeks information about the other. On the basis of the appearance, actions, and manner that each presents, the other makes inferences about what the stranger is like—about identity, age, status, attitudes, and intent. It is this process of impression formation (or more exactly, the way in which individuals manage the impression others form of them) that the dramaturgical model is concerned with.

Goffman stresses the fact that we must constantly act on inferences about other people. On the basis of what others say and do, we infer that they *are* a certain way. We continually make inferences about their personalities, but the particular cues on which we base our inferences are not always clear even to ourselves. Goffman suggests that we use two separate kinds of cues—the expression that people *give* and the expression that they *give off.* The first refers to direct communication, the words people say and the information they are intended to convey. The second refers to indirect communication, the wide range of nonverbal behaviors that we also use to judge people. We generally assume that the expressions given off are not performed for our benefit, and we therefore tend to rely heavily on these cues to make inferences about others. Given that this tendency prevails, we are obviously better off if the indirect information we communicate is consistent with what we verbalize. Thus, if dinner guests want to convey the impression that they enjoy their food, not only must they *say* that it is delicious, but they must also *seem* to enjoy it—have a pleasant look, pick up the food eagerly, chew it with gusto, and finish the serving.

Since indirect behavior is often perceived as more valid communication than words, people develop techniques of *impression management,* or ways of using indirect communication to foster impressions that accomplish their objectives. According to Goffman, the *expression* given off by the performer determines the *impression* left with the audience, and the impression that others get or the definition of the situation they accept determines their responses.

The metaphor inherent in this view of interpersonal behavior is, as we have indicated, the theater. As Goffman notes, it is clear at the onset that the model is inadequate, as all models are; that is, the theater differs from real life in numerous ways. The things presented on stage are make-believe, whereas life is made up of real events, most of which have not been rehearsed. Furthermore, there is no audience for real-life performances, or more accurately the audience and the other characters are not always separate entities in the real-life enactment of events, as they are on the stage. Thus, although the concept of audience is not identical in the theater and in everyday interpersonal contact, we readily make the translation. The other theatrical terms can be similarly translated.

Parts and Routines = Positions and Roles

In Chapter 2 we defined a role as a behavioral component of a position in some social structure. In the same way that social institutions are composed of *positions* with distinctive *roles* or behaviors, a play is made up of a number of parts usually played by different actors. If a presentation consists of comedy sketches, each sketch may be referred to as a *routine* or pre-established action.

Is the suggestion that people put on presentations for others and do routines and engage in impression management a cynical view of behavior? An important dimension in making this judgment is the person's belief in the part being played. A truly cynical con man would neither believe in his own act nor have any concern with the beliefs of his audience except to the extent that those beliefs affected the achievement of his momentary goal. Sincere individuals would also portray themselves to be sincere. In either case, the relationship between what they did and the impression their audience received would be the same.

Scenery and Stage Props = Setting

On stage, scenery and props serve the important functions of fostering a given mood in the audience and of conveying important information, such as the location of the action and the period during which it takes place. Similarly in everyday life, the impression that one desires to make is more likely to be created if the setting is appropriate. For example, if doctors or dentists are to seem professionally abreast of their field in technique and knowledge, they can help to create that image with an array of expensive, spotless, and modern equipment. Indeed, since the patient cannot assess how tirelessly the physician pores over the medical literature in private, the lay person must rely on such public, if superficial, signs of competence.

The use of setting and set design to aid in impression management is apparent in the design of a courtroom. Not only must judges *be* impartial; they must *appear* to be so. The central position of the bench between the prosecution on one side and the defense on the other communicates the impression that the judge is unbiased. Similarly, the physical elevation of the bench, which requires others to speak upwards, supports the impression that judges are morally and ethically above the level of the petty disputants who may appear before them. By virtue of these and other physical aspects of the judge's position in the courtroom, one is apt to ascribe to the judge as a person attributes consistent with the position and role of a judge.

Costumes, Makeup, and Hand Props = Appearance

To supplement the general impression created by the sets, actors convey information to the audience about the characters they play by means of costume, makeup, and any hand props they may carry, such as a scepter, a gun, a book, or a mop.

In real-life situations, appearance is even more important than the settings in determining the inferences we make about the personalities of others.

Special *costumes* or uniforms are widely used to identify people in different positions as they engage in their performances. Among those who wear uniforms are police officers, nurses, soldiers, referees, judges, service people, baseball players, airplane pilots, brides, and nuns. For that matter, business clothing is also a uniform, and as such it communicates to others a variety of information, such as the form of address the wearer is likely to expect and in a general way the wearer's sort of work. The terms *white collar* and *blue collar* when used to describe jobs obviously grew out of the fact that the costumes of people who work in offices are different from those of people who work in factories. The prevalence of this difference allows an individual to use clothing to manage the impression that others form. A blue-collar worker who lives in a certain kind of neighborhood may seize the opportunity to foster a middle-class image of himself by going to work in a business suit while carrying a blue-collar uniform—and perhaps lunch—in a briefcase.

Of course the theatrical performer's use of *makeup* has a very direct application to everyday presentations. Not only do many individuals of both sexes use facial cosmetics, but the use of wigs, toupés, hair dye, padded bras, elevator shoes, and contact lenses attests to the importance of physical appearance in impression management (see Fig. 21.1). The elab-

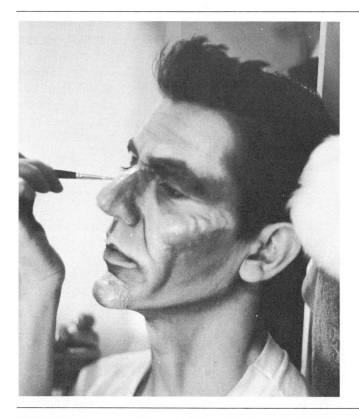

Fig. 21.1. Actor applying makeup for the role of Lincoln. (Photo by Jerry Mitchell. Reprinted from *The Mask of Reality* by Irene Corey, with permission of the publisher, Anchorage Press, Inc., Anchorage, Kentucky.)

orate grooming involved in preparing to start the day or to meet another person regularly involves bathing, brushing the teeth, deodorizing, dressing, combing the hair, and often much, much more. All this activity can be seen as preparation for a performance before others.

Some people more than others put on presentations requiring elaborate costuming, makeup, and preparation. Some find that a few *hand props* or pieces of sign equipment help their role enactment along. On first taking a role, the novice finds props especially helpful in carrying off a convincing portrayal. Ready examples are the tobacco-chewing baseball rookie, the pipe-smoking graduate student, and the briefcase-toting executive trainee. Such newcomers sometimes overact their parts; for example, few people are as ostentatious as the newly rich, as pious as the religious convert, or as strict as the student grader.

Acting = Manner

The characters and their interrelationships are further defined by the actors themselves in what they do and how they do it—in short, in their acting. This element of the presentation includes the way actors interpret their part or play their role.

In real-life situations, people's appearance communicates their general social status, but it is their manner that more particularly informs others of the precise role they expect to play in a given situation. Thus, as Goffman indicates, those who enter a situation with a haughty and aggressive manner give the impression that they expect to initiate and direct the course of the conversation. A meek and apologetic manner, on the other hand, implies to those present that the person expects to follow the lead of others. We forewarn others of our expectations by our manner.

Adopting a certain manner is especially important for service personnel, who need to seize and hold the initiative in their relations with their clients, even though the clients may be of higher status. Whyte (1946) indicates that this process can be seen in the behavior of a waitress:

> The skilled waitress tackles the customer with confidence and without hesitation. For example, she may find that a new customer has seated himself before she could clear off the dirty dishes and change the cloth. He is now leaning on the table studying the menu. She greets him, says, "May I change the cover, please?" and, without waiting for an answer, takes his menu away from him so that he moves back from the table, and she goes about her work. The relationship is handled politely but firmly, and there is never any question as to who is in charge.*

* From "When workers meet" by W. F. Whyte, in *Industry and Society,* W. F. Whyte (ed.). Copyright 1946. Used by permission of McGraw-Hill Book Company.

Dramatic Realization = Showing Off

As a theatrical term, *dramatic realization* has a meaning close to that of *acting* but refers more specifically to actions which communicate key aspects of the story enacted and the character portrayed. For example, if burning a secret note is an important action in the play, the hero does not merely take the note from his pocket and toss it into the fireplace; rather he must occupy the audience's attention with the action, perhaps by withdrawing the note from his pocket, putting it back, taking it out again, holding it up to the light to read it (allowing the audience to see what it is), and only then crumpling the paper and throwing it into the fire. Yet the action must not be *overemphasized*: the audience must be aware of it, but it must not be so blatant that they say to themselves, "He's trying to tell us something."

In everyday speech, the phrase *showing off* has a similar meaning, although it has a judgmental quality and smacks too much of overacting to be a really apt translation. The phenomenon referred to is the tendency in the presence of others to engage in—or to increase the visibility of—actions that confirm a desired impression which might otherwise have remained obscure. For example, if a football player has to leave the field because of pain in his leg, he may as well limp a little to highlight the fact. Or consider the college student who decides to shift the load of books she is carrying so that those around her have a better opportunity to see and be duly impressed by the titles. Such a presentation does not necessarily constitute a falsehood, for she may in fact have been reading books on Zen Buddhism or the theory of relativity. To make the titles visible may merely serve to disclose to others an interesting and easily overlooked aspect of her personality.

In many everyday situations, people may want to demonstrate some aspect of their situation to others. When directly telling them would seem boastful or at best pointless, they may employ a more indirect and seemingly unintentional means of communication. Of course, if the performers overact and members of the audience detect that embellishment is taking place they will label such actors as show-offs and the performance will backfire. At such times, however, especially if the performer is a beginner, the audience may exercise tact in disguising the fact that it has seen through the performance. We shall return to the phenomenon of tact later.

Cast = Team

The members of the cast or troupe of any production are highly dependent on one another for a successful performance. In a tumbling or gymnastic act, each performer must assume that the others will be in the right places at the right time, and similarly, each actor in a dramatic company depends on the others to faithfully deliver the lines which serve as cues for his or her own speeches. A performer who forgets what to do or does something inappropriate may jeopardize the effectiveness of the show.

Like dramatic productions, everyday presentations are often group enterprises. Consequently, the best unit to use in considering the techniques of impression management and the contingencies that arise in their use is the *performance team*. The sense in which an individual's relationship to others constitutes a performance is sometimes difficult to see, but the difference between a team's backstage behavior and the selves they present to others is easier to detect. For example, although open criticism and violent arguments may occur between a husband and a wife when they are alone, before their children they usually try to project a solid front. The same kind of regard for displaying consensus in front of an audience can be seen in the behavior of such teams as army officers before enlisted personnel, doctors and nurses before their patients, and police officers before the public. These cases show a desire among teammates to avoid public disagreement. They also constitute a demonstration that the goal of any performance is to foster in the audience a single definition of the situation, a process which requires suppressing inconsistent information during the performance.

The composition of the teams and the nature of the performance being given can sometimes change rapidly. For example, when a teacher and a class of students confront each other in a schoolroom, each is the audience for the other's presentation. When the teacher is out of the room, the students relax their front and engage in backstage camaraderie; when the teacher returns, they cease behaving in ways that are inconsistent with a presentation of studiousness. But if an outsider, such as the principal, comes onto the scene, teacher and class are suddenly on the same team; they are in collusion to present to the principal, who has become their audience, an exemplary picture of education in progress.

Polite Applause = Tact

The success of a theatrical production is not solely dependent on the performers. In a very real sense, the audience performs for the actors, as well as vice versa. By their response to the action on stage its members communicate to the performers, and their language includes applause, restlessness, and silence. Usually, the audience enters into tacit collusion with the performers to help them put on a good show. Even for mediocre performances audiences always offer at least *polite applause*. Furthermore, if a performer is a beginner or is making a comeback or has overcome some obstacle to give a performance, the audience may tactfully overlook mistakes and even offer pronounced approval.

In everyday interactions the roles of performer and audience are more fluid than they are in the theater. Who is the performer and who is the audience in a typical conversation is arbitrary: as the listener one gives off expressions and has a manner for which the speaker is the audience. So-called good listeners are not considered so because they remain silent and impassive but because they dramatize the fact that they hear and understand what the speaker says; they respond with eye contact, head nods, facial expressions, bodily movements, and verbal comments.

It is clear that the audience is frequently as important to the success of a presentation as the performers themselves. Awareness of this fact may indeed be responsible for the phenomenon of polite applause in the theater and tact in everyday encounters. On the other hand, perhaps we are tactful because we all by turns play the roles of performer and audience. Whatever the explanation, people in the role of audience often attempt to assist performers in their impression management and tactfully avoid opportunities to spoil the show.

The most direct analogy to polite applause lies in the tactful offer to an inadequate performance of a response usually reserved for good ones. As previously mentioned, we sometimes accord this kind of extra consideration to children and beginners. In addition, some people find it in their interest to ingratiate themselves with others by responding in ways analogous to polite applause. For example, the most successful prostitutes are those who give generous approval of their clients' performances, and as Goffman points out, sweethearts and wives sometimes perform a similar role.

Of course, tactful responses carry the danger that the performers will discover that they are being tactfully protected. In addition—to increase the complexity—the audience can become aware that the performer is aware of its tact. When that happens, says Goffman:

> The separateness of the teams will break down and be momentarily replaced by a communion of glances through which each team openly admits to the other its state of information. At such moments the whole dramaturgical structure of social interaction is suddenly and poignantly laid bare, and the line separating the teams momentarily disappears. Whether this close view of things brings shame or laughter, the teams are likely to draw rapidly back into their appointed characters.*

---

* From *The Presentation of Self in Everyday Life* by Erving Goffman, p. 233. Copyright © 1959 by Erving Goffman. Reprinted by permission of Doubleday and Company, Inc.

Speaking out of Character = Treatment of the Absent, High Signs, and Team Collusion

A cast member can engage in various kinds of action to spoil the desired impression. One rather serious kind is speaking out of character. Imagine, for example, an actress playing Joan of Arc. If she were to stub her toe accidentally and burst forth with an exclamation of pain, this petty action would be grossly inconsistent with the image of a martyr about to submit to a painful death for her convictions. There are, of course, many opportunities—usually with less catastrophic results—to speak or act out of character and damage the impression being fostered.

When a team presents itself before an audience of some kind, backstage familiarity among the members is suppressed in the service of a successful performance. However, when teammates think the audience is not paying attention, they sometimes take a chance on speaking out of character for the purpose of derogating the audience. The child who makes faces at the teacher behind his back or who gives a satirical performance of the teacher role for the benefit of her classmates demonstrates this tendency to treat the audience differently when it is attending than when it is not. In a similar manner, employees often refer to their superiors by unflattering nicknames which they would not think of using if the superiors were present. Goffman suggests that such collusive practices help maintain the solidarity of the team by demonstrating mutual regard at the expense of the audience.

Besides tending to treat others differently when they are absent than when they are present, teammates sometimes develop special codes, sign language, or high signs, which enable them to carry on surreptitious communication in the presence of others. This practice is especially common in certain retail sales establishments—jewelry stores, furniture companies, automobile lots—where it may be used to communicate such information as whether the customer's credit rating is good enough to warrant promoting merchandise in a particular price range. In such a situation, the form of communication must be secretive, because the information being transmitted conflicts with the image the salesperson is attempting to convey of a relatively disinterested person who is there merely to help the customer.

Scene Changes = Privacy

Raising and lowering the curtain in a theater serves the same function as opening and closing doors in everyday situations. Doors and curtains often demarcate regions which are temporarily closed off so that preparations for a performance can be made out of sight of the intended audience (see Fig. 21.2). When we invite guests, we usually specify a "curtain time," not merely for the other persons' convenience, but also to make sure the preparation is complete before the performance begins. It is embarrassing to both guest and host for the former to arrive early enough to catch the latter in frenzied preparation. Similarly, the practice of knocking before entering a room minimizes the chances that people will come upon one another too suddenly. It serves no other function than to tell the person within to prepare for meeting someone else.

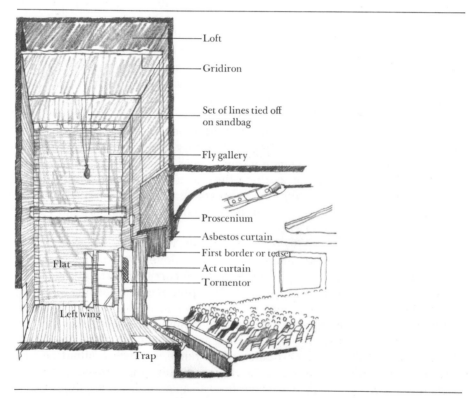

Fig. 21.2. Cutaway drawing of a theater.

Of course, not all people are required to knock before entering or to arrive at a prescribed time. As a way of demonstrating to some friends that we and they have a special relationship with nothing to hide from each other, we let them enter without knocking, or come in through the back door, or arrive early enough to stand around and chat while we are making preparations for the less intimate guests.

The House and the Backstage = Regions

As indicated above, the place where performers give their presentations, whether theatrical or everyday, can generally be curtained off to allow for scene changes. In addition to this temporarily private area, there are other regions which are completely inaccessible to the audience—the regions analogous to backstage. The cast has access to both the house and backstage, but the audience has access only to the house. To understand behavior in everyday settings, we can think of the house and backstage as analogues of any number of front and back regions, such as the workroom of a funeral home versus its reception room. As Goffman indicates:

> If the bereaved are to be given the illusion that the dead one is really in a deep and tranquil sleep, then the undertaker must be able to keep the bereaved from the workroom where the corpses are drained, stuffed, and painted in preparation for their final performance. (p. 114)

The kitchen of a restaurant is another prime example of back and front region contrast. The waiter may enter the dining room of a fine restaurant with a haughty, serene countenance that gives no clue to the steaming pandemonium of the kitchen from which he has just emerged. Indeed, the impression of elegant, personal service would quickly be spoiled if the diner were allowed backstage where dozens of orders are hastily dispatched and smudges on the silver are wiped away on aprons. It is interesting to note in this regard that some short-order eating places without a separate kitchen area attempt to capitalize on their inability to cover up culinary mistakes. One midwestern chain has as its motto, "In sight it must be right."

Thus, despite some exceptions, most settings involve two regions— front and back. Front regions are where the performance occurs and back regions are where actions take place which are relevant to (but inconsistent with) the performance presented to the audience. To these two, Goffman adds a third—*the outside*—a residual region consisting of all places that are not part of the other two regions.

The outside is an important region primarily because people from there, people who are neither part of the audience nor performers, often enter the front or back regions during a performance. These outsiders may well be people for whom the performers will put on a show later, and embarrassment can result if the show they are to view as audience is in conflict with the impression created by the show they interrupt. Such conflict could stem from the fact that the current presentation is either too similar to or too different from the outsiders' show.

To solve this problem, the performers engage in *front-region* control by means of a variety of maneuvers. In the theater the audience's entry is controlled by tickets, and in everyday social events the composition of the group is controlled by invitation. However, some additional staging problems are sometimes encountered, because any general social production may involve a number of small performances for which the roles of audience and outsider change rapidly. For example, if a hostess wants to make more than one of her guests feel that she is especially glad to see them, she had better greet them in the foyer or in some other separated area where her routine will not be overheard by those who have already been performed to. The desired impression is likely to be endangered if a former member of the audience sees the show again. Of course, this kind of problem is by no means peculiar to the role of hostess. Salespeople, insurance agents, doctors, barbers, waitresses, and those in numerous other occupational roles frequently depend on the personal touch to exaggerate the uniqueness of the services they perform for each client.

USE OF THE MODEL IN PERSONALITY STUDY

The foregoing sample of observations about everyday behavior was mediated and given order by thinking within a dramaturgical model, a framework in which the human is viewed as an actor or a player of parts. To the extent that such an analogy provides coherence to previously unordered facts and suggests new insight into the process being modeled, it is a useful tool. Thus the purpose of models is heuristic; it leads investigators to the discovery of similarities between dramatic presentations and personality that were not initially obvious and that suggest hypotheses about the functioning of personality that might never have occurred to them without the mediating analogue. A model is a tool to aid systematic thinking and to help in the construction of an adequate theory, in this case a theory of personality and interpersonal behavior.

Perhaps the chief function of the dramaturgical analogy has been to increase awareness of certain aspects of interpersonal behavior and hence to make them objects of study. Some of the situations Goffman analyzes seem trivial, but he suggests that "it is out of these unpromising materials that the gossamer reality of social occasions is built. We find that our little inhibitions are carefully tied into a network, that the waste products of our serious activities are worked into a pattern, and that this network and this pattern are made to carry important social functions." *

---

* Quoted in *Time*, January 10, 1969, p. 51. Reprinted by permission from *Time*, The Weekly Newsmagazine; copyright Time Inc., 1969.

Before discussing applications of the model in psychological research, we should elaborate two assumptions of Goffman's approach. The first concerns the nature of personality according to the model, and the second concerns the relationship between reality and performances.

The Nature of Personality

As indicated in Chapter 2, role theorists view differences between people as products of the roles they play rather than of traits inherent in the individuals themselves. The dramaturgical model clearly falls within this role-theory view of the nature of individual differences. Goffman suggests that one makes inferences about other people and what they are really like on the basis of cues they intentionally and unintentionally provide. However, he assumes that these cues (which *appear* to be indicative of the person's nature) really tell us about the position the person holds in society and about the demands of the task the person engaged in but nothing about *who* the person is. In terms of the theatrical metaphor, the audience attributes the nature of the character being performed to the person who plays the part although, in fact, the behavior they witness is dictated by the role being played rather than by the player. On the most general level, what the model implies is that one's behavior is largely determined by one's momentary situation and the characteristics of it, as opposed to characteristics which reside within the person. In short, personality does not exist, but roles and people who play them do. The apparent personality is a dramatic effect arising from the manner and appearance of the player, the setting of the performance, and the response of the audience to it.

Reality and Performances

The employment of such concepts as *performances* and *speaking out of character* implies that what is presented to others is unreal and that only what is behind the mask is genuine. However, Goffman assumes that communication out of character, faux pas, and other backstage information have no more claim to reality than do the officially sanctioned presentations with which they are inconsistent. The important point is merely that one frequently finds oneself in the role of performer in the front region at the same time that one is a teammate in the back region and moreover that these two roles are usually incompatible with each other. For example, if one applied for a job and presented oneself as thoroughly qualified, this presentation might be completely accurate; and yet if the employer happened to see evidence of the backstage self-doubts the applicant had, the

"Let there be no doubt, sir, about who is captain."

Drawing by Mulligan; © 1975
The New Yorker Magazine, Inc.

show of competence would be seriously jeopardized. In order to sustain the presented characterization of themselves or their team, people must deal with innumerable sources of information which are potentially destructive to the definition of the situation they are attempting to foster.

The dramaturgical model is easily misunderstood as referring only to those rare occasions when one is blatantly pretending to be something one is not—when one is an out-and-out phony. However, to say that we are all actors is not to say that we are all con men as well. The model implies no condemnation. On the contrary, it merely assumes that part of the human condition comprises communicating with others through words and actions and managing those words and actions to say what we intend. When we tell another our innermost secrets and disclose our most intensely felt fears and desires, this too is a presentation—a presentation of honesty. It may be the truest of truths presented in a completely guileless manner, but if the definition of this scene is to be maintained and we are to communicate our honesty effectively, we must perform well; we must avoid actions and manners which imply dishonesty and deviousness.

PRACTICAL APPLICATIONS

One area of application for the dramaturgical model has been the understanding of schizophrenic behavior. Some investigators (Braginsky, Braginsky, and Ring, 1969) maintain that the sometimes difficult-to-understand behavior of hospitalized schizophrenics is best approached as part of a strategy of impression management.

We shall consider here two experiments which were designed to demonstrate that hospital patients use impression management as a strategy to achieve their personal goals. The assumption underlying this research is that, contrary to the prevailing view, schizophrenics are quite resourceful and effective in governing their own expressions in ways that serve their interests. The more common assumption is that schizophrenics are notably deficient in their ability to carry off a presentation which works to their advantage, but this belief may stem from our ignorance of the mental patient's goals. Although most middle-class individuals find the prospect of life in a hospital rather unappealing, the facilities there offer many persons a more satisfactory life than they could hope to achieve on the outside. What is being suggested is that the aberrant behavior that appears to represent a failure of impression management may often be a successful performance from the patient's standpoint.

The Use of Impression Management to Control One's Hospital Fate

Two kinds of patients that presumably differed in their motivation to remain in the hospital were selected to participate in an experiment. The investigators assumed on the basis of other data that most *newcomers* (those who had been hospitalized for less than three months and for the first time) would be highly motivated to be released from the hospital, whereas the majority of the *oldtimers* (those hospitalized for three months or longer—most of them for more than three years) would prefer to stay. The newcomers were somewhat younger (average age 31) than the oldtimers (40) and a bit better educated (11 versus 9 years of schooling), but the diagnoses of the patients in both groups were comparable, most having been classified as schizophrenic.

The experiment consisted in having the patients fill out a 30-item test under varying instructions. The items were chosen from the Minnesota Multiphasic Personality Inventory and merely required the subject to check as True or False relatively neutral items like "It makes me angry to have people hurry me" and "I gossip a little at times." All subjects took the same test, but for half of them it was entitled "Mental Illness Test" and for the other half, "Self-Insight Test." The instructions for the two groups also differed. In the *mental illness* test condition, the subjects were told:

> This test is designed to measure how severely mentally ill a patient is. We have found that the more items answered True by a patient the more severely ill a patient is and the greater are his chances of remaining in the hospital for a long period of time. Patients who answer many of the items False are less severely mentally ill and will probably remain in the hospital for a short period of time. We would like to find out how ill you are.*

In the *self-insight* test condition, the instructions were:

> This test is designed to measure how much knowledge a patient has about himself. We have found that the more items answered True by a patient the more he knows about himself, the less severely ill he is and the greater are his chances of remaining in the hospital for a short period of time. Patients who answer many of the items as False know less about themselves, are more mentally ill and will probably remain in the hospital for a long period of time. We would like to find out how much you know about yourself. (p. 60)

Both pretest instructions clearly tell the patients how to create an impression of being sick enough to be allowed to stay in the hospital if they choose.

Table 21.1 Mean number of True responses according to treatment condition and status of patient.*

Patient status	Test condition	
	Mental Illness	Self-Insight
Newcomers	13.00	18.80
Old-timers	18.80	9.70

* Adapted from Braginsky, Braginsky, and Ring, 1969, p. 62.

The results (Table 21.1) clearly show the expected effect in the number of True answers given by patients in the different experimental conditions. Newcomers generally gave more False answers on the so-called mental illness test and True answers on the self-insight test, whereas old-timers showed the opposite strategy. In their test responses the patients presented themselves in accordance with the assumptions made initially

---

* From *Methods of Madness: The Mental Hospital as a Last Resort,* by Benjamin M. Braginsky, Dorothea D. Braginsky, and Kenneth Ring, p. 60. Copyright © 1969 by Holt, Rinehart and Winston, Inc. Reprinted by permission.

about their motivations. The interesting aspect of the results is not only that two *different* kinds of patients responded in different directions, but also that the *same* kinds of patients responded in different ways, depending on the apparent implications of their answers.

The investigators designed this experiment to demonstrate in a quantitative way and under controlled conditions the counterpower that patients use to influence the decisions made concerning them. The hypothesized role that the patient's impression management plays in actual staff decisions is summarized in Table 21.2. This study shows that mental patients do attempt to control their own fate by the manner in which they present themselves, but it does not provide any evidence of the actual effectiveness of their presentational strategies. Braginsky and his associates designed a second experiment with that goal in mind.

Table 21.2 The (hypothetical) role of impression management in mediating discharge rates for two classes of mental patients.

Patient class	Ascribed motivation	Appropriate impression to be fostered	Typical discharge decision
Newcomers	I want to leave	I am mentally healthy	Discharged
Old-timers	I want to stay	I am mentally ill	Retained

* From Braginsky, Braginsky, and Ring, 1969, p. 65.

The Effectiveness of Impression Management in the Hospital

In the second study the investigators considered the influence that long-term schizophrenic patients exercised on hospital decisions about themselves. The patients were told two days in advance that they were scheduled to talk with a staff psychologist, and on the appointed day the 30 subjects were all taken to a room to await individual interviews.

Unknown to the patients, they had been randomly divided into two groups whose treatment differed in one important respect. While escorting a patient to the interview, an assistant confided information about the purpose of the interview. In the *discharge* condition he said, "I think the person you are going to see is interested in examining patients to see whether they might be ready for discharge." In the *open-ward* condition he said, "I think the person you are going to see is interested in examining patients to see whether they should be on open or closed wards."

To eliminate possible bias in the interviewer's treatment of the subjects, the interviewer remained ignorant of which group any given subject was in. Each interview lasted only two minutes; it began with the question "How are you feeling?" and continued in the same way for all patients. Afterward the interviewer explained the real purpose of the interview as part of an experiment.

To determine the impression that each patient created by his or her responses to the interview, tape recordings of each session were played at a later time to three staff psychiatrists. They knew nothing about the experiment or the patients who served as subjects; they were merely asked to listen to the tapes and make several ratings including: (1) the degree of illness on a five-point scale ranging from "not at all" to "extremely ill" and (2) the amount of control a patient needed on an eight-point scale from "complete freedom (discharge)" to "maximum control (closed ward and continual observation)."

Since all the patients interviewed were old-timers (as opposed to newcomers), it was assumed that as a group they would be motivated to appear sick enough to remain in the hospital but well enough to enjoy the freedom of an open ward. As expected, the patients who believed the interviewer was considering their discharge presented themselves as quite mentally ill. The three psychiatrists who heard their interviews rated them as significantly less well and as requiring more hospital control and observation than comparable patients in the open-ward condition who thought they might be moved to a closed ward. The open-ward patients made the psychiatrists think that they were reasonably well and that they required little in the way of hospital care.

The investigators made an analysis of the content of the patients' remarks to ascertain which elements influenced the psychiatrists' impression. For example, a count of the symptoms the patients mentioned showed clearly that the patients were quite discriminating as to when they took the role of a crazy person. Not one subject in the open-ward condition mentioned having such serious symptoms as hallucinations and delusions, but nearly half the other patients did. Unlike the schizophrenic in the textbook picture, these patients were quite able to manipulate their own social behavior in accordance with their long-range goals.

SUMMARY

In this chapter we have presented a model of personality which uses the metaphor of the theater. The assumption underlying the model is that everyone acts on the basis of inferences about others which are drawn from observable behavior and that, in partial recognition of this fact, people engage in *impression management,* or attempts to influence the impression that others receive of them. As in the theater, everyday performers learn to make consistent presentations so that not only what they say, but also their *appearance,* their *manner* and the *setting* of their action contribute to the desired impression. Sometimes the success of everyday presentations requires *showing off* a bit or dramatizing some easily overlooked fact about one's self. In life as on the stage, however, enacting a role before others carries with it the possibility that the show will fall flat. Fortunately, members of the audience as well as the performers often have a curious stake in the success of the presentation, and to avoid an embarrassing scene, they exercise *tact* to help save the situation.

The existence of these everyday performances is apparent in the difference in the behavior of *teammates* or partners when they are alone and when they have an audience. In some situations, teammates treat members of their audience with derision in their absence and use *high signs* and other forms of collusive communication in their presence. Frequently, keeping the communication secret is necessary to keep from spoiling the impression being created for others.

According to the model, a basic requirement for convincing impression management, whether on or off stage, is to suppress information which is inconsistent with the definition of the situation one is attempting to foster. Maintaining a consistent presentation requires occasional periods of *privacy* to prepare the scene of the action. In addition, it may be necessary to segregate those who are not teammates for a particular performance into a *front region,* reserving a *back region* (analogous to backstage in a theater) for those "in the know" before whom it is safe to contradict the role played for the audience.

A special view of personality maintained by the model is consistent with the viewpoint of role theory. Specifically, it is assumed that personality depends on the demands of the role one plays rather than on fixed and long-term characteristics of the person. We also discussed an aspect of the approach which invites misinterpretation. The language of role playing suggests that the model applies only to fraudulent presentations and that the real self is different from the presented self. On the contrary, however, the model asserts that people engage in impression management whenever they encounter others, and that this assertion applies to the hygienic acts with which they start every day as well as to whatever outright pretending they may occasionally engage in.

Finally, as examples of the application of the dramaturgical model in psychological research, two experiments were cited which demonstrate that schizophrenics can and do engage in impression management. The first study showed that recently admitted hospital patients (who were motivated to obtain a discharge) and long-term patients (who preferred to stay in the hospital) each answered MMPI items in such a way as to foster in the staff an impression consistent with their personal goals. The second study included a similar demonstration in an interview situation. It also showed that long-term schizophrenic patients used impression management effectively enough to control the judgment of three psychiatrists concerning their extent of illness and need for care.

SUGGESTIONS FOR FURTHER READING

Goffman, E. *The Presentation of Self in Everyday Life.* New York: Doubleday, 1959. The material in Chapter 21 is an extension and elaboration of the position taken by Goffman in this 1959 book. Readers who enjoyed the material will find an endless parade of fascinating insights in this and Goffman's numerous subsequent books.

Brissett, D., and C. Edgley (eds.). *Life as Theatre: A Dramaturgical Sourcebook.* Chicago: Aldine, 1975. A collection of previously published papers on social roles, mental illness, and self-concept. The authors share a common dramaturgical view of personality and social relations.

22
The Human as Computer

22 The Human as Computer

I. **Principal constructs and their translation**
   A. Start = stimuli
   B. Read in data S = recognition
   C. Search = recall
   D. Combine = emotional reaction
   E. Transform = action
   F. Read in data E = environment
   G. Consequences loop = consequences
   H. Modify memory = learning
   I. Print out = introspection

II. **Use of the model in personality study**
   A. Personality development and change
   B. Personality structure
   C. Interpersonal behavior
      1. Effects of initial attitudes
      2. Psychotherapy

III. **Practical applications**
   A. Prediction and diagnosis of personality characteristics
      1. Computer predictions of outcome and performance
      2. Automated personality diagnosis and report writing
      3. Computer simulation and modeling of expert judges
   B. Psychotherapy and attitude change

IV. **Summary**

V. **Suggestions for further reading**

We are living in the Age of the Computer. The application of computer technology to human activities has made possible a whole new range of possibilities which extend from scientific mate selection (computer dating) to travel in outer space. Largely because of the computer, the extent and possibilities of scientific knowledge have enormously multiplied in the last two decades. Given the almost unprecedented contributions of computer technology to science and to human affairs, it was almost inevitable that these awesome machines would attract the attention of personality theorists.

It has become increasingly evident that computers can do many things that were once thought to be the exclusive province of human beings. In fact, there are many processes in which the computer is clearly superior to humans. Computers can play chess, compose music, direct traffic, and perform mathematical feats well outside the range of mere human possibilities. And though occasionally "temperamental" or "stubborn," the computer for the most part can perform such activities endlessly and indefatigably with a docility and dependability that rival the most dedicated people. Small wonder, then, that we should compare ourselves with the computer and see in it many of our own most desirable characteristics.

Although most of us joke about the "humanlike" nature of computers, many personality theorists are beginning to take the analogy quite seriously. This chapter will provide a brief account of the activities of some of the personality theorists who have adopted the model of "the human computer" as the starting point for their scientific investigations. Before starting our discussion, however, we must make a rather fundamental distinction between two views of the human as computer.

In the first view, called the *computer simulation* of personality, the correspondence or analogy between human and computer is direct and quite literal. For example, it might be asserted that the human brain and the computer *operate in the same manner.* Different parts of the brain (known or hypothesized) would then correspond to different parts of the computer, and the rules governing the processes taking place in both systems would be considered identical. With this assumption as a starting point, computers are arranged to operate according to a theory of how the brain operates. When identical problems are given to a computer and to a brain (person) and both systems arrive at the same solution, it is said that the computer has *simulated* (assumed the appearance of) the human brain. Such simulation is taken as evidence of the appropriateness of the original analogy.

In the other view, with which we will be mainly concerned, the computer is a useful device for testing both broad and limited theories of personality. The human characteristics dictated by a particular personality theory are *modeled* on a computer, and the many possible interrelationships and implications of these characteristics are calculated. In *computer modeling* of personality, is it not necessary to assume that the computer is exactly—or even approximately—the same as a person. From this viewpoint, the computer is simply a gigantic calculating machine used to test the many possible implications of a particular theory of personality.

PRINCIPAL CONSTRUCTS AND THEIR TRANSLATION

The basic components of a computer system include facilities for input, output, storage, and control processing. Data and instructions enter the computer as input through the medium of punched cards. Input is transmitted by the control-processing unit to a central storage or "memory" device. The processing unit obtains instructions from a program, stored in memory, and performs the specified operations on the data, which are also stored in memory. The results of the operations are printed out on paper.

The heart of a computer system resides in the *program,* which provides instructions for the numerical, transfer, and logical operations to be performed. And since programs are made by humans, the many ingenious applications of computer technology to human problems must, in the final analysis, be credited to humans rather than to their faithful machine. A computer program, consisting of a series of statements which specify exactly the operations to be performed by the machine, is entered on cards (or tape). The nature of each statement is mechanically detected by the read-punch unit, and the pattern of data triggers the electronic operations of the control-processing unit. The operations dictated by a program may be visualized in terms of a *flow diagram* of the kind illustrated in Fig. 22.1. By tracing the step-by-step operations dictated by a program, we can gain some insight into the manner in which computers work.

Aldous is a computer program named for Aldous Huxley, author of *Brave New World.* He was created by Professor John C. Loehlin of the University of Texas, a pioneer in the computer modeling of personality. When at rest, Aldous is stored in a file as 750 IBM cards, each containing a specific machine instruction. Aldous comes to life as a program stored in a computer with 20 cells available for immediate memory and up to 1,400 cells available for permanent memory. Aldous is perhaps best understood in relation to the computer program described in Fig. 22.1. We will now restate that program, placing a psychological interpretation on each of the steps (Fig. 22.2).

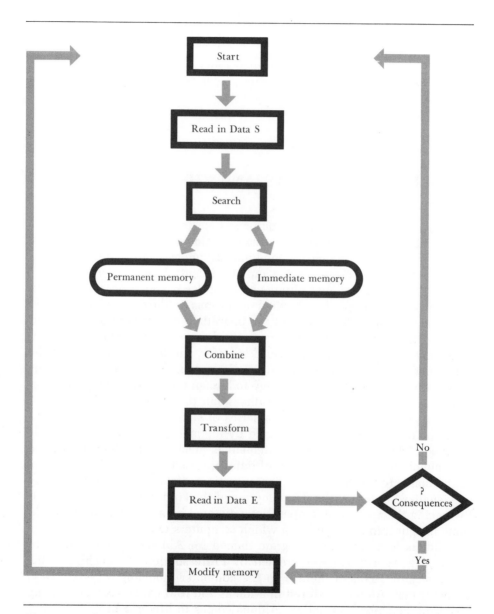

Fig. 22.1.   Flow diagram of a computer program.

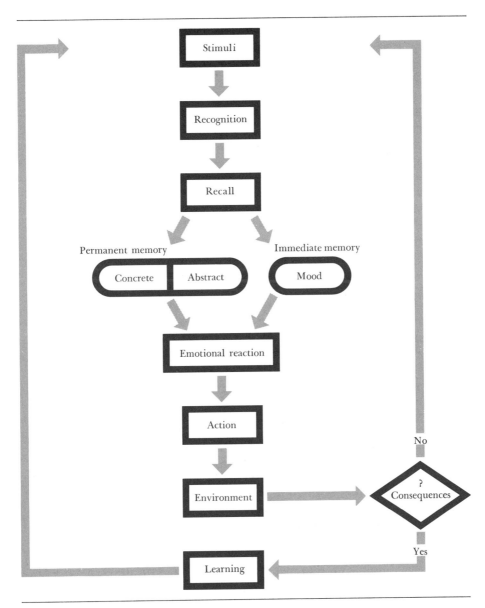

Fig. 22.2. Flow diagram of a computer model of personality.

Start = Stimuli

Assuming that everything is plugged in properly, we must inform the computer that it is time to begin work. A statement on a punched card provides the control-processing unit with a start instruction, and the computer awaits our next command.

In the case of Aldous, the program initiates a sequence of events
which results in the successive presentation of stimuli, i.e., data. The set
of stimuli, designated Data S, represents the *attributes* or characteristics
of the stimulus object. The manner in which these attributes are represented on an IBM card is suggested in Fig. 22.3.

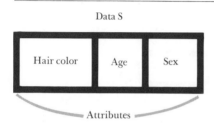

Fig. 22.3. Contents of a stimulus attributes data card.

The three attributes of Data S stimuli specified in the figure are hair
color, age, and sex. Four values each can be assigned for hair color
(blonde = 1, brunet = 2, red = 3, gray = 4) and age (child = 1, teenager = 2,
adult = 3, older adult = 4), and two values define sex (male = 1, female =
2). Together there are 32 possible patterns of stimulus attributes ($4 \times 4 \times 2 = 32$) that Aldous can detect. Note that each possible stimulus object
can be assigned a unique code (blonde, teenage girl would be 122; gray-
haired, old man would be 441). These unique codes can be employed to
specify particular cells in both permanent and immediate memory that
contain information relevant to the specific stimulus objects. In actuality,
Aldous is typically confronted with stimuli that have more varied attributes than those employed in our example. For example, Aldous has
been presented with stimuli that can take on ten values for each of three
attributes, resulting in a total of 1,000 ($10 \times 10 \times 10$) different stimulus
objects that may be discriminated from one another.

Read in Data S = Recognition

The control-processing unit is instructed to read in a set of data from the
read-punch unit. In this instance, we are reading in a specific type of data
(Data S) that is identified in such a way that the unit will recognize it.

Although computers can recognize stimuli with unfailing accuracy, humans cannot. Consequently, Aldous is programmed to "misperceive" on occasion. Misperception occurs infrequently and on a random basis, but when it occurs, Aldous misperceives stimulus objects by ± 1 on one of the three attributes (a blonde, teenage female is seen as a blonde, child female). More typically, Aldous will perceive the stimulus correctly and thus be able to classify it in terms of its numerical code.

Search = Recall

Once a given datum has been read in, the computer is instructed to search its memory cells for information relevant to that particular datum, which has been precoded in such a way that the control-processing unit knows exactly which storage locations are relevant to it. In this instance, information relevant to the datum has been stored in both permanent and immediate memory, both of which are represented by curved boxes in Fig. 22.1 to indicate that they are parts of the computer rather than program instructions.

Having recognized a particular stimulus object, Aldous has two psychological aspects that determine his feelings toward that object: his *attitude* and his current *mood*. Aldous' attitude toward the object in question is stored in a permanent memory cell which has been assigned a code number corresponding to the attributes of the object (e.g., 122 for blonde, teenage girl). The contents of this particular memory cell are illustrated in Fig. 22.4. Note that Cell 122 contains four pieces of information relevant

Fig. 22.4.   Contents of a memory cell.

to Aldous' attitude: the number of previous encounters Aldous has had with objects possessing the attributes in question and the degree of attraction, hostility, and fear he experiences in relation to objects of this kind. To the extent that Aldous' previous encounters have been satisfying, he will feel attraction; if they have been frustrating, he will feel hostility; if the outcomes have been mainly painful, he will experience fear. In sum, Aldous' attitude toward a particular object is represented by a profile of numerical values corresponding to the attraction, hostility, and fear components of his feelings toward that object.

In addition to having specific attitudes toward specific stimulus objects, Aldous has generalized attitudes toward particular *classes* of stimulus objects. Thus, stored in other locations in permanent memory are Aldous' attitudes toward blondes in general, teenagers in general, females in general, etc. Each generalized category is represented by a memory cell of the kind depicted in Fig. 22.4. Aldous' overall feelings are thus jointly determined by both his *concrete* and his *abstract* attitudes toward the object in question.

Aldous' *mood* is stored, appropriately, in immediate memory. There a description of Aldous' emotional reaction to the most recently encountered stimulus object is stored. Mood is described in terms of the categories of attraction, hostility, and fear. As Fig. 22.2 shows, Aldous' reaction to a given stimulus is determined by his current mood, as well as by his abstract and concrete attitudes toward that stimulus.

Combine = Emotional Reaction

The information found located in both permanent and immediate memory is now combined according to a prearranged scheme. The result is a set of values that represents a weighted average of information from both memory sources.

As we have already anticipated, Aldous' emotional response to a particular stimulus is determined by a combination of his concrete attitude, his abstract attitude, and his current mood. But the manner in which these three determinants combine is a function of other aspects of Aldous' personality. Such aspects (traits) must be determined by the programmer. For example, by weighting concrete attitudes more heavily than abstract attitudes, we can program a Concrete Aldous. By giving abstract attitudes more weight, we can program an Abstract ("intellectual") Aldous. Placing heavy weight on current mood results in an Impulsive Aldous. Placing more weight on past experience than on current mood yields a Conservative Aldous. But regardless of which Aldous we are dealing with, a final emotional reaction occurs that may be described by intensities from 0 to 9 for each of the three components of attraction, hostility, and fear.

Transform = Action

The control-processing unit is instructed to evaluate the weighted average of information from the memory units and to transform that information into a new set of values according to a prearranged scheme.

Given an emotional reaction to a stimulus object, what course of action will Aldous take? The first consideration here is the *degree* of action Aldous will take in relation to the *intensity* of his emotional reaction. Typically, Aldous is programmed to take no action in the face of emotional values from 0 to 2; to take mild action in the presence of emotional values from 3 to 5; to take strong action in the presence of values from 6 to 8; and to be "paralyzed" or immobilized if the value is 9. These reaction patterns may be programmed at the discretion of the programmer, however. A Decisive Aldous may be programmed to take strong action in the face of relatively mild emotional stimuli, a Phlegmatic Aldous to respond only to the most intense of emotional stimuli.

Aldous' actions may differ in kind as well as degree. He may *approach, attack,* or *withdraw,* depending on whether his emotional reaction is primarily attraction, hostility, or fear. In general, if his emotional reaction is strong attraction, he will approach strongly; if mild hostility, he will attack mildly. However, two components of high and equal intensity (e.g., strong attraction, strong fear) will place him in conflict, and he may not react at all.

Read in Data E = Environment

At this point, a new set of data is read in from the read-punch unit. The data are coded in such a way that their relation to the transformed data is clear to the machine.

With respect to Aldous, the final course of action chosen takes place in the context of an environment provided by additional data read in as Data E. The input from Data E represents the environmental consequences (for Aldous) of interacting with a particular stimulus object. The manner in which these consequences are represented on an IBM card is suggested in Fig. 22.5. There are three general classes of consequences: satisfying, frustrating, and painful. Since each consequence may take on intensity values from 0 to 9, there are 1,000 ($10 \times 10 \times 10$) possible patterns of con-

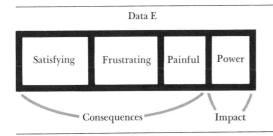

Fig. 22.5. Contents of an environmental consequences data card.

sequences associated with interacting with different stimulus objects. Each pattern of consequences is associated with a specific stimulus object of definite attributes. For example, the consequences of interacting with a blonde, teenage girl (122) may be strongly satisfying, mildly frustrating, and not at all painful (920). A fourth dimension of the Data E input specifies the *power,* or probable impact, of the stimulus object on Aldous. An object of low power will affect Aldous only if he chooses to interact with it. An object of high power will have consequences for Aldous, regardless of how he relates to it.

Consequences Loop = Consequences

The unit is now instructed to make a logical decision about the transformed data in relation to the data read in as Data E. If either of the two data sets exceeds the value of a certain number, the operation will have a consequence; if neither exceeds the value, it will not. Should no consequence occur, the control-processing unit will move on to the next item of input data. Should a consequence occur, the unit will consider the next program instruction. The loop nature of this operation ensures that it will be performed repetitively until all input data are exhausted.

Returning to Aldous, the unit is now instructed to make a logical decision about Aldous' action in relation to the environmental consequences and power of the stimulus object. Recall that there are three consequences to Aldous of any response on his part: satisfaction, frustration, or pain. If an object has primarily satisfying consequences, Aldous is likely to be satisfied; if primarily painful consequences, he is likely to be hurt. But whether or not these possible consequences affect Aldous is also a function of the power of the stimulus object, as determined by the fourth value of Data E. In general, consequences will occur only if the power of the object is greater than 3. If he withdraws or attacks mildly, he will be affected only if the power exceeds 5. And finally, if Aldous withdraws or attacks strongly, he will be affected by consequences only if the power of the stimulus object is greater than 8.

Modify Memory = Learning

In the present example, the consequences of the logical decision involves a numerical modification of memory cells in permanent storage. If no consequence occurs, those memory cells remain unchanged.

If Aldous' actions toward the stimulus object do have consequences, the consequences will be recorded in his permanent memory system. Their extent will, in turn, depend on the amount of previous experience

Aldous has had with that object. If the number of previous encounters with the object (see Fig. 22.4) is small, Aldous' concrete attitudes will be strongly changed. If he has had a large number of previous encounters, the effect of any one encounter will be slight in terms of attitude change. In general, the number of encounters with objects of an abstract class will be greater than the number with a specific object, so that abstract attitudes will be modified less than concrete attitudes. It should also be clear that the experiences of childhood are more formative than those of adulthood.

Print Out = Introspection

This instruction results in the printing out of numerical values that reside in the memory cells. Such values may be printed out before or after a particular input datum has been read in. Values of any cell in permanent or immediate memory may be printed out whenever the program calls for them.

Box 22.1   John C. Loehlin.

Photo by Frank Armstrong, Information Service, University of Texas

John C. Loehlin (holding Aldous) received his undergraduate training at Harvard and his Ph.D. in psychology from the University of California. After a number of years of teaching at the University of Nebraska, he moved to the University of Texas, where he is currently Professor of Psychology. At a conference on Computer Simulation of Personality held at Princeton in 1961, Loehlin presented a paper entitled "A computer program that simulates personality" which aroused considerable interest in what was then a pioneering area of study. Loehlin (1968) has subsequently published a highly readable introduction to both his own work and that of others in the field of computer modeling of personality.

The events we have been describing in Aldous' program are internal to the machine and cannot be observed directly. At any point, however, we can ask Aldous one of three types of questions: (a) "How do you feel about that last object?" (b) "How do you feel about this next object?" (c) "How do you feel about _____?" When asked any of these questions, Aldous will print out the amount of experience he has had with the object and the strengths of his attraction, hostility, and fear toward it. The third type of question may be employed to query Aldous about his generalized or abstract attitudes. Thus one might ask, "How do you feel about blondes?" and he would print out the relevant information.

USE OF THE MODEL IN PERSONALITY STUDY

By human standards, Aldous is admittedly a very simple and incomplete personality. Nevertheless, as Loehlin (1962, 1963, 1965, 1968) has convincingly demonstrated, the study of even such a simple computer model as Aldous may serve to clarify and sharpen the basic constructs of personality theory. Experiments conducted with Aldous have shed light on such diverse areas as personality development and change, personality structure, and interpersonal behavior. We shall now briefly describe the nature of experiments in each of these areas.

Personality Development and Change

The world in which Aldous lives consists of situations which can have satisfying, frustrating, or painful consequences for him. Should Aldous choose to confront such situations directly, he will increase his knowledge of his environment and develop definite attitudes toward a variety of objects in the environment. Should he withdraw, his knowledge of his environment may remain limited in scope and his attitudes toward objects may be prejudiced rather than realistic. Which course of action Aldous chooses will be determined primarily by the nature of the environment in which he lives. Since the nature of the environment is determined by the programmer, it is possible to investigate the influence of different kinds of environment on the development of Aldous' personality.

Aldous' personality development has been studied in two quite different worlds. One was a *benign* world in which situations tended to be satisfying rather than frustrating or painful; the other was a *hostile* world in which situations were mainly frustrating and painful. The course of Aldous' development in each of these environments was studied by periodic administration of a "personality questionnaire" to Aldous. The questionnaire called for a sample of his attitudes toward objects in his environment and thereby provided average scores for his attraction, hostility, and fear. An "adjustment index" was also obtained in order to assess the appropriateness of Aldous' attitudes in relation to the nature of his environment. In like manner, an assessment was made of the appropriateness of his actions, given the nature of his environment.

As might be expected, if Aldous is indeed an adequate model of personality, two quite different Aldouses developed in the two different worlds. In the benign world, Aldous became increasingly outgoing until, after a few hundred trials, he approached the vast majority of situations with confidence and with a benign outlook. In the hostile world, on the other hand, he became increasingly fearful and seclusive and eventually avoided all social contact.

Having demonstrated that Aldous developed in a manner that was consistent with most personality theories, Loehlin (1963) turned his attention to the measurement of attitude change. By changing environments, can one make a Trusting Aldous paranoid or a Withdrawn Aldous outgoing? Loehlin obtained answers to these questions by "raising" Aldous in one type of environment and then placing him in another that was quite different. In one study Aldous stayed in a benign environment through 500 trials and then shifted to a hostile environment. In another he started in a hostile environment and then moved to one that was benign. In both studies, Aldous learned to modify his behaviors in a manner that was compatible with his new environment. In general, the older Aldous was when he moved to a new environment, the longer it took him to adjust to it. Loehlin also found that Trusting Aldous learned the unpleasant nature of his hostile environment faster than Withdrawn Aldous discovered the nature of his new and favorable world. Although Withdrawn Aldous eventually learned to relax, his early bitter experiences prevented him from exploring his new world vigorously.

Personality Structure

Although Aldous' attitudes toward his environment are free to vary with experience, a number of his personality traits are relatively constant throughout his life. Such traits may be thought of as "cognitive," "temperamental," or "expressive" in nature. Thus the experimenter must decide whether Aldous will tend to rely primarily on abstract or on concrete memories. Similarly, he must decide whether Aldous will behave primarily in terms of current mood or past experience. Finally, the experimenter must decide whether Aldous will act strongly on slight emotion or whether he will be sluggish in response to emotional stimuli. To make Aldous abstract or concrete, impulsive or conservative, decisive or phlegmatic, is to impart a "personality structure" that will set limits on the nature of his development.

One can study the manner in which personality traits influence attitude development and change by observing the effects of different trait values on Aldous' personality. In an extensive series of studies, Loehlin (1963) varied one or more trait values and observed their effects on Aldous' development and change in different environments. As would be expected, different personality structures resulted in quite different behavior patterns, which were consistent with the meaning of the traits involved. For example, Phlegmatic Aldous tended to be relatively inert, whereas Decisive Aldous would occasionally "blow his top" in relation to strong emotions. But *all* Aldouses tended eventually to make satisfactory adjustments when shifted from one kind of environment to another. In fact, the similarities in final adjustment among the various Aldouses were more striking than their differences. Loehlin (1963) comments: "In computer models, too, apparently, quite different 'styles of life' may lead to equally satisfactory adjustments." (p. 200)

Interpersonal Behavior

The experiments described thus far have studied the behavior of Aldous in a highly generalized environment on which he had no effect. Such an *impersonal* environment is unrealistic in that our responses to persons in our environment typically influence those persons to respond to us in a definite way. When we attack others, they are likely to attack us in return or to withdraw. Clearly, this *interpersonal* aspect of environments gives them a dynamic quality that is poorly modeled by the computer routines we have considered up to now.

In a more recent series of studies, Loehlin (1965) studied the interpersonal behavior of Aldous by providing him with a "friend" with whom he could interact. Two Aldouses (programs) were stored in the computer in such a way that the responses of each model served as stimuli for the other. Each Aldous was programmed to interpret the responses of a partner in the light of the behavior of his own that had preceded the response. Thus withdrawal by the partner would be satisfying if it occurred in response to attack, but frustrating if in response to approach.

Effects of initial attitudes. In one experiment, both Aldous A and Aldous B were given initial attitudes that were primarily fearful and, to a lesser extent, hostile. Early interaction sequences were brief and were terminated mainly by B's withdrawal from A's attack. As this pattern of inter-action continued, A became less fearful and started attacking B, even when B withdrew. Eventually B became less fearful and began to fight back. From that point on, a relatively stable pattern developed which was characterized by mutual hostility and attack.

In another experiment, A and B were given initial attitudes that were primarily positive and, to a lesser extent, fearful. The early interaction se-quences were characterized by mutual approach and the development of strong positive attitudes—in a pattern that Loehlin called "the honey-moon." Because the honeymooners had not learned how to cope with ag-gression, the first occurrence of an aggressive response provoked a pro-longed "lovers' quarrel." A pattern of mutual affection, punctuated by quarrels, continued until the lovers worked out an arrangement in which each met strong aggression with withdrawal and mild aggression with a positive response. Having worked out patterns for coping with hostility, the lovers eventually developed a long and permanent relationship of an almost exclusively positive nature.

Loehlin performed a number of other experiments using different com-binations of initial attitudes and varying the personality-trait values of the models. In the course of these studies, it became apparent that combina-tions of initial attitude and personality-trait values that result in stable positive relations are extremely difficult to find. The relationships in most of the studies terminated in a state of mutual hostility. Modifying the re-activity to emotional stimuli of one or both participants tended to heighten this effect. Loehlin (1965) comments: "In computer model interpersonal relations, as in other complex systems, there are more ways for things to go wrong than to go right." (p. 581)

Psychotherapy.   In an intriguing series of studies, the behavior of Aldous was again allowed to vary, but the behavior of his partner was prepro-grammed to respond in accordance with different psychotherapeutic pro-cedures. One such therapist ("St. Aldous") was programmed to respond with unconditional positive regard, irrespective of Aldous' behavior. When a primarily negative Aldous was paired with this therapist, the posi-tive actions of the therapist were frustrating to Aldous' attacks, and he rapidly developed a pattern of even more hostile behavior.

Another, more directive therapist achieved some success with a nega-tive Aldous. This therapist was programmed to respond to withdrawal by a mildly positive approach, to meet mild aggression with stronger aggres-sion, and to withdraw mildly in the face of strong aggression. This thera-peutic program brought Aldous' hostility under control and resulted in a marked increase in his positive attitudes. However, when the "cured"

Aldous returned to normal interaction with a free-responding partner, some of his old aggressive patterns returned. Subsequent psychotherapy with the directive therapist was attempted, and that time it had lasting effects. Aldous was finally able to develop effective and positive relationships with free-responding partners.

PRACTICAL APPLICATIONS

Computer modeling of personality is a relatively new field, and foreseeing all of its possible practical applications to human affairs is difficult. From the pioneering work of Loehlin and others, it seems clear that the computer modeling approach will have considerable impact on personality theories, both past and future. Computer modeling is not a theory, but it represents instead an *approach* to the understanding of theories that has considerable analytic possibilities. The most salutary effect of computer modeling on personality theorizing is the increased demand for *explicitness* inherent in the writing of a computer program.

The constructs of traditional personality theory have frequently possessed a rather vague "literary" quality that defied exact interpretation. In translating such constructs into actual computer operations, theorists are forced to become quite concrete concerning the implications of their constructs. In describing Aldous, for example, we have spoken of his "experiences," "attitudes," and "traits." Do we really mean what these words denote? If not, how *should* such constructs be represented in a computer? And finally, as we have already seen, once our constructs are specified in the language of the computer, their interrelationships may be investigated in a way that would not be possible without a computer.

The application of computer technology to the field of personality has not been limited to theoretical issues. In fact, the practical applications have been more extensive than the theoretical. The most prominent applications have occurred in the field of personality assessment, in which computers have come to play an increasingly major role in the prediction and diagnosis of personality characteristics. More recently, serious attention has been given to the possible role of the computer in effecting behavior modification and attitude change.

Prediction and Diagnosis of Personality Characteristics

Computer predictions of outcome and performance.   In applied personality assessment, the psychologist attempts to assign individuals to job categories or training programs in such a manner that the personality characteristics of the candidates match the social, emotional, and skill requirements of the positions. Typically, candidates are subjected to an extensive program of psychological testing involving observational, self-report, and indirect-measurement techniques. The assessment psychologist then tries to integrate the large mass of data obtained into a coherent personality picture of each candidate, and he assigns candidates to positions on that basis.

A number of assessment psychologists (e.g., Meehl, 1954) have criticized this traditional approach on the grounds that the complex integration of psychological test data would be more efficiently executed by a computer than by a psychologist. Given the fact that the assessment psychologist assigns different weights to different aspects of the test data in formulating predictions, it seems logical to assume that such intuitive mathematical operations would be performed more reliably and more accurately by a computer. An extensive series of studies comparing predictions made by assessment psychologists with those made by computers has established, with reasonable certainty, that this assumption is indeed correct (Meehl, 1954; Sawyer, 1966). When large amounts of personality data must be combined in a mathematically optimal fashion, the assessment psychologist is no match for the electronic digital computer.

Automated personality diagnosis and report writing. In hospitals and clinics throughout the country, psychologists routinely administer self-report devices, such as the Minnesota Multiphasic Personality Inventory, score the various scales to form a profile, and then interpret the diagnostic significance of the profile in the form of a clinical report. Some time ago, a group of psychologists at the Mayo Clinic recognized that this relatively routinized procedure might lend itself to automation by means of a computer (Swenson *et al.,* 1965). Consequently, they devised a computer system for automating the entire process of test administration and interpretation from beginning to end.

Patients were administered the MMPI on specially prepared IBM cards that could be directly entered into a computer. The computer converted their responses to scale scores and formed a profile for interpretation. A "library" of interpretive statements, stored in the memory of a computer, represented personality descriptions associated with different patterns of MMPI profiles. A given pattern of MMPI scale scores caused the computer to print out a "psychological report" of the kind illustrated in Fig. 22.6. The procedure is totally automated in the sense that patients are tested and interpretive psychological reports prepared without a psychologist's ever actually seeing the patients or their test responses.

```
                FAIRVIEW COUNTY HOSPITAL
                 PSYCHOLOGICAL REPORT


DOE,JOHN   47 YR OLD WHITE MARRIED MALE
      WARD B12    TESTED 11/02/70


MMPI SCALE SCORES
       L   F   K  HS   D  HY  PD  MF  PA  PT  SC  MA
RAW  05  03  27  14  23  28  24  23  11  23  17  13
  T  53  50  77  72  65  71  75  55  59  68  60  48



BR   3 CONSIDER PSYCHIATRIC EVALUATION.
     K   HIGHLY DEFENSIVE. MINIMIZES OR
         UNDERSTATES PROBLEMS IN SOCIAL
         AND EMOTIONAL ADJUSTMENT.
    PD   SOMEWHAT REBELLIOUS OR NONCONFORMIST.
         AVOIDS CLOSE PERSONAL TIES.
    HS   CONSIDERABLE NUMBER OF PHYSICAL
         COMPLAINTS. PROMINENT CONCERN WITH
         BODILY FUNCTIONS.
    HY   PROBABLY SOMEWHAT IMMATURE, EGOCENTRIC
         SUGGESTIBLE, AND DEMANDING.
    PT   CONSCIENTIOUS,ORDERLY, AND SELF-
         CRITICAL.
     D   MILDLY DEPRESSED OR PESSIMISTIC.
    SC   TENDS TOWARD ABSTRACT INTERESTS
         SUCH AS SCIENCE PHILOSOPHY AND
         RELIGION.
    PA   SENSITIVE. ALIVE TO OPINIONS OF
         OTHERS.
    MF   NORMAL MALE INTEREST PATTERN FOR
         WORK, HOBBIES, ETC.
    MA   LOW ENERGY AND ACTIVITY LEVEL.
         DIFFICULT TO MOTIVATE, APATHETIC.
```

Fig. 22.6. A computer-written psychological report.

Computer simulation and modeling of expert judges. In the practice of personality assessment, expert psychologists frequently have to make highly complex interpretations of personality characteristics on the basis of psychological test data. Such a practice is both time-consuming and very expensive. Recently, psychologists have turned their attention to the possibility of building computer models of such experts in the hope that the models may prove less expensive and possibly even more accurate than the experts themselves.

In one study, Kleinmuntz (1963) asked an expert psychologist to verbalize the logical operations in making judgments of adjustment from MMPI profiles of college students. On the basis of the expert's verbalizations, Kleinmuntz wrote a computer program that provided a partial simulation of the expert's judging behavior. The computer model of the expert was then employed in the "judgment" of adjustment from a new series of MMPI profiles. The model of the expert was found to perform as well as the expert himself or, in some instances, better.

Psychotherapy and Attitude Change

We have already noted conditions which led to maladaptive attitudes and behaviors on Aldous' part and "therapeutic" procedures which appeared to modify such attitudes and behaviors. The theoretical implications of computer modeling for the study of psychotherapeutic transactions should be apparent, even from these brief examples. The possibilities of applying computer modeling procedures to the actual treatment or modification of personality disorders are more remote, although several such applications have been suggested.

Loehlin's (1965) attempts to modify Negative Aldous' attitudes and behavior can be construed as analogues of nondirective and directive psychotherapy. In a more elaborate attempt to simulate a psychotherapeutic technique, Colby (1963) built a computer model designed to simulate the motivational, emotional, and cognitive processes of a neurotic patient during the psychoanalytic hour. Conflicts between acceptable and unacceptable unconscious impulses are resolved by an elaborate program of "defense mechanisms" (e.g., substitution, displacement, projection).

If it were possible for proponents of different techniques of psychotherapy to agree on a common personality model, the relative effectiveness of different treatment procedures could be compared on a computer model of a patient. Unfortunately, different schools of thought in psychotherapy are associated with different theories of personality structure and dynamics, and each would tend to build a model quite different from the others. Nevertheless, the specificity and concreteness demanded by computer modeling could serve to illuminate the underlying assumptions of different schools of thought, as is apparent from the work of Colby.

The greatest potential practical application of computer models to psychotherapy seems to reside in the possibility of representing actual patients by computer models. The extensive data yielded in psychotherapy sessions could be employed in the construction of a computer model of the patient's attitudes, beliefs, and emotions. Should the computer model prove to be an adequate simulation of certain relevant aspects of the patient's personality, a number of promising innovations might be explored. For example, it would be possible for a therapist to estimate the possible effects of a given interpretation on the patient by first trying out the interpretation on the computer model. If the procedure appeared to have beneficial effects for the model, it could then be tried with the patient. Similarly, computer models of actual patients might prove highly effective as training devices in the education of beginning therapists. The inevitable therapeutic mistakes made by the beginning therapist would have less severe consequences for a computer model than they would for a real patient.

SUMMARY

The "humanlike" characteristics of computers have led personality psychologists to give serious consideration to the notion of the human as computer. In computer modeling of personality, the human characteristics dictated by a particular personality theory are used to construct a computer program that calculates the interrelationships and implications of these characteristics. In such a construction, it is not assumed that the computer is exactly or even approximately the same as a person.

In the present chapter, we have described a computer model of personality, which consists of a program of instructions and a number of locations in the memory of the computer. The input data are regarded as stimulus objects with specifiable attributes. Such stimuli are recognized by the model, which then proceeds to search its memory for attitudes toward the objects. On the basis of past attitudes, determined by prior experiences, the model reacts emotionally to the stimuli. Depending on that emotional reaction, the model pursues a course of action toward the stimulus objects. In the light of the environmental context in which such actions occur, there may be consequences for the model which result in modification or expansion of the model's original attitudes toward the objects.

We illustrated the application of such a model to personality study by a series of experiments relating to personality development and change, personality structure, and interpersonal behavior. In general, the computer model behaved in a humanlike fashion. More important, the translation of personality constructs into actual computer operations shed considerable light on the assumptions underlying personality theories in these areas. We concluded that all personality theories would benefit from such a detailed examination of their assumptions and principal constructs.

The practical applications of computer modeling to personality study have occurred primarily in the area of prediction and diagnosis and in that of psychotherapy and attitude change. In the area of prediction, it appears that a computer is more accurate than a psychologist in combining large amounts of personality data for making predictions. Similarly, many current diagnostic procedures which rely on expert psychologists could be executed more efficiently through the use of computer models of experts than of the experts themselves. The possibilities of applying computer modeling procedures to the actual treatment or modification of personality disorders are more remote. Of several such applications that have been suggested, the most promising is the possibility of representing actual patients by computer models.

SUGGESTIONS FOR FURTHER READING

Abelson, R. P. Simulation of social behavior. In G. Lindzey and E. Aronson (eds.), *Handbook of Social Psychology,* Vol. 2. Reading, Mass.: Addison-Wesley, 1968, pp. 274–356. A detailed survey of computer models of social behavior with special interest for students of social psychology.

Loehlin, J. C. *Computer Models of Personality.* New York: Random House, 1968. A highly readable introduction to computer models of personality, written for the beginning student. Aldous is described along with models developed by other authors.

Tomkins, S. S., and S. Messick (eds.). *Computer Simulation of Personality.* New York: Wiley, 1963. A collection of papers from an early conference on computer models of personality. In Chapter 13, George Kelly discusses Aldous and other issues in simulation.

References

Abelson, H., R. Cohen, E. Heaton, and C. Suder. Public attitudes toward and experience with erotic materials. *Technical Reports of the Commission on Obscenity and Pornography*, Vol. 6. Washington, D.C.: U.S. Government Printing Office, 1970.

Abelson, R. P. Simulation of social behavior. In G. Lindzey and E. Aronson (eds.), *Handbook of Social Psychology*, Vol. 2. Reading, Mass.: Addison-Wesley, 1968, pp. 274–356.

Acker, L. E., and A. E. Edwards. Transfer of vasoconstriction over a bipolar meaning dimension. *Journal of Experimental Psychology*, 1964, **67,** 1–6.

Ader, R., and P. M. Conklin. Handling of pregnant rats: effects on emotionality of their offspring. *Science*, 1963, **142,** 411–412.

Ainsworth, M. D. S., and S. M. Bell. Attachment, exploration, and separation: a discussion illustrated by the behavior of one-year-olds in a strange situation. Paper presented at the annual meeting of the American Psychological Association, San Francisco, 1968.

Al-issa, I., and W. Dennis (eds.). *Cross-cultural Studies of Behavior*. New York: Holt, 1970.

Allport, G. W. *Personality: A Psychological Interpretation*. New York: Holt, 1937.

Allport, G. W. Scientific models and human morals. Presidential address to Division of Personality and Social Psychology, 1946. *Psychological Review*, 1947, **54,** 182–192.

Allport, G. W. *Becoming*. New Haven: Yale University Press, 1955.

Allport, G. W. The fruits of eclecticism: Bitter or sweet? In G. W. Allport, *The Person in Psychology*. Boston: Beacon Press, 1968, pp. 3–27.

Amir, Y. Contact hypothesis in ethnic relations. *Psychological Bulletin*, 1969, **71,** 319–342.

Amoroso, D. M., M. Brown, M. Preusse, E. E. Ware, and D. W. Pilkey. An investigation of behavioral, psychological, and physiological reactions to pornographic stimuli.

Technical Reports of the Commission on Obscenity and Pornography, Vol. 8. Washington, D.C.: U.S. Government Printing Office, 1970.

Ardrey, R. A tiger about to stir up a mare's nest. *Life,* June 20, 1969, p. 9.

Aronfreed, J., and A. Reber. Internalized behavioral suppression and the timing of social punishment. *Journal of Personality and Social Psychology,* 1965, **1,** 3–16.

Aronson, E., and D. Linder. Gain and loss of esteem as determinants of interpersonal attraction. *Journal of Experimental Social Psychology,* 1965, **1,** 156–171.

Asch, S. E. *Social Psychology.* New York: Prentice-Hall, 1952.

Ayllon, T., and N. H. Azrin. The measurement and reinforcement of behavior of psychotics. *Journal of the Experimental Analysis of Behavior,* 1965, **8,** 357–383.

Ayllon, T., and N. H. Azrin. *The Token Economy.* New York: Appleton-Century-Crofts, 1968.

Azrin, N. H., and R. R. Hutchinson. Conditioning of the aggressive behavior of pigeons by a fixed-interval schedule of reinforcement. *Journal of Experimental Analysis of Behavior,* 1967, **10,** 395–402.

Azrin, N. H., R. R. Hutchinson, and D. F. Hake. Attack, avoidance, and escape reactions to aversive shock. *Journal of Experimental Analysis of Behavior,* 1967, **10,** 131–148.

Azrin, N. H., R. R. Hutchinson, and R. McLaughlin. The opportunity for aggression as an operant reinforcer during aversive stimulation. *Journal of Experimental Analysis of Behavior,* 1965, **8,** 171–180.

Bagby, J. A cross-cultural study of perceptual predominance in binocular rivalry. *Journal of Abnormal and Social Psychology,* 1959, **54,** 33–34.

Baldwin, A. L. A cognitive theory of socialization. In D. A. Goslin (ed.), *Handbook of Socialization Theory and Research.* Chicago: Rand McNally, 1969, pp. 325–346.

Bandura, A. Influence of models' reinforcement contingencies on the acquisition of imitative responses. *Journal of Personality and Social Psychology,* 1965, **1,** 589–595.

Bandura, A. *Principles of Behavior Modification.* New York: Holt, Rinehart and Winston, 1969.

Bandura, A. *Social Learning Theory.* Morristown, N.J.: General Learning Press, 1971.

Bandura, A. (ed.). *Psychological Modeling: Conflicting Theories.* Chicago: Aldine-Atherton, 1971.

Bandura, A. *Aggression: A Social Learning Analysis.* Englewood Cliffs, N.J.: Prentice-Hall, 1973.

Bandura, A., and F. L. Menlove. Factors determining vicarious extinction of avoidance behavior through symbolic modeling. *Journal of Personality and Social Psychology,* 1968, **8,** 99–108.

Bandura, A., D. Ross, and S. A. Ross. Imitation of film-mediated aggressive models. *Journal of Abnormal and Social Psychology,* 1963, **66,** 3–11. (a)

Bandura, A., D. Ross, and S. A. Ross. A comparative test of the status envy, social power, and the secondary reinforcement theories of identificatory learning. *Journal of Abnormal and Social Psychology,* 1963, **67,** 601–607. (b)

Bandura, A., and R. H. Walters. *Adolescent Aggression.* New York: Ronald Press, 1959.

Bandura, A., and R. H. Walters. *Social Learning and Personality Development*. New York: Holt, Rinehart and Winston, 1963.

Bannister, D. The genesis of schizophrenic thought disorder: a serial invalidation hypothesis. *British Journal of Psychiatry*, 1963, **109**, 680–686.

Bannister, D., and F. Fransella. A grid test of schizophrenic thought disorder. *British Journal of Social and Clinical Psychology*, 1966, **5**, 95–102.

Bannister, D., and F. Fransella. *Inquiring Man: The Theory of Personal Constructs*. Harmondsworth, England: Penguin, 1971.

Bannister, D., and J. M. M. Mair. *The Evaluation of Personal Constructs*. New York: Academic Press, 1968.

Bannister, D., and P. Salmon. Schizophrenic thought disorder: specific or diffuse? *British Journal of Medical Psychology*, 1966, **39**, 215–219.

Bardwick, J. M. *Psychology of Women: A Study of Bio-Cultural Conflicts*. New York: Harper and Row, 1971.

Baron, Robert A. Threatened retaliation from the victim as an inhibitor of physical aggression. *Journal of Research in Personality*, 1973, **7**, 103–115.

Barron, F. *Creativity and Personal Freedom*. Princeton: Van Nostrand, 1968.

Barron, F. *Creative Person and Creative Process*. New York: Holt, Rinehart and Winston, 1969.

Barry, H., I. Child, and M. Bacon. Relation of child training to subsistence economy. *American Anthropologist*, 1959, **61**, 51–63.

Bartlett, F. C. *Remembering*. Cambridge: Cambridge University Press, 1932.

Becker, W. C. *Parents are Teachers*. Champaign, Illinois: Research Press, 1971.

Benedict, R. (1934) *Patterns of Culture*, Cambridge, Mass.: Riverside Press, 1961.

Bentler, P. M. Heterosexual behavior assessment: I. Males. *Behavior Research and Therapy*, 1968, **6**, 21–25.

Bergin, A. E., and R. M. Suinn. Individual psychotherapy and behavior therapy, in *Annual Review of Psychology*. Palo Alto: Annual Reviews, Inc., 1975, **27**, 509–556.

Berkowitz, L. The effects of observing violence. *Scientific American*, 1964, **210**, 35–41.

Berkowitz, L. Simple views of aggression: an essay review. *American Scientist*, 1969, **57**, 372–383.

Bernardin, A. C., and R. Jessor. A construct validation of the EPPS with respect to dependency. *Journal of Consulting Psychology*, 1957, **21**, 63–67.

Berry, T. W. Independence and conformity in subsistence-level societies. *Journal of Personality and Social Psychology*, 1967, **7**, 415–418.

Biber, H., L. B. Miller, and J. L. Dyer. Feminization in preschool. *Developmental Psychology*, 1972, **7**, 86.

Biddle, B. J., and E. J. Thomas (eds.). *Role Theory: Concepts and Research*. New York: Wiley, 1966.

Bishop, J. A., and L. M. Cook. Moths, melanism and clean air. *Scientific American*, 1975, **232**, 90–99.

Boller, P. F. *Quotemanship*. Dallas: S M U Press, 1967.

Boring, E. G. *A History of Experimental Psychology*, 2nd ed. New York: Appleton-Century-Crofts, 1950.

Bowlby, J., M. B. Ainsworth, M. Boston, and D. Rosenbluth. Effects of mother-child separation. *British Journal of Medical Psychology*, 1956, **29**, 211–247.

Brady, J. P., and E. E. Levitt. The relation of sexual preferences to sexual experiences. *Psychological Record*, 1965, **15**, 377–384. (a)

Brady, J. P., and E. E. Levitt. The scalability of sexual experiences. *Psychological Record*, 1965, **15**, 275–279. (b)

Braginsky, B. M., D. D. Braginsky, and K. Ring. *Methods of Madness*, New York: Holt, Rinehart and Winston, 1969.

Bray, R. M., G. L. Clore, S. Itkin, and P. Murphy. Attraction among black and white children under conditions of racial equality: A field study. Paper presented at Southeastern Psychological Association, Atlanta, March, 1975.

Brewer, M. B. Determinants of social distance among East African tribal groups, *Journal of Personality and Social Psychology*, 1968, **10**, 279–289.

Brissett, D., and C. Edgley (eds.). *Life as Theatre: A Dramaturgical Sourcebook*. Chicago: Aldine, 1975.

Broadhurst, P. L. Experiments in psychogenetics: applications of biometrical genetics to the inheritance of behavior. In H. J. Eysenck (ed.), *Experiments in Personality*, Vol. 1: *Psychogenetics and Psychopharmacology*. London: Routledge and Kegan Paul, 1960.

Broadhurst, P. L. Analysis of maternal effects in the inheritance of behavior. *Animal Behavior*, 1961, **9**, 129–141.

Brook, P. Filming a masterpiece. *Observer Weekend Review*, July 26, 1964.

Brown, J. S. Gradients of approach and avoidance responses and their relation to level of motivation. *Journal of Comparative and Physiological Psychology*, 1948, **41**, 450–465.

Byrne, D., and J. Lamberth. The effect of erotic stimuli on sex arousal evaluative responses and subsequent behavior. *Technical Reports of the Commission on Obscenity and Pornography*, Vol. 8. Washington, D.C.: U.S. Government Printing Office, 1970.

Cairns, R. B., and M. Lewis. Dependency and the reinforcement value of a verbal stimulus. *Journal of Consulting Psychology*, 1962, **26**, 1–8.

Campbell, Colen. Transcendence is as American as Ralph Waldo Emerson. *Psychology Today*, April 1974, pp. 37–38.

Campbell, D. T. Distinguishing differences in perception from failures of communication in cross-cultural studies. In F. S. C. Northrop and H. H. Livingston (eds.), *Cross-cultural Understanding: Epistemology and Anthropology*. New York: Harper and Row, 1964, pp. 308–336.

Carthy, J. D., and F. J. Ebling (eds.). *The Natural History of Aggression*. New York: Academic Press, 1965.

Casey, M. D., C. E. Blank, D. R. K. Street, L. J. Segall, J. H. McDougall, P. J. McGrath, and J. L. Skinner. YY chromosomes and antisocial behaviour. *Lancet*, 1966, **2**, 859–860.

Cattell, R. B. *The Scientific Analysis of Personality*. Baltimore: Penguin, 1965.

Chomsky, N. Review of Skinner's *Verbal Behavior*. *Language*, 1959, **35**, 26–58.

Clark, R. A. The projective measurement of experimentally induced levels of sexual motivation. *Journal of Experimental Psychology*, 1952, **44**, 391–399.

Colby, K. M. Computer simulation of a neurotic process. In S. S. Tomkins and S. Messick (eds.), *Computer Simulation of Personality.* New York: Wiley, 1963, pp. 165–179.

Conly, R. L. Porpoises: our friends in the sea. *National Geographic,* 1966, **130,** September, pp. 396–424.

Cook, L. M., R. R. Askew, and J. A. Bishop. Increasing frequency of the typical form of the peppered moth in Manchester. *Nature,* 1970, **227,** 1155.

Cook, R. F., and R. H. Fosen. Pornography and the sex offender: Patterns of exposure and immediate arousal effects of pornographic stimuli. *Technical Reports of the Commission on Obscenity and Pornography,* Vol. 7. Washington, D.C.: U.S. Government Printing Office, 1970.

Court-Brown, W. M. Sex chromosomes and the law. *Lancet,* 1962, **2,** 508.

Court-Brown, W. M. Males with an XYY sex chromosome complement. *Journal of Medical Genetics,* 1968, **5,** 341–359.

Covington, M. V. The cognitive curriculum: a process-oriented approach to education. In J. Hellmuth (ed.), *Cognitive Studies,* Vol. I. New York: Brunner/Mazel, 1970, pp. 491–502.

Crichton, M. *The Terminal Man.* New York: Knopf, 1972.

Cronbach, L. J., and P. E. Meehl. Construct validity in psychological tests. *Psychological Bulletin,* 1955, **52,** 281–302.

Crowe, R. R. The adopted offspring of women criminal offenders: A study of their arrest records. *Archives of General Psychiatry,* 1972, **27,** 600–603.

Dahlstrom, W. G., and G. S. Welsh. *An MMPI Handbook: A Guide to Use in Clinical Research and Practice.* Minneapolis: University of Minnesota Press, 1960.

Daly, R. F. Neurological abnormalities in XYY males. *Nature,* 1969, **221,** 472–473.

D'Andrade, R. G. Sex differences and cultural institutions. In E. E. Maccoby (ed.), *The Development of Sex Differences.* Stanford: Stanford University Press, 1966, pp. 174–204.

Darden, E. Masculinity-femininity body rankings by males and females. *Journal of Psychology,* 1972, **80,** 205–212.

Dart, R. The predatory transition from ape to man. *International Anthropological and Linguistic Review,* 1953, **1,** 201–219.

Darwin, C. R. *On the Origin of Species by Means of Natural Selection, or, the Preservation of Favoured Races in the Struggle for Life.* London: J. Murray, 1859.

Defries, G. C., and G. E. McClearn. Social dominance and Darwinian fitness in the laboratory mouse. *American Naturalist,* 1970, **104,** 408–411.

Denenberg, V. H. Stimulation in infancy, emotional reactivity, and exploratory behavior. In D. C. Glass (ed.), *Neurophysiology and Emotion.* New York: Rockefeller University Press, 1967.

Denenberg, V. H., G. A. Hudgens, and M. X. Zarrow. Mice reared with rats: modification of behavior by early experience with another species. *Science,* 1964, **143,** 380–381.

Denenberg, V. H., R. E. Paschke, and M. X. Zarrow. Killing of mice by rats prevented by early interaction between the two species. *Psychonomic Science,* 1968, **11,** 39.

Denenberg, V. H., K. M. Rosenberg, R. Paschke, and M. X. Zarrow. Mice reared with rat aunts: effects on plasma corticosterone and open field activity. *Nature,* 1969, **221,** 73–74.

Denenberg, V. H., and M. X. Zarrow. Rat pax. *Psychology Today*, 1970, **3**, 45–47; 66–67.

Dibiase W. J., and L. A. Hjelle. Body-image stereotype and body-type preferences among male college students. *Perceptual and Motor Skills*, 1968, **27**, 1143–1146.

Dollard, J., and N. E. Miller. *Personality and Psychotherapy*, New York: McGraw-Hill, 1950.

Dornbusch, S. M. Afterword. In E. E. Maccoby (ed.), *The Development of Sex Differences*. Stanford: Stanford University Press, 1966, pp. 205–219.

Eaton, W. O., and G. L. Clore. Interracial imitation at a summer camp. *Journal of Personality and Social Psychology*, 1976, in press.

Edwards, A. L. *The Social Desirability Variable in Personality Assessment and Research*. New York: Dryden, 1957.

Edwards, A. L. *Edwards Personal Preference Schedule*, New York: Psychological Corporation, 1959.

Edwards, A. L. *The Measurement of Personality Traits by Scales and Inventories*. New York: Holt, 1970.

Edwards, D. A. Mice: fighting by neonatally androgenized females. *Science*, 1968, **161**, 1027–1028.

Edwards, W., H. Lindman, and L. D. Phillips. Emerging technologies for making decisions. *New Directions in Psychology II*. New York: Holt, Rinehart and Winston, 1965, pp. 259–325.

Eichenwald, H. F., and P. C. Fry. Nutrition and learning. *Science*, 1969, **163**, 644–648.

Elkind, D. *Children and Adolescents: Interpretative Essays on Jean Piaget*. New York: Oxford University Press, 1970.

Elkind, D. *Children and Adolescents: Interpretive Essays on Jean Piaget*, 2nd ed. New York: Oxford University Press, 1974.

Ellis, A. *The American Sexual Tragedy*, 2nd ed. New York: Lyle Stuart, 1962.

Epstein, S. The measurement of drive and conflict in humans: theory and experiment. In M. R. Jones (ed.), *Nebraska Symposium on Motivation*. Lincoln: University of Nebraska Press, 1962, pp. 127–206.

Erickson, C. J., and D. S. Lehrman. Effect of castration of male ring doves upon ovarian activity of females. *Journal of Comparative and Physiological Psychology*, 1964, **58**, 164–166.

Erikson, E. H. *Childhood and Society*. New York: Norton, 1950.

Erikson, K. T. Patient role and social uncertainty: a dilemma of the mentally ill. *Psychiatry*, 1957, **20**, 263–274.

"The Facts on Transcendental Meditation," *Psychology Today*, April 1974, pp. 37–46.

Farnsworth, P. R. A social effect on the perception of facial resemblance. *Journal of Social Psychology*, 1965, **65**, 221–223.

Feder, H. H., and R. E. Whalen. Feminine behavior in neonatally castrated and estrogen-treated male rats. *Science*, 1965, **147**, 306–307.

Feffer, M. Symptom expression as a form of primitive decentering. *Psychological Review*, 1967, **74**, 16–28.

Feffer, M. Developmental analysis of interpersonal behavior. *Psychological Review*, 1970, **77**, 197–214.

Fenichel, O. *The Psychoanalytic Theory of Neurosis*. New York: Norton, 1945.

Ferster, C. B., and B. F. Skinner. *Schedules of Reinforcement*. New York: Appleton-Century-Crofts, 1957.

Feshbach, S. The function of aggression and the regulation of aggressive drive. *Psychological Review*, 1964, **71**, 257–272.

Fiske, D. W. *Measuring the Concepts of Personality*. Chicago: Aldine, 1971.

Flanders, J. P. A review of research on imitative behavior. *Psychological Bulletin*, 1968, **69**, 316–337.

Flavell, J. H. *The Developmental Psychology of Jean Piaget*. Princeton: Van Nostrand, 1963.

Ford, C. S., and F. A. Beach. *Patterns of Sexual Behavior*. New York: Harper and Row, 1951.

Forssman, H., and G. Hambert. Chromosomes and antisocial behavior. *Excerpta Criminology*, 1967, **7**, 113–117.

Fox, R. In the beginning: aspects of hominid behavioural evolution. *Man*, 1967, **2**, 415–433.

Freedman, D. An ethological approach to the genetical study of human behavior. In S. G. Vandenberg (ed.), *Methods and Goals in Human Behavior Genetics*. New York: Academic Press, 1965.

Freedman, D. G. Smiling in blind infants and the issue of innate vs. acquired. *Journal of Child Psychology and Psychiatry*, 1964, **5**, 171–184.

Freedman, D. G. *Human Infancy: An Evolutionary Perspective*. Hillsdale, New Jersey: Lawrence Erlbaum Associates, 1974.

Freedman, L. Z., and A. Roe. Evolution and human behavior. In A. Roe and G. G. Simpson (eds.), *Behavior and Evolution*. New Haven: Yale University Press, 1958, pp. 455–479.

Freeman, D. Human aggression in anthropological perspective. In J. D. Carthy and F. J. Ebling (eds.), *The Natural History of Aggression*. New York: Academic Press, 1964, pp. 109–118.

Freud, S. (1895) Project for a scientific psychology. In J. Strachey (ed.), *The Standard Edition of the Complete Psychological Works of Sigmund Freud*, Vol. 1. London: Hogarth Press, 1953, pp. 295–397.

Freud, S. (1900) The interpretation of dreams. *Standard Edition*, Vols. 4 and 5, 1953.

Freud, S. (1905) Three essays on the theory of sexuality. *Standard Edition*, Vol. 7, 1953, pp. 130–243.

Freud, S. (1911) Psychoanalytic notes on an autobiographical account of a case of paranoia (dementia paranoides). *Standard Edition*, Vol. 12, 1958, pp. 3–84.

Freud, S. (1920) Beyond the pleasure principle. *Standard Edition*, Vol. 18, 1955, pp. 7–64.

Freud, S. Why war? In J. Strachey (ed.), *Collected Papers*, Vol. 5. London: Hogarth Press, 1950, pp. 273–287.

Freud, S. *The Standard Edition of the Complete Psychological Works*, J. Strachey (ed.). London: Hogarth Press, 1953-

Freud, S. The interpretation of dreams. *Standard Edition,* Vols. 4 and 5. London: Hogarth Press, 1953.

Freud, S. The psychopathology of everyday life. *Standard Edition,* Vol. 6. London: Hogarth Press, 1960.

Freud, S. The ego and the id. *Standard Edition,* Vol. 19. London: Hogarth Press, 1961.

Freud, S. *The Complete Introductory Lectures on Psychoanalysis* (Translated and edited by James Strachey). New York: Norton, 1966.

Friedan, B. *The Feminine Mystique.* New York: Dell, 1963.

Fuller, J. L., and M. B. Waller. Is early experience different? In E. L. Bliss (ed.), *Roots of Behavior,* New York: Harper and Row, 1962.

Furth, H. G. *Piaget for Teachers.* Englewood Cliffs, N.J.: Prentice-Hall, 1970.

German, J. Studying human chromosomes today. *American Scientist,* 1970, **58,** 182–201.

Gewirtz, J. L. Deprivation and satiation of social stimuli as determinants of their reinforcing efficacy. In J. P. Hill (ed.), *Minnesota Symposium on Child Psychology,* Vol. 1. Minneapolis: University of Minnesota Press, 1967, pp. 3–56.

Gewirtz, J. L. (ed.). *Attachment and Dependency.* New York: Halsted, 1972.

Ginsburg, B. E. Genetic parameters in behavioral research. In J. Hirsch (ed.), *Behavior-Genetic Analysis.* New York: McGraw-Hill, 1967, pp. 135–153.

Ginsburg, H., and S. Opper. *Piaget's Theory of Intellectual Development: An Introduction.* Englewood Cliffs, N.J.: Prentice-Hall, 1969.

Gisvold, D. A validity study of the autonomy and deference subscales of the EPPS. *Journal of Consulting Psychology,* 1958, **22,** 445–447.

Goffman, E. *The Presentation of Self in Everyday Life.* Garden City, N.Y.: Doubleday, 1959.

Goldfarb, W. Variations in adolescent adjustment of institutionally reared children. *American Journal of Orthopsychiatry,* 1947, **17,** 449–457.

Goldstein, K. *The Organism.* New York: American Book, 1939.

Goldstein, M. J., H. S. Kant, L. L. Judd, C. J. Rice, and R. Green. Exposure to pornography and sexual behavior in deviant and normal groups. *Technical Reports of the Commission on Obscenity and Pornography,* Vol. 7. Washington, D.C.: U.S. Government Printing Office, 1970.

Goodwin, D. W., F. Schulsinger, L. Hermanson, S. B. Guze, and G. Winokur. Alcohol problems in adoptees raised apart from alcoholic biological parents. *Archives of General Psychiatry,* 1973, **28,** 238–243.

Gorer, G. Man has no "killer" instinct. *The New York Times Magazine,* Nov. 27, 1966.

Gottesman, I. I. Heritability of personality: a demonstration. *Psychological Monographs,* 1963, **77,** No. 9 (Whole No. 572), pp. 1–21.

Gough, H. G. *California Psychological Inventory.* Palo Alto: Consulting Psychologists Press, 1957.

Goy, R. W., and J. S. Jackway. Inheritance of patterns of mating behavior in the female guinea pig. *Animal Behavior,* 1959, **7,** 142–149.

Goy, R. W., and J. S. Jackway. Role of inheritance in determination of sexual behavior patterns. In E. L. Bliss (ed.), *Roots of Behavior,* New York: Hoeber, 1962.

Gray, P. H. Theory and evidence of imprinting in human infants. *Journal of Psychology,* 1958, **46,** 155–166.

Gray, P. H. Verification of Spalding's method for controlling visual experience by hooding chicks in the shell. *Proceedings of Montana Academy of Sciences,* 1961, **21,** 120–123.

Gray, P. H. *The Comparative Analysis of Behavior.* Dubuque, Iowa: Brown, 1966.

Griffin, J. H. *Black Like Me.* New York: New American Library, 1960.

Guilford, J. P. *Personality.* New York: McGraw-Hill, 1959.

Gumpert, P., M. Deutsch, and Y. Epstein. Effect of incentive magnitude on cooperation in the prisoner's dilemma game. *Journal of Personality and Social Psychology,* 1969, **11,** 66–69.

Guttman, L. The basis for scalogram analysis. In S. A. Stouffer *et al., Measurement and Prediction.* Princeton: Princeton University Press, 1950, pp. 60–90.

Haldane, J. B. S. Introducing Douglas Spalding. *British Journal of Animal Behavior,* 1954, **2,** 1.

Hall, C. S. The inheritance of emotionality. *Sigma Xi Quarterly,* 1938, **26,** 17–27.

Hall, C. S. *A Primer of Freudian Psychology.* New York: World Book, 1954.

Hampson, J. L. Determinants of psychosexual orientation. In F. A. Beach (ed.), *Sex and Behavior.* New York: Wiley, 1965, pp. 108–132.

Hampson, J. L., and J. G. Hampson. The ontogenesis of sexual behavior in man. In W. C. Young (ed.), *Sex and Internal Secretions,* 3rd ed. Baltimore: William and Wilkins, 1961.

Harlow, H. F. The nature of love. *American Psychologist,* 1958, **13,** 673–685.

Harlow, H. F. The heterosexual affectional system in monkeys. *American Psychologist,* 1962, **17,** 1–9.

Harlow, H. F., and M. K. Harlow. The effect of rearing conditions on behavior. *Bulletin of the Menninger Clinic,* 1962, **26,** 213–224.

Harlow, H. F., M. K. Harlow, R. O. Dodsworth, and G. L. Arling. The maternal behavior of rhesus monkeys deprived of mothering and peer associations in infancy. *Proceeding of the American Philosophical Society,* 1966, **110,** 58–66.

Hart, B. M., K. E. Allen, J. S. Buell, F. R. Harris, and M. M. Wolf. Effects of social reinforcement on operant crying. *Journal of Child Psychology,* 1964, **1,** 145–153.

Hartmann, H. (1939) *Ego Psychology and the Problem of Adaptation.* New York: International Universities Press, 1958.

Hathaway, S. R., and J. C. McKinley. *Minnesota Multiphasic Personality Inventory* (Revised Manual). New York: Psychological Corporation, 1951.

Heathers, G. Emotional dependence and independence in a physical threat situation. *Child Development,* 1953, **24,** 169–179.

Heathers, G. Emotional dependence and independence in nursery school children. *Journal of Genetic Psychology,* 1955, **87,** 37–58.

Hebb, D. O. *The Organization of Behavior.* New York: Wiley, 1949.

Helson, H. Current trends and issues in adaptation-level theory. *American Psychologist,* 1964, **19,** 26–38.

Henderson, N. D. Prior treatment effects on open field behaviour of mice—a genetic analysis. *Animal Behaviour,* 1967, **15**, 364–376.

Heston, L. L. Psychiatric disorders in foster home reared children of schizophrenic mothers. *British Journal of Psychiatry,* 1966, **112**, 819–826.

Hilton, I. Differences in the behavior of mothers toward first and later born children. *Journal of Personality and Social Psychology,* 1967, **7**, 282–290.

Himelhoch, J., and S. F. Fava (eds). *Sexual Behavior in American Society.* New York: Norton, 1955.

Hokanson, J. E., M. Burgess, and M. F. Cohen. Effects of displaced aggression on systolic blood pressure. *Journal of Abnormal and Social Psychology,* 1963, **67**, 214–218.

Holland, J. G. Technique for behavioral analysis of human observing. *Science,* 1957, **125**, 348–350.

Hornstein, H. A., E. Fisch, and M. Holmes. Influence of a model's feeling about his behavior and his relevance as a comparison other on observers' helping behavior. *Journal of Personality and Social Psychology,* 1968, **10**, 222–226.

Howard, J. L., C. B. Reifler, and M. B. Liptzin. Effects of exposure to pornography. *Technical Reports of the Commission on Obscenity and Pornography,* Vol. 8. Washington, D.C.: U.S. Government Printing Office, 1970.

Hudgens, G. A., V. H. Denenberg, and M. X. Zarrow. Mice reared with rats: effects of preweaning and postweaning social interactions upon adult behaviour. *Behaviour,* 1968, **30**, 259–274.

Hunt, J. McV. *Intelligence and Experience.* New York: Ronald Press, 1961.

Hunt, J. McV. Environment, development, and scholastic achievement. In M. Deutsch, I. Katz, and A. R. Jensen (eds.), *Social Class, Race, and Psychological Development.* New York: Holt, Rinehart and Winston, 1968, pp. 293–336.

Hunt, J. McV. The impact and limitations of the giant of developmental psychology. In D. Elkind and J. H. Flavell (eds.), *Studies in Cognitive Development: Essays in Honor of Jean Piaget.* London: Oxford University Press, 1969, pp. 3–66.

Ismail, A. A. A., R. A. Harkness, K. E. Kirkham, J. A. Loraine, P. B. Whatmore, and R. P. Brittain. Effect of abnormal sex-chromosome complements on urinary testosterone levels. *Lancet,* 1968, **1**, 220–222.

Jacobs, P. A., M. Brunton, M. M. Melville, R. P. Brittain, and W. F. McClemont. Aggressive behaviour, mental subnormality and the XYY male. *Nature,* 1965, **209**, 1351–1352.

Jacobs, P. A., M. Brunton, M. H. Melville, R. P. Brittain, and P. B. Whatmore. Chromosome studies on men in a maximum security hospital. *Annals of Human Genetics,* 1968, **31**, 339–351.

Jaffe, J. M. *Prenatal Determinants of Behaviour.* Oxford: Pergamon, 1969.

James, M., and D. Jongeward. *Born to Win: Transactional Analysis with Gestalt Experiments.* Reading, Mass.: Addison-Wesley, 1973.

James, W. *The Principles of Psychology.* New York: Dover, 1950, pp. 310–311. Original publication by Henry Holt, 1890.

Jennings, F. G. Jean Piaget: notes on learning. *Saturday Review,* May 20, 1967, pp. 81–83.

Joffe, J. M. *Prenatal Determinants of Behaviour.* Oxford: Pergamon Press, 1969.

Johnson, J. *Disorders of Sexual Potency in the Male.* Oxford: Pergamon Press, 1968.

Johnson, R. W. *Aggression in Man and Animals.* Philadelphia: W. B. Saunders, 1972.

Johnson, W. T., L. Kupperstein, and J. Peters. Sex offenders' experience with erotica. *Technical Reports of the Commission on Obscenity and Pornography,* Vol. 7. Washington, D.C.: U.S. Government Printing Office, 1970.

Jones, E. *The Life and Work of Sigmund Freud,* Vol. I. New York: Basic Books, 1953.

Jones, M. B. Behavior genetics. In P. F. Regan and E. G. Pattishall, Jr. (eds.), *Behavioral Science Contributions to Psychiatry,* International Psychiatry Clinics, **2**. Boston: Little, Brown, 1965.

Jourard, S. M. *Disclosing Man to Himself.* Princeton: Van Nostrand, 1968.

The Journal of Social Issues, 1973, Vol. 29, No. 3.

Kagan, J. The measurement of overt aggression from fantasy. *Journal of Abnormal and Social Psychology,* 1956, **52**, 390–393.

Kagan, J. Socialization of aggression and the perception of parents in fantasy. *Child Development,* 1958, **29**, 311–320.

Kagan, J., and H. A. Moss. The stability of passive and dependent behavior from childhood through adulthood. *Child Development,* 1960, **31**, 577–591.

Kagan, J., and H. A. Moss. *Birth to Maturity.* New York: Wiley, 1962.

Kagan, J., and P. H. Mussen. Dependency themes on the TAT and group conformity. *Journal of Consulting Psychology,* 1956, **20**, 29–32.

Kahn, M. The physiology of catharsis. *Journal of Personality and Social Psychology,* 1966, **3**, 278–286.

Kallmann, F. J., and D. Reisner. Twin studies on genetic variation in resistance and susceptibility to tuberculosis. *Journal of Heredity,* 1943, **43**, 269–276.

Kanfer, F. H. The maintenance of behavior by self-generated stimuli and reinforcement. In A. Jacobs and L. B. Sachs (eds.), *The Psychology of Private Events.* New York: Academic Press, 1971.

Kanfer, F. H., L. E. Cox, J. M. Greiner, and P. Karoly. Contracts, demand characteristics, and self-control. *Journal of Personality and Social Psychology,* 1974, **30**, 605–619.

Kanfer, F. H., and P. Karoly. Self-control: A behavioristic excursion into the lion's den. *Behavior Therapy,* 1972, **3**, 398–416.

Karlins, M., and L. M. Andrews (eds.). *Man Controlled.* New York: The Free Press, 1972.

Karoly, P., and F. H. Kanfer. Effects of prior contractual experiences on self-control in children. *Developmental Psychology,* 1974, **10**, 459–460.

Kauffman, H. *Aggression and Altruism.* New York: Holt, Rinehart and Winston, 1970.

Kaufman, I. C., and L. A. Rosenblum. Depression in infant monkeys separated from their mothers. *Science,* 1967, **155**, 1030–1031.

Kelly, E. L. *Assessment of Human Characteristics.* Belmont, Calif.: Brooks/Cole, 1967.

Kelly, G. A. *The Psychology of Personal Constructs.* New York: Norton, 1955, 2 vols.

Kelly, G. A. Europe's matrix of decision. In M. R. Jones (ed.), *Nebraska Symposium on Motivation.* Lincoln: University of Nebraska Press, 1962.

Kelly, G. A. *A Theory of Personality*. New York: Norton, 1963.

Kessler, S., and R. H. Moos. The XYY karyotype and criminality: a review. *Journal of Psychiatric Research*, 1970, **7**, 153–170.

Kinsey, A. C., W. B. Pomeroy, and C. E. Martin. *Sexual Behavior in the Human Male*. Philadelphia: Saunders, 1948.

Kinsey, A. C., W. B. Pomeroy, C. E. Martin, and P. H. Gebhard. *Sexual Behavior in the Human Female*. Philadelphia: Saunders, 1953.

Kleinmuntz, B. MMPI decision rules for the identification of college maladjustment. *Psychological Monographs*, 1963, **77**, No. 14 (Whole No. 477).

Kohlberg, L. Cognitive stages and preschool education. *Human Development*, 1966, **9**, 5–17. (a)

Kohlberg, L. A cognitive-developmental analysis of children's sex-role concepts and attitudes. In E. Maccoby (ed.), *The Development of Sex Differences*. Stanford: Stanford University Press, 1966, pp. 82–173. (b)

Kohlberg, L. Moral and religious education and the public schools: a developmental view. In T. Sizer (ed.), *Religion and Public Education*. Boston: Houghton Mifflin, 1967, pp. 164–183.

Kohlberg, L. Stage and sequence: the cognitive-developmental approach to socialization. In D. A. Goslin (ed.), *Socialization Theory and Research*. Chicago: Rand McNally, 1969, pp. 347–480.

Korner, A. F. Individual differences at birth: Implications for early experience and later development. *American Journal of Orthopsychiatry*, 1971, **41**, 608–619.

Kuethe, J. L. Social schemas. *Journal of Abnormal and Social Psychology*, 1962, **64**, 31–38. (a)

Kuethe, J. L. Social schemas and the reconstruction of social object displays from memory. *Journal of Abnormal and Social Psychology*, 1962, **65**, 71–75. (b)

Kuethe, J. L. The pervasive influence of social schemata. *Journal of Abnormal and Social Psychology*, 1964, **68**, 248–254.

Kutschinsky, B. The effect of pornography—an experiment on perception, attitudes, and behavior. *Technical Reports of the Commission on Obscenity and Pornography*, Vol. 8. Washington, D.C.: U.S. Government Printing Office, 1970.

Kuo, Z. Y. *The Dynamics of Behavior Development*. New York: Random House, 1967.

Lagerspetz, K. Genetic and social causes of aggressive behaviour in mice. *Scandinavian Journal of Psychology*, 1961, **2**, 167–173.

Lagerspetz, K. Y. H., R. Tirri, and K. M. J. Lagerspetz. Neurochemical and endocrinological studies of mice selectively bred for aggressiveness. *Scandinavian Journal of Psychology*, 1968, **9**, 157–160.

Lagerspetz, K., and K. Wuorinen. A cross-fostering experiment with mice selectively bred for aggressiveness and non-aggressiveness. Institute of Psychology, University of Turku, 1965, Report **17**, 1–6. (Mimeo)

Lang, P. J., and A. D. Lazovik. Personality and hypnotic susceptibility. *Journal of Consulting Psychology*, 1962, **26**, 317–322.

Langer, J. *Theories of Development*, New York: Holt, Rinehart and Winston, 1969.

Lavrakas, P. J. Female preferences for male physiques. *Journal of Research in Personality*, 1975, **9**, 324–334.

Leakey, L. S. B. Development of aggression as a factor in early human and pre-human evolution. In C. D. Clemente and D. B. Lindsley (eds.), *Aggression and Defense: Neural Mechanisms and Social Patterns.* Berkeley: University of California Press, 1967, pp. 1–11.

Lee, P. C., and A. L. Wolinsky. Male teachers of young children: A preliminary empirical study. *Young Children,* 1973, **28,** 342–352.

Lehrman, D. S. Interaction between internal and external environments in the regulation of the reproductive cycle of the ring dove. In F. A. Beach (ed.), *Sex and Behavior.* New York: Wiley, 1965, pp. 355–380.

Lesser, G. S. The relationship between overt and fantasy aggression as a function of maternal response to aggression. *Journal of Abnormal and Social Psychology,* 1957, **55,** 218–221.

Lesser, G. S. Conflict analysis of fantasy aggression. *Journal of Personality,* 1958, **26,** 29–41.

Levine, S. The psychophysiological effects of infantile stimulation. In E. L. Bliss (ed.), *Roots of Behavior.* New York: Harper and Row, 1962.

Levine, S., and R. Mullins, Jr. Estrogen administered neonatally affects adult sexual behavior in male and female rats. *Science,* 1964, **14,** 185–187.

Levitt, E. E., and J. P. Brady. Sexual preferences in young adult males and some correlates. *Journal of Clinical Psychology,* 1965, **21,** 347–354.

Lewis, M. and L. A. Rosenblum (eds.). *The Origins of Human Behavior: The Effect of the Infant on Its Caregiver.* New York: Wiley, 1974.

Lindzey, G., H. Winston, and M. Manosevitz. Social dominance in inbred mouse strains. *Nature,* 1961, **191,** 474–476.

Little, K. B. Cultural variations in social schemata. *Journal of Personality and Social Psychology,* 1968, **10,** 1–7.

Loehlin, J. C. The personality of Aldous. *Discovery,* 1962, **23,** 23–26.

Loehlin, J. C. A computer program that simulates personality. In S. S. Tomkins and S. Messick (eds.), *Computer Simulation of Personality.* New York: Wiley, 1963, pp. 189–211.

Loehlin, J. C. "Interpersonal" experiments with a computer model of personality. *Journal of Personality and Social Psychology,* 1965, **2,** 580–584.

Loehlin, J. C. *Computer Models of Personality.* New York: Random House, 1968.

Lövaas, O. I. Effect of exposure to symbolic aggression on aggressive behavior. *Child Development,* 1961, **32,** 37–44.

Loevinger, J. Objective tests as instruments of psychological theory. *Psychological Reports,* 1957, **3,** 635–694.

Lorenz, K. *On Aggression.* New York: Harcourt, 1966.

McClearn, G. E. Behavior genetic analysis of aggression. In R. E. Whalen (ed.), *The Neuropsychology of Aggression.* (Advances in Behavioral Biology, Vol. **12**) New York: Plenum Press, 1974, pp. 87–97.

McClearn, G. E., and J. C. Defries. *Introduction to Behavioral Genetics.* San Francisco: W. H. Freeman, 1973.

McClelland, D. C., J. W. Atkinson, R. A. Clark, and E. L. Lowell. *The Achievement Motive.* New York: Appleton, 1953.

McClintock, M. Menstrual synchrony and suppression. *Nature,* 1971, **229,** 244–245.

McGill, T. E., and W. C. Blight. Effects of genotype on the recovery of sex drive in the male mouse. *Journal of Comparative and Physiological Psychology,* 1963, **56,** 887–888.

MacCorquodale, K. B. F. Skinner's verbal behavior: a retrospective appreciation. *Journal of the Experimental Analysis of Behavior,* 1969, **12,** 831–841.

Maccoby, E. E. (ed.). *The Development of Sex Differences.* Stanford: Stanford University Press, 1966.

Maccoby, E. E., and C. N. Jacklin. *The Psychology of Sex Differences.* Stanford: Stanford University Press, 1974.

MacLeish, K. Stone age cave men of Mindaneo. *National Geographic,* August 1972.

Maharishi International University Catalogue 1974/75. Los Angeles: Maharishi International University Press, 1974.

Maher, B. (ed.). *Clinical Psychology and Personality: The Selected Papers of George Kelly.* New York: Wiley, 1969.

Mainardi, D., M. Marson, and A. Pasquali. Causation of sexual preferences of the house mouse. The behaviour of mice reared by parents whose odour was artificially altered. *Atti della Societa Italiana di Scienze Naturali e del Museo Civico di Storia Naturali di Milano,* 1965, **104,** 325–338. Cited in P. A. Parsons, *The Genetic Analysis of Behaviour.* London: Methuen, 1967.

Mann, L., and I. L. Janis. A follow-up study of the long-term effects of emotional role playing. *Journal of Personality and Social Psychology,* 1968, **8,** 339–342.

Manning, A. The effects of artificial selection for mating speed in Drosophila melanogaster. *Animal Behavior,* 1961, **9,** 82–92.

Maslow, A. H. *Toward a Psychology of Being.* Princeton: Van Nostrand, 1962.

Maslow, A. H. *Motivation and Personality,* 2nd ed. New York: Harper and Row, 1970.

Masters, W. H., and V. E. Johnson. *Human Sexual Response.* Boston: Little, Brown, 1966.

Masters, W. H. and V. E. Johnson. *Human Sexual Inadequacy.* Boston: Little, Brown, 1970.

Masters, W. H. and V. E. Johnson. *The Pleasure Bond.* Boston: Little, Brown, 1974.

Mead, M. *Sex and Temperament.* New York: Morrow, 1935.

Mead, M. *Culture and Commitment.* New York: Doubleday, 1970.

Meehl, P. E. *Clinical vs. Statistical Prediction.* Minneapolis: University of Minnesota Press, 1954.

Megargee, E. I. Undercontrolled and overcontrolled personality types in extreme antisocial aggression. *Psychological Monographs,* 1966, **80,** No. 3 (Whole No. 611).

Megargee, E. I., and G. A. Mendelsohn. A cross-validation of twelve MMPI indices of hostility and control. *Journal of Abnormal and Social Psychology,* 1962, **65,** 431–438.

Megargee, E. I., and E. S. Menzies. The assessment and dynamics of aggression. In P. McReynolds (ed.). *Advances in Psychological Assessment,* Vol. 2. Palo Alto, Calif.: Science and Behavior Books, 1971, pp. 133–156.

Mehrabian, A. *An Analysis of Personality Theories.* Englewood Cliffs, N.J.: Prentice-Hall, 1968.

Meichenbaum, D. H. Cognitive factors in behavior modification: Modifying what clients say to themselves. *Research Report No. 25.* Waterloo: University of Waterloo, 1971.

Meichenbaum, D., and J. Goodman. Training impulsive children to talk to themselves: A means for developing self-control. *Journal of Abnormal Psychology,* 1971, **77,** 115–126.

Michael, R. P., and J. Herbert. Menstrual cycle influences grooming behavior and sexual activity in the rhesus monkey. *Science,* 1963, **140,** 500–501.

Miller, N. E. Experimental studies of conflict. In J. McV. Hunt (ed.), *Personality and the Behavior Disorders,* Vol. I. New York: Ronald Press, 1944, pp. 431–465.

Miller, N. E., and J. Dollard. *Social Learning and Imitation.* New Haven: Yale University Press, 1941.

Miller, R. E., W. F. Caul, and I. A. Mirsky. Communication of affects between feral and socially isolated monkeys. *Journal of Personality and Social Psychology,* 1967, **7,** 231–239.

Mischel, W. Father-absence and delay of gratification: cross-cultural comparisons. *Journal of Abnormal and Social Psychology,* 1961, **63,** 116–124.

Mischel, W. A social-learning view of sex differences in behavior. In E. E. Maccoby (ed.), *The Development of Sex Differences.* Stanford: Stanford University Press, 1966, pp. 56–81.

Mischel, W. *Personality and Assessment.* New York: Wiley, 1968.

Mischel, W. Continuity and change in personality. *American Psychologist,* 1969, **24,** 1012–1018.

Mischel, W. Toward a cognitive social learning reconceptualization of personality. *Psychological Review,* 1973, **80,** 252–283.

Mischel, W., E. B. Ebbeson, and A. R. Zeiss. Cognitive and attentional mechanisms on delay of gratification. *Journal of Personality and Social Psychology,* 1972, **21,** 204–218.

Mitchell, J. Cons, square-johns, and rehabilitation. In B. J. Biddle and E. J. Thomas (eds.), *Role Theory: Concepts and Research.* New York: Wiley, 1966.

Money, J. Influence of hormones on sexual behavior. *Annual Review of Medicine,* 1965, **16,** 67–82. (a)

Money, J. (ed.). *Sex Research: New Developments.* New York: Holt, Rinehart and Winston, 1965. (b)

Money, J., and A. A. Ehrhardt. *Man & Woman Boy & Girl: The Differentiation and Dimorphism of Gender Identity from Conception to Maturity.* Baltimore: Johns Hopkins, 1972.

Money, J., A. A. Ehrhardt, and D. N. Masica. Fetal feminization induced by androgen insensitivity in the Testicular Feminizing Syndrome: effect on marriage and maternalism. *Johns Hopkins Medical Journal,* 1968, **123,** 105–114.

Montagu, A. (ed.). *Man and Aggression,* 2nd ed. New York: Oxford University Press, 1973.

Montagu, A. Aggression and the evolution of man. In R. S. Whalen (ed.), *The Neuropsychology of Aggression* (Advances in Behavioral Biology, Vol. 12) New York: Plenum Press, 1974, pp. 1–29.

Moore, M. Aggression themes in a binocular rivalry situation. *Journal of Personality and Social Psychology,* 1966, **3,** 685–688.

Moreno, J. L. *Psychodrama.* New York: Beacon Press, 1946.

Morgan, C. D., and H. A. Murray. A method for investigating fantasies: The Thematic Apperception Test. *Archives of Neurology and Psychiatry,* 1935, **34,** 289–306.

Morris, D. *The Naked Ape.* New York: McGraw-Hill, 1967.

Moss, H. A., and J. Kagan. Report on personality consistency and change from the Fels longitudinal study. *Vita Humana,* 1964, **7,** 127–138.

Mowrer, O. H. *Learning Theory and Personality Dynamics.* New York: Ronald Press, 1950.

Murdock, G. P. Comparative data on the division of labor by sex. *Social Forces,* 1937, **15,** 551–553.

Murray, H. A. *Explorations in Personality.* New York: Oxford University Press, 1938.

Murray, H. A. *Thematic Apperception Test.* Cambridge, Mass.: Harvard University Press, 1943.

Murstein, B. I. *Theory and Research in Projective Techniques.* New York: Wiley, 1963.

Nisbett, R. E. Birth order and participation in dangerous sports. *Journal of Personality and Social Psychology,* 1968, **8,** 351–353.

O'Daniel, J. W. This is Moscow today. *Reader's Digest,* 1951, **59,** July, pp. 51–54.

Osgood, C. E., G. J. Suci, and P. H. Tannenbaum. *The Measurement of Meaning.* Urbana: University of Illinois Press, 1957.

Ottinger, D. R., and J. E. Simmons. Behavior of human neonates and pre-natal maternal anxiety. *Psychological Reports,* 1964, **14,** 391–394.

Owen, David R. The 47, XYY male: A review. *Psychological Bulletin,* 1972, **78,** 209–233.

Panton, J. H. Predicting prison adjustment with the MMPI. *Journal of Clinical Psychology,* 1958, **14,** 308–312.

Papanicolaou, A. D., K. E. Kirkham, and J. A. Loraine. Abnormalities in urinary gonadotrophin excretion in men with a 47, XYY sex chromosome constitution. *Lancet,* 1968, **2,** 608–610.

Patterson, G. R., R. A. Littman, and W. Bricker. Assertive behavior in children: a step toward a theory of aggression. *Monographs of the Society for Research in Child Development,* 1967, **32,** No. 5 (serial no. 113).

Paul, G. L. Chronic mental patient: current status—future directions. *Psychological Bulletin,* 1969, **71,** 81–94.

Phillips, J. L., Jr. *The Origins of Intellect: Piaget's Theory.* San Francisco: Freeman, 1969.

Phoenix, C. H., R. W. Goy, A. A. Gerall, and W. C. Young. Organizing action of prenatally administered testosterone propionate on the tissues mediating mating behavior in the female guinea pig. *Endocrinology,* 1959, **65,** 369–382.

Piaget, J. *The Psychology of Intelligence.* London: Routledge and Kegan Paul, 1950.

Pinard, A., and M. Laurendeau. "Stage" in Piaget's cognitive-developmental theory: exegesis of a concept. In D. Elkind and J. H. Flavell (eds.), *Studies in Cognitive De-*

velopment: Essays in Honor of Jean Piaget. London: Oxford University Press, 1969, pp. 121–170.

Podell, L., and J. C. Perkins. A Guttman scale for sexual experience: a methodological note. *Journal of Abnormal and Social Psychology,* 1957, **54,** 420–422.

Pomeroy, W. B. Human sexual behavior. In N. L. Farberow (ed.), *Taboo Topics.* New York: Atherton, 1963.

Pribram, K. H. The neuropsychology of Sigmund Freud. In A. J. Bachrach (ed.), *Experimental Foundations of Clinical Psychology.* New York: Basic Books, 1962, pp. 442–468.

Price, W. H., J. A. Strong, P. B. Whatmore, and W. F. McClemont. Criminal patients with XYY sex-chromosome complement. *Lancet,* 1966, **1,** 565–566.

Price, W. H., and P. B. Whatmore. Behaviour disorders and pattern of crime among XYY males identified at a maximum security hospital. *British Medical Journal,* 1967, **1,** 533–536.

Raine, W. M. *Famous Sheriffs and Western Outlaws.* New York: New Home Library, 1944.

Rasmussen, E. W. The relation between strength of sexual drive and fertility as evident from experimental investigation. *Proceedings 2nd International Congress of Animal Reproduction.* (Copenhagen) 1952, **1,** 188–191.

Reichenbach, H. *Experience and Prediction.* Chicago: University of Chicago Press, 1938.

Reiss, A. J. Police brutality—answers to key questions. *Trans-action,* 1968, July/August, pp. 10–19.

Renner, K. E. Temporal integration: modification of the incentive value of a food reward by early experience with deprivation. *Journal of Experimental Psychology,* 1967, **75,** 400–407.

Renner, K. E. Temporal integration: amount of reward and the relative utility of immediate and delayed outcomes. *Journal of Comparative and Physiological Psychology,* 1968, **65,** 182–186.

Renner, K. E., and J. B. Tinsley. "Self-punitive Behavior," in G. Bower (ed.), *The Psychology of Learning and Motivation,* Vol. 10. New York: Academic Press, 1976.

The Report of the Commission on Obscenity and Pornography. New York: Bantam, 1970.

Rogers, C. R. *Client-centered Therapy.* Boston: Houghton Mifflin, 1951.

Rogers, C. R. A theory of therapy, personality and interpersonal relationships. In S. Koch (ed.), *Psychology: A Study of a Science,* Vol. III, *Formulations of the Person and the Social Context.* New York: McGraw-Hill, 1959, pp. 185–256.

Rogers, C. R. Toward a modern approach to values: the valuing process in the mature person. *Journal of Abnormal and Social Psychology,* 1964, **68,** 160–167.

Rorschach, H. (1921) *Psychodiagnostics.* New York: Grune and Stratton, 1949.

Rosenberg, B. G., and B. Sutton-Smith. *Sex and Identity.* New York: Holt, 1972.

Rosenkrantz, P., S. Vogel, H. Bee, I. Broverman, and D. M. Broverman. Sex-role stereotypes and self-concept in college students. *Journal of Consulting and Clinical Psychology,* 1968, **32,** 287–295.

Rosenthal, D., P. H. Wender, S. S. Kety, F. Schulsinger, J. Welner, and L. Østergaard. Schizophrenics' offspring reared in adoptive homes. In D. Rosenthal and S. Kety (eds.), *The Transmission of Schizophrenia*. Oxford: Pergamon Press, 1968.

Ross, D. Relationship between dependency, intentional learning, and incidental learning in preschool children. *Journal of Personality and Social Psychology*, 1966, **4**, 374–381.

Sackett, G. P. Response of rhesus monkeys to social stimulation presented by means of colored slides. *Perceptual and Motor Skills*, 1965, **20**, 1027–1028.

Sackett, G. P. Monkeys reared in visual isolation with pictures as visual input: evidence for an innate releasing mechanism. *Science*, 1966, **154**, 1468–1472.

Sackett, G. P. Innate mechanisms, differential rearing experiences, and the development of social attachments by rhesus monkeys. Paper presented at the annual meeting of the American Psychological Association, San Francisco, 1968.

Sackett, G. P., M. Porter, and H. Holmes. Choice behavior in rhesus monkeys: effects of stimulation during the first month of life. *Science*, 1965, **147**, 304–306.

Sanford, N. Personality: its place in psychology. In S. Koch (ed.), *Psychology: Study of a Science*, Vol. 5. New York: McGraw-Hill, 1963.

Sanford, R. N. The effects of abstinence from food upon the imaginal processes: a preliminary experiment. *Journal of Psychology*, 1936, **2**, 129–136.

Sarason, I. G., and V. J. Ganzer. Social influence techniques in clinical and community psychology. In C. D. Spielberger (ed.), *Current Topics in Clinical and Community Psychology*. New York: Academic Press, 1969, pp. 1–66.

Sarbin, T. R. Role theoretical interpretation of psychological change. In P. Worchel and D. Byrne (eds.), *Personality Change*. New York: Wiley, 1964, pp. 176–219.

Sawyer, J. Measurement and prediction, clinical and statistical. *Psychological Bulletin*, 1966, **66**, 178–200.

Scarr, S. The origins of individual differences in Adjective Check List scores. *Journal of Consulting Psychology*, 1966, **30**, 354–357.

Scarr, S. Environmental bias in twin studies. *Eugenics Quarterly*, 1968, **15**, 34–40.

Scarr, S. Social introversion-extraversion as a heritable response. *Child Development*, 1969, **40**, 823–832.

Schachter, S. *The Psychology of Affiliation*. Stanford: Stanford University Press, 1959.

Schachter, S. Cognitive effects on bodily functioning: studies of obesity and eating. In D. C. Glass (ed.), *Neurophysiology and Emotion*. New York: Rockefeller University Press, 1967, pp. 117–144.

Schachter, S., and J. E. Singer. Cognitive, social, and physiological determinants of emotional state. *Psychological Review*, 1962, **69**, 379–399.

Schaffer, H. R., and P. E. Emerson. Patterns of response to physical contact in early human development. *Journal of Child Psychology and Psychiatry*, 1964, **5**, 1–13.

Schon, M., and A. M. Sutherland. The relationship of pituitary hormones to sexual behavior in women. In H. G. Beigel (ed.), *Advances in Sex Research*. New York: Harper and Row, Hoeber Medical Division, 1963, pp. 33–47.

Schultz, S. D. A differentiation of several forms of hostility by scales empirically constructed from significant items on the MMPI. *Dissertation Abstracts*, 1955, **17**, 717–720.

Schutz, W. C. *Joy*. New York: Grove Press, 1967.

Schwartz, G. E. TM relaxes some people and makes them feel better. *Psychology Today*, April 1974, pp. 39–44.

Scodel, A. Heterosexual somatic preference and fantasy dependency. *Journal of Consulting Psychology*, 1957, **21**, 371–374.

Scott, J. P. Social behavior, organization, and leadership in a small flock of domestic sheep. *Comparative Psychology Monographs*, 1945, **18** (4), 1–29.

Scott, J. P. *Animal Behavior*. New York: American Museum of Natural History, 1963. Originally published by the University of Chicago Press, 1958.

Scott, J. P. Agonistic behavior in mice and rats: a review. *American Zoologist*, 1966, **6**, 683–701.

Sears, R. R., J. W. M. Whiting, V. Nowlis, and P. S. Sears. Some child-rearing antecedents of aggression and dependency in young children. *Genetic Psychology Monographs*, 1953, **47**, 135–234.

Sears, R. R., and G. W. Wise. Relation of cup feeding in infancy to thumb-sucking and the oral drive. *American Journal of Orthopsychiatry*, 1950, **20**, 123–138.

Seligman, M. E. P. *Helplessness*. San Francisco: W. H. Freeman, 1975.

Shainess, Natalie. How "sex experts" debase sex. *World*, January 2, 1973.

Sigel, I. E. The Piagetian system and the world of education. In D. Elkind and J. H. Flavell (eds.), *Studies in Cognitive Development: Essays in Honor of Jean Piaget*. London: Oxford University Press, 1969, pp. 465–489.

Sikes, M. P., and S. E. Cleveland. Human relations training for police and community. *American Psychologist*, 1968, **23**, 766–769.

Singer, J. L. (ed.). *The Control of Aggression and Violence*. New York: Academic Press, 1971.

Skinner, B. F. Baby in a box. *Ladies Home Journal*, October, 1945.

Skinner, B. F. *Walden Two*. New York: Macmillan, 1948.

Skinner, B. F. How to teach animals. *Scientific American*, 1951, **185**, 26–29.

Skinner, B. F. *Verbal Behavior*. New York: Appleton-Century-Crofts, 1957.

Skinner, B. F. *Cumulative Record*. New York: Appleton-Century-Crofts, 1961.

Skinner, B. F. *The Technology of Teaching*. New York: Appleton-Century-Crofts, 1968.

Skinner, B. F. *Beyond Freedom and Dignity*. New York: Knopf, 1971.

Skinner, B. F. *About Behaviorism*. New York: Knopf, 1974.

Sluckin, W. *Imprinting and Early Learning*. Chicago: Aldine, 1965.

Sluckin, W. *Early Learning in Man and Animal*. Cambridge, Mass.: Schenkmann Publishing Co., 1972.

Smith, R. T. A comparison of socioenvironmental factors in monozygotic and dizygotic twins: testing an assumption. In S. G. Vandenberg (ed.), *Methods and Goals in Human Behavior Genetics*. New York: Academic Press, 1965, pp. 45–61.

Spalding, D. A. Instinct, with original observations on young animals. *Macmillan's Magazine*, 1873, **27**, 282–293. Reprinted in British *Journal of Animal Behavior*, 1954, **2**, 2–11.

Spence, J. T., R. Helmreich, and J. Stapp. A short version of the attitudes toward women scale. *Psychonomic Bulletin*, 1973, **2**, 219–220.

Steffy, R. A., D. Meichenbaum, and J. A. Best. Aversive and cognitive factors in the modification of smoking behavior. *Behavior Research and Therapy*, 1970, **8**, 115–125.

Stendler-Lavatelli, C. B. Environmental intervention in infancy and childhood. In M. Deutsch, I. Katz, and A. R. Jensen (eds.), *Social Class, Race and Psychological Development*. New York: Holt, Rinehart and Winston, 1968, pp. 347–380.

Stephens, W. N. *The Family in Cross-cultural Perspective*. New York: Holt, Rinehart and Winston, 1963.

Storr, A. *Human Aggression*. New York: Atheneum, 1968.

Strickberger, M. W. *Genetics*. New York: Macmillan, 1968.

Strongman, K. T., and C. J. Hart. Stereotyped reactions to body build. *Psychological Reports*, 1968, **23**, 1175–1178.

Suomi, S. J., H. F. Harlow, and W. T. McKinney. Monkey psychiatrists. *American Journal of Psychiatry*, 1972, **128**, 927–932.

Sutton-Smith, B., and B. G. Rosenberg. Age changes on the effects of ordinal position on role identification. *Journal of Genetic Psychology*, 1965, **107**, 61–73.

Swenson, W. M., H. P. Rome, J. S. Pearson, and T. L. Brannick. A totally automated psychological test: experience in a medical center. *Journal of the American Medical Association*, 1965, **191**, 925–927.

Swift, M. S., and G. Spivack. *Alternative Teaching Strategies*. Champaign, Illinois: Research Press, 1975.

Tannenbaum, P. H. Emotional arousal as a mediator of communication effects. *Technical Reports of the Commission on Obscenity and Pornography*, Vol. 8. Washington, D.C.: U.S. Government Printing Office, 1970.

Thompson, T., and T. Sturm. Classical conditioning of aggressive display in Siamese Fighting Fish. *Journal of Experimental Analysis of Behavior*, 1965, **8**, 397–403.

Thompson, W. R. Influence of prenatal maternal anxiety on emotionality in young rats. *Science*, 1957, **126**, 73–74.

Thompson, W. R. Development and the biophysical bases of personality. In E. F. Borgatta and W. W. Lambert (eds.), *Handbook of Personality Theory and Research*. Chicago: Rand McNally, 1968, pp. 149–214.

Tiger, L. Male bonding and the exclusion of females. *New York*, 1969, **2**, No. 27, July 7, pp. 41–45.

Tiger, L. *Men in Groups*. New York: Random House, 1969.

Tinbergen, N. On war and peace in animals and man. *Science*, 1968, **160**, 1411–1418.

Toch, H. H., and W. H. Schulte. Readiness to perceive violence as the result of police training. *British Journal of Psychology*, 1961, **52**, 389–394.

Tomkins, S. S., and S. Messick (eds.). *Computer Simulation of Personality*. New York: Wiley, 1963.

Tridon, A. *Psychoanalysis and Love*. New York: Permabooks, 1949.

Ullmann, L. P. *Institution and Outcome*. New York: Pergamon Press, 1967.

Vale, J. R., Donald Ray, and C. A. Vale. Interaction of genotype and exogenous neonatal androgen: agonistic behavior in female mice. *Behavioral Biology,* 1972, **7.**

Vale, J. R., C. A. Vale, and J. P. Harley. Interaction of genotype and population number with regard to aggressive behavior, social grooming, and adrenal and gonadal weight in male mice. *Communications in Behavioral Biology,* 1971, **6,** 209–221.

Valins, S. Cognitive effects of false heart-rate feedback. *Journal of Personality and Social Psychology,* 1966, **4,** 400–408.

Walters, R. H., and E. Llewellyn Thomas. Enhancement of punitiveness by visual and audiovisual displays. *Canadian Journal of Psychology,* 1963, **17,** 244–255.

Walters, R. H., E. Llewellyn Thomas, and C. W. Acker. Enhancement of punitive behavior by audiovisual displays. *Science,* 1962, **136,** 872–873.

Walters, R. H., and R. D. Parke. Social motivation, dependency, and susceptibility to social influence. In L. Berkowitz (ed.), *Advances in Experimental Social Psychology,* Vol. I. New York: Academic Press, 1964, pp. 231–276.

Walters, R. H., and R. D. Parke. The influence of punishment and related disciplinary techniques on the social behavior of children: theory and empirical findings. In B. A. Maher (ed.), *Progress in Experimental Personality Research,* Vol. 4. New York: Academic Press, 1967, pp. 179–228.

Washburn, S. L. Tools and human evolution. *Scientific American,* 1960, **203,** 63–75.

Washburn, S. L., and V. Avis. Evolution of human behavior. In A. Roe and G. G. Simpson (eds.), *Behavior and Evolution.* New Haven: Yale University Press, 1958, pp. 421–436.

Washburn, S. L., and J. Shirek. Human evolution. In J. Hirsch (ed.), *Behavior-Genetic Analysis,* New York: McGraw-Hill, 1967.

Weinstein, L. Social schemata of emotionally disturbed boys. *Journal of Abnormal Psychology,* 1965, **70,** 457–461.

Weinstein, L. Social experience and social schemata. *Journal of Personality and Social Psychology,* 1967, **6,** 429–434.

Weitzenhoffer, A. M., and E. R. Hilgard, *Stanford Hypnotic Susceptibility Scale.* Palo Alto: Consulting Psychologists' Press, 1959.

Werner, H. The concept of development from a comparative and organismic point of view. In D. B. Harris (ed.), *The Concept of Development.* Minneapolis: University of Minnesota Press, 1957, pp. 125–148.

Wertham, F. *A Sign for Cain.* New York: Macmillan, 1966.

Whalen, R. E. (ed.). *The Neuropsychology of Aggression.* (*Advances in Behavioral Biology,* Vol. 12). New York: Plenum Press, 1974.

Whiting, J. W. M. Resource mediation and learning by identification. In I. Iscoe and H. W. Stevenson (eds.), *Personality Development in Children.* Austin: University of Texas Press, 1960.

Whiting, J. W. M. Methods and problems in cross-cultural research. In G. Lindzey and E. Aronson (eds.), *The Handbook of Social Psychology,* Vol. 2. Reading, Mass.: Addison-Wesley, 1968, pp. 693–728.

Whiting, J. W. M., and I. L. Child. *Child Training and Personality.* New Haven: Yale University Press, 1953.

Whorf, B. L. *Language, Thought, and Reality.* New York: Wiley, 1952.

Whyte, W. F. When workers and customers meet. In W. F. Whyte (ed.), *Industry and Society.* New York: McGraw-Hill, 1946.

Wickler, W. *The Sexual Code: The Social Behavior of Animals and Men.* Garden City: Anchor, 1973.

Wiggins, J. S., N. Wiggins, and J. C. Conger. Correlates of heterosexual somatic preference. *Journal of Personality and Social Psychology,* 1968, **10,** 82–89.

Wiggins, J. S., and C. L. Winder. The Peer Nomination Inventory: an empirically derived sociometric measure of adjustment in preadolescent boys. *Psychological Reports,* 1961, **9,** 643–677 (Monograph Supplement 5-V9).

Wiggins, J. S. *Personality and Prediction: Principles of Personality Assessment.* Reading, Mass.: Addison-Wesley, 1973.

Williams, A. R. Meet the Russian people. *Survey Graphic,* 1944, **33,** 42–45.

Williams, R. J. *Biochemical Individuality.* New York: Wiley, 1956.

Williams, R. J. The biological approach to the study of personality. A paper presented at The Berkeley Conference on Personality Development in Childhood, University of California, May 5, 1960.

Wilson, R. S. Twins: early mental development. *Science,* 1972, **175,** 914–917.

Winder, C. L., and J. S. Wiggins. Social reputation and social behavior: a further validation of the Peer Nomination Inventory. *Journal of Abnormal and Social Psychology,* 1964, **68,** 681–684.

Witkin, H. A., H. B. Lewis, M. Hertzman, K. Machover, P. B. Meissner, and S. Wapner. *Personality Through Perception.* New York: Harper, 1954.

Wolff, P. H. Piaget's sensorimotor theory of intelligence and general developmental psychology. In L. Breger (ed.), *Clinical-Cognitive Psychology: Models and Integrations.* Englewood Cliffs, N.J.: Prentice-Hall, 1969, pp. 228–245.

Wood-Gush, D. G. M. A study of sex drive of two strains of cockerel through three generations. *Animal Behaviour,* 1960, **8,** 43–53.

Wood-Gush, D. G. M., and R. Osborne. A study of differences in the sex drives of cockerels. *British Journal of Animal Behavior,* 1956, **4,** 102–110.

Woodworth, R. S. *Personal Data Sheet.* Chicago: Stoelting, 1920.

Yarrow, M. R., and P. M. Scott. Imitation of nurturant and nonnurturant models. *Journal of Personality and Social Psychology,* 1972, **23,** 259–270.

Yarrow, M. R., P. M. Scott, and C. V. Wexler. Learning concern for others. *Developmental Psychology* **8,** 240–260.

Young, J. Z. *An Introduction to the Study of Man.* New York: Oxford University Press, 1971.

Young, R. K., G. L. Clore, and W. Holtzman. Further change in attitude toward the Negro in a southern university. In D. Byrne and M. Hamilton (eds.), *Personality Research: A Book of Readings.* Englewood Cliffs, N.J.: Prentice-Hall, 1966.

Zamenhof, S., E. Van Marthens, and F. L. Margolis. DNA (cell number) and protein in neonatal brain: alteration by maternal dietary protein restriction. *Science,* 1968, **160,** 322–323.

Zetterberg, H. L. The consumers of pornography where it is easily available: The Swedish experience. *Technical Reports of the Commission on Obscenity and Pornography,* Vol. 9. Washington, D.C.: U.S. Government Printing Office, 1970.

Ziegler, H. P. Displacement activity and motivational theory: a case study in the history of ethology. *Psychological Bulletin,* 1964, **61,** 362–376.

Zucker, R. A., M. Manosevitz, and R. I. Lanyon. Birth order, anxiety, and affiliation during a crisis. *Journal of Personality and Social Psychology,* 1968, **8,** 354–359.

Zuckerman, M., and H. J. Grosz. Suggestibility and dependency. *Journal of Consulting Psychology,* 1958, **22,** 328.

Name Index

Abelson, H., 293
Abelson, R. P., 549
Acker, C. W., 217
Acker, L. E., 38, 39
Ader, R., 33
Adler, A., 354
Ainsworth, M. D. S., 128, 135
Al-Issa, I., 94
Allen, K. E., 124, 126
Allport, G. W., 11, 428, 429, 430, 432
Amir, Y., 228
Amoroso, D. M., 294
Andrews, L. M., 477
Ardrey, R., 303
Aristotle, 353
Arling, G. L., 122
Aronfreed, J., 42
Aronson, E., 46, 549
Asch, S. E., 164
Atkinson, J. W., 90
Avis, V., 174
Ayllon, T., 466, 467, 468, 469, 470
Azrin, N. H., 200, 201, 203, 466, 467, 468, 469, 470

Bacon, M., 147, 148
Bagby, J., 205
Baldwin, A. L., 404, 411
Bandura, A., 53, 54, 94, 138, 200, 202, 208, 209, 212, 213, 230, 298, 299, 377, 378, 379, 381, 382, 385, 386, 390, 393, 395, 396, 397, 398, 399
Bannister, D., 496, 497, 501, 502

Bardwick, J. M., 273
Baron, R. A., 204
Barron, F., 442
Barry, H., 147, 148
Bartlett, F. C., 49, 50, 51
Beach, F. A., 257, 258, 263, 264, 273
Becker, W. C., 393
Bee, H., 336
Bell, S. M., 128
Benedict, R., 4, 64, 223
Bentler, P. M., 327
Bergin, A. E., 469
Berkowitz, L., 192, 214, 216
Bernardin, A. C., 161
Berry, T. W., 147, 148
Best, J. A., 392
Biber, H., 300
Biddle, B. J., 94
Blank, C. E., 181
Blight, W. C., 259
Bogoras, W., 308
Boller, P. E., 227
Boring, E. G., 377
Boxton, M., 128
Bowlby, J., 128
Brady, J. P., 327, 328, 329, 330, 331
Braginsky, B. M., 521, 522, 523
Braginsky, D. D., 521, 522, 523
Brannick, T. L., 545
Bray, R. M., 228
Breuer, J., 347, 354
Brewer, M. B., 224, 225, 226
Bricker, W., 396

Brisset, D., 526
Brittain, R. P., 182, 183
Broadhurst, P. L., 22
Brook, P., 177
Brunton, M., 182
Broverman, D. M., 336
Broverman, I., 336
Brown, J. S., 390
Brown, M., 294
Buell, J. S., 124, 126
Burgess, M., 217
Byrne, D., 292, 294

Cairns, R. B., 135, 161
Campbell, C., 433
Campbell, D. T., 65
Carthy, J. D., 175, 194
Casey, M. D., 181
Cattell, R. B., 94
Caul, W. F., 40, 280
Charcot, J., 346, 347
Child, I., 147, 148
Child, I. L., 68
Clark, R. A., 90, 338, 339, 341
Cleveland, S. E., 440
Clore, G. L., 228
Cohen, M. F., 217
Cohen, R., 293
Colby, K. M., 547
Conger, J. C., 332
Conklin, P. M., 33
Conley, R. L., 452
Cook, R. F., 295
Cooley, C. H., 506
Cornbach, L. J., 74
Court-Brown, W. M., 181, 183
Covington, M. V., 419, 420
Cox, L. E., 391, 392
Crichton, M., 477
Crowe, R. R., 27

Dahlstrom, W. G., 293
Daly, R. F., 184
D'Andrade, R. G., 302
Darden, E., 335
Dart, R., 174
Darwin, C. R., 356, 376
DeFries, G. C., 180
Defries, J. C., 93
Denenberg, V. H., 35, 112, 113, 189, 190, 191, 193, 269

Dennis, W., 94
Dibiase, W. J., 334
Dodsworth, R. O., 122
Dollard, J., 376, 377, 378, 380, 383, 384, 385, 386, 388, 390, 391, 393, 395, 397, 398, 399, 400
Doob, L., 395
Dornbusch, S. M., 306, 307, 308
Dutsch, M., 132
Dyer, J. L., 300

Eaton, W. O., 228
Ebbeson, E. B., 386
Ebling, F. J., 175, 194
Edgley, C., 526
Edwards, A. E., 38, 39
Edwards, A. L., 83, 94
Edwards, D. A., 187, 188
Edwards, W., 49
Ehrhardt, A. A., 261, 265, 273
Eichenwald, H. F., 33
Elkind, D., 405, 408, 413, 414, 416, 424
Ellis, A., 446
Emerson, P. E., 106
Epstein, S., 47, 283
Epstein, Y., 132
Erickson, C. J., 262
Erikson, E. H., 353, 355, 420
Erikson, K. T., 465

Farnsworth, P. R., 227
Fava, S. F., 317
Feder, H. H., 261
Feffer, M., 419
Fenichel, O., 370
Ferster, C. B., 458, 464
Feshback, S., 207
Fisch, E., 57
Fiske, D. W., 94
Flanders, J. P., 58
Flavell, J. H., 413, 414
Ford, C. S., 257, 258, 263, 264, 273
Forssman, H., 184
Fosen, R. H., 295
Fox, R., 175
Fransella, F., 496, 501
Freedman, D. G., 103, 104, 105, 106, 114, 117
Freedman, L. Z., 174
Freeman, D., 175
Freud, A., 354, 355

Freud, S., 8, 34, 87, 166, 207, 208, 230, 297, 309, 334, 346, 348, 349, 350, 351, 352, 353, 354, 355, 356, 357, 359, 360, 363, 367, 369, 370, 371, 372, 373, 377, 378, 383, 385, 389, 395, 397, 400, 405, 407, 408, 420, 429, 432, 480
Friedan, B., 307
Fry, P. C., 33
Fuller, J. L., 34
Furth, H. G., 424

Ganzer, V. J., 397
Gerall, A. A., 260
German, J., 28
Gesell, A., 420
Gewirtz, J. L., 127, 135, 150
Ginsburg, B. E., 180
Ginsburg, H., 424
Gisvold, D., 164
Glass, D. C., 93
Goffman, E., 506, 507, 508, 511, 514, 515, 517, 518, 519, 526
Goldfarb, W., 114
Golding, W., 177
Goldstein, K., 438
Goldstein, M. J., 295
Goodman, J., 387
Goodwin, D. W. F., 27
Gorer, G., 222, 223
Goslin, D. A., 418, 422
Gottesman, I. I., 185
Gough, H. G., 86, 241, 242, 244
Goy, R. W., 259, 260
Gray, P. H., 111, 112, 114, 115, 116
Green, R., 295
Greiner, J. M., 391, 392
Griffin, J. H., 61
Grosz, H. J., 164
Guilford, J. P., 4, 70, 94
Gumpert, P., 132
Guthrie, E. R., 377
Guttman, L., 326, 327, 328, 341, 417
Guze, S. B., 27

Hake, D. F., 200
Haldane, J. B. S., 110
Hall, C. S., 22, 373
Hambert, G., 184
Hampson, J. G., 257
Hampson, J. L., 257, 269
Harkness, R. A., 183

Harley, J. P., 180
Harlow, H. F., 120, 121, 122, 261, 278, 279, 281
Harlow, M. K., 122, 279
Harris, F. R., 124, 126
Hart, B. M., 124, 126
Hart, C. J., 334
Hartmann, H., 351, 352, 354, 355
Hathaway, S. R., 85
Heathers, G., 126, 141
Heaton, E., 293
Hebb, D. O., 35, 36, 404, 405, 406
Helmreich, R., 336
Helson, H., 46
Henderson, N. D., 23
Herbert, J., 257
Hermanson, L., 27
Hertzman, M., 130
Heston, L. L., 26
Hilgard, E. R., 162
Hilton, I., 141, 143, 144
Himelhoch, J., 317
Hjelle, L. A., 334
Hobbes, T., 191
Hokanson, J. E., 217
Holland, J. G., 461
Holmes, H., 113, 114
Holmes, M., 57
Horney, K., 353
Hornstein, H. A., 57
Howard, J. L., 293
Howells, W. H., 17
Hudgens, G. A., 112, 113, 190
Hull, C., 376, 377, 383, 384, 385, 398
Hunt, J. McV., 408, 409, 419
Hutchinson, R. R., 200, 201, 203
Huxley, A., 531

Ismail, A. A. A., 183
Itkin, S., 228

Jacklin, C. N., 310
Jackway, J. S., 259
Jacobs, P. A., 182
Jaffe, J. M., 93
James, M., 448
James, W., 111, 376, 377, 429, 435, 437
Janis, I. L., 63
Jennings, F. G., 411
Jessor, R., 161
Joffe, J. M., 33

Johnson, R. N., 194
Johnson, V. E., 280, 282, 283, 285, 286, 287, 288, 289, 314, 321, 322, 324, 325, 341, 398, 399
Johnson, W. T., 295
Jones, E., 347, 354
Jones, M. B., 23
Jongeward, D., 448
Journard, S. M., 445, 446
Judd, L. L., 295
Jung, C. G., 354

Kagan, J., 108, 109, 110, 165, 167, 168, 185, 186, 247, 248
Kahn, M., 395
Kallmann, F. J., 30
Kanfer, F. H., 391, 392
Kant, H. S., 295
Karlins, M., 477
Karoly, P., 391, 392
Kauffman, H., 191, 192
Kaufman, I. C., 128
Keller, B., 103, 104
Kelley, R., 115
Kelly, E. L., 95
Kelly, G. A., 5, 6, 11, 480, 481, 488, 489, 490, 491, 492, 496, 497, 498, 499, 502, 549
Kessler, S., 184
Kety, S. S., 27
Kinsey, A. C., 314, 315, 316, 317, 318, 319, 321, 325, 328, 331, 341
Kirkham, K. E., 183
Kleinmuntz, B., 546
Kohlberg, L., 301, 407, 416, 417, 418, 419, 420, 421, 422, 423
Korner, A. F., 107
Krafft-Ebing, R. von, 347
Kuethe, J. L., 129, 130
Kuo, Z. Y., 188, 189, 270, 271, 272
Kupperstein, L., 295
Kutchinsky, B., 294

Lagerspetz, K. M. J., 179
Lagerspetz, K. Y. H., 179
Lamberth, J., 292, 294
Lang, P. J., 164
Langer, J., 379, 409, 410
Lanyon, R. I., 146
Lashley, K., 406
Laurendeau, M., 416
Lavrakas, P. J., 335

Lazovik, A. D., 164
Leakey, L. S. B., 175
Lee, P. C., 301
Lehrman, D. S., 262
Leibnitz, G., 353, 355
Lesser, G. S., 246, 250
Levine, S., 35, 261
Levitt, E. E., 327, 328, 329, 330, 331
Lewis, H. B., 130
Lewis, M., 107, 117, 135, 161
Linder, P., 46
Lindman, H., 49
Lindzey, G., 179, 549
Liptzin, M. B., 293
Little, K. B., 66
Littman, R. A., 396
Locke, J., 353, 379
Loehlin, J. C., 539, 540, 541, 542, 543, 544, 547, 549
Loevinger, J., 74
Loraine, J. A., 183
Lorenz, K., 192, 194, 221, 222
Lövaas, O. I., 217
Lowell, E. L., 90

McClearn, G. E., 93, 180, 181
McClelland, D. C., 90
McClemont, W. F., 182
McClintock, M., 263
McDougall, J. H., 181
McGill, T. E., 259
McGrath, P. J., 181
McKinley, J. C., 85
McKinney, W. T., 122
McLaughlin, R., 203
McReynolds, P., 252
Maccoby, E. E., 310
MacCorquodale, K. B. F., 463
Machover, K., 130
MacLeish, K., 192
Maharishi, 431, 433, 439, 445
Maher, B., 480, 502
Mainardi, D. M., 269, 270
Mair, J. M. M., 502
Mann, L., 63, 294
Manning, A., 259
Manosevitz, M., 146, 179
Margolis, F. L., 32
Marsan, M., 269
Martin, C. E., 316, 317, 318, 319, 321, 325, 328, 331

Masica, D. N., 261
Maslow, A. H., 431, 432, 437, 438, 442, 444, 445
Masters, W. H., 280, 282, 283, 285, 286, 287, 288, 289, 314, 321, 322, 324, 325, 341, 397, 398, 399
Mead, G. H., 506
Mead, M., 304, 355, 433
Meehl, P. E., 74, 545
Megargee, E. I., 237, 239, 241, 242, 243, 245, 252
Mehrabian, A., 411, 412, 414, 421
Meichenbaum, D. H., 387, 392
Meissner, P. B., 130
Melville, M. H., 182
Mendelson, G. A., 239
Menlove, F. L., 53–54
Menzies, E. S., 252
Messick, S., 549
Michael, R. P., 257
Miller, L. B., 300
Miller, N. E., 376, 377, 378, 379, 380, 383, 384, 385, 386, 388, 390, 391, 393, 395, 397, 398, 399, 400
Miller, R. E., 40, 280
Mirsky, I. A., 40, 280
Mischel, W., 45, 95, 297, 386, 387
Mitchell, J., 59
Money, J., 260, 261, 265, 269, 273
Montagu, A., 192, 194
Montessori, M., 419
Moore, M., 205, 206, 207
Moos, R. H., 184
Moreno, J. L., 61
Morgan, C. D., 351
Morris, D., 102, 256
Moss, H. A., 108, 109, 110, 185, 186
Mowrer, O. H., 297, 366, 377, 379, 395
Mullins, R., Jr., 261
Murdock, G. P., 302, 303
Murphy, P., 228
Murray, H. A., 47, 89, 159, 351, 355
Murstein, B. I., 48, 252
Mussen, P. H., 165, 167, 168

Nisbett, R. E., 145
Nowlis, V., 393

O'Daniel, J. W., 227
Opper, S., 424
Osborne, R., 259

Osgood, C. E., 333
Ottinger, D. R., 33
Owen, D. R., 184

Panton, J. H., 239
Papanicolaou, A. D., 183
Parke, R. D., 127, 393
Paschke, R. E., 189, 190
Pasquali, A., 269
Patterson, G. R., 396
Paul, G. L., 465, 466
Pavlov, I., 377
Pearson, J. S., 545
Penfield, W., 406
Perkins, J. C., 327
Peters, J., 295
Phillips, J. L., Jr., 414, 424
Phillips, L. D., 49
Phoenix, C. H., 260
Piaget, J., 404, 407, 408, 409, 410, 411, 413, 414, 416, 418, 419, 421, 423, 424
Pilkey, D. W., 294
Pinard, A., 416
Podell, L., 327
Pomeroy, W. B., 316, 317, 318, 319, 321, 325, 328, 331
Porter, M., 113, 114
Preusse, M., 294
Pribram, K. H., 349
Price, W. H., 182

Raine, W. M., 218
Rank, O., 354
Rasmussen, E. W., 259
Ray, D., 187
Reber, A., 42
Reichenbach, H., 485, 486
Reifler, C. B., 293
Reisner, D., 30
Reiss, A., 219, 220
Renner, K. E., 45, 93
Rice, C. J., 295
Ring, K., 521, 522, 523
Roe, A., 174
Rogers, C., 429, 430, 432, 436, 437, 438, 439, 480
Rome, H. P., 545
Rorschach, H., 88, 89, 350
Rosekrans, M. A., 58
Rosenberg, B. G., 274
Rosenberg, K. M., 190

Rosenblum, L. A., 107, 117, 128, 135
Rosenbluth, D., 128
Rosenkrantz, P., 336
Rosenthal, D., 27
Ross, D., 139, 140, 212, 213, 298, 299
Ross, S. A., 212, 213, 298, 299

Sackett, G. P., 113, 114, 122
Salmon, P., 496
Sanford, N., 4
Sanford, R. N., 47
Sarason, I. G., 397
Sarbin, T. R., 61, 64
Sawyer, J., 545
Scarr, S., 26, 107, 108
Schachter, S., 56, 77, 141, 284
Schaffer, H. R., 106
Schon, M., 264
Schulsinger, F., 27
Schulte, W. H., 205, 207
Schultz, S. D., 239
Schutz, W. C., 436, 439
Schwartz, G. E., 443
Scodel, A., 166, 167, 168, 169, 332
Scott, J. P., 179, 192, 214, 280
Sears, P. S., 393
Sears, R. R., 68, 393, 395
Segall, L. J., 181
Seligman, M. E. P., 94
Shainess, N., 287
Shakespeare, W., 506, 507
Shirek, J., 15
Sigel, I. E., 419
Sikes, M. P., 440
Simmons, J. E., 33
Simpson, G. G., 174
Singer, J. E., 56, 77
Singer, J. L., 209
Skinner, B. F., 94, 377, 453, 454, 455, 458,
    460, 461, 462, 463, 464, 466, 469, 470, 471,
    472, 473, 474, 475, 476, 477
Skinner, J. L., 181
Sluckin, W., 111, 117
Smith, R. T., 26
Spalding, D. A., 110, 111
Spence, J. T., 336
Spinoza, B., 52
Spivack, G., 394
Stapp, J., 336
Steffy, R. A., 392
Stendler-Lavatelli, C. B., 419

Stephens, W. N., 305, 308
Storr, A., 191
Strachey, J., 230
Street, D. R. K., 181
Strickberger, M. W., 25
Strong, J. A., 182
Strongman, K. T., 334
Strum, T., 198
Suci, G. J., 333
Suder, C., 293
Suinn, R. M., 469
Suomi, S. J., 122
Sutherland, A. M., 264
Sutton-Smith, B., 274
Swenson, W. M., 545
Swift, M. S., 394

Tannenbaum, P. H., 293, 333
Thomas, E. J., 94
Thomas, L., 217
Thompson, T., 198
Thompson, W. R., 20, 33
Thorndike, E. L., 376, 377
Tiger, L., 177, 178, 303
Tinbergen, N., 176
Tirri, R., 179
Toch, H. H., 205, 207
Tolman, E. C., 377
Tomkins, S. S., 549
Tridon, A., 167

Ullmann, L. P., 465

Vale, J. R., 180, 187
Valins, S., 284
Van Marthens, E., 32
Vogel, S., 336

Waller, M. B., 34
Walters, R. H., 127, 138, 200, 202, 217, 377,
    378, 379, 381, 385, 386, 393, 397, 398, 399
Wapner, S., 130
Ware, E. E., 294
Washburn, S. L., 15, 100, 174
Watson, J. B., 377
Weinstein, L., 130
Weitzenhoffer, A. M., 162
Welner, J., 27
Welsh, G. S., 239
Wender, P. H., 27
Werner, H., 404, 405, 406, 409, 412, 418

Wertham, F., 192
Wexler, C. V., 214
Whalen, R. E., 194, 261
Whatmore, P. B., 182, 183
Whiting, 68, 297, 393
Whorf, B. L., 410
Whyte, W. F., 511
Wickler, W., 106, 274
Winder, C. L., 235, 236, 237
Wiggins, J. W., 95, 154, 158, 234, 235, 236, 237
Wiggins, N., 332
Williams, A. R., 227
Williams, R. J., 4, 18
Wilson, R. S., 105
Winder, C. L., 154, 158, 234
Winokur, G., 27
Winston, H., 179
Wise, G. W., 68

Witkin, H. A., 130
Wolf, M. M., 124, 126
Wolff, P. H., 421
Wolinsky, A. L., 301
Wood-Gush, D. G. M., 259
Woodworth, R. S., 82
Wuorinen, K., 179

Yarrow, M. R., 135, 214
Young, J. Z., 93
Young, W. C., 260

Zamenhof, S., 32
Zarrow, M. X., 112, 113, 189, 190, 191, 193
Zeiss, A. R., 386
Zetterberg, H. L., 293
Ziegler, H. P., 192
Zucker, R. A. M., 146
Zuckerman, M., 164

Subject Index

Abnormal personality: assessment of, 81–82, 85–86, 491–497; maintenance of, in mental hospitals, 465–466; scales of, 71–72

Accommodation, 413–414

Adolescence, 31–32

Adoption: studies of, 26

Affiliation: effect of birth order on, 145–146; effect of fear on, 145–146

Aggression: assaultiveness and degree of control over expression of, 237–239, 241–245; and avoidance learning, 200; and behavior genetics, 178–186; binocular rivalry to measure, 204–207; classical conditioning of, 198–200; and cognitive-development theory, 421–422; in computer simulation of interpersonal interactions, 542; as consequence of threat, 488–489; correlated with other behaviors, 179; CPI as measure of control over, 241–245; cross-fostering, 178–179, 190–191; cultural expression of, 222–223; cultural factors in determining, 223–224; cultural versus instinctual causes of, 221–222; differential reinforcement of, 201–202; and dominance hierarchies, 175–176, 178; effect of early social expression in, 179–181, 187–191; effect of extra Y chromosome on, 181–185; effect of fighting success on, 174–175, 178–179; effect of justifying, 214–217; and ethology, 176–178, 221–222; evolution of, 174–175; genetic determi-nants of, 179–185; hormonal influence on, 183, 188; and imitation, 212–214; influence of age on, 206–207; influence of past experience on, 205; influence of sex role on, 185–186, 205–206; and instinct, 189; instrumental conditioning of, 200–202; intensity of physical, 237–238; MMPI as measure of control over, 239–241; observational learning of, 212–214; Peer Nomination Inventory as measure of, 234–237; perceptual processes, 204–207; and police officer's role, 217–221; psychoanalysis, 352, 362, 369–370; and punishment, 202–203; as reaction to frustration, 199–200, 212–214; reinforcement of, 202–203; reinforcement value of, 192, 200, 203–204, 396–397; relationship between aggression anxiety and fantasy, 249–250; relationship between fantasy and overt, 245–249; relationship between fear of punishment and fantasy, 249–250; as resistance to revision of cognitive structures, 207–208; as self-fulfillment according to self theory, 444–445; social learning theory's interpretation of, 208, 395–397; stability of, 185–186; TAT as measure of, 46–49, 245–246; and territoriality, 178–179; twin studies, 185–186

Anaclitic identification, 297

Anxiety: in Kelly's construct system, 488–489; in psychoanalysis, 360–361, 362, 364, 365

Asch line-judging task, 147–149, 164

Assessment of personality: See Psychological assessment; Psychological tests

Assimilation, 413–414

Atayal: development of the concept of dreams among, 417–418

Australopithecus, 15–18, 175

Avoidance learning: acquisition of, 40–42; and aggression, 200; as an explanation for the development of conscience, 42–43; persistence of, 42, 384–385

Awareness in self theory, 440–441; as means to increased sensitivity, 441; as means to personal satisfaction, 436–437; and self-understanding, 436–437

Barr Body, 265–267

Bayley Infant Behavior Profile, 101–106

Bayley Mental and Motor Scales, 103–104

Behavior genetics, 18–32, 102–110; adoption studies in, 26; and aggression, 178–186; analysis of pure genetic strains in, 21–22, 259; animal research in, 21; chromosome analysis in, 27–28; establishment of genetic differences in, 21–22, 259; experimental methods of, 21–28; genotypic-experiential correlation in, 31–32; genotypic-experiential interaction in, 15, 29; maternal effects in, 21–23; principles of, 28–32; relationship between phenotype and genotype, 19, 20; and sexuality, 259; twin research in, 23–27, 103–108

Behaviorism. See Operant psychology

Binocular rivalry, 204–207

Biological viewpoint, 8, 10, 14–36, 100–117; aggression, 172–194; central assertion, 14; dependency, 100–117; evolutionary perspective, 15, 100; individual differences, 18; psychoanalysis, 348–350; sexuality, 254–274

Birth order: and affiliation to reduce fear, 145–146; and dependency, 141–146; and fear, 145–146

Brain: comparative growth of, 16; evolution of, 16–17; as evolutionary contribution to dependency, 15

California Psychological Inventory, 86–87, 241–246

Child-rearing practices: and aggression, 232–252; cultural influence on, 67–68; and dependence, 100; effect of neoteny on, 17, 100–102; and relationship of emotional disturbance to age of weaning, 68

Chromosomes: extra Y, 181–183; relationship to phenotype, 20. See also Genes; Genotype

Classical conditioning, 37–40, 402–424; of aggression, 198–200; of autonomic functions, 37; description of, 37–39; differential, 39; of fear, 40–42; and feelings of dependency, 122–124; of feelings of security, 123; and sexuality, 278–281; to social cues, 40; stimulus discrimination in, 39, 40; stimulus generalization in, 38, 39

Cognitions: in a child, 409–410; development of, 410; and reality, 410

Cognitive-development theory: and active view of human, 408–409; and adaptation, 413–416; and aggression, 421–422; assumptions of, 404; biological model of, 405; central assertion of, 410–411; cognitive relativity of, 410, 412–413; and dependency, 420–421; developmental orientation of, 404–405; and hierarchical growth, 409; historical perspectives, 404–408; and implications for education, 419–420; and intelligence, 416; interactional perspective of, 409; and morality, 421–422; orthogenetic principle in, 412–413; philosophical perspective of, 408–410; principal constructs of, 411–418; range and focus of, 419–420; and refinement of common sense, 404; relations of structure and function in, 411; sexual identification, 422–423; and sexual identity, 422–423; as stage-sequential development, 416–418, 419

Cognitive processes, 48–51, 131–134; cognitive types, 50–51; decision making, 48–49; and sexuality, 285–288. See also Cognitive structures

Cognitive structures, 49–51, 404; and aggression, 207–208; categorization into schemes, 49, 50; as explanation of personality differences, 50–51; influence of language on, 410; and influence on perception, 49–51, 131, 410; simple versus complex, 50–51; and social origins of a schema, 50; technique of serial reproduction to indicate, 49–50; theoretical need for, 404; used to classify information, 49–50

Cognitive transformations, 386

Communication in Kelly's construct system, 490

Computer model of personality, 528–549; action in a, 536–537; Aldous (a computer program) as a, 531, 534–544; attitudes in a, 535–536, 538–539; consequences, 538; effects of initial attitudes in a, 535, 542–543; emotional reaction in a, 536; environment in a, 537–538; introspection in a, 539–540; learning in a, 538–539; as means to analyze personality theories, 540–544; mood in a, 536; in psychotherapy, 543–544, 547–548; recall in a, 535–536; recognition in a, 534–535; stimuli in a, 534; in study of attitude change, 540–541; in study of interpersonal behavior, 542; as model of personality development, 540–541; in study of personality structure, 541–542; in study of therapy techniques, 547–548; translation of computer constructs into constructs of a, 531–540

Computer program, 531–533; as model of interpersonal behavior, 542; as model of personality (Aldous), 540–544; operations dictated by, 531

Computers: control-processing unit in, 534; input to, 534; output from, 532–533; storage in, 532–533; use of, in assessing psychological test data, 544–545; use of, in predicting performance from personality characteristics, 545; use of, in writing personality descriptions from MMPI, 545–546

Concordance in twins, 24–25, 30

Conflict in Dollard and Miller's social learning theory, 389–390, 397

Conformity: cultural differences in, 147–149, 164; Edwards Personal Preference Schedule as measure of, 164–165; TAT as measure of, 165–166

Conscience: development of, through avoidance learning, 42–43; and the superego, 364–367

Conservation, acquisition of, 414–416

Construct(s), 6–8; cognitive (see Kelly's construct system); in computer model of personality, 531–540; evaluation of, 6; Goffman's dramaturgical model, 507–518; multiple, 6–7; in operant psychology, 453–460; in psychoanalysis, 356–367; traits as, 73–74

Construct systems, 6–8; Kelly's (see Kelly's construct system); relativism of, 8

Construct validity: of California Psychological Inventory, 86–87; of Edwards Personal Preference Schedule, 159–160; external considerations in evaluating, 75; of fantasy measures, 165–169; of MMPI, 84–86; of Peer Nomination Inventory, 156–159; 235–237; structural considerations in evaluating, 75; substantive considerations in evaluating, 74–75; of TAT, 90

Constructive alternativism, 5–8

Contact hypothesis, 226–229

Context of discovery, 485

Context of verification, 486–487

Cooperations: in prisoner's dilemma game, 132–133

Creative people, 441–442

Creative process in Kelly's construct system, 490–491

Creativity as freedom, 442–443

Critical period, 34; and imprinting, 110–116

Cro-Magnon, 16

Cross-cultural research, 64–69; advantages of, 64–65; on differences in sex roles, 302–308; on dreams, 417–418; and Human Relations Area Files, 68–69; multi-culture, multi-observer method of, 65; objective method of, 65–66; on physical contact, 66–67; on relation of emotional disturbance to age of weaning, 68–69; traditional anthropological method of, 64–65

Cross-fostering, 22; and aggression, 178–179; 190–191

Cue in Dollard and Miller's social learning theory, 384

Cue-producing response in Dollard and Miller's social learning theory, 384

Cultures, 64–69; and aggression, 221–229; child training, 67–68; contact, 67; and dependency, 146–149; Human Relations

Cultures (*cont.*)
Area Files, 147–148; methods of study, 65–67; noncontact, 67; objective observation, 64–66; and sexuality, 302–308

Darwinism: and Freud, 355–357
Decision making, 48–49; in prisoner's dilemma games, 132–133
Defense mechanism: against aggression, 370; against dependency, 396; projection as a, 362–363; psychoanalysis, 350, 351; rationalization, 364; reaction formation as a, 363–364; repression as a, 361–362
Delinquency, 31, 32; and extra Y chromosome, 181–183; and muscular physique, 31–32
Deoxyribonucleic acid (DNA), 28–29
Dependency: as acquired drive, 392; and age, 140–141; behavior of mothers, 141–145; and birth order, 141–146; cognitive-developmental approach to, 420–421; as conditioned feelings of attachment, 123; cultural influence on, 146–149; Edwards Personal Preference Schedule as measure of, 82–84, 159–162, 164; and effect on imitation, 138–139, 421; as effect of isolation, 122; evolutionary history of, 100–102; fantasy, 165–169; feelings of, 120–124; forced, 131–134; inability to develop social, 122, 123; influence of breast feeding on, 333–334; influence of sex-role training on, 109–110; in terms of lack of instrumental skills, 123; as learned instrumental responses, 123; measures of, 154–170; and neoteny, 100–102; observational learning of, 138–139; passivity, 108–110; Peer Nomination Inventory as measure of, 80, 154–159; psychoanalysis, 368–369, 421; as reflected in feelings of attachment, 122–124; and relationship to breast size preference, 333–334; and relationship to perceptual processes, 129–130; and relationship to punishment, 126–127; roles, 140–146; self theory's evaluation of, 443–444; social learning theory's interpretation of, 392–395; stability of, 109; summary of biological approach to, 116–117; task-oriented versus person-oriented, 140–141; TAT as measure

of, 165–169; twin research 103–108; values, 127–129
Dependent behaviors: instrumental conditions of, 122, 124–126; and relation to feelings of attachment, 123; as result of isolation, 122
Deprivation: effects of early, 36, 278–280; effects of sexual, 278–280, 282–283; effects of social, 120–122, 278–279; of physical interaction and later maternal behavior, 278–279; of physical interaction and later mating behavior, 278; as used to demonstrate imprinting, 112–113
Determinants of personality. See Personality, determinants of
Diagnosis. See Psychological assessment; Psychological tests
Discordance in twins, 24–25
Discrimination in Dollard and Miller's social learning theory, 388
Discriminative stimulus, 457, 470–471
Dominance: construction of a scale to measure, 86–87; hierarchies, 175–176, 178; and human evolution, 175; selective breeding for social, 178–179; and sexuality, 298–300
Down's syndrome, 28
Dramaturgical model of personality, 504–526; appearance in, 509–510; front, back, and outside regions in, 517–518; heuristic value of, 508; and impression management, 507, 508, 521–524; manner in, 511; nature of personality according to, 519; notion of human as an actor in, 506; performance team in, 512–513; positions and roles, 508; privacy in, 515–516; relationship of reality to role performances in, 519–520; roles in, 506–507; setting in, 509; showing off in, 512; tact in, 513–514; translation of theatrical constructs into everyday experience by, 507–518; treatment of absent and team collusion in, 515
Dreams: in psychoanalysis, 350–351; in cognitive-developmental theory, 416–418
Drive: as defined by Dollard and Miller, 383; dependency as a, 392; reduction, 358–360; secondary, 384
Drosophila, sexual genotypes of, 267

Early experiences, 32; and aggression, 179–181, 186–193; atypical social, 36; environmental deprivation during, 36, 278–280; environmental enrichment during, 35; explanations for effects of, 34–35; and imprinting, 110–112, 269–270; and later choice of sexual mate, 269–270; malnutrition during, 32–33; over-mothering during, 123; postnatal, 33–34, 261–265; prenatal, 32–33, 260–261; rejection during, 278–280; of sexual behavior and sexual behavior after castration, 261

Edwards Personal Preference Schedule, 82–84, 159–162, 164; construct validity, 159–160

Education: implications of sequential-stage development approach for, 419–420; Piaget's view of goal of, 419–420. *See also* Teaching, technology of

Ego, 348, 351–352, 356, 364–368, 419; definition of, 348; and identification, 419. *See also* Defense mechanisms

Ego psychology, 351–352

Ego structures, 352

Emergent evolution, developmental variant of, 409

Emotional arousal and imitation, 56

Emotional disturbance and relation to age of weaning, 68–69

Emotional reactivity in rats, 23

Empathic inference, 405

Eskimos, independence of, 147–149

Events, 5

Evolution: of aggression, 174–175; of behavior, 15; and biological viewpoint, 15, 100–102; bipedalism, 15, 100–102; cultural, 18; definition of, 15; emergent, 409; of family, 17, 102; and gene pool, 15; of human sexual responsiveness, 256–258; and neoteny, 100–102; of sex roles, 17, 256–258; social, 15; social versus organic, 17

Experimental viewpoint, 10, 36–51; and aggression, 196–209; central assertion of, 36; and dependency, 120–135; relationship to psychoanalysis, 351–352; and sexuality, 276–289

Family, evolution of, 17, 100–102

Fantasy: and aggression, 245–250; construct validity, 165–169; and dependency, 165–169; and psychoanalysis, 347; psychosexual orality, 166–168

Fear: and birth order, 145–146; dependency and socialization, 103–106; and effect of affiliation, 145–146; and social learning, 53–55

Fels Child Behavior Scales, 107–108

Field dependency, 130–131; relationship to cognitive style, 130–131; relationship to dependent behaviors, 130–131

Fixed-role therapy, 498–499

Free association, 347

Frigidity, 285–288

Frustration as antecedent of aggression, 199–200, 212–214, 395

Generalization in Dollard and Miller's social learning theory, 388

Gene pool, 15

Genes: and effect on emotionality in rats, 23; in twins, 23–24, 103–108. *See also* Chromosomes; Genotype

Genotype, 15; and adoption studies, 26; and aggression, 180; in behavior-genetic research, 19, 103; and correlation to environmental factors, 31–32; and influence on intelligence, 20; and influence on sexual behavior, 259; and influence on social orientation and fearfulness, 103, 106; and influence on sociability, 103; and interaction with environmental factors, 20; and relationship to phenotype, 19, 20; and sexual identity, 265–267; and twin studies, 23–27, 103–108

Guilt in Kelly's construct system, 489–490

Guttman scale, 326–329

Habit, 376–377

Heritability, 20. *See also* Behavior genetics; Genes; Genotype

Hermaphrodites, 261, 268–269

Higher processes. *See* Cognitive processes

Homosexuality: and psychoanalysis, 363

Id, 348, 350, 356; definition of, 348; and psychoanalysis, 348

Identification, 297–301

Imitation: and aggression, 212–214; fear reduction, 53–55; influence of conse-

Imitation (cont.)
quences to model on, 57; influence of dependency on, 138–140; influence of model's status on, 58; influence of observer's emotional arousal on, 56; influence of similarity between observer and model on, 58; influence of vicarious reinforcement on, 57; and inhibitory or disinhibitory effects, 56; by young boys of father, 422–423; range of, 55; and sexuality, 292–295; in social learning theory, 378. See also Models; Observational learning
Impotence, 278–280, 285–288
Impression management: in Goffman's dramaturgical model, 507, 508; by schizophrenics in hospitals, 521–524
Imprinting: behavior-genetic analysis of, 110–112; characteristics of, 110–111; and effect on later sexual preference, 115–116, 269–270; in humans, 114–115; in mammals, 112; social function of, 111, 113–115; Spalding's initial studies of, 110–111
Incentive learning, 44–45; establishment of outcome values in, 44; relative value of outcomes in, 45
Individual differences: biological, 18–19; in cognitive style, 131–132; determinants of (see Personality, determinants of); as focal point of personality, 4; genetic, 27–28 (see also Behavior genetics; Genes; Genotype); in relation to traits, 70; in sexual identity, 265
Instinct: and imprinting, 110–111
Instinctual drives: classification of, 348; components of, 348; Freud's interest in, 348, 358–359
Instinctual energy: and pleasure principle, 359; and reality principle, 359
Instrumental conditioning, 40–44; of aggression, 200–202; of avoidance responses, 40–43; of dependent behaviors, 122–124; of escape responses, 40–42; of personality, 44; of resistance to temptation, 42–43; of sexual behaviors, 281–283; and shaping, 43–44. See also Operant psychology
Intelligence, 7; genotypic-experiential interaction in determining, 20; as viewed

according to cognitive-developmental theory, 416
Interviews: and role behavior, 60–61; structured, 81; techniques used in, 80–81; unstructured, 80–81

Karyotype analysis: and aggressiveness, 181–185; in determining sexual identity, 27–28, 261, 267–268; neurological abnormalities, 183–184
Kelly's construct system, 5, 478–502; and anxiety, 488–489; assessment of individual in, 491–497; and communication, 490; and creative process, 490–491; and guilt, 489–490; in Kelly's model of personality, 491–497; looseness and inconsistency of schizophrenia in, 495–496; and problem solving, 490–491; and psychotherapy, 498–499; and threat, 488–489
Kelly's model of human the scientist: channelization in, 482, 487–488; circumspection in, 481, 484–485; control in, 481, 486; core personal constructs in, 481, 483–484; examples of constructs of, 481–482; and international understanding, 499–500; personal construct system, 483; personal validation in, 482, 486–487; personality assessment according to, 491–497; preemption in, 481, 485–486; role of past experience in, 481, 482; subordinate personal constructs in, 481, 484; translation of scientific constructs into constructs of, 480–481; as used to provide unique perspectives toward personality, 480. See also Scientific investigation
Kinsey studies: check on accuracy of, 320–321; content of the interviews in, 315–316; establishment of rapport in, 320; hypotheses derived from, 325–328; maintenance of confidentiality of, 318–319; recruitment of interviewers for, 316; recruitment of subjects for, 317–318; and statistics on various sexual behaviors, 327
Kisii, 225–226
Klinefelter's syndrome, 267–268

Language: acquisition of, 462–464; operant

conditioning of, 462–464; and thought processes, 410
Learning dilemma, 384–385
Learning processes, 37–45; in computer model of personality, 538–539; role of drive reduction in, 40–43; role of reinforcement in, 43–44; and sexuality, 278–285; types of, 37
Liking: and perceived similarity, 224–227; use of contact to increase, 227–229
Linguistic reality hypothesis, 410
Lord of the Flies, 177–178
Love: inadequate classical conditioning of, 278–280; importance of physical contact in development of, 278, 282–283, 446

Malnutrition, effects of, 32–33
Masters and Johnson research: laboratory procedures of, 282–283, 323–324; recruitment of samples for, 322–323; significance of, 285, 324–325; on treating sexual inadequacy, 282–283; as social learning theories, 396–397
Maternal behavior in cloth-surrogate-mothered monkeys, 120–122, 279–280
Maturation, 31; in cognitive-developmental theory, 410; cross-species variation in, 100–101; effects of extended duration of, 100–101; effect of infantile stimulation on, 33–34
Mental retardation: mongolism, 28
Minnesota Multiphasic Personality Inventory (MMPI), 84–86, 239–241, 421–522, 545–546
Modeling. See Observational learning
Models, 53–58; of personality, 10–11 (see also Computer model of personality; Dramaturgical model of personality; Kelly's model of the human as scientist; Operant psychology); value of, 488. See also Imitation
Mongolism. See Down's syndrome
Morality, development of, 364–367

Natural selection, 15–17; and dominance, 178–179; man's influence on, 15–17; and territoriality, 178–179
Need achievement: development of fan-

tasy measure of, 89–90; use of TAT in measuring, 89–90
Neo-Freudians, 350, 352–353
Neoteny, 17, 68–69, 100–102
Neurological theory of behavior, Freud's, 349–350
Nonparticipant observation, 77
Norms: cultural variations in dependency on, 147–149; internal, 46–47
Nursing: affective function of, 121; and influence on later life, 167–168

Observation, 76–77; contrived, 77; controlled, 76; naturalistic, 76; nonparticipant, 77; participant, 77
Observational learning, 53–55, 385–386; of aggression, 212–214; of dependency, 138–139; and extinction of fear, 53–55; of fear, 53; and multiple versus single models, 53–55; role of reinforcement in, 57; of sex-appropriate behavior, 295–296; of sexual behavior, 292–295
Oedipus complex, 297–298; and defensive identification, 297; social learning theory approach to, 298
Operant psychology, 450–477; applicability across species of, 453; and cumulative record, 458–460, 460–461; and discriminative learning, 470–471; and discriminative stimuli, 457; and gambling, 464; and hours of deprivation, 454; human as performing animal in, 453; and maintenance of sick behavior, 464–466; and modification of symptomatic behavior through token economy, 466–468; and operant responses, 457; organism or subject in, 453; and pellet dispenser, 455–456; and principal constructs in animal laboratory, 453–460; and reinforcement, 454–455; and schedules of reinforcement, 457–459, 461–462, 471–473; and secondary reinforcer, 456; and shaping, 43–44, 456; and Skinner box, 454; and social planning, 473–476; and socialization, 456; and technology of teaching, 471–473; and verbal behavior, 462–464
Operant responses: in language, 462–464; in token economy, 467
Orality, 166–168

Participant observation, 77
Passivity: and dependency, 108–110
Peer Nomination Inventory, 80; and aggression, 234-237; construct validity of, 156–159; development of, 154–156, 234–235
Perceptions: of conservation, 414–416; social, 129–130
Perceptual processes, 45–48, 49–51, 129–131; adaptation level, 46–47; and aggression, 204–207; and ambiguous stimuli, 47–48; binocular rivalry to study, 204–207; cognitive influence on, 49–51, 410; context in, 46–47; development of, 413; effect of needs on, 47–48; incentive contrasts, 46; influence of past experience on, 46; motivation in, 46, 47–48; and relevance to personality, 47–48; and sexuality, 284–285; social contrasts, 46
Personality: authors' approach toward, 8–10; Goffman's dramaturgical model, 519; and Kelly's construct system, 491–497; models of, 10–11 (see also Computer model of personality; Dramaturgical model of personality; Kelly's model of the human as scientist; Operant psychology); viewpoints of, 8, 10. See also Personality, determinants of
Personality, determinants of: biological, 14, 176–177; birth order as a, 141–146; cognitive structures as, 50–51; cultural, 64–69, 130, 224–227; early experiences as, 110–116; evolutionary, 15, 174–175; genetic, 15, 18–19, 21–23, 27–28, 103–108, 178–186; genetic versus environmental, 23–27, 29–33, 191–193; hormonal, 183, 188; interaction between biological and social, 15–18, 177; modeling as a, 53–55; neurological, 188; prenatal experiences as, 32–33; punishment as a, 43, 202–203; role playing as a, 61; roles as, 60–61; social reinforcements as, 43–44
Phenotype, 19; relationship to genotype, 19–20
Philosophical issues: active versus passive human, 351, 353, 408–409, 433; emergent versus additive development, 409; maturational versus experiential view of development, 409
Philosophy of science: and constructive alternativism, 5–8

Pleasure principle, 359
Police officers: influence of race on inappropriate aggression of, 220; influence of status on inappropriate aggression of, 220–221; role-inappropriate aggression of, 218–220; and sensitivity training, 440
Polyandry, 305
Polygamy and human evolution, 175
Polygyny, 305
Pornography, 292–295
Postural Sway Test, 162
Prenatal experience, 32–33; effects of maternal stress during, 33; effects of protein deficiency during, 32–33; and intelligence, 32–33; and masculinization of female, 263–265
Prejudice, use of contact to reduce, 226–229
Prisoner's dilemma games, 132–133
Problem-solving in Kelly's construct system, 490–491
Projection, 362–367
Projective techniques, 87–90; assumptions behind, 87. See also Rorschach Inkblot Test; Thematic Apperception Test
Psychoanalysis: and aggression, 352, 362, 369–370; and anxiety, 360–361, 364, 365; and biological viewpoint, 348–350; central assertion of, 356; constructs in, 356–367; Darwinism and Freud, 356–357; and defense mechanisms, 350, 351, 361–365; and dependency, 368–369, 421; and dreams, 350–351; drive reduction, 358–360; and ego, 348, 351–352, 356, 364–368; and experimental viewpoint, 351–352; free association, 347; and homosexuality, 363; and id, 348, 350, 356; instinctual drives, 358–359; origins of, 346–348; and origins of hysterical symptoms, 346–347; and passive versus active human, 351, 353; pervasiveness of Freud's influence on, 346; and pleasure principle, 359; and projection, 362–363; and psychometric-trait viewpoint, 350–351; and psychosexual development, 370–371; and psychosocial development, 364–365; range of application of, 346; and rationalization, 364; reaction formation, 363–364; and reality principle, 359; recent systematic formulations of, 355–

Psychoanalysis (*cont.*)
356; repression, 361–362; and sexuality, 347, 370–371; and social viewpoint, 352–353, 364–365; structural constructs of, 351–352, 364–368; and superego, 351–352, 356, 364–368; and talking cure, 347; unconscious processes, 356–358

Psychodrama, 61

Psychological assessment: of abnormal personality, 81–82, 85–86, 491–497; by computer, 544–545; with contrived observation, 77; with controlled observation, 76–77; indirect methods of, 87–90; with interviews, 80–81; in Kelly's construct system, 491–497; with naturalistic observation, 76; nature of, 70; with nonparticipant observation, 77; object of, 70; observational methods of, 76–81; with participant observation, 77; by peers, 79; personality inventories used in, 81–87; projective techniques of, 87–90; scales used in, 71–73; self-report methods of, 81–87, 237–245, 324–337. *See also* Psychological tests

Psychological tests: adjective check list, 107–108; Bayley Infant Behavior Profile, 104–106; Bayley Mental and Motor Scales, 103–104; California Psychological Inventory, 86–87, 241–245; concept-sorting tasks, 492; construct validity of, 74–75; Edwards Personal Preference Schedule, 82–84, 159–162, 164; empirical personality inventories, 84–87; Fels child behavior scales, 107–108; forced-choice personality inventories, 82–84; Guttman scale, 326–329; internal consistency of, 74; measurement models for combining items on, 75; Minnesota Multiphasic Personality Inventory, 84–86, 239–241, 521–522, 545–546; Peer Nomination Inventory, 80, 154–159; 234–237; prediction of behavior from, 75; Postural Sway Test, 162; range of content sampled by, 74; rational personality inventories, 81–82; Role Construct Repertory Test, 492–497; Rorschach Inkblot Test, 88–89, 350–351; social desirability of items on, 83; Stanford Hypnotic Susceptibility Scale, 162–163; Thematic Apperception Test (TAT), 46–49, 89–90, 165–169, 245–246, 337–341, 350–

351; Woodworth Personal Data Sheet, 81–82. *See also individual test listings;* Psychological assessment; Rating scales

Psychometric-trait viewpoint, 10, 70–90; and aggression, 78, 232–252; antecedents of, 70; central assertion, 70; and dependency, 152–170; influence of psychoanalysis on, 350–351; and sexuality, 312–342

Psychosexual development: anal stage of, 370; as extension of Freud's theory, 370–371; infantile sexuality in, 370; oral stage of, 370; urethral stage, 370

Psychotherapy: by computer program, 543–544, 547–548; in Kelly's construct system, 498–499; nondirective, 429–432, 436–437; role playing in, 59–61

Punishment: avoidance of, 43, 204, 297; in controlling human personality, 43; effects on sexual behavior, 270–272; effectiveness of, 43; and influence on expression of aggression, 202–203

Rat as model of personality, 450–477. *See also* Operant psychology

Rating scales, 76–79; bipolar versus unipolar, 71–72; continuous versus discrete, 71; cumulated point, 78; graphic, 78; interval versus ordinal, 72–73; numerical, 78; using peer nominations, 80, 154–159; using trait ratings by peers, 79. *See also* Psychological tests

Reality principle, 359

Reciprocal crossing, 22

Reinforcement: and aggressive behavior, 201–204; in Bandura and Walters' social learning theory, 393; as consequence of genotype, 31–32; in controlling human personality, 43–44; delay of, 386; of dependent behavior, 124–127; in Dollard and Miller's social learning theory, 383–384, 393; as drive reduction, 40–43, 384; influence of dependency on susceptibility to, 125–126; as necessary for learning, 40; in observational learning, 57; in operant psychology, 43–44, 454–455; by reward, 43–44; schedules of, 393–394, 457–458, 458–459, 461–462, 471–473; secondary, 384, 392; social, 44; system in hospitals, 467–469; in token economy, 467–469; vicarious, 57

Reinforcer: aggression as a, 192, 200, 203–204, 396–397; establishment of value of, 44, 45; relative value of, 44–45; secondary, 456

Repression: in psychoanalysis, 361–362

Response: in Dollard and Miller's social learning theory, 384; hierarchy, 384

Reward. See Reinforcement

Role construct repertory test, 492–497; in assessment of thought disorder, 492–496; and test reliability, 496–497

Role enactment, 61–64. See also Role playing

Role expectations, 59

Role playing, 61–64; as agent of personality change, 61; to reduce cigarette consumption, 62–64; in psychodrama, 61; and self-expectations, 59–60; as therapeutic technique, 61

Role taking in communication, 490

Role theory and nature of personality, 61, 519

Roles: age, 140–141; aggression and police officer's, 217–221; as alternative to personality traits, 60–61; analogy of theatrical parts to, 506; and birth order, 141–146; contribution of appearance to defining, 60; contribution of manner to defining, 60; defined, 59; formal, 59; and influence on dependency, 140–146; and influence on aggressiveness, 217–220; informal, 59; of mentally ill, 464–466; relationship between reality and performance of, 519–520; sex (see Sex roles)

Rorschach Inkblot Test, 88–89, 350–351

Scales, 71–73; bipolar versus unipolar, 71–72; continuous versus discrete, 71; interval versus ordinate, 72–73. (See also Rating scales)

Schema. See Cognitive structures

Schizophrenia: assessment of, 26–27; assessment of thought processes in, 495–497; and self-control, 387

Schizophrenics: study of children of, 26–27; use of impression management to control hospital fate by, 521–524

Scientific investigation: central assertions in, 483–484; context of discovery in, 485; context of verification in, 486–487; elaborations of central assertions in, 484; experimentation in, 486; formulation of problem in, 484–485; interpretation in, 487–488; results in, 486–487; role of prior facts in, 481, 482; role of scientist's viewpoint in, 480–481; statement of hypothesis in, 485–486 (See also Kelly's Model of the human as scientist)

Secondary-reward theory of sexual identification, 297

Selective breeding: of animals, 21–23, 178–181; for fighting ability, 23, 179–180; of sexual motivation, 259

Self: empirical, 435–437; self theory's influence on behaviorists' use of concept of, 429, 432–433; valuing, 437. See also Self theory

Self-control, 387–388; CPI as measure of, 241–246; MMPI as measure of, 239–241; and schizophrenia, 387

Self theory, 426–448; absolute state of psychological adjustment in, 437–438; and active view of human, 433; aggression as self-fulfillment in, 444–445; and awareness, 440–441; central assertion of, 434–435; competence as consequence of self-fulfillment in, 435; and creativity, 441–443; empirical, 435–437; evaluation of dependency by, 443–444; humanistic orientation of, 428–429; importance of acceptance of experiences in, 438–439; natural-growth tendency of human in, 435, 438; and nondirective psychotherapy, 429–432, 436–437; principal constructs, 435–438; as reaction to behaviorism, 429; and Science of Creative Intelligence, 443; self as construct of, 435; and self-actualization, 432, 438–439; and sensitivity, 441; and sexuality, 445–446; and softening effect on behaviorism, 432–433; transcendental meditation, 431, 433, 439, 445; and unconditional positive regard, 436, 439

Sensitivity training, 440

Sex roles, 295–301; acquisition of, 423; cultural differences in, 302–308; and double standard of sexual behavior, 305; evolution of, 17; inequality between male and female, 305–308; mass media and female, 308. *See also* Sexual identity

Sexual identification: cognitive-developmental approach to, 301, 422–423; empirical research on theories of, 297–301; social learning theory view of, 297–301; theories of, 297–301

Sexual identity: development of, 265–269; as indicated by chromosome constitution, 265–267; as indicated by nuclear chromatin, 265–267; influence of learning experiences on, 295–296. *See also* Sex roles

Sexual preference, 327–328, 329–331; cognitive influences on, 284–285; effects of early experience in modifying, 269–272; somatic, men, 331–334; somatic, women, 334–337

Sexuality: and arousal, 292–293, 338–341; breast size preference, 333–334; and cognitive processes, 285–288; and correlation to dominance and aggressiveness, 298–300; cumulative nature of experiences of, 325–326; and double standard, 305; and dysfunction, 285–288, 398; effect of early experience on development of, 260–272, 278–280; effect of early sexual experience on, 269–272; effect of sexual deprivation on, 278–280; 282–283; evolutionary background of human, 256–258; and gender, 260–261, 268, 269, 301, 423; genetic influence on, 259; of human female compared to female chimpanzee, 257; importance of early physical contact on, 278–280, 281–283; inadequate, 261; increased freedom in expression of, 287–288; influence of hormones during early experiences c.., 34, 262–265; influence of hormones during prenatal period on, 32, 260–261; influence of hormones on human, 257–258, 260–261, 264–265; instrumental conditioning of, 281–283; interrelationship of external stimuli and hormones on, 258, 262; Kinsey studies of, 314–328 (*see also* Kinsey studies); Masters-Johnson observations of, 280, 282–283, 285–288, 321–325; and perceptual processes, 284–285; possible mechanisms through which genotype influences, 259; preference for various expressions of, 327–

328, 329–331; and psychoanalysis, 347, 370–371; psychological factors in human, 256–257, 284–285, 285–286; and punishment, 270–272; and satiation, 293; and self theory, 445–446; and social learning theory, 397–398; status of women, 304–308; use of TAT in measuring preoccupation with, 337–341

Shaping, 43–44, 456; of annoying behavior in child, 460–462

Similarity: and imitation, 58; liking and perceived, 224–227

Skinner box, 454

Smoking, therapeutic treatment of, 62–64

Social comparison process, 46

Social conformity, 164–165; and fantasy dependency, 165–166

Social distance, cultural factors in determining, 66–67, 130, 224–227

Social exchange, 391–392; alpha variables, 391; beta variables, 391–392; concept of self, 392

Social learning theory: and aggression, 208, 395–397; of Bandura and Walters, 385–388; behavior modification in, 390–391; central assertion of, 382; and concept of habit, 376–377, 391; constructs based on Hull's, 376–377; and dependency, 392–395; of Dollard and Miller, 377–379, 383–385, 388–390; early, 377; Masters-Johnson, 396–397; modern, 377–378; observational learning, 385–386; philosophical perspective of, 379–380; principal constructs, 383–385; and response hierarchies, 384, 390–391; self-control in, 387–388; and sexuality, 397–398; situational specificity of behavior in, 386–387; and symptom substitution, 390–391; as theory versus model, 378–379

Social power theory of sexual identification, 298–300

Social viewpoint, 10, 52–69; and aggression, 210–230; central assertion, 52; cultures, 64–69; and dependency, 136–150; models, 53–58; and psychoanalysis, 352–353, 364–365; roles, 59–64; and sexuality, 292–310

Socialization: of aggression, 205–206; contribution of neoteny to, 17, 68–69, 100–102; effects of atypical early social ex-

Socialization (*cont.*)
periences on, 110–115; effects of imprinting on, 110–115; influence of culture on, 67–68; influence of hereditary factors on, 103–106; and operant psychology, 456; use of punishment in, 44
Stage-sequential development: characteristics of, 416; and cognitive transformations, 416–418; concept of dreams as empirical example of, 416–418; concrete operations stage in, 418; formal operations stage in, 418; and learning, 419; of moral judgment, 421–422; sensorimotor stage in, 418
Stanford Hypnotic Susceptibility Scale, 162–163
Status-envy theory of sexual identification, 297–298
Suggestibility, 162–163
Superego, 348, 351–352; definition of, 348; and psychoanalysis, 351–352, 356, 364–368
Swazi, 50

Tasaday, 192
Teaching, technology of: discriminations in, 470–471; use of schedules of reinforcement in, 472–473. *See also* Education
Temne, dependency in the, 147–149
Territoriality, 178
Theatrical productions: acting in, 511; cast in, 512–513; costumes, makeup, and hand props in, 509–510; dramatic realization in, 512; parts and routines in, 508; polite applause after, 513–514; scene changes in, 515–516; scenery and stage props in, 509; separation of house and backstage during, 517–518; speaking out of character in, 516, 519; staging of, 508
Thematic Apperception Test (TAT) 89–90, 165–169; and aggression, 46–47, 245–

246; construct validity of, 90; as measure of social conformity, 165–166; in measuring need for achievement, 89; in measuring sexual imagery and guilt, 337–341; in testing hypothesis derived from psychoanalytic theory, 167–169, 350–351
Theories: example of the construction of, 480–481; of personality (See Psychoanalysis; Self theory; Social learning theory; Cognitive-developmental theory)
Threat: consequences of, 489; definition of, 489; in Kelly's construct system, 488–489
Token economy, 466–469
Trait attribution, 70
Trait measurement. *See* Psychological assessment; Psychological tests
Traits: in computer model of personality, 541–542; as constructs, 73–74; and correlation to maturation, 31–32; covariation of, 73–74; differing construction of, as function of measurement method, 76; dynamics of, 73–74; nature of, 70; stability of, 73–74; structure of, 73–74
Transcendental meditation, 431, 433, 439; and aggression, 445; and Science of Creative Intelligence, 443
Trauma, susceptibility to, in young animals, 34
Tuberculosis, genetic versus environmental factors in susceptibility to, 29–30
Turner's syndrome, 268–269
Twin studies, 23–27, 30, 103–108, 185–186

Unconditional positive regard: and computer psychotherapist, 543–544; and self theory, 436, 439

Values: and dependency, 127–129

Woodworth Personal Data Sheet, 81–82